THE LONGMAN WRITER

Rhetoric, Reader, Handbook

Judith Nadell

—

Linda McMeniman

—

John Langan

With Business Communications Appendix taken from:
Workplace Communications: The Basics, Second Edition
by George J. Searles

Custom Edition for Westwood College

WESTWOOD COLLEGE

· EST. 1953 ·

PEARSON
Custom
Publishing

PEARSON
Longman

Cover art: *Providence*, by George Delany.

Taken from:

The Longman Writer: Rhetoric, Reader, Handbook, Fifth Edition
by Judith Nadell, Linda McMeniman, and John Langan
Copyright © 2003 by Pearson Education, Inc.
Published by Longman, Inc.
Upper Saddle River, New Jersey 07458

Workplace Communications: The Basics, Second Edition
by George J. Searles
Copyright © 2003 by Pearson Education, Inc.
Published by Longman, Inc.

This special edition published in cooperation with Pearson Custom Publishing.

Printed in the United States of America

10 9 8 7 6 5 4

ISBN 0-536-81530-5

2004240012

AP

Please visit our web site at *www.pearsoncustom.com*

PEARSON CUSTOM PUBLISHING
75 Arlington Street, Suite 300, Boston, MA 02116
A Pearson Education Company

BRIEF CONTENTS

APPENDICES

TAKEN FROM *WORKPLACE COMMUNICATIONS: THE BASICS*, SECOND EDITION
BY GEORGE J. SEARLES

(A Detailed Contents follows this Brief Contents.)

DETAILED CONTENTS

17 CAUSE-EFFECT   378

18 DEFINITION   413

PART V   THE LITERARY PAPER AND EXAM ESSAY   611

22   WRITING ABOUT LITERATURE   613

THE
LONGMAN
WRITER

RHETORIC, READER, HANDBOOK

ABOUT THE AUTHORS

Judith Nadell was until several years ago Associate Professor of Communications at Rowan University (New Jersey). During her eighteen years at Rowan, she coordinated the introductory course in the Freshman Writing Sequence and served as Director of the Writing Lab. In the past several years, she has developed a special interest in grass-roots literacy. Besides designing an adult-literacy project, a children's reading-enrichment program, and a family-literacy initiative, she has worked as a volunteer tutor and a tutor trainer in the programs. A Phi Beta Kappa graduate of Tufts University, she received a doctorate from Columbia University. She is the author of *Becoming a Read-Aloud Coach* (Townsend Press) and coauthor of *Doing Well in College* (McGraw-Hill), *Vocabulary Basics* (Townsend Press), and *The Longman Reader*. The recipient of a New Jersey award for excellence in the teaching of writing, Judith Nadell lives with her coauthor husband, John Langan, near Philadelphia.

Linda McMeniman taught in the College Writing Department in the College of Communication at Rowan University for more than twenty years. At Rowan, she taught courses in composition, research, business writing, advanced writing, and semantics. A Phi Beta Kappa graduate of New York University, she holds a Ph.D. from the University of Pennsylvania. She has been a freelance writer, an editorial consultant, and author of the Longman textbook *From Inquiry to Argument*. Linda McMeniman lives in Pennsylvania with her husband and family.

John Langan has taught reading and writing courses at Atlantic Cape Community College near the New Jersey shore for more than twenty years. He earned an advanced degree in reading at Glassboro State College and another in writing at Rutgers University. Active in a mentoring program, he designed a reading-enrichment program for inner-city high school students and recently wrote a motivational and learning skills guidebook, *Ten Skills You Really Need to Succeed in College* (McGraw-Hill). Coauthor of *The Longman Reader* and author of a series of college textbooks on both reading and writing, he has published widely with McGraw-Hill Book Company, Townsend Press, and Longman. His books include *English Skills*, *Reading and Study Skills*, and *College Writing Skills*.

PREFACE

In our more than sixty years of combined experience teaching composition, the three of us have gathered ideas from colleagues, journals, books, and conferences. Mindful of shifting trends in composition theory and practice, we've experimented with a variety of instructional methods. We've also risked the deflation of our egos as we've tested numerous hunches of our own. And so, when we started thinking about writing the first edition of this book, we looked as objectively as we could at our classroom experiences. Which approaches, we asked ourselves, had truly helped students become more confident, more skilled, more insightful writers?

Like the first four editions, the fifth edition of *The Longman Writer: Rhetoric, Reader, Handbook* represents a distillation of what we've learned about writing these many years. We continue to adopt an eclectic approach in the book, bringing together the best from often conflicting schools of thought, blending in class-tested strategies of our own. The mix we've come up with works for our students; we think it will for yours, too.

In the book, as in our classes, we try to strike a balance between product and process. Stressing the connection between reading and writing, we describe possible sequences and structures. At the same time, we emphasize that these steps and formats shouldn't be viewed as rigid prescriptions but as strategies for helping students discover what works best for them. This flexibility means that the book can fit a wide range of teaching philosophies and learning styles.

The Longman Writer includes everything that instructors and students need in a one- or two-semester first-year college composition course: (1) a comprehensive *rhetoric*, including chapters on each stage of the writing process, discussions of the exam essay and the literary paper, and an in-depth treatment of the research paper; (2) a *reader* with thirty-five *professional selections* and thirteen *student essays* integrated into the rhetoric; plus (3) a concise, easy-to-use *Handbook*. Throughout the text, we aim for a supportive, conversational tone that inspires students' confidence without being patronizing. Numerous *activities* and *writing assignments*—*more than 350 in all*—develop awareness of rhetorical choices and encourage students to explore a range of composing strategies.

THE BOOK'S PLAN

Gratified by the first four editions' warm, enthusiastic reception, we have—once again—decided not to tinker with the book's essential structure. The book's format remains as follows:

Part I, "The Reading Process," provides guided practice in a three-step process for reading with close attention and interpretive skill. An activity at the end of Chapter 1, "Becoming a Strong Reader," gives students a chance to put the sequence to use. First, they read Ellen Goodman's provocative essay "Family Counterculture." The essay has been annotated both to show the reading process in action and to illustrate how close critical reading can suggest promising writing topics.

Students then respond to sample questions and writing assignments, all similar to those that accompany the professional selections in Part III. Part I thus does more than just tell students how to sharpen their reading abilities; it guides them through a clearly sequenced plan for developing critical reading skills.

Part II, "The Writing Process," takes students, step-by-step, through a multi-stage composing sequence. To make the writing process easier for students to understand, we provide a separate chapter for each of the following stages:

- Chapter 2, "Getting Started Through Prewriting"
- Chapter 3, "Identifying a Thesis"
- Chapter 4, "Supporting the Thesis with Evidence"
- Chapter 5, "Organizing the Evidence"
- Chapter 6, "Writing the Paragraphs in the First Draft"
- Chapter 7, "Revising Overall Meaning, Structure, and Paragraph Development"
- Chapter 8, "Revising Sentences and Words"
- Chapter 9, "Editing and Proofreading"

In Chapter 2, we introduce students to a range of prewriting techniques, including brainstorming, mapping, and journal writing. Stressing the need for students to analyze their purpose and audience, we explain how to limit a broad topic and how to generate raw, preliminary material about the topic. Chapter 2, like the other chapters in Part II, ends with an array of practical activities.

At this point, students are ready for our discussion of thesis statements in Chapter 3. Numerous examples illustrate how to frame an effective thesis, how to position it in an essay, and what pitfalls to avoid. The chapter also encourages students to view their first thesis as tentative; they learn that as writing continues, new ideas emerge that may force them to reformulate their initial thesis.

Chapter 4 starts with a description of strategies for gathering evidence to support a thesis. Then we discuss techniques for evaluating the relevance, specificity, accuracy, and persuasiveness of supporting material. Numerous suggestions for organizing evidence are presented in Chapter 5. Besides describing chronological, spatial, emphatic, and simple-to-complex methods for sequencing material, the chapter illustrates various approaches for preparing effective outlines.

In Chapter 6, students learn how to move from an outline to a first draft. Urging students to view the first draft as work in progress, we describe ways to avoid getting bogged down. Plentiful "before" and "after" examples show how to write unified, specific, and coherent paragraphs and essays. The chapter concludes with techniques for writing strong introductions, conclusions, and titles.

Emphasizing how helpful peer review can be, Chapters 7 and 8 introduce students to a multi-stage revising process. In Chapter 7, students learn how to respond to peer and instructor feedback and how to evaluate an essay's overall content and structure. Once they know how to rework an essay at this level, they are ready to move ahead to Chapter 8. This chapter begins with abundant "before" and "after" examples that illustrate strategies for making sentences clear, concise, and emphatic. The chapter then describes approaches for refining word choice, with extensive examples showing how to make language natural, vigorous, and specific. Rounding out the chapter is a section on nonsexist language. Throughout Chapters 7 and 8, handy checklists make revision more manageable by focusing students on one rewriting stage at a time. And a series of structured activities helps them apply the checklists when they revise their own and other students' papers. Chapter 9 offers hints for editing and proofreading.

We continually point out in Part II that the stages in the writing process are fluid. Indeed, the case history of an evolving student paper dramatically illustrates just how recursive and individualized the writing process can be. Similarly, we stress that there's no single correct way to write. Focusing on the excitement and sheer fun of exploring ideas on paper, we explain that everyone must tailor the writing process to fit his or her own needs.

Throughout Part II, three instructional devices are used to strengthen students' understanding of the writing process. *Checklists* summarize key concepts and keep students focused on the essentials. Extensive *end-of-chapter activities* also reinforce pivotal skills. Designed to highlight the way invention and revision come into play throughout the writing process, the activities involve students in making rhetorical decisions about such matters as purpose, audience, tone, point of view, organization, paragraph development, and sentence structure. And numerous *guided exercises* involve students in writing—right from the start—showing them how to take their papers through successive stages in the composing process.

Finally, to illustrate the interdependence of reading and writing, the chapters in Part II present—from prewriting through revision—the progressive stages of a student essay written in response to Ellen Goodman's "Family Counterculture" (the professional selection in Part I). In short, *by the end of Part II, the entire reading-writing process has been illustrated,* from reading a selection to writing about it.

Part III, "The Patterns of Development," opens with Chapter 10, which provides a concise overview that reinforces two key points: that the patterns come into play throughout the writing process and that most writers combine patterns in their work. The rest of Part III consists of nine chapters, each covering a different pattern: description, narration, illustration, division-classification, process analysis, comparison-contrast, cause-effect, definition, and argumentation-persuasion. The first few chapters address the more personal and expressive patterns of development, while later chapters move to the more public and analytic patterns. However, because they are self-contained, the chapters can be covered in any order. Part III's thirty-one professional essays are grouped according to the nine patterns of development.

We recognize that some instructors are reluctant to teach the patterns of development as discrete forms; they fear that doing so implies that writers set out to prepare an essay using a specific pattern and that an essay contains only one pattern. Of course, writing usually doesn't work that way at all. So throughout Parts II and III, we provide numerous examples and activities to illustrate that writers select a pattern because it helps them generate material and organize their ideas—that is, it helps serve their rhetorical purposes. We also show that most writing combines two or more patterns, with one pattern usually providing the organizational framework for a piece.

The nine pattern-of-development chapters also illustrate that the multi-stage composing sequence described in Part II has relevance no matter which pattern or combination of patterns is used in an essay. Each chapter in Part II thus follows the same format:

- *A detailed explanation of the pattern* begins the chapter. The explanation includes these sections: (1) a definition of the pattern, (2) a description of the way the pattern helps writers accommodate their purpose and audience, (3) a Prewriting Checklist to spark creativity and help students get started, (4) step-by-step guidelines for using the pattern, and (5) a Revision/Peer Review Checklist to focus students' efforts when they rework their papers.

  The argumentation-persuasion chapter is even more extensive. Besides the sections described above, it includes a clearly explained section on Toulmin logic, a chart on refutation strategies, and a full discussion of induction, deduction, and logical fallacies.

- Following the explanation of each pattern of development is an *annotated student essay, from prewriting through revision.* Written in response to one of the professional selections in the chapter, each essay clearly illustrates the pattern under discussion. By comparing successive stages of the essay, students come to appreciate the way material is progressively reshaped and refined.

- *Commentary* after the student essay points out the blend of patterns in the paper, identifies the paper's strengths, and pinpoints areas needing improvement. "First draft" and "revised" versions of one section of the essay reveal how the student writer went about revising, thus illustrating the relationship between the final draft and the steps taken to produce it.

- Next come *extensive prewriting and revising activities.* Together, these two sets of activities help students appreciate the distinctive features of the pattern being studied. The first prewriting activity asks students to generate raw material for an essay and helps them see that the essay may include more than one pattern of development. The last revising activity gives students a chance to rework a paragraph that needs strengthening. Other activities encourage students, working alone or in groups, to examine rhetorical options, to anticipate the consequences of such choices, and to experiment with a variety of composing techniques.

- The *professional selections* follow the activities. Representing a variety of subjects, tones, and points of view, the selections include tried-and-true classics like George Orwell's "Shooting an Elephant" and E. B. White's "Once More to the Lake." Other selections have rarely, if ever, been included in a composition text. Among these are Beth Johnson's "Bombs Bursting in Air," Dave Barry's "The Ugly Truth About Beauty," and Ann McClintock's "Propaganda Techniques in Today's Advertising." Of course, each selection clearly illustrates a specific pattern of development or combination of patterns.

    Extensive instructional apparatus accompanies each professional selection:

    1. *A biographical note* and *Pre-Reading Journal Entry* give background on the author and create interest in the piece.

    2. *Questions for Close Reading* help students dig into and interpret the selection. The first question asks them to identify the selection's thesis; the last provides work on vocabulary development.

    3. *Questions About the Writer's Craft* deal with such matters as purpose, audience, tone, point of view, organization, sentence structure, diction, and figurative language. The first question (labeled "The Pattern") focuses on the distinctive features of the pattern(s) used in the selection. And often there's another question (labeled "Other Patterns") that asks students to analyze the writer's use of additional patterns in the piece.

    4. Next come *five writing assignments,* all prompted by the selection and packed with suggestions on how to proceed. The first two assignments ask students to write an essay using the same pattern(s) as the selection; the next two invite students to discover for themselves which pattern(s) would be most appropriate for an essay; the last assignment helps students turn the raw material in their journals into fully considered essays. Frequently, the writing assignments are preceded by a special symbol (**∞**), indicating a cross-reference to another professional selection in the book. By encouraging students to make connections between selections, these assignments broaden students' perspectives and give them additional material to draw upon when they write. Such paired assignments will be especially welcome to instructors stressing recurring ideas and themes.

- At the end of each pattern-of-development chapter are two sets of Additional Writing Topics: *General Assignments* and *Assignments with a Specific Purpose, Audience, and Point of View.* The first set provides open-ended topics that prompt students to discover for themselves the best way to use a specific pattern. The second set, problem-solving in nature, develops students' sensitivity to rhetorical context by asking them to apply the pattern in three different real-world settings: "On Campus," "At Home or in the Community," and "On the Job."

Part IV consists of two chapters on **"The Research Paper."** In this practical, comprehensive guide, we demonstrate how to tailor the multi-stage composing process described in Part II to the demands of writing a research paper. This section is filled with hints on all of the following: using the library, drawing upon the

Internet, taking notes, introducing quoted material, interpreting statistics, evaluating conflicting sources, documenting material, and avoiding plagiarism. The critical link between taking effective notes and writing a strong research paper is also underscored through a series of notecards based on an article pertinent to the essay's topic. A fully annotated research paper illustrates MLA documentation, while a separate section provides guidelines for using the APA system. Activities at the end of both chapters help ensure mastery of key research skills.

Part V includes two chapters, **"Writing About Literature"** and **"Writing Exam Essays."** Besides showing students how to adapt the composing process to fit the requirements of these highly specific writing situations, each chapter includes a student essay and commentary, as well as helpful end-of-chapter activities.

The book concludes with **Part VI, "A Concise Handbook."**[1] Detailed and user-friendly, the Handbook offers easy-to-grasp explanations of those areas that most often give students trouble. Boxed *"Cautions"* help students focus on the essentials. When appropriate, alternative correction strategies are presented so that students come to see that there may be more than one way to remedy a problem. Plentiful *practice activities* encourage mastery of important skills.

What's New in the Fifth Edition

Before beginning work on the fifth edition of *The Longman Writer*, we looked closely at the questionnaires completed by instructors using the book. Their comments, always discerning and constructive, helped us identify additional material the book might include. Indeed, even a quick glance at the fifth edition of *The Longman Writer* reveals that this is a significant revision. Here are some of the new features of the fifth edition:

- Most importantly, *every selection in the book* (both new and retained) *is framed by a new set of assignments: a "Pre-Reading Journal Entry" assignment before the piece and a "Writing Assignment Using a Journal Entry as a Starting Point" after the piece. Taken together, these two "bookend" assignments illustrate not only the connection between reading and writing but also the process involved in shaping a piece of writing.* The pre-reading journal assignment "primes" students for the selection by encouraging them to explore—in a loose, unpressured way—their thoughts about an issue that will be raised in the selection. The journal entry thus motivates students to read the piece with extra care, attention, and personal investment. This assignment also paves the way to the "Writing Assignment Using a Journal Entry as a Starting Point." This latter assignment helps students translate the raw material in their journals into a full-length essay. By the time students reach this final assignment, the rough ideas in their journal entry will have been enriched by a careful reading of the selection. This work will have set the stage for a more rigorously conceived essay.

---

[1]Note: Part VI is *not* included in *The Longman Writer, Fifth Edition/Brief Edition*. The *Brief Edition* is appropriate in those classes where students are likely to have purchased a separate English handbook.

- *More than one-third of the selections are new.* Many of these readings were suggested by instructors across the country; others were chosen after a lengthy search through magazines, nonfiction collections, newspapers, autobiographies, and the like. Whether written by a well-known figure such as Stephen King ("Why We Crave Horror Movies") or a relative newcomer such as Beth Johnson ("Bombs Bursting in Air"), the new selections are bound to stimulate strong writing on a variety of topics—gender, education, race, mass culture, family life, and morality, to name a few. When selecting new readings, we took special care to include humorous pieces (for example, Bill Bryson's "Your New Computer") as well as those written from the third-person point of view (for example, James Gleick's "Life As Type A"). Honoring the requests of many instructors, we also made an effort to find compelling pieces on the way technology affects our everyday lives. Clifford Stoll's "Why Computers Don't Belong in the Classroom" is one of several such pieces.

- *Additional attention is given to the concept of peer review, including the use of e-mail to facilitate students' responses to one another's work.* An expanded discussion provides students with guidelines for reacting to other students' work and for responding to the feedback they themselves receive. This emphasis on peer review encourages students to work together and learn from one another; it also helps students evaluate their own writing more incisively. In addition to emphasizing the usefulness of e-mail in exchanging student writing, this section also offers practical suggestions for exactly how students can go about using this technology to respond to each other's work.

- *Many assignments* (signaled by 🖳) *suggest that students might want to conduct research in the library and/or on the Internet as part of their preparation for an essay.* Most of these assignments are worded in such a way that the essay can be written without visiting the library or going online, but the research option is there for instructors and students who think an essay would benefit from the citation of outside sources. The Companion Website provides links to Internet sites that students will find helpful if they supplement an essay with research.

- *Writing in non-academic contexts receives greater emphasis.* The "Assignments with a Specific Purpose, Audience, and Point of View" sections at the end of each pattern chapter have been revised to focus on how a particular pattern can be used in three different real-life writing contexts: "On Campus," "At Home or in the Community," and "On the Job."

- *The value of collaborative learning is underscored more than ever.* Many assignments encourage students to investigate various sides of an issue by brainstorming with classmates, questioning friends, speaking with family members, or interviewing "experts." Such assignments help students formulate sound, well-reasoned opinions and steer them away from reflexive, off-the-cuff positions.

- *A greater number of linked assignments* (indicated by ∞) *help students make connections between selections*, thus broadening their perspectives and giving them additional material to draw upon when they write.

- *The argumentation-persuasion chapter, already more comprehensive than that of any comparable text, expands the discussion of refutation strategies* by presenting *a provocative new pair of professional essays, with one essay having been written in rebuttal to the other.*

- The *research paper* has been *updated* to reflect the *most recent guidelines regarding the use of electronic sources.*

- *The chapters on research and documentation have been updated as well as streamlined.* These chapters now include *up-to-date information on both library and Internet research, highlighting the most useful and authoritative research tools and sources.* The sample MLA and APA bibliographic entries have also been revised to exemplify—in a highly user-friendly manner—the most recent guidelines regarding the documentation of print and electronic sources.

- *A Companion Website* (at *www.ablongman.com/nadell*) *by Karen Grandy (University of Windsor) offers a number of helpful features,* including the addresses of relevant Websites for assignments calling for Internet research, as well as a variety of supplementary activities.

TEACHING ANCILLARIES

An Instructor's Edition of *The Longman Writer,* Fifth Edition, includes a comprehensive Instructor's Manual. The manual includes the following: a thematic table of contents; lists of the book's collaborative and/or problem-solving exercises; pointers about using the book; suggested activities; a detailed syllabus; answers to the Handbook exercises; and in-depth responses to the end-of-chapter activities, Questions for Close Reading, and Questions About the Writer's Craft.

A separate Instructor's Manual is available for instructors of this edition.

ACKNOWLEDGMENTS

Throughout our teaching and certainly in writing this book, we've drawn upon the expertise and wisdom of many composition scholars and practitioners. Although we cannot list all those who have influenced us, we owe a special debt to James Britton, Kenneth Bruffee, Frances Christensen, Edward P. J. Corbett, Peter Elbow, Janet Emig, Linda Flower, Donald Hall, Ken Macrorie, James Moffett, Donald Murray, Frank O'Hare, Mina Shaughnessy, Nancy Sommers, and W. Ross Winterowd.

Over the years, many writing instructors have reviewed *The Longman Writer.* These colleagues' hard-hitting, practical comments guided our work every step of the way. To the following reviewers we are indeed grateful: John C. Baker, Concord College; Thomas G. Beverage, Coastal Carolina Community College; Barry Brunetti, Gulf Coast Community College; Joyce L. Cherry, Albany State

University; Tony C. Clark, Scottsdale Community College; Bruce Coad, Mountain View College; Beatrice I. Curry, Columbia State Community College; Juanita Davis, Columbia State Community College; William Dyer, Mankato State University; Jo Nell Farrar, San Jacinto College Central; Adam Fischer, Coastal Carolina Community College; Andrea Glebe, University of Nevada, Las Vegas; Linda Hasley, Redlands Community College; M. Jean Jones, Columbia State Community College; Rowena R. Jones, Northern Michigan University; Leela Kapai, University of the District of Columbia; Anne M. Kuhta, Northern Virginia Community College; William B. Lalicker, West Chester University of Pennsylvania; Joe Law, Wright State University; Carol Owen Lewis, Trident Technical College; James L. Madachy, Gallaudet University; Jeffrey Maxson, Rowan University; Nancy McGee, Detroit College of Business; Rita M. Mignacca, State University of New York at Brockport; Margaret Kissam Morris, Mercy College; Betty P. Nelson, Volunteer State Community College; Douglas L. Okey, Spoon River College; Doris Osborn, Northern Oklahoma College; Mack A. Perry, Jackson State Community College; John S. Ramsey, State University of New York at Fredonia; Clay Randolph, Oklahoma City Community College; Gladys C. Rosser, Fayetteville Technical Community College; Peggy Ruff, DeVry Institute of Technology; Elizabeth Sarcone, Delta State University; Laura A. Scibona, State University of New York at Brockport; Marilyn Segal, California State University at Northridge; Rodger Slater, Scottsdale Community College; Richard Stoner, Broome Community College; Martha Coultas Strode, Spoon River College; Carole F. Taylor, University of Dayton; Delores Waters, Delgado Community College; Wendy F. Weiner, Northern Virginia Community College; Carol Wershoven, Palm Beach Community College; Stephen Wilhoit, University of Dayton; Gene Young, Morehead State University; and Richard C. Zath, DeVry Institute of Technology.

For help in preparing the fifth edition, we owe thanks to the perceptive comments of these reviewers: Michael Cronin, Northern Oklahoma College; Kathryn Henkins, Mt. San Antonio College; Tamara M. Karn, Chapman University; Austin Straus, Mt. San Antonio College; and Ellen K. Straw, Mt. San Antonio College.

At Longman, our thanks go to Eben Ludlow, who has played a key role in helping to shape the book from the very start. We're also indebted to Douglas Bell for skillfully handling the complex details of the production process.

Thanks go to the very knowledgeable librarians at the Camden County Library in Voorhees, New Jersey, for sharing their expertise on library and Internet research.

Several individuals from our in-home office deserve special thanks. Karen Beardslee and Frank Smigiel—two talented composition instructors—helped us with instructional apparatus. Janet M. Goldstein provided invaluable assistance when it came time to refine the journal-to-essay writing assignments. And special thanks go to Eliza A. Comodromos, new coauthor of *The Longman Reader*. Her insights and hard work influenced every phase of this edition.

Of course, much appreciation goes to our families. To both sides of Judy Nadell and John Langan's family go affectionate thanks for being so supportive of our work. To Linda McMeniman's husband, Larry Schwab, and their children, Laurel,

Emily, and Jeremy, much love and thanks for their charm, playfulness, patience, and support.

Finally, we're grateful to our students. Their candid reactions to various drafts of the text sharpened our thinking and kept us honest. We're especially indebted to the thirteen students whose work is included in the book. Their essays illustrate dramatically the potential and the power of student writing.

Judith Nadell
Linda McMeniman
John Langan

THE
LONGMAN
WRITER

RHETORIC, READER, HANDBOOK

THE
READING
PROCESS

PART I

1
BECOMING
A STRONG
READER

More than two hundred years ago, essayist Joseph Addison commented, "Of all the diversions of life, there is none so proper to fill up its empty spaces as the reading of useful and entertaining authors." Addison might have added that reading also challenges our beliefs, deepens our awareness, and stimulates our imagination.

Why, then, don't more people delight in reading? After all, most children feel great pleasure and pride when they first learn to read. As children grow older, though, the initially magical world of books is increasingly associated with homework, tests, and grades. Reading turns into an anxiety-producing chore. Also, as demands on a person's time accumulate throughout adolescence and adulthood, reading often gets pushed aside in favor of something that takes less effort. It's easier simply to switch on the television and passively view the ready-made images that flash across the screen. In contrast, it's almost impossible to remain passive while reading. Even a slick best-seller requires that the reader decode, visualize, and interpret what's on the page. The more challenging the materials, the more actively involved the reader must be.

The essays we selected for Part III of this book call for active reading. Representing a broad mix of styles and subjects, the essays range from the classic to the contemporary. They contain language that will move you, images that will enlarge your understanding of other people, ideas that will transform your views on complex issues.

The selections in Part III serve other purposes as well. For one thing, they'll help you develop a repertoire of reading skills—abilities that will benefit you throughout life. Second, as you become a better reader, your own writing style will become more insightful and polished. Increasingly, you'll be able to draw on the ideas presented in the selections and employ the techniques that professional writers use to express such ideas. As novelist Saul Bellow has observed, "A writer is a reader moved to emulation."

In the pages ahead, we outline a three-stage approach for getting the most out of this book's selections. Our suggestions will enhance your understanding of the book's essays, as well as help you read other material with greater ease and assurance.

STAGE 1: GET AN OVERVIEW OF THE SELECTION

Ideally, you should get settled in a quiet place that encourages concentration. If you can focus your attention while sprawled on a bed or curled up in a chair, that's fine. But if you find that being very comfortable is more conducive to day-dreaming and dozing off than it is to studying, avoid getting too relaxed.

Once you're settled, it's time to read the selection. To ensure a good first reading, try the following hints:

- Get an overview of the essay and its author. Start by reading the biographical note that precedes the selection. By providing background information about the author, the note helps you evaluate the writer's credibility as well as his or her slant on the subject. For example, if you know that Deborah Tannen is a widely published linguistics professor at Georgetown University, you can better assess whether she is a credible source for the analysis she presents in her essay "But What Do You Mean?" (see page 288).

- Do the *Pre-Reading Journal Entry* assignment, which precedes the selection. This assignment prepares you for the piece by helping you to explore—in an easy, unpressured way—your thoughts about a key point raised in the selection. By preparing the journal entry, you're inspired to read the selection with special care, attention, and personal investment. (For more on pre-reading journal entries, see pages 19–20.)

- Consider the selection's title. A good title often expresses the essay's main idea, giving you insight into the selection even before you read it. For example, the title of Ann McClintock's essay, "Propaganda Techniques in Today's Advertising," (Chapter 14) suggests that the piece will examine the dark side of the advertising world. A title may also hint at a selection's tone. The title of Robert Barry's piece, "Becoming a Videoholic," (the student essay in Chapter 15) points to an essay that's light in spirit, whereas George Orwell's "Shooting an Elephant" (Chapter 12) suggests a piece with a serious mood.

- Read the selection straight through purely for pleasure. Allow yourself to be drawn into the world the author has created. Just as you first see a painting from the doorway of a room and form an overall impression without perceiving the details, you can have a preliminary, subjective feeling about a reading selection. Moreover, because you bring your own experiences and viewpoints to the piece, your reading will be unique. As Emerson said, "Take the book, my friend, and read your eyes out; you will never find there what I find."

- After this initial reading of the selection, focus your first impressions by asking yourself whether you like the selection. In your own words, briefly describe the piece and your reaction to it.

STAGE 2: DEEPEN YOUR SENSE OF THE SELECTION

At this point, you're ready to move further into the selection. A second reading will help you identify the specific features that triggered your initial reaction. Here are some suggestions on how to proceed:

- Mark off the selection's main idea, or thesis, often found near the beginning or end. If the thesis isn't stated explicitly, write down your own version of the selection's main idea.
- Locate the main supporting evidence used to develop the thesis. You may even want to number in the margin each key supporting point.
- Take a minute to write "Yes" or "No" beside points with which you strongly agree or disagree. Your reaction to these points often explains your feelings about the aptness of the selection's ideas.
- Return to any unclear passages you encountered during the first reading. The feeling you now have for the piece as a whole will probably help you make sense of initially confusing spots. However, this second reading may also reveal that, in places, the writer's thinking isn't as clear as it could be.
- Use your dictionary to check the meanings of any unfamiliar words.
- Ask yourself if your initial impression of the selection has changed in any way as a result of this second reading. If your feelings *have* changed, try to determine why you reacted differently on this reading.

STAGE 3: EVALUATE THE SELECTION

Now that you have a good grasp of the selection, you may want to read it a third time, especially if the piece is long or complex. This time, your goal is to make judgments about the essay's effectiveness. Keep in mind, though, that you shouldn't evaluate the selection until after you have a strong hold on it. A negative, even a positive reaction is valid only if it's based on an accurate reading.

At first, you may feel uncomfortable about evaluating the work of a professional writer. But remember: Written material set in type only *seems* perfect; all writing can be finetuned. By identifying what does and doesn't work in others' writing, you're taking an important first step toward developing your own power as a writer. You might find it helpful at this point to get together with other students to discuss the selection. Comparing viewpoints often opens up a piece, enabling you to gain a clearer perspective on the selection and the author's approach.

To evaluate the essay, ask yourself the following questions:

Questions for Evaluating a Selection

1. *Where does support for the selection's thesis seem logical and sufficient? Where does support seem weak?* Which of the author's supporting facts, arguments, and examples seem pertinent and convincing? Which don't?

2. *Is the selection unified? If not, why not?* Where does something in the selection not seem relevant? Where are there any unnecessary digressions or detours?

3. *How does the writer make the selection move smoothly from beginning to end?* How does the writer create an easy flow between ideas? Are any parts of the essay abrupt and jarring? Which ones?

4. *Which stylistic devices are used to good effect in the selection?* Which pattern of development or combination of patterns does the writer use to develop the piece? Why do you think those patterns were selected? How do paragraph development, sentence structure, and word choice (diction) contribute to the piece's overall effect? What tone does the writer adopt? Where does the writer use figures of speech effectively? (The terms *patterns of development, sentence structure, diction,* and the like are explained in Chapter 2.)

5. *How does the selection encourage further thought?* What new perspective on an issue does the writer provide? What ideas has the selection prompted you to explore in an essay of your own?

It takes some work to follow the three-stage approach just described, but the selections in Part III make it worth the effort. Bear in mind that none of the selections you'll read in Part III sprang full-blown from the pen of its author. Rather, each essay is the result of hours of work—hours of thinking, writing, rethinking, and revising. As a reader, you should show the same willingness to work with the selections, to read them carefully and thoughtfully. Henry David Thoreau, an avid reader and prolific writer, emphasized the importance of this kind of attentive reading when he advised that "books must be read as deliberately and unreservedly as they were written."

To illustrate the multi-stage reading process, we've annotated the professional essay that follows: Ellen Goodman's "Family Counterculture." Note that annotations are provided in the margin of the essay as well as at the end of the essay. As you read Goodman's essay, try applying the three-stage sequence. You can measure your ability to dig into the selection by making your own annotations on Goodman's essay and then comparing them to ours. You can also see how well you evaluated the piece by answering the preceding five questions and then comparing your responses to ours on pages 9–11.

ELLEN GOODMAN

The recipient of a Pulitzer Prize, Ellen Goodman (1941–) worked for *Newsweek* and the *Detroit Free Press* before joining the staff of *The Boston Globe* in the mid-1970s. A resident of the Boston area, Goodman writes a popular syndicated column that provides insightful commentary on life in the United States. Her pieces have appeared in a number of national publications, including *The Village Voice* and *McCall's*. Collections of her columns have been published in *Close to Home* (1979), *Turning Points* (1979), *At Large* (1981), *Keeping in Touch* (1985), *Making Sense* (1989), and *Value Judgments* (1993). Most recently, she coauthored *I Know Just What You Mean* (1999), a book that examines the complex nature of women's friendships. The following selection is from *Value Judgments*.

Pre-Reading Journal Entry

Television is often blamed for having a harmful effect on children. Do you think this criticism is merited? In what ways does TV exert a negative influence on children? In what ways does TV exert a positive influence on youngsters? Take a few minutes to respond to these questions in your journal.

FAMILY COUNTERCULTURE

1   Sooner or later, most Americans become card-carrying members of the counterculture. This is not an underground holdout of hippies. No beads are required. All you need to join is a child.

2   At some point between Lamaze and the PTA, it becomes clear that one of your main jobs as a parent is to counter the culture. What the media delivers to children by the masses, you are expected to rebut one at a time.

3   The latest evidence of this frustrating piece of the parenting job description came from pediatricians. This summer, the American Academy of Pediatrics called for a ban on television food ads. Their plea was hard on the heels of a study showing that one Saturday morning of TV cartoons contained 202 junk-food ads.

4   The kids see, want, and nag. That is, after all, the theory behind advertising to children, since few six-year-olds have their own trust funds. The end result, said the pediatricians, is obesity and high cholesterol.

5   Their call for a ban was predictably attacked by the grocers' association. But it was also attacked by people assembled under the umbrella marked "parental responsibility." We don't need bans, said these "PR" people, we need parents who know how to say "no."

Margin annotations:

- Interesting take on the term *counterculture*
- Time frame established
- Light humor. Easy, casual tone
- Time frame picked up
- Thesis, developed overall by cause-effect pattern
- First research-based example to support thesis

Relevant paragraph? Identifies Goodman as a parent, but interrupts flow	Well, I bow to no one in my capacity for naysaying. I agree that it's a well-honed skill of child raising. By the time my daughter was seven, she qualified as a media critic. 6
Transition doesn't work but would if ¶6 cut.	But it occurs to me now that the call for "parental responsibility" is increasing in direct proportion to the irresponsibility of the marketplace. Parents are expected to protect their children from an increasingly hostile environment. 7
Series of questions and brief answers consistent with overall casual tone	Are the kids being sold junk food? Just say no. Is TV bad? Turn it off. Are there messages about sex, drugs, violence all around? Counter the culture. 8
Brief real-life examples support thesis.	Mothers and fathers are expected to screen virtually every aspect of their children's lives. To check the ratings on the movies, to read the labels on the CDs, to find out if there's MTV in the house next door. All the while keeping in touch with school and, in their free time, earning a living. 9
Fragments	
More examples	In real life, most parents do a great deal of this monitoring and just-say-no-ing. Any trip to the supermarket produces at least one scene of a child grabbing for something only to have it returned to the shelf by a frazzled parent. An extraordinary number of the family arguments are over the goodies—sneakers, clothes, games—that the young know only because of ads. 10
Another weak transition—no contrast	But at times it seems that the media have become the mainstream culture in children's lives. Parents have become the alternative. 11
Restatement of thesis	
Second research-based example to support thesis	Barbara Dafoe Whitehead, a research associate at the Institute for American Values, found this out in interviews with middle-class parents. 12
Citing an expert reinforces thesis.	"A common complaint I heard from parents was their sense of being overwhelmed by the culture. They felt their voice was a lot weaker. And they felt relatively more helpless than their parents.
Restatement of thesis	"Parents," she notes, "see themselves in a struggle for the hearts and minds of their own children." It isn't that they can't say no. It's that there's so much more to say no to. 13
Comparison-contrast pattern—signaled by *Today, Once,* and *Now*	Without wallowing in false nostalgia, there has been a fundamental shift. Americans once expected parents to raise their children in accordance with the dominant cultural messages. Today they are expected to raise their children in opposition. 14
	Once the chorus of cultural values was full of ministers, teachers, neighbors, leaders. They demanded more conformity, but offered more support. 15

Now the messengers are Ninja Turtles, Madonna, rap groups, and celebrities pushing sneakers. Parents are considered "responsible" only if they are successful in their resistance. ——————————————————— Restatement of thesis

16 It's what makes child raising harder. It's why parents feel more isolated. It's not just that American families have less time with their kids. It's that we have to spend more of this time doing battle with our own culture.

17 It's rather like trying to get your kids to eat their green beans after ——— Conveys the challenges they've been told all day about the wonders of Milky Way. Come to think   that parents face of it, it's exactly like that.

Thesis: First stated in paragraph 2 ("... it becomes clear that one of your main jobs as a parent is to counter the culture. What the media delivers to children by the masses, you are expected to rebut one at a time.") and then restated in paragraphs 11 ("the media have become the mainstream culture in children's lives. Parents have become the alternative."); 13 (Parents are frustrated, not because "... they can't say no. It's that there's so much more to say no to."); and 16 ("It's not just that American families have less time with their kids. It's that we have to spend more of this time doing battle with our own culture.").

First Reading: A quick take on a serious subject. Informal tone and to-the-point style get to the heart of the media vs. parenting problem. Easy to relate to.

Second and Third Readings:

1. Uses the findings of the American Academy of Pediatrics, a statement made by Barbara Dafoe Whitehead, and a number of brief examples to illustrate the relentless work parents must do to counter the culture.
2. Uses cause-effect overall to support thesis and comparison/contrast to show how parenting nowadays is more difficult than it used to be.
3. Not everything works (reference to her daughter as a media critic, repetitive and often inappropriate use of *but* as a transition), but overall the essay succeeds.
4. At first, the ending seems weak. But it feels just right after an additional reading. Shows how parents' attempts to counter the culture are as commonplace as their attempts to get kids to eat vegetables. It's an ongoing and constant battle that makes parenting more difficult than it has to be and less enjoyable than it should be.
5. Possible essay topics: A humorous paper about the strategies kids use to get around their parents' saying "no" or a serious paper on the negative effects on kids of another aspect of television culture (cable television, MTV, tabloid-style talk shows, and so on).

The following answers to the questions on page 6 will help crystalize your reaction to Goodman's essay.

1. **Where does support for the selection's thesis seem logical and sufficient? Where does support seem weak?** Goodman begins to provide evidence for her thesis when she cites the American Academy of Pediatrics's call for a "ban on television food ads" (paragraphs 3–5). The ban followed a study showing that kids are exposed to 202 junk-food ads during a single Saturday morning

of television cartoons. Goodman further buoys her thesis with a list of brief "countering the culture" examples (8–10) and a slightly more detailed example (10) describing the parent-child conflicts that occur on a typical trip to the supermarket. By citing Barbara Dafoe Whitehead's findings (12–13) later on, Goodman further reinforces her point that the need for constant rebuttal makes parenting especially frustrating: Because parents have to say "no" to virtually everything, more and more family time ends up being spent "doing battle" with the culture (16).

2. **Is the selection unified? If not, why not?** In the first two paragraphs, Goodman identifies the problem and then provides solid evidence of its existence (3–4, 8–10). But Goodman's comments in paragraph 6 about her daughter's skill as a media critic seem distracting. Even so, paragraph 6 serves a purpose because it establishes Goodman's credibility by showing that she, too, is a parent and has been compelled to be a constant naysayer with her child. From paragraph 7 on, the piece stays on course by focusing on the way parents have to compete with the media for control of their children. The concluding paragraphs (16–17) reinforce Goodman's thesis by suggesting that parents' struggle to counteract the media is as common—and as exasperating—as trying to get children to eat their vegetables when all the kids want is to gorge on candy.

3. **How does the writer make the selection move smoothly from beginning to end?** The first two paragraphs of Goodman's essay are clearly connected: The phrase "sooner or later" at the beginning of the first paragraph establishes a time frame that is then picked up at the beginning of the second paragraph with the phrase "at some point between Lamaze and the PTA." And Goodman's use in paragraph 3 of the word *this* ("The latest evidence of *this* frustrating piece of the parenting job description . . .") provides a link to the preceding paragraph. Other connecting strategies can be found in the piece. For example, the words *Today, Once,* and *Now* in paragraphs 14–15 provide an easy-to-follow contrast between parenting in earlier times and parenting in this era. However, because paragraph 6 contains a distracting aside, the contrast implied by the word *But* at the beginning of paragraph 7 doesn't work. Nor does Goodman's use of the word *But* at the beginning of paragraph 11 work; the point there emphasizes rather than contrasts with the one made in paragraph 10. From this point on, though, the essay is tightly written and moves smoothly along to its conclusion.

4. **Which stylistic devices are used to good effect in the selection?** Goodman uses several patterns of development in her essay. The selection as a whole shows the *effect* of the mass media on kids and their parents. In paragraphs 3 and 12, Goodman provides *examples in the form of research data* to support her thesis, while paragraphs 8–10 provide a series of *brief real-life examples*. Paragraphs 12–15 use a *contrast,* and paragraph 17 makes a *comparison* to punctuate Goodman's concluding point. Throughout, Goodman's *informal, conversational tone* draws readers in, and her *no-holds-barred style* drives her point home forcefully. In paragraph 8, she uses a *question and answer format* ("Are the kids being sold junk food? Just say no.") *and short sentences* ("Turn it

off" and "Counter the culture") to illustrate how pervasive the situation is. And in paragraph 9, she uses *fragments* ("To check the ratings . . ." and "All the while keeping in touch with school . . .") to focus attention on the problem. These varied stylistic devices help make the essay a quick, enjoyable read. Finally, although Goodman is concerned about the corrosive effects of the media, she leavens her essay with dashes of *humor*. For example, the image of parents as card-carrying hippies (1) and the comments about green beans and Milky Ways (17) probably elicit smiles or gentle laughter from most readers.

5. **How does the selection encourage further thought?** Goodman's essay touches on a problem most parents face at some time or another—having to counter the culture in order to protect their children. Her main concern is how difficult it is for parents to say "no" to virtually every aspect of the culture. Although Goodman offers no immediate solutions, her presentation of the issue urges us to decide for ourselves which aspects of the culture should be countered and which should not.

If, for each essay you read in this book, you consider the preceding questions, you'll be able to respond thoughtfully to the *Questions for Close Reading* and *Questions About the Writer's Craft* presented after each selection. Your responses will, in turn, prepare you for the writing assignments that follow the questions. Interesting and varied, the assignments invite you to examine issues raised by the selections and encourage you to experiment with various writing styles and organizational patterns.

Following are some sample questions and writing assignments based on the Goodman essay; all are similar to the sort that appear later in this book. Note that the final writing assignment paves the way for the successive stages of a student essay presented in Part II, "The Writing Process." (The final version of the essay appears on pages 137–139.)

Questions for Close Reading

1. According to Goodman, what does it mean to "counter the culture"? Why is it harder now than ever before?

2. Which two groups, according to Goodman, protested the American Academy of Pediatrics's ban on television food ads? Which of these two groups does she take more seriously? Why?

Questions About the Writer's Craft

1. What audience do you think Goodman had in mind when she wrote this piece? How do you know? Where does she address this audience directly?

2. What word appears four times in paragraph 16? Why do you think Goodman repeats this word so often? What is the effect of this repetition?

Writing Assignments

1. Goodman believes that parents are forced to say "no" to almost everything the media offer. Write an essay supporting the idea that not everything the media present is bad for children.

2. Goodman implies that, in some ways, today's world is hostile to children. Do you agree? Drawing upon but not limiting yourself to the material in your pre-reading journal, write an essay in which you support or reject this viewpoint.

The benefits of active reading are many. Books in general and the selections in Part III in particular will bring you face to face with issues that concern all of us. If you study the selections and the questions that follow them, you'll be on your way to discovering ideas for your own papers. Part II offers practical suggestions for turning those ideas into well-organized, thoughtful essays.

THE WRITING PROCESS

2

GETTING STARTED THROUGH PREWRITING

OBSERVATIONS ABOUT THE WRITING PROCESS

Not many people retire at age thirty-eight. But Michel Montaigne, a sixteenth-century French attorney, did exactly that. Montaigne retired at a young age because he wanted to read, think, and write about all the subjects that interested him. After spending years getting his ideas down on paper, Montaigne finally published his short prose pieces. He called them *essais*—French for "trials" or "attempts."

In fact, all writing is an attempt to transform ideas into words, thus giving order and meaning to life. By using the term *essais,* Montaigne acknowledged that a written piece is never really finished. Of course, writers have to stop at some point, especially if they have deadlines to meet. But, as all experienced writers know, even after they dot the final *i,* cross the final *t,* and say "That's it," there's always something that could have been explored further or expressed a little better.

When we read a piece of writing, we see only the finished product. Not being privy to the writer's effort to convey meaning, we may hold a romanticized notion of what it means to be a writer. We may imagine the writer transported by flashes of creativity, polished prose appearing—as if by magic—on the page. In practice, though, most writers do anything but pour out well-formed thoughts.

Rather, they stare into space, dash off a few pages, crumple them up, and start all over. Even E. B. White, the American essayist celebrated for his eloquent, seemingly effortless prose, confessed, "Writing . . . is a hell of a chore for me, closely related to acid indigestion."

If White, who made his living as a writer, admitted such anxiety, you shouldn't be surprised if you feel some apprehension when it's time to write a paper. Your uneasiness may stem in part from your belief that some people are born writers, others are not—and that you're one of the latter. Some people *do* seem to be born with a gift for language, just as some people seem to be born with a gift for athletics or music. But with practice, just about anyone can learn to play a solid game of tennis or to sing on key. And that's what most of us are aiming for—not to be the Venus Williamses, the Pavarottis, or the E. B. Whites of the world, but to perform skillfully and confidently.

As with singing or playing tennis, learning to write well is a challenge. Shaky starts and changes in direction aren't uncommon. Although there's no way to eliminate the work needed to write effectively, certain approaches can make the process more manageable and rewarding. In Chapters 2–9, we describe a sequence of steps for writing essays. Familiarity with a specific sequence develops your awareness of strategies and choices, making you feel more confident when it comes time to write. You're less likely to look at a blank piece of paper and think, "Help! Now what do I do?" During the sequence, you do the following:

- Prewrite
- Identify your thesis
- Support the thesis with evidence
- Organize the evidence
- Write the paragraphs of the first draft
- Revise meaning, structure, and paragraph development
- Revise sentences and words
- Edit and proofread

Even though we present the sequence as a series of steps, it's not a rigid formula that you must follow step by unchanging step. Somewhere in school we were taught that a straight line is the shortest distance between two points. But writing isn't as simple or tidy as that. Most people develop personalized approaches to the writing process. Some writers mull over a topic in their heads and then move quickly into a promising first draft; others outline their essays in detail before beginning to write. Between these two extremes are any number of effective approaches.

Most of us tend to be creatures of habit; we feel secure and comfortable doing things the way we always have. You've probably approached writing in much the same way for many years. At first, you may be reluctant to try the techniques we describe here and in the following chapters. That's understandable. But we urge you to experiment with the strategies we present. Try them, use what works, discard what doesn't. And always feel free to streamline or alter the steps in the sequence to suit your individual needs and the requirements of specific writing assignments.

USE PREWRITING TO GET STARTED

Prewriting refers to strategies you can use to generate ideas *before* starting the first draft of a paper. Prewriting techniques are like the warm-ups you do before going out to jog—they loosen you up, get you moving, and help you to develop a sense of well-being and confidence. Since prewriting techniques encourage imaginative exploration, they also help you discover what interests you most about your subject. Having such a focus early in the writing process keeps you from plunging into your initial draft without first giving some thought to what you want to say. Prewriting thus saves you time in the long run by keeping you on course.

Prewriting can help in other ways, too. When we write, we often sabotage our ability to generate material because we continually critique what we put down on paper. "This makes no sense," "This is stupid," "I can't say that," and other critical thoughts pop into our minds. Such negative, self-critical comments stop the flow of our thoughts and reinforce the fear that we have nothing to say and aren't very good at writing. During prewriting, you deliberately ignore your internal critic. Your purpose is simply to get ideas down on paper *without evaluating* their effectiveness. Writing without immediately judging what you produce can be liberating. Once you feel less pressure, you'll probably find that you can generate a good deal of material. And that can make your confidence soar.

One final advantage of prewriting: The random associations typical of prewriting tap the mind's ability to make unusual connections. When you prewrite, you're like an archaeologist going on a dig. On the one hand, you may not unearth anything; on the other hand, you may stumble upon one interesting find after another. Prewriting helps you appreciate—right from the start—this element of surprise in the writing process.

Keep a Journal

Of all the prewriting techniques, keeping a **journal** (daily or almost daily) is the one most likely to make writing a part of your life. If you prefer keeping a handwritten journal, consider using a small notebook that you can carry with you for on-the-spot writing. If you feel more comfortable working at a computer, keep your journal printouts in a loose-leaf notebook. No matter how you proceed, be sure to date all entries.

Some journal entries focus on a single theme; others wander from topic to topic. Your starting point may be a dream, a snippet of overheard conversation, a video on MTV, a political cartoon, an issue raised in class or in your reading—anything that surprises, interests, angers, depresses, confuses, or amuses you. You may also use a journal to experiment with your writing style—say, to vary your sentence structure if you tend to use predictable patterns.

Here is a fairly focused excerpt from a student's journal:

```
Today I had to show Paul around school. He and Mom got here
by 9. I didn't let on that this was the earliest I've gotten up
all semester! He got out of the car looking kind of nervous.
Maybe he thought his big brother would be different after a
couple of months of college. I walked him around part of the
campus and then he went with me to Am. Civ. and then to lunch. He
met Greg and some other guys. Everyone seemed to like him. He's
got a nice, quiet sense of humor. When I went to Bio., I told him
that he could walk around on his own since he wasn't crazy about
sitting in on a science class. But he said "I'd rather stick with
you." Was he flattering me or was he just scared? Anyway it made
me feel good. Later when he was leaving, he told me he's
definitely going to apply. I guess that'd be kind of nice,
having him here. Mom thinks it's great and she's pushing it. I
don't know. I feel kind of like it would invade my privacy. I
found this school and have made a life for myself here. Let him
find his own school! But it could be great having my kid brother
here. I guess this is a classic case of what my psych teacher
calls ambivalence. Part of me wants him to come, and part of me
doesn't. (November 10)
```

The journal is a place for you to get in touch with the writer inside you. Although some instructors collect students' journals, you needn't be overly concerned with spelling, grammar, sentence structure, or organization. While journal writing is typically more structured than freewriting (see page 29), you don't have to strive for entries that read like mini-essays. On the contrary, sometimes you may find it helpful to use a simple list (see the journal entry on pages 19–20) when recording your thoughts about a subject. You may leave loose ends, drift to new topics, and evoke the personal and private without fully explaining or describing. The most important thing is to let your journal writing prompt reflection and insights.

Writing openly and fluently doesn't happen overnight; you need to keep at it. Try to complete a page-long journal entry three to five times a week. It's also a good idea to reread each week's entries to identify recurring themes and concerns. Keep a list of these issues at the back of your journal, under a heading like "Possible Essay Subjects." Here, for instance, are a few topics suggested by the preceding journal entry: deciding which college to attend, leaving home, sibling rivalry. Each of these topics could be developed in a full-length essay.

Using the journal to identify potential essay subjects helps you see that everyday life can be the source of meaningful writing. Most of us have become so accustomed to the routines of our lives that we cannot see the interesting in the ordinary. In *Walden*, a collection of journal entries, Henry David Thoreau wrote that our lives would be enriched immeasurably if we "employ[ed] a certain portion of each day looking back upon the time which has passed and in writing down . . . [our] thoughts and feelings." Keeping a journal does indeed foster an awareness of our own lives. It prevents us from thinking of ourselves as dull, dreary people to whom nothing happens. And it provides a wealth of material to draw on in our writing.

The Pre-Reading Journal Entry

To reinforce the value of journal writing, we've included a journal assignment before every selection in the book. This assignment, called the *Pre-Reading Journal Entry*, gets you ready for the piece by encouraging you to explore—in a tentative fashion—your thoughts about an issue that will be raised in the selection. Here, once again, is the *Pre-Reading Journal Entry* assignment that precedes Ellen Goodman's "Family Counterculture" (see page 7):

> Television is often blamed for having a harmful effect on children. Do you think this criticism is merited? In what ways does TV exert a negative influence on children? In what ways does TV exert a positive influence on youngsters? Take a few minutes to respond to these questions in your journal.

The following journal entry shows how one student, Harriet Davids, responded to the journal assignment. A thirty-eight-year-old college student and mother of two young teenagers, Harriet was understandably intrigued by the assignment. As you'll see, Harriet used a listing strategy to prepare her journal entry. She found that lists were perfect for dealing with the essentially "for or against" nature of the journal assignment.

TV's Negative Influence on Kids	TV's Positive Influence on Kids
Teaches negative behaviors (violence, sex, swearing, drugs, alcohol, etc.)	Teaches important educational concepts (Sesame Street, shows on The Learning Channel, etc.)
Cuts down on imagination and creativity	Exposes kids to new images and worlds (Reading Rainbow, Mister Rogers' Neighborhood)
Cuts down on time spent with parents (talking, reading, playing games together)	Can inspire important discussions (about morals, sexuality, drugs, etc.) between kids and parents
Encourages parents' lack of involvement with kids	Gives parents a needed break from kids
Frightens kids excessively by showing images of real-life violence (terrorist attacks, war, murders, etc.)	Educates kids about the painful realities in the world

Encourages isolation (watching screen rather than interacting with other kids)	Creates common ground among kids, basis of conversations and games
De-emphasizes reading and creates need for constant stimulation	Encourages kids to slow down and read books based on a TV series or show (the Arthur and the Clifford, the Big Red Dog series, The Bookworm Bunch, etc.)
Promotes materialism (commercials)	Can be used by parents to teach kids that they can't have everything they see

The journal assignment and subsequent journal entry do more than prepare you to read a selection with extra care and attention; they also pave the way to a full-length essay. Here's how. The final assignment following each selection is called *Writing Assignment Using a Journal Entry as a Starting Point.* This assignment helps you to translate the raw material in your journal entry into a thoughtful, well-considered essay. By the time you get to the assignment, the rough ideas in your journal entry will have been enriched by your reading of the selection. (For an example of a writing assignment that draws upon material in a pre-reading journal entry, turn to page 177.)

As you've just seen, journal writing can stimulate thinking in a loose, unstructured way; journal writing can also prompt the focused thinking required by a specific writing assignment. When you have a specific piece to write, you should approach prewriting in a purposeful, focused manner. You need to:

- Understand the boundaries of the assignment
- Determine your purpose, audience, tone, and point of view
- Discover your essay's limited subject
- Generate raw material about your limited subject
- Organize the raw material

We'll discuss each of these steps in turn. But first, here's a practical tip: If you don't use a word processor during the prewriting stage, try using a pencil and scrap paper. They're less intimidating than pen, typewriter, and "official" paper; they also reinforce the notion that prewriting is tentative and exploratory.

Understand the Boundaries of the Assignment

Most likely, you'll find considerable variety in your college writing assignments. Sometimes a professor will indicate that you can write on a topic of your own choosing; other times you may be given a highly specific assignment. Most assignments, though, will fit somewhere in between. In any case, you shouldn't start writing a paper until you know what's expected. First, clarify the *kind of paper* the instructor has in mind. Assume the instructor asks you to discuss the key ideas in an assigned reading. What exactly does the instructor want you to do? Should you include a brief summary of the selection? Should you compare the author's ideas with your own view of the subject? Should you determine if the author's view is supported by valid evidence? If you're not sure about an assignment, ask your instructor—not the student next to you, who may be as confused as you—to make the requirements clear. Most instructors are more than willing to provide an explanation. They would rather take a few minutes of class time to explain the assignment than spend hours reading dozens of student essays that miss the mark.

Second, find out *how long* the paper is expected to be. Many instructors will indicate the approximate length of the papers they assign. If no length requirements are provided, discuss with the instructor what you plan to cover and indicate how long you think your paper will be. The instructor will either give you the go-ahead or help you refine the direction and scope of your work.

Determine Your Purpose, Audience, Tone, and Point of View

Once you understand the requirements for a writing assignment, you're ready to begin thinking about the essay. What is its *purpose*? For what *audience* will it be written? What *tone* and *point of view* will you use? Later on, you may modify your decisions about these issues. That's fine. But you need to understand the way these considerations influence your work in the early phases of the writing process.

Purpose

Start by clarifying to yourself the essay's broad **purpose.** What do you want the essay to accomplish? The papers you write in college are usually meant to *inform* or *explain*, to *convince* or *persuade*, and sometimes to *entertain*.

In practice, writing often combines purposes. You might, for example, write an essay trying to *convince* people to support a new trash recycling program in your community. But before you win readers over, you most likely would have to *explain* something about current waste-disposal technology.

When purposes blend in this way, the predominant one influences the essay's content, organization, pattern of development, emphasis, and language. Assume you're writing about a political campaign. If your primary goal is to *entertain*, to take a gentle poke at two candidates, you might use the comparison-contrast pattern to organize your essay. You might, for example, start with several accounts of one candidate's "foot-in-mouth disease" and then describe the attempts of the other candidate, a multimillionaire, to portray himself as an average Joe. Your language, full of exaggeration, would reflect your objective. But if your primary purpose is to *persuade* readers that the candidates are incompetent and shouldn't be elected, you might adopt a serious, straightforward style. Selecting the argumentation-persuasion pattern to structure the essay, you might use one candidate's gaffes and the other's posturings to build a case that neither is worthy of public office.

Audience

Writing is a social act and thus implies a reader or an **audience.** To write effectively, you need to identify who your readers are and to take their expectations and needs into account. An essay about the artificial preservatives in the food served by the campus cafeteria would take one form if submitted to your chemistry professor and a very different form if written for the college newspaper. The chemistry paper would probably be formal and technical, complete with chemical formulations and scientific data: "Distillation revealed sodium benzoate particles suspended in a gelatinous medium." But such technical material would be inappropriate in a newspaper column intended for general readers. In this case, you might provide specific examples of cafeteria foods containing additives—"Those deliciously smoky cold cuts are loaded with nitrates and nitrites, both known to cause cancer in laboratory animals"—and suggest ways to eat more healthfully—"Pass by the deli counter and fill up instead on vegetarian pizza and fruit juices."

If you forget your readers, your essay can run into problems. Consider what happened when one student, Roger Salucci, submitted a draft of his essay to his instructor for feedback. The assignment was to write about an experience that demonstrated the value of education. Here's the opening paragraph from Roger's first draft:

```
 When I received my first page as an EMT, I realized pretty quickly
that all the weeks of KED and CPR training paid off. At first, when
the call came in, it was nerve city for this guy, I can tell you. When
the heat is on, my mind tends to go as blank as a TV screen at 2:00
a.m. in the morning. But I beat it to the van right away. After a
couple of false turns, my partner and I finally got the right house
and found a woman fibrillating and suffering severe myocardial
arrhythmia. Despite our anxiety, our heads were on straight; we knew
exactly what to do.
```

Roger's instructor found his essay unclear because she knew nothing about being an EMT (Emergency Medical Technician). When writing the essay, Roger neglected to consider his audience; specifically, he forgot that college instructors are no more knowledgeable than anyone else about subjects outside their special-ty. Roger's instructor also commented that she was thrown off guard by the paper's casual, slangy approach ("it was nerve city for this guy, I can tell you"; "I beat it to the van right away"). Roger used a breezy, colloquial style—almost as though he were chatting about the experience with friends—but the instructor had expected a more formal approach.

The more you know about your readers, the more you can adapt your writing to fit their needs and expectations. The accompanying checklist will help you analyze your audience.

☑ ANALYZING YOUR AUDIENCE: A CHECKLIST

☐ What are my readers' age, sex, and educational levels? How do these factors affect what I need to tell and don't need to tell my readers?

☐ What are my readers' political, religious, and other beliefs? How do these beliefs influence their attitudes and actions?

☐ What interests and needs motivate my audience?

☐ How much do my readers already know about my subject? Do they have any misconceptions?

☐ What biases do they have about me, my subject, and my opinion?

☐ How do my readers expect me to relate to them?

☐ What values do I share with my readers that will help me communicate with them?

Tone

Just as your voice may project a range of feelings, your writing can convey one or more **tones**, or emotional states: enthusiasm, anger, resignation, and so on. Tone isn't a decorative adornment tacked on as an afterthought. Rather, tone is integral to meaning. It permeates writing and reflects your attitude toward yourself, your purpose, your subject, and your readers.

In everyday conversation, vocal inflections, facial expressions, and body gestures help convey tone. In writing, how do you project tone without these aids? You pay close attention to *sentence structure* and *word choice*. In Chapter 8, we present detailed strategies for finetuning sentences and words during the revision stage. Here we simply want to help you see that determining your tone should come early in the writing process because the tone you select influences the sentences and words you use later.

Sentence structure refers to the way sentences are shaped. Although the two paragraphs that follow deal with exactly the same subject, note how differences in sentence structure create sharply dissimilar tones:

> During the 1960s, many inner-city minorities considered the police an occupying force and an oppressive agent of control. As a result, violence grew against police in poorer neighborhoods, as did the number of residents killed by police.

> An occupying force. An agent of control. An oppressor. That's how many inner-city minorities in the '60s viewed the police. Violence against police soared. Police killings of residents mounted.

Informative in its approach, the first paragraph projects a neutral, almost dispassionate tone. The sentences are fairly long, and clear transitions ("During the 1960s"; "As a result") mark the progression of thought. But the second paragraph, with its dramatic, almost alarmist tone, seems intended to elicit a strong emotional response; its short sentences, fragments, and abrupt transitions reflect the turbulence of earlier times.

Word choice also plays a role in establishing the tone of an essay. Words have **denotations,** neutral dictionary meanings, as well as **connotations,** emotional associations that go beyond the literal meaning. The word *beach*, for instance, is defined in the dictionary as "a nearly level stretch of pebbles and sand beside a body of water." This definition, however, doesn't capture individual responses to the word. For some, *beach* suggests warmth and relaxation; for others, it calls up images of hospital waste and sewage washed up on a once-clean stretch of shoreline.

Since tone and meaning are tightly bound, you must be sensitive to the emotional nuances of words. Think about some of the terms denoting *adult human female: woman, chick, broad, member of the fair sex*. While all of these words denote the same thing, their connotations—the pictures they call up—are sharply different. Similarly, in a respectful essay about police officers, you wouldn't refer to *cops, narcs,* or *flatfoots;* such terms convey a contempt inconsistent with the tone intended. Your words must also convey tone clearly; otherwise, meaning is lost. Suppose you're writing a satirical piece criticizing a local beauty pageant. Dubbing the participants "livestock on view" leaves no question about your tone. But if you simply referred to the participants as "attractive young women," readers might be unsure of your attitude. Remember, readers can't read your mind, only your paper.

Point of View

When you write, you speak to your audience as a unique individual. **Point of view** reveals the person you decide to be as you write. Like tone, point of view is closely tied to your purpose, audience, and subject. Imagine you want to convey to students in your composition class the way your grandfather's death—on your eighth birthday—impressed you with life's fragility. To capture that day's impact on you, you might tell what happened from the point of view of a child: "Today is my birthday. I'm eight. Grandpa died an hour before I was supposed to have my party." Or you might choose instead to recount the event speaking as the adult you are today: "My grandfather died an hour before my eighth birthday party." Your point of view will obviously affect the essay's content and organization.

The most strongly individualized point of view is the **first person** (*I, me, mine, we, us, our*). Because it focuses on the writer, the first-person point of view is appropriate in narrative and descriptive essays based on personal experience. It also suits other types of essays (for example, causal analyses and process analyses) when the bulk of evidence presented consists of personal observation. In such essays, avoiding the first person often leads to stilted sentences like "There was strong parental opposition to the decision" or "Although Organic Chemistry had been dreaded, it became a passion." In contrast, the sentences sound much more natural when the first person is used: "*Our* parents strongly opposed the decision" and "Although *I* had dreaded Organic Chemistry, it became *my* passion."

Like many students, you may feel that a lightning bolt will strike you if you use the first person when writing. Indeed, in high school, you may have been warned away from (even forbidden to use) the first person. And it does have its dangers. For one thing, in essays voicing an opinion, most first-person expressions ("I believe that . . ." and "In my opinion . . .") are unnecessary; the point of view stated is assumed to be the writer's unless another source is indicated. Second, in a paper intended to be an objective presentation of an issue, the first person distracts from the issue by drawing unwarranted attention to the writer: "I think it's important to realize that most violent crime in this country is directly related to substance abuse." By way of contrast, note how the matter under discussion is clearly highlighted when the first person is omitted: "Most violent crime in this country is directly related to substance abuse."

In some situations, writers use the **second person** (*you, your, yours*), alone or in combination with the first person. In fact, we frequently use forms of *you* in this book. For instance, we write, "If *you're* the kind of person who doodles while thinking, *you* may want to try mapping . . ." rather than "If a *writer* is the kind of person who doodles while thinking, *he* or *she* may want to try mapping. . . ." As you can see, the second person simplifies style and involves the reader in a more personal way. You'll also find that the *imperative* form of the verb ("*Send* letters of protest to the television networks") engages readers in much the same way. The implied *you* speaks to the audience directly and lends immediacy to the directions. Despite these advantages, the second-person point of view often isn't appropriate in many college courses where more formal, less conversational writing is called for.

The **third-person** point of view is by far the most common in academic writing. The third person gets its name from the stance it conveys—that of an outsider or "third person" observing and reporting on matters of primarily public rather than private importance: "The international team of negotiators failed to resolve the border dispute between the two nations." In discussions of historical events, scientific phenomena, works of art, and the like, the third-person point of view conveys a feeling of distance and objectivity. When you write in the third person, though, don't adopt such a detached stance that you end up using a stiff, artificial style: "On this campus, approximately two-thirds of the student body is dependent on bicycles as the primary mode of transportation to class." Aim instead for a more natural and personable quality: "Two-thirds of the students on campus ride their bikes to class." (For a more detailed discussion of levels of formality, see pages 119–121 in Chapter 8.)

Discover Your Essay's Limited Subject

Once you have a firm grasp of the assignment's boundaries and have determined your purpose, audience, tone, and point of view, you're ready to focus on a **limited subject** of the general assignment. Because too broad a subject can result in a diffuse, rambling essay, be sure to restrict your general subject before starting to write.

The following examples show the difference between general subjects that are too broad for an essay and limited subjects that are appropriate and workable. The examples, of course, represent only a few among many possibilities.

General Subject	Less General	Limited Subject
Education	Computers in education	Computers in elementary school arithmetic classes
	High school education	High school electives
Transportation	Low-cost travel	Hitchhiking
	Getting around a metropolitan area	The transit system in a nearby city
Work	Planning for a career	College internships
	Women in the work force	Women's success as managers

How do you move from a general to a narrow subject? Imagine that you're asked to prepare a straightforward, informative essay for your writing class. The assignment, prompted by Ellen Goodman's essay "Family Counterculture" (page 7), is an extension of the journal-writing assignment on page 12.

> Goodman implies that, in some ways, today's world is hostile to children. Do you agree? Drawing upon but not limiting yourself to the material in your pre-reading journal, write an essay in which you support or reject this viewpoint.

You might feel unsure about how to proceed. But two techniques can help you limit such a general assignment. Keeping your purpose, audience, tone, and point of view in mind, you may **question** or **brainstorm** the general subject. These two techniques have a paradoxical effect. Although they encourage you to roam freely over a subject, they also help restrict the discussion by revealing which aspects of the subject interest you most.

Question the General Subject

One way to narrow a subject is to ask a series of *who, how, why, where, when,* and *what* questions. The following example shows how Harriet Davids, the mother of two young teenagers, used this technique to limit the Goodman assignment.

> Student essay in progress

You may recall that, before reading Goodman's essay, Harriet had used her journal to explore TV's effect on children (see pages 19–20). After reading "Family Counterculture," Harriet concluded that she essentially agreed with Goodman; like Goodman, she felt that parents nowadays are indeed forced to raise their children in an "increasingly hostile environment." She was pleased that the writing assignment gave her an opportunity to expand preliminary ideas she had jotted down in her journal.

Harriet realized that she had to narrow the Goodman assignment. She started by asking a number of pointed questions about the general topic. As she proceeded, she was aware that the same questions could have led to different limited subjects—just as other questions would have.

General Assignment: We live in a world that is difficult, even hostile toward children.

Question	Limited Subject
<u>Who</u> is to blame for the difficult conditions under which children grow up?	Parents' casual attitude toward child rearing
<u>How</u> have schools contributed to the problems children face?	Not enough counseling programs for kids in distress
<u>Why</u> do children feel frightened?	Divorce
<u>Where</u> do kids go to escape?	Television, which makes the world seem even more dangerous
<u>When</u> are children most vulnerable?	The special problems of adolescents
<u>What</u> dangers or fears should parents discuss with their children?	AIDS, drugs, alcohol, war, terrorism

Brainstorm the General Subject

Another way to focus on a limited subject is to list quickly everything about the general topic that pops into your mind. Working vertically down the page, jot down brief words, phrases, and abbreviations to capture your free-floating thoughts. Writing in complete sentences will slow you down. Don't try to organize or censor your ideas. Even the most fleeting, random, or seemingly outrageous thoughts can be productive.

Here's an example of the brainstorming that Harriet Davids decided to do in an effort to gather even more material for the Goodman assignment:

> Student essay in progress

General Subject: We live in a world that is difficult, even hostile toward children.

TV--shows corrupt politicians, casual sex, drugs, alcohol, foul language, violence

Real-life violence on TV, esp. terrorist attacks and war, scares kids--have nightmares!

Kids babysat by TV

Not enough guidance from parents

Kids raise selves

Too many divorces

Parents squabbling over material goods in settlements

Money too important

Kids feel unimportant

Families move a lot

I moved in fourth grade--hated it

Rootless feeling

Nobody graduates from high school in the same district in
which they went to kindergarten

Drug abuse all over, in little kids' schools

Pop music glorifies drugs

Kids not innocent--know too much

Single-parent homes

Day-care problems

Abuse of little kids in day care

TV coverage of day-care abuse frightens kids

Perfect families on TV make kids feel inadequate

As you can see, questioning and brainstorming suggest many possible limited
subjects. To identify especially promising ones, reread your material with pen or
pencil in hand. What arouses your interest, anger, or curiosity? What themes seem
to dominate and cut to the heart of the matter? Star or circle ideas with potential.
Be sure to pay close attention to material generated at the end of your questioning
and brainstorming. Often your mind takes a few minutes to warm up, with the
best ideas popping out last.

<table>
<tr><td>Student
essay in
progress</td></tr>
</table>

After marking the material, write several phrases or sentences summarizing
the most promising limited subjects. These, for example, are just a few that
emerged from Harriet Davids's questioning and brainstorming the Goodman
assignment:

TV partly to blame for children having such a hard time

Relocation stressful to children

Schools also at fault

The special problems that parents face raising children today

Harriet decided to write on the last of these limited subjects. This topic, in turn,
is the focus of our discussion on the pages ahead.

Generate Raw Material About Your Limited Subject

When a limited subject strikes you as having possibilities, your next step is to
begin generating material about that topic. If you do this now, in the prewriting
stage, you'll find it easier to write the paper later on. Since you'll already have
amassed much of the material for your essay, you'll be able to concentrate on other
matters—say, finding just the right words to convey your ideas. Taking the time
to sound out your limited subject during the prewriting stage also means you
won't find yourself halfway through the first draft without much to say.

To generate raw material, you may use *freewriting, brainstorming, mapping,* and
other techniques.

Freewrite on Your Limited Subject

Although freewriting can help you narrow a general subject, it's more valuable once you have limited your topic. **Freewriting** means jotting down in rough sentences or phrases everything that comes to mind. Although freewriting looks like regular prose because it is recorded horizontally, from margin to margin, it's much more fragmented. As you freewrite, you get swept along and go wherever your thoughts take you. You may skip back and forth between ideas, taking off in a more focused manner when you stumble across something interesting.

To capture this continuous stream of thought, write nonstop for ten minutes or more. Don't censor anything; put down whatever pops into your head. Don't reread, edit, or pay attention to organization, spelling, or grammar. If your mind goes blank, repeat words until another thought emerges.

Consider part of the freewriting that Harriet Davids generated about her limited subject, "The special problems that parents face raising children today":

> Student essay in progress

```
Parents today have tough problems to face. Lots of dangers.
Drugs and alcohol for one thing. Also crimes of violence against
kids. Parents also have to keep up with cost of living, everything
costs more, kids want and expect more. Television? Another thing
is Playboy, Penthouse. Sexy ads on TV, movies deal with sex. Kids
grow up too fast, too fast. Drugs. Witness real-life violence on
TV, like terrorist attacks. Little kids can't handle knowing too
much at an early age. Both parents at work much of the day.
Finding good day care a real problem. Lots of latchkey kids.
Another problem is getting kids to do homework, lots of other
things to do. Especially like going to the mall! When I was young,
we did homework after dinner, no excuses accepted by my parents.
```

Brainstorm Your Limited Subject

Let your mind wander freely, as you did when narrowing your general subject. This time, though, list every idea, fact, and example that occurs to you about your limited subject. Use brief words and phrases, so you don't get bogged down writing full sentences. For now, don't worry whether ideas fit together or whether the points listed make sense.

To gather additional material on her limited subject for the Goodman assignment ("The special problems that parents face raising children today"), Harriet brainstormed the following list:

> Student essay in progress

```
Trying to raise kids when both parents work
Prices of everything outrageous, even when both parents work
Commercials make everyone want more of everything
```

```
Clothes so important
Day care not always the answer--cases of abuse
Day care very expensive
Sex everywhere--TV, movies, magazines, Internet
Sexy clothes on little kids. Absurd!
Sexual abuse of kids
Violence on TV, esp. images of real-life terrorist attacks
--scary for kids!
Violence against kids when parents abuse drugs
Acid, "Ecstasy," heroin, cocaine, AIDS
Schools have to teach kids about these things
Schools doing too much--not as good as they used to be
Not enough homework assigned--kids unprepared
Distractions from homework--malls, TV, phones, stereos, MTV,
Internet, computer games
```

Use Group Brainstorming

Brainstorming can also be conducted as a group activity. Thrashing out ideas with other people stretches the imagination, revealing possibilities you may not have considered on your own. Group brainstorming doesn't have to be conducted in a formal classroom situation. You can bounce ideas around with friends and family anywhere—over lunch, at the student center, and so on.

Map Out the Limited Subject

If you're the kind of person who doodles while thinking, you may want to try **mapping,** sometimes called **diagraming** or **clustering.** Like other prewriting techniques, mapping proceeds rapidly and encourages the free flow of ideas.

Begin by expressing your limited subject in a crisp phrase and placing it in the center of a blank sheet of paper. As ideas come to you, put them along lines or in boxes or circles around the limited subject. Draw arrows and lines to show the relationships among ideas. Don't stop there, however. Focus on each idea; as subpoints and details come to you, connect them to their source idea, again using boxes, lines, circles, or arrows to clarify how everything relates.

On the next page is an example of the kind of map that Harriet Davids could have drawn to generate material for her limited subject based on the Goodman assignment.

There's no right or wrong way to do mapping. Sometimes you'll move from the limited subject to a key related idea and all the details it prompts before moving to the next key idea; other times you'll map all the major divisions of a limited subject before mapping the details of any one idea.

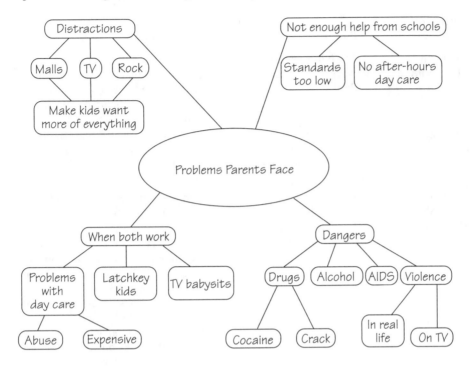

Use the Patterns of Development

Throughout this book, we show how writers use various **patterns of development,** singly or in combination, to develop and organize their ideas. Because each pattern has its own distinctive logic, the patterns encourage you to think about a limited subject in surprising new ways.

The various patterns of development are discussed in detail in Chapters 10–19 of Part III. At this point, though, you should find the following chart helpful. It not only summarizes the broad purpose of each pattern but also shows the way each pattern could generate different raw material for the limited subject of Harriet Davids's essay.

Limited Subject: The special problems that parents face raising children today.

Pattern of Development	Purpose	Raw Material
Description	To detail what a person, place, or object is like	Detail the sights and sounds of a glitzy mall that attracts lots of kids
Narration	To relate an event	Recount what happened when neighbors tried to forbid their kids to go to a rock concert
Illustration	To provide specific instances or examples	Offer examples of family arguments nowadays: Can a friend known to use drugs visit? Will permission be given to go to a party where alcohol will be served? Can parents outlaw MTV?

Pattern of Development	Purpose	Raw Material
Division-classification	To divide something into parts or to group related things into categories	Identify the components of a TV commercial that distorts kids' values Classify the kinds of commercials that make it difficult to teach kids values
Process analysis	To explain how something happens or how something is done	Explain step by step how family life can disintegrate when parents have to work all the time to make ends meet
Comparison-contrast	To point out similarities and/or dissimilarities	Contrast families today with those of a generation ago
Cause-effect	To analyze reasons and consequences	Explain why parents are not around to be with their kids: industry's failure to provide day care and its inflexibility about granting time off for parents with sick kids Explain the consequences of absentee parents: Kids feel unloved; they turn to TV for role models; they're undisciplined; they take on adult responsibility too early
Definition	To explain the meaning of a term or concept	What is meant by "tough love"
Argumentation-persuasion	To win people over to a point of view	Convince parents that they must work with the schools to develop programs that make kids feel safer and more secure

(For more on ways to use the patterns of development in different phases of the writing process, see pages 40, 47–48, 54–55, 67–68, and Chapter 10.)

Conduct Research

Some limited subjects (for example, "Industry's day-care policies") can be developed only if you do some research. You may conduct **primary research,** in which you interview experts, conduct your own studies, compile your own statistics, and the like. Or you may conduct **secondary research,** in which you visit the library and/or go online to identify books and articles about your limited subject. (See pages 519–521 in Part IV on how to conduct research.) At this point, you don't need to read closely the material you find. Just skim and perhaps take a few brief notes on ideas and points that could be useful.

In researching the Goodman assignment, for instance, Harriet Davids could look under the following headings and subheadings:

> Student essay in progress

Day care
Drug abuse
Family
Parent-child relationship
    Child abuse
    Children of divorced parents
    Children of working mothers
School and home

Organize the Raw Material

Some students prefer to wait until after they have formulated a thesis to shape their prewriting material. (For information on thesis statements, see Chapter 3.) But if you find that imposing a preliminary order on your prewriting provides the focus needed to devise an effective thesis, you'll probably want to prepare a **scratch list** or **outline** at this point. In Chapter 5, we talk about the more formal outline you may need later on in the writing process (pages 57–60). Here we show how a rough outline or scratch list can help shape the tentative ideas generated during prewriting.

As you reread your exploratory thoughts about the limited subject, keep the following questions in mind: What *purpose* have you decided on? What are the characteristics of your *audience?* What *tone* will be effective in achieving your purpose with your audience? What *point of view* will you adopt? Record your responses to these questions at the top of your prewriting material.

Now go to work on the raw material itself. Cross out anything not appropriate for your purpose, audience, tone, and point of view; add points that didn't originally occur to you. Star or circle compelling items that warrant further development. Then draw arrows between related items, your goal being to group such material under a common heading. Finally, determine what seems to be the best order for the headings.

By giving you a sense of the way your free-form material might fit together, a scratch outline makes the writing process more manageable. You're less likely to feel overwhelmed once you actually start writing because you'll already have some idea about how to shape your material into a meaningful statement. Remember, though, the scratch outline can, and most likely will, be modified along the way.

Harriet Davids's handwritten annotations on her brainstormed list (page 34) illustrate the way Harriet began shaping her raw prewriting material. Note how she started by recording at the top her limited subject as well as her decisions about purpose, audience, tone, and point of view. Next, she crossed out the material she didn't want to use. For instance, Harriet decided that the example of violence, such as terrorism, on TV was too complex to include it in her essay, so she crossed it out. Note how clear supporting points emerged after she grouped together similar ideas.

Student essay in progress

Purpose: To inform

Audience: Instructor as well as class members, most of
whom are 18-20 years old

Tone: Serious and straightforward

Point of view: Third person (mother of two teenage girls)

Limited subject: The special problems that parents face raising children today

① Day Care

Trying to raise kids when both parents work

Prices of everything outrageous, even when both parents work

Commercials make everyone want more of everything

Clothes so important

Day care not always the answer--cases of abuse *problems—before and after school*

Day care very expensive

③ Sexual
material
everywhere

Sex everywhere--TV, movies, magazines, Internet

Sexy clothes on little kids. Absurd!

Sexual abuse of kids

④ Dangers

Violence on TV, esp. images of real-life terrorist attacks
--scary for kids!

Violence against kids when parents abuse drugs

Acid, "Ecstasy," heroin, cocaine, AIDS—*also drinking*

Schools have to teach kids about these things

Schools doing too much--not as good as they used to be

Not enough homework assigned--kids unprepared

② Homework
distractions

Distractions from homework--malls, TV, phones, stereos, MTV,
Internet, computer games *video arcades, rock concerts*

The following scratch outline shows how Harriet began to shape her prewriting into a more organized format. (If you'd like to see Harriet's more formal
outline and her first draft, turn to pages 59–60 and 83–84.)

Purpose: To inform

Audience: Instructor as well as class members, most of whom
are 18-20 years old

Tone: Serious and straightforward

Point of view: Third person (mother of two teenage girls)

Limited subject: The special problems that parents face raising children today

1. Day care for two-career families

   • Expensive

   • Before-school problems

   • After-school problems

2. Distractions from homework

   • Stereos, televisions, computers, phones in room at home

- Places to go--malls, video arcades, fast-food restaurants, rock concerts

3. Sexually explicit materials
   - Magazines and books
   - Internet
   - Television shows
   - MTV
   - Movies

4. Life-threatening dangers
   - Drugs
   - Drinking
   - AIDS
   - Violence against children (by sitters, in day care, etc.)

Continues on page 39

The prewriting strategies described in this chapter provide a solid foundation for the next stages of your work. But invention and imaginative exploration don't end when prewriting is completed. As you'll see, remaining open to new ideas is crucial during all phases of the writing process.

ACTIVITIES: GETTING STARTED THROUGH PREWRITING

1. Number the items in each set from 1 (*broadest subject*) to 5 (*most limited subject*):

   Set A
   Abortion
   Controversial social issue
   Cutting state abortion funds
   Federal funding of abortions
   Social issues

   Set B
   Business majors
   Students' majors
   College students
   Kinds of students on campus
   Why students major in business

2. Which of the following topics are too broad for an essay of two to five type-written pages: soap operas' appeal to college students; day care; trying to "kick" junk food; male and female relationships; international terrorism?

3. Assume you're writing essays on two of the topics below. For each one, explain how you might adapt your purpose, tone, and point of view to the audiences indicated in parentheses. (You may find it helpful to work with others on this activity.)

   a. Overcoming shyness (ten-year-olds; teachers of ten-year-olds; young singles living in large apartment buildings)
   b. Telephone solicitations (people training for a job in this field; homeowners; readers of a humorous magazine)
   c. Smoking (people who have quit; smokers; elementary school children)

4. Choose one of the following general topics for a roughly five-hundred-word essay. Then use the prewriting technique indicated in parentheses to identify several limited topics. Next, with the help of one or more patterns of development, generate raw material on the limited subject you consider most interesting.

   a. Friendship (*journal writing*)
   b. Malls (*mapping*)
   c. Leisure (*freewriting*)
   d. Television (*brainstorming*)
   e. Required courses (*group brainstorming*)
   f. Manners (*questioning*)

5. For each set of limited subjects and purposes that follows, determine which pattern(s) of development would be most useful. (Save this material so you can work with it further after reading the next chapter.)

   a. The failure of recycling efforts on campus
      Purpose: to explain why students and faculty tend to disregard recycling guidelines
   b. The worst personality trait that a teacher, parent, boss, or friend can have
      Purpose: to poke fun at this personality trait
   c. The importance of being knowledgeable about national affairs
      Purpose: to convince students to stay informed about current events

6. Select *one* of the following limited subjects. Then, given the purpose and audience indicated, draft a paragraph using the first-, second-, or third-person point of view. Next, rewrite the paragraph two more times, each time using a different point of view. What differences do you see in the three versions? Which version do you prefer? Why?

   a. American action movies like *The Terminator* and *Lethal Weapon*
      Purpose: to defend the enjoyment of such films
      Audience: those who like foreign "art" films

b. Senioritis

Purpose: to explain why high school seniors lose interest in school
Audience: parents and teachers

c. Television commercials aimed at teens and young adults

Purpose: to make fun of the commercials' persuasive appeals
Audience: advertising executives

7. Select *one* of the following general subjects. Keeping in mind the indicated purpose, audience, tone, and point of view, use a prewriting technique to limit the subject. Next, by means of another prewriting strategy, generate relevant information about the restricted topic. Finally, shape your raw material into a scratch outline—crossing out, combining, and adding ideas as needed. (Save your scratch outline so you can work with it further after reading the next chapter.)

a. Rock music

Purpose: to explain its attraction
Audience: classical music fans
Tone: playful
Writer's point of view: a rock fan

b. Becoming a volunteer

Purpose: to recruit
Audience: ambitious young professionals
Tone: straightforward
Writer's point of view: head of a volunteer organization

c. Sexist attitudes in music videos

Purpose: to inform
Audience: teenagers of both sexes
Tone: objective but with some emotion
Writer's point of view: a teenage male

d. Major problems in high school education

Purpose: to create awareness of the problems
Audience: teachers
Tone: serious and concerned
Writer's point of view: a former high school student

3
IDENTIFYING
A THESIS

The process of prewriting—discovering a limited subject and generating ideas about it—prepares you for the next stage in writing an essay: identifying the paper's *thesis,* or controlling idea.

WHAT IS A THESIS?

Presenting your position on a subject, the **thesis** should focus on an interesting and significant issue, one that engages your energies and merits your consideration. You may think of the thesis as the essay's hub—the central point around which all the other material revolves. Your thesis determines what does and does not belong in the essay. The thesis, especially when it occurs early in an essay, also helps focus the reader on the piece's central point and thus helps you achieve your writing purpose.

FINDING A THESIS

Sometimes the thesis emerges early in the prewriting stage, particularly if a special angle on your limited topic sparks your interest or becomes readily apparent. Often, though, you'll need to do some work to determine your thesis. For some topics, you may need to do some library research. For other subjects, the best way to identify a promising thesis is to look through your prewriting and ask yourself questions like these: "What statement does all this prewriting support? What aspect of the limited subject is covered in most detail? What is the focus of the most provocative material?"

For a look at the process of finding the thesis within prewriting material, glance back in Chapter 2 at the annotated brainstorming (page 34) and the resulting scratch outline (pages 34–35) that Harriet Davids prepared for her limited subject, "The special problems that parents face raising children today." Harriet eventually devised the following thesis to capture the focus of her prewriting: "Being a parent today is much more difficult than it was a generation ago." (For more on how Harriet arrived at her thesis, see page 42.)

Student essay in progress

Sometimes the thesis won't be easy to pinpoint. Indeed, you may find that you need to refocus your thesis as you move through the stages of the writing process. To see how this progressive clarification might work, imagine you're writing a paper about adjusting to the academic demands of college life. After looking over your prewriting, you might identify this preliminary thesis: "Many college students flounder during the first semester because they have trouble adjusting to the amount of work required by their professors." However, once you start writing the essay, you might realize that students' increased personal freedom, not their increased workload, is the primary problem. You would revise your thesis accordingly: "Many college students flounder the first semester because they become so distracted by new freedoms in their personal lives that they don't give enough attention to academics."

WRITING AN EFFECTIVE THESIS

What makes a thesis effective? Generally expressed in one or two sentences, a thesis statement often has two parts. One part presents your paper's *limited subject*; the other presents your *point of view*, or *attitude*, about that subject. Here are some examples of the way you might move from general subject to limited subject to thesis statement. In each thesis statement, the limited subject is underlined once and the attitude twice.

General Subject	Limited Subject	Thesis Statement
Education	Computers in elementary school arithmetic classes	Computer programs in arithmetic can individualize instruction more effectively than the average elementary school teacher can.
Transportation	A metropolitan transit system	Although the city's transit system still has problems, it has become safer and more efficient in the last two years.
Work	College internships	The college internship program has had positive consequences for students.
Drugs	Driving while intoxicated	Individuals found guilty of drunk driving should have their licenses revoked for five years.

Tone and Point of View

An effective thesis establishes a tone and point of view suitable for a given purpose and audience. If you're writing an essay arguing that multimedia equipment can never replace a live teacher in the classroom, you need to frame a thesis that matches your and your readers' concerns about the subject. Instead of breezily writing, "Parents, schoolboards, principals: ditch the boob tube and the cutesy interactive computer and put the bucks where it counts—in teachers," you would aim for a more thoughtful and serious tone: "Education won't be improved by purchasing more electronic teaching tools but by allocating more money to hire and develop good teachers."

Implied Pattern of Development

On page 21, we show how an essay's purpose may suggest a pattern of development. In the same way, an effective thesis may point the way to a pattern of development that would be appropriate for developing the essay. Consider the thesis statements in the preceding list. The first thesis might use *comparison-contrast*; the second *illustration*; the third *cause-effect*; and the fourth *argumentation-persuasion*. (For more information about the relationship between an essay's purpose and its pattern of development, see the chart on pages 31–32.)

Including a Plan of Development

Sometimes a thesis will include a **plan of development:** a concise *overview of the essay's main points in the exact order* in which those points will be discussed. To incorporate a plan of development into your thesis, use single words or brief phrases that convey—in a nutshell—your essay's key points; then add those summarized points to the end of the thesis, being sure to present them in the order they will appear in the essay. Note, for example, the way a plan of development (in italics) is included in the following thesis: "Baseball's inflated salaries hurt *the fans, the sport, and most of all, the athletes.*"

A thesis with a plan of development is an effective strategy for keeping readers focused on an essay's main points. If you decide to prepare such a thesis, be careful not to overload it with too much information. Rather than writing "An after-school job can promote a sense of responsibility in young people, teach important human-relations skills, and create awareness of career options," tighten the plan of development so it reads more crisply: "An after-school job develops responsibility, human-relations skills, and an awareness of career options."

If the essay's key points resist your efforts to reduce them to crisp phrases, you can place the plan of development in a separate sentence, directly *after* the thesis. Consider the plan of development (in italics) that comes after the following thesis: "Many parents have unrealistic expectations for their children. These parents want their children to *accept their values, follow their paths, and succeed where they have failed.*" Note that the points in a plan of development are expressed in grammatically parallel terms: The plan of development for the paper on baseball salaries contains nouns in series ("the fans," "the sport," "the athletes"), while the plan of development for the paper on parental expectations contains verb phrases ("accept their values," "follow their paths," "succeed where they have failed").

Because preparing an effective thesis is such a critical step in writing a sharply focused essay, you need to avoid the following four common problems.

1. Don't Write a Highly Opinionated Statement

Although your thesis should express your attitude toward your subject, don't go overboard and write a dogmatic, overstated thesis: "With characteristic clumsiness, campus officials bumbled their way through the recent budget crisis." A more moderate thesis can make the same point, *without alienating readers:* "Campus officials had trouble managing the recent budget crisis effectively."

2. Don't Make an Announcement

Some writers use the thesis statement merely to announce the limited subject of their paper and forget to indicate their attitude toward the subject. Such statements are announcements of intent, not thesis statements.

Compare the following three announcements with the thesis statements beside them:

Announcement	Thesis Statement
My essay will discuss whether a student pub should exist on campus.	This college should not allow a student pub on campus.
Handgun legislation will be the subject of my paper.	Banning handguns is the first step toward controlling crime in America.
I want to discuss cable television.	Cable television has not delivered on its promise to provide an alternative to network programming.

3. Don't Make a Factual Statement

Your thesis and thus your essay should focus on an issue capable of being developed. If a fact is used as a thesis, you have no place to go; a fact generally doesn't invite much discussion.

Notice the difference between the following factual statements and thesis statements:

Factual Statement	Thesis Statement
Many businesses pollute the environment.	Tax penalties should be levied against businesses that pollute the environment.
Movies nowadays are often violent.	Movie violence provides a healthy outlet for aggression.
America's population is growing older.	The aging of the American population will eventually create a crisis in the delivery of health-care services.

4. Don't Make a Broad Statement

Avoid stating your thesis in vague, general, or sweeping terms. Broad statements make it difficult for readers to grasp your essay's point. Moreover, if you start with a broad thesis, you're saddled with the impossible task of trying to develop a book-length idea with an essay that runs only several pages.

The following examples contrast thesis statements that are too broad with effectively focused statements:

Broad Statement	Thesis Statement
Nowadays, high school education is often meaningless.	High school diplomas have been devalued by grade inflation.
Newspapers cater to the taste of the American public.	The success of *USA Today* indicates that people want newspapers that are easy to read and entertaining.
The computer revolution is not all that we have been led to believe it is.	Home computers are still an impractical purchase for many people.

ARRIVING AT AN EFFECTIVE THESIS

Student essay in progress

On pages 38–39, we discussed the basic process for finding a thesis; we also pointed out how Harriet Davids—after reviewing her prewriting—identified her paper's thesis: "Being a parent today is much more difficult than it was a generation ago." But Harriet didn't discover her thesis immediately; she went through several stages before she came up with the final wording. The following paragraph describes the steps Harriet took when formulating her essay's central point. In all likelihood, you too will need to experiment a bit before arriving at an effective thesis.

Starting with her limited subject ("The special problems that parents face raising children today"), Harriet at first worded her thesis to read "My essay will show that raising children today is a horror show compared to how it was when my parents raised me." As soon as she read what she had written, Harriet saw that she had prepared an *announcement* rather than a thesis. Rephrasing the statement to do away with the announcement, she next wrote "Raising children today is a horror show compared to how it was when my parents raised me." When Harriet read this version out loud, she was pleased to hear that the rewording eliminated the announcement—but she was surprised to discover that the rephrasing highlighted two problems she hadn't detected earlier. For one thing, her statement was *highly opinionated* and *slangy* ("horror show"). Second, the statement *misrepresented* what she intended to do by suggesting—incorrectly—that she was going to (1) discuss the child-rearing process and (2) contrast her parents' and her own child-raising experiences. She planned to do neither. Instead, she intended to (1) emphasize parenthood's challenges and (2) address—in a general way—the difference between parenting today and parenting years ago. So, recasting her statement

Continues on page 49

one more time to eliminate these problems, Harriet arrived at the final wording of her thesis: "Being a parent today is much more difficult than it was a generation ago."

PLACING THE THESIS IN AN ESSAY

The thesis is often located in the middle or at the end of the introduction. But considerations about audience, purpose, and tone should always guide your decision about its placement. You may, for example, choose to delay the thesis if you feel that background information needs to be provided before readers can fully understand your key point—especially if the concept is complex and best taken in slowly. Similarly, if you sense your audience is resistant to your thesis, you may wish to lead readers to it gradually. Conversely, if you feel that readers would appreciate a direct, forthright approach, you might place the thesis early in the essay—perhaps even at the very beginning of the introduction.

Sometimes the thesis is reiterated—using fresh words—in the essay's conclusion or elsewhere. If done well, this repetition keeps readers focused on the essay's key point. You may even leave the thesis implied, relying on strong support, tone, and style to convey the essay's central idea.

One final point: Once you start writing your first draft, some feelings, thoughts, and examples may emerge that modify, even contradict, your initial thesis. Don't resist these new ideas. Keep them in mind as you revise the thesis and—in the process—move toward a more valid and richer view of your subject.

ACTIVITIES:
IDENTIFYING
A THESIS

1. For each of the following limited subjects, four possible thesis statements are given. Indicate whether each thesis is an announcement (A), a factual statement (FS), too broad a statement (TB), or an acceptable thesis (OK). Revise the flawed statements. Then, for each effective thesis statement, identify a possible purpose, audience, tone, and point of view.

   a. *Limited subject:* The ethics of treating severely disabled infants

   • Some babies born with severe disabilities have been allowed to die.

   • There are many serious issues involved in the treatment of newborns with disabilities.

- The government should pass legislation requiring medical treatment for newborns with disabilities.
- This essay will analyze the controversy surrounding the treatment of severely disabled babies who would die without medical care.

  b. *Limited subject:* Privacy and computerized records

- Computers raise some significant questions for all of us.
- Computerized records keep track of consumer spending habits, credit records, travel patterns, and other personal information.
- Computerized records have turned our private lives into public property.
- In this paper, the relationship between computerized records and the right to privacy will be discussed.

2. Turn back to activity 5 on page 36. For each set of limited subjects listed there, develop an effective thesis. Select *one* of the thesis statements. Then, keeping in mind the purpose indicated and the pattern of development you identified earlier, draft a paragraph developing the point expressed in the thesis. (Save the paragraph so you can work with it further after reading the next chapter.)

3. Following are four pairs of general and limited subjects. Generate an appropriate thesis for each pair. Select one of the thesis statements, and determine which pattern of development would support the thesis most effectively. Use that pattern to draft a paragraph developing the thesis. (Save the paragraph so you can work with it further after reading the next chapter.)

General Subject	Limited Subject
Psychology	The power struggles in a classroom
Health	Doctors' attitudes toward patients
The elderly	Television's depiction of the elderly
Work	Minimum-wage jobs for young people

4. Each set that follows lists the key points for an essay. Based on the information provided, prepare a possible thesis for each essay. Then propose a possible purpose, audience, tone, and point of view.

   Set A

- One evidence of this growing conservatism is the re-emerging popularity of fraternities and sororities.
- Beauty contests, ROTC training, and corporate recruiting—once rejected by students on many campuses—are again popular.
- Most important, many students no longer choose possibly risky careers that enable them to contribute to society but instead select safe fields with money-making potential.

   Set B

- We do not know how engineering new forms of life might affect the earth's delicate ecological balance.

- Another danger of genetic research is its potential for unleashing new forms of disease.
- Even beneficial attempts to eliminate genetic defects could contribute to the dangerous idea that only perfect individuals are entitled to live.

5. Keep a journal for several weeks. Then reread a number of entries, identifying two or three recurring themes or subjects. Narrow the subjects and, for each one, generate possible thesis statements. Finally, using an appropriate pattern of development, draft a paragraph for one of the thesis statements. (Save the paragraph so you can work with it further after reading the next chapter.)

6. Select a broad topic—either your own or one of the following: animals, popularity, the homeless, money, fashion trends, race relations, parties. Working with a partner, use a prewriting technique to narrow the topic so that it's suitable for an essay of two to five typed pages. Using another prewriting strategy, generate details on the limited topic. Next, examine the material and identify at least two possible thesis statements. Then, for each thesis, reshape your prewriting, determining which items are appropriate, which are not, and where more material is needed.

7. Return to the scratch outline you prepared in response to activity 7 on page 37. After examining the outline, identify a thesis that conveys the central idea behind most of the raw material. Then, ask others to evaluate your thesis in light of the material in your scratch outline. Finally, keeping the thesis—as well as your purpose, audience, and tone—in mind, refine the scratch outline by deleting inappropriate items, adding relevant ones, and indicating where more material is needed. (Save your refined scratch outline and thesis so you can work with them further after reading the next chapter.)

4
SUPPORTING THE THESIS WITH EVIDENCE

After identifying a preliminary thesis, you should develop the evidence need-ed to support that central idea. This supporting material grounds your essay, showing readers you have good reason for feeling as you do about your subject. Your evidence also adds interest and color to your writing.

In college essays of 500 to 1,500 words, you usually need at least three major points of evidence to develop your thesis. These major points—each focusing on related but separate aspects of the thesis—eventually become the supporting paragraphs (see pages 65–75) in the body of the essay.

WHAT IS EVIDENCE?

By **evidence,** we mean a number of different kinds of support. *Reasons* are just one option. To develop your thesis, you might also include *examples, facts, details, statistics, personal observation* or *experience, anecdotes,* and *expert opinions* and *quota-tions* (gathered from books, articles, interviews, documentaries, and the like). Imagine you're writing an essay with the thesis, "People normally unconcerned about the environment can be galvanized to constructive action if they feel per-sonally affected by an environmental problem." You could support this thesis with any combination of the following types of evidence:

- *Reasons* why people become involved in the environmental movement: they believe the situation endangers the health of their families; they fear the value of their homes will plummet; they feel deceived by officials' assurances that there's nothing to worry about.

- *Examples* of neighborhood recycling efforts succeeding in communities once plagued by trash-disposal problems.

- *Facts* about residents' efforts to preserve the quality of well water in a community undergoing widespread industrial development.

- *Details* about the specific steps the average person can take to get involved in environmental issues.

- *Statistics* showing the growing number of Americans concerned about the environment.

- A *personal experience* telling about the way you became involved in an effort to stop a local business from dumping waste into a neighborhood stream.

- An *anecdote* about an ordinarily apathetic friend who protested the commercial development of a wooded area where he jogs.

- A *quotation* from a well-known scientist about the considerable impact that well-organized, well-informed citizens can have on environmental legislation.

HOW DO YOU FIND EVIDENCE?

Where do you find the examples, anecdotes, details, and other types of evidence needed to support your thesis? As you saw when you followed Harriet Davids's strategies for gathering material for an essay (pages 26–35), a good deal of information is generated during the prewriting stage. In this phase of the writing process, you tap into your personal experiences, draw upon other people's observations, perhaps interview a person with special knowledge about your subject. The library and the Internet, with their abundant material, are another rich source of supporting evidence. (For information on using the library and the Internet, see Chapter 20.) In addition, the various patterns of development are a valuable source of evidence.

How the Patterns of Development Help Generate Evidence

In Chapter 2, we discussed how the patterns of development could help generate material about Harriet Davids's limited subject (pages 30–32). The same patterns also help develop support for a thesis. The following chart shows how they generate evidence for this thesis: "To those who haven't done it, babysitting looks easy. In practice, though, babysitting can be difficult, frightening, even dangerous."

Pattern of Development	Evidence Generated
Description	Details about a child who, while being babysat, was badly hurt playing on a backyard swing.
Narration	Story about the time a friend babysat a child who became seriously ill and whose condition was worsened by the babysitter's remedies.
Illustration	Examples of potential babysitting problems: an infant who rolls off a changing table; a toddler who sticks objects into an electric outlet; a school-age child who is bitten by a neighborhood dog.
Division-classification	A typical babysitting evening divided into stages: playing with the kids; putting them to bed; dealing with their nighttime fears once they're in bed.
	Classify kids' nighttime fears: of monsters under their beds; of bad dreams; of being abandoned by their parents.
Process analysis	Step-by-step account of what a babysitter should do if a child becomes ill or injured.
Comparison-contrast	Contrast between two babysitters: one well-prepared, the other unprepared.
Cause-effect	Why children have temper tantrums; the effect of such tantrums on an unskilled babysitter.
Definition	What is meant by a *skilled* babysitter?
Argumentation-persuasion	A proposal for a babysitting training program to be offered by the local community center.

(For further discussion of ways to use the patterns of development in different phases of the writing process, see pages 31–32, 40, 54–55, 67–68, and Chapter 10.)

CHARACTERISTICS OF EVIDENCE

No matter how it is generated, all types of supporting evidence share the characteristics described in the following sections. You should keep these characteristics in mind as you review your thesis and scratch list. That way, you can make the changes needed to strengthen the evidence gathered earlier. As you'll see shortly, Harriet Davids focused on many of these issues as she worked with the evidence she collected during the prewriting phase.

The Evidence Is Relevant and Unified

All the evidence in an essay must clearly support the thesis. It makes no difference how riveting material might be; if it doesn't *relate directly* to the essay's central point, the evidence should be eliminated. Irrelevant material can weaken your position by implying that no relevant support exists. It also distracts readers from your controlling idea, thus disrupting the paper's overall unity.

Suppose you want to write an essay with the thesis "Fairly fought arguments can strengthen relationships." To support your thesis, you could adapt prewriting material about an argument you had with a friend: how the disagreement started, how you and your friend worked out your differences, how your friendship deepened because of what you learned about each other. Also to the point would be statements from your sister who found, after reading a book on conflict management, that her relationship with her co-workers improved significantly. Similarly relevant would be an account of a conflict-ridden family whose tensions eased once a counselor taught them how to air their differences. It would *not* serve your thesis, however, to include details about the way negotiating strategies can backfire. This material wouldn't be appropriate because it contradicts the point you want to make.

Early in the writing process, Harriet Davids was aware of the importance of relevant evidence. Take a moment to review Harriet's annotated prewriting (page 34). Even though Harriet hadn't yet identified her thesis, she realized she should delete a number of items on the reshaped version of her brainstormed list—for example, "prices of everything outrageous . . ." and "Not enough homework assigned—kids unprepared." Harriet eliminated these points because they weren't consistent with the focus of her limited subject.

> Student
> essay in
> progress

The Evidence Is Specific

When evidence is vague and general, readers lose interest in what you're saying, become skeptical of your ideas' validity, and feel puzzled about your meaning. In contrast, *specific, concrete evidence* provides sharp *word pictures* that engage your readers, persuade them that your thinking is sound, and clarify meaning.

Consider a paper with this thesis: "College students should not automatically dismiss working in fast-food restaurants; such jobs can provide valuable learning experiences." Here's how you might go wrong trying to support the thesis: Suppose you begin with the broad claim that these admittedly lackluster jobs can teach students a good deal about themselves. In a similarly abstract fashion, you go on to say that such jobs can affect students' self-concepts in positive ways. You end by declaring that such changes in self-perception lead to greater maturity.

To prevent readers from thinking "Who cares?" or "Who says?" you need to replace these vague generalities with specific, concrete evidence. For example, focusing on your own experience working at a fast-food restaurant, you might start by describing how you learned to control your sarcasm; such an attitude, you discovered, alienated co-workers and almost caused your boss to fire you. You could also recount the time you administered the Heimlich maneuver to a choking customer; your quick thinking and failure to panic increased your self-esteem. Finally, you could explain that the job encouraged you to question some of your values; you became close friends with a bookish, introspective co-worker—the kind of person you used to spurn. This specific, particularized evidence would support your thesis and help readers "see" the point you're making. (Pages 69–71 describe strategies for making evidence specific.)

Student
essay in
progress

At this point, it will be helpful to look once again at the annotations that Harriet Davids entered on her prewriting material (page 34). Note the way she jotted down new details to make her prewriting more specific. For instance, to the item "Distractions from homework," she added the examples "video arcades" and "rock concerts." And once Harriet arrived at her thesis ("Being a parent today is much more difficult than it was a generation ago"), she realized that she needed to provide even more specifics. With her thesis firmly in mind, she expanded her prewriting material—for instance, the point about sexuality on television. To develop that item, she specified three kinds of TV programming that depict sexuality offensively: soap operas, R-rated comedians, R-rated cable movies. And, as you'll soon discover, Harriet added many more specific details when she prepared her final outline (pages 59–60) and her first and final drafts (pages 83–84 and 137–139).

The Evidence Is Adequate

Readers won't automatically accept your thesis; you need to provide *enough specific evidence* to support your viewpoint. On occasion, a single extended example will suffice. Generally, though, you'll need a variety of evidence: facts, examples, reasons, personal observations, expert opinion, and so on.

Assume you want to write an essay arguing that "college students living on campus should register and vote where they attend school." Hoping the essay will be published in the campus newspaper, you write it in the form of an open letter to the student body. One reason in support of your thesis strikes you immediately: that eighteen-year-olds should act as the adults they are and become involved in the electoral process. You also present as evidence a description of how good you felt during the last election when you walked into the voting booth set up in the student center. If this is all the support you provide, students probably won't be convinced; you haven't offered *sufficient* evidence. You need to present additional material—statistics on the shockingly low number of students registered to vote at your school; an account of a voter-registration drive at a nearby university that got students involved in the community and thus reduced traditional "town-grown" tensions; quotations from several students who voted against an anti-student housing ordinance and saw the ordinance defeated; an explanation of how easy it is to register.

Student
essay in
progress

Now take a final look at Harriet's annotations on her prewriting (page 34). As you can see, Harriet realized she needed more than one block of supporting material to develop her limited subject; that's why she identified four separate blocks of evidence (day care, homework distractions, sexual material, and dangers). As soon as Harriet formulated her thesis, she reexamined her prewriting to see if it provided sufficient support for her essay's central point. Luckily, Harriet recognized that these four blocks of evidence needed to be developed further. She thus decided to enlarge the "Distractions from homework" block by drawing upon her daughters' love affair with MTV and the "Life-threatening dangers" block by including details about the way peer pressure to experiment with drugs and alcohol endangers young people. Harriet's final outline (pages 59–60) reflects these decisions. When you look at the outline, you'll also note that Harriet ended up eliminating one of the four blocks of evidence ("Day care") she had identified earlier. But she added so many specific and dramatic details when writing her first and final drafts (pages 83–84 and 137–139) that her evidence was more than sufficient.

Continues on page 59

The Evidence Is Dramatic

The most effective evidence enlarges the reader's experience by *dramatizing reality.* Say you plan to write an essay with the thesis "People who affirm the value of life refuse to wear fur coats." If, as support, you state only that most animals killed for their fur are caught in leg-hold traps, your readers will have little sense of the suffering involved. But if you write that steel-jaw, leg-hold traps snap shut on an animal's limb, crushing tissue and bone and leaving the animal to die, in severe pain, from exposure or starvation, your readers can better envision the animal's plight.

The Evidence Is Accurate

Make your evidence as dramatic as you can, but be sure it is *accurate.* When you have a strong belief and want readers to see things your way, you may be tempted to overstate or downplay facts, disregard information, misquote, or make up details. Suppose you plan to write an essay making the point that dormitory security is lax. You begin supporting your thesis by narrating the time you were nearly mugged in your dorm hallway. Realizing the essay would be more persuasive if you also mentioned other episodes, you decide to invent some material. Perhaps you describe several supposed burglaries on your dorm floor or exaggerate the amount of time it took campus security to respond to an emergency call from a residence hall. Yes, you've supported your point—but at the expense of truth.

The Evidence Is Representative

Using *representative* evidence means that you rely on the *typical,* the *usual,* to show that your point is valid. Contrary to the maxim, exceptions don't prove the rule. Perhaps you plan to write an essay contending that the value of seat belts has been exaggerated. To support your position, you mention a friend who survived a head-on collision without wearing a seat belt. Such an example isn't representative because the facts and figures on accidents suggest your friend's survival was a fluke.

Borrowed Evidence Is Documented

If you include evidence from outside sources (books, articles, interviews), you need to *acknowledge* where that information comes from. If you don't, readers may consider your evidence nothing more than your point of view, or they may regard as dishonest your failure to cite your indebtedness to others for ideas that obviously aren't your own.

The rules for crediting sources in informal writing are less established than they are for formal research. Follow any guidelines your instructor provides, and try to keep your notations, like those that follow, as simple as possible.

```
Business Life (March 16, 2002) reports that corporate
wrongdoing has led to a rash of consumer protests.

    Science writer Natalie Angier believes that private zoos may be
the only hope for some endangered species.
```

In formal research, you need to provide much more detailed documentation of sources. For information on formal documentation, see Chapter 21.

Strong supporting evidence is at the heart of effective writing. Without it, essays lack energy and fail to project the writer's voice and perspective. Such lifeless writing is also more apt to put readers to sleep than to engage their interest and convince them that the points being made are valid. Taking the time to accumulate solid supporting material is, then, a critical step in the writing process. (If you'd like to read more about the characteristics of strong evidence, see pages 69–73. If you'd like suggestions for organizing an essay's evidence, see the diagram on page 82.)

ACTIVITIES: SUPPORTING THE THESIS WITH EVIDENCE

1. Imagine you're writing an essay with the following thesis in mind. Which of the statements in the list support the thesis? Label each statement acceptable (OK), irrelevant (IR), inaccurate (IA), or too general (TG).

   Thesis: Colleges should put less emphasis on sports.

   a. High-powered athletic programs can encourage grade fixing.
   b. Too much value is attached to college sports.
   c. Athletics have no educational value.
   d. Competitive athletics can lead to extensive and expensive injuries.
   e. Athletes can spend too much time on the field and not enough on their studies.
   f. Good athletic programs create a strong following among former undergraduates.

2. For each of the following thesis statements, list at least three supporting points that convey vivid word pictures.

a. Rude behavior in movie theaters seems to be on the rise.

b. Recent television commercials portray men as incompetent creatures.

c. The local library fails to meet the public's needs.

d. People often abuse public parks.

3. Turn back to the paragraphs you prepared in response to activity 2, activity 3, or activity 5 in Chapter 3 (pages 44 and 45). Select one paragraph and strengthen its evidence, using the guidelines presented in this chapter.

4. Choose one of the following thesis statements. Then identify an appropriate purpose, audience, tone, and point of view for an essay with this thesis. Using freewriting, mapping, or the questioning technique, generate at least three supporting points for the thesis. Last, write a paragraph about one of the points, making sure your evidence reflects the characteristics discussed in this chapter. Alternatively, you may go ahead and prepare the first draft of an essay having the selected thesis. (If you choose the second option, you may want to turn to page 82 to see a diagram showing how to organize a first draft.) Save whatever you prepare so you can work with it further after reading the next chapter.

a. Winning the lottery may not always be a blessing.

b. All of us can take steps to reduce the country's trash crisis.

c. Drug education programs in public schools are (or are not) effective.

5. Select one of the following thesis statements. Then determine your purpose, audience, tone, and point of view for an essay with this thesis. Next, use the patterns of development to generate at least three supporting points for the thesis. Finally, write a paragraph about one of the points, making sure that your evidence demonstrates the characteristics discussed in this chapter. Alternatively, you may go ahead and prepare a first draft of an essay having the thesis selected. (If you choose the latter option, you may want to turn to page 82 to see a diagram showing how to organize a first draft.) Save whatever you prepare so you can work with it further after reading the next chapter.

a. Teenagers should (or should not) be able to obtain birth-control devices without their parents' permission.

b. The college's system for awarding student loans needs to be overhauled.

c. VCRs have changed for the worse (or the better) the way Americans entertain themselves.

6. Look at the thesis and refined scratch outline you prepared in response to activity 7 in Chapter 3 (page 45). Where do you see gaps in the support for your thesis? By brainstorming with others, generate material to fill these gaps. If some of the new points generated suggest that you should modify your thesis, make the appropriate changes now. (Save this material so you can work with it further after reading the next chapter.)

(For more activities on generating evidence, see pages 86–89 in Chapter 6 as well as pages 129–132 in Chapter 8.)

5

ORGANIZING THE EVIDENCE

Once you've generated supporting evidence, you're ready to *organize* that material. Even highly compelling evidence won't illustrate the validity of your thesis or achieve your purpose if it isn't organized properly. Some writers can move quickly from generating support to writing a clearly structured first draft. (They usually say they have sequenced their ideas in their heads.) Most, however, need to spend some time sorting out their thoughts on paper before starting the first draft; otherwise, they tend to lose their way in a tangle of ideas.

When moving to the organizing stage, you should have in front of you your scratch list (see pages 34–35) and thesis, plus any supporting material you've accumulated since you did your prewriting. To find a logical framework for all this material, you'll need to (1) determine which pattern of development is implied in your evidence, (2) select one of four basic approaches for organizing your evidence, and (3) outline your evidence. These issues are discussed in the following sections.

USE THE PATTERNS OF DEVELOPMENT

As you saw on pages 31–32 and 47–48, the patterns of development (definition, narration, process analysis, and others) can help you develop prewriting material and generate evidence for a thesis. In the organizing stage, the patterns provide frameworks for presenting the evidence in an orderly, accessible way. Here's how.

Each pattern of development has its own internal logic that makes it appropriate for some writing purposes but not for others. (You may find it helpful at this point to turn to pages 31–32 so you can review the broad purpose of each pattern.) Imagine that you want to write an essay *explaining why* some students drop out of college during the first semester. If your essay consisted only of a lengthy narrative of two friends floundering through the first month of college, you wouldn't achieve your purpose. A condensed version of the narrative might be appropriate at some point in the essay, but—to meet your objective—most of the paper would have to focus on *causes* and *effects.*

Once you see which pattern (or combination of patterns) is implied by your purpose, you can block out your paper's general structure. For instance, in the preceding example, you might organize the essay around a three-part discussion of the key reasons that students have difficulty adjusting to college: (1) they miss friends and family, (2) they take inappropriate courses, and (3) they experience conflicts with roommates. As you can see, your choice of pattern of development significantly influences your essay's content and organization.

Some essays follow a single pattern, but most blend them, with a predominant pattern providing the piece's organizational framework. In our example essay, you might include a brief *description* of an overwhelmed first-year college student; you might *define* the psychological term *separation anxiety;* you might end the paper by briefly explaining a *process* for making students' adjustment to college easier. Still, the essay's overall organizational pattern would be *cause-effect* because the paper's primary purpose is to explain why students drop out of college. (See pages 67–68 and Chapter 10 for more information on the way patterns often mix.)

Although writers often combine the patterns of development, your composition instructor may ask you to write an essay organized according to a single pattern. Such an assignment helps you understand a particular pattern's unique demands. Keep in mind, though, that most writing begins not with a specific pattern but with a specific *purpose.* The pattern or combination of patterns used to develop and organize an essay evolves out of that purpose.

SELECT AN ORGANIZATIONAL APPROACH

No matter which pattern(s) of development you select, you need to know four general approaches for organizing the supporting evidence in an essay: chronological, spatial, emphatic, and simple-to-complex.

Chronological Approach

When an essay is organized **chronologically,** supporting material is arranged in a clear time sequence, usually starting with what happened first and ending with what happened last. Occasionally, chronological arrangements can be resequenced to create flashback or flashforward effects, two techniques discussed in Chapter 12 on narration.

Essays using narration (for example, an experience with prejudice) or process analysis (for instance, how to deliver an effective speech) are most likely to be organized chronologically. The paper on public speaking might use a time sequence to present its points: how to prepare a few days before the presentation is due; what to do right before the speech; what to concentrate on during the speech itself. (For examples of chronologically arranged student essays, turn to pages 204–205 in Chapter 12 and pages 313–316 in Chapter 15.)

Spatial Approach

When you arrange supporting evidence **spatially,** you discuss details as they occur in space, or from certain locations. This strategy is particularly appropriate for description. Imagine that you plan to write an essay describing the joyous times you spent as a child playing by a towering old oak tree in the neighborhood park. Using spatial organization, you start by describing the rich animal life (the plump earthworms, swarming anthills, and numerous animal tracks) you observed while hunkered down *at the base* of the tree. Next, you re-create the contented feeling you experienced sitting on a branch *in the middle* of the tree. Finally, you describe the glorious view of the world you had *from the top* of the tree.

Although spatial arrangement is flexible (you could, for instance, start with a description from the top of the tree), you should always proceed systematically. And once you select a particular spatial order, you should usually maintain that sequence throughout the essay; otherwise, readers may get lost along the way. (A spatially arranged student essay appears in Chapter 11 on pages 164–166.)

Emphatic Approach

In **emphatic** order, the most compelling evidence is saved for last. This arrangement is based on the psychological principle that people remember best what they experienced most recently. Emphatic order has built-in momentum because it starts with the least important point and builds to the most significant. This method is especially effective in argumentation-persuasion essays, in papers developed through examples, and in pieces involving comparison-contrast, division-classification, or causal analysis.

Consider an essay analyzing the negative effect that workaholic parents can have on their children. The paper might start with a brief discussion of relatively minor effects, such as the family's eating mostly frozen or take-out foods. Paragraphs on more serious effects might follow: children get no parental help with homework; they try to resolve personal problems without parental advice. Finally, the essay might close with a detailed discussion of the most significant effect—children's lack of self-esteem because they feel unimportant in their parents' lives. (The student essays on pages 238–240 in Chapter 13, pages 355–357 in Chapter 16, and pages 421–423 in Chapter 18 all use an emphatic arrangement.)

Simple-to-Complex Approach

A final way to organize an essay is to proceed with relatively **simple** concepts to more **complex** ones. By starting with easy-to-grasp, generally accepted evidence, you establish rapport with your readers and assure them that the essay is firmly grounded in shared experience. In contrast, if you open with difficult or highly technical material, you risk confusing and alienating your audience.

Assume you plan to write a paper arguing that your college has endangered students' health by not making an all-out effort to remove asbestos from dormitories and classroom buildings. It probably wouldn't be a good idea to begin with a medically sophisticated explanation of precisely how asbestos damages lung tissue. Instead, you might start with an observation that is likely to be familiar to your readers—one that is part of their everyday experience. You could, for example, open with a description of asbestos—as readers might see it— wrapped around air ducts and furnaces or used as electrical insulation and fireproofing material. Having provided a basic, easy-to-visualize description, you could then go on to explain the complicated process by which asbestos can cause chronic lung inflammation. (See pages 389–392 in Chapter 17 for an example of a student essay using the simple-to-complex arrangement.)

Depending on your purpose, any one of these four organizational approaches might be appropriate. For example, assume you planned to write an essay developing Harriet Davids's thesis: "Being a parent today is much more difficult than it was a generation ago." To emphasize that the various stages in children's lives present parents with different difficulties, you'd probably select a *chronological* sequence. To show that the challenges parents face vary depending on whether children are at home, at school, or in the world at large, you'd probably choose a *spatial* sequence. To stress the range of problems that parents face (from less to more serious), you'd probably use an *emphatic* sequence. Finally, to illustrate today's confusing array of theories for raising children, you might take a *simple-to-complex* approach, moving from the basic to the most sophisticated theory.

PREPARE AN OUTLINE

Do you, like many students, react with fear and loathing to the dreaded word *outline?* Do you, if asked to submit an outline, prepare it *after* you've written the essay? If you do, we hope to convince you that having an outline—a skeletal version of your paper—*before* you begin the first draft makes the writing process much more manageable. The outline helps you organize your thoughts beforehand, and it guides your writing as you work on the draft. Even though ideas continue to evolve during the draft, an outline clarifies how ideas fit together, which points are major, which should come first, and so on. An outline may also reveal places where evidence is weak, prompting you to eliminate the material altogether, retain it in an unemphatic position, or do more prewriting to generate additional support.

Like previous stages in the writing process, outlining is individualized. Some people prepare highly structured, detailed outlines; others make only a few informal jottings. Sometimes outlining will go quickly, with points falling easily into place; at other times you'll have to work hard to figure out how points are related. If that happens, be glad you caught the problem while outlining, rather than while writing or revising.

To prepare an effective outline, you should reread and evaluate your scratch list and thesis as well as any other evidence you've generated since the prewriting stage. Then decide which pattern of development (description, cause-effect, and so on) seems to be suggested by your evidence. Also determine whether your evidence lends itself to a chronological, a spatial, an emphatic, or a simple-to-complex order. Having done all that, you're ready to identify and sequence your main and supporting points.

The amount of detail in an outline will vary according to the paper's length and the instructor's requirements. A scratch outline consisting of words or phrases (such as the one on pages 34–35 in Chapter 2) is often sufficient, but for longer papers, you'll probably need a more detailed and formal outline. In such cases, the suggestions in the accompanying checklist will help you develop a sound plan. Feel free to modify these guidelines to suit your needs.

☑ GUIDELINES FOR OUTLINING: A CHECKLIST

- ☐ Write your purpose, audience, tone, point of view, and thesis at the top of the outlining page.
- ☐ Below the thesis, enter the pattern of development that seems to be implied by the evidence you've accumulated.
- ☐ Also record which of the four organizational approaches would be most effective in sequencing your evidence.
- ☐ Reevaluate your supporting material. Delete anything that doesn't develop the thesis or that isn't appropriate for your purpose, audience, tone, and point of view.
- ☐ Add any new points or material.
- ☐ Group related items together. Give each group a heading that represents a main topic in support of your thesis.
- ☐ Label these main topics with roman numerals (I, II, III, and so on). Let the order of numerals indicate the best sequence.
- ☐ Identify subtopics and group them under the appropriate main topics. Indent and label these subtopics with capital letters (A, B, C, and so on). Let the order of the letters indicate the best sequence.
- ☐ Identify supporting points (often reasons and examples) and group them under the appropriate subtopics. Indent and label these supporting points with arabic numbers (1, 2, 3, and so on). Let the numbers indicate the best sequence.

□ Identify specific details (secondary examples, facts, statistics, expert opinions, quotations) and group them under the appropriate supporting points. Indent and label these specific details with lowercase letters (a, b, c, and so on). Let the letters indicate the best sequence.

□ Examine your outline, looking for places where evidence is weak. Where appropriate, add new evidence.

□ Double-check that all main topics, subtopics, supporting points, and specific details develop some aspect of the thesis. Also confirm that all items are arranged in the most logical order.

The sample outline that starts below and continues on the next page develops the thesis "Being a parent today is much more difficult than it was a generation ago." You may remember that this is the thesis that Harriet Davids devised for the essay she planned to write in response to the assignment on page 26. Harriet's scratch list, based on her brainstorming, appears on pages 27–28. (You may want to review pages 34–35 to see how Harriet later reconsidered material on the scratch list in light of her thesis.) When you compare Harriet's scratch list and outline, you'll find some differences. On the one hand, the outline tends to contain more specifics (for instance, the details about sexually explicit materials—in magazines and books, in movies, on television, and on the Internet). On the other hand, the outline doesn't include all the material in the scratch list. For example, after reconsidering her purpose, audience, tone, point of view, and thesis, Harriet decided to omit from her outline the section on day care and the points about AIDS and rock posters.

Harriet's outline is called a **topic outline** because it uses phrases, or topics, for each entry. (See pages 312–313, 354, and 467–468 for other examples of topic outlines.) For a more complex paper, a **sentence outline** might be more appropriate (see pages 237 and 595–597). You can also mix phrases and sentences (see pages 388–389), as long as you are consistent about where you use each.

In Harriet's outline, note that indentations signal the relationships among the essay's points and that the same grammatical form is used to begin each entry on a particular level. For instance, since a noun phrase ("Distractions from homework") follows roman numeral I, noun phrases also follow subsequent roman numerals. Such consistency helps writers see if items at a particular level are comparable.

Student essay in progress

Purpose: To inform

Audience: Instructor as well as class members, most of whom are 18-20 years old

Tone: Serious and straightforward

Point of view: Third person (mother of two teenage girls)

Thesis: Being a parent today is much more difficult than it
was a generation ago.

Pattern of development: Illustration

Organizational approach: Emphatic order

I. Distractions from homework

    A. At home

        1. Stereos, radios, CDs

        2. Television--esp. on MTV

        3. Computers--Internet, computer games

    B. Outside home

        1. Malls

        2. Video arcades

        3. Fast-food restaurants

II. Sexually explicit materials

    A. In print

        1. Sex magazines--<u>Playboy</u>, <u>Penthouse</u>

        2. Pornographic books

    B. In movies

        1. Seduction scenes

        2. Casual sex

    C. On television

        1. Soap operas

        2. R-rated comedians

        3. R-rated movies on cable

    D. Internet

        1. Easy-to-access adult chat rooms

        2. Easy-to-access pornographic websites

III. Increased dangers

    A. Drugs--peer pressure

    B. Alcohol--peer pressure

    C. Violent crimes against children

Hints for moving from an outline to a first draft appear on pages 63–65. For additional suggestions on organizing a first draft, see the diagram on page 82.

Before starting to write your first draft, show your outline to several people (your instructor, friends, classmates). Their reactions will indicate whether your proposed organization is appropriate for your thesis, purpose, audience, tone, and point of view. Their comments can also highlight areas needing additional work. After making whatever changes are needed, you're in a good position to go ahead and write the first draft of your essay.

ACTIVITIES: ORGANIZING THE EVIDENCE

1. The following thesis statement is accompanied by a scrambled list of supporting points. Prepare a topic outline for a potential essay, being sure to distinguish between major and secondary points.

   Thesis: Our schools, now in crisis, could be improved in several ways.

   Certificate requirements for teachers
   Schedules
   Teachers
   Longer school year
   Merit pay for outstanding teachers
   Curriculum
   Better textbooks
   Longer school days
   More challenging course content

2. For each of the following thesis statements, there are two purposes given. Determine whether each purpose suggests an emphatic, chronological, spatial, or simple-to-complex approach. Note the way the approach varies as the purpose changes.

   a. *Thesis:* Traveling in a large city can be an unexpected education.
      Purpose 1: To explain, in a humorous way, the stages in learning to cope with the city's cab system
      Purpose 2: To describe, in a serious manner, the vastly different sections of the city as viewed from a cab

   b. *Thesis:* The student government seems determined to improve its relations with the college administration.
      Purpose 1: To inform readers by describing efforts that student leaders took, month by month, to win administrative support
      Purpose 2: To convince readers by explaining straightforward as well as intricate pro-administration resolutions that student leaders passed

   c. *Thesis:* Supermarkets use sophisticated marketing techniques to prod consumers into buying more than they need
      Purpose 1: To inform readers that positioning products in certain locations encourages impulse buying

Purpose 2: To persuade readers not to patronize those chains using especially objectionable sales strategies

3. Return to the paragraph or first draft you prepared in response to activity 4 or activity 5 in Chapter 4. Applying the principles discussed in Chapter 5, strengthen the organization of the evidence you generated. (If you rework a first draft, save the draft so you can refine it further after reading the next chapter.)

4. Each of the following brief essay outlines consists of a thesis and several points of support. Which pattern of development would you probably use to develop the overall organizational framework for each essay? Which pattern(s) would you use to develop each point of support? Why?

   a. *Thesis:* Friends of the opposite sex fall into one of several categories: the pal, the confidante, or the pest.

   Points of Support

   - Frequently, an opposite-sex friend is simply a "pal."
   - Sometimes, though, a pal turns, step by step, into a confidante.
   - If a confidante begins to have romantic thoughts, he or she may become a pest, thus disrupting the friendship.

   b. *Thesis:* What happens when a child gets sick in a two-income household? Numerous problems occur.

   Points of Support

   - Parents often encounter difficulties as they take steps to locate a babysitter or make other child-care arrangements.
   - If no child-care helper can be found, a couple must decide which parent will stay at home—a decision that may create conflict between husband and wife.
   - No matter what they do, parents inevitably will incur at least one of several kinds of expenses.

5. For one of the thesis statements given in activity 4, identify a possible purpose, audience, tone, and point of view. Then, use one or more patterns to generate material to develop the points of support listed. Get together with someone else to review the generated material, deleting, adding, combining, and arranging ideas in logical order. Finally, make an outline for the body of the essay. (Save your outline. After reading the next chapter, you can use it to write the essay's first draft.)

6. Look again at the thesis and scratch outline you refined and elaborated in response to activity 6 in Chapter 4. Reevaluate this material by deleting, adding, combining, and rearranging ideas as needed. Then, in preparation for writing an essay, outline your ideas. Consider whether an emphatic, chronological, spatial, or simple-to-complex approach will be most appropriate. Finally, ask at least one other person to evaluate your organizational plan. (Save your outline. After reading the next chapter, you can use it to write the essay's first draft.)

6
WRITING THE PARAGRAPHS IN THE FIRST DRAFT

After prewriting, deciding on a thesis, and developing and organizing evidence, you're ready to write a first draft—a rough, provisional version of your essay. Some people work slowly as they prepare their drafts, while others quickly dash off their drafts. No matter how you proceed, you should concentrate on providing paragraphs that support your thesis. Also try to include all relevant examples, facts, and opinions, sequencing this material as effectively as you can.

Because of your work in the preceding stages, the first draft may flow quite smoothly. But don't be discouraged if it doesn't. You may find that your thesis has to be reshaped, that a point no longer fits, that you need to return to a prewriting activity to generate additional material. Such stopping and starting is to be expected. Writing the first draft is a process of discovery, involving the continual clarification and refining of ideas.

HOW TO MOVE FROM OUTLINE TO FIRST DRAFT

There's no single right way to prepare a first draft. With experience, you'll undoubtedly find your own basic approach, adapting it to suit each paper's length, the time available, and the instructor's requirements. Some writers rely heavily on their scratch lists or outlines; others glance at them only occasionally. Some people write the first draft in longhand; others use a typewriter or computer.

However you choose to proceed, consider the following general suggestions when moving from an outline or scratch list to a first draft:

- Make the outline's *main topics* (I, II, III) the *topic sentences* of the essay's supporting paragraphs. (Topic sentences are discussed later in this chapter.)
- Make the outline's *subtopics* (A, B, C) the *subpoints* in each paragraph.
- Make the outline's *supporting points* (1, 2, 3) the *key examples* and *reasons* in each paragraph.
- Make the outline's *specific details* (a, b, c) the *secondary examples,* facts, statistics, expert opinion, and quotations in each paragraph.

(To see how one student, Harriet Davids, moved from outline to first draft, turn to pages 83–84.)

GENERAL SUGGESTIONS ON HOW TO PROCEED

Although outlines and lists are valuable for guiding your work, don't be so dependent on them that you shy away from new ideas that surface during your writing of the first draft. It's during this time that promising new thoughts often pop up; as they do, jot them down. Then, at the appropriate point, go back and evaluate them: Do they support your thesis? Are they appropriate for your essay's purpose, audience, tone, and point of view? If so, go ahead and include the material in your draft.

It's easy to get stuck while preparing the first draft if you try to edit as you write. Remember: A draft isn't intended to be perfect. For the time being, adopt a relaxed, noncritical attitude. Working as quickly as you can, don't stop to check spelling, correct grammar, or refine sentence structure. Save these tasks for later. One good way to help remind you that the first draft is tentative is to prepare it in longhand, using scrap paper and pencil. Writing on alternate lines also underscores your intention to revise later on, when the extra space will make it easier to add and delete material. Similarly, writing on only one side of the paper can prove helpful if, during revision, you decide to move a section to another part of the paper.

IF YOU GET BOGGED DOWN

All writers get bogged down now and then. The best thing to do is accept that sooner or later it will happen to you. When it does, keep calm and try to write something—no matter how awkward or imprecise it may seem. Just jot a reminder to yourself in the margin ("Fix this," "Redo," or "Ugh!") to finetune the section later. Or leave a blank space to hold a spot for the right words when they finally break loose. It may also help to reread—out loud is best—what you've already written. Regaining a sense of the larger context is often enough to get you moving again. You might also try talking your way through a troublesome section. Like most people, you probably speak more easily than you write; by speaking aloud, you tap this oral fluency and put it to work in your writing.

If a section of the essay strikes you as particularly difficult, don't spend time struggling with it. Move on to an easier section, write that, and then return to the challenging part. If you're still getting nowhere, take a break. Watch television, listen to music, talk with friends. While you're relaxing, your thoughts may loosen up and untangle the knotty section. If, on the other hand, an obligation such as a class or an appointment forces you to stop writing when the draft is going well, jot down a few notes in the margin to remind yourself of your train of thought. The notes will keep you from getting stuck when you pick up the draft later.

A SUGGESTED SEQUENCE FOR WRITING THE FIRST DRAFT

Because you read essays from beginning to end, you may assume that writers work the same way, starting with the introduction and going straight through to the conclusion. Often, however, this isn't the case. In fact, since an introduction depends so heavily on everything that follows, it's usually best to write the introduction *after* the essay's body.

When preparing your first draft, you may find it helpful to follow this sequence:

1. Write the essay's supporting paragraphs.
2. Write the other paragraphs in the essay's body.
3. Write the introduction.
4. Write the conclusion.

Write the Supporting Paragraphs

Before starting to write the essay's **supporting paragraphs,** enter your thesis at the top of the page. You might even underline key words in the thesis to keep yourself focused on the central ideas you plan to develop. Also, now that you've planned the essay's overall organization, you may want to add to your thesis a **plan of development:** a brief *overview* of the essay's *major points in the exact order* in which you will discuss those points. (For more on plans of development, see pages 40–41.)

Not every essay needs a plan of development. In a brief paper, readers can often keep track of ideas without this extra help. But in a longer, more complex essay, a plan of development helps readers follow the progression of main points

in the supporting paragraphs. Whether or not you include a plan of development, always keep in mind that writing the draft often leads to new ideas; you
may have to revise your thesis, plan of development, and supporting paragraphs
as the draft unfolds.

Drawn from the main sections in your outline or scratch list, each supporting
paragraph should develop an aspect of your essay's thesis or plan of development.
Although there are no hard-and-fast rules, strong supporting paragraphs are
(1) often focused by topic sentences, (2) organized around one or more patterns of
development, (3) unified, (4) specific, (5) adequately supported, and (6) coherent.
Aim for as many of these qualities as you can in the first draft. The material on the
following pages will help keep you focused on your goal. But don't expect the draft
paragraphs to be perfect; you'll have the chance to revise them later on.

Use Topic Sentences

Frequently, each supporting paragraph in an essay is focused by a **topic sentence.**
This sentence usually states a main point in support of the thesis. In a formal outline,
such a point customarily appears, often in abbreviated form, as a *main topic* marked
with a roman numeral (I, II, III).

Student
essay in
progress

The transformation of an outline's main topic to a paragraph's topic sentence is
often a matter of stating your attitude toward the outline topic. When changing
from main outline topic to topic sentence, you may also add details that make the
topic sentence more specific and concrete. Compare, for example, Harriet
Davids's outline on pages 59–60 with her first draft on pages 83–84. You'll see that
the outline entry "I. Distractions from homework" turned into the topic sentence
"Parents have to control all the new distractions/temptations that turn kids away
from schoolwork" (paragraph 2). The difference between the outline topic and the
topic sentence is thus twofold: The topic sentence has an *element of opinion* ("have
to control"), and it is focused by *added details* (in this case, the people involved—
parents and children).

The topic sentence functions as a kind of mini-thesis for the paragraph.
Generally one or two sentences in length, the topic sentence usually appears at or
near the beginning of the paragraph. However, it may also appear at the end, in
the middle, or—with varied wording—several times within the paragraph. In still
other cases, a single topic sentence may state an idea developed in more than one
paragraph. When a paragraph is intended primarily to clarify or inform, you may
want to place its topic sentence at the beginning; that way, readers are prepared to
view everything that follows in light of that main idea. If, though, you intend a
paragraph to heighten suspense or to convey a feeling of discovery, you may
prefer to delay the topic sentence until the end.

Regardless of its length or location, the topic sentence states the paragraph's
main idea. The other sentences in the paragraph provide support for this central
point in the form of examples, facts, expert opinion, and so on. Like a thesis statement, the topic sentence *signals the paragraph's subject* and frequently *indicates the
writer's attitude* toward that subject. In the topic sentences that follow, the subject
of the paragraph is underlined once and the attitude toward that subject is
underlined twice:

Topic Sentences

Some students select a particular field of study for the wrong reasons.

The ocean dumping of radioactive waste is a ticking time bomb.

Several contemporary rock groups show unexpected sensitivity to social issues.

Political candidates are sold like slickly packaged products.

As you work on the first draft, you may find yourself writing paragraphs without paying too much attention to topic sentences. That's fine, as long as you remember to evaluate the paragraphs later on. When revising, you can provide a topic sentence for a paragraph that needs a sharper focus, recast a topic sentence for a paragraph that ended up taking an unexpected turn, even eliminate a topic sentence altogether if a paragraph's content is sufficiently unified to imply its point.

With experience, you'll develop an instinct for writing focused paragraphs without having to pay such close attention to topic sentences. A good way to develop such an instinct is to note how the writers in this book use topic sentences to shape paragraphs and clarify meaning. (If you'd like some practice in identifying topic sentences, see pages 85–86.)

Use the Patterns of Development

As you saw on pages 54–55, an entire essay can be organized around one or more patterns of development. These patterns can also provide the organizational framework for an essay's supporting paragraphs. Assume you're writing an article for your town newspaper with the thesis "Year-round residents of an ocean community must take an active role in safeguarding the seashore environment." As the following examples indicate, your supporting paragraphs could develop this thesis through a variety of patterns, with each paragraph's topic sentence suggesting a specific pattern or combination of patterns.

Topic Sentence	Possible Pattern of Development
In a nearby ocean community, signs of environmental damage are everywhere.	*Description* of a seaside town with polluted waters, blighted trees, and diseased marine life
Typically, residents blame industry or tourists for such damage.	*Narration* of a conversation among seaside residents
Residents' careless behavior is also to blame, however.	*Illustrations* of residents' littering the beach, injuring marine life while motor boating, walking over fragile sand dunes
Even environmentally concerned residents may contribute to the problem.	*Cause-effect* explanation of the way Styrofoam packaging and plastic food wrap, even when properly disposed of in a trash can, can harm scavenging seagulls
Fortunately, not all seaside towns are plagued by such environmental problems.	*Comparison-contrast* of one troubled shore community with another more ecologically sound one

Topic Sentence	Possible Pattern of Development
It's clear that shore residents must become "environmental activists."	*Definition* of an *environmental activist*
Residents can get involved in a variety of pro-environmental activities.	*Division-classification* of activities at the neighborhood, town, and municipal levels
Moreover, getting involved is an easy matter.	*Process analysis* of the steps for getting involved at the various levels
Such activism yields significant rewards.	A final *argumentation-persuasion* pitch showing residents the benefits of responsible action

Of course, each supporting paragraph in an essay doesn't have to be organized according to a different pattern of development; several paragraphs may use the same pattern. Nor is it necessary for any one paragraph to be restricted to a single pattern; supporting paragraphs often combine patterns. For example, the topic sentence "Fortunately, not all seaside towns are plagued by such environmental problems" might be developed primarily through *comparison-contrast*, but the paragraph would need a fair amount of *description* to clarify the differences between towns. (For more on the way the patterns of development come into play throughout the writing process, see pages 30–32, 40, 47–48, 54–55, and Chapter 10.)

Make the Paragraphs Unified

Just as overall evidence must support an essay's thesis (pages 46–47), the facts, opinions, and examples in each supporting paragraph must have *direct bearing* on the paragraph's topic sentence. If the paragraph has no topic sentence, the supporting material must be *consistent* with the paragraph's *implied focus*. A paragraph is **unified** when it meets these requirements.

Consider the following sample paragraph, taken from an essay illustrating recent changes in Americans' television-viewing habits. The paragraph focuses on people's reasons for switching from network to cable television. As you'll see, though, the paragraph lacks unity because it contains points (underlined) unrelated to its main idea. Specifically, the criticism of cable's foul language contradicts the paragraph's topic sentence—"Many people consider cable TV an improvement over network television." To present a balanced view of cable versus network television, the writer should discuss these points, but in *another paragraph*.

Nonunified Support

Many people consider cable TV an improvement over network television. For one thing, viewers usually prefer the movies on cable. Unlike network films, cable movies are often only months old, they have not been edited by censors, and they are not interrupted by commercials. Growing numbers of people also feel that cable specials are superior to the ones the networks grind

out. Cable viewers may enjoy such performers as U2, Madonna, or
Chris Rock in concert, whereas the networks continue to broadcast
tired, look-alike sit-coms and boring awards ceremonies. <u>There
is, however, one problem with cable comedians. The foul language
many of them use makes it hard to watch these cable specials with
children. The networks, in contrast, generally present "clean"
shows that parents and children can watch together</u>. Then, too,
cable TV offers viewers more flexibility since it schedules shows
at various times over the month. People working night shifts or
attending evening classes can see movies in the afternoon, and
viewers missing the first twenty minutes of a show can always
catch them later. It's not surprising that cable viewership is
growing while network ratings have taken a plunge.

Make the Paragraphs Specific

If your supporting paragraphs are vague, readers will lose interest, remain
unconvinced of your thesis, even have trouble deciphering your meaning. In contrast, paragraphs filled with **concrete, specific details** engage readers, lend force
to ideas, and clarify meaning.

Following are two versions of a paragraph from an essay about trends in the
business community. Although both paragraphs focus on one such trend—
flexible working hours—note how the first version's vague generalities leave
meaning unclear. *What,* for example, is meant by "flex-time scheduling"? *Which*
companies have tried it? *Where,* specifically, are these companies located? *How,*
exactly, does flex-time increase productivity, lessen conflict, and reduce
accidents? The second paragraph answers these questions with specifics and, as
a result, is more informative and interesting.

Nonspecific Support

More and more companies have begun to realize that flex-time
scheduling offers advantages. Several companies outside Boston
have tried flex-time scheduling and are pleased with the way the
system reduces the difficulties their employees face getting to
work. Studies show that flex-time scheduling also increases
productivity, reduces on-the-job conflict, and minimizes work-
related accidents.

Specific Support

More and more companies have begun to realize that flex-time
scheduling offers advantages over a rigid 9-to-5 routine. Along
suburban Boston's Route 128, such companies as Compugraphics and

Consolidated Paper now permit employees to schedule their arrival any time between 6 a.m. and 11 a.m. The corporations report that the number of rush-hour jams and accidents has fallen dramatically. As a result, employees no longer arrive at work weighed down by tension induced by choking clouds of exhaust fumes and the blaring horns of gridlocked drivers. Studies sponsored by the journal *Business Quarterly* show that this more mellow state of mind benefits corporations. Traffic-stressed employees begin their workday anxious and exasperated, still grinding their teeth at their fellow commuters, their frustration often spilling over into their performance at work. By contrast, stress-free employees work more productively and take fewer days off. They are more tolerant of co-workers and customers, and less likely to balloon minor irritations into major confrontations. Perhaps most important, employees arriving at work relatively free of stress can focus their attention on working safely. They rack up significantly fewer on-the-job accidents, such as falls and injuries resulting from careless handling of dangerous equipment. Flex-time improves employee well-being, and as well-being rises, so do company profits.

Five Strategies for Making Paragraphs Specific.   How can you make the evidence in your paragraphs specific? the following techniques should help.

1. **Provide examples that answer** *who, which, what,* **and similar questions.** In contrast to the vague generalities in the first paragraph on flex-time scheduling, the second paragraph provides examples that answer a series of basic questions. For instance, the general comment "Several companies outside Boston" (*which* companies?) is replaced by "Compugraphics and Consolidated Paper." The vague phrase "difficulties their employees face getting to work" (*what* difficulties?) is dramatized with the examples "rush-hour jams and accidents." Similarly, "work-related accidents" (*which* accidents?) is illustrated with "falls and injuries resulting from careless handling of dangerous equipment."

2. **Replace general nouns and adjectives with precise ones.** In the following sentences, note how much sharper images become when exact nouns and adjectives replace imprecise ones:

General	More Specific	Most Specific
A *man* had trouble lifting the *box* out of the *old* car.	A *young man, out of shape,* struggled to lift the *heavy crate* out of the *beat-up sports* car.	*Joe, only twenty years old but more than fifty pounds overweight,* struggled to lift the *heavy wooden crate* out of the *rusty and dented Mustang.*

3. **Replace abstract words with concrete ones.** Notice the way the example on the right, firmly grounded in the physical, clarifies the intangible concepts in the example on the left:

Abstract	Concrete
The fall day had great *beauty,* despite its *dreariness.*	*Red, yellow,* and *orange* leaves *gleamed wetly* through the *gray mist.*

(For more on making abstract language concrete, see pages 121–122 in Chapter 8.)

4. **Use words that appeal to the five senses (sight, touch, taste, smell, sound).** The sentence on the left lacks impact because it fails to convey any sensory impressions; the sentence on the right, though, gains power through the use of sensory details:

Without Sensory Images	With Sensory Images
The computer room is eerie.	In the computer room, keys *click* and printers *grate* while row after row of students stare into screens that *glow without shedding any light.* (sound and sight)

(For more on sensory language, see pages 160–161 in Chapter 11.)

5. **Use vigorous verbs.** Linking verbs (such as *seem* and *appear*) and *to be* verbs (such as *is* and *were*) paint no pictures. Strong verbs, however, create sharp visual images. Compare the following examples:

Weak Verbs	Strong Verbs
The spectators *seemed* pleased and *were* enthusiastic when the wheelchair marathoners *went* by.	The spectators *cheered* and *whistled* when the wheelchair marathoners *whizzed* by.

(For more on strong verbs, see pages 122–123 in Chapter 8.)

Provide Adequate Support

Each supporting paragraph should also have **adequate support** so that your readers can see clearly the validity of the topic sentence. At times, a single extended example is sufficient; generally, however, an assortment of examples, facts, personal observations, and so forth is more effective.

Following are two versions of a paragraph from a paper showing how difficult it is to get personal, attentive service nowadays at gas stations, supermarkets, and department stores. Both paragraphs focus on the problem at gas stations, but one paragraph is much more effective. As you'll see, the first paragraph starts with good specific support, yet fails to provide enough of it. The second paragraph offers additional examples, descriptive details, and dialog—all of which make the writing stronger and more convincing.

Inadequate Support

Gas stations are a good example of this impersonal attitude. At many stations, attendants have even stopped pumping gas. Motorists pull up to a combination convenience store and gas island where an attendant is enclosed in a glass booth with a tray for taking money. The driver must get out of the car, pump the gas, and walk over to the booth to pay. That's a real inconvenience, especially when compared with the way service stations used to be run.

Adequate Support

Gas stations are a good example of this impersonal attitude. At many stations, attendants have even stopped pumping gas. Motorists pull up to a combination convenience store and gas island where an attendant is enclosed in a glass booth with a tray for taking money. The driver must get out of the car, pump the gas, and walk over to the booth to pay. Even at stations that still have "pump jockeys," employees seldom ask, "Check your oil?" or wash windshields, although they may grudgingly point out the location of the bucket and squeegee. And customers with a balky engine or a nonfunctioning heater are usually out of luck. Why? Many gas stations have eliminated on-duty mechanics. The skillful mechanic who could replace a belt or fix a tire in a few minutes has been replaced by a teenager in a jumpsuit who doesn't know a carburetor from a charge card and couldn't care less.

Make the Paragraphs Coherent

A jigsaw puzzle with all the pieces heaped on a table remains a baffling jumble unless it's clear how the pieces fit together. Similarly, paragraphs can be unified, specific, and adequately supported, yet—if internally disjointed or inadequately connected to each other—leave readers feeling confused. Readers need to be able to follow with ease the progression of thought within and between paragraphs. One idea must flow smoothly and logically into the next; that is, your writing must be **coherent.**

The following paragraph lacks coherence for two main reasons. First, it sequences ideas improperly. (The idea about toll attendants' being cut off from co-workers is introduced, dropped, then picked up again. References to motorists are similarly scattered throughout the paragraph.) Second, it doesn't indicate how individual ideas are related. (What, for example, is the connection between drivers who pass by without saying anything and attendants who have to work at night?)

Incoherent Support

Collecting tolls on the turnpike must be one of the loneliest jobs in the world. Each toll attendant sits in his or her booth, cut off from other attendants. Many drivers pass by each booth. None stays long enough for a brief "hello." Most don't acknowledge the attendant at all. Many toll attendants work at night, pushing them "out of sync" with the rest of the world. The attendants have to deal with rude drivers who treat them like non-people, swearing at them for the long lines at the tollgate. Attendants dislike how cut off they feel from their co-workers. Except for infrequent breaks, they have little chance to chat with each other and swap horror stories--small pleasures that would make their otherwise routine jobs bearable.

Coherent Support

Collecting tolls on the turnpike must be one of the loneliest jobs in the world. First of all, although many drivers pass by the attendants, none stays long enough for more than a brief "hello." Most drivers, in fact, don't acknowledge the toll collectors at all, with the exception of those rude drivers who treat the attendants like non-people, swearing at them for the long lines at the tollgate. Then, too, many toll attendants work at night, pushing them further "out of sync" with the rest of the world. Worst of all, attendants say, is how isolated they feel from their co-workers. Each attendant sits in his or her booth, cut off from other attendants. Except for infrequent breaks, they have little chance to chat with each other and swap horror stories--small pleasures that would make their otherwise routine jobs bearable.

To avoid the kinds of problems found in the incoherent paragraph, use—as the revised version does—two key strategies: (1) a clearly *chronological, spatial,* or *emphatic order* ("*Worst of all,* attendants say . . .") and (2) *signal devices* ("*First of all,* although many drivers pass by . . .") to show how ideas are connected. The following sections discuss these two strategies.

Chronological, Spatial, and Emphatic Order. As you learned in Chapter 5, an entire essay can be organized using chronological, spatial, or emphatic order (pages 55–56). These strategies can also be used to make a paragraph coherent.

Imagine you plan to write an essay showing the difficulties many immigrants face when they first come to this country. Let's consider how you might structure the essay's supporting paragraphs, particularly the way each paragraph's organizational approach can help you arrange ideas in a logical, easy-to-follow sequence.

One paragraph, focused by the topic sentence "The everyday life of a typical immigrant family is arduous," might be developed through a **chronological** account of the family's daily routine: purchasing, before dawn, fruits and vegetables for their produce stand; setting up the stand early in the morning; working there for ten hours; attending English class at night. Another paragraph might develop its topic sentence—"Many immigrant families get along without the technology that others take for granted"—through **spatial** order, taking readers on a brief tour of an immigrant family's rented home: the kitchen lacks a dishwasher or microwave; the living room has no stereo, computer, or VCR, only a small black-and-white TV; the basement has just a washtub and clothesline instead of a washer and dryer. Finally, a third paragraph with the topic sentence "A number of worries typically beset immigrant families" might use an **emphatic** sequence, moving from less significant concerns (having to wear old, unfashionable clothes) to more critical issues (having to deal with isolation and discrimination).

Signal Devices.   Once you determine a logical sequence for your points, you need to make sure that readers can follow the progression of those points within and between paragraphs. **Signal devices** provide readers with cues, reminding them where they have been and indicating where they are going.

Try to include some signals—however awkward or temporary—in your first draft. If you find you *can't,* that's probably a warning that your ideas may not be arranged logically—in which case, it's better to find that out now rather than later on.

Useful signal devices include *transitions, bridging sentences, repeated words, synonyms,* and *pronouns.* Keep in mind, though, that a light touch should be your goal with such signals. Too many call attention to themselves, making the essay mechanical and plodding.

1. **Transitions.**   Words and phrases that ease readers from one idea to another are called **transitions.** Among such signals are the following:

Time	Space	Addition	Examples
first	above	moreover	for instance
next	below	also	for example
during	next to	furthermore	to illustrate
finally	behind	in addition	specifically

Contrast	Comparison	Summary
but	similarly	therefore
however	also	thus
in contrast	likewise	in short
on the one/ other hand	too	in conclusion

Note how the underlined transitions in the following paragraph provide clear cues to readers, showing how ideas fit together:

> Although the effect of air pollution on the human body is distressing, its effect on global ecology is even more troubling. In the Bavarian, French, and Italian Alps, <u>for example</u>, once magnificent forests are slowly being destroyed by air pollution. Trees dying from pollution lose their leaves or needles, allowing sunlight to reach the forest floor. <u>During</u> this process, grass prospers in the increased light and pushes out the native plants and moss that help hold rainwater. The soil <u>thus</u> loses absorbency and becomes hard, causing rain and snow to slide over the ground instead of sinking into it. This, <u>in turn</u>, leads to erosion of the soil. <u>After</u> a heavy rain, the eroded land <u>finally</u> falls away in giant rockslides and avalanches, destroying entire villages and causing life-threatening floods.

2. **Bridging sentences.** Although **bridging sentences** may be used within a paragraph, they are more often used to move readers from one paragraph to the next. Look again at the first sentence in the preceding paragraph on pollution. Note that the sentence consists of two parts: The first part reminds readers that the previous discussion focused on pollution's effect on the body; the second part tells readers that the focus will now be pollution's effect on ecology.

3. **Repeated words, synonyms, and pronouns.** The **repetition** of important words maintains continuity, reassures readers that they are on the right track, and highlights key ideas. **Synonyms**—words similar in meaning to key words or phrases—also provide coherence, while making it possible to avoid unimaginative and tedious repetitions. Finally, **pronouns** (*he, she, it, they, this, that*) enhance coherence by causing readers to think back to the original word (antecedent) the pronoun replaces. When using pronouns, however, be sure there is no ambiguity about antecedents. (See pages 673–674 in the Handbook.)

   The following paragraph uses repeated words (underlined once), synonyms (underlined twice), and pronouns (underlined three times) to integrate ideas:

> <u>Studies</u> have shown that color is also an important part of the way <u>people</u> experience <u>food</u>. In one <u>study</u>, <u>individuals</u> fed a rich red tomato sauce didn't notice <u>it</u> had no flavor until <u>they</u> were nearly <u>finished</u> eating. Similarly, in another <u>experiment</u>, <u>people</u> were offered strangely colored <u>foods</u>: gray pork chops, lavender mashed potatoes, dark blue peas, dessert topped with yellow whipped cream. Not one of the <u>subjects</u> would eat the strange-looking <u>food</u>, even though <u>it</u> smelled and tasted normal.

Write Other Paragraphs in the Essay's Body

Paragraphs supporting the thesis are not necessarily the only kind in the body of an essay. You may also include paragraphs that give background information or provide transitions.

Background Paragraphs

Usually found near the essay's beginning, **background paragraphs** provide information that doesn't directly support the thesis but that helps the reader understand or accept the discussion that follows. Such paragraphs may consist of a definition, brief historical overview, or short description. For example, in the student essay "Salt Marsh" on pages 164–166 the paragraph following the introduction defines a salt marsh and summarizes some of its features. This background information serves as a lead-in to the detailed description that makes up the rest of the essay.

Because you don't want to distract readers from your essay's main point, background paragraphs should be kept as brief as possible. In a paper outlining a program that you believe your college should adopt to beautify its grounds, you would probably need a background paragraph describing typical campus eyesores. Too lengthy a description, though, would detract from the presentation of your step-by-step program.

Transitional Paragraphs

Another kind of paragraph, generally one to three sentences long, may appear between supporting paragraphs to help readers keep track of your discussion. Like the bridging sentences discussed earlier in the chapter, **transitional paragraphs** usually sum up what has been discussed so far and then indicate the direction the essay will take next.

Although too many transitional paragraphs make writing stiff and mechanical, they can be effective when used sparingly, especially in essays with sharp turns in direction. For example, in a paper showing how to purchase a car, you might start by explaining the research a potential buyer should do beforehand: Consult publications like *Consumer Reports;* check performance records published by the automotive industry; call several dealerships for price information. Then, as a transition to the next section—how to negotiate at the dealership—you might provide the following paragraph:

```
Once you have armed yourself with the necessary information,
you are ready to meet with a salesperson at the showroom. Your
experience at the dealership should not be intimidating as long
as you follow the guidelines below.
```

Write the Introduction

Many writers don't prepare an **introduction** until they have started to revise; others feel more comfortable if their first draft includes in basic form all parts of the final essay. If that's how you feel, you'll probably write the introduction as you

complete your first draft. No matter when you prepare it, keep in mind how crucial the introduction is to your essay's success. First impressions count heavily.
More specifically, the introduction serves three distinct functions: It arouses
readers' interest, introduces your subject, and presents your thesis.

Introductions are difficult to write—so difficult, in fact, that you may be tempted
to take the easy way out and use a stale beginning like "According to Webster. . . ."
Equally yawn-inducing are sweeping generalizations that sound grand but say
little: "Throughout human history, people have waged war" or "Affection is
important in all our lives." Don't, however, go too far in the other direction and
come up with a gimmicky opening: "I don't know about you, but in my life, love
is the next best thing to being there. Where? Heaven, that's where!" Contrived and
coy, such introductions are bound to be inconsistent with your essay's purpose,
tone, and point of view. Remember, the introduction's style and content should
flow into the rest of the essay.

The length of your introduction will vary according to your paper's scope and
purpose. Most essays you write, however, will be served best by a one- or two-
paragraph beginning. To write an effective introduction, use any of the following
methods, singly or in combination. The thesis statement in each sample introduction
is underlined. Note, too, that the first thesis includes a plan of development, whereas
the last thesis is followed by a plan of development (see pages 40–41).

Broad Statement Narrowing to a Limited Subject

For generations, morality has been molded primarily by parents,
religion, and schools. Children traditionally acquired their
ideas about what is right and wrong, which goals are important in
life, and how others should be treated from these three sources
collectively. But in the past few decades, a single force--
television--has undermined the beneficial influence that parents,
religion, and school have on children's moral development.
Indeed, <u>television often implants in children negative values
about sex, work, and family life</u>.

Brief Anecdote

At a local high school recently, students in a psychology
course were given a hint of what it is like to be the parents of
a newborn. Each "parent" had to carry a raw egg around at all
times to symbolize the responsibilities of parenthood. The egg
could not be left alone; it limited the "parents'" activities; it
placed a full-time emotional burden on "Mom" and "Dad." This
class exercise illustrates a common problem facing the majority
of new mothers and fathers. <u>Most people receive little
preparation for the job of being parents</u>.

Starting with an Idea That Is the Opposite of the One Actually Developed

We hear a great deal about divorce's disastrous impact on children. We are deluged with advice on ways to make divorce as painless as possible for youngsters; we listen to heartbreaking stories about the confused, grieving children of divorced parents. Little attention has been paid, however, to a different kind of effect that divorce may have on children. <u>Children from divorced families may become skilled manipulators, playing off one parent against the other, worsening an already painful situation.</u>

Series of Short Questions

What happens if a child is caught vandalizing school property? What happens if a child goes for a joyride in a stolen car and accidentally hits a pedestrian? Should parents be liable for their children's mistakes? Should parents have to pay what might be hundreds of thousands of dollars in damages? Adults have begun to think seriously about such questions because the laws concerning the limits of parental responsibility are changing rapidly. <u>With unfortunate frequency, courts have begun to hold parents legally and financially responsible for their children's misbehavior.</u>

Quotation

Educator Neil Postman believes that television has blurred the line between childhood and adulthood. According to Postman, "All the secrets that a print culture kept from children . . . are revealed all at once by media that do not, and cannot, exclude any audience." <u>This media barrage of information, once intended only for adults, has changed childhood for the worse.</u>

Brief Background on the Topic

For a long time, adults believed that "children should be seen, not heard." On special occasions, youngsters were dressed up and told to sit quietly while adults socialized. Even when they were alone with their parents, children were not supposed to bother adults with their concerns. However, beginning with psychologist Arnold Gesell in the 1940s, child-raising experts began to question the wisdom of an approach that blocked communication. In 1965, Haim Ginott's ground-breaking book *Between Parent and Child* stressed the importance of conversing with children. More recently, two of Ginott's disciples, Adele Sager and Elaine Mazlich, wrote a book on this subject: *How to Talk So Children Will Listen and Listen So Children Will Talk*. <u>These days, experts agree, successful parents are those who encourage their children to share their thoughts and concerns</u>.

Refutation of a Common Belief

Adolescents care only about material things; their lives revolve around brand-name sneakers, designer jeans, the latest fad in stereo equipment. They resist education, don't read, barely know who is president, mainline rock 'n' roll, experiment with drugs, and exist on a steady diet of Ring-Dings, nachos, and beer. This is what many adults, including parents, seem to believe about the young. <u>The reality is, however, that young people today show more maturity and common sense than most adults give them credit for</u>.

Dramatic Fact or Statistic

Seventy percent of the respondents in a poll conducted by columnist Ann Landers stated that, if they could live their lives over, they would choose not to have children. This startling statistic makes one wonder what these people believed parenthood would be like. <u>Many parents have unrealistic expectations for their children</u>. Parents want their children to accept their values, follow their paths, and succeed where they failed.

Write the Conclusion

You may have come across essays that ended with jarring abruptness because they had no conclusions at all. Other papers may have had conclusions, but they sputtered to a weak close, a sure sign that the writers had run out of steam and wanted to finish as quickly as possible. Just as satisfying closes are an important part of everyday life (we feel cheated if dinner doesn't end with dessert or if a friend leaves without saying goodbye), a strong **conclusion** is an important part of an effective essay.

However important conclusions may be, they're often difficult to write. When it comes time to write one, you may feel you've said all there is to say. To prevent such an impasse, you can try saving a compelling statistic, quotation, or detail for the end. Just make sure that this interesting item fits in the conclusion and that the essay's body contains sufficient support without it.

Occasionally, an essay doesn't need a separate conclusion. This is often the case with narration or description. For instance, in a narrative showing how a crisis can strengthen a faltering friendship, your point will probably be made with sufficient force without a final "this is what the narrative is all about" paragraph.

Usually, though, a conclusion is necessary. Generally one or two paragraphs in length, the conclusion should give the reader a feeling of completeness and finality. One way to achieve this sense of "rounding off" is to return to an image, idea, or anecdote from the introduction.

Because people tend to remember most clearly the points they read last, the conclusion is also a good place to remind readers of your thesis, phrasing this central idea somewhat differently than you did earlier in the essay. You may also use the conclusion to make a final point about your subject. This way, you leave your readers with something to mull over. Be careful, though, not to open an entirely new line of thought at the essay's close. If you do, readers may feel puzzled and frustrated, wishing you had provided evidence for your final point. And, of course, always be sure that concluding material fits your thesis and is consistent with your purpose, tone, and point of view.

In your conclusion, it's best to steer away from stock phrases like "In sum," "In conclusion," and "This paper has shown that. . . ." Also avoid lengthy conclusions. As in everyday life, prolonged farewells are tedious.

Following are examples of some of the techniques you can use to write effective conclusions. These strategies may be used singly or in combination. The first strategy, the *summary conclusion*, can be especially helpful in long, complex essays since readers may appreciate a review of your points. Tacked onto a short essay, though, a summary conclusion often seems boring and mechanical.

Summary

    Contrary to what many adults think, most adolescents are not only aware of the important issues of the times but also deeply concerned about them. They are sensitive to the plight of the homeless, the destruction of the environment, and the pitfalls of rampant materialism. Indeed, today's young people are not less mature and sensible than their parents were. If anything, they are more so.

Prediction

    The growing tendency on the part of the judicial system to hold parents responsible for the actions of their delinquent children can have a disturbing impact on all of us. Parents will feel bitter toward their own children and cynical about a system that holds them accountable for the actions of minors. Children, continuing to escape the consequences of their actions, will become even more lawless and destructive. Society cannot afford two such possibilities.

Quotation

The comic W. C. Fields is reputed to have said, "Anyone who hates children and dogs can't be all bad." Most people do not share Fields's cynicism. Viewing childhood as a time of purity, they are alarmed at the way television exposes children to the seamy side of life, stripping youngsters of their innocence and giving them a glib sophistication that is a poor substitute for wisdom.

Statistic

Granted, divorce may, in some cases, be the best thing for families torn apart by parents battling one another. However, in longitudinal studies of children from divorced families, psychologist Judith Wallerstein found that only 10 percent of the youngsters felt relief at their parents' divorce; the remaining 90 percent felt devastated. Such statistics surely call into question parents' claims that they are divorcing for their children's sake.

Recommendation or Call for Action

It is a mistake to leave parenting to instinct. Instead, we should make parenting skills a required course in schools. In addition, a nationwide hotline should be established to help parents deal with crises. Such training and continuing support would help adults deal more effectively with many of the problems they face as parents.

Write the Title

Some writers say that they often begin a piece with only a title in mind. But for most, writing the **title** is the finishing touch. Although creating a title is usually one of the last steps in writing an essay, it shouldn't be done haphazardly. It may take time to write an effective title—one that hints at the essay's thesis and snares the reader's interest.

Good titles may make use of the following techniques: *repetition of sounds* ("The Plot Against People"), *humor* ("Neat People Versus Sloppy People"), and *questions* ("Am I Blue?"). More often, though, titles are straightforward phrases derived from the essay's subject or thesis: "Shooting an Elephant" and "Why Computers Don't Belong in the Classroom," for example.

PULLING IT ALL TOGETHER

Now that you know how to prepare a first draft, you might find it helpful to examine the illustration below to see how the different parts of a draft can fit together. Keep in mind that not every essay you write will take this shape. As your purpose, audience, tone, and point of view change, so will your essay's structure. An introduction or conclusion, for instance, may be developed in more than one paragraph; the thesis statement may be implied or delayed until the essay's middle or end; not all paragraphs may have topic sentences; and several supporting paragraphs may be needed to develop a single topic sentence. Even so, the basic format presented here offers a strategy for organizing a variety of writing assignments—from term papers to lab reports. Once you feel comfortable with the structure, you have a foundation on which to base your variations. (This book's student and professional essays illustrate some possibilities.) Even when using a specific format, you always have room to give your spirit and imagination free play. The language you use, the details you select, the perspective you offer are uniquely yours. They are what make your essay different from anyone else's.

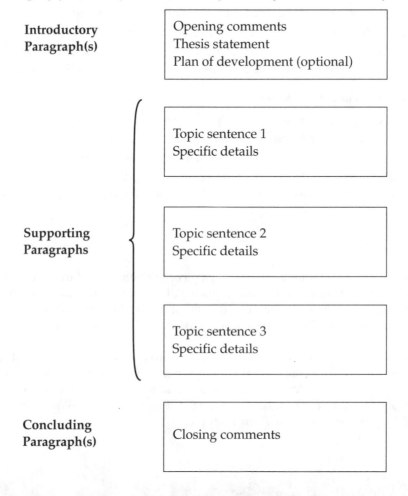

Introductory Paragraph(s)
- Opening comments
- Thesis statement
- Plan of development (optional)

Supporting Paragraphs
- Topic sentence 1
  Specific details

- Topic sentence 2
  Specific details

- Topic sentence 3
  Specific details

Concluding Paragraph(s)
- Closing comments

SAMPLE FIRST DRAFT

Here is the first draft of Harriet Davids's essay. (You saw Harriet's prewriting scratch list on pages 34–35, her thesis on page 39, and so on.) Harriet wrote the draft in one sitting. Working at a computer, she started by typing her thesis at the top of the first page. Then, following the guidelines on pages 63–64, she moved the material in her outline (pages 59–60) to her draft. (See page 66 for an explanation of the differences between her outline and draft.) Harriet worked rapidly; she started with the first body paragraph and wrote straight through to the last supporting paragraph.

By moving quickly, Harriet got down her essay's basic text rather easily. Once she felt she had captured in rough form what she wanted to say, she reread her draft to get a sense of how she might open and close the essay. Then she drafted her introduction and conclusion; both appear here, together with the body of the essay. (The commentary following the draft will give you an even clearer sense of how Harriet proceeded.)

> Student essay in progress

Challenges for Today's Parents
by Harriet Davids

Thesis: Being a parent today is much more difficult than it was a generation ago.

Raising children used to be much simpler in the '50s and '60s. I remember TV images from that era showing that parenting involved simply teaching kids to clean their rooms, do their homework, and ____. But being a parent today is much more difficult because nowadays parents have to shield/protect kids from lots of things, like distractions from schoolwork, from sexual material, and from dangerous situations.

Add specifics

Parents have to control all the new distractions/temptations that turn kids away from schoolwork. These days many kids have stereos, computers, and televisions in their rooms. Certainly, my girls can't resist the urge to watch MTV and go online, especially if it's time to do homework. Unfortunately, though, kids aren't assigned much homework and what is assigned too often is busywork. And there are even more distractions outside the home. Teens no longer hang out/congregate on the corner where Dad and Mom can yell to them to come home and do homework. Instead they hang out at the mall, in video arcades, and at fast-food restaurants. Obviously, parents and school can't compete with all this.

Weak transition   (Also) parents have to help kids develop responsible sexual
values even though sex is everywhere. Kids see sex magazines and
dirty paperbacks in the corner store where they used to get candy
and comic books. And instead of the artsy nude shots of the past,
kids see ronchey (sp?), explicit shots in <u>Playboy</u> and <u>Penthouse</u>.
And movies have sexy stuff in them today. Teachers seduce
students and people treat sex casually/as a sport. Not exactly
traditional values. TV is no better. Kids see soap-opera
characters in bed and cable shows full of nudity by just flipping
the dial (FIX). Even worse is what's on the Internet. Too easy
for kids to access chat rooms and websites dealing with adult,
sometimes pornographic material. The situation has gotten so out
of hand that maybe the government should establish guidelines on
what's permissible.

   Worst of all are the life-threatening dangers that parents must
help children fend off over the years. With older kids, drugs
fall into place as a main concern (Awk). Peer pressure to try
drugs is bigger (wrong word) to kids than their parents'
warnings. Other kinds of warnings are common when children are
small. Then parents fear violence since news shows constantly
report stories of little children being abused (add specifics).
And when kids aren't much older, they have to resist the pressure
Redo   to drink. (Alcohol has always attracted kids, but nowadays they
are drinking more and this can be deadly, especially when
drinking is combined with driving.)

   Most adults love their children and want to be good parents.
But it's difficult because the world seems stacked against
young people. Even Holden Caufield (sp?) had trouble dealing
with society's confusing pressures. Parents must give their
children some freedom but not so much that the kids lose sight
of what's important.

Commentary

   As you can see, Harriet's draft is rough. Because she knew she would revise later
on (pages 101 and 129), she "zapped out" the draft in an informal, colloquial style.
For example, she occasionally expressed her thoughts in fragments ("Not exactly
traditional values"), relied heavily on "and" as a transition, and used slangy
expressions such as "kids," "dirty paperbacks," and "lots of things." Similarly,
rather than finetuning, Harriet simply made marginal or parenthetical notes to
herself: "redo" or "fix" to signal awkward sentences; "add specifics" to mark

overly general statements; "wrong word" after an imprecise word; "sp" to remind herself to check spelling in the dictionary; "weak transition" to indicate where a stronger signaling device was needed. Note, too, that she used slashes between alternative word choices and left a blank space when wording just wouldn't come. (Harriet's final draft appears on pages 137–139.)

Continues on page 101

Writing a first draft may seem like quite a challenge, but the tips offered in this chapter should help you proceed with confidence. Indeed, as you work on the draft, you may be surprised by how much you enjoy writing. After all, this is your chance to get down on paper something you want to say.

ACTIVITIES: WRITING THE PARAGRAPHS IN THE FIRST DRAFT

1. For each paragraph that follows, determine whether the topic sentence is stated or implied. If the topic sentence is explicit, indicate its location in the paragraph (beginning, end, middle, or both beginning and end). If the topic sentence is implied, state it in your own words.

    a.   In 1902, a well-known mathematician wrote an article "proving" that no airplane could ever fly. Just a year later, the Wright brothers made their first flight. In the 1950s, a famed British astronomer said in an interview that the idea of space travel was "utter bilge." Similarly, noted scholars in this country and abroad claimed that automobiles would never replace the trolley car and that the electric light was an impractical gimmick. Clearly, being an expert doesn't guarantee a clear vision of the future.

    b.   Motorists in Caracas, Venezuela, must follow an odd/ even license-number system for driving their cars on any given day. Cars with license plates ending in even numbers can drive downtown only on even-numbered days. Similarly, in Los Angeles several summers ago, an experimental program required businesses with more than one hundred employees to form "Don't drive to work" programs. Such programs established ride-sharing schedules and offered employees incentives for using mass transportation. Even more extreme is Singapore's method for limiting downtown traffic--most private vehicles are completely banned from central sections of the city.

c.   A small town in Massachusetts that badly needed extra space for grade school classes found it in an unlikely spot. Most of the town's available buildings were too far from the main school or too small. One building, however, was nearby and spacious; it even offered excellent lunch-room and recreation facilities. Despite some objections, the building was chosen--a former saloon, complete with bar, bar stools, cocktail lounge, and pool hall.

d.   The physical complaints of neurotics--people who are exceptionally anxious, pessimistic, hostile, or tense-- were once largely ignored by physicians. Many doctors believed that neurotics' frequent health complaints sim-ply reflected their emotional distress. New research, though, shows that neurotics are indeed likely to have physical problems. Specifically, researchers have found that neurotics stand a greater chance of suffering from arthritis, asthma, ulcers, headaches, and heart disease. In addition, there is growing evidence that people who were chronically anxious or depressed in their teens and twenties are more likely to become ill, even die, in their forties.

e.   Many American companies have learned the hard way that they need to know the language of their foreign customers. When Chevrolet began selling its Nova cars in Latin America, hardly anyone would buy them. The company finally realized that Spanish speakers read the car's name as the Spanish phrase "no va," meaning "doesn't go." When Pepsi-Cola ran its "Pepsi gives you life" ads in China, con-sumers either laughed or were offended. The company hadn't translated its slogan quite right. In Chinese, the slogan came out "Pepsi brings your ancestors back from the dead."

2. Using the strategies described on pages 70–71, strengthen the following vague paragraphs. Elaborate each one with striking specifics that clarify meaning and add interest. As you provide specifics, you may need to break each paragraph into several.

a.   Other students can make studying in the college library difficult. For one thing, they take up so much space that they leave little room for anyone else. By being inconsiderate in other ways, they make it hard to concentrate on the task at hand. Worst of all, they do things that make it almost impossible to find needed books and magazines.

b.   Some people have dangerous driving habits. They act as though there's no one else on the road. They also seem unsure of where they're going. Changing their minds from second to second, they leave it up to others to figure out what they're going to do. Finally, too many people drive at speeds that are either too slow or too fast, creating dangerous situations for both drivers and pedestrians.

c.   Things people used to think were safe are now considered dangerous. This goes for certain foods that are now considered unhealthy. Similarly, some habits people thought were harmless have been found to be risky. Even things in the home, in the workplace, and in the air have been found to cause harm. So much has been discovered in recent years about what is harmful that it makes you wonder: What additional dangers lurk in the environment?

d.   Society encourages young people to drink. For one thing, youngsters learn early that alcohol plays a prominent role in family and business celebrations. Children also see that liquor is an important part of adults' celebration of national holidays. But the place where youngsters see alcohol depicted most enticingly is on TV. Prime-time shows and beer commercials imply that alcohol is an essential part of a good life.

3. Using the designations indicated in parentheses, identify the flaw(s) in the development of each of the following paragraphs. The paragraphs may lack one or more of the following: unity (U), specific and sufficient support (S), coherence (C). The paragraphs may also needlessly repeat a point (R). Revise the paragraphs, deleting, combining, and rearranging material. Also, add supporting evidence and signal devices where needed.

a.   Studies reveal that individuals' first names can influence other people's perceptions. Some names reflect favorably on individuals. For example, a survey conducted by Opinion Masters, Inc., showed that male business executives thought the names Dorothy and Katherine conveyed competence and professionalism. And participants in a British study reported that names like Richard and Charles commanded respect and sounded "classy." Of course, participants' observations also reflect the fairly rigid stratification of British society. Other names, however, can have a negative impact. In one study, for instance, teachers gave lower grades to essays supposedly written by boys named Hubert and Elmer than to the very same essays when credited to boys with more popular names. Another study found that girls with unpopular names (like Gertrude or Gladys) did worse on tests than girls with more appealing names. Such findings underscore the arbitrary nature of the grading process.

b.   This "me first" attitude is also behind the cheating that seems prevalent nowadays. School is perhaps the first place where widespread cheating occurs, with students devising shrewd strategies to do well--often at the expense of others. And since schools are reluctant to teach morality, children grow up with distorted values. The same exaggerated self-interest often causes people, once they reach adulthood, to cheat their companies and co-workers. It's no wonder American business is in such trouble.

c.   Despite widespread belief to the contrary, brain size within a species has little to do with how intelligent a particular individual is. A human brain can range from 900 cubic centimeters to as much as 2,500 cubic centimeters, but a large brain does not indicate an equally large degree of intelligence. If humans could see the size of other people's brains, they would probably judge each other accordingly, even though brain size has no real significance.

d.   For the 50 percent of adult Americans with high cholesterol, heart disease is a constant threat. Americans can reduce their cholesterol significantly by taking a number of easy steps. Since only foods derived from animals contain

cholesterol, eating a strict vegetarian diet is the best way
to beat the cholesterol problem. Also, losing weight is
known to reduce cholesterol levels--even in those who were
as little as ten pounds overweight. Physicians warn, though,
that quick weight loss almost always leads to an equally
rapid regaining of the lost pounds. For those unwilling to
try a vegetarian diet, poultry, fish, and low-fat dairy
products can substitute for such high-cholesterol foods as
red meat, eggs, cream, and butter. Adding oat bran to the
diet has been shown to lower cholesterol. The bran absorbs
excess cholesterol in the blood and removes it from the
body through waste matter.

4. Strengthen the coherence of the following paragraphs by providing a clear
organizational structure and by adding appropriate signal devices. To improve
the flow of ideas, you may also need to combine and resequence sentences.

I was a camp counselor this past summer. I learned that
leading young children is different from leading people your
own age. I was president of my high school Ecology Club. I
ran it democratically. We wanted to bring a speaker to the
school. We decided to do a fund-raiser. I solicited ideas
from everybody. We got together to figure out which was best.
It became obvious which was the most profitable and workable
fund-raiser. Everybody got behind the effort. The discussion
showed that the idea of a raffle with prizes donated by local
merchants was the most profitable.

I learned that little kids operate differently. I had to be
more of a boss rather than a democratic leader. I took
suggestions from the group on the main activity of the day.
Everyone voted for the best suggestion. Some kids got
especially upset. There a problem with kids whose ideas
were voted down. I learned to make the suggestions myself. The
children could vote on my suggestions. No one was overly
attached to any of the suggestions. They felt that the outcome
of the voting was fair. Basically, I got to be in charge.

5. For an essay with the thesis shown here, indicate the implied pattern(s) of
development for each topic sentence that follows.

Thesis: The college should make community service a requirement for
graduation.

Topic Sentences

a. "Mandatory community service" is a fairly new and often misunderstood concept.

b. Certainly, the conditions in many communities signal serious need.

c. Here's the story of one student's community involvement.

d. There are, though, many other kinds of programs in which students can become involved.

e. Indeed, a single program offers students numerous opportunities.

f. Such involvement can have a real impact on students' lives.

g. This is the way mandatory community service might work on this campus.

h. However, the college could adopt two very different approaches—one developed by a university, the other by a community college.

i. In any case, the college should begin exploring the possibility of making community service a graduation requirement.

6. Select one of the topic sentences listed in activity 5. Use individual or group brainstorming to generate support for it. After reviewing your raw material, delete, add, and combine points as needed. Finally, with the thesis in mind, write a rough draft of the paragraph.

7. Imagine you plan to write a serious essay on one of the following thesis statements. The paper will be read by students in your composition class. After determining your point of view, use any prewriting techniques you want to identify the essay's major and supporting points. Arrange the points in order and determine where background and/or transitional paragraphs might be helpful.

a. Society needs stricter laws against noise pollution.

b. The traditional lecture format used in many large colleges and universities discourages independent thinking.

c. Public buildings in this town should be redesigned to accommodate the disabled.

d. Long-standing discrimination against women in college athletics must stop.

8. Use any of the techniques described on pages 76–81 to revise the opening and closing paragraphs of two of your own papers. When rewriting, don't forget to keep your purpose, audience, tone, and point of view in mind.

9. Reread Harriet Davids's first draft on pages 83–84. Overall, does it support Harriet's thesis? Which topic sentences focus paragraphs effectively? Where is evidence specific, unified, and coherent? Where does Harriet run into some problems? Make a list of the draft's strengths and weaknesses. Save your list for later review. (In the next chapter, you'll be asked to revise Harriet's draft.)

10. Freewrite or write in your journal about a subject that's been on your mind lately. Reread your raw material to see what thesis seems to emerge. What might your purpose, audience, tone, and point of view be if you wrote an essay with this thesis? What primary and secondary points would you cover? Prepare an outline of your ideas. Then draft the essay's body, providing background and transitional paragraphs if appropriate. Finally, write a rough

version of the essay's introduction, conclusion, and title. (Save your draft so you can revise it after reading the next chapter.)

11. If you prepared a first draft in response to activity 3 in Chapter 5 (page 62), work with at least one other person to strengthen that early draft by applying the ideas presented in this chapter. (Save this stronger version of your draft so you can refine it further after reading the next chapter.)

12. Referring to the outline you prepared in response to activity 5 or activity 6 in Chapter 5 (page 62), draft the body of an essay. After reviewing the draft, prepare background and transitional paragraphs as needed. Then draft a rough introduction, conclusion, and title. Ask several people to react to what you've prepared, and save your draft so you can work with it further after reading the next chapter.

7
REVISING OVERALL MEANING, STRUCTURE, AND PARAGRAPH DEVELOPMENT

By now, you've probably abandoned any preconceptions you might have had about good writers sitting down and creating a finished product in one easy step. Alexander Pope's comment that "true ease in writing comes from art, not chance" is as true today as it was more than two hundred years ago. Writing that seems effortlessly clear is often the result of sustained work, not of good luck or even inborn talent. And much of this work takes place during the final stage of the writing process, when ideas, paragraphs, sentences, and words are refined and reshaped.

You've most likely seen cartoons picturing writers plugging away at their typewriters, filling their wastebaskets with sheet after sheet of crumpled paper. It's true. Professional writers—novelists, journalists, textbook authors—seldom submit a piece of writing that hasn't been revised. They recognize that rough, unpolished work doesn't do them justice. What's more, they often look forward to revising. Columnist Ellen Goodman puts it this way: "What makes me happy is rewriting. . . . It's like cleaning house, getting rid of all the junk, getting things in the right order, tightening up."

In a sense, revision occurs throughout the writing process: At some earlier stage, you may have dropped an idea, overhauled your thesis, or shifted paragraph order. What, then, is different about the rewriting that occurs in the revision stage? The answer has to do with the literal meaning of the word *revision*—reseeing, or seeing again. Genuine revision involves casting clear eyes on your work, viewing it as though you're a reader rather than the writer. Revision is not, as some believe, simply touch-up work—changing a sentence here, a word there, eliminating spelling errors, typing a neat final copy. Revision means that you go through your paper looking for trouble, ready to pick a fight with your own writing. And then you must be willing to sit down and make the changes needed for your writing to be as effective as possible.

Throughout this book, we emphasize that everyone approaches early stages in the writing process differently. The same is true for the revision stage. Some people dash off a draft, knowing they'll spend hours reworking it later. Others find that writing the first draft slowly yields such good results that wholesale revision isn't necessary. Some writers revise neatly, while others fill their drafts with messily scribbled changes. Then there are those who find that the more they revise, the more they overcomplicate their writing and rob it of spontaneity. So, for each writer and for each piece of writing, the amount and kind of revision will vary.

Because revision is hard work, you may resist it. After putting the final period in your first draft, you may feel done and have trouble accepting that more work remains. Or, as you read the draft, you may see so many weak spots that you view revision as punishment for not getting things right the first time. And, if you feel shaky about how to proceed, you may be tempted to skip revising altogether.

If all this sounds as though we're talking about you, don't give up. Here are seven strategies to help you get going if you balk at or feel overwhelmed by revising.

STRATEGIES TO MAKE REVISION EASIER

Keep in mind that the revision strategies discussed here should be adapted to each writing situation. Revising an answer on an essay exam is quite different from revising a paper you've spent several weeks preparing. Other considerations include your professor's requirements and expectations, the time available, and the paper's bearing on your grade. In any case, the following strategies will help you approach revision more confidently.

Set Your First Draft Aside for a While

When you pick up your draft after having set it aside for a time, you'll approach it with a fresh, more objective point of view. How much of an interval to leave depends on the time available to you. In general, though, the more time between finishing the draft and starting to revise, the better.

Work from Typed or Printed Text

Working with an essay in impersonal typewritten form, instead of in your own familiar handwriting, helps you see the paper impartially, as if someone else had written it. Each time you make major changes, try to retype your essay so that you can see it anew. Using a word processor makes it easy to prepare successive copies. If, however, you work from handwritten drafts, don't boldly strike out or erase as you revise. Instead, lightly cross out material, in case you want to retrieve it later on.

Read the Draft Aloud

Hearing how your writing sounds helps you pick up problems that might otherwise go undetected: places where sentences are awkward, meaning is ambiguous, words are imprecise. Even better, have another person read your draft aloud to you. The thought of this probably makes you shudder, but it's worth the risk. Someone else doesn't have—as you do—a vested interest in making your writing sound good. If a reader slows to a crawl over a murky paragraph or trips over a convoluted sentence, you know where you have to do some rewriting.

Participate in Peer Review

Writing is social and interactive; it promotes dialog. For this reason, many instructors include in-class or at-home peer review as a regular part of a composition course. Peer review—the critical reading of another person's writing with the intention of suggesting changes—accomplishes several important goals. First, peer review helps you gain a more objective perspective on your work. When you write something, you're often too close to what you've prepared to evaluate it fairly; you may have trouble seeing where the writing is strong and where it needs to be strengthened. Peer review supplies the fresh, neutral perspective you need. Second, reviewing your classmates' work broadens your own composing options. You may be inspired to experiment with a technique you admired in a classmate's writing but wouldn't have thought of on your own. Finally, peer review trains you to be a better reader and critic of your *own* writing. When you get into the habit of critically reading other students' writing, you become more adept at critiquing your own.

Preparing a helpful peer review is a skill that takes time to develop. At first, you, like many students, may be too easy or too critical. Effective peer review calls for rigor and care; you should give classmates the conscientious feedback that you hope for in return. Peer review also requires tact and kindness; feedback should always be constructive and include observations about what works well in a piece of writing. People have difficulty mustering the energy to revise if they feel there's nothing worth revising.

If your instructor doesn't require peer review, you can set up peer review sessions on your own, adapting the suggestions here to fit your needs. Start by selecting readers who are objective (not a love-struck admirer or a doting grandparent) and skilled enough to provide useful commentary. It's a good idea to provide each reviewer with a copy of your paper, allowing them to read, reread, and write on it at their own pace.

To ensure that you leave peer review sessions with specific observations about what does and doesn't work in your writing, give your readers a clear sense of what you want from them. If you simply ask, "How's this?", you may receive a vague comment like "It's not very effective." What you want are *concrete observations and suggestions:* "I'm confused because what you say in the fifth sentence contradicts what you say in the second" or "You make the same point in the second and fourth paragraphs. Shouldn't the paragraphs be combined?"

To promote such specific responses, ask your readers targeted (preferably written) questions like "My introduction seems bland. What ideas do you have for perking it up?" or "I'm having trouble moving from my second to my third point. How can I make the transition smoother?" Such questions require more than "yes" or "no" responses; they encourage readers to dig into your writing where you sense it needs work. You may develop your own questions, or you may adapt the revision checklists in this and the following chapter (pages 98–99, 100–101, 118 and 128). (If it's feasible, encourage readers to *write* their responses to your questions.)

If you and your peer reviewer(s) can't meet in person, **e-mail** can provide a crucial means of contact. With a couple of clicks, you can simply send each other computer files of your work. Before you do so, determine whether your word-processing software is compatible; that will dictate whether you should send each other your computerized drafts as file attachments or as cut-and-pasted text insertions in the e-mail message box. You and your reviewers also need to decide exactly how to exchange comments about each other's drafts. You might conclude, for example, that you'll type your responses, perhaps in bold capitals, into the file itself. Or you might decide to print out the drafts and reply to them in writing, later exchanging the annotated drafts in person. No matter what you and your peers decide, you'll probably find e-mail an invaluable tool in the writing process.

Evaluate and Respond to Peer Review

Accepting criticism isn't easy (even if you asked for it), and not all peer reviewers will be tactful. Even so, try to listen with an open mind to those giving you feedback. Take notes on their oral observations and/or have them fill out the checklist described above. Later, when you're ready to revise your paper, reread your notes. Which reviewer remarks seem valid? Which recommendations are workable? Which are not? In addition, try using a feedback chart or a system of marginal annotations to help you evaluate and remedy any perceived weaknesses in your draft.

Here's how to use a three-column **feedback chart.** In the first column, list the major problems you and your readers see in the draft. Next, rank the problems, designating the most critical as "1." Then in the second column, jot down possible solutions—your own as well as your readers'. Finally, in the third column, briefly describe what action you'll take to correct each problem. Here is a sample chart:

Problems	Suggestions	Decisions
④ Informal expressions in paragraph 3 seem out of keeping with the rest of the essay.	Lighten language elsewhere. Make the language in paragraph 3 less slangy.	Make language in paragraph 3 a bit more formal. Also make overall language less stiff, especially in paragraphs 2 and 5.
① Thesis in introduction contradicted by paragraph 2.	Delete paragraph 2. Qualify the thesis so that there's no contradiction.	Qualify thesis.
② Chronological order used until paragraph 4. That background paragraph breaks the flow.	Delete background paragraph. Move paragraph to beginning. Add transition so paragraph fits more easily.	Delete background paragraph--not needed, except for definition, which can be added to introduction.
③ Too many long sentences	Eliminate some prepositional phrases. Break up long sentences into shorter ones.	Take out some prepositional phrases.

Whether or not you decide to use a feedback chart, be sure to enter **marginal annotations** on your draft (preferably a clean copy of it) before revising it. In the margins, jot down any major problems, numbered in order of importance, along with possible remedies. Marking your paper this way, much as an instructor might, helps you view your paper as though it were written by someone else. Then, keeping the draft's problems in mind, start revising. You may make changes directly above the appropriate line or, when necessary, rework sections on a separate sheet of paper. To see how such marginal annotations work, turn to page 101 or look at the sample first drafts of student essays in Chapters 11–19.

If you've been working on a computer, type in your changes, or handwrite changes directly on the draft above the appropriate line. (Rework extensive sections on a separate sheet of paper.) When revising, always keep in mind that you may not agree with every reviewer suggestion. That's fine. It's *your* paper, and it's *your* decision to implement or reject the suggestions made by your peers.

Evaluate and Respond to Your Instructor's Comments

Most likely, your peers won't be the only ones giving you feedback. Your instructor will also react to your early or final draft. Like many students, you may be tempted to look only briefly at your instructor's comments. Perhaps you've "had it" with the essay and don't want to think about revising it to reflect the instructor's remarks. And if there's a grade on the essay, you may think that's the only thing that counts.

But remember: Although grades are important, comments are even more so. They can help you *improve* your writing—if not in this paper, then in the next one. If you're reading or listening to your instructor's feedback, pay close attention and take notes. Then use a modified version of the feedback chart or a system of marginal annotations (see page 96) to help you evaluate and react to the instructor's comments. If you don't understand or don't agree with the instructor's observations, you shouldn't hesitate to request a conference. Be sure to go to the conference prepared. You might, for example, put a check next to the instructor's comments you want to discuss. Your instructor will appreciate your thoughtful planning; getting together gives both you and the instructor a chance to clarify your respective points of view.

View Revision as a Series of Steps

The six revision techniques described so far will help you approach revision with more confidence. We've saved for last, though, the strategy we consider most critical: dividing revision into steps.

You can overcome a bad case of revision jitters simply by viewing revision as a process. Instead of trying to tackle all of a draft's problems at once, proceed step by step. (The feedback chart and annotation system will help you do just that.) If time allows, read your essay several times. Move from a broad overview (the *macro* level) to an up-close look at mechanics (the *micro* level). With each reading, focus on different issues and ask different questions about the draft.

Here is a recommended series of revision steps:

First step: Revise overall meaning and structure.
Second step: Revise paragraph development.
Third step: Revise sentences and words.

At first, the prospect of reading and rewriting a paper several times may seem to make revision more, not less, overwhelming. Eventually, though, you'll become accustomed to revision as a process, and you'll appreciate the way such an approach improves your writing.

Ernest Hemingway once told an interviewer that he had revised the last page of one of his novels thirty-nine times. When the interviewer asked, "What was it that had you stumped?", Hemingway answered, "Getting the words right." We don't expect you to revise your paper thirty-nine times. Whenever possible, though, you should aim for three readings. Resist the impulse to tinker with, say, an unclear sentence until you're sure the essay as a whole makes its point clearly. After all, it can be difficult to rephrase a muddy sentence until you have the essay's overall meaning well in hand.

Remember, though: There are no hard-and-fast rules about the revision steps. For one thing, there are bound to be occasions when you have time for, at best, only one quick pass over a draft. Moreover, as you gain experience revising, you'll probably streamline the process or shift the steps around. Assume, for example, that you get bogged down trying to recast the thesis so it more accurately reflects the draft's overall meaning (the first step). You might take a break by fastforwarding to the final stage and using the dictionary to check the spelling of several words. Or, while reorganizing a paragraph (the second step), you might realize you need to rephrase some sentences (the third step).

The remainder of this chapter discusses the first and second steps in the revision process—revising overall meaning and structure and paragraph development. Chapter 8 focuses on the third step—revising sentences and words.

REVISING OVERALL MEANING AND STRUCTURE

During this first step in the revision process, you (and any readers you may have) should read the draft quickly to assess its *general effect* and *clarity*. Does the draft accomplish what you set out to do? Does it develop a central point clearly and logically? Does it merit and hold the reader's attention?

It's not uncommon when revising at this stage to find that the draft doesn't fully convey what you had in mind. Perhaps your intended thesis ends up being overshadowed by another idea. (If that happens, you have two options: (1) you may pursue the new line of thought as your revised thesis, or (2) you may bring the paper back into line with your original thesis by deleting extraneous material.) Another problem might be that readers miss a key point. Perhaps you initially believed the point could be implied, but you now realize it needs to be stated explicitly.

Preparing a *brief outline* of a draft can help evaluate the essay's overall structure. Either you or a reader can prepare the outline. In either case, your thesis, reflecting any changes made during the first draft, should be written at the top of the outline page. Then you or your readers jot down in brief outline form the paper's basic structure. With the draft pared down to its essentials, you can see more easily how parts contribute to the whole and how points do or do not fit together. This barebones rendering often reveals the changes needed to remedy any fuzziness or illogic in the development of the draft's central idea and key supporting points.

The following checklist is designed to help you and your readers evaluate a draft's overall meaning and structure. As with other checklists in the book, you may either use all the checklist questions or focus only on those especially relevant to a particular essay. (Activities at the end of the chapter will refer you to this checklist when you revise several essays.) To see how one student used the checklist when revising, turn to page 101.

> ☑ REVISING OVERALL MEANING AND STRUCTURE:
>   A CHECKLIST
>
> ☐ What is your initial reaction to the draft? What do you like and dislike?
> ☐ What audience does the essay address? How suited to this audience are the essay's purpose, tone, and point of view?

> ☐ What is the essay's thesis? Is it explicitly stated or implied? If the perceived thesis isn't what was intended, what changes need to be made?
> ☐ What are the essay's main points? If any stray from or contradict the thesis, what changes need to be made?
> ☐ According to what organizing principle(s)—spatial, chronological, emphatic, simple to complex—are the main points arranged? How does this organizational scheme reinforce the thesis?
> ☐ Which patterns of development (narration, description, comparison-contrast, and so on) help shape the draft? How do these patterns reinforce the thesis?
> ☐ Where would background information, definition of terms, or additional material clarify meaning?

You are now ready to focus on the second step in the revising process.

REVISING PARAGRAPH DEVELOPMENT

After you use feedback to refine the paper's fundamental meaning and structure, it's time to look closely at the essay's paragraphs. At this point, you and those giving you feedback should read the draft more slowly. How can the essay's paragraphs be made more unified (see pages 68–69) and more specific (pages 69–71)? Which paragraphs seem to lack sufficient support (pages 71–72)? Which would profit from more attention to coherence (pages 72–75)?

At this stage, you may find that a paragraph needs more examples to make its point or that a paragraph should be deleted because it doesn't develop the thesis. Or perhaps you realize that a paragraph should be placed earlier in the essay because it defines a term that readers need to understand from the outset.

Here's a strategy to help assess your paragraphs' effectiveness. In the margin next to each paragraph, make a brief notation that answers these two questions: (1) What is the paragraph's *purpose?* and (2) What is its *content?* Then skim the marginal notes to see if each paragraph does what you intended.

During this stage, you should also examine the *length of your paragraphs.* Here's why.

You know how boring it can be to travel long stretches of unvarying highway. Without interesting twists and turns, sweeping views, and occasional rest stops, you struggle to stay awake. The same is true in writing. Paragraphs all the same length dull your readers' response, while variations encourage them to sit up and take notice. (We imagine, for example, that the two-sentence paragraph above got your attention.)

If your paragraphs tend to run long, try breaking some of them into shorter, crisper chunks. Be sure, however, not to break paragraphs just anywhere. To preserve the paragraphs' logic, you may need to reshape and add material, always keeping in mind that each paragraph should have a clear and distinctive focus.

However, don't go overboard and break up all your paragraphs. Too many short paragraphs become as predictable as too many long ones. An abundance of brief paragraphs also makes it difficult for readers to see how points are related. (In such cases, you might combine short paragraphs containing similar ideas.) Furthermore, overreliance on short paragraphs may mean that you haven't provided sufficient evidence for your ideas. Finally, a succession of short paragraphs (as in a newspaper article) encourages readers to skim when, of course, you want them to consider carefully what you have to say. So use short paragraphs, but save them for places in the essay where you want to introduce variation or achieve emphasis.

The following checklist is designed to help you and your readers evaluate a draft's paragraph development. (Activities at the end of the chapter will refer you to the checklist when you revise several essays.) To see how a student used the checklist when revising, turn to page 101.

> ✔ REVISING PARAGRAPH DEVELOPMENT: A CHECKLIST
>
> ☐ In what way does each supporting paragraph develop the essay's thesis? Which paragraphs fail to develop the thesis? Should they be deleted or revised?
>
> ☐ What is each paragraph's central idea? If this idea is expressed in a topic sentence, where is this sentence located? Where does something stray from or contradict the paragraph's main idea? How could the paragraph's focus be sharpened?
>
> ☐ Where in each paragraph does support seem irrelevant, vague, insufficient, inaccurate, nonrepresentative, or disorganized? What could be done to remedy these problems? Where would additional sensory details, examples, facts, statistics, expert authority, and personal observations be appropriate?
>
> ☐ By what organizational principle (spatial, chronological, or emphatic) are each paragraph's ideas arranged? Why is this the most effective order?
>
> ☐ How could paragraph coherence be strengthened? What signal devices are used to relate ideas within and between paragraphs? Where are there too few signals? Too many?
>
> ☐ Where do too many paragraphs of the same length dull interest? Where would a short paragraph be more effective? A long one?
>
> ☐ How could the introduction be strengthened? What striking anecdote, fact, or statistic elsewhere in the essay might be moved to the introduction? How does the introduction establish the essay's purpose, audience, tone, and point of view? What strategy links the introduction to the essay's body?

□ How could the conclusion be strengthened? What striking anecdote, fact, or statistic elsewhere in the essay might be moved to the conclusion? Would echoing something from the introduction help round off the essay more effectively? How has the conclusion been made an integral part of the essay?

SAMPLE STUDENT REVISION OF OVERALL MEANING, STRUCTURE, AND PARAGRAPH DEVELOPMENT

The introduction to Harriet Davids's first draft that we saw in Chapter 6 (pages 83–84) is reprinted here with Harriet's revisions. In the margin, numbered in order of importance, are the problems with the introduction's meaning, structure, and paragraph development—as noted by Harriet's editing group. (The group used the checklists on pages 98–99 and 100–101 to focus their critique.) The above-line changes show Harriet's first efforts to eliminate these problems through revision.

> Student essay in progress

In the '50s and '60s, parents had it easy, TV comedies of that period show the
~~Raising children used to be much simpler in the 50s and 60s. I~~

Cleavers scolding Beaver about his dirty hands, the Andersons telling Bud to do his
~~remember TV images from that era showing that parenting involved~~
homework, and the Nelsons telling Ricky to clean his room.
~~simply teaching kids to clean their rooms, do their homework,~~

B
~~and~~ _____ . ~~But~~ ᵇeing a parent today is much more difficult꜀
                                ^
                        N   must   their children   many
~~because~~ ᵑowadays parents ~~have to shield/~~protect ~~kids~~ from ~~lots of~~
          ^
       —from a growing number of   ly explicit
things ~~like~~ distractions ~~from schoolwork,~~ from sexual ᵐaterial, and
      ^   ^
from dangerous situations.

> ② Take out personal reference
> ③ Give specific TV shows
>
> ① Thesis too long. Make plan of development separate sentence.

Continues on page 128

(If you'd like to see Harriet's final draft, turn to page 137.)

There's no doubt about it: As Harriet's reworked introduction shows, revision is challenging. But once you learn how to approach it step by step, you'll have the pleasure of seeing a draft become sharper and more focused. The rather global work you do early in the revision process puts you in a good position to concentrate on sentences and words—our focus in the following chapter.

ACTIVITIES:
REVISING OVERALL
MEANING, STRUCTURE,
AND PARAGRAPH
DEVELOPMENT

An important note: When revising essay drafts in activities 1–3, don't worry too much about sentence structure and word choice. However, do save your revisions so you can focus on these matters after you read the next chapter.

1. On page 101, you saw the marginal notes and above-line changes that Harriet Davids added to her first draft introduction. Now look at the draft's other paragraphs on pages 38–39 and identify problems in overall meaning, structure, and paragraph development. Working alone or in a group, start by asking questions like these: "Where does the essay stray from the thesis?" and "Where does a paragraph fail to present points in the most logical and compelling order?" (The critique you prepared for activity 9 in Chapter 6 should help.) For further guidance, refer to the checklists on pages 98–99 and 100–101. Summarize and rank the perceived problems in marginal annotations or on a feedback chart. Then type your changes (into a word processor, if you use one), or enter them between the lines of the draft (work on a newly typed copy, a photocopy, or the textbook pages themselves). Don't forget to save your revision.

2. Retrieve the draft you prepared in response to activity 12 in Chapter 6 (page 91). Outline the draft. Does your outline reveal any problems in the draft's overall meaning and structure? If it does, make whatever changes are needed. The checklists on pages 98–99 and 100–101 will help focus your revising efforts. (Save your revised draft so you can work with it further after reading the next chapter.)

3. On the next page is the first draft of an essay advocating a longer elementary school day. Read it closely. Are tone and point of view consistent throughout? Is the thesis clear? Is the support in each body paragraph relevant, specific, and adequate? Are ideas arranged in the most effective order? Working alone or in a group, use the checklists on pages 98–99 and 100–101 to identify problems with the draft's overall meaning, structure, and paragraph development. Summarize and rank the perceived problems on a feedback chart or in marginal annotations. Then revise the draft by typing a new version or by entering your changes by hand (on a photocopy of the draft, a typed copy, or the textbook pages themselves). Don't forget to save your revision.

The Extended School Day

Imagine a seven-year-old whose parents work until five each night. When she arrives home after school, she is on her own. She's a good girl, but still a lot of things could happen. She could get into trouble just by being curious. Or something could happen through no fault of her own. All over the country, there are many "latchkey" children like this little girl. Some way must be found to deal with the problem. One suggestion is to keep elementary schools open longer than they now are. There are many advantages to this idea.

Parents wouldn't have to be in a state of uneasiness about whether their child is safe and happy at home. They wouldn't get uptight about whether their child's needs are being met. They also wouldn't have to feel guilty because they are not able to help a child with homework. The longer day would make it possible for the teacher to provide such help. Extended school hours would also relieve families of the financial burden of hiring a home sitter. As my family learned, having a sitter can wipe out the budget. And having a sitter doesn't necessarily eliminate all problems. Parents still have the hassle of worrying whether the person will show up and be reliable.

It's a fact of life that many children dislike school, which is a sad commentary on the state of education in this country. Even so, the longer school day would benefit children as well. Obviously, the dangers of their being home alone after school would disappear because by the time the bus dropped them off after the longer school day, at least one parent would be home. The unnameable horrors feared by parents would not have a chance to happen. Instead, the children would be in school, under trained supervision. There, they would have a chance to work on subjects that give them trouble. In contrast, when my younger brother had difficulty with subtraction in second grade, he had to struggle along because there wasn't enough time to give him the help he needed. The longer day would also give children a chance to participate in extracurricular activities. They could join a science club, play on a softball team, sing in a school chorus, take an art class. Because school districts are trying to save money, they often cut back on such extracurricular activities. They don't realize how important such experiences are.

Finally, the longer school day would also benefit teachers. Having more hours in each day would relieve them of a lot of pressure. This longer workday would obviously require schools to increase teachers' pay. The added salary would be an incentive for teachers to stay in the profession.

Implementing an extended school day would be expensive, but I feel that many communities would willingly finance its costs because it provides benefits to parents, children, and even teachers. Young children, home alone, wondering whether to watch another TV show or to wander outside to see what's happening, need this longer school day now.

4. Look closely at your instructor's comments on an ungraded draft of one of your essays. Using a feedback chart, summarize and evaluate your instructor's comments. That done, rework the essay. Type your new version, or make your changes by hand. In either case, save the revision so you can work with it further after reading the next chapter.

5. Return to the draft you wrote in response to activity 10 or activity 11 in Chapter 6 (pages 90–91). To identify any problems, meet with several people and request that one of them read the draft aloud. Then ask your listeners focused questions about the areas you sense need work. Alternatively, you may use the checklists on pages 98–99 and 100–101 to focus the group's feedback. In either case, summarize and rank the comments on a feedback chart or in marginal annotations. Then, using the comments as a guide, revise the draft. Either type a new version or do your revising by hand. (Save your revision so you can work with it further after reading the next chapter.)

8
REVISING
SENTENCES
AND WORDS

REVISING SENTENCES

Having refined your essay's overall meaning, structure, and paragraph development, you can concentrate on sharpening individual sentences. Although polishing sentences inevitably involves decisions about individual words, for now focus on each sentence as a whole; you can evaluate individual words later. At this point, work to make your sentences:

- Consistent with your intended tone
- Economical
- Varied in type
- Varied in length
- Emphatic

Make Sentences Consistent with Your Tone

In Chapter 2, we saw how integral **tone** is to meaning (pages 23–24). As you revise, be sure each sentence's **content** (its images and ideas) and **style** (its structure and length) reinforce your intended tone: Both *what* you say and *how* you say it should support the essay's overall mood.

Consider the following excerpt from a piece by *Philadelphia Inquirer* columnist Melissa Dribben. Responding to the ongoing debate over gun control, Dribben supports legislation sought by the mayor of Philadelphia to limit handgun purchases to one per person per month. She writes:

> There are people who buy a new toothbrush every month. A new vacuum-cleaner bag. A fresh box of baking soda. A pair of $5 sunglasses. This you understand. You can never have too many.

> But when you reach the point where you have a stash of .38-caliber pistols bigger than your supply of clean underwear, you have a problem. And it isn't a shopping addiction.

Dribben's tone here is biting and sarcastic, her attitude exasperated and mocking. She establishes this tone partly through sentence content (what she says). For example, to her it is outrageous that people would want to buy guns more frequently than they purchase basic household and personal necessities. Dribben's style (how she says it) also contributes to her overall tone. The three fragments in the first paragraph convey an attitude of angry disbelief. These fragments, followed by two brief but complete sentences, build to the longer, climactic sentence at the beginning of the second paragraph. That sentence, especially when combined with the crisp last sentence, delivers a final, quick jab to those opposed to the proposed legislation. In short, content and style help express Dribben's impassioned attitude toward her subject.

Make Sentences Economical

Besides reinforcing your tone, your sentences should be **economical** rather than wordy. Use as few, not as many, words as possible. Students sometimes pad their writing because they think the longer a paper is, the higher the grade it will receive. Most instructors, though, are skilled at spotting wordiness intended only to fill pages. Your sentences won't be wordy if you (1) eliminate redundancy, (2) delete weak phrases, and (3) remove unnecessary *who, which,* and *that* clauses.

Eliminate Redundancy

Redundancy means unnecessary repetition. Sometimes words are repeated exactly; sometimes they are repeated by way of *synonyms,* other words or phrases that mean the same thing. When writing is redundant, words can be trimmed away without sacrificing meaning or effect. Why, for example, write "In the expert opinion of one expert" and needlessly repeat the word *expert?* Similarly, "They found it difficult to get consensus or agreement about the proposal" contains an unnecessary synonym (*agreement*) for *consensus.*

Redundancy isn't the same as repetition for dramatic emphasis. Consider the following excerpt from an address to the United Nations by John F. Kennedy:

> Unconditional war can no longer lead to unconditional victory. It can no longer serve to settle disputes. It can no longer be of concern to great powers alone. . . .

Here the repetition of *unconditional* and *can no longer* drives home the urgency of Kennedy's message. Repetition used, in this way, to underscore the relationship among sentences or ideas is called *parallelism*. (For more on parallelism, see pages 115–116.)

When not used as a stylistic device, however, repetition weakens prose. Take a look at the sentence pairs below. Note how the revised versions are clearer and stronger because the redundancy in the original sentences (italicized) has been eliminated:

Original While under the *influence* of alcohol, many people insist they are not under the *influence* and *swear* they are sober.

Revised While under the influence of alcohol, many people insist they are sober.

Original *They designed a computer program* that increased sales by 50 percent. The *computer program they designed* showed how the TRS-80 can be *used* and *implemented* in small *businesses* and *firms*.

Revised Their program, which showed how the TRS-80 computer can be used in small businesses, increased sales by 50 percent.

Delete Weak Phrases

In addition to eliminating redundancy, you can make sentences more economical by **deleting the three types of weak phrases** described here.

1. Empty Phrases. In speaking, we frequently use empty phrases that give us time to think but don't add to our message—expressions such as "Okay?" and "You know what I mean?" In writing, though, we have the chance to eliminate such deadwood. Here are some common culprits—expressions that are needlessly awkward and wordy—along with their one-word alternatives:

Wordy Expressions	Revised
due to the fact that	because
in light of the fact that	since
regardless of the fact that	although
in the event that	if
in many cases	often
in that period	then
at the present time	now
at this point in time	now
in the not-too-distant future	soon
for the purpose of	to
has the ability to	can
be aware of the fact that	know
is necessary that	must

Notice the improvement in the following sentences when wordy, often awkward phrases are replaced with one-word substitutes:

Original   *It is necessary that* the government outlaw the production of carcinogenic pesticides.
Revised   The government *must* outlaw the production of carcinogenic pesticides.

Original   Student leaders were upset by *the fact that* no one in the administration consulted them.
Revised   Student leaders were upset *because* no one in the administration consulted them.

Some phrases don't even call for concise substitutes. Because they add nothing at all to a sentence's meaning, they can simply be deleted. Here are some examples: "shy *type of* child," "*kind of* person," "*field of* communications," "small *in size*." The revised sentence that follows has exactly the same meaning as the original, but the meaning is expressed without the empty phrase *in color:*

Original   The hybrid azaleas were light blue *in color.*
Revised   The hybrid azaleas were light blue.

Other times, to avoid an empty phrase, you may need to recast a sentence slightly:

Original   The midterm assessment is *for the purpose of letting* students know if they are failing a course.
Revised   The midterm assessment *lets* students know if they are failing a course.

2. Roundabout Openings with *There, It,* and Question Words Like *How* and *What*. At the beginning of a sentence, you're formulating a new thought, so you may grope around a bit before pinning down what you want to say. For this reason, the openings of sentences are especially vulnerable to unnecessary phrases. Common culprits include phrases beginning with *There* and *It* (when *It* does not refer to a specific noun), and words like *How* and *What* (when they don't actually ask a question). In the following examples, note that trimming away excess words highlights the subject and verb, thus clarifying meaning:

Original   It was their belief that the problem had been solved.
Revised   They believed the problem had been solved.

Original   There are now computer courses offered by many high schools.
Revised   Many high schools now offer computer courses.

Original   What should be done in this crisis is to transport food to the victims' homes.
Revised   Food must be transported to the victims' homes.

Original   How to simplify the college's registration process should be a priority.
Revised   Simplifying the college's registration process should be a priority.

Of course, feel free to open with *There* or *It* when some other construction would be less clear or effective. For example, don't write "Many reasons can be cited why students avoid art courses" when you can say "There are many reasons why students avoid art courses."

3. Excessive Prepositional Phrases. Strings of prepositional phrases (word groups beginning with *at, on,* and the like) tend to make writing choppy; they weigh sentences down and hide main ideas. Note how much smoother and clearer sentences become when prepositional phrases (italicized in the following examples) are eliminated:

Original Growth *in the greenhouse effect* may result *in increases in the intensity of hurricanes.*
Revised   The growing greenhouse effect may intensify hurricanes.

Original The reassurance *of a neighbor* who was the owner *of a pit bull* that his dog was incapable *of harm* would not be sufficient to prevent most parents *from calling* the authorities if the dog ran loose.
Revised   Despite a neighbor's reassurance that his pit bull was harmless, most parents would call the authorities if the dog ran loose.

These examples show that prepositional phrases can sometimes be eliminated by substituting one strong verb (*intensify*) or by using the possessive form (*neighbor's reassurance, his pit bull*) rather than an *of* phrase.

Remove Unnecessary *Who, Which,* and *That* Clauses

Often *who, which,* or *that* clauses can be removed with no loss of meaning. Consider the tightening possible in these sentences:

Original The townsfolk misunderstood the main point *that the developer made.*
Revised   The townsfolk misunderstood *the developer's main point.*

Original The employees *who protested* the restrictions went on strike, *which was a real surprise to management.*
Revised   The employees *protesting* the restrictions *surprised management* by going on strike.

Vary Sentence Type

Another way to invigorate writing is to **vary sentence type.** Since the predictable soon becomes dull, try to offer a mixture of simple, compound, complex, and compound-complex sentences.

Simple Sentences

A **clause** is a group of words with both a subject and a verb. Clauses can be **independent** (able to stand alone) or **dependent** (unable to stand alone). A **simple sentence** consists of a single independent clause (whose subject and verb are italicized here):

The *president serves* four years.

Marie Curie investigated radioactivity and *died* from its effects.

Unlike most mammals, *birds* and *fish see* color.

Notice that a simple sentence can have more than one verb (sentence 2) or more than one subject (sentence 3). In addition, any number of modifying phrases (such as *Unlike most mammals*) can extend the sentence's length and add information. What distinguishes a simple sentence is its single *subject-verb combination*.

Simple sentences can convey dramatic urgency:

> Suddenly we heard the screech of brakes. Across the street, a small boy lay sprawled in front of a car. We started to run toward the child. Seeing us, the driver sped away.

Simple sentences are also excellent for singling out a climactic point: "They found the solution." In a series, however, they soon lose their impact and become boring. Also, because simple sentences highlight one idea at a time, they don't clarify the relationships among ideas. Consider these two versions of a passage:

Original

> Many first-year college students are apprehensive. They won't admit it to themselves. They hesitate to confide in their friends. They never find out that everyone else is anxious, too. They are nervous about being disliked and feeling lonely. They fear not "knowing the ropes."

Revised

> Many first-year college students are apprehensive, but they won't admit it to themselves. Because they hesitate to confide in their friends, they never find out that everyone else is anxious, too. Being disliked, feeling lonely, not "knowing the ropes"—these are what beginning college students fear.

In addition to sounding repetitive and childish, the simple sentences in the original version fragment the passage into a series of disconnected ideas. In contrast, the revised version includes a variety of sentence types and patterns, all of which are discussed on the pages ahead. This variety clarifies the relationships among ideas, so that the passage reads more easily.

Compound Sentences

Compound sentences consist of two or more independent clauses. There are four types of compound sentences. The most basic type consists of two simple sentences joined by a *coordinating conjunction* (*and, but, for, nor, or, so,* or *yet*). Here's an example:

> Chimpanzees and gorillas can learn sign language, *and* they have been seen teaching this language to others.

Another type of compound sentence has a semicolon (;), rather than a comma and coordinating conjunction, between the two simple sentences:

Yesterday, editorials attacked the plan; a week ago, they praised it.

A third type of compound sentence links two simple sentences with a semicolon plus a *conjunctive adverb* such as *however, moreover, nevertheless, therefore,* and *thus:*

Every year billions of U.S. dollars go to researching AIDS; *however,* recent studies show that a large percentage of the money has been mismanaged.

A final type of compound sentence consists of two simple sentences connected by a *correlative conjunction,* a word pair such as *either . . . or, neither . . . nor,* or *not only . . . but also:*

Either the litigants will win the lawsuit, *or* they will end up in debt from court costs.

Compound sentences help clarify the relationship between ideas. Similarities are signaled by such words as *and* and *moreover,* contrasts by *but* and *however,* cause-effect by *so* and *therefore.* When only a semicolon separates the two parts of a compound sentence, the relationship between those two parts is often a contrast. ("Yesterday, editorials attacked the plan; a week ago, they praised it.")

Complex Sentences

In a **complex sentence,** a dependent (subordinate) clause is joined to an independent clause. Sometimes the dependent clause (italicized in the following examples) is introduced by a subordinating conjunction such as *although, because, if, since,* or *when:*

Since they have relatively small circulations, specialty magazines tend to be expensive.

We knew there had been a power failure *because all the clocks in the building were two hours slow.*

Other dependent clauses are introduced by a relative pronoun such as *that, which,* or *who:*

Several celebrities revealed *that they have been stalked by delusional fans.*

Fame and wealth from his writings had little effect on author J. R. R. Tolkien, *who continued to teach until reaching retirement age.*

As you can see, the order of the dependent and independent clause isn't fixed. The dependent clause may come first, last, or even in the middle of the independent clause, as in this example:

Nurses' uniforms, *although they are no longer the norm,* are still required by some hospitals.

Whether to use a comma between a dependent and an independent clause depends on a number of factors, including the location of the dependent clause and whether it's *restrictive* (essential for identifying the thing it modifies) or *nonrestrictive.* (For more information on punctuating clauses, see page 654 in the Handbook.)

Because a dependent clause is subordinate to an independent one, complex sentences can clarify the relationships among ideas. Consider the two paragraphs that follow. The first merely strings together a series of simple and compound sentences, all of them carrying roughly the same weight. In contrast, the complex sentences in the revised version use subordination to connect ideas and signal their relative importance.

Original

Are you the "average American"? Then take heed. Here are the results of a time-management survey. You might want to budget your time differently. According to the survey, you spend six years of your life eating. Also, you're likely to spend two years trying to reach people by telephone, so you should convince your friends to get answering machines. Finally, you may be married and expect long conversations with your spouse to occur spontaneously, but you'll have to make a special effort. Ordinarily, your discussions will average only four minutes a day.

Revised

If you're the "average American," take heed. After you hear the results of a time-management survey, you might want to budget your time differently. According to the survey, you spend six years of your life eating. Also, unless you convince your friends to get an answering machine, you're likely to spend two years trying to reach them by telephone. Finally, if you're married, you shouldn't expect long conversations with your spouse to occur spontaneously. Unless you make a special effort, your discussions will average only four minutes a day.

If you find that the original paragraph resembles your writing more than the revised, don't despair. With experience, you'll develop a strong sense of how to connect and rank ideas through subordination. For now, just remember the following: Expressed as a dependent clause, an idea is relegated to a position of secondary importance; expressed as an independent clause, it's emphasized. So reserve for the independent clause the point you want to highlight.

The following sentences illustrate how meaning shifts depending on what is put in the main clause and what is subordinated:

Although most fraternities and sororities no longer have hazing, pledging is still a big event on many campuses.

Although pledging is still a big event on many campuses, most fraternities and sororities no longer have hazing.

In the first sentence, the focus is on *pledging;* in the second, it is on the *discontinuation of hazing.*

Compound-Complex Sentences

A **compound-complex sentence** connects one or more dependent clauses to two or more independent clauses. In the following example, the two independent clauses are underscored once and the two dependent clauses twice:

The Procrastinators' Club, <u>which is based in Philadelphia</u>, <u>issues a small magazine</u>, <u>but it appears infrequently</u>, <u>only when members get around to writing it</u>.

Go easy on the number of compound-complex sentences you use. Because they tend to be long, a string of them is likely to overwhelm the reader and cloud meaning.

Vary Sentence Length

You've probably noticed that simple sentences tend to be short, compound and complex sentences tend to be of medium length, and compound-complex sentences tend to be long. Generally, by varying sentence type, a writer automatically **varies sentence length** as well. However, sentence type doesn't always determine length. In this example, the simple sentence is longer than the complex one:

Simple Sentence

Hot and thirsty, exhausted from the effort of carrying so many groceries, I desired nothing more than an ice-cold glass of lemonade.

Complex Sentence

Because I was hot and thirsty, I craved lemonade.

The difference lies in the number of **modifiers**—words or groups of words used to describe another word or group of words. So, besides considering sentence type, check on sentence length when revising.

Short Sentences

Too many short sentences, like too many simple ones, can sound childish and create a choppy effect that muddies the relationship among ideas. Used wisely, though, a series of short sentences gives writing a staccato rhythm that carries more punch and conveys a faster pace than the same number of words gathered into longer sentences. As you read the two passages that follow, note how the first version's clipped rhythms are more effective for conveying a rush of terrifying events:

Witches bring their faces close. Goblins glare with fiery eyes. Fiendish devils stealthily approach to claw a beloved stuffed bear. The toy recoils in horror. These are among the terrifying happenings in the world of children's nightmares.

Witches bring their faces close as goblins glare, their eyes fiery. Approaching stealthily, fiendish devils come to claw a beloved stuffed bear that recoils in horror. These are among the terrifying happenings in the world of children's nightmares.

Brevity also highlights a sentence, especially when surrounding sentences are longer. Consider the dramatic effect of the final sentence in this paragraph:

Starting in June, millions of Americans pour onto the highways, eager to begin vacation. At the same time, city, state, and federal agencies deploy hundreds, even thousands of workers to repair roads that have, until now, managed to escape bureaucratic attention. Chaos results.

The short sentence "Chaos results" stands out because it's so much shorter than the preceding sentences. The emphasis is appropriate because, in the writer's view, chaos is the dramatic consequence of prolonged bureaucratic inertia.

Long Sentences

Long sentences often convey a leisurely pace and establish a calm tone:

As I look across the lake, I see the steady light of a campfire at the water's edge, the flames tinting to copper an aluminum rowboat tied to the dock, the boat glimmering in the darkness.

However, as with short sentences, don't overdo it. Too many long sentences can be hard to follow. And remember: A sentence stands out most when it differs in length from surrounding sentences. Glance back at the first paragraph on children's nightmares (page 113). The final long sentence stands in contrast to the preceding short ones. The resulting emphasis works because the final sentence is also the paragraph's topic sentence.

Make Sentences Emphatic

The previous section shows how sentence length affects meaning by highlighting some sentences in a paragraph but not others. Within a single sentence, you can use a number of techniques to make parts of the sentence stand out from the rest. To achieve such **emphasis,** you can: (1) place key ideas at the beginning or end, (2) set them in parallel constructions, (3) express them as fragments, or (4) express them in inverted word order.

Place Key Points at the Beginning or End

A sentence's start and close are its most prominent positions. So, keeping your overall meaning in mind, use those two spots to highlight key ideas.

Let's look first at the **beginning** position. Here are two versions of a sentence; the meanings differ because the openers differ.

The potentially life-saving drug, developed by junior researchers at the medical school, will be available next month.

Developed by junior researchers at the medical school, the potentially life-saving drug will be available next month.

In the first version, the emphasis is on the life-saving potential of a drug. Reordering the sentence shifts attention to those responsible for discovering the drug.

An even more emphatic position than a sentence's beginning is its **end.** Put at the close of a sentence whatever you want to emphasize:

Kindergarten is wasted on the young—especially the co-ed naptime.

Now look at two versions of another sentence, each with a slightly different meaning because of what's at the end:

Increasingly, overt racism is showing up in—of all places—popular song lyrics.

Popular song lyrics are showing—of all things—increasingly overt racism.

In the first version, the emphasis is on lyrics; in the second, it's on racism.

Be sure, though, that whatever you place in the climactic position merits the emphasis. The following sentence is so anticlimactic that it's unintentionally humorous:

The family, waiting anxiously for the results of the medical tests, sat.

Similarly, don't build toward a strong climax only to defuse it with some less important material:

On the narrow parts of the trail, where jagged cliffs drop steeply from the path, keep your eyes straight ahead and don't look down, toward the town of Belmont in the east.

In the preceding sentence, "toward the town of Belmont in the east" should be deleted. The important point surely isn't Belmont's location but how to avoid an accident.

Use Parallelism

Parallelism occurs when ideas of comparable weight are expressed in the same grammatical form, thus underscoring their equality. Parallel elements may be words, phrases, clauses, or full sentences. Here are some examples:

Parallel Nouns

We bought *pretzels, nachos,* and *candy bars* to feed our pre-exam jitters.

Parallel Adverbs

Smoothly, steadily, quietly, the sails tipped toward the sun.

Parallel Verbs

The guest lecturer *spoke* to the group, *showed* her slides, and then *invited* questions.

Parallel Adjective Phrases

Playful as a kitten but *wise as a street Tom,* the old cat played with the string while keeping a watchful eye on his surroundings.

Parallel Prepositional Phrases

Gloomy predictions came *from political analysts, from the candidate's staff,* and, surprisingly, *from the candidate herself.*

Parallel Dependent Clauses

Since our rivals were in top form, since their top player would soon come up to bat, we knew that all was lost.

As you can see, the repetition of grammatical forms creates a pleasing symmetry that emphasizes the sequenced ideas. Parallel structure also conveys meaning economically. Look at the way the following sentences can be tightened using parallelism:

Nonparallel

Studies show that most women today are different from those in the past. They want to have their own careers. They want to be successful. They also want to enjoy financial independence.

Parallel

Studies show that most women today are different from those in the past. They want to have careers, be successful, and enjoy financial independence.

Parallel constructions are often signaled by word pairs (correlative conjunctions) such as *either . . . or, neither . . . nor,* and *not only . . . but also.* To maintain parallelism, the same grammatical form must follow each half of the word pair.

Either professors are too rigorous, *or* they are too lax.

The company is interested in *neither* financing the project *nor* helping locate other funding sources.

When my roommate argues, she tends to be *not only* totally stubborn *but also* totally wrong.

Parallelism can create elegant and dramatic writing. Too much, though, seems artificial, so use it sparingly. Save it for your most important points.

Use Fragments

A **fragment** is part of a sentence punctuated as if it were a whole sentence—that is, with a period at the end. A sentence fragment consists of words, phrases, and/or dependent clauses, *without an independent clause.* Here are some examples:

Resting quietly.

Except for the trees.
Because they admired her.

A demanding boss who accepted no excuses.

Ordinarily, we advise students to stay clear of fragments. However, like most rules, this one may at times be broken—*if* you do so intentionally and skillfully. To be on the safe side, ask your composition instructor whether an occasional fragment—used as a stylistic device—will be considered acceptable. Here's an example showing the way fragments (underlined) can be used effectively for emphasis:

```
One of my aunt's eccentricities is her belief that only
personally made gifts show the proper amount of love. Her gifts
are often strange. Hand-drawn calendars. Home-brewed cologne that
smells like jam. Crocheted washcloths. Frankly, I'd rather
receive a gift certificate from a department store.
```

Notice how the three fragments focus attention on the aunt's charmingly offbeat gifts. Remember, though: When overused, fragments lose their effect, so draw on them sparingly. (See pages 650–655 in the Handbook.)

Use Inverted Word Order

In most English sentences, the subject comes before the verb. When you use **inverted word order,** however, at least part of the verb comes before the subject. The resulting sentence is so atypical that it automatically stands out.

Inverted statements, like those that follow, are used to emphasize an idea:

Normal	My Uncle Bill is a strange man.
Inverted	A strange man is my Uncle Bill.

Normal	Their lies about the test scores were especially brazen.
Inverted	Especially brazen were their lies about the test scores.

Normal	The age-old tree would never again bear fruit.
Inverted	Never again would the age-old tree bear fruit.

A note of caution: Inverted statements should be used infrequently and with special care. Bizarre can they easily sound.

Another form of inversion, the question, also acts as emphasis. A question may be a genuine inquiry, one that focuses attention on the issue at hand, as in the following example:

> Since the 1960s, only about half of this country's eligible voters have gone to the polls during national elections. *Why are Americans so apathetic?* Let's look at some of the reasons.

Or a question may be *rhetorical;* that is, one that implies its own answer and encourages the reader to share the writer's view:

> Yesterday, there was yet another accident at the intersection of Fairview and Springdale. Given the disproportionately high number of collisions at that crossing, *can anyone question the need for a traffic light?*

The following checklist is designed to help you and your readers evaluate the sentences in a first draft. (Activities at the end of the chapter will refer you to this checklist when you revise several essays.) To see how one student, Harriet Davids, used the checklist when revising, turn to page 129.

☑ REVISING SENTENCES: A CHECKLIST

☐ Which sentences are inconsistent with the essay's intended tone? How could the problem be corrected?

☐ Which sentences could be more economical? Where could unnecessary repetition, empty phrases, and weak openings be eliminated? Which prepositional phrases could be deleted? Where are there unnecessary *who*, *which*, and *that* clauses?

☐ Where should sentence type be more varied? Where would subordination clarify the connections among ideas? Where would simpler sentences make the writing less inflated and easier to understand?

☐ Where does sentence length become monotonous? Which short sentences should be connected to enhance flow and convey a more leisurely pace? Which long sentences would be more effective if broken into crisp, short ones?

☐ Where would a different sentence pattern add variety? Better highlight key sentence elements? Seem more natural?

☐ Which sentences could be more emphatic? Which strategy would be most effective—expressing the main point at the beginning or end, using parallelism, or rewriting the sentence as a fragment, question, or inverted-word-order statement?

REVISING WORDS

After refining the sentences in your first draft, you're in a good position to look closely at individual words. During this stage, you should aim for:

- words consistent with your intended tone
- an appropriate level of diction
- words that neither overstate nor understate
- words with appropriate connotations
- specific rather than general words
- strong verbs
- no unnecessary adverbs
- original figures of speech
- nonsexist language

Make Words Consistent with Your Tone

Like full sentences, individual words and phrases should also reinforce your intended tone. Reread the Melissa Dribben excerpt on gun control (see page 106). Earlier we discussed how sentence structure and length contribute to the excerpt's biting tone. Word choice also plays an important role. The word *stash* mocks the impulse to hoard guns as if they were essential but depletable goods—like clean underwear. And the specific phrase *.38-caliber pistols* evokes the image of a weapon with frightening lethal power. Such word choices reinforce the overall tone Dribben wants to convey.

Use an Appropriate Level of Diction

Diction refers to the words a writer selects. Those words should be appropriate for the writer's purpose, audience, point of view, and tone. If, for example, you are writing a straightforward, serious piece about on-the-job incompetence, you would be better off saying that people "don't concentrate on their work" and they "make frequent errors," rather than saying they "screw up" or "goof off."

There are three broad levels of diction: *formal, popular,* and *informal.* To describe feelings of pervasive sadness, clinical psychologists might use the highly formal term *dysthymia,* while the popular term for such emotions is *depression.* At the other end of the continuum, someone might use the informal phrase *down in the dumps.* Within each level of diction, there are degrees of formality and informality: *Down in the dumps* and *bummed out* are both informal, but *bummed out* is the slangier expression.

Formal Diction

Impersonal and distant in tone, **formal diction** is the type of language found in scholarly journals. Contractions are rare; long, specialized, technical words are common. Unfortunately, many people mistakenly equate word length with education: The longer the words, they think, the more impressed readers will be. So rather than using the familiar and natural words *improve* and *think,* they thumb through a thesaurus (literally or figuratively) for such fancy-sounding alternatives as *ameliorate* and *conceptualize.* They write "That is the optimum consequence we have the expectation of attaining" rather than "That is the best result we can expect." Remember: It's a word's ability to convey meaning clearly that counts, not its number of syllables.

Similarly, when writing for a general audience, don't show off specialized knowledge by throwing in **jargon,** insiders' terms from a particular area of expertise (say, a term like *authorial omniscience* from literary theory). Such "shop-talk" should be used only when less specialized words would lack the necessary precision. If readers are apt to be unfamiliar with a term, provide a definition.

Some degree of formality is appropriate—when, for example, you write up survey results for a sociology class. In such a case, your instructor may expect you to avoid the pronoun *I* (see page 24). Other instructors may think it's pretentious for a student to refer to himself or herself in the third person ("The writer observed that..."). These instructors may be equally put off by the artificiality of the passive voice (pages 123–124): "It was observed that. . . ." To be safe, find out what your instructors expect. If possible, use *I* when you mean "I." Your writing will be no less objective—unless using *I* tempts you to highly personal remarks and opinions. Even in more formal situations, resist the temptation to dazzle readers by piling up multisyllable words. (For more on avoiding pretentious language, see below.)

Popular Diction

Popular, or **mainstream,** diction is found in most magazines, newspapers, books, and texts (including this one). In such prose, the writer may use the first person and address the reader as "you." Contractions appear frequently; special-ized vocabulary is kept to a minimum.

You should aim for popular diction in most of the writing you do—in and out of college. Also keep in mind that an abrupt downshift to slang (*freaked out* instead of *lost control*) or a sudden turn to highly formal language (*myocardial infarction* instead of *heart attack*) will disconcert readers and undermine your credibility.

Informal Diction

Informal diction, which conveys a sense of everyday speech, is friendly and casu-al. First-person and second-person pronouns are common, as are contractions and fragments. Colloquial expressions (*rub the wrong way*) and slang (*you wimp*) are used freely. Informal diction isn't appropriate for academic papers, except where it is used to indicate *someone else's* speech.

Avoid Words That Overstate or Understate

When revising, be on the lookout for **doublespeak,** language that deliberately overstates or understates reality. Here's an example of each.

In their correspondence, Public Works Departments often refer to "ground-mounted confirmatory route markers"—a grandiose way of saying "road signs." Other organizations go to the other extreme and use **euphemisms,** words that minimize something's genuine gravity or importance. Hospital officials, for instance, sometimes call deaths resulting from staff negligence "unanticipated therapeutic misadventures." When revising, check that you haven't used words that exaggerate or downplay something's significance.

Select Words with Appropriate Connotations

Mark Twain once said, "The difference between the right word and the almost right word is the difference between lightning and the lightning bug." Even two words listed as synonyms in a dictionary or thesaurus can differ in meaning in important ways.

The dictionary meaning of a word is its **denotation.** The word *motorcycle,* for example, is defined as "a two- or three-wheeled vehicle propelled by an internal-combustion engine that resembles a bicycle, but is usually larger and heavier, and often has two saddles." Yet how many of us think of a motorcycle in these terms? Certainly, there is more to a word than its denotation. A word also comes surrounded by **connotations**—associated sensations, emotions, images, and ideas. For some, the word *motorcycle* probably calls to mind danger and noise. For motorcyclists themselves, the word most likely summons pleasant memories of high-speed movement through the open air.

Given the wide range of responses that any one word can elicit, you need to be sensitive to each word's shades of meaning so you can judge when to use it rather than some other word. Examine the following word series to get a better feel for the subtle but often critical differences between similar words:

contribution, donation, handout

quiet, reserved, closemouthed

everyday, common, trite

follower, disciple, groupie

Notice the extent to which words' connotations create different impressions in these two examples:

The young woman emerged from the interview, her face *aglow*. Moving *briskly* to the coatrack, she *tossed* her raincoat over one arm. After a *carefree* "Thank you" to the receptionist, she *glided* from the room.

The young woman emerged from the interview, her face *aflame*. Moving *hurriedly* to the coatrack, she *flung* her raincoat over one arm. After a *perfunctory* "Thank you" to the receptionist, she *bolted* from the room.

In the first paragraph, the words *aglow, carefree,* and *glided* have positive connotations, so the reader surmises that the interview was a success. In contrast, the second paragraph contains words loaded with negative connotations: *aflame, perfunctory,* and *bolted.* Reading this paragraph, the reader assumes something went awry.

A thesaurus can help you select words with the right connotations. Just look up any word with which you aren't satisfied, and you'll find a list of synonyms. To be safe, stay away from unfamiliar words. Otherwise, you stand a good chance of using a word incorrectly and creating a howler. Several years ago, one of our students wrote in an essay, "I wanted to *bequeath* the party by midnight." What he meant was that he wanted to "*leave* the party by midnight." He had, though, already used the word *leave* several times, so, looking for a synonym, he turned to the thesaurus, where he came across the word *bequeath.* But writing "I wanted to *bequeath* the party by midnight" doesn't work because *bequeath* means to leave property or goods by means of a will. Our advice? Choose only those words whose nuances you understand.

Use Specific Rather Than General Words

Besides carrying the right connotations, words should be **specific** rather than general. That is, they must avoid vagueness and ambiguity by referring to *particular* people, animals, events, objects, and phenomena. If they don't, readers may misinterpret what you mean.

Assume you're writing an essay about the demise of neighborhood movie houses. If, at one point, you refer to the "theaters' poor facilities," readers may imagine you're referring to faulty sound quality and projection. If you mean the theaters' messy physical surroundings, you need specific language to send the right message: wads of gum stuck under the seats, crushed popcorn tubs everywhere, a sticky film coating the floor. Precise words like these eliminate confusion.

Besides clarifying meaning, specific words enliven writing and make it more convincing. Compare these two paragraphs:

Original

> Sponsored by a charitable organization, a group of children from a nearby town visited a theme park. The kids had a great time. They went on several rides and ate a variety of foods. Reporters and a TV crew shared in the fun.

Revised

> Sponsored by the United Glendale Charities, twenty-five underprivileged Glendale grade-schoolers visited the Universe of Fun Themepark. The kids had a great time. They roller-coastered through a meteor shower on the Space Probe, encountered a giant squid on the Submarine Voyage, and screamed their way past coffins and ghosts in the House of Horrors. At the International Cuisine arcade, they sampled foods ranging from Hawaiian poi to German strudel. Reporters from the *Texas Herald* and a camera crew from WGLD, the Glendale cable station, shared in the fun.

You may have noticed that the specific words in the second paragraph provide answers to "which," "how," and similar questions. In contrast, when reading the first paragraph, you probably wondered, "*Which* charitable organization? *Which* theme park? *Which* rides?" Similarly, you may have asked, "*How* large a group? *How* young were the kids?" Specific language also answers "In what way?" The revised paragraph details *in what way* the children "had a great time." They didn't just eat "a variety of foods." Rather, they "sampled foods ranging from Hawaiian poi to German strudel." So, when you revise, check to make sure that your wording doesn't leave unanswered questions like "How?", "Why?", and "In what way?" (For more on making writing specific, see pages 49–50 and 69–71.)

Use Strong Verbs

Because a verb is the source of action in a sentence, it carries more weight than any other element. Replacing weak verbs and nouns with **strong verbs** is, then, another way to tighten and energize language. Consider the following strategies.

Replace *To Be* and Linking Verbs with Action Verbs

Overreliance on *to be* verbs (*is, were, has been*, and so on) tends to stretch sentences, making them flat and wordy. The same is true of motionless **linking verbs** such as *appear, become, sound, feel, look,* and *seem.* Since these verbs don't communicate any action, more words are required to complete their meaning and explain what is happening. Even *to be* verb forms combined with present participles (*is laughing, were running*) are weaker than bare **action verbs** (*laughs, ran*). Similarly, linking verbs combined with adjectives (*becomes shiny, seemed offensive*) aren't as vigorous as the action verb alone (*shines, offended*). Look how much more effective a paragraph becomes when weak verbs are replaced with dynamic ones:

Original

> The waves *were* so high that the boat *was* nearly *tipping* on end. The wind *felt* rough against our faces, and the salt spray *became* so strong that we *felt* our breath *would be* cut off. Suddenly, in the air *was* the sound I had dreaded most—the snap of the rigging. I *felt* panicky.

Revised

> The waves *towered* until the boat nearly *tipped* on end. The wind *lashed* our faces, while the salt spray *clogged* our throats and *cut* off our breath. Suddenly, the sound I had dreaded most *splintered* the air—the snap of the rigging. Panic *gripped* me.

The second paragraph is not only less wordy; it's also more vivid.

When you revise, look closely at your verbs. If you find too many *to be* and linking verb forms, ask yourself, "What's happening in the sentence?" Your response will help you substitute stronger verbs that will make your writing more compelling.

Change Passive Verbs to Active Ones

To be verb forms (*is, has been,* and so on) may also be combined with a past participle (*cooked, stung*), resulting in a **passive verb.** A passive verb creates a sentence structure in which the subject is *acted on* and, therefore, is placed in a secondary or passive position. In contrast, the subject of an **active verb** *performs* the action. Consider the following active and passive forms:

Passive	Active
A suggestion was made by the instructor that the project plan be revised by the students.	The instructor suggested that the students revise the project plan.
The employees' grievances will be considered by the union-management team when contract terms are being negotiated.	The union-management team will consider employees' grievances when negotiating contract terms.

Although they're not grammatically incorrect, passive verbs generally weaken writing, making it wordy and stiffly formal. Sometimes, though, it makes sense to use the passive voice. Perhaps you don't know who performed an action. ("When I returned to my car, I noticed the door had been dented.") Or you may want to emphasize an event, not the agent responsible for the event. For example, in an article about academic dishonesty on your campus, you might deliberately use the passive voice: "Every semester, research papers are plagiarized and lab reports falsified."

Unfortunately, corporations, government agencies, and other institutions often use the passive voice to avoid taking responsibility for controversial actions. Notice how easily the passive conceals the agent: "The rabbits were injected with a cancer-causing chemical."

Because the passive voice *is* associated with "official" writing, you may think it sounds scholarly and impressive. It doesn't. Unless you have good reason for deemphasizing the agent, change passive verbs to active ones.

Replace Weak Verb-Noun Combinations

Just as *to be,* linking, and passive verbs tend to lengthen sentences needlessly, so do weak verb-noun combinations. Whenever possible, replace such combinations with their strong verb counterparts. Change "made an estimate" to "estimated," "gave approval" to "approved." Notice how revision tightens these sentences, making them livelier and less pretentious:

Original   They *were* of the *belief* that the report was due next week.
Revised   They *believed* the report was due next week.

Original   The technical adviser *effected a replacement* of the system.
Revised   The technical adviser *replaced* the system.

Delete Unnecessary Adverbs

Strong verbs can further tighten your writing by ridding it of unnecessary adverbs. "She *strolled* down the path" conveys the same message as "She *walked slowly* and *leisurely* down the path"—but more economically. Similarly, why write "The crime was *extremely difficult* for the police to solve" when you can simply write "The crime *mystified* the police"?

Adverbs such as *extremely, really,* and *very* usually weaken writing. Although they are called "intensifiers," they make writing less, not more, intense. Notice that the following sentence reads more emphatically *without* the intensifier:

Original   Although the professor's lectures are controversial, no one denies that they are *really* brilliant.
Revised   Although the professor's lectures are controversial, no one denies that they are brilliant.

"Qualifiers" such as *quite, rather,* and *somewhat* also tend to weaken writing. When you spot one, try to delete it:

Original   When planning a summer trip to the mountains, remember to pack warm clothes; it turns *quite* cool at night.
Revised   When planning a summer trip to the mountains, remember to pack warm clothes; it turns cool at night.

Use Original Figures of Speech

Another strategy for adding vitality to your writing is to create imaginative, nonliteral comparisons, called **figures of speech.** For example, you might describe midsummer humidity this way: "Going from an air-conditioned building to the street is like being hit in the face with peanut butter." Or you might describe someone's raw, sunburned face by saying it is "as red as a skinned tomato." Notice that in both cases the comparisons yoke essentially dissimilar things (humidity and peanut butter, a face and a tomato). Such unexpected connections surprise readers and help keep their interest.

Figures of speech also tighten writing. Since they create sharp images in the reader's mind, you don't need many words to convey as much information. If someone writes "My teenage years were like a perpetual root canal," the reader immediately knows how painful and never-ending the author found adolescence.

Similes, Metaphors, Personification

Figures of speech come in several varieties. A **simile** is a direct comparison of two unlike things using the words *like* or *as:* "The moon brightened the yard *like* a floodlight." In a **metaphor,** the comparison is implied rather than directly stated: "The girl's *barbed-wire hair* set off *electric shocks* in her parents." In **personification,** an inanimate object is given human characteristics: "The couple robbed the store without noticing a silent, hidden eyewitness who later would tell all—a video camera." (For more on figures of speech, see page 161.)

Avoid Clichés

Trite and overused, some figures of speech signal a lack of imagination: *a tough nut to crack, cool as a cucumber, green with envy.* Such expressions, called **clichés,** are so predictable that you can hear the first few words (*Life is a bowl of . . .*) and fill in the rest (*cherries*). Clichés lull writer and reader alike into passivity since they encourage rote, habitual thinking.

When revising, either eliminate tired figures of speech or give them an unexpected twist. For example, seeking a humorous effect, you might write "Beneath his rough exterior beat a heart of lead" (instead of "gold"); rather than "Last but not least," you might write "Last but also least."

Two Other Cautions

First, if you include figures of speech, *don't pile one on top of another,* as in the following sentence:

Whenever the dorm residents prepared for the first party of the season, hairdryers howled like a windstorm, hairspray rained down in torrents, stereos vibrated like an earthquake, and shouts of excitement shook the walls like an avalanche.

Second, guard against *illogical* or *mixed* figures of speech. In the following example, note the ludicrous and contradictory comparisons:

They rode the roller coaster of high finance, dodging bullets and avoiding ambushes from those trying to lasso their streak of good luck.

To detect outlandish comparisons, visualize each figure of speech. If it calls up some unintentionally humorous or impossible image, revise or eliminate it.

Avoid Sexist Language

Sexist language gives the impression that one sex is more important, powerful, or valuable than the other. You may have noticed such language in certain reading selections in this book—for example, selections that refer to the average person as *he*. Some of these essays were written before people became alert to sexist overtones; others reveal the tenacity of long-standing habits and attitudes. Fortunately, a growing number of writers—female and male—are replacing sexist language with **gender-neutral** or **nonsexist** terms that convey no sexual prejudice. You, too, can avoid sexist language. But to do so, you need to be aware of the situations in which it is apt to occur.

Sexist Vocabulary

Using nonsexist vocabulary means staying away from terms that demean or exclude one of the sexes. Such slang words as *stud, jock, chick,* and *fox* portray people as one-dimensional. Just as adult males should be called *men,* adult females should be referred to as *women,* not *girls.* Similarly, men shouldn't be empowered with professional and honorary titles while professional women are assigned only personal titles. Why, for example, years ago should Ronald Reagan have been referred to as *President* Reagan while the Prime Minister of England, Margaret Thatcher, was called *Mrs.* Thatcher? In addition, consider replacing *Mrs.* and *Miss* with *Ms.;* like *Mr., Ms.* doesn't indicate marital status.

Be alert as well to the fact that words not inherently sexist can become so in certain contexts. Asking "What does the *man* in the street think of the teachers' strike?" excludes the possibility of asking women for their reactions.

Because language in our culture tends to exclude women rather than men, we list here a number of common words that exclude women. When you write (or speak), make an effort to use the more inclusive alternatives given.

Sexist	Nonsexist
the average guy	the average person
chairman	chairperson, chair
congressman	congressional representative
fireman	fire fighter
foreman	supervisor
layman	layperson
mailman	mail carrier, letter carrier
mankind, man	people, humans, human beings
policeman	police officer
salesman	salesperson
statesman	diplomat
spokesman	spokesperson
workmen	workers

Also, be on the lookout for phrases that suggest a given profession or talent is unusual for someone of a particular sex: *woman judge, woman doctor, male secretary, male nurse.*

Sexist Pronoun Use

Indefinite singular nouns—those representing a general group of people consisting of both genders—can lead to **sexist pronoun use**: "On *his* first day of school, a young child often experiences separation anxiety," or "Each professor should be responsible for monitoring *his* own students' progress." These sentences exclude female children and female professors from consideration, although the situations being described apply equally to them. But writing "On *her* first day of school, a young child often experiences separation anxiety" or "Each professor should be responsible for monitoring *her* own students' progress" is similarly sexist because the language excludes males.

Indefinite *pronouns* such as *anyone, each,* and *everybody* may also pave the way to sexist language. Although such pronouns often refer to a number of individuals, they are considered singular. So, wanting to be grammatically correct, you may write a sentence like the following: "Everybody wants *his* favorite candidate to win." The sentence, however, is sexist because *everybody* is certainly not restricted to men. But writing "Everybody wants *her* candidate to win" is equally sexist because now males aren't included.

Here's one way to avoid these kinds of sexist constructions: Use *both* male and female pronouns, instead of just one or the other. For example, you could write "On *his or her* first day of school, a young child often experiences separation anxiety" or "Everybody wants *his or her* favorite candidate to win." If you use both pronouns, you might try to vary their order; that is, alternate *his or her* with *her or his,* and so on. Another approach is to use the gender-neutral pronouns *they, their,* or *themselves:* "Everybody wants *their* favorite candidate to win." Be warned, though. Some people object to using these plural pronouns with singular indefinite pronouns, even though the practice is common in everyday speech. To be on the safe side, ask your instructors if they object to any of the approaches described here. If not, feel free to choose whichever nonsexist construction seems most graceful and least obtrusive.

If you're still unhappy with the result, two alternative strategies enable you to eliminate the need for *any* gender-marked singular pronouns. First, you can change singular general nouns or indefinite pronouns to their plural equivalents and then use nonsexist plural pronouns:

Original   A *workaholic* feels anxious when *he* isn't involved in a task-related project.
Revised   *Workaholics* feel anxious when *they're* not involved in task-related projects.

Original   *Everyone* in the room expressed *his* opinion freely.
Revised   *Those* in the room expressed *their* opinions freely.

Second, you can recast the sentence to omit the singular pronoun:

Original   A *manager* usually spends part of each day settling squabbles among *his* staff.
Revised   A manager usually spends part of each day settling *staff squabbles.*

Original   No *one* wants *his* taxes raised.
Revised   No one wants *to pay more taxes.*

The following checklist is designed to help you and your readers evaluate the words in a draft. (Activities at the end of the chapter will refer you to this checklist when you revise several essays.) To see how one student, Harriet Davids, used the checklist when revising, turn to page 129.

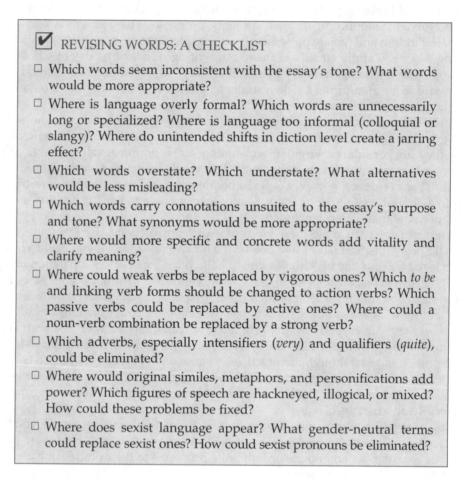

☑ REVISING WORDS: A CHECKLIST

☐ Which words seem inconsistent with the essay's tone? What words would be more appropriate?

☐ Where is language overly formal? Which words are unnecessarily long or specialized? Where is language too informal (colloquial or slangy)? Where do unintended shifts in diction level create a jarring effect?

☐ Which words overstate? Which understate? What alternatives would be less misleading?

☐ Which words carry connotations unsuited to the essay's purpose and tone? What synonyms would be more appropriate?

☐ Where would more specific and concrete words add vitality and clarify meaning?

☐ Where could weak verbs be replaced by vigorous ones? Which *to be* and linking verb forms should be changed to action verbs? Which passive verbs could be replaced by active ones? Where could a noun-verb combination be replaced by a strong verb?

☐ Which adverbs, especially intensifiers (*very*) and qualifiers (*quite*), could be eliminated?

☐ Where would original similes, metaphors, and personifications add power? Which figures of speech are hackneyed, illogical, or mixed? How could these problems be fixed?

☐ Where does sexist language appear? What gender-neutral terms could replace sexist ones? How could sexist pronouns be eliminated?

SAMPLE STUDENT REVISION OF SENTENCES AND WORDS

Student essay in progress

Reprinted here is the introduction to Harriet Davids's first draft—as it looked after she entered on a word processor the changes she made in overall meaning, structure, and paragraph development (see page 101). To help identify problems with words and sentences, Harriet asked someone in her editing group to read the revised version aloud. Then she asked the group to comment on her paper, using the checklists on pages 118 and 128. The marginal notes indicate her ranking of the group's comments in order of importance. The above-line changes show how Harriet revised in response to these suggestions for improving the paragraph's sentences and words.

Reruns of   from the

~~In the 50s and 60s, parents had it easy,~~ TV comedies ~~of that~~
'50s and '60s dramatize the kinds of problems that parents used to have.
~~period show~~ the Cleavers scolding Beaver about his dirty hands;

ground   for not
the Andersons ~~telling~~ Bud to do his homework, ~~and~~ the Nelsons

dock   's allowance because he forgets
~~telling~~ Ricky to clean his room. Being a parent today is much

than it was a generation ago.
more difficult. Nowadays parents must protect their children from

many things--from a growing number of distractions, from sexually

life-threatening
explicit material, and from ~~dangerous~~ situations.

① Combine into one sentence idea of '50s/'60s parents and TV shows

② Make each family's problems a separate sentence

③ Use stronger verbs (not "telling")

④ Make "dangerous situations" more specific

Continues on page 137

Once you, like Harriet, have carefully revised sentences and words, your essay needs only to be edited (for errors in grammar, punctuation, and spelling) and proofread. In the next chapter, you'll read about these final steps. You'll also see a student essay that has gone through all phases of the writing process.

ACTIVITIES: REVISING SENTENCES AND WORDS

1. Revise the following wordy, muddy sentences, making them economical and clear.

   a. What a person should do before subletting a rental apartment is make sure to have the sublet agreement written up in a formal contract.

b. In high school, it often happens that young people deny liking poetry because of the fact that they fear running the risk of having people mock or make fun of them because they actually enjoy poetry.

c. In light of the fact that college students are rare in my home neighborhood, being a college student gives me immediate and instant status.

d. There were a number of people who have made the observation that the new wing of the library looks similar in appearance to several nearby buildings with considerable historical significance.

e. It was, in my opinion, an apt comment when the professor noted that most of the students who complain about how demanding the requirements of a course are tend to work at part-time or even full-time jobs.

2. Using only simple or simple and compound sentences, write a paragraph based on one of the following topic sentences. Then rewrite the paragraph, making some of the sentences complex and others compound-complex. Examine your two versions of the paragraph. What differences do you see in meaning and emphasis?

a. The campus parking lot is dangerous at night.

b. Some students have trouble getting along with their roommates.

c. Silent body language speaks loudly.

d. Getting on a teacher's good side is an easily mastered skill.

3. The following sentences could be more emphatic. Examine each one to determine its focus; then revise the sentence, using one of the following strategies: placing the most important item first or last, parallelism, inverted word order, a fragment. Try to use a different strategy in each sentence.

a. The old stallion's mane was tangled, and he had chipped hooves, and his coat was scraggly.

b. Most of us find rude salespeople difficult to deal with.

c. The politician promises, "I'll solve all your problems."

d. We meet female stereotypes such as the gold digger, the dangerous vixen, and the "girl next door" in the movies.

e. It's a wise teacher who encourages discussion of controversial issues in the classroom.

4. The following paragraph is pretentious and murky. Revise to make it crisp and clear.

    Since its founding, the student senate on this campus has maintained essentially one goal: to upgrade the quality of its student-related services. Two years ago, the senate, supported by the opinions of three consultants provided by the National Council of Student Governing Boards, was confident it was operating from a base of quality but felt that, if given additional monetary support from the administration, a significant improvement in student services would be facilitated. This was a valid prediction, for that is exactly what transpired in the past fifteen months once additional monetary resources were, in fact, allocated by the administration to the senate and its activities.

5. Write a sentence for each word in the series that follows, making sure your details reinforce each word's connotations:

   a. chubby, voluptuous, portly
   b. stroll, trudge, loiter
   c. turmoil, anarchy, hubbub

6. Write three versions of a brief letter voicing a complaint to a store, a person, or an organization. One version should be charged with negative connotations; another should "soft pedal" the problem. The final version should present your complaint using neutral, objective words. Which letter do you prefer? Why?

7. Describe each of the following in one or two sentences, using a creative figure of speech to convey each item's distinctive quality:

   a. a baby's hand
   b. a pile of dead leaves
   c. a sophisticated personal computer
   d. an empty room
   e. an old car

8. Enliven the following dull, vague sentences. Use your knowledge of sentence structure to dramatize key elements. Also, replace weak verbs with vigorous ones and make language more specific.

   a. I got sick on the holiday.
   b. He stopped the car at the crowded intersection.
   c. A bird appeared in the corner of the yard.
   d. The class grew restless.
   e. The TV broadcaster put on a concerned air as she announced the tragedy.

9. The following paragraph contains too many linking verbs, passives, adverbs, and prepositions. In addition, noun forms are sometimes used where their verb counterparts would be more effective. Revise the paragraph by eliminating unnecessary prepositions and providing more vigorous verbs. Then add specific, concrete words that dramatize what is being described.

   The farmers in the area conducted a meeting during which they formulated a discussion of the vandalism problem in the county in which they live. They made the estimate that, on the

average, each of them had at least an acre of crops destroyed
the past few weekends by gangs of motorcyclists who have been
driving maliciously over their land. The increase in such
vandalism has been caused by the encroachment of the suburbs on
rural areas.

10. Revise the following sentences to eliminate sexist language.

    a. The manager of a convenience store has to guard his cash register carefully.
    b. When I broke my arm in a car accident, a male nurse, aided by a physician's assistant, treated my injury.
    c. All of us should contact our congressman if we're not satisfied with his performance.
    d. The chemistry professors agree that nobody should have to buy her own Bunsen burner.

An important note: When revising essay drafts in activities 11 and 12, don't worry too much about grammar, punctuation, and spelling. However, do save your revisions, so you can focus on these matters after reading the next chapter.

11. In response to activity 1 in Chapter 7 (page 102), you revised the overall meaning, structure, and paragraph development of Harriet Davids's first draft. Find that revision so that you can now focus on its sentences and words. Get together with at least one other person and ask yourselves questions like these: "Where should sentence type, length, or pattern be more varied?" and "Where would more specific and concrete words add vitality and clarify meaning?" For further guidance, refer to the checklists on pages 118 and 128. Summarize and rank any perceived problems in marginal annotations or a feedback chart. Then type your changes into a word processor or enter them between the lines of the draft. (Save your revision so you can edit and proofread it after reading the next chapter.)

12. Return to the draft you prepared in response to activity 2, activity 3, activity 4, or activity 5 in Chapter 7 (pages 102–104). Get together with several people and request that one of them read the draft aloud. Then, using the checklists on pages 118 and 128, ask the group members focused questions about any sentences and words that you feel need sharpening. After evaluating the feedback, revise the draft. Either key your changes into a word processor or do your revising by hand. (Save your revision so you can edit and proofread it after reading the next chapter.)

9
EDITING AND PROOFREADING

It happens all too often. A student works hard to revise an essay—reading it over, making changes (some of them extensive), refining sentences and words—all to arrive at the best version possible. Then the student types the paper and hands it in without even a glance.

Wanting to get a piece of writing off your desk is a normal human response to so much work. But if you don't edit and proofread—that is, closely check your writing for grammar, spelling, and typographical errors—you run the risk of sabotaging your previous efforts. Readers may assume that a piece of writing isn't worth their time if they're jolted by surface flaws that make it difficult to read. So, to make sure that your good ideas get a fair hearing, you should do the following:

- Edit
- Use the appropriate manuscript format
- Proofread

EDIT CAREFULLY

When revising the paper, you probably spotted some errors in grammar, punctuation, or spelling, perhaps flagging them for later correction. Now—after you're satisfied with the essay's organization, development, and style—it's time to fix these errors. It's also time to search for and correct errors that have slipped by you so far.

If you're working with pen and paper or on a typewritten or word-processed draft with handwritten annotations, use a different color ink, so your new corrections will stand out. Because most writers find it easier to locate errors on a clean copy of their text, consider retyping your draft before editing it. If you use a word processor, search for errors both on the screen and on a printout. If your software includes a spelling check, your search for misspellings will be greatly simplified. Be aware, however, that such programs may not find errors in the spelling of proper nouns, and that they won't flag errors that constitute legitimate words (for example, *he* when you meant *the* or *their* when you meant *there*).

To be a successful editor of your own work, you need two standard tools: a grammar handbook (like the one on pages 645–709) and a good dictionary. One way to keep track of the errors you're prone to make is to record them on a simple chart. Divide the chart into three columns: (1) *Error,* (2) *Rules for Correcting Error,* and (3) *Error Corrected.* When your instructor returns an essay, copy representative mistakes you've made into the first column. Look up in a handbook the rules that apply and enter them in the second column. Then, in the last column, rewrite the phrase or sentence from your paper with the error corrected. As the semester goes on, you'll develop a *personalized inventory* of writing errors to use in checking your own work.

If you're weak in spelling, make a similar inventory of spelling errors and corrections. Use four columns for this list: (1) *Word Misspelled,* (2) *Part of Word Misspelled,* (3) *Spelling Rule,* and (4) *Word Corrected.* (For more on spelling, see pages 706–709 in the Handbook.)

USE THE APPROPRIATE MANUSCRIPT FORMAT

After correcting all grammar and spelling problems, you're ready to produce the final copy. In doing so, you should follow accepted academic practice, adapted to your instructor's requirements. Most instructors will require that you type your papers. Even if this isn't the case, typed or computer-printed papers look neater, are easier to grade, and show that you have made the transition to college-level format.

The following checklist on manuscript format describes the basic rules for college essays as well as special rules for typed, computer-generated, and handwritten papers.

☑ APPROPRIATE MANUSCRIPT FORMAT: A CHECKLIST

Computer-Generated Papers

☐ Use good-quality white paper.

☐ Never hand in a written piece on spread-sheet paper. Tear off sheet edges at the perforations, separate the pages, and arrange them in correct order. Don't rip the paper from the printer, rush to class, and hand in the accordion-folded sheets!

☐ Double-space throughout the paper, and make sure your printer uses legible, easy-to-read characters. An ink-jet, daisy wheel, or laser printer is best, but a dot-matrix printer that approximates "letter quality" is also acceptable.

Typed Papers

☐ Use standard-sized (8-½ by 11 inches), good-quality white typing paper. Don't use "erasable" paper or onion skin. The result is often a smudged look, and the instructor may have a difficult time getting the paper to accept inked-in comments.

☐ Use a typewriter with a standard typestyle. Avoid script or other hard-to-read typefaces.

☐ Make sure the typewriter prints in dark black ink. Keep the type clean and change the ribbon as needed.

☐ Double-space throughout the paper, and type on only one side of the page.

Handwritten Papers

☐ Use white, lined paper with a margin rule on the left side. The paper may have holes for insertion in a notebook, but don't rip pages out of a spiral notebook unless there are perforations that permit you to do so neatly.

☐ Use only standard-sized paper: 8-½ by 10 or 11 inches.

☐ Write on only one side of the page, using dark blue or black ink, never pencil.

☐ Don't skip lines, except between paragraphs.

☐ Write legibly and carefully, in a moderate size. Eliminate exaggerated mannerisms from your handwriting, such as curlicues and extreme slants.

All Papers

☐ Leave adequate margins: one inch at the top and bottom and right and left of each page should be sufficient.

☐ If you include a title page, place the title about one-third of the way down the page. Enter the title, and double-space between lines of the title and your name. Course and section, instructor's name, and date, on separate lines, are double-spaced and centered.

☐ If you don't include a title page, use a standard heading, as specified by your instructor, at the top of the first page. One standard format for the heading consists of your name, the instructor's name, the course title and number, and the date on double-spaced lines in the upper-left corner, an inch from the top.

☐ Center the title of your paper one double space below the heading. Capitalize only the first letters of all main words. Don't use all caps, underlining, or quotation marks. Double-space a title having more than one line.

☐ Double-space between the title and the first paragraph of your essay.

☐ With the exception of the title page, number each page, including the first, by putting an Arabic numeral in the upper-right corner one-half inch below the top of the page. Avoid putting p. or page with the page number. Include your last name before each page number, in case pages become separated.

☐ Indent the first line of each paragraph five spaces.

☐ Paper clip or staple your essay's pages, placing the outline wherever your instructor requests. Don't use the corner "rip and fold" method; it doesn't hold, and it spoils the look of a carefully typed paper.

☐ Don't use a report cover unless your instructor requests it.

(For examples of correct manuscript format, see pages 137 and 593–594.)

PROOFREAD CLOSELY

Proofreading means checking your final copy carefully for "typos" or other mistakes. One trick is to read your material backward: If you read from the end of each paragraph to the beginning, you can focus on each word individually to make sure no letters have been left out or transposed. This technique prevents you from getting caught up in the flow of ideas and missing small defects, which is easy to do when you've read your own words many times.

What should you do when you find a typo? Simply use a pen with dark ink to make an above-line correction. The following standard proofreader's marks will help you indicate some common types of corrections:

Proofreader's Mark	Meaning	Example
∧	insert missing letter or word	televsion
ℓ	delete	reports the the findings
∼	reverse order	the gang's here all
¶	start new paragraph	to dry. Next, put
#	add space	the girls
⌒	close up space	boy cott

If you make so many corrections on a page that it begins to look like a draft, retype the page. If you're using a computer, make the corrections on the disk and reprint the page.

STUDENT ESSAY: FROM PREWRITING THROUGH PROOFREADING

Student essay in progress

In the last several chapters, we've taken you through the various stages in the writing process—from prewriting to proofreading. You've seen how Harriet Davids used prewriting (pages 25–33) and outlining (pages 33–35) to arrive at her thesis (pages 39 and 42–43) and her first draft (pages 83–84). You also saw how Harriet revised, first, her draft's overall meaning and paragraph development (page 101) and, second, its sentences and words (pages 128–129). In this chapter, you'll look at Harriet's final draft—the paper she submitted to her instructor after completing all the stages of the writing process.

Harriet, a thirty-eight-year-old college student and mother of two teenagers, wanted to write an informative paper with a straightforward, serious tone. While preparing her essay, she kept in mind that her audience would include her course instructor as well as her classmates, many of them considerably younger than she. This is the assignment that prompted Harriet's essay:

> Goodman implies that, in some ways, today's world is hostile to children. Do you agree? Drawing upon but not limiting yourself to the material in your pre-reading journal, write an essay in which you support or reject this viewpoint.

Harriet's essay is annotated so you can see how it illustrates the essay format described in Chapter 6 (page 82). As you read the essay, try to determine how well it reflects the principles of effective writing. The commentary following the paper will help you look at the essay more closely and give you some sense of the way Harriet went about revising her first draft.

Harriet Davids
Professor Kinne
College Composition, Section 203
October 4, 2002

Challenges for Today's Parents

1   Reruns of situation comedies from the 1950s and early 1960s dramatize the kinds of problems that parents used to have with their children. The Cleavers scold Beaver for not washing his hands before dinner; the Andersons ground Bud for not doing his homework; the Nelsons dock little Ricky's allowance because he keeps forgetting to clean his room. But times have changed

Introduction

Thesis ─────┐
            │ dramatically. Being a parent today is much more difficult than it
Plan of   was a generation ago. Parents nowadays must protect their
development ───┘ children from a growing number of distractions, from sexually
               explicit material, and from life-threatening situations.

First supporting ┌─→Today's parents must try, first of all, to control all the new   2
paragraph   distractions that tempt children away from schoolwork. At home, a
Topic sentence ──┘ child may have a room furnished with a stereo, television, and
                 computer. Not many young people can resist the urge to listen to
                 a CD, go online, play computer games, or watch MTV--especially if
                 it is time to do schoolwork. Outside the home, the distractions
                 are even more alluring. Children no longer "hang out" on a
                 neighborhood corner within earshot of Mom or Dad's reminder to
                 come in and do homework. Instead, they congregate in vast
                 shopping malls, buzzing video arcades, and gleaming fast-food
                 restaurants. Parents and school assignments have obvious
                 difficulty competing with such enticing alternatives.

Second supporting   Besides dealing with these distractions, parents have to shield   3
paragraph   their children from a flood of sexually explicit materials.
                 Today, children can find sex magazines and pornographic
Topic sentence ──┐ paperbacks in the same corner store that once offered only comics
with link to   and candy. Children will not see the fuzzily photographed nudes
previous   that a previous generation did but will encounter the hard-core
paragraph   raunchiness of Playboy or Penthouse. Moreover, the movies young
                 people rent from the neighborhood video store or see at the local
                 theater often focus on highly sexual situations. It is difficult
                 to teach children traditional values when films show teachers
                 seducing students and young people treating sex as a casual
                 sport. Unfortunately, television, with its often heavily sexual
                 content, is no better. With just a flick of the dial, children
                 can see soap-opera stars cavorting in bed or watch cable programs
                 where nudity is common. But the sexually graphic content of TV
                 shows is nothing compared with the seamy material on the
                 Internet. Many parents report that their children, sometimes
                 without intending to, access pornographic chat rooms and websites
                 that haunt the youngsters for months afterward.

Third supporting   Most disturbing to parents today, however, is the increase in   4
paragraph   life-threatening dangers that face young people. When children are
                 small, parents fear that their youngsters may be victims of
Topic sentence ──┘ violence. Every news program seems to carry a report about a mass
with emphasis   murderer who preys on young girls, a deviant who has buried six boys
signal

in his backyard, or an organized child pornography ring that molests preschoolers. When children are older, parents begin to worry about their kids' use of drugs. Peer pressure to experiment with drugs is often stronger than parents' warnings. This pressure to experiment can be fatal. Finally, even if young people escape the hazards associated with drugs, they must still resist the pressure to drink. Although alcohol has always held an attraction for teenagers, reports indicate that they are drinking more than ever before. As many parents know, the consequences of this attraction can be deadly--especially when drinking is combined with driving.

5   Within one generation, the world as a place to raise children has changed dramatically. One wonders how yesterday's parents would have dealt with today's problems. Could the Andersons have kept Bud away from MTV? Could the Nelsons have shielded little Ricky from sexually explicit material? Could the Cleavers have protected Beaver from drugs and alcohol? Parents must be aware of all these distractions and dangers yet be willing to give their children the freedom they need to become responsible adults. It is not an easy task.

Conclusion

References to TV shows recall introduction

Commentary

Introduction and Thesis

The opening paragraph attracts readers' interest by recalling several vintage television shows that have almost become part of our cultural heritage. Harriet begins with these examples from the past because they offer such a sharp contrast to the present, thus underscoring the idea expressed in her *thesis:* "Being a parent today is much more difficult than it was a generation ago." Opening in this way, with material that serves as a striking contrast to what follows, is a common and effective strategy. Note, too, that Harriet's thesis states the paper's subject (being a parent) as well as her attitude toward the subject (the job is more demanding than it was years ago).

Student essay in progress

Plan of Development

Harriet follows her thesis with a *plan of development* that anticipates the three major points to be covered in the essay's supporting paragraphs. Unfortunately, this particular plan of development is somewhat mechanical, with the major points being trotted past the reader in one long, awkward sentence. To deal with the problem, Harriet could have rewritten the sentence or eliminated the plan of development altogether, ending the introduction with her thesis.

Patterns of Development

Although Harriet develops her thesis primarily through *examples,* she also draws on two other patterns of development. The whole paper implies a *contrast* between the way life and parenting are now and the way they used to be. The essay also contains an element of *causal analysis* since all the factors that Harriet cites affect children and the way they are raised.

Purpose, Audience, Tone, and Point of View

Given the essay's *purpose* and *audience*, Harriet adopts a serious *tone*, providing no-nonsense evidence to support her thesis. Note, too, that she uses the *third-person point of view*. Although she writes from the perspective of a mother of two teenage daughters, she doesn't write in the first person or refer specifically to her own experiences and those of her daughters. She adopts this objective stance because she wants to keep the focus on the issue rather than on her family.

What if Harriet had been asked by her daughters' school newspaper to write a humorous column about the trials and tribulations that parents face raising children? Aiming for a different tone, purpose, and audience, Harriet probably would have taken another approach. Drawing upon her personal experience, she might have confessed how she survives MTV's flash and dazzle, as well as the din of stereos blasting rock music at all hours: she stuffs her ears with cotton, hides her daughters' CDs, and cuts off the electricity. This material—with its first-person perspective, exaggeration, and light tone—would be appropriate.

Organization

Structuring the essay around a series of *relevant* and *specific examples,* Harriet uses *emphatic order* to sequence the paper's three main points: that a growing number of distractions, sexually explicit materials, and life-threatening situations make parenting difficult nowadays. The third supporting paragraph begins with the words "Most disturbing to parents today . . . ," signaling that Harriet feels particular concern about the physical dangers children face. Moreover, she uses basic organizational strategies to sequence the supporting examples within each paragraph. The details in the first supporting paragraph are organized *spatially*, starting with distractions at home and moving to those outside the home. The second supporting paragraph arranges examples *emphatically*. Harriet starts with sexually explicit publications and ends with the "seamy material on the Internet," which is even more disturbing than TV's "heavily sexual content." The third and final supporting paragraph is organized *chronologically*; it begins by discussing dangers to small children and concludes by talking about teenagers.

The essay also displays Harriet's familiarity with other kinds of organizational strategies. Each supporting paragraph opens with a *topic sentence*. Further, *signal devices* are used throughout the paper to show the relationship among ideas: *transitions* ("*Instead,* they congregate in vast shopping malls"; "*Moreover,* the movies young people rent from the neighborhood video store or see at the local theater often focus on highly sexual situations"); *repetition* ("*sexual* situations" and "*sexual* content"); *synonyms* ("distractions . . . enticing alternatives" and "life-threatening . . . fatal"); *pronouns* ("young people . . . *they*"); and *bridging sentences* ("Besides dealing with these distractions, parents have to shield their children from a flood of sexually explicit materials").

Two Minor Problems

Harriet's efforts to write a well-organized essay result in a somewhat predictable structure. It might have been better had she rewritten one of the paragraphs, perhaps embedding the topic sentence in the middle of the paragraph or saving it for the end. Similarly, Harriet's signal devices are a little heavy-handed. Even so, an essay with a sharp focus and clear signals is preferable to one with a confusing or inaccessible structure. As she gains more experience, Harriet can work on making the structure of her essays more subtle.

Conclusion

Harriet brings the essay to a satisfying *close* by reminding readers of the paper's central idea and three main points. The final paragraph also extends the essay's scope by introducing a new but related issue: that parents have to strike a balance between their need to provide limitations and their children's need for freedom.

Revising the First Draft

As you saw on pages 101 and 128–129, Harriet reworked her essay a number of times. For a clearer sense of her revision process, compare the final version of her conclusion (on page 139) with the original version reprinted here. Harriet wisely waited to rework her conclusion until after she had finetuned the rest of the essay. The marginal annotations, ranked in order of importance, indicate the problems that Harriet and her editing group detected in the conclusion:

	Student essay in progress

Original Conclusion

① Paragraph seems tacked on

    Most adults love their children and want to be good parents.
But it's difficult because the world seems stacked against young
people. Even Holden Caulfield had trouble dealing with society's
pressures. Parents must give their children some freedom but not
so much that kids lose sight of what's important.

③ Boring sentence— too vague

② Inappropriate reference to Holden

As soon as Harriet heard her paper read aloud during a group session, she realized her conclusion didn't work at all. Rather than bringing the essay to a pleasing finish, the final paragraph seemed like a tired afterthought. A classmate also pointed out that her allusion to *The Catcher in the Rye* misrepresented the essay's focus since Harriet discusses children of all ages, not just teens.

Keeping these points in mind, Harriet decided to scrap her original conclusion. Working at a word processor, she prepared a new, much stronger concluding paragraph. Besides eliminating the distracting reference to Holden Caulfield, she replaced the shopworn opening sentence ("Most adults love their children....") with three interesting and rhythmical questions ("Could the Andersons ... Could the Nelsons ... Could the Cleavers ...?"). Because these questions recall the essay's main points and echo the introduction's reference to vintage television shows, they help unify Harriet's paper and bring it to a satisfying close.

These are just a few of the changes Harriet made when reworking her essay. Realizing that writing is a process, she left herself enough time to revise. She was gratified by her classmates' responses to what she had written and pleased by the lively discussion her essay provoked. Early in her composition course, Harriet learned that attention to the various stages in the writing process yields satisfying results, for writer and reader alike.

ACTIVITIES: EDITING AND PROOFREADING

1. Applying for a job, a student wrote the following letter. Edit and proofread it carefully, as if it were your own. If you have trouble spotting many grammar, spelling, and typing errors, that's a sign you need to review the appropriate sections of the Handbook (page 645).

Dear Mr. Eno:

I am a sophomore at Harper College who will be returning home to Brooktown this June, hopefully, to fine a job for the the summer. One that would give me further experience in the retail field. I have heard from my freind, Sarah Snyder, that your hiring college studnets as assistant mangers, I would be greatly intrested in such a postion.

I have quite a bit of experience in retail sales. Having worked after school in a "Dress Place" shop at Mason Mall, Pennsylvania. I started their as a sales clerk, by my second year I was serving as assistant manger.

I am reliable and responsible, and truely enjoy sales work. Mary Carver, the owner of the "Dress Place," can verify my qualifications, she was my supervisor for two years.

I will be visiting Brooktown from April 25 to 30. I hope to have an oppurtunity to speak to you about possible summer jobs at that time, and will be available for interview at your convience. Thank-you for you're consideration.

Sincerley,

Joan Ackerman

Joan Ackerman

2. Retrieve the revised essay you prepared in response to either activity 11 or activity 12 in Chapter 8 (page 132). Following the guidelines described on the preceding pages, edit and proofread your revision. After making the needed changes, prepare your final draft of the essay, using the appropriate manuscript format. Before submitting your paper to your instructor, ask someone to check it for grammar, spelling, and typographical errors that may have slipped by you undetected.

THE PATTERNS OF DEVELOPMENT

10
AN OVERVIEW OF THE PATTERNS OF DEVELOPMENT

Throughout Part II, you saw how the patterns of development—narration, process analysis, definition, and so on—are used as strategies for generating, developing, and organizing ideas for essays. You also learned that, in practice, most types of writing combine two or more patterns. This chapter, the first in Part III, provides additional information about these important points. Once you have a clear understanding of the patterns in general, you'll be ready to move on to the remaining chapters in Part III. There you'll learn more about the unique characteristics of each pattern.

THE PATTERNS IN ACTION: DURING THE WRITING PROCESS

As you know, the patterns of development come into play throughout the composing process. In the prewriting stage, awareness of the patterns encourages you to think about your subject in fresh, new ways. Assume, for example, that you've been asked to write an essay about the way children are disciplined in school. However, you draw a blank as soon as you try to limit this general subject. To break the logjam, you could apply one or more patterns of development to your subject. *Comparison-contrast* might prompt you to write an essay investigating the differences between your parents' and your own feelings about school discipline.

147

Division-classification might lead you to another paper—one that categorizes the kinds of discipline used in school. And *cause-effect* might point to still another essay—one that explores the way students react to being suspended.

Further along in the writing process—after you've identified your limited subject and your thesis—the patterns of development can help you generate your paper's evidence. Imagine that your thesis is "Teachers shouldn't discipline students publicly just to make an example of them." You're not sure, though, how to develop this thesis. Calling on the patterns might spark some promising possibilities. *Narration* might encourage you to recount the disastrous time you were singled out and punished for the misdeeds of an entire class. Using *definition,* you might explain what is meant by an *autocratic* disciplinary style. *Argumentation-persuasion* might prompt you to advocate a new plan for disciplining students fairly and effectively.

The patterns of development also help you organize your ideas by pointing the way to an appropriate framework for a paper. Suppose you plan to write an essay for the campus newspaper about the disturbingly high incidence of shoplifting among college students; your purpose is to *persuade* young people not to get involved in this tempting, supposedly victimless crime. You believe that many readers will be deterred from shoplifting if you tell them about the harrowing *process* set in motion once a shoplifter is detected. With this step-by-step explanation in mind, you can now map out the essay's content: what happens when a shoplifter is detained by a salesperson, questioned by store security personnel, led to a police car, booked at the police station, and tried in a courtroom.

THE PATTERNS IN ACTION: IN AN ESSAY

Although Part III devotes a separate chapter to each of the nine patterns of development, all chapters emphasize the same important point: Most writing consists of several patterns, with the dominant pattern providing the piece's organizational framework. To reinforce this point, each chapter contains a section, "How [the Pattern] Fits Your Purpose and Audience," that shows how a writer's purpose often leads to a blending of patterns. You'll also notice that one of the "Questions About the Writer's Craft" following each professional selection often asks you to analyze the piece's combination of patterns. Further, the "Writing Assignments Using Other Patterns of Development" encourage you to discover for yourself which mix of patterns would work best in a given piece of writing. In short, all through *The Longman Writer,* we emphasize that the patterns of development are far from being mechanical formulas. On the contrary: They are practical strategies that open up options in every stage of the composing process.

Before studying how the writers in Part III combine patterns of development, you'll probably find it helpful to glance back at pages 31–32 so you can review the broad purpose of each pattern. That done, you'll be ready to analyze the selections in this part of the book. The following checklist will help you look more closely at the selections.

☑ ANALYZING HOW A WRITER COMBINES PATTERNS:
A CHECKLIST

☐ What are the writer's purpose and thesis?

☐ Which pattern of development dominates this essay? How does this pattern help the writer support the essay's thesis and fulfill the essay's purpose?

☐ What other patterns appear in the essay? How do these secondary patterns help the writer support the essay's thesis and fulfill the essay's purpose?

Your responses to these three questions will reward you with a richer understanding of the way skilled prose stylists use the patterns of development in their work. To give you an even clearer sense of how writers mix patterns, we have annotated the essay "The Death of the Moth" by Virginia Woolf, using the preceding three questions as a guide. By making your own annotations on Woolf's essay and then comparing them to ours, you can measure your ability to analyze Woolf's use of the patterns. You can further evaluate your analysis of the piece by answering the three questions on your own and then comparing your responses to ours on pages 152–154.

VIRGINIA WOOLF

Virginia Woolf (1882–1941) is considered one of the most innovative writers of the twentieth century. Born in London, Woolf became a key member of the Bloomsbury Group, a circle of writers and artists committed to the highest standards in art and literature. Woolf's works include the novels *Mrs. Dalloway* (1923) and *To the Lighthouse* (1927), as well as the collection of essays *A Room of One's Own* (1920). Although her work met with critical acclaim, Woolf was troubled all her life by severe depression and committed suicide in 1941. The following selection first appeared in the volume *The Death of the Moth and Other Essays* (1948).

THE DEATH OF THE MOTH

1   Moths that fly by day are not properly to be called moths; they do not excite that pleasant sense of dark autumn nights and ivy-blossom which the commonest yellow-underwing asleep in the shadow of the curtain never fails to rouse in us. They are hybrid creatures, neither gay like butterflies nor sombre like their own species. Nevertheless the present specimen, with his narrow hay-coloured wings, fringed with a tassel of the same

Description of the moth

Definition (by negation): How this moth differs from the usual kind colour, seemed to be content with life. It was a pleasant morning, mid-September, mild, benignant, yet with a keener breath than that of the summer months. The plough was already scoring the field opposite the window, and where the share had been, the earth was pressed flat and gleamed with moisture. Such vigour came rolling in from the fields and the down beyond that it was difficult to keep the eyes strictly turned upon the book. The rooks too were keeping one of their annual festivities; soaring round the tree tops until it looked as if a vast net with thousands of black knots in it had been cast up into the air; which, after a few moments, sank slowly down upon the trees until every twig seemed to have a knot at the end of it. Then, suddenly, the net would be thrown into the air again in a wider circle this time, with the utmost clamour and vociferation, as though to be thrown into the air and settle slowly down upon the tree tops were a tremendously exciting experience.

The same energy which inspired the rooks, the ploughmen, the horses,   2
and even, it seemed, the lean bare-backed downs, sent the moth fluttering from side to side of his square of the windowpane. One could not help watching him. One was, indeed, conscious of a queer feeling of pity for him. The possibilities of pleasure seemed that morning so enormous and so various that to have only a moth's part in life, and a day moth's at that, appeared a hard fate, and his zest in enjoying his meagre opportunities to the full, pathetic. He flew vigorously to one corner of his compartment, and, after waiting there a second, flew across to the other. What remained for him but to fly to a third corner and then to a fourth? That was all he could do, in spite of the size of the downs, the width of the sky, the far-off smoke of houses, and the romantic voice, now and then, of a steamer out at sea. What he could do he did. Watching him, it seemed as if a fibre, very thin but pure, of the enormous energy of the world had been thrust into his frail and diminutive body. As often as he crossed the pane, I could fancy that a thread of vital light became visible. He was little or nothing but life.

Yet, because he was so small, and so simple a form of the energy that   3
was rolling in at the open window and driving its way through so many narrow and intricate corridors in my own brain and in those of other human beings, there was something marvellous as well as pathetic about

Part of implied pur-
pose/thesis: Nature's
energy

Description of nature's
energy here *contrasts*
with *description* of
nature in ¶5 (part of
purpose/thesis).

Comparison between
nature's energy and the
moth's strong life force
(part of purpose/thesis)

Start of *narrative* (main
pattern) about the
moth's plight

Start of *narrative* about
Woolf's reaction to the
moth's plight

Description of moth's
strong life force—
despite his small size
(these two contrasting
qualities are part of
purpose/thesis)

Part of purpose/thesis:
The moth represents
life.

Narrative about Woolf's
reaction continues.

Restatement of part of
purpose/thesis: The
moth's two contrasting
qualities

him. It was as if someone had taken a tiny bead of pure life and decking it
as lightly as possible with down and feathers, had set it dancing and zigzag-
ging to show us the true nature of life. Thus displayed one could not get
over the strangeness of it. One is apt to forget all about life, seeing it
humped and bossed and garnished and cumbered so that it has to move
with the greatest circumspection and dignity. Again, the thought of all that
life might have been had he been born in any other shape caused one to
view his simple activities with a kind of pity.

Restatement of part of purpose/thesis: The moth represents life.

4   After a time, tired by his dancing apparently, he settled on the window
ledge in the sun, and, the queer spectacle being at an end, I forgot about
him. Then, looking up, my eye was caught by him. He was trying to resume
his dancing, but seemed either so stiff or so awkward that he could only
flutter to the bottom of the window-pane; and when he tried to fly across
it he failed. Being intent on other matters I watched these futile attempts
for a time without thinking, unconsciously waiting for him to resume his
flight, as one waits for a machine, that has stopped momentarily, to start
again without considering the reason of its failure. After perhaps a seventh
attempt he slipped from the wooden ledge and fell, fluttering his wings, on
to his back on the window sill. The helplessness of his attitude roused me.
It flashed upon me that he was in difficulties; he could no longer raise himself; his legs struggled vainly. But, as I stretched out a pencil, meaning to
help him to right himself, it came over me that the failure and awkward-
ness were the approach of death. I laid the pencil down again.

Narrative about the moth's plight continues: tension builds.

Narrative about Woolf's reaction continues.

Hint of the resolution of the narrative about the moth

5   The legs agitated themselves once more. I looked as if for the enemy
against which he struggled. I looked out of doors. What had happened
there? Presumably it was midday, and work in the fields had stopped.
Stillness and quiet had replaced the previous animation. The birds had
taken themselves off to feed in the brooks. The horses stood still. Yet the
power was there all the same, massed outside, indifferent, impersonal, not
attending to anything in particular. Somehow it was opposed to the little
hay-coloured moth. It was useless to try to do anything. One could only
watch the extraordinary efforts made by those tiny legs against an oncoming doom which could, had it chosen, have submerged an entire city, not
merely a city, but masses of human beings; nothing, I knew, had any chance

Narrative about Woolf's reaction continues.

Description of nature's indifference here con-trasts with description of nature in ¶1 (part of purpose/thesis).

Restatement of part of purpose/thesis: The strength of the moth's life force—despite small size

Part of purpose/thesis: Death's inevitability

Narrative about moth continues.

against death. Nevertheless after a pause of exhaustion the legs fluttered again. It was superb, this last protest, and so frantic that he succeeded at

Narrative about Woolf's reaction continues.

last in righting himself. One's sympathies, of course, were all on the side of life. Also, when there was nobody to care or to know, this gigantic effort

Narrative about Woolf's reaction continues.

on the part of an insignificant little moth, against a power of such magnitude, to retain what no one else valued or desired to keep, moved one

Restatement of part of purpose/thesis: The strength of the moth's life force—despite his size

strangely. Again, somehow, one saw life, a pure bead. I lifted the pencil again, useless though I knew it to be. But even as I did so, the unmistakable tokens of death showed themselves. The body relaxed, and instantly grew stiff. The struggle was over. The insignificant little creature now knew

Resolution of the *narrative* about the moth

death. As I looked at the dead moth, this minute wayside triumph of so great a force over so mean an antagonist filled me with wonder. Just as life had been strange a few minutes before, so death was now as strange. The

Restatement of part of purpose/thesis: Death's inevitability

moth having righted himself now lay most decently, and uncomplainingly composed. O yes, he seemed to say, death is stronger than I am.

The following answers to the questions on page 149 will help you analyze Virginia Woolf's use of the patterns of development in the essay "The Death of the Moth."

1. What are the writer's purpose and thesis? *Woolf's purpose* is to show that the tiny moth's courageous but ultimately futile battle to cling to life embodies the struggle at the very heart of all existence. Woolf achieves her purpose by relating the story of the moth's efforts to resist death. Her *thesis* might be expressed this way: Although living creatures may make "extraordinary efforts" (paragraph 5) to hold on to life, these attempts aren't strong enough to defy death. Nothing, Woolf writes, has "any chance against death" (5).

Woolf's purpose and thesis first become apparent at the end of paragraph 2. There she shows that the moth, with his "frail and diminutive body," represents "nothing but life." Although "small . . . and simple" (3), the moth is suffused with the same extraordinary energy that is evident in the natural world beyond Woolf's window. This energy, combined with the moth's tiny size, makes the creature both "marvellous" and "pathetic" (3)—two qualities that are particularly apparent during the moth's final struggles. During those moments, the moth makes a final "superb" (5) protest against death, but ultimately the "insignificant" (5) creature—like all forms of life—must cease his valiant struggle and die.

2. Which pattern of development dominates the essay? How does this pattern help the writer support the essay's thesis and fulfill the essay's purpose? Although the essay's first paragraph is largely descriptive, it becomes clear by paragraph 2 that the description is in service of a larger *narrative* about the moth's struggles. It's this narrative that dominates the essay.

At the beginning, the moth is imbued with vitality, as he flies "vigorously" (paragraph 2) and with "zest" (2) from one side of the window to the other. But narrative tension begins to build in paragraph 4. There Woolf writes that the moth tries once again to cross the windowpane, fails repeatedly, and slips "onto his back," seemingly defeated. However, even then, the moth doesn't abandon his hold on life, for—as Woolf relates in paragraph 5—he tries, despite exhaustion, to right himself. Against all odds, he finally succeeds, but his frantic struggle to hold on to life takes its toll, and the tiny creature soon dies. This detailed story of the moth's futile battle against death is presented as an emblem of the fate of all life. Through this narrative, Woolf achieves her purpose and thesis: to convey the power of nature and the inability of living creatures—despite heroic efforts—to defy this power.

Paralleling the tale of the moth's struggle is another *narrative:* the story of Woolf's changing understanding of the event that unfolds before her. When the moth is "dancing" (3), energetic, and vital, Woolf "can't help watching him" (2) and feels a kind of wonderment at this "tiny bead of pure life" (3). Then in paragraph 4, Woolf writes that she forgets about the moth for a while until she happens to look up and see his "futile attempts" to "resume dancing." For a few moments, she watches the moth's "stiff" and "awkward" efforts to fly, expecting him to demonstrate the same vitality as before. Suddenly, she understands that the moth is "in difficulties" and can no longer lift himself up. She tries to help but abandons her efforts when she realizes that the moth's labored efforts signify the "approach of death." Paragraph 5 presents the final stage of Woolf's interior narrative. She looks outside her window for an explanation of the moth's plight. But now she finds that the forces of nature—earlier so exuberant and vibrant—are, if anything, "opposed to the little hay-coloured moth." With that, her attention is once again drawn to the moth and the fluttering of his legs. Although drained, the tiny creature makes one last effort to resist death—and, improbably enough, picks himself up one more time. Struck by the sheer power of the moth's life force, Woolf is prompted, as before, to help the creature, even though she recognizes the futility. But then the "unmistakable" tokens of death appear, and the moth gives up his struggle, succumbing—as all forms of life must—to the forces of nature. With the moth lying "uncomplainingly composed," Woolf comes to accept the fact that "death is stronger than life."

3. What other patterns appear in the essay? How do these secondary patterns help the writer support the essay's thesis and fulfill the essay's purpose? Although the essay is predominantly a narrative, it also contains other patterns. The *descriptive* passage at the beginning of the essay includes a brief *definition by negation* in which Woolf explains how the creature she is observing differs from the usual, more colorful night moth. The rest of paragraph 1 draws upon description to evoke the sense of early autumn and nature's extraordinary energy. This description of the natural world's vibrancy and abundance, exemplified by the rooks and plowed earth, *contrasts* with Woolf's later characterization of the natural world in paragraph 5. There she writes, "Stillness and quiet . . . replaced the previous animation," and she senses not that nature fosters vitality, but that it is "indifferent, impersonal, not attending to anything in particular."

Shifting her focus in paragraph 2 from the natural world to the moth, Woolf exercises her *descriptive* powers to convey the moth's extraordinary zest as he flies across the windowpane. In this paragraph, Woolf also draws upon *comparison-contrast* to show that despite *differences* in their sizes, the tiny moth and the vast natural world embody the *same* primal energy. Woolf's consideration of this elemental similarity leads her to the basic *contrast* at the heart of the essay: While the moth's tiny size makes him "pathetic," his formidable life spirit makes him "marvellous." He may be small and lightweight, but he is abuzz with vitality. When contrasted to the enormous power of nature, the moth—like all forms of life—may be puny, but his impulse to defy such power inspires awe and reverence.

11
DESCRIPTION

WHAT IS DESCRIPTION?

All of us respond in a strong way to sensory stimulation. The sweet perfume of a candy shop takes us back to childhood; the blank white walls of the campus infirmary remind us of long vigils at a hospital where a grandmother lay dying; the screech of a subway car sets our nerves on edge.

Without any sensory stimulation, we sink into a less-than-human state. Neglected babies, left alone with no human touch, no colors, no lullabies, become withdrawn and unresponsive. And prisoners dread solitary confinement, knowing that the sensory deprivation can be unbearable, even to the point of madness.

Because sensory impressions are so potent, descriptive writing has a unique power and appeal. **Description** can be defined as the expression, in vivid language, of what the five senses experience. A richly rendered description freezes a subject in time, evoking sights, smells, sounds, textures, and tastes in such a way that readers become one with the writer's world.

How description fits your purpose and audience

Description can be a supportive technique that develops part of an essay, or it can be the dominant technique used throughout an essay. Here are some examples of the way description can help you meet the objective of an essay developed chiefly through another pattern of development:

- In a *causal analysis* showing the *consequences* of pet overpopulation, you might describe the desperate appearance of a pack of starving stray dogs.
- In an *argumentation-persuasion essay* urging more rigorous handgun control, you might start with a description of a violent family confrontation that ended in murder.
- In a *process analysis* explaining the pleasure of making ice cream at home, you might describe the beauty of an old-fashioned, hand-cranked ice cream maker.
- In a *narrative essay* recounting a day in the life of a street musician, you might describe the musician's energy and the joyous appreciation of passersby.

In each case, the essay's overall purpose would affect the amount of description needed.

Your readers also influence how much description to include. As you write, ask yourself, "What do my particular readers need to know to understand and experience keenly what I'm describing? What descriptive details will they enjoy most?" Your answers to these and similar questions will help you tailor your description to specific readers. Consider an article intended for professional horticulturists; its purpose is to explain a new technique for controlling spider mites. Because of readers' expertise, there would be little need for a lengthy description of the insects. Written for a college newspaper, however, the article would probably provide a detailed description of the mites so student gardeners could spot them with ease.

While your purpose and audience define *how much* to describe, you have great freedom deciding *what* to describe. Description is especially suited to objects (your car or desk, for example), but you can also describe a person, an animal, a place, a time, and a phenomenon or concept. You might write an effective description about a friend who runs marathons (person), a pair of ducks that returns each year to a neighbor's pond (animals), the kitchen of a fast-food restaurant (place), a period when you were unemployed (time), the "fight or flight" response to danger (phenomenon or concept).

Description can be divided into two types: objective and subjective. In an **objective description,** you describe the subject in a straightforward and literal way, without revealing your attitude or feelings. Reporters, as well as technical and scientific writers, specialize in objective description; their jobs depend on their ability to detail experiences without emotional bias. For example, a reporter may write an unemotional account of a township meeting that ended in a fistfight. Or a marine biologist may write a factual report describing the way sea mammals are killed by the plastic refuse (sandwich wrappings, straws, fishing lines) that humans throw into the ocean.

In contrast, when writing a **subjective description,** you convey a highly personal view of your subject and seek to elicit a strong emotional response from your readers. Such subjective descriptions often take the form of reflective pieces or character studies. For example, in an essay describing the rich plant life in an inner-city garden, you might reflect on people's longing to connect with the soil and express admiration for the gardeners' hard work—an admiration you'd like readers to share. Or, in a character study of your grandfather, you might describe his stern appearance and gentle behavior, hoping that the contradiction will move readers as much as it moves you.

The *tone* of a subjective description is determined by your purpose, your attitude toward the subject, and the reader response you wish to evoke. Consider an essay about a dynamic woman who runs a center for disturbed children. If your goal is to make readers admire the woman, your tone will be serious and appreciative. But if you want to criticize the woman's high-pressure tactics and create distaste for her management style, your tone will be disapproving and severe.

The language of a descriptive piece also depends, to a great extent, on whether your purpose is primarily objective or subjective. If the description is objective, the language is straightforward, precise, and factual. Such *denotative* language consists of neutral dictionary meanings. If you want to describe as dispassionately as possible fans' violent behavior at a football game, you might write about the "large crowd" and its "mass movement onto the field." But if you are shocked by the fans' behavior and want to write a subjective piece that inspires similar outrage in readers, then you might write about the "swelling mob" and its "rowdy stampede onto the field." In the latter case, the language used would be *connotative* and emotionally charged so that readers would share your feelings. (For more on denotation and connotation, see page 24 and pages 120–121.)

Subjective and objective descriptions often overlap. Sometimes a single sentence contains both objective and subjective elements: "Although his hands were large and misshapen by arthritis, they were gentle to the touch, inspiring confidence and trust." Other times, part of an essay may provide a factual description (the physical appearance of a summer cabin your family rented), while another part of the essay may be highly subjective (how you felt in the cabin, sitting in front of a fire on a rainy day).

PREWRITING STRATEGIES

The following checklist shows how you can apply to description some of the prewriting strategies discussed in Chapter 2.

☑ DESCRIPTION: A PREWRITING CHECKLIST

Choose a Subject to Describe

☐ Might a photograph, postcard, prized possession, or journal entry suggest a subject worth describing?

☐ Will you describe a person, animal, object, place, time period, or phenomenon? Is the subject readily observable, or will you have to reconstruct it from memory?

Determine Your Purpose, Audience, Tone, and Point of View

☐ Is your purpose to inform or to evoke an emotional response? If you want to do both, which is your predominant purpose?

☐ What audience are you writing for? How much does the audience already know about the subject you plan to describe?

☐ What tone and point of view will best serve your purpose and make readers receptive to your description?

Use Prewriting to Generate Details About the Subject

☐ How could freewriting, journal entries, or brainstorming help you gather sensory specifics about your subject?

☐ What relevant details about your subject come to mind when you apply the questioning technique to each of the five senses? What sounds (pitch, volume, and quality) predominate? What can you touch and how does it feel (temperature, weight, texture)? What do you see (color, pattern, shape, size)? What smells (pleasant, unpleasant) can't you forget? What tastes (agreeable, disagreeable) remain memorable?

STRATEGIES FOR USING DESCRIPTION IN AN ESSAY

After prewriting, you're ready to draft your essay. The following suggestions will be helpful whether you use description as a dominant or supportive pattern of development.

1. Focus a descriptive essay around a dominant impression. Like other kinds of writing, a descriptive essay must have a thesis, or main point. In a descriptive essay with a subjective slant, the thesis usually centers on the **dominant impression** you have about your subject. Suppose you decide to write an essay on your ninth-grade history teacher, Ms. Hazzard. You want the paper to convey how unconventional and flamboyant she was. The essay could, of course, focus on a different dominant impression—how insensitive she could be to students, for example. What's important is that you establish—early in the paper—the dominant impression you intend to convey. Although descriptive essays often imply, rather than explicitly state, the dominant impression, that impression should be unmistakable.

2. Select the details to include. The prewriting techniques discussed on pages 25–32 can help you develop heightened powers of observation and recall. Practice in noting significant details can lead you to become—in the words of novelist Henry James—"one of those people on whom nothing is lost." The power of description hinges on your ability to select from all possible details *only those that support the dominant impression*. All others—no matter how vivid or interesting—must be left out. If you were describing how flamboyant Ms. Hazzard could be, the details in the following paragraph would be appropriate:

> A large-boned woman, Ms. Hazzard wore her bright red hair piled on top of her head, where it perched precariously. By the end of class, wayward strands of hair tumbled down and fell into eyes fringed by spiky false eyelashes. Ms. Hazzard's nails, filed into crisp points, were painted either bloody burgundy or neon pink. Plastic bangle bracelets, also either burgundy or pink, clattered up and down her ample arms as she scrawled on the board the historical dates that had, she claimed, "changed the world."

Such details—the heavy eye makeup, stiletto nails, gaudy bracelets—contribute to the impression of a flamboyant, unusual person. Even if you remembered times that Ms. Hazzard seemed perfectly conventional and understated, most likely you wouldn't describe those times because they would contradict the dominant impression.

You must also be selective in the *number of details* you include. Having a dominant impression helps you eliminate many details gathered during prewriting, but there still will be choices to make. For example, it would be inappropriate to describe in exhaustive detail everything in a messy room:

> The brown desk, made of a grained plastic laminate, is directly under a small window covered by a torn yellow-and-gold plaid curtain. In the left corner of the desk are four crumbled balls of blue-lined yellow paper, three red markers (all without caps), two fine-point blue pens, a crumbling pink eraser, and four letters, two bearing special wildlife stamps. A green down-filled vest and an out-of-shape red cable-knit sweater are thrown over the back of the bright blue metal bridge chair pushed under the desk. Under the chair is an oval braided rug, its once brilliant blues and greens spotted by soda and coffee stains.

Readers will be reluctant to wade through such undifferentiated specifics. Even more important, such excessive detailing dilutes the essay's focus. You end up with a seemingly endless list of specifics, rather than with a carefully crafted word picture. In this regard, sculptors and writers are similar—what they take away is as important as what they leave in.

3. Organize the descriptive details.   It's important to select the organizational pattern (or combination of patterns) that best supports your dominant impression. The paragraphs in a descriptive essay are usually sequenced *spatially* (from top to bottom, interior to exterior, near to far) or *chronologically* (as the subject is experienced in time). But the paragraphs can also be ordered *emphatically* (ending with your subject's most striking elements) or by *sensory impression* (first smell, then taste, then touch, and so on).

You might, for instance, use a *spatial* pattern to organize a description of a large city as you viewed it from the air, a taxi, or a subway car. A description of your first day on a new job might move *chronologically,* starting with how you felt the first hour on the job and proceeding through the rest of the day. In a paper describing a bout with the flu, you might arrange details *emphatically,* beginning with a description of your low-level aches and pains and concluding with an account of your raging fever. An essay about a neighborhood garbage dump could be organized by *sensory impressions:* the sights of the dump, its smells, its sounds. Regardless of the organizational pattern you use, provide enough *signal devices* (for example, *about, next, worst of all*) so that readers can follow the description easily.

Finally, although descriptive essays don't always have conventional topic sentences, each descriptive paragraph should have a clear focus. Often this focus is indicated by a sentence early in the paragraph that names the scene, object, or individual to be described. Such a sentence functions as a kind of *informal topic sentence;* the paragraph's descriptive details then develop that topic sentence.

4. Use vivid sensory language and varied sentence structure.   The connotative language typical of subjective description should be richly evocative. The words you select must etch in readers' minds the same picture that you have in yours. For this reason, rather than relying on vague generalities, you must use language that involves readers' senses. Consider the difference between the following paired descriptions:

Vague	**Vivid**
The food was unappetizing.	The stew congealed into an oval pool of muddy-brown fat.
The toothpaste was refreshing.	The toothpaste, minty sweet, tingled against my bare teeth, finally free from braces.
Filled with passengers and baggage, the car moved slowly down the road.	Burdened with its load of clamoring children and bulging suitcases, the car labored down the interstate on bald tires and worn shocks, emitting puffs of blue exhaust and an occasional backfire.

Unlike the *concrete, sensory-packed* sentences on the right, the sentences on the left fail to create vivid word pictures that engage readers. While all good writing blends abstract and concrete language, descriptive writing demands an abundance of specific sensory language. (For more on specific language, see pages 121–122 in Chapter 8.)

Although you should aim for rich, sensory images, avoid overloading your sentences with *too many adjectives:* "A stark, smooth, blinding glass cylinder, the fifty-story skyscraper dominated the crowded city street." Delete unnecessary words, retaining only the most powerful: "A blinding glass cylinder, the skyscraper dominated the street."

Remember, too, that *verbs pack more of a wallop* than adverbs. The following sentence has to rely on adverbs (italicized) because its verbs are so weak: "She walked *casually* into the room and *deliberately* tried not to pay attention to their stares." Rewritten, so that verbs (italicized), not adverbs, do the bulk of the work, the sentence becomes more powerful: "She *strolled* into the room and *ignored* their stares." *Onomatopoetic* verbs, like *buzz, sizzle,* and *zoom,* can be especially effective because their sounds convey their meaning. (For more on vigorous verbs, see pages 122–124 in Chapter 8.)

Figures of speech—nonliteral, imaginative comparisons between two basically dissimilar things—are another way to enliven descriptive writing. *Similes* use the word *like* or *as* when comparing; *metaphors* state or imply that the two things being compared are alike; and *personification* attributes human characteristics to inanimate things. (For further discussion of figures of speech, refer to pages 125–126 in Chapter 8.)

The examples that follow show how effective figurative language can be in descriptive writing:

Simile

Moving as jerkily as a marionette on strings, the old man picked himself up off the sidewalk and staggered down the street.

Metaphor

Stalking their prey, the hall monitors remained hidden in the corridors, motionless and ready to spring on any unsuspecting student who tried to sneak into class late.

Personification

The scoop of vanilla ice cream, plain and unadorned, cried out for hot fudge sauce and a sprinkling of sliced pecans.

(For suggestions on avoiding clichéd figures of speech, see page 125 in Chapter 8.)

Finally, when writing descriptive passages, you need to *vary sentence structure.* Don't use the same subject-verb pattern in all sentences. The second example above, for instance, could have been written as follows: "The hall monitors stalked their prey. They hid in the corridors. They remained motionless and ready to spring on any unsuspecting student who tried to sneak into class late." But the sentence is richer and more interesting when the descriptive elements are embedded, eliminating what would otherwise have been a clipped and predictable subject-verb pattern. (For more on sentence variety, see pages 109–114 in Chapter 8.)

REVISION STRATEGIES

Once you have a draft of the essay, you're ready to revise. The following checklist will help you and those giving you feedback apply to description some of the revision techniques discussed in Chapters 7 and 8.

☑ DESCRIPTION: A REVISION/PEER REVIEW CHECKLIST

Revise Overall Meaning and Structure

☐ What dominant impression does the essay convey? Is the dominant impression stated or implied? Where? Should it be made more obvious or more subtle? Why?

☐ Is the essay primarily objective or subjective? Should the essay be more personal and emotionally charged or less so?

☐ Which descriptive details don't support the dominant impression? Should they be deleted, or should the dominant impression be adjusted to encompass the details?

Revise Paragraph Development

☐ How are the essay's descriptive paragraphs (or passages) organized—spatially, chronologically, emphatically, or by sensory impressions? Would another organizational pattern be more effective? Which one(s)? Why?

☐ Which paragraphs lack a distinctive focus?

☐ Which descriptive paragraphs (or passages) deteriorate into a mere list of sensory impressions?

☐ Which descriptive paragraphs (or passages) are too abstract or general? Which fail to engage the reader's senses? How could they be made more concrete and specific?

Revise Sentences and Words

☐ What signal devices (such as *above, next, worst of all*) guide readers through the description? Are there enough signals? Too many?

☐ Where should sentence structure be varied so that it is less predictable and monotonous?

☐ Which sentences lack sensory images? How could they be made more evocative?

☐ Where should flat verbs and adverbs be replaced with vigorous verbs? Where would onomatopoeia enliven a sentence?

☐ Where are there too many adjectives? Which could be deleted?

☐ What figures of speech appear in the essay? Which seem contrived or trite?

STUDENT ESSAY: FROM PREWRITING THROUGH REVISION

The student essay that follows was written by Marie Martinez in response to this assignment:

> The essay "Once More to the Lake" is an evocative piece about a spot that had special meaning in E. B. White's life. Write an essay about a place that holds rich significance for you, centering the description on a dominant impression.

After deciding to write about the salt marsh near her grandparents' home, Marie used the prewriting technique of *questioning* to gather sensory details about this special place. To enhance her power of recall, she focused, one at a time, on each of the five senses. Then, typing as quickly as she could, she listed the sensory specifics that came to mind.

When Marie later reviewed the details listed under each sensory heading, she concluded that her essay's dominant impression should be the marsh's peaceful beauty. With that dominant impression in mind, she added some details to her prewriting and deleted others. Below is Marie's original prewriting; the handwritten insertions indicate her later efforts to develop the material:

Questioning Technique

See: What do I see at the marsh?

- line of tall, waving reeds *bordering the creek*
- path--flattened grass
- spring--bright green (*brilliant green*)
- autumn--gold (*tawny*)
- winter--gray
- soil--spongy
- dark soil
- blue crabs
- creek--narrow, sinuous, can't see beginning or end *less than 15' wide*

- birds--little, brown
- low tide--steep bank of creek
- ~~an occasional beer can or potato chip bag~~
- grass under the water--green waves, shimmers
- fish--tiny, with silvery (minnows) sides, dart through water and vegetation *and underwater tangles*
- center of creek--everything water and sky

Hear: How does it sound there?

- chirping of birds (*"tweep, tweep"*)
- splash of turtle or otter
- mainly silent

Smell: Why can't I forget its smell?

- salt
- soil

Feel: How does it feel?

- soil--spongy
- water--warmer than ocean; rub
- my face and neck; mucky *and oily*
- mud--slimy (*through toes*)
- crabs brush my legs
- feel buoyant, weightless

When Marie reviewed her annotated prewriting, she decided that, in the essay, she would order her brainstormed impressions by location rather than by sensory type. Using a spatial method of organization, she would present details as she moved from place to place—from her grandparents' home to the creek. The arrangement of details was now so clear to Marie that she felt comfortable moving to a first draft without further shaping her prewriting or preparing an outline. As she wrote, though, she frequently referred to her prewriting to retrieve sensory details about each location.

Now read Marie's paper, "Salt Marsh," noting the similarities and differences between her prewriting and final essay. You'll see that the essay's introduction and conclusion weren't drawn from the prewriting material, whereas most of the sensory details were. Notice, too, that when she wrote the essay, Marie expanded these details by adding more specifics and providing several powerful similes. Finally, consider how well the essay applies the principles of description discussed in this chapter. (The commentary that follows the paper will help you look at the essay more closely and will give you some sense of how Marie went about revising her first draft.)

Salt Marsh

by Marie Martinez

Introduction

1 In one of his journals, Thoreau told of the difficulty he had escaping the obligations and cares of society: "It sometimes happens that I cannot easily shake off the village. The thought of some work will run in my head and I am not where my body is--I am out of my senses. In my walks I . . . return to my senses." All of us feel out of our senses at times. Overwhelmed by problems or everyday annoyances, we lose touch with sensory pleasures as we spend our days in noisy cities and stuffy classrooms. Just as Thoreau walked in the woods to return to his senses, I have a special place where I return to mine: the salt marsh behind my grandparents' house.

Dominant impression (thesis)

2 My grandparents live on the East Coast, a mile or so inland from the sea. Between the ocean and the mainland is a wide fringe of salt marsh. A salt marsh is not a swamp, but an expanse of dark, spongy soil threaded with saltwater creeks and clothed in a kind of grass called salt meadow hay. All the water in the marsh rises and falls daily with the ocean tides, an endless cycle that changes the look of the marsh--partly flooded or mostly dry--as the day progresses.

Informal topic sentence: Definition paragraph

3   Heading out to the marsh from my grandparents'
house, I follow a short path through the woods. As I
walk along, a sharp smell of salt mixed with the rich
aroma of peaty soil fills my nostrils. I am always
amazed by the way the path changes with the seasons.
Sometimes I walk in the brilliant green of spring,
sometimes in the tawny gold of autumn, sometimes in
the grayish-tan of winter. No matter the season, the
grass flanking the trail is often flattened into
swirls, like thick Van Gogh brush strokes that curve
and recurve in circular patterns. No people come here.
The peacefulness heals me like a soothing drug.

Informal topic sentence: First paragraph in a four-part spatial sequence

Simile

4   After a few minutes, the trail suddenly opens up to a
view that calms me no matter how upset or discouraged I
might be: a line of tall waving reeds bordering and
nearly hiding the salt marsh creek. To get to the creek,
I part the reeds.

Informal topic sentence: Second paragraph in the spatial sequence

5   The creek is a narrow body of water no more than
fifteen feet wide, and it ebbs and flows as the ocean
currents sweep toward the land or rush back toward the
sea. The creek winds in a sinuous pattern so that I
cannot see its beginning or end, the places where it
trickles into the marsh or spills into the open ocean.
Little brown birds dip in and out of the reeds on the
far shore of the creek, making a special "tweep-tweep"
sound peculiar to the marsh. When I stand at low tide on
the shore of the creek, I am on a miniature cliff, for
the bank of the creek falls abruptly and steeply into
the water. Below me, green grasses wave and shimmer
under the water while tiny minnows flash their silvery
sides as they dart through the underwater tangles.

Informal topic sentence: Third paragraph in the spatial sequence

6   The creek water is often much warmer than the ocean,
so I can swim there in three seasons. Sitting on the
edge of the creek, I scoop some water into my hand, rub
my face and neck, then ease into the water. Where the
creek is shallow, my feet sink into a foot of muck that
feels like mashed potatoes mixed with motor oil. But
once I become accustomed to it, I enjoy squishing the
slimy mud through my toes. Sometimes I feel brushing
past my legs the blue crabs that live in the creek.

Informal topic sentence: Last paragraph in the spatial sequence

Simile

Other times, I hear the splash of a turtle or an otter
as it slips from the shore into the water. Otherwise,
it is silent. The salty water is buoyant and lifts my
spirits as I stroke through it to reach the middle of
the creek. There in the center, I float weightlessly,
surrounded by tall reeds that reduce the world to water
and sky. I am at peace.

Conclusion   The salt marsh is not the kind of dramatic landscape   7
found on picture postcards. There are no soaring
mountains, sandy beaches, or lush valleys. The marsh is
a flat world that some consider dull and uninviting. I
am glad most people do not respond to the marsh's subtle
beauty because that means I can be alone there. Just as
the rising tide sweeps over the marsh, floating debris
out to the ocean, the marsh washes away my concerns and

Echo of idea in
introduction ──────→ restores me to my senses.

Commentary

The Dominant Impression

Marie responded to the assignment by writing a moving tribute to a place having special meaning for her—the salt marsh near her grandparents' home. Like
most descriptive pieces, Marie's essay is organized around a *dominant impression:*
the marsh's peaceful solitude and gentle, natural beauty. The essay's introduction
provides a context for the dominant impression by comparing the pleasure Marie
experiences in the marsh to the happiness Thoreau felt in his walks around
Walden Pond.

Other Patterns of Development

Before developing the essay's dominant impression, Marie uses the second
paragraph to *define* a salt marsh. An *objective description,* the definition clarifies
that a salt marsh—with its spongy soil, haylike grass, and ebbing tides—is not to
be confused with a swamp. Because Marie offers such a factual definition, readers have the background needed to enjoy the personalized view that follows.

Besides the definition paragraph and the comparison in the opening paragraph, the essay contains a strong element of *causal analysis:* Throughout, Marie
describes the marsh's effect on her.

Sensory Language

At times, Marie develops the essay's dominant impression explicitly, as when
she writes "No people come here" (paragraph 3) and "I am at peace" (6). But
Marie generally uses the more subtle techniques characteristic of *subjective*

description to convey the dominant impression. First of all, she fills the essay with strong *connotative language*, rich with *sensory images*. The third paragraph describes what she smells (the "sharp smell of salt mixed with the rich aroma of peaty soil") and what she sees ("brilliant green," "tawny gold," and "grayish-tan"). In the fifth paragraph, she uses *onomatopoeia* ("tweep-tweep") to convey the birds' chirping sound. And the sixth paragraph includes vigorous descriptions of how the marsh feels to Marie's touch. She splashes water on her face and neck; she digs her toes into the mud at the bottom of the creek; she delights in the delicate brushing of crabs against her legs.

Figurative Language, Vigorous Verbs, and Varied Sentence Structure

You might also have noted that *figurative language, energetic verbs,* and *varied sentence patterns* contribute to the essay's descriptive power. Marie develops a simile in the third paragraph when she compares the flattened swirls of swamp grass to the brush strokes in a painting by Van Gogh. Later she uses another simile when she writes that the creek's thick mud feels "like mashed potatoes mixed with motor oil." Moreover, throughout the essay, she uses lively verbs ("shimmer,""flash") to capture the marsh's magical quality. Similarly, Marie enhances descriptive passages by varying the length of her sentences. Long, fairly elaborate sentences are interspersed with short, dramatic statements. In the third paragraph, for example, the long sentence describing the circular swirls of swamp grass is followed by the brief statement "No people come here." And the sixth paragraph uses two short sentences ("Otherwise, it is silent" and "I am at peace") to punctuate the paragraph's longer sentences.

Organization

We can follow Marie's journey through the marsh because she uses an easy-to-follow combination of *spatial, chronological,* and *emphatic* patterns to sequence her experience. The essay relies primarily on a spatial arrangement since the four body paragraphs focus on the different spots that Marie reaches: first, the path behind her grandparents' house (paragraph 3); then the area bordering the creek (4); next, her view of the creek (5); last, the creek itself (6). Each stage of her walk is signaled by an *informal topic sentence* near the start of each paragraph. Furthermore, *signal devices* (marked by italics here) indicate not only her location but also the chronological passage of time: "*As* I walk along, a sharp smell . . . fills my nostrils" (3); "*After* a few minutes, the trail suddenly opens up . . ." (4); "*Below* me, green grasses wave . . ." (5). And to call attention to the creek's serene beauty, Marie saves for last the description of the peace she feels while floating in the creek.

An Inappropriate Figure of Speech

Although the four body paragraphs focus on the distinctive qualities of each location, Marie runs into a minor problem in the third paragraph. Take a moment to reread that paragraph's last sentence. Comparing the peace of the marsh to the effect of a "soothing drug" is jarring. The effectiveness of Marie's essay hinges on her ability to create a picture of a pure, natural world. A reference to drugs is inappropriate. Now, reread the paragraph aloud, stopping after "No people come here." Note how much more in keeping with the essay's dominant impression the paragraph is when the reference to drugs is omitted.

Conclusion

The concluding paragraph brings the essay to a graceful close. The powerful *simile* found in the last sentence contains an implied reference to Thoreau and to Marie's earlier statement about the joy to be found in special places having restorative powers. Such an allusion echoes, with good effect, the paper's opening comments.

Revising the First Draft

When Marie met with some classmates during a group feedback session, the students agreed that Marie's first draft was strong and moving. But they also said that they had difficulty following her route through the marsh; they found her third paragraph especially confusing. Marie kept track of her classmates' comments on a separate piece of paper and then entered them, numbered in order of importance, in the margin of her first draft. Reprinted here is the original version of Marie's third paragraph, along with her annotations:

Original Version of Third Paragraph

① Chronology is confusing

③ Make more specific

② Develop more fully—maybe use a simile

As I head out to the marsh from the house, I follow a short trail through the woods. A smell of salt and soil fills my nostrils. The end of the trail suddenly opens up to a view that calms me no matter how upset or discouraged I might be: a line of tall, waving reeds bordering the salt marsh creek. Civilization seems far away as I walk the path of flattened grass and finally reach my goal, the salt marsh creek hidden behind the tall, waving reeds. The path changes with the seasons; sometimes I walk in the brilliant green of spring, sometimes in the tawny gold of autumn, sometimes in the gray of winter. In some areas, the grass is flattened into swirls that make the marsh resemble one of those paintings by Van Gogh. No people come here. The peacefulness heals me like a soothing drug. The path stops at the line of tall, waving reeds standing upright at the border of the creek. I part the reeds to get to the creek.

When Marie looked more carefully at the paragraph, she agreed it was confusing. For one thing, the paragraph's third and fourth sentences indicated that she had come to the path's end and had reached the reeds bordering the creek. In the following sentences, however, she was on the path again. Then, at the end, she was back at the creek, as if she had just arrived there. Marie resolved this confusion by breaking the single paragraph into two separate ones—the first describing the walk along the path, the second describing her arrival at the creek.

This restructuring, especially when combined with clearer transitions, eliminated the confusion.

While revising her essay, Marie also intensified the sensory images in her original paragraph. She changed the "smell of salt and soil" to the "sharp smell of salt mixed with the rich aroma of peaty soil." And when she added the phrase "thick Van Gogh brush strokes that curve and recurve in circular patterns," she made the comparison between the marsh grass and a Van Gogh painting more vivid.

These are just some of the changes Marie made while rewriting the paper. Her skillful revisions provided the polish needed to make an already strong essay even more evocative.

ACTIVITIES: DESCRIPTION

Prewriting Activities

1. Imagine you're writing two essays: One explains how students get "burned out"; the other contends that being a spendthrift is better (or worse) than being frugal. Jot down ways you might use description in each essay.

2. Go to a place on campus where students congregate. In preparation for an *objective* description of this place, make notes of various sights, sounds, smells, and textures, as well as the overall "feel" of the place. Then, in preparation for a *subjective* description, observe and take notes on another sheet of paper. Compare the two sets of material. What differences do you see in word choice and selection of details?

3. Prepare to interview an interesting person by outlining several questions ahead of time. When you visit that person's home or workplace, bring a notebook in which to record his or her responses. During the interview, observe the person's surroundings, voice, body language, dress, and so on. As soon as the interview is over, make notes on these matters. Then review your notes and identify your dominant impression of the person. With that impression in mind, which details would you omit if you were writing an essay? Which would you elaborate? Which organizational pattern (spatial, emphatic, chronological, or sensory) would you select to organize your description? Why?

Revising Activities

4. Revise each of the following sentence sets twice. The first time, create an unmistakable mood; the second time, create a sharply contrasting mood. To

convey atmosphere, vary sentence structure, use vigorous verbs, provide rich sensory details, and pay special attention to words' connotations.

a. The card players sat around the table. The table was old. The players were, too.

b. A long line formed outside the movie theater. People didn't want to miss the show. The movie had received a lot of attention recently.

c. A girl walked down the street in her first pair of high heels. This was a new experience for her.

5. The following sentences contain clichés. Rewrite each sentence, supplying a fresh and imaginative figure of speech. Add whatever descriptive details are needed to provide a context for the figure of speech.

a. They were as quiet as mice.

b. My brother used to get green with envy if I had a date and he didn't.

c. The little girl is proud as a peacock of her Girl Scout uniform.

d. The professor is as dull as dishwater.

6. The following descriptive paragraph is from the first draft of an essay showing that personal growth may result when romanticized notions and reality collide. How effective is the paragraph in illustrating the essay's thesis? Which details are powerful? Which could be more concrete? Which should be deleted? Where should sentence structure be more varied? How could the description be made more coherent? Revise the paragraph, correcting any problems you discover and adding whatever sensory details are needed to enliven the description. Feel free to break the paragraph into two or more separate ones.

As a child, I was intrigued by stories about the farm in Harrison County, Maine, where my father spent his teens. Being raised on a farm seemed more interesting than growing up in the suburbs. So about a year ago, I decided to see for myself what the farm was like. I got there by driving on Route 334, a surprisingly easy-to-drive, four-lane highway that had recently been built with matching state and federal funds. I turned into the dirt road leading to the farm and got out of my car. It had been washed and waxed for the occasion. Then I headed for a dirt-colored barn. Its roof was full of huge, rotted holes. As I rounded the bushes, I saw the house. It too was dirt-colored. Its paint must have worn off decades ago. A couple of dead-looking old cars were sprawled in front of the barn. They were dented and windowless. Also by the barn was an ancient refrigerator, crushed like a discarded accordion. The porch steps to the house were slanted and wobbly. Through the open windows came a stale smell and the sound of television. Looking in the front door screen, I could see two chickens jumping

around inside. Everything looked dirty both inside and out.
Secretly grateful that no one answered my knock, I bolted down
the stairs, got into my clean, shiny car, and drove away.

PROFESSIONAL SELECTIONS: DESCRIPTION

E. B. WHITE

Recipient of the Presidential Medal of Freedom and the National Medal for
Literature, Elwyn Brooks White (1899–1985) is considered one of America's foremost
essayists. Known for his graceful prose, White wrote *The New Yorker's* "Talk of the
Town" column for many years. He also authored, with William Strunk, Jr., the
renowned guide for writers, *The Elements of Style.* White's books for children include
the beloved classic *Charlotte's Web* (1952). This selection is taken from *The Essays of
E. B. White* (1977).

Pre-Reading Journal Entry

In your journal, list at least two occasions—either serious or humorous—that
made you keenly aware that you were growing older. What was it about each
situation that forced this realization upon you? How did the realization affect
you? Did it please or distress you? Jot down as many details about each instance
as you can.

ONCE MORE TO THE LAKE

1   One summer, along about 1904, my father rented a camp on a lake in Maine and
took us all there for the month of August. We all got ringworm from some kittens and
had to rub Pond's Extract on our arms and legs night and morning, and my father
rolled over in a canoe with all his clothes on; but outside of that the vacation was a
success and from then on none of us ever thought there was any place in the world
like that lake in Maine. We returned summer after summer—always on August 1 for
one month. I have since become a salt-water man, but sometimes in summer there
are days when the restlessness of the tides and the fearful cold of the sea water and
the incessant wind that blows across the afternoon and into the evening make me
wish for the placidity of a lake in the woods. A few weeks ago this feeling got so strong
I bought myself a couple of bass hooks and a spinner and returned to the lake where
we used to go, for a week's fishing and to revisit old haunts.

I took along my son, who had never had any fresh water up his nose and who   2
had seen lily pads only from train windows. On the journey over to the lake I began
to wonder what it would be like. I wondered how time would have marred this
unique, this holy spot—the coves and streams, the hills that the sun set behind, the
camps and the paths behind the camps. I was sure that the tarred road would have
found it out, and I wondered in what other ways it would be desolated. It is strange
how much you can remember about places like that once you allow your mind to
return into the grooves that lead back. You remember one thing, and that suddenly reminds you of another thing. I guess I remembered clearest of all the early
mornings, when the lake was cool and motionless, remembered how the bedroom
smelled of the lumber it was made of and of the wet woods whose scent entered
through the screen. The partitions in the camp were thin and did not extend clear
to the top of the rooms, and as I was always the first up I would dress softly so as
not to wake the others, and sneak out into the sweet outdoors and start out in the
canoe, keeping close along the shore in the long shadows of the pines. I remembered being very careful never to rub my paddle against the gunwale for fear of disturbing the stillness of the cathedral.

The lake had never been what you would call a wild lake. There were cottages   3
sprinkled around the shores, and it was in farming country although the shores of
the lake were quite heavily wooded. Some of the cottages were owned by nearby
farmers, and you would live at the shore and eat your meals at the farmhouse.
That's what our family did. But although it wasn't wild, it was a fairly large and
undisturbed lake and there were places in it that, to a child at least, seemed infinitely remote and primeval.

I was right about the tar: it led to within half a mile of the shore. But when I got   4
back there, with my boy, and we settled into a camp near a farmhouse and into the
kind of summertime I had known, I could tell that it was going to be pretty much the
same as it had been before—I knew it, lying in bed the first morning, smelling the bedroom and hearing the boy sneak quietly out and go off along the shore in a boat. I
began to sustain the illusion that he was I, and therefore, by simple transposition, that
I was my father. This sensation persisted, kept cropping up all the time we were there.
It was not an entirely new feeling, but in this setting it grew much stronger. I seemed
to be living a dual existence. I would be in the middle of some simple act, I would be
picking up a bait box or laying down a table fork, or I would be saying something, and
suddenly it would be not I but my father who was saying the words or making the gesture. It gave me a creepy sensation.

We went fishing the first morning. I felt the same damp moss covering the worms   5
in the bait can, and saw the dragonfly alight on the tip of my rod as it hovered a few
inches from the surface of the water. It was the arrival of this fly that convinced me
beyond any doubt that everything was as it always had been, that the years were a
mirage and that there had been no years. The small waves were the same, chucking
the rowboat under the chin as we fished at anchor, and the boat was the same boat,
the same color green and the ribs broken in the same places, and under the floorboards
the same fresh-water leavings and débris—the dead helgramite, the wisps of moss, the
rusty discarded fishhook, the dried blood from yesterday's catch. We stared silently at
the tips of our rods, at the dragonflies that came and went. I lowered the tip of mine
into the water, tentatively, pensively dislodging the fly, which darted two feet away,

poised, darted two feet back, and came to rest again a little farther up the rod. There had been no years between the ducking of this dragonfly and the other one—the one that was part of memory. I looked at the boy, who was silently watching his fly, and it was my hands that held his rod, my eyes watching. I felt dizzy and didn't know which rod I was at the end of.

6   We caught two bass, hauling them in briskly as though they were mackerel, pulling them over the side of the boat in a businesslike manner without any landing net, and stunning them with a blow on the back of the head. When we got back for a swim before lunch, the lake was exactly where we had left it, the same number of inches from the dock, and there was only the merest suggestion of a breeze. This seemed an utterly enchanted sea, this lake you could leave to its own devices for a few hours and come back to, and find that it had not stirred, this constant and trustworthy body of water. In the shallows, the dark, water-soaked sticks and twigs, smooth and old, were undulating in clusters on the bottom against the clean ribbed sand, and the track of the mussel was plain. A school of minnows swam by, each minnow with its small individual shadow, doubling the attendance, so clear and sharp in the sunlight. Some of the other campers were in swimming, along the shore, one of them with a cake of soap, and the water felt thin and clear and unsubstantial. Over the years there had been this person with the cake of soap, this cultist, and here he was. There had been no years.

7   Up to the farmhouse to dinner through the teeming, dusty field, the road under our sneakers was only a two-track road. The middle track was missing, the one with the marks of the hooves and the splotches of dried, flaky manure. There had always been three tracks to choose from in choosing which track to walk in; now the choice was narrowed down to two. For a moment I missed terribly the middle alternative. But the way led past the tennis court, and something about the way it lay there in the sun reassured me; the tape had loosened along the backline, the alleys were green with plantains and other weeds, and the net (installed in June and removed in September) sagged in the dry noon, and the whole place steamed with midday heat and hunger and emptiness. There was a choice of pie for dessert, and one was blueberry and one was apple, and the waitresses were the same country girls, there having been no passage of time, only the illusion of it as in a dropped curtain—the waitresses were still fifteen; their hair had been washed, that was the only difference—they had been to the movies and seen the pretty girls with the clean hair.

8   Summertime, oh, summertime, pattern of life indelible, the fade-proof lake, the woods unshatterable, the pasture with the sweetfern and the juniper forever and ever, summer without end; this was the background, and the life along the shore was the design, the cottagers with their innocent and tranquil design, their tiny docks with the flagpole and the American flag floating against the white clouds in the blue sky, the little paths over the roots of the trees leading from camp to camp and the paths leading back to the outhouses and the can of lime for sprinkling, and at the souvenir counters at the store the miniature birch-bark canoes and the postcards that showed things looking a little better than they looked. This was the American family at play, escaping the city heat, wondering whether the newcomers in the camp at the head of the cove were "common" or "nice," wondering whether it was true that the people who drove up for Sunday dinner at the farmhouse were turned away because there wasn't enough chicken.

It seemed to me, as I kept remembering all this, that those times and those sum-   9
mers had been infinitely precious and worth saving. There had been jollity and peace
and goodness. The arriving (at the beginning of August) had been so big a business in
itself, at the railway station the farm wagon drawn up, the first smell of the pine-laden
air, the first glimpse of the smiling farmer, and the great importance of the trunks and
your father's enormous authority in such matters, and the feel of the wagon under you
for the long ten-mile haul, and at the top of the last long hill catching the first view of
the lake after eleven months of not seeing this cherished body of water. The shouts and
cries of the other campers when they saw you, and the trunks to be unpacked, to give
up their rich burden. (Arriving was less exciting nowadays, when you sneaked up in
your car and parked it under a tree near the camp and took out the bags and in five
minutes it was all over, no fuss, no loud wonderful fuss about trunks.)

Peace and goodness and jollity. The only thing that was wrong now, really, was   10
the sound of the place, an unfamiliar nervous sound of the outboard motors. This
was the note that jarred, the one thing that would sometimes break the illusion and
set the years moving. In those other summertimes all motors were inboard; and
when they were at a little distance, the noise they made was a sedative, an ingredient of summer sleep. They were one-cylinder and two-cylinder engines, and some
were make-and-break and some were jump-spark, but they all made a sleepy sound
across the lake. The one-lungers throbbed and fluttered, and the twin-cylinder ones
purred and purred, and that was a quiet sound, too. But now the campers all had
outboards. In the daytime, in the hot mornings, these motors made a petulant, irri-
table sound; at night, in the still evening when the afterglow lit the water, they
whined about one's ears like mosquitoes. My boy loved our rented outboard, and his
great desire was to achieve single-handed mastery over it, and authority, and he soon
learned the trick of choking it a little (but not too much), and the adjustment of the
needle valve. Watching him I would remember the things you could do with the old
one-cylinder engine with the heavy flywheel, how you could have it eating out of
your hand if you got really close to it spiritually. Motorboats in those days didn't have
clutches, and you would make a landing by shutting off the motor at the proper time
and coasting in with a dead rudder. But there was a way of reversing them, if you
learned the trick, by cutting the switch and putting it on again exactly on the final
dying revolution of the flywheel, so that it would kick back against compression and
begin reversing. Approaching a dock in a strong following breeze, it was difficult to
slow up sufficiently by the ordinary coasting method, and if a boy felt he had complete mastery over his motor, he was tempted to keep it running beyond its time and
then reverse it a few feet from the dock. It took a cool nerve, because if you threw
the switch a twentieth of a second too soon you would catch the flywheel when it
still had speed enough to go up past center, and the boat would leap ahead, charg-
ing bull-fashion at the dock.

We had a good week at the camp. The bass were biting well and the sun shone end-   11
lessly, day after day. We would be tired at night and lie down in the accumulated heat
of the little bedrooms after the long hot day and the breeze would stir almost imper-
ceptibly outside and the smell of the swamp drift in through the rusty screens. Sleep
would come easily and in the morning the red squirrel would be on the roof, tapping
out his gay routine. I kept remembering everything, lying in bed in the mornings—the
small steamboat that had a long rounded stern like the lip of a Ubangi, and how quietly she ran on the moonlight sails, when the older boys played their mandolins and

the girls sang and we ate doughnuts dipped in sugar, and how sweet the music was on the water in the shining night, and what it had felt like to think about girls then. After breakfast we would go up to the store and the things were in the same place—the minnows in a bottle, the plugs and spinners disarranged and pawed over by the youngsters from the boys' camp, the Fig Newtons and the Beeman's gum. Outside, the road was tarred and cars stood in front of the store. Inside, all was just as it had always been, except there was more Coca-Cola and not so much Moxie and root beer and birch beer and sarsaparilla. We would walk out with the bottle of pop apiece and sometimes the pop would backfire up our noses and hurt. We explored the streams, quietly, where the turtles slid off the sunny logs and dug their way into the soft bottom; and we lay on the town wharf and fed worms to the tame bass. Everywhere we went I had trouble making out which was I, the one walking at my side, the one walking in my pants.

12   One afternoon while we were there at the lake a thunderstorm came up. It was like the revival of an old melodrama that I had seen long ago with childish awe. The second-act climax of the drama of the electrical disturbance over a lake in America had not changed in any important respect. This was the big scene, still the big scene. The whole thing was so familiar, the first feeling of oppression and heat and a general air around camp of not wanting to go very far away. In midafternoon (it was all the same) a curious darkening of the sky, and a lull in everything that had made life tick; and then the way the boats suddenly swung the other way at their moorings with the coming of a breeze out of the new quarter, and the premonitory rumble. Then the kettle drum, then the snare, then the bass drum and cymbals, then crackling light against the dark, and the gods grinning and licking their chops in the hills. Afterward the calm, the rain steadily rustling in the calm lake, the return of light and hope and spirits, and the campers running out in joy and relief to go swimming in the rain, their bright cries perpetuating the deathless joke about how they were getting simply drenched, and the children screaming with delight at the new sensation of bathing in the rain, and the joke about getting drenched linking the generations in a strong indestructible chain. And the comedian who waded in carrying an umbrella.

13   When the others went swimming, my son said he was going in, too. He pulled his dripping trunks from the line where they had hung all through the shower and wrung them out. Languidly, and with no thought of going in, I watched him, his hard little body, skinny and bare, saw him wince slightly as he pulled up around his vitals the small, soggy, icy garment. As he buckled the swollen belt, suddenly my groin felt the chill of death.

Questions for Close Reading

1. What is the selection's thesis (or dominant impression)? Locate the sentence(s) in which White states his main idea. If he doesn't state the thesis explicitly, express it in your own words.

2. Why does White return to the lake in Maine he had visited as a child? Why do you think he has waited to revisit it until he has a young son to bring along?

3. Several times in the essay, White notes that he felt as if he were his own father—and that his son became his childhood self. What event first prompts this sensation? What actions and thoughts cause it to recur?

4. How is the latest visit to the lake similar to White's childhood summers? What differences does White notice? What effects do the differences have on him?

5. Refer to your dictionary as needed to define the following words used in the selection: *incessant* (paragraph 1), *placidity* (1), *primeval* (3), *transposition* (4), *undulating* (6), *indelible* (8), *petulant* (10), and *languidly* (13).

Questions About the Writer's Craft

1. **The pattern.** Through vivid language, descriptive writing evokes sensory experiences. In "Once More to the Lake," White overlays two sets of sensory details: those of the present-day lake and those of the lake as it was in his boyhood. Which set of details is more objective? Which seems sharper and more powerful? Why?

2. To describe the lake, White chooses many words and phrases with religious connotations. Give some examples. What might have been his purpose in using such language?

3. **Other patterns.** In paragraph 12, White uses a metaphor to describe a thunderstorm. To what does he compare a thunderstorm? Why does he make this comparison?

4. White refers to "the chill of death" in the final paragraph. What brings on this feeling? Why does he feel it "in his groin"? Where has this idea been hinted at previously in the essay?

Writing Assignments Using Description as a Pattern of Development

1. Write a descriptive essay about a special place in your life. The place need not be a natural setting like White's lake; it could be a city or building that has meant a great deal to you. Use sensory details and figurative language, as White does, to enliven your description and convey the place's significance for you.

∞ 2. White was fortunate that his lake had remained virtually unchanged. But many other special spots have been destroyed or are threatened with destruction. Write a descriptive essay about a place (a park, a school, an old-fashioned ice cream parlor) that is "infinitely precious and worth saving." For your dominant theme, show which aspects of your subject make it worthy of being preserved for future generations. Joseph H. Suina's "And Then I Went to School" (page 371) may spark some helpful ideas since it details the special qualities of a place threatened with extinction.

Writing Assignments Using Other Patterns of Development

∞ 3. Sometimes, we, like White, are suddenly reminded of the nearness of death: a crushed animal lies in the road, a politician is assassinated, a classmate is killed in a car crash. Write an essay about a time you were forced to think about mortality. Explain what happened and describe your thoughts and feelings afterward. Before writing your essay, be sure to read Beth Johnson's "Bombs Bursting in Air" (page 245), a powerful account of the author's reaction to the tragedies she's encountered in her life.

∞ 4. Have your older relatives attempted to share with you some special experiences of their younger years? Have you done the same thing with your own children, nephews, or nieces? You may have taken loved ones to a special place, as White did, or listened to stories or looked at photographs. Write an essay recounting such an experience. Explain the motivations of the older generation and the effects on the younger one. Before planning your paper, you may want to read Toni Morrison's "A Slow Walk of Trees" (page 362); it depicts two generations' views of the past as well as the effect of those views on the present.

Writing Assignment Using a Journal Entry as a Starting Point

5. Write an essay narrating an incident that reminded you that you weren't as young as you used to be. Review your pre-reading journal entry, selecting the *one* occasion you would most enjoy writing about. Draw upon the specifics in your journal, providing additional details about both external circumstances and your internal state of mind. End your essay by discussing how your realization affected your subsequent thoughts and actions.

MAYA ANGELOU

Born Marguerite Johnson in 1928, Maya Angelou rose from a difficult childhood in Stamps, Arkansas, to become a multitalented performer and writer. A professor at Wake Forest University since 1991, she has danced professionally; starred in an off-Broadway play; acted on television; and become a prolific, highly regarded writer. Her work includes several volumes of poetry, such as *Oh Pray My Wings Are Gonna Fit Me Well* (1975), *Now Sheba Sings the Song* (1988), and *A Brave and Startling Truth* (1995); collections of essays, the latest of which is *Even the Stars Look Lonesome* (1997); and a series of autobiographical books, beginning with *I Know Why the Caged Bird Sings* (1969), from which the following selection is taken. Raped at the age of eight in St. Louis, Angelou responded by speaking to no one but her brother, Bailey. She and Bailey were soon sent to Stamps to live with their grandmother (Momma), at which point this excerpt begins.

Pre-Reading Journal Entry

Growing up isn't easy. In your journal, list several challenges you've had to face in your life. In each case, was there someone who served as a "life line," providing you with crucial guidance and support? Who was that individual? How did this person steer your through the difficulty?

SISTER FLOWERS

For nearly a year [after I was raped], I sopped around the house, the Store, the school and the church, like an old biscuit, dirty and inedible. Then I met, or rather got to know, the lady who threw me my first life line.   1

Mrs. Bertha Flowers was the aristocrat of Black Stamps. She had the grace of control to appear warm in the coldest weather, and on the Arkansas summer days it seemed she had a private breeze which swirled around, cooling her. She was thin without the taut look of wiry people, and her printed voile dresses and flowered hats were as right for her as denim overalls for a farmer. She was our side's answer to the richest white woman in town.   2

Her skin was a rich black that would have peeled like a plum if snagged, but then no one would have thought of getting close enough to Mrs. Flowers to ruffle her dress, let alone snag her skin. She didn't encourage familiarity. She wore gloves too.   3

I don't think I ever saw Mrs. Flowers laugh, but she smiled often. A slow widening of her thin black lips to show even, small white teeth, then the slow effortless closing. When she chose to smile on me, I always wanted to thank her. The action was so graceful and inclusively benign.   4

She was one of the few gentlewomen I have ever known, and has remained throughout my life the measure of what a human being can be.   5

Momma had a strange relationship with her. Most often when she passed on the road in front of the Store, she spoke to Momma in that soft yet carrying voice, "Good day, Mrs. Henderson." Momma responded with "How you, Sister Flowers?"   6

Mrs. Flowers didn't belong to our church, nor was she Momma's familiar. Why on earth did she insist on calling her Sister Flowers? Shame made me want to hide my face. Mrs. Flowers deserved better than to be called Sister. Then, Momma left out the verb. Why not ask, "How *are* you, *Mrs.* Flowers?" With the unbalanced passion of the young, I hated her for showing her ignorance to Mrs. Flowers. It didn't occur to me for many years that they were as alike as sisters, separated only by formal education.   7

Although I was upset, neither of the women in the least shaken by what I thought an unceremonious greeting. Mrs. Flowers would continue her easy gait up the hill to her little bungalow, and Momma kept on shelling peas or doing whatever had brought her to the front porch.   8

Occasionally, though, Mrs. Flowers would drift off the road and down to the Store and Momma would say to me, "Sister, you go on and play." As she left I would hear the beginning of an intimate conversation. Momma persistently using the wrong verb, or none at all.   9

"Brother and Sister Wilcox is sho'ly the meanest—" "Is," Momma? "Is"? Oh, please, not "is," Momma, for two or more. But they talked, and from the side of the building where I waited for the ground to open up and swallow me, I heard the soft-voiced Mrs.   10

Flowers and the textured voice of my grandmother merging and melting. They were interrupted from time to time by giggles that must have come from Mrs. Flowers (Momma never giggled in her life). Then she was gone.

11   She appealed to me because she was like people I had never met personally. Like women in English novels who walked the moors (whatever they were) with their loyal dogs racing at a respectful distance. Like the women who sat in front of roaring fireplaces, drinking tea incessantly from silver trays full of scones and crumpets. Women who walked over the "heath" and read morocco-bound books and had two last names divided by a hyphen. It would be safe to say that she made me proud to be Negro, just by being herself.

12   She acted just as refined as whitefolks in the movies and books and she was more beautiful, for none of them could have come near that warm color without looking gray by comparison.

13   It was fortunate that I never saw her in the company of powhitefolks. For since they tend to think of their whiteness as an evenizer, I'm certain that I would have had to hear her spoken to commonly as Bertha, and my image of her would have been shattered like the unmendable Humpty-Dumpty.

14   One summer afternoon, sweet-milk fresh in my memory, she stopped at the Store to buy provisions. Another Negro woman of her health and age would have been expected to carry the paper sacks home in one hand, but Momma said, "Sister Flowers, I'll send Bailey up to your house with these things."

15   She smiled that slow dragging smile, "Thank you, Mrs. Henderson. I'd prefer Marguerite, though." My name was beautiful when she said it. "I've been meaning to talk to her, anyway." They gave each other age-group looks.

16   Momma said, "Well, that's all right then. Sister, go and change your dress. You going to Sister Flowers's."

17   The chifforobe was a maze. What on earth did one put on to go to Mrs. Flowers's house? I knew I shouldn't put on a Sunday dress. It might be sacrilegious. Certainly not a house dress, since I was already wearing a fresh one. I chose a school dress, naturally. It was formal without suggesting that going to Mrs. Flowers's house was equivalent to attending church.

18   I trusted myself back into the Store.

19   "Now, don't you look nice." I had chosen the right thing, for once. . . .

20   There was a little path beside the rocky road, and Mrs. Flowers walked in front swinging her arms and picking her way over the stones.

21   She said, without turning her head, to me, "I hear you're doing very good school work, Marguerite, but that it's all written. The teachers report that they have trouble getting you to talk in class." We passed the triangular farm on our left and the path widened to allow us to walk together. I hung back in the separate unasked and unanswerable questions.

22   "Come and walk along with me, Marguerite." I couldn't have refused even if I wanted to. She pronounced my name so nicely. Or more correctly, she spoke each word with such clarity that I was certain a foreigner who didn't understand English could have understood her.

23   "Now no one is going to make you talk—possibly no one can. But bear in mind, language is man's way of communicating with his fellow man and it is language alone which separates him from the lower animals." That was a totally new idea to me, and I would need time to think about it.

"Your grandmother says you read a lot. Every chance you get. That's good, but not   24
good enough. Words mean more than what is set down on paper. It takes the human
voice to infuse them with the shades of deeper meaning."

I memorized the part about the human voice infusing words. It seemed so valid and   25
poetic.

She said she was going to give me some books and that I not only must read them,   26
I must read them aloud. She suggested that I try to make a sentence sound in as many
different ways as possible.

"I'll accept no excuse if you return a book to me that has been badly handled." My   27
imagination boggled at the punishment I would deserve if in fact I did abuse a book of
Mrs. Flowers's. Death would be too kind and brief.

The odors in the house surprised me. Somehow I had never connected Mrs.   28
Flowers with food or eating or any other common experience of common people.
There must have been an outhouse, too, but my mind never recorded it.

The sweet scent of vanilla had met us as she opened the door.   29

"I made tea cookies this morning. You see, I had planned to invite you for cookies   30
and lemonade so we could have this little chat. The lemonade is in the icebox."

It followed that Mrs. Flowers would have ice on an ordinary day, when most fami-   31
lies in our town bought ice late on Saturdays only a few times during the summer to
be used in the wooden ice-cream freezers.

She took the bags from me and disappeared through the kitchen door. I looked   32
around the room that I had never in my wildest fantasies imagined I would see.
Browned photographs leered or threatened from the walls and the white, freshly done
curtains pushed against themselves and against the wind. I wanted to gobble up the
room entire and take it to Bailey, who would help me analyze and enjoy it.

"Have a seat, Marguerite. Over there by the table." She carried a platter covered   33
with a tea towel. Although she warned that she hadn't tried her hand at baking sweets
for some time, I was certain that like everything else about her the cookies would
be perfect.

They were flat round wafers, slightly browned on the edges and butter-yellow in the   34
center. With the cold lemonade they were sufficient for childhood's lifelong diet.
Remembering my manners, I took nice little lady-like bites off the edges. She said she
had made them expressly for me and that she had a few in the kitchen that I could
take home to my brother. So I jammed one whole cake in my mouth and the rough
crumbs scratched the insides of my jaws, and if I hadn't had to swallow, it would have
been a dream come true.

As I ate she began the first of what we later called "my lessons in living." She said   35
that I must always be intolerant of ignorance but understanding of illiteracy. That
some people, unable to go to school, were more educated and even more intelligent
than college professors. She encouraged me to listen carefully to what country people
called mother wit. That in those homely sayings was couched the collective wisdom
of generations.

When I finished the cookies she brushed off the table and brought a thick, small   36
book from the bookcase. I had read *A Tale of Two Cities* and found it up to my standards as a romantic novel. She opened the first page and I heard poetry for the first
time in my life.

"It was the best of times and the worst of times . . ." Her voice slid in and curved   37
down through and over the words. She was nearly singing. I wanted to look at the

pages. Were they the same that I had read? Or were there notes, music, lined on the pages, as in a hymn book? Her sounds began cascading gently. I knew from listening to a thousand preachers that she was nearing the end of her reading, and I hadn't really heard, heard to understand, a single word.

38   "How do you like that?"

39   It occurred to me that she expected a response. The sweet vanilla flavor was still on my tongue and her reading was a wonder in my ears. I had to speak.

40   I said, "Yes, ma'am." It was the least I could do, but it was the most also.

41   "There's one more thing. Take this book of poems and memorize one for me. Next time you pay me a visit, I want you to recite."

42   I have tried often to search behind the sophistication of years for the enchantment I so easily found in those gifts. The essence escapes but its aura remains. To be allowed, no, invited, into the private lives of strangers, and to share their joys and fears, was a chance to exchange the Southern bitter wormwood for a cup of mead with Beowulf[1] or a hot cup of tea and milk with Oliver Twist.[2] When I said aloud, "It is a far, far better thing that I do, than I have ever done . . ."[3] tears of love filled my eyes at my selflessness.

43   On that first day, I ran down the hill and into the road (few cars ever came along it) and had the good sense to stop running before I reached the Store.

44   I was liked, and what a difference it made. I was respected not as Mrs. Henderson's grandchild or Bailey's sister but for just being Marguerite Johnson.

45   Childhood's logic never asks to be proved (all conclusions are absolute). I didn't question why Mrs. Flowers had singled me out for attention, nor did it occur to me that Momma might have asked her to give me a little talking to. All I cared about was that she had made tea cookies for *me* and read to *me* from her favorite book. It was enough to prove that she liked me.

---

[1]The hero of an Old English epic poem dating from the eighth century (editors' note).

[2]The main character in Charles Dickens's novel *Oliver Twist* (1837) (editors' note).

[3]The last words of Sydney Carton, the selfless hero of Charles Dickens's novel *A Tale of Two Cities* (1859) (editors' note).

Questions for Close Reading

1. What is the selection's thesis (or dominant impression)? Locate the sentence(s) in which Angelou states her main idea. If she doesn't state the thesis explicitly, express it in your own words.

2. Angelou states that Mrs. Flowers "has remained throughout my life the measure of what a human being can be" (5). What does Angelou admire about Mrs. Flowers?

3. Why is young Angelou so ashamed of Momma when Mrs. Flowers is around? How do Momma and Mrs. Flowers behave with each other?

4. What are the "lessons in living" that Angelou receives from Mrs. Flowers during their first visit? How do you think these lessons might have subsequently influenced Angelou?

5. Refer to your dictionary as needed to define the following words used in the selection: *taut* (paragraph 2), *voile* (2), *benign* (4), *unceremonious* (8), *gait* (8), *moors* (11), *incessantly* (11), *scones* (11), *crumpets* (11), *heath* (11), *chifforobe* (17), *sacrilegious* (17), *infuse* (24), *couched* (35), and *aura* (42).

Questions About the Writer's Craft

1. **The pattern.** Reread the essay, focusing on the descriptive passages first of Mrs. Flowers and then of Angelou's visit to Mrs. Flowers's house. To what senses does Angelou appeal in these passages? What method of organization (see page 160) does she use to order these sensory details?

2. To enrich the description of her eventful encounter with Mrs. Flowers, Angelou draws upon figures of speech (see pages 125–126). Consider, for example, the similes in paragraphs 1 and 11. How do these figures of speech contribute to the essay's dominant impression?

3. **Other patterns.** Because Angelou's description has a strong narrative component, it isn't surprising that there's a considerable amount of dialog in the selection. For example, in paragraphs 7 and 10, Angelou quotes Momma's incorrect grammar. She then provides an imagined conversation in which the young Angelou scolds Momma and corrects her speech. What do these imagined scoldings of Momma reveal about young Angelou? How do they relate to Mrs. Flowers's subsequent "lessons in life"?

4. Although it's not the focus of this selection, the issue of race remains in the background of Angelou's portrait of Mrs. Flowers. Where in the selection does Angelou imply that race was a fact of life in her town? How does this specter of racism help Angelou underscore the significance of her encounter with Mrs. Flowers?

Writing Assignments Using Description as a Pattern of Development

1. At one time or another, just about all of us have met someone who taught us to see ourselves more clearly and helped us understand what we wanted from life. Write an essay describing such a person. Focus on the individual's personal qualities, as a way of depicting the role he or she played in your life. Be sure not to limit yourself to an objective description. Subjective description, filled with lively language and figures of speech, will serve you well as you provide a portrait of this special person.

∞ 2. Thrilled by the spectacle of Mrs. Flowers's interesting home, Angelou says she wanted to "gobble up the room entire" and share it with her brother. Write an essay describing in detail a place that vividly survives in your memory. You may describe a setting that you visited only once or a familiar setting that holds a special place in your heart. Before you write, list the qualities and sensory impressions you associate with this special place; then refine the list so that all details support your dominant impression. You may want to read E. B. White's "Once More to the Lake" (page 171), and Joseph H. Suina's "And Then I Went to School" (page 371) to see how two very different writers evoke the qualities of special places in their lives.

Writing Assignments Using Other Patterns of Development

∞ 3. When the young Angelou discovers, thanks to Mrs. Flowers, the thrill of acceptance, she experiences a kind of *epiphany*—a moment of enlightenment. Write an essay about an event in your life that represented a kind of epiphany. You might write about a positive discovery, such as when you realized you had a special talent for something, or about a negative discovery, such as when you realized that a beloved family member had a serious flaw. To make the point that the moment was a turning point in your life, start by describing what kind of person you were before the discovery. Then narrate the actual incident, using vivid details and dialogue to make the event come alive. End by discussing the importance of this epiphany in your life. For additional accounts of personal epiphanies, read Audre Lorde's "The Fourth of July" (page 216) and Beth Johnson's "Bombs Bursting in Air" (page 245).

4. Think of an activity that engages you completely, one that provides—as reading does for Angelou—an opportunity for growth and expansion. Possibilities include reading, writing, playing an instrument, doing crafts, dancing, hiking, playing a sport, cooking, or traveling. Write an essay in which you argue the merits of your chosen pastime. Assume that some of your readers are highly skeptical. To win them over, you'll need to provide convincing examples that demonstrate the pleasure and benefits you have discovered in the activity.

Writing Assignment Using a Journal Entry as a Starting Point

5. Write an essay about a time when someone threw you a much-needed "life line" at a challenging time. Review your pre-reading journal entry, selecting *one* time when a person's encouragement and support made a great difference in your life. Be sure to describe the challenge you faced before recounting the specific details of the person's help. Dialog and descriptive details will help you recreate the power of the experience.

GORDON PARKS

The son of deeply religious tenant farmers, Gordon Parks (1912–) grew up in Kansas knowing both the comforts of familial love and the torments of poverty and racism. A series of odd jobs when he was a teenager gave Parks the means to buy his first camera. So evocative were his photographic studies that both *Life* and *Vogue* brought him on staff, the first black photographer to be hired by the two magazines. Parks's prodigious creativity has found expression in filmmaking (*Shaft* in 1971), musical composition (both classical and jazz), fiction, nonfiction, and poetry (titles include *The Learning Tree, A Choice of Weapons, To Smile in Autumn, Arias in Silence,* and *Glimpses Toward Infinity,* published, respectively, in 1986, 1987, 1988, 1994, and 1996). In the following essay, taken from his 1990 autobiography, *Voices in the Mirror,* Parks tells the story behind one of his most memorable photographic works—that of a twelve-year-old boy and his family, living in the slums of Rio de Janeiro.

Pre-Reading Journal Entry

The problem of poverty has provoked a wide array of proposed solutions. One controversial proposal argues that the government should pay poor women financial incentives to use birth control. What do you think of this proposal? Why is such a policy controversial? Use your journal to explore your thinking on this issue.

FLAVIO'S HOME

I've never lost my fierce grudge against poverty. It is the most savage of all human   1
afflictions, claiming victims who can't mobilize their efforts against it, who often lack strength to digest what little food they scrounge up to survive. It keeps growing, multiplying, spreading like a cancer. In my wanderings I attack it wherever I can—in barrios, slums and favelas.

Catacumba was the name of the favela[1] where I found Flavio da Silva. It was wick-   2
edly hot. The noon sun baked the mud-rot of the wet mountainside. Garbage and human excrement clogged the open sewers snaking down the slopes. José Gallo, a *Life* reporter, and I rested in the shade of a jacaranda tree halfway up Rio de Janeiro's most infamous deathtrap. Below and above us were a maze of shacks, but in the distance alongside the beach stood the gleaming white homes of the rich.

Breathing hard, balancing a tin of water on his head, a small boy climbed toward us.   3
He was miserably thin, naked but for filthy denim shorts. His legs resembled sticks covered with skin and screwed into his feet. Death was all over him, in his sunken eyes, cheeks and jaundiced coloring. He stopped for breath, coughing, his chest heaving as water slopped over his bony shoulders. Then jerking sideways like a mechanical toy, he smiled a smile I will never forget. Turning, he went on up the mountainside.

---

[1]Slums on the outskirts of Rio de Janeiro, Brazil, inhabited by seven hundred thousand people (editors' note).

4   The detailed *Life* assignment in my back pocket was to find an impoverished father with a family, to examine his earnings, political leanings, religion, friends, dreams and frustrations. I had been sent to do an essay on poverty. This frail boy bent under his load said more to me about poverty than a dozen poor fathers. I touched Gallo, and we got up and followed the boy to where he entered a shack near the top of the mountainside. It was a leaning crumpled place of old plankings with a rusted tin roof. From inside we heard the babblings of several children. José knocked. The door opened and the boy stood smiling with a bawling naked baby in his arms.

5   Still smiling, he whacked the baby's rump, invited us in and offered us a box to sit on. The only other recognizable furniture was a sagging bed and a broken baby's crib. Flavio was twelve, and with Gallo acting as interpreter, he introduced his younger brothers and sisters: "Mario, the bad one; Baptista, the good one; Albia, Isabel and the baby Zacarias." Two other girls burst into the shack, screaming and pounding on one another. Flavio jumped in and parted them. "Shut up, you two." He pointed at the older girl. "That's Maria, the nasty one." She spit in his face. He smacked her and pointed to the smaller sister. "That's Luzia. She thinks she's pretty."

6   Having finished the introductions, he went to build a fire under the stove—a rusted, bent top of an old gas range resting on several bricks. Beneath it was a piece of tin that caught the hot coals. The shack was about six by ten feet. Its grimy walls were a patchwork of misshapen boards with large gaps between them, revealing other shacks below stilted against the slopes. The floor, rotting under layers of grease and dirt, caught shafts of light slanting down through spaces in the roof. A large hole in the far corner served as a toilet. Beneath that hole was the sloping mountainside. Pockets of poverty in New York's Harlem, on Chicago's south side, in Puerto Rico's infamous El Fungito seemed pale by comparison. None of them had prepared me for this one in the favela of Catacumba.

7   Flavio washed rice in a large dishpan, then washed Zacarias's feet in the same water. But even that dirty water wasn't to be wasted. He tossed in a chunk of lye soap and ordered each child to wash up. When they were finished he splashed the water over the dirty floor, and, dropping to his knees, he scrubbed the planks until the black suds sank in. Just before sundown he put beans on the stove to warm, then left, saying he would be back shortly. "Don't let them burn," he cautioned Maria. "If they do and Poppa beats me, you'll get it later." Maria, happy to get at the licking spoon, switched over and began to stir the beans. Then slyly she dipped out a spoonful and swallowed them. Luzia eyed her. "I see you. I'm going to tell on you for stealing our supper."

8   Maria's eyes flashed anger. "You do and I'll beat you, you little bitch." Luzia threw a stick at Maria and fled out the door. Zacarias dropped off to sleep. Mario, the bad one, slouched in a corner and sucked his thumb. Isabel and Albia sat on the floor clinging to each other with a strange tenderness. Isabel held onto Albia's hair and Albia clutched at Isabel's neck. They appeared frozen in an act of quiet violence.

9   Flavio returned with wood, dumped it beside the stove and sat down to rest for a few minutes, then went down the mountain for more water. It was dark when he finally came back, his body sagging from exhaustion. No longer smiling, he suddenly had the look of an old man and by now we could see that he kept the family going. In the closed torment of that pitiful shack, he was waging a hopeless battle against starvation. The da Silva children were living in a coffin.

10   When at last the parents came in, Gallo and I seemed to be part of the family. Flavio had already told them we were there. "Gordunn Americano!" Luzia said, pointing at me.

José, the father, viewed us with skepticism. Nair, his pregnant wife, seemed tired beyond speaking. Hardly acknowledging our presence, she picked up Zacarias, placed him on her shoulder and gently patted his behind. Flavio scurried about like a frightened rat, his silence plainly expressing the fear he held of his father. Impatiently, José da Silva waited for Flavio to serve dinner. He sat in the center of the bed with his legs crossed beneath him, frowning, waiting. There were only three tin plates. Flavio filled them with black beans and rice, then placed them before his father. José da Silva tasted them, chewed for several moments, then nodded his approval for the others to start. Only he and Nair had spoons; the children ate with their fingers. Flavio ate off the top of a coffee can. Afraid to offer us food, he edged his rice and beans toward us, gesturing for us to take some. We refused. He smiled, knowing we understood.

Later, when we got down to the difficult business of obtaining permission from José   11
da Silva to photograph his family, he hemmed and hawed, wallowing in the pleasant authority of the decision maker. He finally gave in, but his manner told us that he expected something in return. As we were saying good night Flavio began to cough violently. For a few moments his lungs seemed to be tearing apart. I wanted to get away as quickly as possible. It was cowardly of me, but the bluish cast of his skin beneath the sweat, the choking and spitting were suddenly unbearable.

Gallo and I moved cautiously down through the darkness trying not to appear as   12
strangers. The Catacumba was no place for strangers after sundown. Desperate criminals hid out there. To hunt them out, the police came in packs, but only in daylight. Gallo cautioned me. "If you get caught up here after dark it's best to stay at the da Silvas' until morning." As we drove toward the city the large white buildings of the rich loomed up. The world behind us seemed like a bad dream. I had already decided to get the boy Flavio to a doctor, and as quickly as possible.

The plush lobby of my hotel on the Copacabana waterfront was crammed with people   13
in formal attire. With the stink of the favela in my clothes, I hurried to the elevator hoping no passengers would be aboard. But as the door was closing a beautiful girl in a white lace gown stepped in. I moved as far away as possible. Her escort entered behind her, swept her into his arms and they indulged in a kiss that lasted until they exited on the next floor. Neither of them seemed to realize that I was there. The room I returned to seemed to be oversized; the da Silva shack would have fitted into one corner of it. The steak dinner I had would have fed the da Silvas for three days.

Billowing clouds blanketed Mount Corcovado as we approached the favela the   14
following morning. Suddenly the sun burst through, silhouetting Cristo Redentor, the towering sculpture of Christ with arms extended, its back turned against the slopes of Catacumba. The square at the entrance to the favela bustled with hundreds of favelados. Long lines waited at the sole water spigot. Others waited at the only toilet on the entire mountainside. Women, unable to pay for soap, beat dirt from their wash at laundry tubs. Men, burdened with lumber, picks and shovels and tools important to their existence threaded their way through the noisy throngs. Dogs snarled, barked and fought. Woodsmoke mixed with the stench of rotting things. In the mist curling over the higher paths, columns of favelados climbed like ants with wood and water cans on their heads.

We came upon Nair bent over her tub of wash. She wiped away sweat with her   15
apron and managed a smile. We asked for her husband and she pointed to a tiny shack off to her right. This was José's store, where he sold kerosene and bleach. He was sitting on a box, dozing. Sensing our presence, he awoke and commenced complaining about his back. "It kills me. The doctors don't help because I have no money. Always

talk and a little pink pill that does no good. Ah, what is to become of me?" A woman came to buy bleach. He filled her bottle. She dropped a few coins and as she walked away his eyes stayed on her backside until she was out of sight. Then he was complaining about his back again.

16   "How much do you earn a day?" Gallo asked.

17   "Seventy-five cents. On a good day maybe a dollar."

18   "Why aren't the kids in school?"

19   "I don't have money for the clothes they need to go to school."

20   "Has Flavio seen a doctor?"

21   He pointed to a one-story wooden building. "That's the clinic right there. They're mad because I built my store in front of their place. I won't tear it down so they won't help my kids. Talk, talk, talk and pink pills." We bid him good-bye and started climbing, following mud trails, jutting rock, slime-filled holes and shack after shack propped against the slopes on shaky pilings. We sidestepped a dead cat covered with maggots. I held my breath for an instant, only to inhale the stench of human excrement and garbage. Bare feet and legs with open sores climbed above us—evils of the terrible soil they trod every day, and there were seven hundred thousand or more afflicted people in favelas around Rio alone. Touching me, Gallo pointed to Flavio climbing ahead of us carrying firewood. He stopped to glance at a man descending with a small coffin on his shoulder. A woman and a small child followed him. When I lifted my camera, grumbling erupted from a group of men sharing beer beneath a tree.

22   "They're threatening," Gallo said. "Keep moving. They fear cameras. Think they're evil eyes bringing bad luck." Turning to watch the funeral procession, Flavio caught sight of us and waited. When we took the wood from him he protested, saying he was used to carrying it. He gave in when I hung my camera around his neck. Then, beaming, he climbed on ahead of us.

23   The fog had lifted and in the crisp morning light the shack looked more squalid. Inside the kids seemed even noisier. Flavio smiled and spoke above their racket. "Someday I want to live in a real house on a real street with good pots and pans and a bed with sheets." He lit the fire to warm leftovers from the night before. Stale rice and beans—for breakfast and supper. No lunch; midday eating was out of the question. Smoke rose and curled up through the ceiling's cracks. An air current forced it back, filling the place and Flavio's lungs with fumes. A coughing spasm doubled him up, turned his skin blue under viscous sweat. I handed him a cup of water, but he waved it away. His stomach tightened as he dropped to his knees. His veins throbbed as if they would burst. Frustrated, we could only watch; there was nothing we could do to help. Strangely, none of his brothers or sisters appeared to notice. None of them stopped doing whatever they were doing. Perhaps they had seen it too often. After five interminable minutes it was over, and he got to his feet, smiling as though it had all been a joke. "Maria, it's time for Zacarias to be washed!"

24   "But there's rice in the pan!"

25   "Dump it in another pan—and don't spill water!"

26   Maria picked up Zacarias, who screamed, not wanting to be washed. Irritated, Maria gave him a solid smack on his bare bottom. Flavio stepped over and gave her the same, then a free-for-all started with Flavio, Maria and Mario slinging fists at one another. Mario got one in the eye and fled the shack calling Flavio a dirty son-of-a-bitch. Zacarias wound up on the floor sucking his thumb and escaping his washing. The black bean and rice breakfast helped to get things back to normal. Now it was time to get Flavio to the doctor.

The clinic was crowded with patients—mothers and children covered with open sores,   27
a paralytic teenager, a man with an ear in a state of decay, an aged blind couple holding
hands in doubled darkness. Throughout the place came wailings of hunger and hurt. Flavio
sat nervously between Gallo and me. "What will the doctor do to me?" he kept asking.

"We'll see. We'll wait and see."   28

In all, there were over fifty people. Finally, after two hours, it was Flavio's turn and he   29
broke out in a sweat, though he smiled at the nurse as he passed through the door to the
doctor's office. The nurse ignored it; in this place of misery, smiles were unexpected.

The doctor, a large, beady-eyed man with a crew cut, had an air of impatience.   30
Hardly acknowledging our presence, he began to examine the frightened Flavio.
"Open your mouth. Say 'Ah.' Jump up and down. Breathe out. Take off those pants.
Bend over. Stand up. Cough. Cough louder. Louder." He did it all with such cold efficiency. Then he spoke to us in English so Flavio wouldn't understand. "This little chap
has just about had it." My heart sank. Flavio was smiling, happy to be over with the
examination. He was handed a bottle of cough medicine and a small box of pink pills,
then asked to step outside and wait.

"This the da Silva kid?"   31

"Yes."   32

"What's your interest in him?"   33

"We want to help in some way."   34

"I'm afraid you're too late. He's wasted with bronchial asthma, malnutrition and, I   35
suspect, tuberculosis. His heart, lungs and teeth are all bad." He paused and wearily
rubbed his forehead. "All that at the ripe old age of twelve. And these hills are packed
with other kids just as bad off. Last year ten thousand died from dysentery alone. But
what can we do? You saw what's waiting outside. It's like this every day. There's hardly enough money to buy aspirin. A few wealthy people who care help keep us going."
He was quiet for a moment. "Maybe the right climate, the right diet, and constant
medical care might. . . ." He stopped and shook his head. "Naw. That poor lad's finished. He might last another year—maybe not." We thanked him and left.

"What did he say?" Flavio asked as we scaled the hill.   36

"Everything's going to be all right, Flav. There's nothing to worry about."   37

It had clouded over again by the time we reached the top. The rain swept in, clearing   38
the mountain of Corcovado. The huge Christ figure loomed up again with clouds swirling
around it. And to it I said a quick prayer for the boy walking beside us. He smiled as if
he had read my thoughts. "Papa says 'El Cristo' has turned his back on the favela."

"You're going to be all right, Flavio."   39

"I'm not scared of death. It's my brothers and sisters I worry about. What would   40
they do?"

"You'll be all right, Flavio."[2]   41

---

[2]Parks's photo-essay on Flavio generated an unprecedented response from *Life* readers.
Indeed, they sent so much money to the da Silvas that the family was able to leave the
favela for better living conditions. Parks brought Flavio to the United States for medical
treatment, and the boy's health was restored. However, Flavio's story didn't have an
unqualified happy ending. Although he overcame his illness and later married and had a
family, Flavio continuously fantasized about returning to the United States, convinced
that only by returning to America could he improve his life. His obsession eventually
eroded the promise of his life in Brazil (editors' note).

Questions for Close Reading

1. What is the selection's thesis (or dominant impression)? Locate the sentence(s) in which Parks states his main idea. If he doesn't state the thesis explicitly, express it in your own words.

2. What is Flavio's family like? Why does Flavio have so much responsibility in the household?

3. What are some of the distinctive characteristics of Flavio's neighborhood and home?

4. What seems to be the basis of Flavio's fear of giving food to Parks and Gallo? What did Parks and Gallo understand that led them to refuse?

5. Refer to your dictionary as needed to define the following words used in the selection: *barrios* (paragraph 1), *jacaranda* (2), *jaundiced* (3), and *spigot* (14).

Questions About the Writer's Craft

1. **The pattern.** Without stating it explicitly, Parks conveys a dominant impression about Flavio. What is that impression? What details create it?

2. **Other patterns.** When relating how Flavio performs numerous household tasks, Parks describes several processes. How do these step-by-step explanations reinforce Parks's dominant impression of Flavio?

3. Parks provides numerous sensory specifics to depict Flavio's home. Look closely, for example, at the description in paragraph 6. Which words and phrases convey strong sensory images? How does Parks use transitions to help the reader move from one sensory image to another?

4. Paragraph 13 includes a scene that occurs in Parks's hotel. What's the effect of this scene? What does it contribute to the essay that the most detailed description of the *favela* could not?

Writing Assignments Using Description as a Pattern of Development

∞ 1. Parks paints a wrenching portrait of a person who remains vibrant and hopeful even though he is suffering greatly—from physical illness, poverty, overwork, and worry. Write a description about someone you know who has shown courage or other positive qualities during a time of personal trouble. Include, as Parks does, plentiful details about the person's appearance and behavior so that you don't have to state directly what you admire about the person. Maya Angelou's "Sister Flowers" (page 178) shows how one writer conveys the special quality of an admirable individual.

2. Parks presents an unforgettable description of the *favela* and the living conditions there. Write an essay about a region, city, neighborhood, or building that also projects an overwhelming negative feeling. Include only those details that convey your dominant impression, and provide—as Parks does—vivid sensory language to convey your attitude toward your subject.

Writing Assignments Using Other Patterns of Development

3. The doctor reports that a few wealthy people contribute to the clinic, but the reader can tell from the scene in Parks's hotel that most people are insensitive to those less fortunate. Write an essay describing a specific situation that you feel reflects people's tendency to ignore the difficulties of others. Analyze why people distance themselves from the problem; then present specific steps that could be taken to sensitize them to the situation. Diane Cole's "Don't Just Stand There" (page 322) and John M. Darley and Bibb Latané's, "Why People Don't Help in a Crisis" (page 401) will provide some perspective on the way people harden themselves to the pain of others.

4. Although Parks celebrates Flavio's generosity of spirit, the writer also illustrates the brutalizing effect of an impoverished environment. Prepare an essay in which you also show that setting, architecture, even furnishings can influence mood and behavior. You may, as Parks does, focus on the corrosive effect of a negative environment, or you may write about the nurturing effect of a positive environment. Possible subjects include a park in the middle of a city, a bus terminal, and a college library.

Writing Assignment Using a Journal Entry as a Starting Point

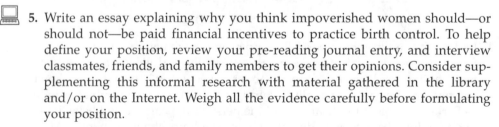

5. Write an essay explaining why you think impoverished women should—or should not—be paid financial incentives to practice birth control. To help define your position, review your pre-reading journal entry, and interview classmates, friends, and family members to get their opinions. Consider supplementing this informal research with material gathered in the library and/or on the Internet. Weigh all the evidence carefully before formulating your position.

ADDITIONAL WRITING TOPICS: DESCRIPTION

General Assignments

Write an essay using description to develop one of the following topics. Remember that an effective description focuses on a dominant impression and arranges details in a way that best supports that impression. Your details—vivid and appealing to the senses—should be carefully chosen so that the essay isn't overburdened with material of secondary importance. When writing, keep in mind that varied sentence structure and imaginative figures of speech are ways to make a descriptive piece compelling.

1. A favorite item of clothing

2. A school as a young child sees it

3. A hospital room you have visited or stayed in

4. An individualist's appearance

5. A coffee shop, bus shelter, newsstand, or some other small place

6. A parade or victory celebration

7. A banana, squash, or other fruit or vegetable

8. A particular drawer

9. A houseplant

10. A "media event"

11. A dorm room

12. An elderly person

13. An attractive man or woman

14. A prosthetic device or wheelchair

15. A TV, film, or music celebrity

16. A student lounge

17. A once-in-a-lifetime event

18. The inside of something, such as a cave, boat, car, shed, or machine

19. A friend, roommate, or other person you know well

20. An essential gadget or a useless gadget

Assignments with a Specific Purpose, Audience, and Point of View

On Campus

1. For an audience of incoming first-year students, prepare a speech describing registration day at your college. Use specific details to help prepare students for the actual event. Choose an adjective that represents your dominant impression of the experience, and keep that word in mind as you write.

2. Your college has decided to replace an old campus structure (for example, a dorm or dining hall) with a new version. Write a letter of protest to the administration, describing the place so vividly and appealingly that its value and need for preservation are unquestionable.

3. As a staff member of the campus newspaper, you have been asked to write a weekly column of social news and gossip. For your first column, you plan to describe a recent campus event—a dance, party, concert, or other social activity. With a straightforward or tongue-in-cheek tone, describe where the event was held, the appearance of the people who attended, and so on.

At Home or in the Community

4. As a subscriber to a community-wide dating service, you've been asked to submit a description of the kind of person you'd like to meet. Describe your ideal date. Focus on specifics about physical appearance, personal habits, character traits, and interests.

5. As a resident of a particular town, you're angered by the appearance of a certain spot and by the activities that take place there. Write a letter to the town council, describing in detail the undesirable nature of this place (a video arcade, an adult bookstore, a bar, a bus station, a neglected park or beach). End with some suggestions about ways to improve the situation.

On the Job

6. You've noticed a recurring problem in your workplace and want to bring it to the attention of your boss, who is typically inattentive. Write a letter to your boss describing the problem. Your goal is not to provide solutions, but rather, to provide vivid description—complete with sensory details—so that your boss can no longer deny the problem.

12
NARRATION

WHAT IS NARRATION?

Human beings are instinctively storytellers. In prehistoric times, our ancestors huddled around campfires to hear tales of hunting and magic. In ancient times, warriors gathered in halls to listen to bards praise in song the exploits of epic heroes. Things are no different today. Boisterous children invariably settle down to listen when their parents read to them; millions of people tune in day after day to the ongoing drama of their favorite soap operas; vacationers sit motionless on the beach, caught up in the latest best-sellers; and all of us enjoy saying, "Just listen to what happened to me today." Our hunger for storytelling is basic.

Narration means telling a single story or several related stories. The story can be a means to an end, a way to support a main idea or thesis. To demonstrate that television has become the constant companion of many children, you might narrate a typical child's day in front of the television—starting with cartoons in the morning and ending with situation comedies at night. Or to support the point that the college registration process should be reformed, you could tell the tale of a chaotic morning spent trying to enroll in classes.

Narration is powerful. Every public speaker, from politician to classroom teacher, knows that stories capture the attention of listeners as nothing else can. We want to know what happened to others, not simply because we're curious, but also because their experiences shed light on our own lives. Narration lends force to opinion, triggers the flow of memory, and evokes places, times, and people in ways that are compelling and affecting.

HOW NARRATION FITS YOUR PURPOSE AND AUDIENCE

Since narratives tell a story, you may think they're found only in novels or short stories. But narration can also appear in essays, sometimes as a supplemental pattern of development. For example, if your purpose in a paper is to *persuade* apathetic readers that airport security regulations must be followed strictly, you might lead off with a brief account of armed terrorists who easily boarded planes on September 11. In a paper *defining* good teaching, you might keep readers engaged by including satirical anecdotes about one hapless instructor, the antithesis of an effective teacher. An essay on the *effects* of an overburdened judicial system might provide—in an attempt to involve readers—a dramatic account of the way one clearly guilty murderer plea-bargained his way to freedom.

In addition to providing effective support in one section of your paper, narration can also serve as an essay's dominant pattern of development. In fact, most of this chapter shows you how to use a single narrative to convey a central point and share with readers your view of what happened. You might choose to narrate the events of an afternoon spent with your three-year-old nephew as a way of revealing how you rediscovered the importance of family life. Or you might relate the story of your roommate's mugging, evoking the powerlessness and terror of being a victim.

Although some narratives relate unusual experiences, most tread familiar ground, telling tales of joy, love, loss, frustration, fear—all common emotions experienced during life. Narratives can take the ordinary and transmute it into something significant, even extraordinary. As Willa Cather, the American novelist, wrote: "There are only two or three human stories and they go on repeating themselves as fiercely as if they had never happened before." The challenge lies in applying your own vision to a tale, thereby making it unique.

PREWRITING STRATEGIES

The following checklist shows how you can apply to narration some of the prewriting strategies discussed in Chapter 2.

NARRATION: A PREWRITING CHECKLIST

Select Your Narrative Event(s)

☐ What event evokes strong emotion in you and is likely to have a powerful effect on your readers?

☐ Does your journal suggest any promising subjects—for example, an entry about a bully's surprisingly respectful behavior toward a disabled student or a painful encounter with racial prejudice?

☐ Does a scrapbook souvenir, snapshot, old letter, or prized object (an athletic trophy, a political button) point to an event worth writing about?

☐ Will you focus on a personal experience (your high school graduation ceremony), an incident in someone else's life (a friend's battle with chronic illness), or a public event (a community effort to save a beached whale)?

☐ Can you recount your story effectively, given the length of a typical college essay? If not, will relating one key incident from the fuller, more complete event enable you to convey the point and feeling of the entire experience?

☐ If you write about an event in someone else's life, will you have time to interview the person? ("Why did you cross the picket line?" "What did you do when your boss told you to lie?")

Focus on the Conflict in the Event

☐ What is the source of tension in the event: one person's internal dilemma, a conflict between characters, or a struggle between a character and a social institution or natural phenomenon?

☐ Will the conflict create enough tension to "hook" readers and keep them interested?

☐ What point does the conflict and its resolution convey to readers?

☐ What tone is appropriate for recounting the conflict?

Use Prewriting to Generate Specifics About the Conflict

☐ Would the questioning technique ("Why did the argument occur?"), brainstorming, freewriting, mapping, or interviewing help you generate details about the conflict? Does your journal suggest ways to explore aspects of the conflict? ("When my friends participated in the violence at the rock concert, why didn't I try to stop them?")

STRATEGIES FOR USING NARRATION IN AN ESSAY

After prewriting, you're ready to draft your essay. The following suggestions will be helpful whether you use narration as a dominant or supportive pattern of development.

1. Identify the point of the narrative conflict.   As you know, most narratives center around a conflict (see the preceding checklist). When you relate a story, it's up to you to convey the *significance* or *meaning* of the event's conflict. In *The Adventures of Huckleberry Finn*, Mark Twain warned: "Persons attempting to find a motive in this narrative will be prosecuted; persons attempting to find a moral in it will be banished. . . ." Twain was, of course, being ironic; his novel's richness lies in its "motives" and "morals." Similarly, when recounting your narrative, be sure to begin with a clear sense of your *narrative point,* or *thesis.* Then either state that point directly or select details and a tone that imply the point you want readers to take away from your story.

For example, suppose you decide to write about the time you got locked in a mall late at night. Your narrative might focus on the way the mall looked after hours and the way you struggled with mounting terror. But you would also use the narrative to make a point. Perhaps you want to emphasize that fear can be instructive. Or your point might be that malls have a disturbing, surreal underside. You could state this thesis explicitly. ("After hours, the mall shed its cheerful daytime demeanor and took on a more sinister quality.") Or you could refrain from stating the thesis directly, relying on your details and language to convey the point of the narrative: "The mannequins stared at me with glazed eyes and frozen smiles" and "The steel grates pulled over each store entrance glinted in the cold light, making each shop look like a prison cell."

2. Develop only those details that advance the narrative point. Nothing is more boring than a storyteller who gets sidetracked and drags out a story with nonessential details. When telling a story, you maintain an effective narrative pace by focusing on your point and eliminating any details that don't support it. A good narrative depends not only on what is included, but also on what has been left out.

How do you determine which specifics to omit, which to treat briefly, and which to emphasize? Having a clear sense of your narrative point and knowing your audience are crucial. Assume you're writing a narrative about a disastrous get-acquainted dance sponsored by your college the first week of the academic year. In addition to telling what happened, you also want to make a point; perhaps you want to emphasize that, despite the college's good intentions, such "official" events actually make it difficult to meet people. With this purpose in mind, you might write about how stiff and unnatural students seemed, all dressed up in their best clothes; you might narrate snatches of strained conversation you overheard; you might describe the way males gathered on one side of the room, females on the other—reverting to behaviors supposedly abandoned in fifth grade. All these details would support your narrative point.

Because you don't want to lead away from that point, you would leave out details about the top-notch band and the appetizing refreshments at the dance. The music and food may have been surprisingly good, but since these details don't advance the point you want to make, they should not be included in your narrative.

You also need to keep your audience in mind when selecting narrative details. If the audience consists of your instructor and other students—all of them familiar with the new student center where the dance was held—specific details about the center probably wouldn't have to be provided. But imagine that the essay is going to appear in the quarterly magazine published by the college's community relations office. Many of the magazine's readers are former graduates who haven't been on campus for several years. They may need additional specifics about the student center: its location, how many people it holds, how it is furnished.

As you write, keep asking yourself, "Is this detail or character or snippet of conversation essential? Does my audience need this detail to understand the conflict in the situation? Does this detail advance or intensify the narrative action?" Summarize details that have some importance but do not deserve lengthy treatment ("Two hours went by . . ."). And try to limit *narrative commentary*—statements that tell rather than show what happened—since such remarks interrupt the narrative flow. Focus instead on the specifics that propel action forward in a vigorous way.

Sometimes, especially if the narrative re-creates an event from the past, you won't be able to remember what happened detail for detail. In such a case, you should take advantage of what is called **dramatic license.** Using your current perspective as a guide, feel free to add or reshape details to suit your narrative point.

3. Organize the narrative sequence. All of us know the traditional beginning of fairy tales: "Once upon a time. . . ." Every narrative begins somewhere, presents a span of time, and ends at a certain point. Frequently, you will want to use a straightforward time order, following the event *chronologically* from beginning to end: first this happened, next this happened, finally this happened.

But sometimes a strict chronological recounting may not be effective—especially if the high point of the narrative gets lost somewhere in the middle of the time sequence. To avoid that possibility, you may want to disrupt chronology, plunge the reader into the middle of the story, and then return in a **flashback** to the tale's beginning. You are probably familiar with the way flashback is used on television and in film. You see someone appealing to the main characters for financial help, then return in a flashback to an earlier time when both were students in the same class. Narratives can also use **flashforward**—you give readers a glimpse of the future (the main character being jailed) before the story continues in the present (the events leading to the arrest). These techniques shift the story onto several planes and keep it from becoming a step-by-step, predictable account. Reserve flashforwards and flashbacks, however, for crucial incidents only, since breaking out of chronological order acts as emphasis. Here are examples of how flashback and flashforward can be used in narrative writing:

Flashback

```
    Standing behind the wooden counter, Greg wielded his knife
expertly as he shucked clams--one every ten seconds--with
practiced ease. The scene contrasted sharply with his first day
on the job, when his hands broke out in blisters and when
splitting each shell was like prying open a safe.
```

Flashforward

> Rushing to move my car from the no-parking zone, I waved a
> quick good-bye to Karen as she climbed the steps to the bus. I
> didn't know then that by the time I picked her up at the bus
> station later that day, she had made a decision that would affect
> both our lives.

Whether or not you choose to include flashbacks or flashforwards in an essay, remember to limit the time span covered by the narrative. Otherwise, you'll have trouble generating the details needed to give the story depth and meaning. Also, regardless of the time sequence you select, organize the tale so it drives toward a strong finish. Be careful that your story doesn't trail off into minor, anticlimactic details.

4. Make the narrative easy to follow.   Describing each distinct action in a separate paragraph helps readers grasp the flow of events. Although narrative essays don't always have conventional topic sentences, each narrative paragraph should have a clear focus. Often this focus is indicated by a sentence early in the paragraph that directs attention to the action taking place. Such a sentence functions as a kind of *informal topic sentence;* the rest of the paragraph then develops that topic sentence. You should also be sure to use time signals when narrating a story. Words like *now, then, next, after,* and *later* ensure that your reader won't get lost as the story progresses.

5. Make the narrative vigorous and immediate.   A compelling narrative provides an abundance of specific details, making readers feel as if they're experiencing the story being told. Readers must be able to see, hear, touch, smell, and taste the event you're narrating. *Vivid sensory description* is, therefore, an essential part of an effective narrative. (See page 71 in Chapter 6 and pages 121–122 in Chapter 8 for more on concrete, sensory language.) Not only do specific sensory details make writing a pleasure to read—we all enjoy learning the particulars about people, places, and things—but they also give the narrative the stamp of reality. The specifics convince the reader that the event being described actually did, or could, occur.

Compare the following excerpts from a narrative essay. The first version is lifeless and dull; the revised version, packed with sensory images, grabs readers with its sense of foreboding:

Original Version

> That eventful day started out like every other summer day. My
> sister Tricia and I made several elaborate mud pies that we
> decorated with care. A little later on, as we were spraying each
> other with the garden hose, we heard my father walk up the path.

Revised

That sad summer day started out uneventfully enough. My sister
Tricia and I spent a few hours mixing and decorating mud pies. Our
hands caked with dry mud, we sprinkled each lopsided pie with
alternating rows of dandelion and clover petals. Later, when the
sun got hotter, we tossed our white T-shirts over the red picket
fence--forgetting my grandmother's frequent warnings to be more
ladylike. Our sweaty backs bared to the sun, we doused each other
with icy sprays from the garden hose. Caught up in the primitive
pleasure of it all, we barely heard my father as he walked up the
garden path, the gravel crunching under his heavy work boots.

A caution: Sensory language enlivens narration, but it also slows the pace. Be
sure that the slower pace suits your purpose. For example, a lengthy description
fits an account of a leisurely summer vacation but is inappropriate in a tale about
a frantic search for a misplaced wallet.

Another way to create an aura of narrative immediacy is to use **dialog** while
telling a story. Our sense of other people comes, in part, from what they say and
the way they sound. Conversational exchanges allow the reader to experience
characters directly. Compare the following fragments of a narrative, one with dialog and one without, noting how much more energetic the second version is.

Original

As soon as I found my way back to the campsite, the trail guide
commented on my disheveled appearance. I explained that I had heard
some gunshots and had run back to camp as soon as I could.

Revised

As soon as I found my way back to the campsite, the trail
guide took one look at me and drawled, "What on earth happened to
you, Daniel Boone? You look as though you've been dragged through
a haystack backwards."

"I'd look a lot worse if I hadn't run back here. When a bullet
whizzes by me, I don't stick around to see who's doing the
shooting."

Note that, when using dialog, you generally begin a new paragraph to indicate
a shift from one person's speech to another's (as in the second example above).
Dialog can also be used to convey a person's inner thoughts. Like conversation
between people, such interior dialog is enclosed in quotation marks.

The challenge in writing dialog, both exterior and interior, is to make each character's speech distinctive and convincing. Reading the dialog aloud—even asking friends or family members to speak the lines—will help you develop an ear for authentic speech. What sounds most natural is often a compressed and reshaped version of what was actually said. As with other narrative details, include only those portions of dialog that serve your purpose, fit the mood you want to create, and reveal character. (For guidelines on punctuating dialog, see pages 688–691 of the Handbook.)

Another way to enliven narratives is to use *varied sentence structure.* Sentences that plod along with the same predictable pattern put readers to sleep. Experiment with your sentences by varying their length and type; mix long and short sentences, simple and complex. (For more on sentence structure, see pages 109–114 in Chapter 8.) Compare the following original and revised versions to get an idea of how effective varied sentence structure can be in narrative writing:

Original

```
    The store manager went to the walk-in refrigerator every day.
The heavy metal door clanged shut behind her. I had visions of
her freezing to death among the hanging carcasses. The shiny door
finally swung open. She waddled out.
```

Revised

```
    Each time the store manager went to the walk-in refrigerator,
the heavy metal door clanged shut behind her. Visions of her
freezing to death among the hanging carcasses crept into my mind
until, finally, the shiny door swung open and out she waddled.
```

Original

```
    The yellow-and-blue striped fish struggled on the line. Its
scales shimmered in the sunlight. Its tail waved frantically. I
saw its desire to live. I decided to let it go.
```

Revised

```
    Scales shimmering in the sunlight, tail waving frantically, the
yellow-and-blue striped fish struggled on the line. Seeing its
desire to live, I let it go.
```

Finally, *vigorous verbs* lend energy to narratives. Use active verb forms ("The boss *yelled at* him") rather than passive ones ("He *was yelled at* by the boss"), and try to replace anemic *to be* verbs ("She *was* a good basketball player") with more dynamic constructions ("She *played* basketball well"). (For more on strong verbs, see pages 122–124 in Chapter 8.)

6. Keep your point of view and verb tense consistent.   All stories have a *narrator,* the person who tells the story. If you, as narrator, tell a story as you experienced it, the story is written in the *first-person point of view* ("I saw the dog pull loose"). But if you observed the event (or heard about it from others) and want to tell how someone else experienced the incident, you would use the *third-person point of view* ("Anne saw the dog pull loose"). Each point of view has advantages and limitations. First person allows you to express ordinarily private thoughts and to re-create an event as you actually experienced it. This point of view is limited, though, in its ability to depict the inner thoughts of other people involved in the event. By way of contrast, third person makes it easier to provide insight into the thoughts of all the participants. However, its objective, broad perspective may undercut some of the subjective immediacy typical of the "I was there" point of view. No matter which point of view you select, stay with that vantage point throughout the entire narrative. (For more on point of view, see pages 24–25 in Chapter 2.)

Knowing whether to use the *past* or *present tense* ("I *strolled* into the room" as opposed to "I *stroll* into the room") is important. In most narrations, the past tense predominates, enabling the writer to span a considerable period of time. Although more rarely used, the present tense can be powerful for events of short durations—a wrestling match or a medical emergency, for instance. A narrative in the present tense prolongs each moment, intensifying the reader's sense of participation. Be careful, though; unless the event is intense and fast-paced, the present tense can seem contrived. Whichever tense you choose, avoid shifting midstream—starting, let's say, in the past tense ("she skated") and switching to the present tense ("she runs").

REVISION STRATEGIES

Once you have a draft of the essay, you're ready to revise. The following checklist will help you and those giving you feedback apply to narration some of the revision techniques discussed in Chapters 7 and 8.

☑ NARRATION: A REVISION/PEER REVIEW CHECKLIST

Revise Overall Meaning and Structure

☐ What is the essay's narrative point? Is it stated explicitly? If so, where? If not, where is it implied? Could the point be conveyed more clearly? How?

☐ What is the narrative's conflict? Is it stated explicitly? If so, where? If not, where is it implied? Could the conflict be made more dramatic? How?

☐ From what point of view is the narrative told? Is that the most effective point of view for this essay? Why or why not?

Revise Paragraph Development

☐ Which paragraphs (or passages) fail to advance the action, reveal character, or contribute to the story's mood? Should these sections be condensed or eliminated?

☐ Where do commentary and description slow the narrative pace? Is such an effect intended? If not, should the sections be tightened or eliminated?

☐ Where is it difficult to follow the chronology of events? Where should paragraph order be changed? Why? Where would chronology be clearer if there were separate paragraphs for distinct time periods? Where would additional time signals help?

☐ How could flashback or flashforward paragraphs (or passages) be used to highlight key events?

☐ What can be done to make the essay's opening paragraph more compelling? Would a dramatic bit of dialog or a mood-setting descriptive passage help?

☐ What could be done to make the essay's closing paragraph more effective? If the final paragraph seems anticlimactic, would it help to end earlier? If the ending doesn't round off the essay in a satisfying way, what could be added that would echo an idea or image in the opening?

Revise Sentences and Words

☐ Where is sentence structure monotonous? How would combining sentences, mixing sentence type, and alternating sentence length help?

☐ Where should the narrative pace be slowed down with long sentences or quickened with short ones?

☐ Where could dialog effectively convey character and propel the story forward? Where could dialog replace commentary?

☐ Which sentences and words are inconsistent with the essay's tone?

☐ Which sentences would benefit from sensory details that heighten the narrative mood?

☐ Where do vigorous verbs convey action? Where could active verbs ("Many of us made the same error") replace passive ones ("The same error was made by many of us")? Where could dull *to be* verbs ("The room was dark") be converted to more dynamic forms ("The room darkened")?

☐ Where are there inappropriate shifts in point of view or verb tense?

STUDENT ESSAY: FROM PREWRITING THROUGH REVISION

The student essay that follows was written by Paul Monahan in response to this assignment:

> In "Shooting an Elephant," George Orwell tells about an incident that forced him to act in a manner contrary to his better instincts. Write a narrative about a time you faced a disturbing conflict and ended up doing something you later regretted.

After deciding to write about an encounter he had with an elderly woman in the store where he worked, Paul did some *freewriting* on a word processor to gather material on his subject. When he later reviewed this freewriting, he crossed out unnecessary commentary, wrote notes signaling where dialog and descriptive details were needed, and indicated where paragraph breaks might occur. After annotating his freewriting in this manner, Paul felt comfortable launching into his first draft, without further shaping his freewriting or preparing an outline. As he wrote, though, he frequently referred to his warm-up material to organize his narrative and retrieve details. Paul's original freewriting is shown here; the handwritten marks indicate Paul's later efforts to shape and develop this material:

Freewriting

An (old woman) entered the (store.) She pushed the door, hobbled in, coughed, and seemed to be in pain. She wore a faded dress and a sweater that was much too small for her. The night was cold, but she didn't wear any stockings. You could see her veins. She strolled around the store, sneezing and hacking. She picked up a can of corn and stared at it. ~~She made me nervous~~. I walked over to see what was going on. Asked if she needed help. — *Set up contrast*

Give details about her appearance

Add dialog

I was the one to do this because I was on duty. Had worked at 7-11 for two years. Felt confident. Always tried to be friendly and polite. Hadn't had any trouble. ~~But the old woman worried me~~.

Background information—move to first paragraph

"I need food," she said. I told her how much the corn cost and also that the bologna was on sale (what a stupid, insensitive thing to do!). She said she couldn't pay. I almost told her to take the can of corn, but all the rules stopped me. Be polite, stay in control. I told her I couldn't give anything away. ¶Her face looked even

Add dialog

More specifics

more saggy. She kind of shook and put the can back. <u>She</u>
<u>left. I rushed out</u> after her. Too late. Felt ashamed
about acting like a robot. Mad at myself. ⟨If only I'd

Good title?

acted differently.⟩

Now read Paul's paper, "If Only," noting the similarities and differences between his prewriting and final essay. You'll notice, for example, that Paul decided to move background information to the essay's opening, and that he ended up using as his title a shortened version of the final sentence in his prewriting. Finally, consider how well the essay applies the principles of narration discussed in this chapter. (The commentary that follows the paper will help you look at Paul's essay more closely and will give you some sense of how he went about revising his first draft.)

If Only

by Paul Monahan

Introduction

Having worked at a 7-Eleven store for two years, I   1
thought I had become successful at what our manager
calls "customer relations." I firmly believed that a
friendly smile and an automatic "sir," "ma'am," and
"thank you" would see me through any situation that
might arise, from soothing impatient or unpleasant people

Narrative point (thesis)

to apologizing for giving out the wrong change. But the
other night an old woman shattered my belief that a glib
response could smooth over the rough spots of dealing
with other human beings.

*Informal topic
sentence*

The moment she entered, the woman presented a sharp   2
contrast to our shiny store with its bright lighting and
neatly arranged shelves. Walking as if each step were
painful, she slowly pushed open the glass door and
hobbled down the nearest aisle. She coughed dryly,

Sensory details

wheezing with each breath. On a forty-degree night, she
was wearing only a faded print dress, a thin, light-
beige sweater too small to button, and black vinyl
slippers with the backs cut out to expose calloused
heels. There were no stockings or socks on her splotchy,
blue-veined legs.

After strolling around the store for several minutes,   3
the old woman stopped in front of the rows of canned
vegetables. She picked up some corn niblets and stared
with a strange intensity at the label. At that point, I

Informal topic sentence

decided to be a good, courteous employee and asked her

if she needed help. As I stood close to her, my smile
became harder to maintain; her red-rimmed eyes were   ———Sensory details
partially closed by yellowish crusts; her hands were
covered with layer upon layer of grime, and the stale smell
of sweat rose in a thick vaporous cloud from her clothes.

4   "I need some food," she muttered in reply to my bright   ———Start of dialog
"Can I help you?"

5   "Are you looking for corn, ma'am?"

6   "I need some food," she repeated. "Any kind."

7   "Well, the corn is ninety-five cents," I said in my
most helpful voice. "Or, if you like, we have a special
on bologna today."

8   "I can't pay," she said.

9   For a second, I was tempted to say, "Take the corn."←———Conflict established
But the employee rules flooded into my mind: Remain
polite, but do not let customers get the best of you. Let
them know that you are in control. For a moment, I even
entertained the idea that this was some sort of test, and
that this woman was someone from the head office, testing
my loyalty. I responded dutifully, "I'm sorry, ma'am, but
I can't give away anything for free."

10   The old woman's face collapsed a bit more, if that were
possible, and her hands trembled as she put the can back   ———Informal topic sentence
on the shelf. She shuffled past me toward the door, her
torn and dirty clothing barely covering her bent back.

11   Moments after she left, I rushed out the door with the   Conclusion
can of corn, but she was nowhere in sight. For the rest of
my shift, the image of the woman haunted me. I had been
young, healthy, and smug. She had been old, sick, and
desperate. Wishing with all my heart that I had acted like
a human being rather than a robot, I was saddened to   ———Echoing of narrative
realize how fragile a hold we have on our better   point in the introduction
instincts.

Commentary

Point of View, Tense, and Conflict

Paul chose to write "If Only" from the *first-person point of view,* a logical choice
because he appears as a main character in his own story. Using the *past tense,* Paul
recounts an incident filled with *conflict*—between him and the woman and between
his fear of breaking the rules and his human instinct to help someone in need.

Narrative Point

It isn't always necessary to state the *narrative point* of an essay; it can be implied. But Paul decided to express the controlling idea of his narrative in two places—in the introduction ("But the other night an old woman shattered my belief that a glib response could smooth over the rough spots of dealing with other human beings") and again in the conclusion, where he expands his idea about rote responses overriding impulses of independent judgment and compassion. All of the essay's *narrative details* contribute to the point of the piece; Paul does not include any extraneous information that would detract from the central idea he wants to convey.

Organization and Other Patterns of Development

The narrative is *organized chronologically,* from the moment the woman enters the store to Paul's reaction after she leaves. Paul limits the narrative's time span. The entire incident probably occurs in under ten minutes, yet the introduction serves as a kind of *flashback* by providing some necessary background about Paul's past experiences. To help the reader follow the course of the narrative, Paul uses *time signals: "The moment* she entered, the woman presented a sharp contrast" (paragraph 2); "*At that point,* I decided to be a good, courteous employee" (3); "*For the rest of my shift,* the image of the woman haunted me" (11).

The paragraphs (except for those consisting solely of dialog) also contain *informal topic sentences* that direct attention to the specific stage of action being narrated. Indeed, each paragraph focuses on a distinct event: the elderly woman's actions when she first enters the store, the encounter between Paul and the woman, Paul's resulting inner conflict, the woman's subsequent response, and Paul's delayed reaction.

This chain of events, with one action leading to another, illustrates that the *cause-effect* pattern underlies the essay's basic structure. And another pattern—*description*—gives dramatic immediacy to the events being recounted. Throughout, rich sensory details engage the reader's interest. For instance, the sentence "her red-rimmed eyes were partially closed by yellowish crusts" (3) vividly re-creates the woman's appearance while also suggesting Paul's inner reaction to the woman.

Dialog and Sentence Structure

Paul uses other techniques to add energy and interest to his narrative. For one thing, he dramatizes his conflict with the woman through *dialog* that crackles with tension. And he achieves a vigorous narrative pace by *varying the length and structure of his sentences.* In the second paragraph, a short sentence ("There were no stockings or socks on her splotchy, blue-veined legs") alternates with a longer one ("On a forty-degree night, she was wearing only a faded print dress, a thin, light-beige sweater too small to button, and black vinyl slippers with the backs cut out to expose calloused heels"). Some sentences in the essay open with a subject and verb ("She coughed dryly"), while others start with dependent clauses or participial phrases ("As I stood close to her, my smile became harder to maintain"; "Walking as if each step were painful, she slowly pushed open the glass door") or with a prepositional phrase ("For a second, I was tempted").

Revising the First Draft

To get a sense of how Paul went about revising his essay, take a moment to look at the original version of his third paragraph shown here. The handwritten annotations, numbered in order of importance, represent Paul's ideas for revision. Compare this preliminary version with the final version in the full essay:

Original Version of Third Paragraph

③Inappropriate words—sound humorous

```
    After (sneezing) and (hacking) her way around the store,
the old woman stopped in front of the vegetable shelves.
(She) picked up a can of corn and stared at the label. (She)
stayed like this for several minutes. Then I walked over
to her and asked if I could be of help.
```

①Boring—not enough details

②Choppy sentences

As you can see, Paul realized the paragraph lacked power, so he decided to add compelling descriptive details about the woman ("the stale smell of sweat," for example). When revising, he also worked to reduce the paragraph's choppiness. By expanding and combining sentences, he gave the paragraph an easier, more graceful rhythm. Much of the time, revision involves paring down excess material. In this case, though, Paul made the right decision to elaborate his sentences. Furthermore, he added the following comment to the third paragraph: "I decided to be a good, courteous employee." These few words introduce an appropriate note of irony and serve to echo the essay's controlling idea.

Finally, Paul decided to omit the words "sneezing and hacking" because he realized they were too comic or light for his subject. Still, the first sentence in the revised paragraph is somewhat jarring. The word *strolling* isn't quite appropriate since it implies a leisurely grace inconsistent with the impression he wants to convey. Replacing *strolling* with, say, *shuffling* would bring the image more into line with the essay's overall mood.

Despite this slight problem, Paul's revisions are right on the mark. The changes he made strengthened his essay, turning it into a more evocative, more polished piece of narrative writing.

ACTIVITIES: NARRATION

Prewriting Activities

1. Imagine you're writing two essays: One analyzes the effect of insensitive teachers on young children; the other argues the importance of family

traditions. With the help of your journal or freewriting, identify different narratives you could use to open each essay.

2. Use brainstorming or any other prewriting technique to generate narrative details about *one* of the following events. After examining your raw material, identify two or three narrative points (thesis statements) that might focus an essay. Then edit the prewriting material for each narrative point, noting which items would be appropriate, which would be inappropriate, and which would have to be developed more fully.

   a. An injury you received
   b. The loss of an important object
   c. An event that made you wish you had a certain skill

3. For each of the following situations, identify two different conflicts that would make a story worth relating:

   a. Going to the supermarket with a friend
   b. Telling your parents which college you've decided to attend
   c. Participating in a demonstration
   d. Preparing for an exam in a difficult course

4. Prepare six to ten lines of vivid and natural-sounding dialog to convey the conflict in *two* of the following situations:

   a. One member of a couple trying to break up with the other
   b. A ten-year-old brother and a teenage sister shopping for a parent's birthday present
   c. A teacher talking to a student who plagiarized a paper
   d. A young person talking to his or her parents about dropping out of college for a semester

Revising Activities

5. Revise each of the following narrative sentence groups twice: once with words that carry negative connotations, and again with words that carry positive connotations. Use varied sentence structure, sensory details, and vigorous verbs to convey mood.

   a. The bell rang. It rang loudly. Students knew the last day of class was over.
   b. Last weekend, our neighbors burned leaves in their yard. We went over to speak with them.
   c. The sun shone in through my bedroom window. It made me sit up in bed. Daylight was finally here, I told myself.

6. The following paragraph is the introduction from the first draft of an essay proposing harsher penalties for drunk drivers. Revise this narrative paragraph to make it more effective. How can you make sentence structure less predictable?

Which details should you delete? As you revise, provide language that conveys the event's sights, smells, and sounds. Also, clarify the chronological sequence.

```
    As I drove down the street in my bright blue sports car, I saw
a car coming rapidly around the curve. The car didn't slow down
as it headed toward the traffic light. The light turned yellow
and then red. A young couple, dressed like models, started
crossing the street. When the woman saw the car, she called out
to her husband. He jumped onto the shoulder. The man wasn't hurt
but, seconds later, it was clear the woman was. I ran to a nearby
emergency phone and called the police. The ambulance arrived, but
the woman was already dead. The driver, who looked terrible,
failed the sobriety test, and the police found out that he had
two previous offenses. It's apparent that better ways have to be
found for getting drunk drivers off the road.
```

PROFESSIONAL SELECTIONS: NARRATION

GEORGE ORWELL

Born Eric Blair in the British colony of India, George Orwell (1903–50) is best known for his two novels *Animal Farm* (1946) and *1984* (1949)—both searing depictions of totalitarian societies. A fierce critic of political and economic injustice, Orwell also wrote a number of essays about the desperate lives of English factory workers and miners. Orwell's position with the Indian Imperial Police provided the basis for the following essay, which is taken from the collection *"Shooting an Elephant" and Other Essays* (1950).

Pre-Reading Journal Entry

Think of times when you were keenly aware of institutional injustice—an action, law, or regulation that is legally in the right but that you felt was wrong. In your journal, record several such examples. Why do you consider them wrong? Have you always felt that way? If not, what changed your opinion?

SHOOTING AN ELEPHANT

In Moulmein, in Lower Burma, I was hated by large numbers of people—the only   1
time in my life that I have been important enough for this to happen to me. I was sub-
divisional police officer of the town, and in an aimless, petty kind of way

anti-European feeling was very bitter. No one had the guts to raise a riot, but if a European woman went through the bazaars alone somebody would probably spit betel juice over her dress. As a police officer I was an obvious target and was baited whenever it seemed safe to do so. When a nimble Burman tripped me up on the football field and the referee (another Burman) looked the other way, the crowd yelled with hideous laughter. This happened more than once. In the end the sneering yellow faces of young men that met me everywhere, the insults hooted after me when I was at a safe distance, got badly on my nerves. The young Buddhist priests were the worst of all. There were several thousand of them in the town and none of them seemed to have anything to do except stand on street corners and jeer at Europeans.

All this was perplexing and upsetting. For at that time I had already made up my   2
mind that imperialism was an evil thing and the sooner I chucked up my job and got out of it the better. Theoretically—and secretly, of course—I was all for the Burmese and all against their oppressors, the British. As for the job I was doing, I hated it more bitterly than I can perhaps make clear. In a job like that you see the dirty work of Empire at close quarters. The wretched prisoners huddling in the stinking cages of the lock-ups, the grey, cowed faces of the long-term convicts, the scarred buttocks of the men who had been flogged with bamboos—all these oppressed me with an intolerable sense of guilt. But I could get nothing into perspective. I was young and ill-educated and I had to think out my problems in the utter silence that is imposed on every Englishman in the East. I did not even know that the British Empire is dying, still less did I know that it is a great deal better than the younger empires that are going to supplant it. All I knew was that I was stuck between my hatred of the empire I served and my rage against the evil-spirited little beasts who tried to make my job impossible. With one part of my mind I thought of the British Raj as an unbreakable tyranny, as something clamped down, *in saecula saeculorum,*[1] upon the will of prostrate peoples; with another part I thought that the greatest joy in the world would be to drive a bayonet into a Buddhist priest's guts. Feelings like these are the normal by-products of imperialism; ask any Anglo-Indian official, if you can catch him off duty.

One day something happened which in a roundabout way was enlightening. It was   3
a tiny incident in itself, but it gave me a better glimpse than I had had before of the real nature of imperialism—the real motives for which despotic governments act. Early one morning the sub-inspector at a police station the other end of the town rang me up on the 'phone and said that an elephant was ravaging the bazaar. Would I please come and do something about it? I did not know what I could do, but I wanted to see what was happening and I got onto a pony and started out. I took my rifle, an old .44 Winchester and much too small to kill an elephant, but I thought the noise might be useful *in terrorem.*[2] Various Burmans stopped me on the way and told me about the elephant's doings. It was not, of course, a wild elephant, but a tame one which had gone "must." It had been chained up, as tame elephants always are when their attack of "must" is due, but on the previous night it had broken its chain and escaped. Its mahout, the only person who could manage it when it was in that state, had set out in pursuit, but had taken the wrong direction and was now twelve hours' journey away, and in the morning the elephant had suddenly reappeared in the town. The Burmese population had no weapons and were quite helpless against it. It had already destroyed

[1]Latin phrase meaning "for ever and ever" (editors' note).
[2]Latin phrase meaning "as a warning" (editors' note).

somebody's bamboo hut, killed a cow and raided some fruit-stalls and devoured the stock; also it had met the municipal rubbish van and, when the driver jumped out and took to his heels, had turned the van over and inflicted violences upon it.

4   The Burmese sub-inspector and some Indian constables were waiting for me in the quarter where the elephant had been seen. It was a very poor quarter, a labyrinth of squalid bamboo huts, thatched with palm-leaf, winding all over a steep hillside. I remember that it was a cloudy, stuffy morning at the beginning of the rains. We began questioning the people as to where the elephant had gone and, as usual, failed to get any definite information. That is invariably the case in the East; a story always sounds clear enough at a distance, but the nearer you get to the scene of events the vaguer it becomes. Some of the people said that the elephant had gone in one direction, some said that he had gone in another, some professed not even to have heard of any elephant. I had almost made up my mind that the whole story was a pack of lies, when we heard yells a little distance away. There was a loud, scandalized cry of 'Go away, child! Go away this instant!' and an old woman with a switch in her hand came round the corner of a hut, violently shooing away a crowd of naked children. Some more women followed, clicking their tongues and exclaiming; evidently there was something that the children ought not to have seen. I rounded the hut and saw a man's dead body sprawling in the mud. He was an Indian, a black Dravidian coolie, almost naked, and he could not have been dead many minutes. The people said that the elephant had come suddenly upon him round the corner of the hut, caught him with its trunk, put its foot on his back and ground him into the earth. This was the rainy season and the ground was soft, and his face had scored a trench a foot deep and a couple of yards long. He was lying on his belly with arms crucified and head sharply twisted to one side. His face was coated with mud, the eyes wide open, the teeth bared and grinning with an expression of unendurable agony. (Never tell me, by the way, that the dead look peaceful. Most of the corpses I have seen looked devilish.) The friction of the great beast's foot had stripped the skin from his back as neatly as one skins a rabbit. As soon as I saw the dead man I sent an orderly to a friend's house nearby to borrow an elephant rifle. I had already sent back the pony, not wanting it to go mad with fright and throw me if it smelt the elephant.

5   The orderly came back in a few minutes with a rifle and five cartridges, and meanwhile some Burmans had arrived and told us that the elephant was in the paddy fields below, only a few hundred yards away. As I started forward practically the whole population of the quarter flocked out of the houses and followed me. They had seen the rifle and were all shouting excitedly that I was going to shoot the elephant. They had not shown much interest in the elephant when he was merely ravaging their homes, but it was different now that he was going to be shot. It was a bit of fun to them, as it would be to an English crowd; besides they wanted the meat. It made me vaguely uneasy. I had no intention of shooting the elephant—I had merely sent for the rifle to defend myself if necessary—and it is always unnerving to have a crowd following you. I marched down the hill looking and feeling a fool, with the rifle over my shoulder and an ever-growing army of people jostling at my heels. At the bottom, when you got away from the huts, there was a metalled road and beyond that a miry waste of paddy fields a thousand yards across, not yet ploughed but soggy from the first rains and dotted with coarse grass. The elephant was standing eight yards from the road, his left side towards us. He took not the slightest notice of the crowd's approach. He was tearing up bunches of grass, beating them against his knees to clean them and stuffing them into his mouth.

I had halted on the road. As soon as I saw the elephant I knew with perfect certain- 6
ty that I ought not to shoot him. It is a serious matter to shoot a working elephant—it
is comparable to destroying a huge and costly piece of machinery—and obviously one
ought not to do it if it can possibly be avoided. And at that distance, peacefully eating,
the elephant looked no more dangerous than a cow. I thought then and I think now that
his attack of "must" was already passing off; in which case he would merely wander
harmlessly about until the mahout came back and caught him. Moreover, I did not in
the least want to shoot him. I decided that I would watch him for a little while to make
sure that he did not turn savage again, and then go home.

But at that moment I glanced round at the crowd that had followed me. It was an 7
immense crowd, two thousand at the least and growing every minute. It blocked the
road for a long distance on either side. I looked at the sea of yellow faces above the
garish clothes—faces all happy and excited over this bit of fun, all certain that the elephant was going to be shot. They were watching me as they would watch a conjurer
about to perform a trick. They did not like me, but with the magical rifle in my hands
I was momentarily worth watching. And suddenly I realized that I should have to shoot
the elephant after all. The people expected it of me and I had got to do it; I could feel
their two thousand wills pressing me forward, irresistibly. And it was at this moment,
as I stood there with the rifle in my hands, that I first grasped the hollowness, the futility of the white man's dominion in the East. Here was I, the white man with his gun,
standing in front of the unarmed native crowd—seemingly the leading actor of the
piece; but in reality I was only an absurd puppet pushed to and fro by the will of those
yellow faces behind. I perceived in this moment that when the white man turns tyrant
it is his own freedom that he destroys. He becomes a sort of hollow, posing dummy,
the conventionalized figure of a sahib. For it is the condition of his rule that he shall
spend his life in trying to impress the "natives," and so in every crisis he has got to do
what the "natives" expect of him. He wears a mask, and his face grows to fit it. I had
got to shoot the elephant. I had committed myself to doing it when I sent for the rifle.
A sahib has got to act like a sahib; he has got to appear resolute, to know his own mind
and do definite things. To come all that way, rifle in hand, with two thousand people
marching at my heels, and then to trail feebly away, having done nothing—no, that
was impossible. The crowd would laugh at me. And my whole life, every white man's
life in the East, was one long struggle not to be laughed at.

But I did not want to shoot the elephant. I watched him beating his bunch of grass 8
against his knees, with that preoccupied grandmotherly air that elephants have. It
seemed to me that it would be murder to shoot him. At that age I was not squeamish
about killing animals, but I had never shot an elephant and never wanted to.
(Somehow it always seems worse to kill a *large* animal.) Besides, there was the beast's
owner to be considered. Alive, the elephant was worth at least a hundred pounds;
dead, he would only be worth the value of his tusks, five pounds, possibly. But I had
got to act quickly. I turned to some experienced-looking Burmans who had been there
when we arrived, and asked them how the elephant had been behaving. They all said
the same thing: he took no notice of you if you left him alone, but he might charge if
you went too close to him.

It was perfectly clear to me what I ought to do. I ought to walk up to within, say, 9
twenty-five yards of the elephant and test his behavior. If he charged, I could shoot; if
he took no notice of me, it would be safe to leave him until the mahout came back.
But also I knew that I was going to do no such thing. I was a poor shot with a rifle and

the ground was soft mud into which one would sink at every step. If the elephant charged and I missed him, I should have about as much chance as a toad under a steam-roller. But even then I was not thinking particularly of my own skin, only of the watchful yellow faces behind. For at that moment, with the crowd watching me, I was not afraid in the ordinary sense, as I would have been if I had been alone. A white man mustn't be frightened in front of "natives"; and so, in general he isn't frightened. The sole thought in my mind was that if anything went wrong those two thousand Burmans would see me pursued, caught, trampled on and reduced to a grinning corpse like that Indian up the hill. And if that happened it was quite probable that some of them would laugh. That would never do. There was only one alternative. I shoved the cartridges into the magazine and lay down on the road to get a better aim.

10   The crowd grew very still, and a deep, low, happy sigh, as of people who see the theatre curtain go up at last, breathed from innumerable throats. They were going to have their bit of fun after all. The rifle was a beautiful German thing with cross-hair sights. I did not then know that in shooting an elephant one would shoot to cut an imaginary bar running from ear-hole to ear-hole. I ought, therefore, as the elephant was sideway on, to have aimed straight at his ear-hole; actually I aimed several inches in front of this, thinking the brain would be further forward.

11   When I pulled the trigger I did not hear the bang or feel the kick—one never does when a shot goes home—but I heard the devilish roar of glee that went up from the crowd. In that instant, in too short a time, one would have thought, even for the bullet to get there, a mysterious, terrible change had come over the elephant. He neither stirred nor fell, but every line of his body had altered. He looked suddenly stricken, shrunken, immensely old, as though the frightful impact of the bullet had paralyzed him without knocking him down. At last, after what seemed a long time—it might have been five seconds, I dare say—he sagged flabbily to his knees. His mouth slobbered. An enormous senility seemed to have settled upon him. One could have imagined him thousands of years old. I fired again into the same spot. At the second shot he did not collapse but climbed with desperate slowness to his feet and stood weakly upright, with legs sagging and head drooping. I fired a third time. That was the shot that did for him. You could see the agony of it jolt his whole body and knock the last remnant of strength from his legs. But in falling he seemed for a moment to rise, for as his hind legs collapsed beneath him he seemed to tower upward like a huge rock toppling, his trunk reaching skywards like a tree. He trumpeted, for the first and only time. And then down he came, his belly towards me, with a crash that seemed to shake the ground even where I lay.

12   I got up. The Burmans were already racing past me across the mud. It was obvious that the elephant would never rise again, but he was not dead. He was breathing very rhythmically with long rattling gasps, his great mound of a side painfully rising and falling. His mouth was wide open—I could see far down into caverns of pale pink throat. I waited a long time for him to die, but his breathing did not weaken. Finally I fired my two remaining shots into the spot where I thought his heart must be. The thick blood welled out of him like red velvet, but still he did not die. His body did not even jerk when the shots hit him, the tortured breathing continued without a pause. He was dying, very slowly and in great agony, but in some world remote from me where not even a bullet could damage him further. I felt that I had got to put an end to that dreadful noise. It seemed dreadful to see the great beast lying there, powerless to move and yet powerless to die, and not even to be able to finish him. I sent back for my small rifle

and poured shot after shot into his heart and down his throat. They seemed to make no impression. The tortured gasps continued as steadily as the ticking of a clock.

In the end I could not stand it any longer and went away. I heard later that it took   13
him half an hour to die. Burmans were bringing dahs and baskets even before I left, and I was told they had stripped the body almost to the bones by the afternoon.

Afterwards, of course, there were endless discussions about the shooting of the ele-   14
phant. The owner was furious, but he was only an Indian and could do nothing. Besides, legally I had done the right thing, for a mad elephant has to be killed, like a mad dog, if its owner fails to control it. Among the Europeans opinion was divided. The older men said I was right, the younger men said it was a damn shame to shoot an elephant for killing a coolie, because an elephant was worth more than any damn Coringhee coolie. And afterwards I was very glad that the coolie had been killed; it put me legally in the right and it gave me a sufficient pretext for shooting the elephant. I often wondered whether any of the others grasped that I had done it solely to avoid looking a fool.

Questions for Close Reading

1. What is the selection's thesis (or narrative point)? Locate the sentence(s) in which Orwell states his main idea. If he doesn't state the thesis explicitly, express it in your own words.

2. How does Orwell feel about the Burmans? What words does he use to describe them?

3. What reasons does Orwell give for shooting the elephant?

4. In paragraph 3, Orwell says that the elephant incident gave him a better understanding of "the real motives for which despotic governments act." What do you think he means? Before you answer, reread paragraph 7 carefully.

5. Refer to your dictionary as needed to define the following words used in the selection: *imperialism* (paragraph 2), *prostrate* (2), *despotic* (3), *mahout* (3), *miry* (5), *conjurer* (7), *futility* (7), and *sahib* (7).

Questions About the Writer's Craft

1. **The pattern.** Most effective narratives encompass a restricted time span. How much time elapses from the moment Orwell gets his gun to the death of the elephant? What time signals does Orwell provide to help the reader follow the sequence of events in this limited time span?

2. Orwell doesn't actually begin his narrative until the third paragraph. What purposes do the first two paragraphs serve?

3. In paragraph 6, Orwell says that shooting a working elephant "is comparable to destroying a huge and costly piece of machinery." This kind of comparison is called an *analogy*—describing something unfamiliar, often abstract, in terms of something more familiar and concrete. Find at least three additional analogies in Orwell's essay. What effect do they have?

4. **Other patterns.** Much of the power of Orwell's narrative comes from his ability to convey sensory impressions—what he saw, heard, smelled. Orwell's description becomes most vivid when he writes about the elephant's death in paragraphs 11 and 12. Find some evocative words and phrases that give the description its power.

Writing Assignments Using Narration as a Pattern of Development

∞ 1. Orwell recounts a time he acted under great pressure. Write a narrative about an action you once took simply because you felt pressured. Perhaps you were attempting to avoid ridicule or to fulfill someone else's expectations. Like Orwell, use vivid details to bring the incident to life and to convey its effect on you. Reading Sophronia Liu's "So Tsi-fai" (page 221) will help you see the sometimes disastrous consequence of the pressure to conform.

∞ 2. Write a narrative essay about an experience that gave you, like Orwell, a deeper insight into your own nature. You may have discovered, for instance, that you can be surprisingly naive, compassionate, petty, brave, rebellious, or good at something. Your essay may be serious or light in tone. Consider first reading Diane Cole's "Don't Just Stand There" (page 322), an essay showing how the author's response to a challenge revealed much about her character.

Writing Assignments Using Other Patterns of Development

3. Was Orwell justified in shooting the elephant? Write an essay arguing either that Orwell was justified *or* that he was not. To develop your thesis, cite several specific reasons, each supported by details drawn from the essay. Here are some points you might consider: the legality of Orwell's act, the elephant's temperament, the crowd's presence, the aftermath of the elephant's death, the death itself.

4. Orwell's essay concerns, in part, the tendency to conceal indecision and confusion behind a facade of authority. Focusing on one or two groups of people (parents, teachers, doctors, politicians, and so on), write an essay about the way people in authority sometimes *pretend* to know what they are doing so that subordinates won't suspect their insecurity or incompetence. Part of your essay should focus on the consequences of such behaviors.

Writing Assignment Using a Journal Entry as a Starting Point

5. Review your pre-reading journal entry, and select *one* action, law, or regulation that you consider indefensible. Interview friends, family, and classmates in an

effort to gather views on all sides of the issue. Also consider supplementing this informal research with information gathered in the library and/or on the Internet. After weighing all your material, formulate a thesis; then write an essay convincing readers of the validity of your position.

AUDRE LORDE

Named poet laureate of the state of New York in 1991, Audre Lorde (1934–92) was a New Yorker born of African-Caribbean parents. Lorde taught at Hunter College for many years and published numerous poems and nonfiction pieces in a variety of magazines and literary journals. Her books include *A Burst of Light* (1988), *Sister Outsider: Essays and Speeches* (1984), and *The Black Unicorn: Poems* (1978). "The Fourth of July" is an excerpt from her autobiography, *Zami: A New Spelling of My Name* (1982).

Pre-Reading Journal Entry

When you were a child, what beliefs about the United States did you have? List these beliefs. For each, indicate whether subsequent experience maintained or shattered your childhood understanding of these beliefs. Take a little time to explore these issues in your journal.

THE FOURTH OF JULY

The first time I went to Washington, D.C., was on the edge of the summer when I 1
was supposed to stop being a child. At least that's what they said to us all at graduation from the eighth grade. My sister Phyllis graduated at the same time from high school. I don't know what she was supposed to stop being. But as graduation presents for us both, the whole family took a Fourth of July trip to Washington, D.C., the fabled and famous capital of our country.

It was the first time I'd ever been on a railroad train during the day. When I was lit- 2
tle, and we used to go to the Connecticut shore, we always went at night on the milk train, because it was cheaper.

Preparations were in the air around our house before school was even over. We 3
packed for a week. There were two very large suitcases that my father carried, and a box filled with food. In fact, my first trip to Washington was a mobile feast; I started eating as soon as we were comfortably ensconced in our seats, and did not stop until somewhere after Philadelphia. I remember it was Philadelphia because I was disappointed not to have passed by the Liberty Bell.

My mother had roasted two chickens and cut them up into dainty bite-size pieces. 4
She packed slices of brown bread and butter and green pepper and carrot sticks. There were little violently yellow iced cakes with scalloped edges called "marigolds," that came from Cushman's Bakery. There was a spice bun and rock-cakes from Newton's, the West Indian bakery across Lenox Avenue from St. Mark's School, and iced tea in a wrapped mayonnaise jar. There were sweet pickles for us and dill pickles for my father, and peaches with the fuzz still on them, individually wrapped to keep them from bruising. And, for neatness, there were piles of napkins and a little tin box with a washcloth dampened with rosewater and glycerine for wiping sticky mouths.

5   I wanted to eat in the dining car because I had read all about them, but my mother reminded me for the umpteenth time that dining car food always cost too much money and besides, you never could tell whose hands had been playing all over that food, nor where those same hands had been just before. My mother never mentioned that Black people were not allowed into railroad dining cars headed south in 1947. As usual, whatever my mother did not like and could not change, she ignored. Perhaps it would go away, deprived of her attention.

6   I learned later that Phyllis's high school senior class trip had been to Washington, but the nuns had given her back her deposit in private, explaining to her that the class, all of whom were white, except Phyllis, would be staying in a hotel where Phyllis "would not be happy," meaning, Daddy explained to her, also in private, that they did not rent rooms to Negroes. "We will take you to Washington, ourselves," my father had avowed, "and not just for an overnight in some measly fleabag hotel."

7   American racism was a new and crushing reality that my parents had to deal with every day of their lives once they came to this country. They handled it as a private woe. My mother and father believed that they could best protect their children from the realities of race in america and the fact of american racism by never giving them name, much less discussing their nature. We were told we must never trust white people, but *why* was never explained, nor the nature of their ill will. Like so many other vital pieces of information in my childhood, I was supposed to know without being told. It always seemed like a very strange injunction coming from my mother, who looked so much like one of those people we were never supposed to trust. But something always warned me not to ask my mother why she wasn't white, and why Auntie Lillah and Auntie Etta weren't, even though they were all that same problematic color so different from my father and me, even from my sisters, who were somewhere in-between.

8   In Washington, D.C., we had one large room with two double beds and an extra cot for me. It was a back-street hotel that belonged to a friend of my father's who was in real estate, and I spent the whole next day after Mass squinting up at the Lincoln Memorial where Marian Anderson[1] had sung after the D.A.R.[2] refused to allow her to sing in their auditorium because she was Black. Or because she was "Colored," my father said as he told us the story. Except that what he probably said was "Negro," because for his time, my father was quite progressive.

9   I was squinting because I was in that silent agony that characterized all of my childhood summers, from the time school let out in June to the end of July, brought about by my dilated and vulnerable eyes exposed to the summer brightness.

10   I viewed Julys through an agonizing corolla of dazzling whiteness and I always hated the Fourth of July, even before I came to realize the travesty such a celebration was for Black people in this country.

11   My parents did not approve of sunglasses, nor of their expense.

12   I spent the afternoon squinting up at monuments to freedom and past presidencies and democracy, and wondering why the light and heat were both so much stronger in Washington, D.C., than back home in New York City. Even the pavement on the streets was a shade lighter in color than back home.

---

[1]An acclaimed African-American opera singer (1902–93), famed for her renderings of Black spirituals.

[2]Daughters of the American Revolution. A society, founded in 1890, for women who can prove direct lineage to soldiers or others who aided in winning American independence from Great Britain during the Revolutionary War (1775–83).

Late that Washington afternoon my family and I walked back down Pennsylvania   13
Avenue. We were a proper caravan, mother bright and father brown, the three of us
girls step-standards in-between. Moved by our historical surroundings and the heat of
the early evening, my father decreed yet another treat. He had a great sense of history, a flair for the quietly dramatic and the sense of specialness of an occasion and a trip.

"Shall we stop and have a little something to cool off, Lin?"   14

Two blocks away from our hotel, the family stopped for a dish of vanilla ice cream   15
at a Breyer's ice cream and soda fountain. Indoors, the soda fountain was dim and fan-
cooled, deliciously relieving to my scorched eyes.

Corded and crisp and pinafored, the five of us seated ourselves one by one at the   16
counter. There was I between my mother and father, and my two sisters on the other
side of my mother. We settled ourselves along the white mottled marble counter, and
when the waitress spoke at first no one understood what she was saying, and so the
five of us just sat there.

The waitress moved along the line of us closer to my father and spoke again. "I said 17
I kin give you to take out, but you can't eat here. Sorry." Then she dropped her eyes
looking very embarrassed, and suddenly we heard what it was she was saying all at the
same time, loud and clear.

Straight-backed and indignant, one by one, my family and I got down from the   18
counter stools and turned around and marched out of the store, quiet and outraged, as
if we had never been Black before. No one would answer my emphatic questions with
anything other than a guilty silence. "But we hadn't done anything!" This wasn't right
or fair! Hadn't I written poems about Bataan and freedom and democracy for all?

My parents wouldn't speak of this injustice, not because they had contributed to it, 19
but because they felt they should have anticipated it and avoided it. This made me
even angrier. My fury was not going to be acknowledged by a like fury. Even my two
sisters copied my parents' pretense that nothing unusual and anti-american had
occurred. I was left to write my angry letter to the president of the united states all by
myself, although my father did promise I could type it out on the office typewriter next
week, after I showed it to him in my copybook diary.

The waitress was white, and the counter was white, and the ice cream I never ate   20
in Washington, D.C., that summer I left childhood was white, and the white heat and
the white pavement and the white stone monuments of my first Washington summer
made me sick to my stomach for the whole rest of that trip and it wasn't much of a
graduation present after all.

Questions for Close Reading

1. What is the selection's thesis (or narrative point)? Locate the sentence(s) in
which Lorde states her main idea. If she doesn't state the thesis explicitly,
express it in your own words.

2. In paragraph 4, Lorde describes the elaborate picnic her mother prepared for
the trip to Washington, D.C. Why did Lorde's mother make such elaborate
preparations? What do these preparations tell us about Lorde's mother?

3. Why does Lorde have trouble understanding her parents' dictate that she
"never trust white people" (paragraph 7)?

4. In general, how do Lorde's parents handle racism? How does the family as a whole deal with the racism they encounter in the ice cream parlor? How does the family's reaction to the ice cream parlor incident make Lorde feel?

5. Refer to your dictionary as needed to define the following words used in the selection: *fabled* (paragraph 1), *injunction* (7), *progressive* (8), *dilated* (9), *vulnerable* (9), *travesty* (10), *decreed* (13), *pretense* (19).

Questions About the Writer's Craft

1. **The pattern.** What techniques does Lorde use to help readers follow the unfolding of the story as it occurs in both time and space?

2. When telling a story, skilled writers limit narrative commentary—statements that tell rather than show what happened—because such commentary tends to interrupt the narrative flow. Lorde, however, provides narrative commentary in several spots. Find these instances. How is the information she provides in these places essential to her narrative?

3. In paragraphs 7 and 19, Lorde uses all lowercase letters when referring to America/American and to the President of the United States. Why do you suppose she doesn't follow the rules of capitalization? In what ways does her rejection of these rules reinforce what she is trying to convey through the essay's title?

4. What key word does Lorde repeat in paragraph 20? What effect do you think she hopes the repetition will have on readers?

Writing Assignments Using Narration as a Pattern of Development

∞ 1. Lorde recounts an incident during which she was treated unfairly. Write a narrative about a time when either you were treated unjustly or you treated someone else in an unfair manner. Like Lorde, use vivid details to make the incident come alive and to convey how it affected you. Essays including George Orwell's "Shooting an Elephant" (page 209), Sophronia Liu's "So Tsi-fai" (page 221), and Brent Staples's "Black Men and Public Space" (page 407) will prompt some ideas worth exploring.

∞ 2. Write a narrative about an experience that dramatically changed your view of the world. The experience might have been jarring and painful, or it may have been positive and uplifting. In either case, recount the incident with compelling narrative details. To illustrate the shift in your perspective, begin with a brief statement of the way you viewed the world before the experience. The following essays provide insight into the way a single experience can alter one's understanding of the world: Maya Angelou's "Sister Flowers" (page 178), Diane Cole's "Don't Just

Stand There" (page 322), Richard Rhodes's "Watching the Animals" (page 334), and Joseph H. Suina's "And Then I Went to School" (page 371).

Writing Assignments Using Other Patterns of Development

3. Lorde suggests that her parents use the coping mechanism of denial to deal with life's harsh realities. For example, she writes that whatever her mother "did not like and could not change, she ignored." Refer to a psychology textbook to learn more about denial as a coping mechanism. When is it productive? When is it counterproductive? Drawing upon your own experiences as well as those of friends, family, and classmates, write an essay contrasting effective and ineffective uses of denial. Near the end of the paper, present brief guidelines that will help readers identify when denial may be detrimental.

 4. In her essay, Lorde decries and by implication takes a strong stance against racial discrimination. Brainstorm with friends, family members, and classmates to identify other injustices in American society. To prompt discussion, you might begin by considering attitudes toward the elderly, the overweight, the physically disabled; the funding of schools in poor and affluent neighborhoods; the portrayal of a specific ethnic group on television; and so on. Focusing on *one* such injustice, write an essay arguing that such an injustice indeed exists. To document the nature and extent of the injustice, use library and/or Internet research as well as your own and other people's experiences. Acknowledge and, when you can, dismantle the views of those who think there isn't a problem.

Writing Assignment Using a Journal Entry as a Starting Point

5. Write an essay comparing and/or contrasting the beliefs you had about the United States as a child with those you have as an adult. Review your pre-reading journal entry, and select *one* American belief to focus on. Provide strong, dramatic examples that show why your childhood belief in this concept has been strengthened or weakened. Before writing, you should consider reading Joseph H. Suina's "And Then I Went to School" (page 371) and Juh Ji-Yeon's "Let's Tell the Story of All America's Cultures" (page 499), two powerful accounts of personal disillusionment with American ideals.

SOPHRONIA LIU

In 1973, at the age of twenty, Sophronia Liu came to the United States from her native Hong Kong. She earned a bachelor's degree and then a master's degree in English from the University of South Dakota. She now makes her home in the Minneapolis–St. Paul area. An actress as well as a writer, Liu is a founding member of

The Asian American Renaissance, an organization dedicated to building the Asian-American community through the arts. Liu's writing has appeared in *Colors Magazine, Making More Waves, Asian American Renaissance Journal,* and other publications. Initially written in response to a class assignment, the selection below was published in the feminist journal *Hurricane Alice* in 1986.

Pre-Reading Journal Entry

Think of at least two times in your childhood or adolescence when you witnessed—as an observer, participant, or victim—someone being bullied. In each case, reflect, in your journal, on these questions: What do you think made the person a target for bullying? Who were the offenders? What do you think provoked the bullying? What impact did this incident have on the people involved?

SO TSI-FAI

1   Voices, images, scenes from the past—twenty-three years ago, when I was in sixth grade:

2   "Let us bow our heads in silent prayer for the soul of So Tsi-fai. Let us pray for God's forgiveness for this boy's rash taking of his own life . . ." Sister Marie (Mung Gu-liang). My sixth-grade English teacher. Missionary nun from Paris. Principal of The Little Flower's School. Disciplinarian, perfectionist, authority figure: awesome and awful in my ten-year-old eyes.

3   "I don't need any supper. I have drunk enough insecticide." So Tsi-fai. My fourteen-year-old classmate. Daredevil; good-for-nothing lazybones (according to Mung Gu-liang). Bright black eyes, disheveled hair, defiant sneer, creased and greasy uniform, dirty hands, careless walk, shuffling feet. Standing in the corner for being late, for forgetting his homework, for talking in class, for using foul language. ("Shame on you! Go wash your mouth with soap!" Mung Gu-liang's sharp command. He did, and came back with a grin.) So Tsi-fai: Sticking his tongue out behind Mung Gu-liang's back, passing secret notes to his friends, kept behind after school, sent to the Principal's office for repeated offenses. So Tsi-fai: incorrigible, hopeless, and without hope.

4   It was a Monday in late November when we heard of his death, returning to school after the weekend with our parents' signatures on our midterm reports. So Tsi-fai also showed his report to his father, we were told later. He flunked three out of the fourteen subjects: English Grammar, Arithmetic, and Chinese Dictation. He missed each one by one to three marks. That wasn't so bad. But he was a hopeless case. Overaged, stubborn, and uncooperative; a repeated offender of school rules, scourge of all teachers; who was going to give him a lenient passing grade? Besides, being a few months over the maximum age—fourteen—for sixth graders, he wasn't even allowed to sit for the Secondary School Entrance Exam.

5   All sixth graders in Hong Kong had to pass the SSE before they could obtain a seat in secondary school. In 1964 when I took the exam, there were more than twenty thousand candidates. About seven thousand of us passed: four thousand were sent to government and subsidized schools, the other three thousand to private and grant-in-aid schools. I came in around no. 2000; I was lucky. Without the public exam, there would be no secondary school for So Tsi-fai. His future was sealed.

Looking at the report card with three red marks on it, his father was furious. So Tsi-   6
fai was the oldest son. There were three younger children. His father was a vegetable
farmer with a few plots of land in Wong Juk-hang, by the sea. His mother worked in a
local factory. So Tsi-fai helped in the fields, cooked for the family, and washed his own
clothes. ("Filthy, dirty boy!" gasped Mung Gu-liang. "Grime behind the ears, black
rims on the fingernails, dirty collar, crumpled shirt. Why doesn't your mother iron your
shirt?") Both his parents were illiterate. So Tsi-fai was their biggest hope: He made it
to the sixth grade.

Who woke him up for school every morning and had breakfast waiting for him?   7
Nobody. ("Time for school! Get up! Eat your rice!" Ma nagged and screamed. The
aroma of steamed rice and Chinese sausages spread all over the house. "Drink your
tea! Eat your oranges! Wash your face! And remember to wash behind your ears!") And
who helped So Tsi-fai do his homework? Nobody. Did he have older brothers like mine
who knew all about the arithmetic of rowing a boat against the currents or with the
currents, how to count the feet of chickens and rabbits in the same cage, the present
perfect continuous tense of "to live" and the future perfect tense of "to succeed"?
None. Nil. So Tsi-fai was a lost cause.

I came in first in both terms that year, the star pupil. So Tsi-fai was one of the last   8
in the class. He was lazy; he didn't care. Or did he?

When his father scolded him, So Tsi-fai left the house. When he showed up again,   9
late for supper, he announced, "I don't need any supper. I have drunk enough insecticide." Just like another one of his practical jokes. The insecticide was stored in the field
for his father's vegetables. He was rushed to the hospital; dead upon arrival.

"He gulped for a last breath and was gone," an uncle told us at the funeral. "But his   10
eyes wouldn't shut. So I said in his ear, 'You go now and rest in peace.' And I smoothed
my hand over his eyelids. His face was all purple."

His face was still purple when we saw him in his coffin. Eyes shut tight, nostrils   11
dilated and white as if fire and anger might shoot out, any minute.

In class that Monday morning, Sister Marie led us in prayer. "Let us pray that God   12
will forgive him for his sins." We said the Lord's Prayer and the Hail Mary. We bowed
our heads. I sat in my chair, frozen and dazed, thinking of the deadly chill in the
morgue, the smell of disinfectant, ether, and dead flesh.

"Bang!" went a gust of wind, forcing open a leaf of the double door leading to the back   13
balcony. "Flap, flap, flap." The door swung in the wind. We could see the treetops by the
hillside rustling to and fro against a pale blue sky. An imperceptible presence had drifted
in with the wind. The same careless walk and shuffling feet, the same daredevil air—
except that the eyes were lusterless, dripping blood; the tongue hanging out, gasping for
air. As usual, he was late. But he had come back to claim his place.

"I died a tragic death," his voice said. "I have as much right as you to be here. This   14
is my seat." We heard him; we knew he was back.

. . . So Tsi-fai: Standing in the corner for being late, for forgetting his homework, for   15
talking in class, for using foul language. So Tsi-fai: Palm outstretched, chest sticking
out, holding his breath: "Tat. Tat. Tat." Down came the teacher's wooden ruler, twenty times on each hand. Never batting an eyelash: then back to facing the wall in the
corner by the door. So Tsi-fai: grimy shirt, disheveled hair, defiant sneer. So Tsi-fai.
Incorrigible, hopeless, and without hope.

The girls in front gasped and shrank back in their chairs. Mung Gu-liang went to   16 the door, held the doorknob in one hand, poked her head out, and peered into the empty balcony. Then, with a determined jerk, she pulled the door shut. Quickly crossing herself, she returned to the teacher's desk. Her black cross swung upon the front of her gray habit as she hurried across the room. "Don't be silly!" she scolded the frightened girls in the front row.

17   What really happened? After all these years, my mind is still haunted by this scene. What happened to So Tsi-fai? What happened to me? What happened to all of us that year in sixth grade, when we were green and young and ready to fling our arms out for the world? All of a sudden, death claimed one of us and he was gone.

18   Who arbitrates between life and death? Who decides which life is worth preserving and prospering, and which to nip in its bud? How did it happen that I, at ten, turned out to be the star pupil, the lucky one, while my friend, a peasant's son, was shoveled under the heap and lost forever? How could it happen that this world would close off a young boy's life at fourteen just because he was poor, undisciplined, and lacked the training and support to pass his exams? What really happened?

19   Today, twenty-three years later, So Tsi-fai's ghost still haunts me. "I died a tragic death. I have as much right as you to be here. This is my seat." The voice I heard twenty-three years ago in my sixth-grade classroom follows me in my dreams. Is there anything I can do to lay it to rest?

Questions for Close Reading

1. What is the selection's thesis (or narrative point)? Locate the sentence(s) in which Liu states her main idea. If she doesn't state the narrative point explicitly, express it in your own words.

2. What is the immediate cause of So Tsi-fai's suicide? What other factors also come into play? Why might he have chosen the method to kill himself that he did?

3. How did Liu's home life compare to that of So Tsi-fai? What connections do you see between each one's family life and academic progress?

4. What does So Tsi-fai say when he returns as a ghost? What do his words indicate about his perception of the educational system—and of his place in it?

5. Refer to your dictionary as needed to define the following words used in the selection: *defiant* (paragraph 3), *incorrigible* (3), *scourge* (4), *subsidized* (5), *dilated* (11), *ether* (12), *imperceptible* (13), *lusterless* (13), and *arbitrates* (18).

Questions About the Writer's Craft

1. **The pattern.**   Most narratives establish a conflict and then move to its resolution. In "So Tsi-fai," however, the reader knows by paragraph 2 that the boy will commit suicide; flashbacks and flashforwards comprise the rest of the essay. Locate these flashbacks and flashforwards. How does Liu signal these time shifts?

2. Liu describes a number of relationships filled with conflict. Identify as many of these conflicted relationships as you can. How do they heighten the essay's narrative tension?

3. In paragraphs 3, 6, and 7, Liu calls attention to certain conversations by placing quotations in parentheses. How do these parenthetical quotations reinforce the contrast between the different ways the author and So Tsi-fai were treated?

4. Throughout the essay, Liu repeats significant material. For example, she repeats the boy's last words twice (3 and 9) as well as whole passages of description (3 and 15). What effect do you think Liu intended these repetitions to have? How do they support her narrative point?

Writing Assignments Using Narration as a Pattern of Development

∞ 1. The death of So Tsi-fai marks the end of the author's childhood, the end of the time when she was "green and young and ready to fling [her] arms out for the world." Write an essay about a time when you were forced to grow up suddenly or were faced with a sobering reality. Your moment of lost innocence might have occurred when you were a child; perhaps you had to cope with illness or divorce. Or your moment of loss may have come when you were an adult; maybe you learned about a relative's unsavory business practices or a respected boss's discriminatory hiring practices. Use vivid description and revealing dialog to convey the tension and conflict you felt in the moment of discovery. Remember, though, to include only those details that reinforce your narrative point. Before writing, you may want to read Audre Lorde's "The Fourth of July" (page 216) and Beth Johnson's "Bombs Bursting in Air" (page 245) for their powerful depiction of lost innocence.

2. Liu depicts the unfairness of an educational system that penalizes children simply because they are disadvantaged. Brainstorm with others to identify injustices that exist in our educational system. You might, for example, decide that teachers single out males for discipline, that students with learning disabilities get a second-rate education, that student athletes receive preferential treatment at grading time. Focusing on a specific educational level, select *one* such type of unfairness, and write an essay recounting two or three dramatic incidents of this inequity. To depict each incident fully, you'll need to reconstruct conversations and provide vivid narrative details, always keeping in mind the narrative point you want to make.

Writing Assignments Using Other Patterns of Development

3. Liu writes, "After all these years, my mind is still haunted by this scene." All of us have witnessed dramatic events that continue to exert power over us even

though they occurred in the past. Write an essay showing the effects of such an event on your life, behavior, attitudes, and values. Begin with a brief account of the event; then explain its consequences for you, making sure your discussion honors the inevitable complexity of cause-effect relationships.

4. Liu's teacher clearly has no concern for her students' self-esteem, a factor that many consider crucial to children's well-being and success. Brainstorm with others to identify as many strategies as possible that elementary school teachers could use to strengthen students' self-image. Select what you consider to be the most compelling strategies, and categorize them into types, such as "group work," "independent study," "leadership experiences," "teacher-student conferences," and so on. Then write an essay explaining the techniques and their value. Be sure to illustrate the strategies with specific examples drawn from your own and other people's experiences. Maya Angelou's "Sister Flowers" (page 178) and Mary Sherry's "In Praise of the 'F' Word" (page 480), will provide insight into the development of a healthy self-esteem.

Writing Assignment Using a Journal Entry as a Starting Point

5. Review your pre-reading journal entry, and select the most dramatic instance of bullying you witnessed as a child or adolescent. Then write an essay in which you analyze the causes and effects of the bullying incident. At the end of the essay, suggest ways that the bullying might have been prevented. To deepen your understanding of the bullying phenomenon, consider doing some research in the library and/or on the Internet.

ADDITIONAL
WRITING
TOPICS:
NARRATION

General Assignments

Write an essay on any of the following topics, using narration as the paper's dominant method of development. Be sure to select details that advance the essay's narrative purpose; you may even want to experiment with flashback or flashforward. In any case, keep the sequence of events clear by using transitional cues. Within the limited time span covered, use vigorous details and varied sentence structure to enliven the narrative. Tell the story from a consistent point of view.

1. An emergency that brought out the best or worst in you

2. The hazards of taking children out to eat

3. An incident that made you believe in fate

4. Your best or worst day at school or work

5. A major decision

6. An encounter with a machine

7. An important learning experience

8. A narrow escape

9. Your first date, first day on the job, or first anything

10. A memorable childhood experience

11. A fairy tale the way you would like to hear it told

12. A painful moment

13. An incredible but true story

14. A significant family event

15. An experience in which a certain emotion (pride, anger, regret, or some other) was dominant

Assignments with a Specific Purpose, Audience, and Point of View

On Campus

1. Write an article for your old high school newspaper. The article will be read primarily by seniors who are planning to go away to college next year. In the article, narrate a story that points to some truth about the "breaking away" stage of life.

2. A friend of yours has seen someone cheat on a test, plagiarize an entire paper, or seriously violate some other academic policy. In a letter, convince this friend to inform the instructor or a campus administrator by narrating an incident in which a witness did (or did not) speak up in such a situation. Tell what happened as a result.

At Home or in the Community

3. You have had a disturbing encounter with one of the people who seems to have "fallen through the cracks" of society—a street person, an unwanted child, or anyone else who is alone and abandoned. Write a letter to the local newspaper describing this encounter. Your purpose is to arouse people's indignation and compassion and to get help for such unfortunates.

4. Your younger brother, sister, relative, or neighborhood friend can't wait to be your age. Write a letter in which you narrate a dramatic story that shows the young person that your age isn't as wonderful as he or she thinks. Be sure to select a story that the person can understand and appreciate.

On the Job

5. As fund-raiser for a particular organization (for example, Red Cross, SPCA, Big Brothers/Big Sisters), you're sending a newsletter to contributors. Support your cause by telling the story of a time when your organization made all the difference—the blood donation that saved a life, the animal that was rescued from abuse, and so on.

6. A customer has written a letter to you (or your boss) telling about a bad experience that he or she had with someone in your workplace. On the basis of that single experience, the customer now regards your company and its employees with great suspicion. It's your responsibility to respond to this complaint. Write a letter to the customer balancing his or her negative picture by narrating a story that shows the "flip side" of your company and its employees.

13
ILLUSTRATION

WHAT IS ILLUSTRATION?

If someone asked you, "Have you been to any good restaurants lately?" you probably wouldn't answer "Yes" and then immediately change the subject. Most likely, you would go on to **illustrate** with examples. Perhaps you'd give the names of restaurants you've enjoyed and talk briefly about the specific things you liked: the attractive prices, the tasty main courses, the pleasant service, the tempting desserts. Such examples and details are needed to convince others that your opinion—in this or any matter—is valid. Similarly, when you talk about larger and more important issues, people won't pay much attention to your opinion if all you do is string together vague generalizations: "We have to do something about acid rain. It's had disastrous consequences for the environment. Its negative effects increase every year. Action must be taken to control the problem." To be taken seriously and convince others that your point is well founded, you must provide specific supporting examples: "The forests in the Adirondacks are dying"; "yesterday's rainfall was fifty times more acidic than normal"; "Pine Lake, in the northern part of the state, was once a great fishing spot but now has no fish population."

Examples are equally important when you write an essay. It's not vague generalities and highfalutin abstractions that make writing impressive. Just the opposite is true. Facts, details, anecdotes, statistics, expert opinion, and personal observations are at the heart of effective writing, giving your work substance and solidity.

HOW ILLUSTRATION FITS YOUR PURPOSE AND AUDIENCE

The wording of assignments and essay exam questions may signal the need for illustration:

> Soap operas, whether shown during the day or in the evening, are among the most popular television programs. Why do you think this is so? Provide specific examples to support your position.

> Some observers claim that college students are less interested in learning than in getting ahead in their careers. Cite evidence to support or refute this claim.

> A growing number of people feel that parents should not allow young children to participate in highly competitive team sports. Basing your conclusion on your own experiences and observations, indicate whether you think this point of view is reasonable.

Such phrases as "Provide specific examples," "Cite evidence," and "Basing your conclusion on your own experiences and observations" signal that each essay would be developed through illustration.

Usually, though, you won't be told so explicitly to provide examples. Instead, as you think about the best way to achieve your essay's purpose, you'll see the need for illustrative details—no matter which patterns of development you use. For instance, to *persuade* skeptical readers that the country needs a national health system, you might mention specific cases to dramatize the inadequacy of our current health-care system: a family bankrupted by medical bills; an uninsured accident victim turned away by a hospital; a chronically ill person rapidly deteriorating because he didn't have enough money to visit a doctor. Or imagine a lightly satiric piece that pokes fun at cat lovers. Insisting that "cat people" are pretty strange creatures, you might make your point—and make readers chuckle—with a series of examples *contrasting* cat lovers and dog lovers: the qualities admired by each group (loyalty in dogs versus independence in cats) and the different expectations each group has for its pets (dog lovers want Fido to be obedient and lovable, whereas cat lovers are satisfied with Felix's occasional spurts of docility and affection). Similarly, you would supply examples in a *causal analysis* speculating on the likely impact of a proposed tuition hike at your college. To convince the college administration of the probable negative effects of such a hike, you might cite the following examples: articles reporting a nationwide upswing in student transfers to less expensive schools; statistics indicating a significant drop in grades among already employed students forced to work more hours to pay increased tuition costs; interviews with students too financially strapped to continue their college education.

Whether you use illustration as a primary or supplemental method of development, it serves a number of important purposes. For one thing, illustrations make writing *interesting*. Assume you're writing an essay showing that television commercials are biased against women. Your essay would be lifeless and boring if all it did was repeat, in a general way, that commercials present stereotyped views of women:

Original

An anti-female bias is rampant in television commercials. It is very much alive, yet most viewers seem to take it all in stride. Few people protest the obviously sexist characters and statements on such commercials. Surely, these commercials misrepresent the way most of us live.

Without interesting particulars, readers may respond, "Who cares?" But if you provide specific examples, you'll attract your readers' attention:

Revised

An anti-female bias is rampant in television commercials. Although millions of women hold responsible jobs outside the home, commercials continue to portray women as simple creatures who spend much of their time thinking about wax buildup, cottony-soft bathroom tissue, and static-free clothes. Men, apparently, have better things to do than fret over such mundane household matters. How many commercials can you recall that depict men proclaiming the virtues of squeaky-clean dishes or sparkling bathrooms? Not many.

Illustrations also make writing *persuasive*. Most writing conveys a point, but many readers are reluctant to accept someone else's point of view unless evidence demonstrates its validity. Imagine you're writing an essay showing that latchkey children are more self-sufficient and emotionally secure than children who return from school to a home where a parent awaits them. Your thesis is obviously controversial. Without specific examples—from your own experience, personal observations, or research studies—your readers would undoubtedly question your position's validity.

Further, illustrations help *explain* difficult, abstract, or unusual ideas. Suppose you're assigned an essay on a complex subject such as inflation, zero population growth, or radiation exposure. As a writer, you have a responsibility to your readers to make these difficult concepts concrete and understandable. If writing an essay on radiation exposure in everyday life, you might start by providing specific examples of home appliances that emit radiation—color televisions, computers, and microwave ovens—and tell exactly how much radiation we absorb in a typical day from such equipment. To illustrate further the extent of our radiation exposure, you could also provide specifics about unavoidable sources of natural radiation (the sun, for instance) and details about the widespread use of radiation in medicine (X rays, radiation therapy). These examples would ground your discussion, making it immediate and concrete, preventing it from flying off into the vague and theoretical.

Finally, examples help *prevent unintended ambiguity*. All of us have experienced the frustration of having someone misinterpret what we say. In face-to-face communication, we can provide on-the-spot clarification. In writing, however, instantaneous feedback isn't available, so it's crucial that meaning be as unambiguous as possible. Illustrations will help. Assume you're writing an essay asserting that ineffective teaching is on the rise in today's high schools. To clarify what you mean by "ineffective," you provide illustrations: the instructor who spends so much time disciplining unruly students that he never gets around to teaching; the moonlighting teacher who is so tired in class that she regularly takes naps during tests; the teacher who accepts obviously plagiarized reports because he's grateful that students hand in something. Without such concrete examples, your readers will supply their own ideas—and these may not be what you had in mind. Readers might imagine "ineffective" to mean harsh and punitive, whereas concrete examples would show that you intend it to mean out of control and irresponsible.

Prewriting strategies

The following checklist shows how you can apply to illustration some of the prewriting techniques discussed in Chapter 2.

☑ ILLUSTRATION: A PREWRITING CHECKLIST

Choose a Subject to Illustrate

☐ What general situation or phenomenon (for example, campus apathy, organic farming) can you depict through illustration?

☐ What difficult or misunderstood concept (nuclear winter, passive aggression) would examples help to explain and make concrete?

Determine Your Purpose, Audience, Tone, and Point of View

☐ What is your purpose in writing?

☐ What audience do you have in mind?

☐ What tone and point of view will best serve your purpose and lead readers to adopt the desired attitude toward the subject being illustrated?

Use Prewriting to Generate Examples

☐ How can brainstorming, freewriting, journal entries, or mapping help you generate relevant examples (events, facts, anecdotes, quotations) from your own or others' experiences?

☐ How could library research help you gather pertinent examples (expert opinion, case studies, statistics)?

Strategies for Using Illustration in an Essay

After prewriting, you're ready to draft your essay. The following suggestions will be helpful whether you use illustration as a dominant or supportive pattern of development.

1. Select the examples to include.   Examples can take several forms, including specific names (of people, places, products, and so on), anecdotes, personal observations, expert opinion, as well as facts, statistics, and case studies gathered through research. Once you've used prewriting to generate as many examples as possible, you're ready to limit your examples to the strongest. Keeping your thesis, audience, tone, and point of view in mind, ask yourself several key questions: "Which examples support my thesis? Which do not? Which are most convincing? Which are most likely to interest readers and clarify meaning?"

You may include several brief examples within a single sentence:

> The French people's fascination with some American literary figures, such as Poe and Hawthorne, is understandable, but their great respect for "artists" like comedian Jerry Lewis is a mystery.

Or you may develop a paragraph with a number of "for instances":

> A uniquely American style of movie-acting reached its peak in the 1950s. Certain charismatic actors completely abandoned the stage techniques and tradition that had been the foundation of acting up to that time. Instead of articulating their lines clearly, the actors mumbled; instead of making firm eye contact with their colleagues, they hung their heads, shifted their eyes, even talked with their eyes closed. Marlon Brando, Montgomery Clift, and James Dean were three actors who exemplified this new trend.

As the preceding paragraph shows, *several examples* are usually needed to achieve your purpose. An essay with the thesis "Rock videos are dangerously violent" wouldn't be convincing if you gave only one example of a violent rock video. Several strong examples would be needed for readers to feel you had illustrated your point sufficiently.

As a general rule, you should strive for variety in the kinds of examples you include. For instance, you might choose a *personal-experience example* drawn from your own life or from the life of someone you know. Such examples pack the wallop of personal authority and lend drama to writing. Or you might include a *typical-case example,* an actual event or situation that did occur—but not to you or to anyone you know. (Perhaps you learned about the event through a magazine article, newspaper account, or television report.) The objective nature of such cases makes them especially convincing. You might also include a speculative or *hypothetical example* ("Imagine how difficult it must be for an elderly person to carry bags of groceries from the market to a bus stop several blocks away"). You'll find that hypothetical cases are effective for clarifying and dramatizing key points, but be sure to acknowledge that the example is indeed invented ("*Suppose* that . . ." or "Let's for a moment *assume* that . . ."). Make certain, too, that the invented situation is easily imagined and could conceivably happen. Finally, you might create a *generalized example*—one that is a composite of the typical or usual. Such generalized examples are often signaled by words that involve the reader ("*All of us*, at one time or another, have been driven to distraction by a trivial annoyance like the buzzing of a fly or the sting of a papercut"), or they may refer to humanity in general ("When *most people* get a compliment, they perk up, preen, and think the praise-giver is blessed with astute powers of observation").

Occasionally, *one extended example*, fully developed with many details, can support an essay. It might be possible, for instance, to support the thesis "Federal legislation should raise the legal drinking age to twenty-one" with a single compelling, highly detailed example of the effects of one teenager's drunken-driving spree.

The examples you choose must also be *relevant*; that is, they must have direct bearing on the point you want to make. You would have a hard time convincing readers that Americans have callous attitudes toward the elderly if you described the wide range of new programs, all staffed by volunteers, at a well-financed center for senior citizens. Because these examples *contradict*, rather than support, your thesis, readers are apt to dismiss what you have to say.

In addition, try to select *dramatic* examples. Say you're writing an essay to show that society needs to take more steps to protect children from abuse. Simply stating that many parents hit their children isn't likely to form a strong impression in the reader's mind. However, graphic examples (children with stab wounds, welts, and burn marks) are apt to create a sense of urgency in the reader.

Make certain, too, that your examples are *accurate*. Exercise special caution when using statistics. An old saying warns that there are lies, damned lies, and statistics— meaning that statistics can be misleading. A commercial may claim, "In a taste test, eighty percent of those questioned indicated that they preferred Fizzy Cola." Impressed? Don't be—at least, not until you find out how the test was conducted. Perhaps the participants had to choose between Fizzy Cola and battery acid, or perhaps there were only five participants, all Fizzy Cola vice presidents.

Finally, select *representative* examples. Picking the oddball, one-in-a-million example to support a point—and passing it off as typical—is dishonest. Consider an essay with the thesis "Part-time jobs contribute to academic success." Citing only one example of a student who works at a job twenty-five hours a week while earning straight A's isn't playing fair. Why not? You've made a *hasty generalization* based on only one case. To be convincing, you need to show how holding down a job affects *most* students' academic performance. (For more on hasty generalizations, see page 458.)

2. Develop your examples sufficiently. To ensure that you get your ideas across, your examples must be *specific*. An essay on the types of heroes in American movies wouldn't succeed if you simply strung together a series of undeveloped examples in paragraphs like this one:

Original

Heroes in American movies usually fall into types. One kind of hero is the tight-lipped loner, men like Clint Eastwood and Humphrey Bogart. Another movie hero is the quiet, shy, or fumbling type who has appeared in movies since the beginning. The main characteristic

of this hero is lovableness, as seen in actors like Jimmy Stewart.
Perhaps the most one-dimensional and predictable hero is the
superman who battles tough odds. This kind of hero is best
illustrated by Sylvester Stallone as Rocky and Rambo.

If you developed the essay in this way—moving from one undeveloped example
to another—you would be doing little more than making a list. To be effective, key
examples must be expanded in sufficient detail. The examples in the preceding
paragraph could be developed in paragraphs of their own. You could, for
instance, develop the first example this way:

Revised

    Heroes can be tight-lipped loners who appear out of nowhere, form no
permanent attachments, and walk, drive, or ride off into the sunset. In
most of his Westerns, from the low-budget "spaghetti Westerns" of the
1960s to Unforgiven in 1992, Clint Eastwood personifies this kind of
hero. He is remote, mysterious, and untalkative. Yet he guns down an
evil sheriff, runs other villains out of town, and helps a handicapped
girl--acts that cement his heroic status. The loner might also be Sam
Spade as played by Humphrey Bogart. Spade solves the crime and sends
the guilty off to jail, yet he holds his emotions in check and has no
permanent ties beyond his faithful secretary and shabby office. One gets
the feeling that he could walk away from these, too, if necessary. Even
in The Right Stuff, an account of America's early astronauts, the
scriptwriters mold Chuck Yeager, the man who broke the sound barrier,
into a classic loner. Yeager, portrayed by the aloof Sam Shepherd, has
a wife, but he is nevertheless insular. Taking mute pride in his ability to distance himself from politicians, bureaucrats, even colleagues,
he soars into space, dignified and detached.

(For hints on making evidence specific, see pages 69–72 in Chapter 6.)

3. Organize the examples. If, as is usually the case, several examples support your
point, be sure to present the examples in an *organized* manner. Often you'll find that
other *patterns of development* (cause-effect, comparison-contrast, definition, and so on)
suggest ways to sequence examples. Let's say you're writing an essay showing that stay-
at-home vacations offer numerous opportunities to relax. You might begin the essay
with examples that *contrast* stay-at-home and get-away vacations. Then you might
move to a *process analysis* that illustrates different techniques for unwinding at home.
The essay might end with examples showing the *effect* of such leisurely at-home breaks.

    Finally, you need to select an *organizational approach consistent* with your *purpose*
and *thesis*. Imagine you're writing an essay about students' adjustment during the
first months of college. The supporting examples could be arranged *chronological-*
ly. You might start by illustrating the ambivalence many students feel the first day
of college when their parents leave for home; you might then offer an anecdote or

two about students' frequent calls to Mom and Dad during the opening weeks of the semester; the essay might close with an account of students' reluctance to leave campus at the midyear break.

Similarly, an essay demonstrating that a room often reflects the character of its occupant might be organized *spatially:* from the empty soda cans on the floor to the spitballs on the ceiling. In an essay illustrating the kinds of skills taught in a composition course, you might move from *simple* to *complex* examples: starting with relatively matter-of-fact skills like spelling and punctuation and ending with more conceptually difficult skills like formulating a thesis and organizing an essay. Last, the *emphatic sequence*—in which you lead from your first example to your final, most significant one—is another effective way to organize an essay with many examples. A paper about Americans' characteristic impatience might progress from minor examples (dependence on fast food, obsession with ever-faster mail delivery) to more disturbing manifestations of impatience (using drugs as quick solutions to problems, advocating simple answers to complex international problems: "Bomb them!").

4. Choose a point of view.   Many essays developed by illustration place the subject in the foreground and the writer in the background. Such an approach calls for the *third-person point of view.* For example, even if you draw examples from your own personal experience, you can present them without using the *first-person* "I." You might convert such personal material into generalized examples (see page 233), or you might describe the personal experience as if it happened to someone else. Of course, you may use the first person if the use of "I" will make the example more believable and dramatic. But remember: Just because an event happened to you personally doesn't mean you have to use the first-person point of view.

REVISION STRATEGIES

Once you have a draft of the essay, you're ready to revise. The following checklist will help you and those giving you feedback apply to illustration some of the revision techniques discussed in Chapters 7 and 8.

 ILLUSTRATION: A REVISION/PEER REVIEW CHECKLIST

Revise Overall Meaning and Structure

☐ What thesis is being advanced? Which examples don't support the thesis? Should these examples be deleted, or should the thesis be reshaped to fit the examples? Why?

☐ Which patterns of development and methods of organization (chronological, spatial, simple-to-complex, emphatic) provide the essay's framework? Would other ordering principles be more effective? If so, which ones?

Revise Paragraph Development

☐ Which paragraphs contain too many or too few examples? Which contain examples that are too brief or too extended? Which include insufficiently or overly detailed examples?

☐ Which paragraphs rely on predictable examples? How could the examples be made more compelling?

☐ Which paragraphs include examples that are atypical or inaccurate?

Revise Sentences and Words

☐ What signal devices (*for example, for instance, in particular, such as*) introduce examples and clarify the line of thought? Where are there too many or too few of these devices?

☐ Where would more varied sentence structure heighten the effect of the essay's illustrations?

☐ Where would more concrete and specific words make the examples more effective?

STUDENT ESSAY: FROM PREWRITING THROUGH REVISION

The student essay that follows was written by Michael Pagano in response to this assignment:

> One implication in Beth Johnson's "Bombs Bursting in Air" is that, given life's unantici-pated tragedies, people need to focus on what's really important rather than on trivial com-plications and distractions. Observe closely the way you and others conduct your daily lives. Use your observations for an essay that supports or refutes Johnson's point of view.

After deciding to write an essay on the way possessions complicate life, Michael sat down at his word processor and did some *freewriting* to generate material on the topic. His original freewriting follows; the handwritten comments indicate Michael's later efforts to develop and shape this material. Note that Michael deleted some points, added others, and made several items more specif-ic; he also labeled and sequenced key ideas. These annotations paved the way for a sentence outline, which is presented after the freewriting.

Freewriting

① Buying

I shop too much. So do my parents--practically every weekend ~~and nearly every holiday except Christmas and Easter. All those Washington's Birthday sales.~~ Then they yell at us kids for watching so much TV, although they're not around to do much with us. In fact, Mom and

④ Discarding items

Dad were the ones who thought our old TV wasn't good [19-inch] [35-inch] enough anymore so they replaced it with a huge color set. I remember all those annoying phone calls when they *classified section* put the ad in the paper to sell the old set. People coming and going. Then Mom and Dad only got $25 for it anyway. It wasn't worth paying for the ad. ~~They never seem to come out ahead.~~ No wonder Mom works part-time at the *2nd job* library and Dad stays so late at the office. I'm getting *overtime* into the same situation. Already up to my ears in debt, *time payments* paying off the car. I spend hours washing it and waxing it, *③ vacuuming car—maintenance* and it doesn't even fit into the garage, which is loaded with discarded junk. The whole house is cluttered. Maybe that's why people move so much--to escape the clutter. There was hardly room for my new word processor in my room. I also have to shove my new clothes into the closets and drawers. My snazzy new pants get all wrinkled. They shrank when I washed them. Now they're too tight. I should have sent them to the dry cleaners. But I'd already paid enough for them. *My computer's giving me trouble* ~~Well, everything's shoddy nowadays.~~ Possessions don't hold *conclusion?* up. So what lasts? Basic values--love, family, friends.

⑤ Running into debt

② Running out of room

③ Having maintenance problems

Outline

Thesis: We clutter our lives with material goods.
  I. We waste a lot of time deciding what to buy.
     A. We window-shop for good-looking footwear.
     B. We look through magazines for stereos and exercise equipment.
     C. Family life suffers when everyone is out shopping.
 II. Once we take our new purchases home, we find we don't have enough room for them.
     A. We stack things in crowded closets, garages, and basements.
     B. When things get too cluttered, we simply move.
III. Our possessions require continual maintenance.
     A. Cars have to be washed and waxed.
     B. New pants have to go to the cleaners.
     C. Word processors and other items break down and have to be replaced.
 IV. Before we replace broken items, we try to get rid of them by placing ads in the classified section.
     A. We have to deal with annoying phone calls.
     B. We have to deal with people coming to the house to see the items.
  V. Our mania for possessions puts us in debt.
     A. We accumulate enormous credit-card balances.
     B. We take second jobs or work overtime to make time payments.

Now read Michael's paper, "Pursuit of Possessions," noting the similarities and differences among his freewriting, outline, and final essay. You'll see, for example, that Michael changed the "I" of his freewriting to the more general "We" in the outline and essay. He made this change because he wanted readers to see themselves in the situations being illustrated. In addition, Michael's outline, while more detailed than his freewriting, doesn't include highly concrete examples, but the essay does. In the outline, for instance, he simply states, "Word processors and other items break down. . . ." In the essay, though, he spins out this point with vivid details: "The home computer starts to lose data, the microwave has to have its temperature controls adjusted, and the DVD player has to be serviced when a disc becomes jammed."

As you read Michael's essay, also consider how well it applies the principles of illustration. (The commentary that follows the paper will help you look at the essay more closely and will give you some sense of how Michael went about revising his first draft.)

Pursuit of Possessions

By Michael Pagano

Introduction	In the essay "Bombs Bursting in Air," Beth Johnson develops the extended metaphor of bombs exploding unexpectedly to represent the tragedies that occur without warning in our daily lives. Herself a survivor of innumerable life bombs, Johnson suggests that in light of life's fragility, we need to remember and appreciate what's really important to us. But very often, we lose sight of what really matters in our lives, instead occupying ourselves with trivial distractions. In

Thesis ⟶ particular, many of us choose to spend our lives in pursuit of material possessions. Much of our time goes

Plan of development ⟶ into buying new things, dealing with the complications they create, and working madly to buy more things or pay for the things we already have.

Topic sentence ⟶ We devote a great deal of our lives to acquiring the material goods we imagine are essential to our well-being. Hours are spent planning and thinking about our future purchases. We window-shop for designer running shoes; we leaf through magazines looking at ads for elaborate stereo equipment; we research back issues of

The first of three paragraphs in a chronological sequence
Consumer Reports to find out about recent developments in exercise equipment. Moreover, once we find what we are looking for, more time is taken up when we decide to actually buy the items. How do we find this time? That's easy. We turn evenings, weekends, and holidays--times that

1

2

used to be set aside for family and friends--into shopping expeditions. No wonder family life is deteriorating
and children spend so much time in front of television
sets. Their parents are seldom around.

3   As soon as we take our new purchases home, they begin ⟵— Topic sentence
to complicate our lives. A sleek new sports car has to
be washed, waxed, and vacuumed. A fashionable pair of
overpriced dress pants can't be thrown in the washing
machine but has to be taken to the dry cleaner. New
stereo equipment has to be connected with a tangled network of cables to the TV, computer, radio, and cassette
deck. Eventually, of course, the inevitable happens. Our
indispensable possessions break down and need to be
repaired. The home computer starts to lose data, the
microwave has to have its temperature controls adjusted,
and the DVD player has to be serviced when a disc
becomes jammed in the machine.

The second paragraph
in the chronological
sequence

A paragraph with many
specific examples

4   After more time has gone by, we sometimes discover ⟵———Topic sentence
that our purchases don't suit us anymore, and so we
decide to replace them. Before making our replacement
purchases, though, we have to find ways to get rid of the
old items. If we want to replace our 19-inch television
set with a 35-inch color set, we have to find time to put
an ad in the classified section of the paper. Then we
have to handle phone calls and set up times people can
come to look at the old TV. We could store the set in the
basement--if we are lucky enough to find a spot that
isn't already filled with other discarded purchases.

The third paragraph in
the chronological
sequence

5   Worst of all, this mania for possessions often influ- ⟵——————— Topic sentence with
ences our approach to work. It is not unusual for people   emphasis signal
to take a second or even a third job to pay off the debt
they fall into because they have overbought. After paying
for food, clothing, and shelter, many people see the rest
of their paycheck go to Visa, MasterCard, department
store charge accounts, and time payments. Panic sets in
when they realize there simply is not enough money to
cover all their expenses. Just to stay afloat, people may
have to work overtime or take on additional jobs.

6   It is clear that many of us have allowed the pursuit   Conclusion
of possessions to dominate our lives. We are so busy

buying, maintaining, and paying for our worldly goods that
we do not have much time to think about what is really
important. We should try to step back from our compulsive
need for more of everything and get in touch with the
basic values that are the real point of our lives.

Commentary

Thesis, Other Patterns of Development, and Plan of Development

In "Pursuit of Possessions," Michael analyzes the mania for acquiring material goods that permeates our society. He begins by addressing an implication conveyed in Beth Johnson's "Bombs Bursting in Air"—that life's fragility dictates that we need to focus on what really matters in our lives. This reference to Johnson gives Michael a chance to contrast the reflective way she suggests we should live with the acquisitive and frenzied way many people lead their lives. This contrast leads to the essay's thesis: "[M]any of us choose to spend our lives in pursuit of material possessions."

Besides introducing the basic contrast at the heart of the essay, Michael's opening paragraph helps readers see that the essay contains an element of *causal analysis*. The final sentence of the introductory paragraph lays out the effects of our possession obsession. This sentence also serves as the essay's *plan of development* and reveals that Michael feels the pursuit of possessions negatively affects our lives in three key ways.

Essays of this length often don't need a plan of development. But since Michael's paper is filled with many *examples*, the plan of development helps readers see how all the details relate to the essay's central point.

Evidence

Support for the thesis consists of numerous examples presented in the *first-person plural point of view* ("*We* lose sight . . .," "*We* devote a great deal of our lives . . .," and so on). Many of these examples seem drawn from Michael's, his friends', or his family's experiences; however, to emphasize the events' universality, Michael converts these essentially personal examples into generalized ones that "we" all experience.

These examples, in turn, are organized around the three major points signaled by the plan of development. Michael uses one paragraph to develop his first and third points and two paragraphs to develop his second point. Each of the four supporting paragraphs is focused by a *topic sentence* that appears at the beginning of the paragraph. The transitional phrase "Worst of all" (paragraph 5) signals that Michael has sequenced his major points *emphatically*, saving for last the issue he considers most significant: how the "mania for possessions . . . influences our approach to work."

Organizational Strategies

Emphatic order isn't Michael's only organizational technique. When reading the paper, you probably felt that there was an easy flow from one supporting paragraph to the next. How does Michael achieve such *coherence between paragraphs?* For one thing, he sequences paragraphs 2–4 *chronologically:* what happens before a purchase is made; what happens afterward. Secondly, topic sentences in paragraphs 3 and 4 include *signal devices* that indicate this passage of time. The topic sentences also strengthen coherence by *linking back* to the preceding paragraph: "*As soon as we take our new purchases home, they* . . . complicate our lives" and "*After more time has gone by,* we . . . discover that our purchases don't suit us anymore."

The same organizing strategies are used *within paragraphs* to make the essay coherent. Details in paragraphs 2–4 are sequenced *chronologically,* and to help readers follow the chronology, Michael uses *signal devices:* "*Moreover, once* we find what we are looking for, more time is taken up . . ." (2); "*Eventually,* of course, the inevitable happens" (3); "*Then* we have to handle phone calls . . ." (4).

Problems with Paragraph Development

You probably recall that an essay developed primarily through illustration must include examples that are *relevant, interesting, convincing, representative, accurate,* and *specific.* On the whole, Michael's examples meet these requirements. The third and fourth paragraphs, especially, include vigorous details that show how our mania for buying things can govern our lives. We may even laugh with self-recognition when reading about "overpriced dress pants that can't be thrown in the washing machine" or a basement "filled . . . with discarded purchases."

The fifth paragraph, however, is underdeveloped. We know that this paragraph presents what Michael considers his most significant point, but the paragraph's examples are rather *flat* and *unconvincing.* To make this final section more compelling, Michael could mention specific people who overspend, revealing how much they are in debt and how much they have to work to become solvent again. Or he could cite a television documentary or magazine article dealing with the issue of consumer debt. Such specifics would give the paragraph the solidity it now lacks.

Shift in Tone

The fifth paragraph has a second, more subtle problem: a *shift in tone.* Although Michael has, up to this point, been critical of our possession-mad culture, he has poked fun at our obsession and kept his tone conversational and gently satiric. In this paragraph, though, he adopts a serious tone, and, in the next paragraph, his tone becomes even weightier, almost preachy. It is, of course, legitimate to have a serious message in a lightly satiric piece. In fact, most satiric writing has such an additional layer of meaning. But because Michael has trouble blending these two moods, there's a jarring shift in the essay.

Shift in Focus

The second paragraph shows another kind of shift—in *focus.* The paragraph's controlling idea is that too much time is spent acquiring possessions. However, starting with "No wonder family life is deteriorating," Michael includes two sentences that introduce a complex issue beyond the scope of the essay. Since the sentences disrupt the paragraph's unity, they should be deleted.

Revising the First Draft

Although the final version of the essay needs work in spots, it's much stronger than Michael's first draft. To see how Michael went about revising the draft, compare his paper's second and third supporting paragraphs with his draft version reprinted here. The annotations, numbered in order of importance, show the ideas Michael hit upon when he returned to his first draft and reworked this section.

Original Version of the Second Paragraph

② Awkward first sentence

① Paragraph goes in too many directions. Cut idea about moving since not enough space.

③ Make problem with pants more specific

④ Develop more fully

> Our lives are spent not only buying things but in dealing with the inevitable complications that are created by our newly acquired possessions. First, we have to find places to put all the objects we bring home. More clothes demand more closets; a second car demands more garage space; a home-entertainment center requires elaborate shelving. We shouldn't be surprised that the average American family moves once every three years. A good many families move simply because they need more space to store all the things they buy. In addition, our possessions demand maintenance time. A person who gets a new car will spend hours washing it, waxing it, and vacuuming it. A new pair of pants has to go to the dry cleaners. New stereo systems have to be connected to already existing equipment. Eventually, of course, the inevitable happens. Our new items need to be repaired. Or we get sick of them and decide to replace them. Before making our replacement purchases, though, we have to get rid of the old items. That can be a real inconvenience.

Referring to the revision checklist on pages 235–236 helped Michael see that the paragraph rambled and lacked energy. He started to revise by tightening the first sentence, making it more focused and less awkward. Certainly, the revised sentence ("As soon as we take our new purchases home, they begin to complicate our lives") is crisper than the original. Next, he decided to omit the discussion about finding places to put new possessions; these sentences about inadequate closet, garage, and shelf space were so exaggerated that they undercut the valid point he wanted to make. He also chose to eliminate the sentences about the mobility of American families. This was, he felt, an interesting point, but it introduced an issue too complex to be included in the paragraph.

Michael strengthened the rest of the paragraph by making his examples more specific. A "new car" became a "sleek new sports car," and a "pair of pants" became a "fashionable pair of overpriced dress pants." Michael also realized he had to do more than merely write, "Eventually, . . . our new items need to be repaired." This point had to be dramatized by sharp, convincing details.

Therefore, Michael added lively examples to describe how high-tech possessions—microwaves, home computers, DVD players—break down. Similarly,
Michael realized it wasn't enough simply to say, as he had in the original, that we
run into problems when we try to replace out-of-favor purchases. Vigorous details
were again needed to illustrate the point. Michael thus used a typical "replace-
able" (an old TV) as his key example and showed the annoyance involved in
handling phone calls and setting up appointments so that people could see the TV.

After adding these specifics, Michael realized that he had enough material to
devote a separate paragraph to the problems associated with replacing old purchases. By dividing his original paragraph, Michael ended up with two well-
focused paragraphs, rather than a single rambling one.

In short, Michael strengthened his essay through substantial revision. Another
round of rewriting would have made the essay stronger still. Even without this
additional work, Michael's essay provides an interesting perspective on a current
social preoccupation.

ACTIVITIES: ILLUSTRATION

Prewriting Activities

1. Imagine you're writing two essays: One is a serious paper analyzing why large
   numbers of public school teachers leave the profession each year; the other is
   a light essay defining *preppie, thug,* or some other slang term used to describe
   a kind of person. Jot down ways you might use examples in each essay.

2. Use mapping or another prewriting technique to gather examples illustrating
   the truth of *one* of the following familiar sayings. Then, using the same or a different prewriting technique, accumulate examples that counter the saying.
   Weigh both sets of examples to determine the saying's validity. After developing
   an appropriate thesis, decide which examples you would elaborate in an essay.

   a. Haste makes waste.

   b. There's no use crying over spilled milk.

   c. A bird in the hand is worth two in the bush.

3. Turn back to activity 4 and activity 5 in Chapter 4, and select *one* thesis statement for which you didn't develop supporting evidence earlier. Identify a purpose, audience, tone, and point of view for an essay with this thesis. Then meet
   with at least one other person to generate as many examples as possible to support the thesis. Next, evaluate the material to determine which examples
   should be eliminated. Finally, from the remaining examples, take the strongest
   one and develop it as fully as you can.

4. Freewrite or use your journal to generate examples illustrating how widespread a recent fad or trend has become. After reviewing your prewriting to determine a possible thesis, narrow the examples to those you would retain for an essay. How might the patterns of development or a chronological, emphatic, spatial, or simple-to-complex approach help you sequence the examples?

Revising Activities

5. The following paragraph is from the first draft of an essay about the decline of small-town shopping districts. The paragraph is meant to show what small towns can do to revitalize business. Revise the paragraph, strengthening it with specific and convincing examples.

> A small town can compete with a large new mall for shoppers.
> But merchants must work together, modernizing the stores and
> making the town's main street pleasant, even fun to walk. They
> should also copy the malls' example by including attention-
> getting events as often as possible.

6. The paragraph that follows is from the first draft of an essay showing how knowledge of psychology can help us understand behavior that might otherwise seem baffling. The paragraph is intended to illustrate the meaning of the psychological term *superego*. Revise the paragraph, replacing its vague, unconvincing examples with one extended example that conveys the meaning of *superego* clearly and dramatically.

> The superego is the part of us that makes us feel guilty
> when we do something that we know is wrong. When we act
> foolishly or wildly, we usually feel qualms about our actions
> later on. If we imagine ourselves getting revenge, we most
> likely discover that the thoughts make us feel bad. All of
> these are examples of the superego at work.

7. Reprinted here is a paragraph from the first draft of a light-spirited essay showing that Americans' pursuit of change for change's sake has drawbacks. The paragraph is meant to illustrate that infatuation with newness costs consumers money yet leads to no improvement in product quality. How effective is the paragraph? Which examples are specific and convincing? Which are not? Do any seem nonrepresentative, offensive, or sexist? How could the paragraph's organization be improved? Consider these questions as you rewrite the paragraph. Add specific examples where needed. Depending on the way you revise, you may want to break this one paragraph into several.

> We end up paying for our passion for the new and improved.
> Trendy clothing styles convince us that last year's outfits are
> outdated, even though our old clothes are fine. Women are

especially vulnerable in this regard. What, though, about items
that have to be replaced periodically, like shampoo? Even slight
changes lead to new formulations requiring retooling of the
production process. That means increased manufacturing costs per
item--all of which get passed on to us, the consumer. Then
there are those items that tout new, trend-setting features that
make earlier versions supposedly obsolete. Some manufacturers,
for example, boast that their stereo sound systems transmit an
expanded-frequency range. The problem is that humans can't even
hear such frequencies, But the high-tech feature dazzles men who
are too naive to realize they're being hoodwinked.

PROFESSIONAL SELECTIONS: ILLUSTRATION

BETH JOHNSON

Beth Johnson (1956–) is a writer, occasional college teacher, and freelance editor.
A graduate of Goshen College and Syracuse University, Johnson is the author of several college texts, including *Everyday Heroes* (1996), and is coauthor of *Voices and Values* (2002). Containing profiles of men and women who have triumphed over obstacles to achieve personal and academic success, the book has provided a motivational boost to college students nationwide. She lives with her husband and three children in Lederach, Pennsylvania. The following piece is one of several that Johnson has written about the complexities and wonders of life.

Pre-Reading Journal Entry

When you were young, did adults acknowledge the existence of life's tragedies, or did they deny such harsh truths? In your journal, list several difficult events that you observed or experienced firsthand as a child. How did the adults in your life explain these hardships? In each case, do you think the adults acted appropriately? If not, how should they have responded?

BOMBS BURSTING IN AIR

1   It's Friday night and we're at the Olympics, the Junior Olympics, that is. My son is on a relay-race team competing against fourth-graders from all over the school district.

His little sister and I sit high in the stands, trying to pick Isaac out from the crowd of figures milling around on the field during these moments of pre-game confusion. The public address system sputters to life and summons our attention. "And now," the tinny voice rings out, "please join together in the singing of our national anthem."

"Oh saaay can you seeeeee," we begin. My arm rests around Maddie's shoulders. I   2
am touching her a lot today, and she notices. "Mom, you're *squishing* me," she chides, wriggling from my grip. I content myself with stroking her hair. News that reached me today makes me need to feel her near. We pipe along, squeaking out the impossibly high note of "land of the freeeeeeeee." Maddie clowns, half-singing, half-shouting the lyrics, hitting the "b's" explosively on "bombs bursting in air."

Bombs indeed, I think, replaying the sound of my friend's voice over the phone that   3
afternoon: "Bumped her head sledding. Took her in for an x-ray, just to make sure. There was something strange, so they did more tests . . . a brain tumor . . . Children's Hospital in Boston Tuesday . . . surgery, yes, right away. . . ." Maddie's playmate Shannon, only five years old. We'd last seen her at Halloween, dressed in her blue princess costume, and we'd talked of Furby and Scooby-Doo and Tootsie Rolls. Now her parents were hurriedly learning a new vocabulary—CAT scans, glioma, pediatric neurosurgery, and frontal lobe.[1] A bomb had exploded in their midst, and, like troops under attack, they were rallying in response.

The games over, the children and I edge our way out of the school parking lot,   4
bumper to bumper with other parents ferrying their families home. I tell the kids as casually as I can about Shannon. "She'll have to have an operation. It's lucky, really, that they found it by accident this way while it's small."

"I want to send her a present," Maddie announces. "That'd be nice," I say, glad to   5
keep the conversation on a positive note.

But my older son is with us now. Sam, who is thirteen, says, "She'll be OK, though,   6
right?" It's not a question, really; it's a statement that I must either agree with or contradict. I want to say yes. I want to say of course she'll be all right. I want them to inhabit a world where five-year-olds do not develop silent, mysterious growths in their brains, where "malignancy" and "seizure" are words for *New York Times* crossword puzzles, not for little girls. They would accept my assurance; they would believe me and sleep well tonight. But I can't; the bomb that exploded in Shannon's home has sent splinters of shrapnel into ours as well, and they cannot be ignored or lied away. "We hope she'll be just fine," I finally say. "She has very good doctors. She has wonderful parents who are doing everything they can. The tumor is small. Shannon's strong and healthy."

"*She'll* be OK," says Maddie matter-of-factly. "In school we read about a little boy   7
who had something wrong with his leg and he had an operation and got better. Can we go to Dairy Queen?"

Bombs on the horizon don't faze Maddie. Not yet. I can just barely remember from   8
my own childhood the sense that still surrounds her, that feeling of being cocooned within reassuring walls of security and order. Back then, Monday meant gym, Tuesday was pizza in the cafeteria, Wednesday brought clarinet lessons. Teachers stood in their familiar spots in the classrooms, telling us with reassuring simplicity that World War II

---

[1]A CAT scan is a computerized cross-sectional image of an internal body structure; a glioma is a tumor in the brain or spinal cord; pediatric neurosurgery is surgery performed on the nerves, brain, or spinal cord of a child; the frontal lobe is the largest section of the brain (editors' note).

happened because Hitler, a very bad man, invaded Poland. Midterms and report cards, summer vacations and new notebooks in September gave a steady rhythm to the world. It wasn't all necessarily happy—through the years there were poor grades, grouchy teachers, exclusion from the desired social group, dateless weekends when it seemed the rest of the world was paired off—but it was familiar territory where we felt walled off from the really bad things that happened to other people.

9   There were hints of them, though, even then. Looking back, I recall the tiny shock waves, the tremors from far-off explosions that occasionally rattled our shelter. There was the little girl who was absent for a week and when she returned wasn't living with her mother and stepfather anymore. There was a big girl who threw up in the bathroom every morning and then disappeared from school. A playful, friendly custodian was suddenly fired, and it had something to do with an angry parent. A teacher's husband had a heart attack and died. These were interesting tidbits to report to our families over dinner, mostly out of morbid interest in seeing our parents bite their lips and exchange glances.

10   As we got older, the bombs dropped closer. A friend's sister was arrested for selling drugs; we saw her mother in tears at church that Sunday. A boy I thought I knew, a school clown with a sweet crooked grin, shot himself in the woods behind his house. A car full of senior boys, going home from a dance where I'd been sent into ecstasy when the cutest of them all greeted me by name, rounded a curve too fast and crashed, killing them. We wept and hugged each other in the halls. Our teachers listened to us grieve and tried to comfort us, but their words came out impatient and almost angry. I realize now that what sounded like anger was a helplessness to teach us lessons we were still too young or too ignorant to learn. For although our sorrow was real, we still had some sense of a protective curtain between us and the bombs. If only, we said. If only she hadn't used drugs. If only he'd told someone how depressed he was. If only they'd been more careful. *We* weren't like them; we were careful. Like magical incantations, we recited the things that we would or wouldn't do in order to protect ourselves from such sad, unnecessary fates.

11   And then my best friend, a beautiful girl of sixteen, went to sleep one January night and never woke up. I found myself shaken to the core of my being. My grief at the loss of my vibrant, laughing friend was great. But what really tilted my universe was the nakedness of my realization that there was no "if only." There were no drugs, no careless action, no crime, no accident, nothing I could focus on to explain away what had happened. She had simply died. Which could only mean that there was no magic barrier separating me and my loved ones from the bombs. We were as vulnerable as everyone else. For months the shock stayed with me. I sat in class watching my teachers draw diagrams of Saturn, talk about Watergate,[2] multiply fractions, and wondered at their apparent cheer and normalcy. Didn't they *know* we were all doomed? Didn't they know it was only a matter of time until one of us took a direct hit? What was the point of anything?

12   But time moved on, and I moved with it. College came and went, graduate school, adulthood, middle age. My heightened sense of vulnerability began to subside, though I could never again slip fully into the soothing security of my younger days. I became more aware of the intertwining threads of joy, pain, and occasional tragedy that weave

---

[2]In June 1972, supporters of Republican President Richard Nixon were caught breaking into the Democratic campaign headquarters in the Watergate office complex in Washington, DC. The resulting investigation of the White House connection to the break-in led to President Nixon's eventual resignation in August 1974 (editors' note).

through all our lives. College was stimulating, exciting, full of friendship and challenge. I fell in love for the first time, reveled in its sweetness, then learned the painful lesson that love comes with no guarantee. A beloved professor lost two children to leukemia, but continued with skill and passion to introduce students to the riches of literature. My father grew ill, but the last day of his life, when I sat by his bed holding his hand, remains one of my sweetest memories. The marriage I'd entered into with optimism ended in bitter divorce, but produced three children whose existence is my daily delight. At every step along the way, I've seen that the most rewarding chapters of my life have contained parts that I not only would not have chosen, but would have given much to avoid. But selecting just the good parts is not an option we are given.

The price of allowing ourselves to truly live, to love and be loved, is (and it's the ultimate irony) the knowledge that the greater our investment in life, the larger the target we create. Of course, it is within our power to refuse friendship, shrink from love, live in isolation, and thus create for ourselves a nearly impenetrable bomb shelter. There are those among us who choose such an existence, the price of intimacy being too high. Looking about me, however, I see few such examples. Instead, I am moved by the courage with which most of us, ordinary folks, continue soldiering on. We fall in love, we bring our children into the world, we forge our friendships, we give our hearts, knowing with increasing certainty that we do so at our own risk. Still we move ahead with open arms, saying yes, yes to life.   13

Shannon's surgery is behind her; the prognosis is good. Her mother reports that the family is returning to its normal routines, laughing again and talking of ordinary things, even while they step more gently, speak more quietly, are more aware of the precious fragility of life and of the blessing of every day that passes without explosion.   14

Bombs bursting in air. They can blind us, like fireworks at the moment of explosion. If we close our eyes and turn away, all we see is their fiery image. But if we have the courage to keep our eyes open and welcoming, even bombs finally fade against the vastness of the starry sky.   15

Questions for Close Reading

1. What is the selection's thesis? Locate the sentence(s) in which Johnson states her main idea. If she doesn't state the thesis explicitly, express it in your own words.

2. In paragraph 2, Johnson describes her "need to feel her [daughter] near." What compels her to want to be physically close to her daughter? Why do you think Johnson responds this way?

3. In describing her family's responses to Shannon's illness, Johnson presents three reactions: Maddie's, Sam's, and her own. How do these responses differ? In what ways do Maddie's, Sam's, and Johnson's reactions typify the age groups to which they belong?

4. In paragraph 13, Johnson describes two basic ways people respond to life's inevitable "bombs." What are these ways? Which response does Johnson endorse?

5. Refer to your dictionary as needed to define the following words used in the selection: *ferrying* (paragraph 4), *shrapnel* (6), *faze* (8), *cocooned* (8), *tremors* (9), *incantations* (10), *vulnerable* (11), *intertwining* (12), *impenetrable* (13), *soldiering on* (13), *prognosis* (14), and *fragility* (14).

Questions About the Writer's Craft

1. **The pattern.** Although Johnson provides many examples of life's "bombs," she gives more weight to some examples than to others. Which examples does she emphasize? Which ones receive less attention? Why?

2. **Other patterns.** What important contrast does Johnson develop in paragraph 6? How does this contrast reinforce the essay's main idea?

3. Writers generally vary sentence structure in an effort to add interest to their work. But in paragraphs 9 and 10, Johnson employs a repetitive sentence structure. Where is the repetition in these two paragraphs? Why do you think she uses this technique?

4. Johnson develops her essay by means of an extended metaphor (see pages 89–90), using bombs as her central image. Identify all the places where Johnson draws upon language and imagery related to bombs and battles. What do you think Johnson hopes to achieve with this sustained metaphor?

Writing Assignments Using Illustration as a Pattern of Development

1. In paragraphs 9 and 10, Johnson catalogues a number of events that made her increasingly aware of life's bombs. Write an essay of your own, illustrating how you came to recognize the inevitability of painful life events. Start by listing the difficult events you've encountered. Select the three most compelling occurrences, and do some freewriting to generate details about each. Before writing, decide whether you will order your examples chronologically or emphatically; use whichever illustrates more effectively your dawning realization of life's complexity. End with some conclusions about your ability to cope with difficult times.

∞ 2. Johnson describes her evolving understanding of life. In an essay of your own, show the way several events combined to change your understanding of a specific aspect of your life. Perhaps a number of incidents prompted you to reconsider career choices, end a relationship, or appreciate the importance of family. Cite only those events that illustrate your emerging understanding. Your decision to use either chronological or emphatic sequence depends on which illustrates more dramatically the change in your perception. To see how other writers describe their journeys of self-discovery, read Maya Angelou's

"Sister Flowers" (page 178), Joseph H. Suina's "And Then I Went to School" (page 371), and Brent Staples's "Black Men and Public Space" (page 407).

Writing Assignments Using Other Patterns of Development

∞ 3. Johnson explores the lasting impact the death of her friend had on her life. Write an essay about the effect of a *single* bomb on your life. You might discuss getting left back in school, losing a loved one, seeing the dark side of someone you admired, and so on. Your causal analysis should make clear how the event affected your life. Perhaps the event had painful short-term consequences but positive long-term repercussions. Maya Angelou's "Sister Flowers" (page 178), Audre Lorde's "The Fourth of July" (page 216), and Sophronia Liu's "So Tsi-Fai" (page 221), provide helpful models for examining the effects of a life-changing event.

4. In an essay, offer readers a guide to surviving a specific life calamity. You might, for instance, explain how to survive a pet's death, a painful breakup, a financial hardship. Consider doing some library and/or Internet research on your subject. Combining your own insights with any material gathered through research, describe fully the steps readers should take to recover from the devastating events.

Writing Assignment Using a Journal Entry as a Starting Point

∞ 5. Johnson asserts that painful truths shouldn't "be ignored or lied away" by adults. Do you agree? Write an essay explaining why you think adults should protect children from harsh realities—or why they should present the whole truth, even when it's painful. Review your pre-reading journal entry, searching for strong examples to support your position. Discussing this topic with others will also help you shape your point of view, as will reading Audre Lorde's "The Fourth of July" (page 216), Toni Morrison's "A Slow Walk of Trees" (page 362), and Yuh Ji-Yeon's "Let's Tell the Story of All America's Cultures" (page 499).

SUSAN DOUGLAS

Susan J. Douglas (1950–), professor of communication studies at the University of Michigan, is the media critic for *The Progressive*. She was written for *The Village Voice* and *The Nation* and is the author of three books—*Inventing American Broadcasting: 1899–1922* (1987), *Where the Girls Are: Growing Up Female with the Mass Media* (1994), and *Listening In: Radio and the American Imagination* (1999). "Managing Mixed Messages" is an excerpt from *Where the Girls Are*.

Pre-Reading Journal Entry

Some people think that the roles of men and women have drastically changed during the last few decades. Do you agree? Use your journal to record your responses to the following questions about gender roles in society: Based on what you have observed in your parents' generation as well as in your own, what do you think has changed about women's place in society? About men's place in society? For each, what seems to have remained the same?

MANAGING MIXED MESSAGES

1   "Mommy, Mommy, hurry, come quickly, *now!*" implores my daughter at 8:16 a.m. on Saturday. This is the one time of the week she's allowed to watch commercial television, and the price is heavy. I drag my hungover and inadequately caffeinated butt over to the TV set. Her eyes shine like moonstones as I see what's on the screen. "Can I get that, Mommy, can I, puleeze? Please, Mommy." I see before me some hideous plastic doll, or pony, or troll, being pitched by a combination of elated little girls, flashing lights, and rap music. Everything seems to be colored hot pink or lilac. Sometimes it's one of these dolls you can put fake jewels all over, other times it's a troll doll in a wedding dress, or it's something really bad, like Kitty Surprise or Cheerleader Skipper. It is always something specifically targeted to little girls. She is four years old, and she understands, completely, the semiotics of gender differentiation. She never calls me when they're selling Killer Commando Unit, G.I. Joe, and all the other Pentagon-inspired stuff obviously for boys. She knows better. She knows she's a girl, and she knows what's for her. Twenty years of feminist politics and here I am, with a daughter who wants nothing more in the whole wide world than to buy Rollerblade Barbie.

2   Having grown up with the mass media myself, and considering what that has done for me and to me, I bring all that to bear as I raise my own little girl, who will, in her own way, and with her own generation, have her hopes and fears shaped by the mass media too. Ever since she was old enough to understand books, kids' movies, and *Sesame Street,* I have looked, in vain, for strong and appealing female characters for her to identify with. With a few exceptions, like *The Paperbag Princess,* shrewd, daring girls who outsmart monsters and value their freedom and self-esteem more than marrying some prince are hard to find. There's Maria, who knows how to fix toasters and stereos, on *Sesame Street.* But little kids are, at first, most drawn to the Muppets, and until recently, not one of the main stars—Big Bird, Kermit, the Count, Elmo, Snuffy, or Oscar—was female. Children's books are not much better. Even if they feature animals as the main protagonists, stories for kids too readily assume, automatically, that the main actor is male. Television cartoons, from Winnie the Pooh (no females except Kanga, and she's always doing laundry or cooking), to Garfield to Doug, not to mention the more obnoxious superhero action ones, still treat females either as nonexistent or as ancillary afterthoughts. We have the cartoon *James Bond, Jr.,* but no *Emma Peel, Jr.* And it goes without saying that nearly all the little girls she sees on TV and elsewhere are white.

3   And then there are the movies. When mothers cling to *The Little Mermaid* as one of the few positive representations of girls, we see how far we have not come. Ariel, the little mermaid in question, is indeed brave, curious, feisty, and defiant. She stands up to her father, saves Prince Eric from drowning, and stares down great white sharks as she

hunts for sunken treasure. But her waist is the diameter of a chive, and her salvation comes through her marriage—at the age of sixteen, no less—to Eric. And the sadistic, consummately evil demon in the movie is, you guessed it, an older, overweight woman with too much purple eyeshadow and eyeliner, a female octopus who craves too much power and whose nether regions evoke the dreaded vagina dentate.[1]

Belle, in *Beauty and the Beast,* dreams of escaping from the narrow confines of her small town, of having great adventures, and has nothing but contempt for the local cleft-chinned lout and macho beefcake Gaston. Her dreams of a more interesting, exciting life, however, are also fulfilled through marriage alone. The most important quality of these characters remains their beauty, followed closely by their selflessness and the ability to sing. There are gestures to feminism—Ariel's physical courage, Belle's love of books, and, in *Aladdin,* Jasmine's defiance of an arbitrary law that dictates when and whom she must marry. These are welcome flourishes, and many of us milk them for all they're worth— "See how *strong* she is, honey?"—but they are still only flourishes, overwhelmed by the age-old narrative that selfless, beautiful girls are rewarded by the love of a prince they barely know. Nonanimated movies for kids are no better. Hollywood simply takes it for granted that little heroes, like big ones, are always boys. So little girls get *Home Alone* and who knows how many sequels, *Cop and a Half, The Karate Kid, Rookie of the Year, Free Willy,* and *Dennis the Menace,* all with little boy leads, little boy adventures, and little boy heroism, while gutsy, smart, enterprising, and sassy little girls remain, after all this time, absent, invisible, denied. Even my daughter, at the age of four, volunteered one day, "Mommy, there should be more movies with girls."

The one movie that I was happy to have my daughter embrace was made over fifty years ago, and judging from anecdotal evidence, it's been enjoying an enormous resurgence among the preschool set. No narrative has gripped my daughter's imagination more than *The Wizard of Oz.* And why not? Finally, here's a *girl* who has an adventure and doesn't get married at the end. She runs away from home, flies to Oz in a cyclone, kills one wicked witch and then another—although never on purpose—and helps Scarecrow get a brain, Tin Man get a heart, and Lion get some courage, all of which Dorothy already has in spades. Throughout the movie, Dorothy is caring, thoughtful, nurturing, and empathetic, but she's also adventuresome, determined, and courageous. She tells off Miss Gulch, slaps the lion while her male friends cower in the bushes, refuses to give the witch her slippers, and chastises the Wizard himself when she feels he is bullying her friends. Of course, when she's older, my daughter will learn the truth about Dorothy: that Judy Garland had to have her breasts strapped down for the part and was fed bucketfuls of amphetamines so she'd remain as slim as the studio wanted. This, too, I think, will speak to my daughter.

Shortly after seeing a few of the Disney fairy tales, both old and new, my daughter announced, at age three and a half, that she would no longer wear the unisex sweat suits and overalls I'd been dressing her in. It was dresses or nothing. Her favorite pretend games became "wedding" and "family," with her as either the bride or the mom. She loved playing Wizard of Oz—she was always Dorothy, of course—but she also loved playing Snow White, dropping like a sack of onions to the kitchen floor after she'd bitten into the pretend apple. The blocks, the Tinkertoys, and the trucks I had gotten her lay neglected, while the Barbie population began to multiply like fruit flies.

One of the things that feminist moms, and dads, for that matter, confront is the force of genetics. In the 1970s, I was convinced that most of the differences between men

4

5

6

7

---

[1]Toothed vagina. Refers to the mythical fear of women's destructive sexual power (editors' note).

and women were the results of socialization. In the nature-nurture debate, I gave nature very little due. But now, as a parent, I have seen my daughter, long before she ever watched television, prefer dolls to trucks, use blocks to build enclosures instead of towers, and focus on interpersonal relationships in her play rather than on hurling projectiles into things. But at the same time, I have seen children's television (which, if anything, is even more retrograde than it was in the 1970s) reinforce and exaggerate these gender differences with a vengeance as if there were no overlap of traits at all between boys and girls . . .

8   In fact, kids' TV is worse than ever, and certainly more crass, more sexist . . . than much of the programming pitched to adults. In addition to all the war toys that train little boys to be cannon fodder and/or gun collectors, and the makeup kits and dolls that train little girls to be sex objects and/or moms, the overall message is about regarding yourself and everyone else you know as a commodity to be bought and sold. Ads geared to each gender encourage kids to dehumanize themselves and one another, to regard people as objects to be acquired or discarded. "Get the right boyfriend! Get the right friends!" commands an ad for a game for girls, Spring Valley High School (or maybe it was called Shop 'Til You Drop). To be a desirable commodity, a little girl must herself consume the right goods so she can make herself pretty and ornament herself properly. Being able to sing and smile admiringly at boys is highly desirable. Being smart, brave, or assertive isn't. On Saturday morning, boys are "cool"; girls are their mirrors, flat, shiny surfaces whose function is to reflect all this coolness back to them and on them. Girls watch boys be "awesome" and do "awesome" things. Girls aren't awesome; they're only spectators.

9   Already I see my little girl, at the age of four, managing the mixed messages around her. I see her process them, try to control them, and allow them into her sense of her place in the world. She wants to be at the center of the action, and she dictates the precise direction of her pretend games with the authority of a field marshal. In the books she has about rabbits, cats, alligators, and the like, she insists that I change all the pronouns from *he* to *she* so the story will be about a girl, not a boy. Already, she is resisting, without yet knowing it, certain sexist presumptions of the media. But she succumbs to them too. For it is also important to her that she be pretty, desired, and the one who beats out the ugly stepsisters for the prince's attention. She wants control and she wants love, and she is growing up in a culture as confused about how much of each a woman can have as it was in the 1950s and '60s. So she will be surrounded by media imagery that holds out promises of female achievement with one hand and slaps her down with the other.

10   One recourse we . . . have is to teach our daughters how to talk back to and make fun of the mass media. This is especially satisfying since, thanks to Nickelodeon, we sometimes see them watching the same stuff we grew up with. In an episode of *Lassie* my daughter and I watched one morning, a ranger comes to the house to warn the mom that there are some mountain lions in the area. As he tries to show her, on a map, where they'd been spotted, she demurs, confessing that she can't read maps and they just confuse her. Then, on her way to meet Dad and Timmy at a Grange dinner, she gets a flat—which, of course, she hasn't a clue how to change—and then gets caught in one of the traps set for the mountain lions. Lassie—a dog—has more brains than she does and has to save her. Such scenes provide the feminist mom with an opportunity to impart a few words of wisdom about how silly and unrealistic TV can be when it comes to women.

11   But . . . I don't want to monitor my daughter's TV viewing on Saturday morning, I want to go back to bed. How many mothers have the time or the energy for such

interventions? Why should such interventions be so constantly necessary? And even the most conscientious and unharried mom can't compensate for the absences, the erasures, of what their daughters don't see, may never see, about women and bravery, intelligence, and courage. . . . Of one thing I am certain. Like us, our daughters will make their own meanings out of much that they see, reading between the lines, absorbing exhortations to be feisty side by side with exhortations to be passive. Like us, they will have to work hard to fend off what cripples them and amplify what empowers them. But why, after all these years, should they still have to work so hard and to resist so much?

Questions for Close Reading

1. What is the selection's thesis? Locate the sentence(s) in which Douglas states her main idea. If she doesn't state the thesis explicitly, express it in your own words.

2. What, according to Douglas, is good about animated movies like *The Little Mermaid* and *Beauty and the Beast?* What is bad about both these animated movies and nonanimated movies like *Home Alone* and *Free Willy?*

3. Why is Douglas happy to have her daughter "embrace" (5) *The Wizard of Oz?* What makes this movie different from the others she mentions earlier? What, if anything, does she find problematic about it?

4. How does Douglas's daughter react to the media presentation of gender roles? How does the girl's reaction reinforce Douglas's thesis?

5. Refer to your dictionary as needed to define the following words used in the selection: *implores* (paragraph 1), *semiotics* (1), *consummately* (3), *nether* (3), *arbitrary* (4), *flourishes* (4), *resurgence* (5), *retrograde* (7), *succumbs* (9), *demurs* (10), *impart* (10), *unharried* (11), *exhortations* (11).

Questions About the Writer's Craft

1. **The pattern.** In the course of her essay, Douglas cites television commercials, books, television shows, and movies to support her thesis. How does she signal movement from one medium to the other?

2. How would you characterize Douglas's tone in the first paragraph of the essay? What words and phrases reveal this tone? How does this tone help Douglas reinforce her thesis?

3. **Other patterns.** The brief personal narrative that opens the essay lets us hear the voice of Douglas's daughter. Where in the essay do we hear Douglas herself speaking? What do these two instances of dialog contribute to the essay?

4. Why do you think Douglas ends her essay with a question? What effect do you think she wanted the question to have on her readers?

Writing Assignments Using Illustration as a Pattern of Development

∞ 1. Douglas provides numerous examples to show how media messages shape her daughter's understanding of what it means to be female. Write an essay in which you cite the experiences and sources of information that shaped your understanding of your gender. Before writing your paper, you may want to read the following essays, all of which provide insight into gender expectations: Maya Angelou's "Sister Flowers" (page 178), Deborah Tannen's "But What Do You Mean?" (page 288), Joyce Garity's "Is Sex All That Matters?" (page 256), and Dave Barry's "The Ugly Truth About Beauty" (page 367).

∞ 2. Douglas claims that the media glorify males at the expense of females. Are there other aspects of our culture that value the behavior and attitudes of males more than those of females? With friends, classmates, and relatives, discuss other areas, such as dating, marriage, academics, athletics, and friendships. Then, focusing on *one* area, write an essay illustrating that a particular aspect of contemporary society values one sex more than the other. To support your point of view, draw upon others' experiences as well as your own. If appropriate, include points made in any of the following essays: Deborah Tannen's "But What Do You Mean?" (page 288), Dave Barry's "The Ugly Truth About Beauty" (page 367), Camille Paglia's "Rape: A Bigger Danger Than Feminists Know" (page 489), and Susan Jacoby's "Common Decency" (page 494).

Writing Assignments Using Other Patterns of Development

3. In paragraph 7, Douglas alludes to the "nature-nurture" debate—in this case, whether the gender differences are a result of primarily genetics or socialization. To gain insight into the complexities of the nature-nurture debate, brainstorm with others. You might also benefit from conducting research in the library and/or on the Internet. Then write an essay arguing your position about the controversy: Is it biology or the environment that plays the predominant role in determining sex-role attitudes and behavior? Remember to defend your viewpoint with plentiful examples based on research as well as your own and other people's experiences. Acknowledge the opposing viewpoint, dismantling as much of it as you can.

4. Douglas asserts that TV is "more sexist" than ever and complains that she has "looked, in vain, for strong and appealing female characters" on TV and in the movies for young girls. Write an essay in which you disagree with Douglas's assertions and instead illustrate that there *are* indeed positive female role models for young girls in children's television and/or film. To support your claim, provide specific examples to prove the existence of positive female protagonists for girls. You might, for example, look at female characters that Douglas neglected to consider or at characters who've emerged since the

publication of Douglas's essay in 1994. In addition, you might do some library and/or Internet research to gain further insight into the issue.

Writing Assignment Using a Journal Entry as a Starting Point

5. In paragraph 9, Douglas says that her daughter wants love and control but is growing up in a culture "as confused about how much of each a woman can have as . . . in the 1950s and '60s." Interview several people who grew up in that period to gather information on gender expectations a generation ago. Using their observations as well as the ones you generated in your pre-reading journal entry, write an essay comparing and contrasting gender expectations now and in the past. Focus your discussion on *either* men *or* women (not both), and reach some conclusions about how much or how little has changed since that earlier time.

JOYCE GARITY

Social worker Joyce Garity (1955–) has served as the supervisor of county foster-child services in two Midwestern states. Garity derived her essay "Is Sex All That Matters?" from a highly regarded presentation she made several years ago at a social workers' conference on teenage parenthood.

Pre-Reading Journal Entry

Whether—and how—schools educate students about sex is a subject of much recent debate. Do you think schools should educate students about sex? What has been your own experience with sex education courses? In your journal, write about the kinds of information, if any, you've received about sex during the course of elementary, middle, and high school. Was the sex education curriculum appropriate? Was it pertinent and informative to students? Explain.

IS SEX ALL THAT MATTERS?

A few years ago, a young girl lived with me, my husband, and our children for several months. The circumstances of Elaine's coming to us don't matter here; suffice it to say that she was troubled and nearly alone in the world. She was also pregnant—hugely, clumsily pregnant with her second child. Elaine was seventeen. Her pregnancy, she said, was an accident; she also said she wasn't sure who had fathered her child. There had been several sex partners and no contraception. Yet, she repeated blandly, gazing at me with clear blue eyes, the pregnancy was an accident, and one she would certainly never repeat.   1

Eventually I asked Elaine, after we had grown to know each other well enough for such conversations, why neither she nor her lovers had used birth control. She blushed—this porcelain-skinned girl with one child in foster care and another swelling the bib of her   2 fashionably faded overalls—she stammered, she blushed some more. Birth control, she finally got out, was "embarrassing." It wasn't "romantic." You couldn't be really passionate, she explained, and worry about birth control at the same time.

3   I haven't seen Elaine for quite a long time. I think about her often, though. I think of her as I page through teen fashion magazines in the salon where I have my hair cut. Although intended to be mainstream and wholesome, these magazines trumpet sexuality page after leering page. On the inside front cover, an advertisement for Guess jeans features junior fashion models in snug denim dresses, their legs bared to just below the crotch. An advertisement for Liz Claiborne fragrances shows a barely clad young couple sprawled on a bed, him painting her toenails. An advertisement for Obsession cologne displays a waif-thin girl draped stomach-down across a couch, naked, her startled expression suggesting helplessness against an unseen yet approaching threat.

4   I think of Elaine because I know she would love these ads. "They're so beautiful," she would croon, and of course they are. The faces and bodies they show are lovely. The lighting is superb. The hair and makeup are faultless. In the Claiborne ad, the laughing girl whose toenails are being painted by her handsome lover is obviously having the time of her life. She stretches luxuriously on a bed heaped with clean white linen and fluffy pillows. Beyond the sheer blowing curtains of her room, we can glimpse a graceful wrought-iron balcony. Looking at the ad, Elaine could only want to be her. Any girl would want to be her. Heck, *I* want to be her.

5   But my momentary desire to move into the Claiborne picture, to trade lives with the exquisite young creature pictured there, is just that—momentary. I've lived long enough to know that what I see is a marketing invention. I know that a moment after the photo shoot was over, the beautiful room was dismantled, the models moved on to their next job, and the technicians took over the task of doctoring the photograph until it reached full-blown fantasy proportions. I know all that.

6   Not so Elaine. After months of living together and countless hours of watching her yearn after magazine images, soap-opera heroines, and rock goddesses, I have a pretty good idea of why she likes ads such as Claiborne's. She sees the way life—her life—is *supposed* to be. She sees a world characterized by sexual spontaneity, playfulness, and abandon. She sees people who don't worry about such unsexy details as birth control. Nor, apparently, do they spend much time thinking about such pedestrian topics as commitment or whether they should act on their sexual impulses. Their clean sunlit rooms are never invaded by the fear of AIDS, of unwanted pregnancy, of shattered lives. For all her apparent lack of defense, the girl on the couch in the Obsession ad will surely never experience the brutality of rape.

7   Years of exposure to this media-invented, sex-saturated universe have done their work on Elaine. She is, I'm sure, completely unaware of the irony in her situation: She melts over images from a sexual Shangri-la, never realizing that her attempts to mirror those images left her pregnant, abandoned, living in the spare bedroom of a stranger's house, relying on charity for rides to the welfare office and supervised visits with her toddler daughter.

8   Of course, Elaine is not the first to be suckered by the cynical practice of using sex to sell underwear, rock groups, or sneakers. Using sex as a sales tool is hardly new. At the beginning of this century, British actress Lily Langtry shocked her contemporaries by posing, clothed somewhat scantily, with a bar of Pear's soap. Advertisers have always known that the masses are susceptible to the notion that a particular product will make

them more sexually attractive. In the past, though, ads used euphemisms, claiming that certain products would make people "more lovable" or "more popular." What is a recent development is the abandonment of any such polite double talk. Advertising today leaves no question about what is being sold along with the roasted peanuts or artificial sweetener. "Tell us about your first time," coyly invites the innuendo-filled magazine advertisement for Campari liquor. A billboard for Levi's shows two jeans-clad young men on the beach, hoisting a girl in the air. The boys' perfect, tan bodies are matched by hers, although we see a lot more of hers: bare midriff, short shorts, cleavage. She caresses their hair; they stroke her legs. A jolly gang-bang fantasy in the making . . .

. . . Studies show that by the age of 20, 75 percent of Americans have lost their   9
virginity. In many high schools—and an increasing number of junior highs—virginity is regarded as an embarrassing vestige of childhood, to be disposed of as quickly as possible. Young people are immersed from their earliest days in a culture that parades sexuality at every turn and makes heroes of the advocates of sexual excess. Girls, from toddlerhood on up, shop in stores packed with clothing once thought suitable only for streetwalkers—lace leggings, crop tops, and wedge-heeled boots. Parents drop their children off at Madonna or Michael Jackson concerts, featuring simulated on-stage masturbation, or at Bobby Brown's show, where a fan drawn out of the audience is treated to a pretended act of copulation. Young boys idolize sports stars like Wilt Chamberlain, who claims to have bedded 20,000 women. And when the "Spur Posse," eight California high school athletes, were charged with systematically raping girls as young as 10 as part of a "scoring" ritual, the beefy young jocks were rewarded with a publicity tour of talk shows, while one father boasted to reporters about his son's "manhood."

In a late, lame attempt to counterbalance this sexual overload, most schools offer   10
sex education as part of their curriculums. (In 1995, forty-seven states recommended or required such courses.) But sex ed classes are heavy on the mechanics of fertilization and birth control—sperm, eggs, and condoms—and light on any discussion of sexuality as only one part of a well-balanced life. There is passing reference to abstinence as a method of contraception, but little discussion of abstinence as an emotionally or spiritually satisfying option. Promiscuity is discussed for its role in spreading sexually transmitted diseases. But the concept of rejecting casual sex in favor of reserving sex for an emotionally intimate, exclusive, trusting relationship—much less any mention of waiting until marriage—is foreign to most public school settings. "Love and stuff like that really wasn't discussed" is the way one Spur Posse member remembers his high school sex education class.

Surely teenagers need the factual information provided by sex education courses.   11
But where is "love and stuff like that" talked about? Where can teens turn for a more balanced view of sexuality? Who is telling young people like Elaine, my former houseguest, that sex is not an adequate basis for a healthy, respectful relationship? Along with warnings to keep condoms on hand, is anyone teaching kids that they have a right to be valued for something other than their sexuality? Madison Avenue, Hollywood, and the TV, music, and fashion industries won't tell them that. Who will?

No one has told Elaine—at least, not in a way she comprehends. I haven't seen her   12
for a long time, but I hear of her occasionally. The baby boy she bore while living in my house is in a foster home, a few miles from his older half-sister, who is also in foster care. Elaine herself is working in a local convenience store—and she is pregnant again. This time, I understand, she is carrying twins.

Questions for Close Reading

1. What is the selection's thesis? Locate the sentence(s) in which Garity states her main idea. If she doesn't state the thesis explicitly, express it in your own words.

2. Why would Elaine love the ads in the teen fashion magazines at Garity's beauty salon? Why doesn't Garity react to the ads as Elaine would? What, according to Garity, *don't* the ads tell us?

3. In Garity's opinion, how does our culture reinforce advertisements' sexually explicit messages?

4. Why, according to Garity, don't sex education courses refute our culture's distorted messages about sex and relationships? What does she believe schools *should* teach about sex?

5. Refer to your dictionary as needed to define the following words used in the selection: *waif* (paragraph 3), *croon* (4), *spontaneity* (6), *abandon* (6), *pedestrian* (6), *irony* (7), *euphemisms* (8), *innuendo* (8), *vestige* (9), *simulated* (9), *copulation* (9), *abstinence* (10), and *exclusive* (10).

Questions About the Writer's Craft

1. **The pattern.**   The numerous examples that Garity provides in paragraphs 3–6 and 8–9 would have been sufficient to convey her central point. Why, then, do you think she decided to include the extended example about Elaine? What does this lengthy example add to the essay?

2. **Other patterns.**   Garity reinforces her thesis by highlighting a number of contrasts. Identify three of these contrasts and explain how they underscore the author's central point.

3. **Other patterns.**   Several cause-effect chains underlie Garity's essay. Identify some of these chains. How do they help Garity convey her thesis?

4. How would you characterize Garity's tone—and her attitude—toward her subject? How do Garity's sentence structure and word choices help to create this tone?

Writing Assignments Using Illustration as a Pattern of Development

∞ 1. Select a single aspect of American popular culture—for example, TV commercials, movies, magazine advertisements, or rock music—and write an essay supporting Garity's point that our society helps create irresponsible sexuality. Like Garity, provide a number of specific, highly detailed examples to illustrate your thesis. Before writing, read Ellen Goodman's "Family Counterculture" (page 7), Susan Douglas's "Managing Mixed Messages" (page 251), and Ann McClintock's "Propaganda Techniques in Today's Advertising" (page 281); these essays will deepen your understanding of popular culture.

∞ **2.** Look closely at and reach some conclusions about the way advertisements and commercials depict a subject other than sex. You might, for example, examine media messages about any of the following: alcohol, academic success, the world of work, or parent-child relationships. Are the media images accurate, or are they distorted? Including persuasive examples of different ads and commercials, write an essay supporting your conclusion. To lend credibility to your analysis of advertising strategies, cite some points raised by Ann McClintock in "Propaganda Techniques in Today's Advertising" (page 281) and/or William Lutz in "Doublespeak" (page 295).

Writing Assignments Using Other Patterns of Development

3. Although she doesn't provide all the details, Garity indicates that Elaine and her children are on welfare. Recently, there has been strong sentiment nationwide to deny welfare payments to unmarried teenagers with more than one child. Read about this controversial issue in the library and/or on the Internet, and discuss it with friends, classmates, and family members. Then determine your position and support it in a persuasive essay. Try to refute as many of the opposing views as you can.

4. Brainstorm with others to discover ways our society might counteract the influence of what Garity calls our "sex-saturated" culture. Then write an essay showing the specific steps that parents or schools or communities or religious organizations could take to provide youngsters with a more balanced view of relationships and sex. Describe the steps in enough detail so that readers can fully understand the potentially positive effects these steps would have on children—and on society at large.

Writing Assignment Using a Journal Entry as a Starting Point

5. The issue of what kinds of subject matter should be included in school sex education curricula has been deliberated by parents, teachers, school administrators, and students. Write an essay in which you argue that the particular sex education (if any) you received in school was *or* was not appropriate and useful to students. As you make your claims, be specific in your analysis of your school's sex education curriculum, examining particular areas of teen sexuality (peer pressure, disease prevention, contraception, and so on) that were—or were not—properly addressed in the classroom. If sex education courses were not offered in your school, discuss whether they should have been and why. In any case, you might do some research in the library and/or on the Internet to provide support, such as statistics or expert opinions, for your position.

ADDITIONAL WRITING TOPICS: ILLUSTRATION

General Assignments

Use illustration to develop one of the following topics into a well-organized essay. When writing the paper, choose enough relevant examples to support your thesis. Organize the material into a sequence that most effectively illustrates the thesis, keeping in mind that emphatic order is often the most compelling way to present specifics.

1. Many of today's drivers have dangerous habits.

2. Drug and alcohol abuse is (or is not) a serious problem among many young people.

3. One rule of restaurant dining is, "Management often seems oblivious to problems that are perfectly obvious to customers."

4. Children today are not encouraged to use their imaginations.

5. The best things in life are definitely not free.

6. A part-time job is an important experience that every college student should have.

7. Television commercials stereotype the elderly (or another minority group).

8. Today, salespeople act as if they're doing you a favor by taking your money.

9. Most people behave decently in their daily interactions with each other.

10. You can tell a lot about people by observing what they eat.

Assignments with a Specific Purpose, Audience, and Point of View

On Campus

1. Lately, many people at your college have been experiencing stress. As a member of the Student Life Committee, you've been asked to prepare a pamphlet illustrating strategies for reducing different kinds of stress. Decide which stresses to discuss and explain coping strategies for each, providing helpful examples as you go.

2. A friend of yours will be going away to college in an unfamiliar environment—in a bustling urban setting or in a quiet rural one. To help your friend prepare for this new environment, write a letter giving examples of what life on an urban or a rural campus is like. You might focus on the benefits and dangers with which your friend is unlikely to be familiar.

At Home or in the Community

3. Shopping for a new car, you become annoyed at how many safety features are available only as expensive options. Write a letter of complaint to the auto manufacturer, citing at least three examples of such options. Avoid sounding hostile.

4. A pet food company is having an annual contest to choose a new animal to feature in its advertising. To win the contest, you must convince the company that your pet is personable, playful, unique. Write an essay giving examples of your pet's special qualities.

On the Job

5. Assume that you're an elementary school principal planning to give a speech in which you'll try to convince parents that television distorts children's perceptions of reality. Write the speech, illustrating your point with vivid examples.

6. The online publication you work for has asked you to write an article on what you consider to be the "three best consumer products of the past twenty-five years." Support your opinion with lively, engaging specifics that are consistent with the website's offbeat and slightly ironic tone.

14

DIVISION-CLASSIFICATION

WHAT IS DIVISION-CLASSIFICATION?

Imagine what life would be like if this were how an average day unfolded:

You plan to stop at the supermarket for only a few items, but your marketing takes over an hour because all the items in the store are jumbled together. Clerks put new shipments anywhere they please; milk is with vegetables on Monday but with laundry detergent on Thursday. Next, you go to the drugstore to pick up some photos you left to be developed. You don't have time, though, to wait while the cashier roots through the large carton into which all the pick-up envelopes have been thrown. You return to your car and decide to stop at the town hall to pay a parking ticket. But the town hall baffles you. The offices are unmarked, and there isn't even a directory to tell you on which floor the Violations Bureau can be found. Annoyed, you get back into your car and, minutes later, end up colliding with another car that was driving toward you in your lane. When you wake up in the hospital, you find there are three other patients in your room: a middle-aged man with a heart problem, a young boy ready to have his tonsils removed, and a woman about to go into labor.

Such a muddled world, lacking the most basic forms of organization, would make daily life chaotic. All of us instinctively look for ways to order our environment. Without systems, categories, or sorting mechanisms, we would be overwhelmed by life's complexity. An organization like a college or university, for example, is made manageable by being divided into various schools (Liberal Arts, Performing Arts, Engineering, and so on). The schools are then separated into departments (English, History, Political Science), and each department's offerings are grouped into distinct categories—English, for instance, into Literature and Composition—before being further divided into specific courses.

The kind of ordering system we've been discussing is called **division-classification,** a way of thinking that allows us to make sense of a complex world. Division and classification, though separate processes, often complement each other. **Division** involves taking a single unit or concept, breaking it down into parts, and then analyzing the connection among the parts and between the parts and the whole. For instance, if we wanted to organize the chaotic hospital described at the beginning of the chapter, we might think about how the single concept **hospital** could be broken down into its components. We might come up with the following breakdown: pediatric wing, cardiac wing, maternity wing,

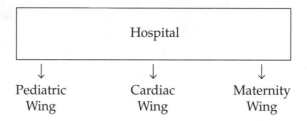

and so on. What we have just done involves division: We've taken a single entity (a hospital) and divided it into some of its component parts (wings), each with its own facilities and patients.

In contrast, **classification** brings two or more related items together and categorizes them according to type or kind. If the disorganized supermarket described earlier were to be restructured, the clerks would have to classify the separate items arriving at the store. Cartons of lettuce, tomatoes, cucumbers, butter, yogurt, milk, shampoo, conditioner, and hair gel would be assigned to the appropriate categories:

HOW DIVISION–CLASSIFICATION FITS YOUR PURPOSE AND AUDIENCE

The reorganized hospital and supermarket show the way division and classification work in everyday life. But division and classification also come into play during the writing process. Because division involves breaking a subject into parts, it can be a helpful strategy during prewriting, especially if you're analyzing a broad, complex subject: the structure of a film; the motivation of a character in a novel; the problem your community has with vandalism; the controversy surrounding school prayer. An editorial examining a recent hostage crisis, for example, might divide the crisis into three areas: how the hostages were treated by (1) their captors, (2) the governments negotiating their release, and (3) the media. The purpose of the editorial might be to show readers that the governments' treatment of the hostages was particularly exploitative.

Classification can be useful for imposing order on the hodgepodge of ideas generated during prewriting. You examine that material to see which of your rough ideas are alike and which are dissimilar, so that you can cluster related items in the same category. Classification would, then, be a helpful strategy when analyzing topics like these: techniques for impressing teachers; comic styles of talk-show hosts; views on abortion; reasons for the current rise in volunteerism. You might, for instance, use classification in a paper showing that Americans are undermining their health through their obsessive pursuit of various diets. Perhaps you begin by brainstorming all the diets that have gained popularity in recent years (the Zone, Slim-Fast, whatever). Then you categorize the diets according to type: high fiber, low protein, high carbohydrate, and so on. Once the diets are grouped, you can discuss the problems within each category, demonstrating to readers that none of the diets is safe or effective.

Division-classification can be crucial when responding to college assignments like the following:

> Based on your observations, what kinds of appeals do television advertisers use when selling automobiles? In your view, are any of these appeals morally irresponsible?

> Analyze the components that go into being an effective parent. Indicate those you consider most vital for raising confident, well-adjusted children.

> Describe the hierarchy of the typical high school clique, identifying the various parts of the hierarchy. Use your analysis to support or refute the view that adolescence is a period of rigid conformity.

> Many social commentators have observed that discourtesy is on the rise. Indicate whether you think this is a valid observation by characterizing the types of everyday encounters you have with people.

These assignments suggest division-classification through the use of such words as *kinds*, *components*, *parts*, and *types*. Generally, though, you won't receive such clear signals to use division-classification. Instead, the broad purpose of the essay—and the point you want to make—will lead you to the analytical thinking characteristic of division-classification.

Sometimes division-classification will be the dominant technique for structuring an essay; other times it will be used as a supplemental pattern in an essay organized primarily according to another pattern of development. Let's look at some examples. Say you want to write a paper *explaining a process* (surviving divorce; creating a hit recording; shepherding a bill through Congress; using the Heimlich maneuver on people who are choking). You could *divide* the process into parts or stages, showing, for instance, that the Heimlich maneuver is an easily mastered skill that readers should acquire. Or imagine you plan to write a light-spirited essay analyzing the *effect* that increased awareness of sexual stereotypes has had on college students' social lives. In such a case, you might use *classification.* To show readers that shifting gender roles make young men and women comically self-conscious, you could categorize the places where students scope out each other in class, at the library, at parties, in dorms. You could then show how students—not wishing to be macho or coyly feminine—approach each other with laughable tentativeness in these four environments.

Now imagine that you're writing an *argumentation-persuasion* essay urging that the federal government prohibit the use of growth-inducing antibiotics in live-stock feed. The paper could begin by *dividing* the antibiotics cycle into stages: the effects of antibiotics on livestock; the short-term effects on humans who consume the animals; the possible long-term effects of consuming antibiotic-tainted meat. To increase readers' understanding of the problem, you might also discuss the antibiotics controversy in terms of an even larger issue: the dangerous ways food is treated before being consumed. In this case, you would consider the various procedures (use of additives, preservatives, artificial colors, and so on), *classifying* these treatments into several types—from least harmful (some additives or artificial colors, perhaps) to most harmful (you might slot the antibiotics here). Such an essay would be developed using both division *and* classification: first, the division of the antibiotics cycle and then the classification of the various food treatments. Frequently, this interdependence will be reversed, and classification will precede rather than follow division.

PREWRITING STRATEGIES

The following checklist shows how you can apply to division-classification some of the prewriting techniques discussed in Chapter 2.

 DIVISION-CLASSIFICATION: A PREWRITING CHECKLIST

Choose a Subject to Analyze

☐ What fairly complex subject (sibling rivalry, religious cults) can be made more understandable through division-classification?

□ Will you divide a single entity or concept (domestic violence) into parts (toward spouse, parent, or child)? Will you classify a number of similar things (college courses) into categories (easy, of average difficulty, tough)? Or will you use both division and classification?

Determine Your Purpose, Audience, Tone, and Point of View

□ What is the purpose of your analysis?

□ Toward what audience will you direct your explanations?

□ What tone and point of view will make readers receptive to your explanation?

Use Prewriting to Generate Material on Parts or Types

□ How can brainstorming, mapping, or any other prewriting technique help you divide your subject into parts? What differences or similarities among parts will you emphasize?

□ How can brainstorming, mapping, or any other prewriting technique help you categorize your subjects? What differences or similarities among categories will you emphasize?

□ How can the patterns of development help you generate material about your subjects' parts or categories? How can you describe the parts or categories? What can you narrate about them? What examples illustrate them? What process do they help explain? How can they be compared or contrasted? What causes them? What are their effects? How can they be defined? What arguments do they support?

STRATEGIES FOR USING DIVISION-CLASSIFICATION IN AN ESSAY

After prewriting, you're ready to draft your essay. The following suggestions will be helpful whether you use division-classification as a dominant or supportive pattern of development.

1. Select a principle of division-classification consistent with your purpose. Most subjects can be divided or classified according to *several different principles*. For example, when writing about an ideal vacation, you could divide your subject according to any of these principles: location, cost, recreation available. Similarly, when analyzing students at your college, you could base your classification on a variety of principles: students' majors, their racial or ethnic background, whether they belong to a fraternity or sorority. In all cases, though, the principle of division-classification you select must meet one stringent requirement: It must help you meet your overall purpose and reinforce your central point.

Sometimes a principle of division-classification seems so attractive that you latch on to it without examining whether it's consistent with your purpose.

Suppose you want to write a paper asserting that several episodes of a new television comedy are destined to become classics. Here's how you might go wrong. You begin by doing some brainstorming about the episodes. Then, as you start to organize the prewriting material, you hit upon a possible principle of classification: grouping the characters in the show according to the frequency with which they appear (main characters appearing in every show, supporting characters appearing in most shows, and guest characters appearing once or twice). You name the characters and explain which characters fit where. But is this principle of classification significant? Has it anything to do with why the shows will become classics? No, it hasn't. Such an essay would be little more than a meaningless exercise.

In contrast, a significant principle of classification might involve categorizing a number of shows according to the easily recognized human types portrayed: the Pompous Know-It-All, the Boss Who's Out of Control, the Lovable Grouch, the Surprisingly Savvy Innocent. You might illustrate the way certain episodes offer delightful twists on these stock figures, making such shows models of comic plotting and humor.

When you write an essay that uses division-classification as its primary method of development, a *single principle* of division-classification provides the foundation for each major section of the paper. Imagine you're writing an essay showing that the success of contemporary music groups has less to do with musical talent than with the group's ability to market themselves to a distinct segment of the listening audience. To develop your point, you might categorize several performers according to the age ranges they appeal to (preteens, adolescents, people in their late twenties) and then analyze the marketing strategies the musicians use to gain their fans' support. The essay's logic would be undermined if you switched, in the middle of your analysis, to another principle of classification—say, the influence of earlier groups on today's music scene.

Don't, however, take this caution to mean that essays can never use more than one principle of division-classification as they unfold. They can—as long as the *shift from one principle to another* occurs in *different parts* of the paper. Imagine you want to write about widespread disillusionment with student government leaders at your college. You could develop this point by breaking down the dissatisfaction into the following: disappointment with the students' qualifications for office; disenchantment with their campaign tactics; frustration with their performance once elected. That section of the essay completed, you might move to a second principle of division—how students can get involved in campus government. Perhaps you break the proposed involvement into the following possibilities: serving on nominating committees; helping to run candidates' campaigns; attending open sessions of the student government.

2. Apply the principle of division-classification logically. In an essay using division-classification, you need to demonstrate to readers that your analysis is the result of careful thought. First of all, your division-classification should be as *complete* as possible. Your analysis should include—within reason—all the parts into which you can divide your subject, or all the types into which you can categorize your subjects. Let's say you're writing an essay showing that where college students live is an important factor in determining how satisfied they are with college life. Keeping your purpose in mind, you classify students according to where they live: with parents, in dorms, in fraternity and sorority houses. But what about all the students who live in rented apartments, houses, or rooms off campus? If these places of residence are ignored, your classification won't be complete; you will lose credibility with your readers because they'll probably realize that you have overlooked several important considerations.

Your division-classification should also be *consistent:* the parts into which you break your subject or the groups into which you place your subjects should be as mutually exclusive as possible. The parts or categories should not be mixed, nor should they overlap. Assume you're writing an essay describing the animals at the zoo in a nearby city. You decide to describe the zoo's mammals, reptiles, birds, and endangered species. But such a classification is inconsistent. You begin by categorizing the animals according to scientific class (mammals, birds, reptiles), then switch to another principle when you classify some animals according to whether they are endangered. Because you drift over to a different principle of classification, your categories are no longer mutually exclusive: endangered species could overlap with any of the other categories. In which section of the paper, for instance, would you describe an exotic parrot that is obviously a bird but is also nearly extinct? And how would you categorize the zoo's rare mountain gorilla? This impressive creature is a mammal, but it is also an endangered species. Such overlapping categories undercut the logic that gives an essay its integrity.

3. Prepare an effective thesis.   If your essay uses division-classification as its dominant method of development, it might be helpful to prepare a thesis that does more than signal the paper's subject and suggest your attitude toward that subject. You might also want the thesis to state the principle of division-classification at the heart of the essay. Furthermore, you might want the thesis to reveal which part or category you regard as most important.

Consider the two thesis statements that follow:

Thesis 1

As the observant beachcomber moves from the tidal area to the upper beach to the sandy dunes, rich variations in marine life become apparent.

Thesis 2

Although most people focus on the dangers associated with the disposal of toxic waste in the land and ocean, the incineration of toxic matter may pose an even more serious threat to human life.

The first thesis statement makes clear that the writer will organize the paper by classifying forms of marine life according to location. Since the purpose of the essay is to inform as objectively as possible, the thesis doesn't suggest the writer's opinion about which category is most significant.

The second thesis signals that the essay will evolve by dividing the issue of toxic waste according to methods of disposal. Moreover, because the paper takes a stance on a controversial subject, the thesis is worded to reveal which aspect of the topic the writer considers most important. Such a clear statement of the writer's position is an effective strategy in an essay of this kind.

You may have noted that each thesis statement also signals the paper's plan of development. The first essay, for example, will use specific facts, examples, and details to describe the kinds of marine life found in the tidal area, upper beach, and dunes. However, thesis statements in papers developed primarily through division-classification don't have to be so structured. If a paper is well written, your principle of division-classification, your opinion about which part or category is most important, and the essay's plan of development will become apparent as the essay unfolds.

4. Organize the paper logically. Whether your paper is developed wholly or in part by division-classification, it should have a logical structure. As much as possible, you should try to discuss *comparable points* in each section of the paper. In the essay on seashore life, for example, you might describe life in the tidal area by discussing the mollusks, crustaceans, birds, and amphibians that live or feed there. You would then follow through, as much as possible, with this arrangement in the paper's other sections (upper beach and dunes). Forgetting to describe the birdlife thriving in the dunes, especially when you had discussed birdlife in the tidal and upper-beach areas, would compromise the paper's structure. Of course, perfect parallelism is not always possible—there are no mollusks in the dunes, for instance. You should also use *signal devices* to connect various parts of the paper: "*Another* characteristic of marine life battered by the tides"; "A *final* important trait of both tidal and upper-beach crustaceans"; "*Unlike* the creatures of the tidal area and the upper beach." Such signals clarify the connections among the essay's ideas.

5. State any conclusions or recommendations in the paper's final section. The analytic thinking that occurs during division-classification often leads to surprising insights. Such insights may be introduced early on, or they may be reserved for the end, where they are stated as conclusions or recommendations. A paper might categorize different kinds of coaches—from inspiring to incompetent—and make the point that athletes learn a great deal about human relations simply by having to get along with their coaches, regardless of the coaches' skills. Such a paper might conclude that participation in a team sport teaches more about human nature than several courses in psychology. Or the essay might end with a proposal: Rookies and seasoned team members should be paired, so that novice players can get advice on dealing with coaching eccentricities.

REVISION STRATEGIES

Once you have a draft of the essay, you're ready to revise. The following checklist will help you and those giving you feedback apply to division-classification some of the revision techniques discussed in Chapters 7 and 8.

✔ DIVISION-CLASSIFICATION: A REVISION/PEER REVIEW
   CHECKLIST

Revise Overall Meaning and Structure

☐ What is the principle of division-classification at the heart of the
essay? How does this principle contribute to the essay's overall purpose and thesis?

☐ Does the thesis state the essay's principle of division-classification?
Should it? Does the thesis signal which part or category is most
important? Should it? Does the thesis reveal the essay's plan of
development? Should it?

☐ Is the essay organized primarily through division, classification, or a
blend of both?

☐ If the essay is organized mainly through division, is the subject sufficiently broad and complex to be broken down into parts? What are
the parts?

☐ If the essay is organized mainly through classification, what are the
categories? How does this categorizing reveal similarities and/or
differences that would otherwise not be apparent?

Revise Paragraph Development

☐ Are comparable points discussed in each of the paper's sections?
What are these points?

☐ In which paragraphs does the division-classification seem illogical,
incomplete, or inconsistent? In which paragraphs are parts or categories not clearly explained?

☐ Are the subject's different parts or categories discussed in separate
paragraphs? Should they be?

☐ What conclusions or recommendations are stated or implied in the
closing paragraph(s)?

Revise Sentences and Words

☐ What signal devices ("Another characteristic"; "A third type"; "The
most important trait") help integrate the paper? Are there enough
signals? Too many?

☐ Where should sentences and words be made more concrete and specific in order to clarify the parts and categories being discussed?

STUDENT ESSAY: FROM PREWRITING THROUGH REVISION

The student essay that follows was written by Gail Oremland in response to
this assignment:

In "Propaganda Techniques in Today's Advertising," Ann McClintock describes the flaws in many of the persuasive strategies used by advertisers. Choose another group of people whose job is also to communicate—for example, parents, bosses, teachers. Then, in an essay of your own, divide the group into types according to the flaws they reveal when communicating.

Gail wanted to prepare a light-spirited paper about college professors' foibles. Right from the start, she decided to focus on three kinds of professors: the "Knowledgeable One," the "Leader of Intellectual Discussion," and the "Buddy." She used the *patterns of development* to generate prewriting material about each kind, typing whatever ideas came to mind as she focused on one pattern at a time. Reprinted here is Gail's prewriting for the Knowledgeable One. Note that not every pattern sparked ideas. When Gail later reviewed her prewriting, she added some details and deleted others. The handwritten marks on the prewriting indicate Gail's later efforts to refine her rough material.

After annotating her prewriting for all the categories, Gail prepared her first draft, without shaping her prewriting further or making an outline. As she wrote, though, she frequently referred to her warm-up material to retrieve specifics about each professorial type.

Prewriting Using the Patterns of Development

```
                         Knowledgeable One
```

Even in a blizzard or hurricane

Narration: Enters, walks to podium, puts notes on stand, begins lecture exactly on schedule. Talks on and on, stating facts. ~~Even when she had a cold, she kept on lecturing, although we could hardly hear her and her voice kept cracking.~~ Always ends lecture exactly on time. Packs her notes. Hurries away. *Shoots out the back door. Back to the privacy of her office, away from students.*

Description: Self-important air, yellowed notes, all weather, drones, students' glazed eyes, yawns

Doesn't stop, so students feel they can't interrupt

Cause-Effect: Thinks she's an expert and that students are ignorant, so students are intimidated. States one dry fact after another, so students get bored. Addresses students as "Mr." or "Miss," so she establishes distance.

Definition: A fact person

Illustration: History prof who knows death toll of every battle; biology prof who knows all the molecules; accounting prof who knows every clause of tax form

Comparison-Contrast: Interest in specialized academic
area vs. no interest in students

    Now read Gail's paper, "The Truth About College Teachers," noting the similarities and differences between her prewriting and final essay. As you may imagine, the patterns of development that yielded the most details during prewriting became especially prominent in the final essay. Note, too, that Gail's prewriting consisted of unconnected details within each pattern, whereas the essay flows easily. To achieve such coherence, Gail used commentary and transitional phrases to connect the prewriting details. As you read the essay, also consider how well it applies the principles of division-classification discussed in this chapter. (The commentary that follows the paper will help you look at the essay more closely and will give you some sense of how Gail went about revising her first draft.)

The Truth About College Teachers

by Gail Oremland

1   A recent TV news story told about a group of
college professors from a nearby university who were
hired by a local school system to help upgrade the
teaching in the community's public schools. The
professors were to visit classrooms, analyze teachers'
skills, and then conduct workshops to help the
teachers become more effective at their jobs. But
after the first round of workshops, the superintendent
of schools decided to cancel the whole project. He
fired the learned professors and sent them back to
their ivory tower. Why did the project fall apart?
There was a simple reason. The college professors, who
were supposedly going to show the public school
teachers how to be more effective, were themselves
poor teachers. Many college students could have
predicted such a disastrous outcome. They know,
firsthand, that college teachers are strange. They
know that professors often exhibit bizarre behaviors,
relating to students in ways that make it difficult
for students to stay awake, or--if awake--to learn.

Introduction

Thesis

2   One type of professor assumes, legitimately enough,
that her function is to pass on to students the vast
store of knowledge she has acquired. But because the
"Knowledgeable One" regards herself as an expert and her
students as the ignorant masses, she adopts an elitist

Topic sentence

The first of three paragraphs on the first category of teacher

The first paragraph in a three-part chronological sequence: What happens *before* class

approach that sabotages learning. The Knowledgeable One enters a lecture hall with a self-important air, walks to the podium, places her yellowed-with-age notes on the stand, and begins her lecture at the exact second the class is officially scheduled to begin. There can be a blizzard or hurricane raging outside the lecture hall; students can be running through freezing sleet and howling winds to get to class on time. Will the Knowledgeable One wait for them to arrive before beginning her lecture? Probably not. The Knowledgeable One's time is precious. She's there, set to begin, and that's what matters.

Topic Sentence ——————→

The second paragraph on the first category of teacher

The second paragraph in the chronological sequence: What happens *during* class

Once the monologue begins, the Knowledgeable One drones on and on. The Knowledgeable One is a fact person. She may be the history prof who knows the death toll of every Civil War battle, the biology prof who can diagram all the common biological molecules, the accounting prof who enumerates every clause of the federal tax form. Oblivious to students' glazed eyes and stifled yawns, the Knowledgeable One delivers her monologue, dispensing one dry fact after another. The only advantage to being on the receiving end of this boring monologue is that students do not have to worry about being called on to question a point or provide an opinion; the Knowledgeable One is not willing to relinquish one minute of her time by giving students a voice. Assume for one improbable moment that a student actually manages to stay awake during the monologue and is brave enough to ask a question. In such a case, the Knowledgeable One will address the questioning student as "Mr." or "Miss." This formality does not, as some students mistakenly suppose, indicate respect for the student as a fledgling member of the academic community. Not at all. This impersonality represents the Knowledgeable One's desire to keep as wide a distance as possible between her and her students.

3

Topic sentence ——————→

The Knowledgeable One's monologue always comes to a close at the precise second the class is scheduled to end. No sooner has she delivered her last forgettable

4

word than the Knowledgeable One packs up her notes and
shoots out the door, heading back to the privacy of her
office, where she can pursue her specialized academic
interests--free of any possible interruption from
students. The Knowledgeable One's hasty departure from
the lecture hall makes it clear she has no desire to
talk with students. In her eyes, she has met her
obligations; she has taken time away from her research
to transmit to students what she knows. Any closer
contact might mean she would risk contagion from
students, that great unwashed mass. Such a danger is to
be avoided at all costs.

5   Unlike the Knowledgeable One, the "Leader of
Intellectual Discussion" seems to respect students.
Emphasizing class discussion, the Leader encourages
students to confront ideas ("What is Twain's view of
morality?" "Was our intervention in Vietnam justified?"
"Should big business be given tax breaks?") and discover
their own truths. Then, about three weeks into the
semester, it becomes clear that the Leader wants
students to discover <u>his</u> version of the truth. Behind
the Leader's democratic guise lurks a dictator. When a
student voices an opinion that the Leader accepts, the
student is rewarded by hearty nods of approval and "Good
point, good point." But if a student is rash enough to
advance a conflicting viewpoint, the Leader responds with
killing politeness: "Well, yes, that's an interesting
perspective. But don't you think that . . . ?" Grade-
conscious students soon learn not to chime in with their
viewpoint. They know that when the Leader, with seeming
honesty, says, "I'd be interested in hearing what you
think. Let's open this up for discussion," they had
better figure out what the Leader wants to hear before
advancing their own theories. "Me-tooism" rather than
independent thinking, they discover, guarantees good
grades in the Leader's class.

6   Then there is the professor who comes across as the
students' "Buddy." This kind of professor does not see
himself as an imparter of knowledge or a leader of

The third paragraph on the first category of teacher

The final paragraph in the chronological sequence: What happens *after* class

Topic sentence

Paragraph on the second category of teacher

Topic sentence

Paragraph on the third
category of teacher

discussion but as a pal, just one in a community of
equals. The Buddy may start his course this way: "All of
us know that this college stuff--grades, degrees, exams,
required reading--is a game. So let's not play it,
okay?" Dressed in jeans, sweatshirt, and scuffed
sneakers, the Buddy projects a relaxed, casual attitude.
He arranges the class seats in a circle (he would never
take a position in front of the room) and insists that
students call him by his first name. He uses no syllabus
and gives few tests, believing that such constraints
keep students from directing their own learning. A free
spirit, the Buddy often teaches courses like "The
Psychology of Interpersonal Relations" or "The Social
Dynamics of the Family." If students choose to use class
time to discuss the course material, that's fine. If
they want to discuss something else, that's fine, too.
It's the self-expression, the honest dialog, that counts.
In fact, the Buddy seems especially fond of digressions
from academic subjects. By talking about his political
views, his marital problems, his tendency to drink one
too many beers, the Buddy lets students see that he is a
regular guy--just like them. At first, students look
forward to classes with the Buddy. They enjoy the
informality, the chitchat, the lack of pressure. But
after a while, they wonder why they are paying for a
course where they learn nothing. They might as well stay
home and watch talk shows.

Conclusion

Echoes opening
anecdote

Obviously, some college professors are excellent. They   7
are learned, hardworking, and imaginative; they enjoy
their work and like being with students. On the whole,
though, college professors are a strange lot. Despite
their advanced degrees and their own exposure to many
different kinds of teachers, they do not seem to
understand how to relate to students. Rather than being
hired as consultants to help others upgrade their teaching
skills, college professors should themselves hire
consultants to tell them what they are doing wrong and
how they can improve. Who should these consultants be?
That's easy: the people who know them best--their
students.

Commentary

Introduction and Thesis

After years of being graded by teachers, Gail took special pleasure in writing an essay that gave her a chance to evaluate her teachers—in this case, her college professors. Even the essay's title, "The Truth About College Teachers," implies that Gail is going to have fun knocking profs down from their ivory towers. To introduce her subject, she uses a timely news story. This brief anecdote leads directly to the essay's *thesis:* "Professors often exhibit bizarre behaviors, relating to students in ways that make it difficult for students to stay awake, or—if awake—to learn." Note that Gail's thesis isn't highly structured; it doesn't, for example, name the specific categories to be discussed. Still, her thesis suggests that the essay is going to *categorize* a range of teaching behaviors, using as a *principle of classification* the strange ways that college profs relate to students.

Purpose

As with all good papers developed through division-classification, Gail's essay doesn't use classification as an end in itself. Gail uses classification because it helps her achieve a broader *purpose*. She wants to *convince* readers—without moralizing or abandoning her humorous tone—that such teaching styles inhibit learning. In other words, there's a serious undertone to her essay. This additional layer of meaning is characteristic of satiric writing.

Categories and Topic Sentences

The essay's body, consisting of five paragraphs, presents the three categories that make up Gail's analysis. According to Gail, college teachers can be categorized as the Knowledgeable One (paragraphs 2–4), the Leader of Intellectual Discussion (5), or the Buddy (6). Obviously, there are other ways professors might be classified. But given Gail's purpose, audience, tone, and point of view, her categories are appropriate; they are reasonably *complete, consistent,* and *mutually exclusive.* Note, too, that Gail uses *topic sentences* near the beginning of each category to help readers see which professorial type she's discussing.

Overall Organization and Paragraph Structure

Gail is able to shift smoothly and easily from one category to the next. How does she achieve such graceful transitions? Take a moment to reread the sentences that introduce her second and third categories (paragraphs 5 and 6). Look at the way each sentence's beginning (in italics here) links back to the preceding category or categories: "*Unlike the Knowledgeable One,* the 'Leader of Intellectual Discussion' seems to respect students"; and the "Buddy . . . *does not see himself as an imparter of knowledge or a leader of discussion* but as a pal. . . ."

Gail is equally careful about providing an easy-to-follow structure within each section. She uses a *chronological sequence* to organize her three-paragraph discussion of the Knowledgeable One. The first paragraph deals with the beginning of the Knowledgeable One's lecture; the second, with the lecture itself; the third, with the end of the lecture. And the paragraphs' *topic sentences* clearly indicate this passage of time. Similarly, *transitions* are used in the paragraphs on the Leader of Intellectual Discussion and the Buddy to ensure a logical progression of points: "*Then,* about three weeks into the semester, it becomes clear that the Leader wants students to discover *his* version of the truth" (5), and "*At first,* students look forward to classes with the Buddy. . . . But *after a while,* they wonder why they are paying for a course where they learn nothing" (6).

Tone

The essay's unity can also be traced to Gail's skill in sustaining her satiric tone. Throughout the essay, Gail selects details that fit her gently mocking attitude. She depicts the Knowledgeable One lecturing from "yellowed-with-age notes . . . , oblivious to students' glazed eyes and stifled yawns," unwilling to wait for students who "run . . . through freezing sleet and howling winds to get to class on time." Then she presents another tongue-in-cheek description, this one focusing on the way the Leader of Intellectual Discussion conducts class: "Good point, good point. . . . Well, yes, that's an interesting perspective. But don't you think that . . . ?" Finally, with similar killing accuracy, Gail portrays the Buddy, democratically garbed in "jeans, sweatshirt, and scuffed sneakers."

Other Patterns of Development

Gail's satiric depiction of her three professorial types employs a number of techniques associated with *narrative* and *descriptive writing:* vigorous images, highly connotative language, and dialog. *Definition, illustration, causal analysis,* and *comparison-contrast* also come into play. Gail defines the characteristics of each type of professor; she provides numerous examples to support her categories; she explains the effects of the different teaching styles on students; and, in her description of the Leader of Intellectual Discussion, she contrasts the appearance of democracy with the dictatorial reality.

Unequal Development of Categories

Although Gail's essay is unified, organized, and well developed, you may have felt that the first category outweighs the other two. There is, of course, no need to balance the categories exactly. But Gail's extended treatment of the first category sets up an expectation that the others will be treated as fully. One way to remedy this problem would be to delete some material from the discussion of the Knowledgeable One. Gail might, for instance, omit the first five sentences in the third paragraph (about the professor's habit of addressing students as Mr. or Miss). Such a change could be made without taking the bite out of her portrayal. Even better, Gail could simply switch the order of her sections, putting the portrait of the Knowledgeable One at the essay's end. Here, the extended discussion wouldn't seem out of proportion. Instead, the sections would appear in *emphatic order,* with the most detailed category saved for last.

Revising the First Draft

It's apparent that an essay as engaging as Gail's must have undergone a good deal of revising. Along the way, Gail made many changes in her draft, but it's particularly interesting to see how she changed her original introduction (reprinted here). The annotation represents her general impressions of the paragraph's problems.

Original Version of the Introduction

Despite their high IQs, advanced degrees, and published papers, *Too serious.*
some college professors just don't know how to teach. Found *Doesn't fit*
almost in any department, in tenured and untenured positions, *rest*
they prompt student apathy. They fail to convey ideas effectively *of essay.*
and to challenge or inspire students. Students thus finish their
courses having learned very little. Contrary to popular opinion,
these professors' ineptitude is not simply a matter of delivering
boring lectures or not caring about students. Many of them care a
great deal. Their failure actually stems from their unrealistic
perceptions of what a teacher should be. Specifically, they adopt
teaching styles or roles that alienate students and undermine
learning. Three of the most common ones are "The Knowledgeable
One," "The Leader of Intellectual Discussion," and "The Buddy."

When Gail showed the first draft of the essay to her composition instructor, he laughed—and occasionally squirmed—as he read what she had prepared. He was enthusiastic about the paper but felt there was a problem with the introduction's tone; it was too serious when compared to the playful, lightly satiric mood of the rest of the essay. When Gail reread the paragraph, she agreed, but she was uncertain about the best way to remedy the problem. After revising other sections of the essay, she decided to let the paper sit for a while before going back to rewrite the introduction.

In the meantime, Gail switched on the TV. The timing couldn't have been better; she tuned into a news story about several supposedly learned professors who had been fired from a consulting job because they had turned out to know so little about teaching. This was exactly the kind of item Gail needed to start her essay. Now she was able to prepare a completely new introduction, making it consistent in spirit with the rest of the paper.

With this stronger introduction and the rest of the essay well in hand, Gail was ready to write a conclusion. Now, as she worked on the concluding paragraph, she deliberately shaped it to recall the story about the fired consultants. By echoing the opening anecdote in her conclusion, Gail was able to end the paper with another poke at professors—a perfect way to close her clever and insightful essay.

ACTIVITIES:
DIVISION-
CLASSIFICATION

Prewriting Activities

1. Imagine you're writing two essays: One is a humorous paper showing how to impress college instructors; the other is a serious essay explaining why volunteerism is on the rise. What about the topics might you divide and/or classify?

2. Use group brainstorming to identify at least three possible principles of division for *one* of the following topics. For each principle, determine what your thesis might be if you were writing an essay.

   a. Prejudice
   b. Rock music
   c. A shopping mall
   d. A good horror movie

3. Through group brainstorming, identify three different principles of classification that might provide the structure for an essay about the possible effects of a controversial decision to expand your college's enrollment. Focusing on one of the principles, decide what your thesis might be. How would you sequence the categories?

Revising Activities

4. Following is a scratch outline for an essay developed through division-classification. On what principle of division-classification is the essay based? What problem do you see in the way the principle is applied? How could the problem be remedied?

   Thesis: The same experience often teaches opposite things to different people.

   • What working as a fast-food cook teaches: Some learn responsibility; others learn to take a "quick and dirty" approach.
   • What a negative experience teaches optimists: Some learn from their mistakes; others continue to maintain a positive outlook.
   • What a difficult course teaches: Some learn to study hard; others learn to avoid demanding courses.
   • What the breakup of a close relationship teaches: Some learn how to negotiate differences; others learn to avoid intimacy.

5. Following is a paragraph from the first draft of an essay urging that day-care centers adopt play programs tailored to children's developmental needs. What principle of division-classification focuses the paragraph? Is the principle applied consistently and logically? Are parts/categories developed sufficiently? Revise the paragraph, eliminating any problems you discover and adding specific details where needed.

   Within a few years, preschool children move from self-absorbed to interactive play. Babies and toddlers engage in solitary play. Although they sometimes prefer being near other children, they focus primarily on their own actions. This is very different from the highly interactive play of the elementary school years. Sometime in children's second year, solitary play is replaced by parallel play, during which children engage in similar activities near one another. However, they interact only occasionally. By age three, most children show at least some cooperative play, a form that involves interaction and cooperative role-taking. Such role-taking can be found in the "pretend" games that children play to explore adult relationships (games of "Mommy and Daddy") and anatomy (games of "Doctor"). Additional signs of youngsters' growing awareness of peers can be seen at about age four. At this age, many children begin showing a special devotion to one other child and may want to play only with that child. During this time, children also begin to take special delight in physical activities such as running and jumping, often going off by themselves to expend their abundant physical energy.

PROFESSIONAL SELECTIONS: DIVISION-CLASSIFICATION

ANN McCLINTOCK

Formerly director of Occupational Therapy at Ancora State Hospital in New Jersey, Ann McClintock (1946–) has also worked as a freelance writer and editor. She speaks frequently to community groups about the effects of advertising on American life. The following essay, revised for this collection, is part of a work-in-progress about the use of propaganda techniques in the marketing of products and candidates.

Pre-Reading Journal Entry

How susceptible are you to ads and commercials? Do you consider yourself an easy target, or are you a "hard sell"? Have you purchased any products simply because you were won over by effective advertising strategies? What products have you not purchased because you deliberately didn't let yourself be swayed by advertisers' tactics? In your journal, reflect on these questions.

PROPAGANDA TECHNIQUES IN
TODAY'S ADVERTISING

Americans, adults and children alike, are being seduced. They are being brain-   1
washed. And few of us protest. Why? Because the seducers and the brainwashers are
the advertisers we willingly invite into our homes. We are victims, content—even
eager—to be victimized. We read advertisers' propaganda messages in newspapers and
magazines; we watch their alluring images on television. We absorb their messages
and images into our subconscious. We all do it—even those of us who claim to see
through advertisers' tricks and therefore feel immune to advertising's charm.
Advertisers lean heavily on propaganda to sell their products, whether the "products"
are a brand of toothpaste, a candidate for office, or a particular political viewpoint.

Propaganda is a systematic effort to influence people's opinions, to win them over   2
to a certain view or side. Propaganda is not necessarily concerned with what is true or
false, good or bad. Propagandists simply want people to believe the messages being
sent. Often propagandists will use outright lies or more subtle deceptions to sway people's opinions. In a propaganda war, any tactic is considered fair.

When we hear the word "propaganda," we usually think of a foreign menace: anti-   3
American radio programs broadcast by a totalitarian regime or brainwashing tactics
practiced on hostages. Although propaganda may seem relevant only in the political
arena, the concept can be applied fruitfully to the way products and ideas are sold in
advertising. Indeed, the vast majority of us are targets in advertisers' propaganda war.
Every day, we are bombarded with slogans, print ads, commercials, packaging claims,
billboards, trademarks, logos, and designer brands—all forms of propaganda. One
study reports that each of us, during an average day, is exposed to over *five hundred*
advertising claims of various types. This saturation may even increase in the future
since current trends include ads on movie screens, shopping carts, video cassettes,
even public television.

What kind of propaganda techniques do advertisers use? There are seven basic types: 4

1. *Name Calling*   Name calling is a propaganda tactic in which negatively charged   5
names are hurled against the opposing side or competitor. By using such names, propagandists try to arouse feelings of mistrust, fear, and hate in their audiences. For
example, a political advertisement may label an opposing candidate a "loser," "fence-
sitter," or "warmonger." Depending on the advertiser's target market, labels such as "a
friend of big business" or "a dues-paying member of the party in power" can be the
epithets that damage an opponent. Ads for products may also use name calling. An
American manufacturer may refer, for instance, to a "foreign car" in its commercial—
not an "imported" one. The label of foreignness will have unpleasant connotations in
many people's minds. A childhood rhyme claims that "names can never hurt me," but
name calling is an effective way to damage the opposition, whether it is another car
maker or a congressional candidate.

2. *Glittering Generalities*   Using glittering generalities is the opposite of name call-   6
ing. In this case, advertisers surround their products with attractive—and slippery—
words and phrases. They use vague terms that are difficult to define and that may have
different meanings to different people: *freedom, democratic, all-American, progressive, Christian,* and *justice.* Many such words have strong, affirmative overtones. This

kind of language stirs positive feelings in people, feelings that may spill over to the product or idea being pitched. As with name calling, the emotional response may overwhelm logic. Target audiences accept the product without thinking very much about what the glittering generalities mean—or whether they even apply to the product. After all, how can anyone oppose "truth, justice, and the American way"?

7   The ads for politicians and political causes often use glittering generalities because such "buzz words" can influence votes. Election slogans include high-sounding but basically empty phrases like the following:

"He cares about people." (That's nice, but is he a better candidate than his opponent?)
"Vote for progress." (Progress by *whose* standards?)
"They'll make this country great again." (What does "great" mean? Does "great" mean the same thing to others as it does to me?)
"Vote for the future." (What kind of future?)
"If you love America, vote for Phyllis Smith." (If I don't vote for Smith, does that mean I don't love America?)

8   Ads for consumer goods are also sprinkled with glittering generalities. Product names, for instance, are supposed to evoke good feelings: *Luvs* diapers, *New Freedom* feminine hygiene products, *Joy* liquid detergent, *Loving Care* hair color, *Almost Home* cookies, *Yankee Doodle* pastries. Product slogans lean heavily on vague but comforting phrases: . . . General Electric "brings good things to life," and Dow Chemical "lets you do great things." Chevrolet, we are told, is the "heartbeat of America," and Chrysler boasts cars that are "built by Americans for Americans."

9   3. *Transfer* In transfer, advertisers try to improve the image of a product by associating it with a symbol most people respect, like the American flag or Uncle Sam. The advertisers hope that the prestige attached to the symbol will carry over to the product. Many companies use transfer devices to identify their products: Lincoln Insurance shows a profile of the President; Continental Insurance portrays a Revolutionary War minuteman; Amtrak's logo is red, white, and blue; Liberty Mutual's corporate symbol is the Statue of Liberty; Allstate's name is cradled by a pair of protective, fatherly hands.

10   Corporations also use the transfer technique when they sponsor prestigious shows on radio and television. These shows function as symbols of dignity and class. Kraft Corporation, for instance, sponsored a "Leonard Bernstein Conducts Beethoven" concert, while Gulf Oil is the sponsor of *National Geographic* specials and Mobil supports public television's *Masterpiece Theatre.* In this way, corporations can reach an educated, influential audience and, perhaps, improve their public image by associating themselves with quality programming.

11   Political ads, of course, practically wrap themselves in the flag. Ads for a political candidate often show either the Washington Monument, a Fourth of July parade, the Stars and Stripes, a bald eagle soaring over the mountains, or a white-steepled church on the village green. The national anthem or "America the Beautiful" may play softly in the background. Such appeals to Americans' love of country can surround the candidate with an aura of patriotism and integrity.

12   4. *Testimonial* The testimonial is one of advertisers' most-loved and most-used propaganda techniques. Similar to the transfer device, the testimonial capitalizes on the

admiration people have for a celebrity to make the product shine more brightly—even though the celebrity is not an expert on the product being sold.

Print and television ads offer a nonstop parade of testimonials: here's William 13 Shatner for Priceline.com; here's basketball star Michael Jordan eating Wheaties; a slew of well-known people (including rap star LL Cool J and the rock group Aerosmith) advertise clothing from the Gap; and Jerry Seinfeld assures us he never goes anywhere without his American Express card. Testimonials can sell movies too; newspaper ads for films often feature favorable comments by well-known reviewers. And, in recent years, testimonials have played an important role in pitching books; the backs of paperbacks frequently list complimentary blurbs by celebrities.

Political candidates, as well as their ad agencies, know the value of testimonials. 14 Barbra Streisand lent her star appeal to the presidential campaign of Bill Clinton, while Arnold Schwarzenegger endorsed George Bush. Even controversial social issues are debated by celebrities. The nuclear freeze debate, for instance, starred Paul Newman for the pro side and Charlton Heston for the con.

As illogical as testimonials sometimes are (Pepsi's Michael Jackson, for instance, is 15 a health-food adherent who does not drink soft drinks), they are effective propaganda. We like the *person* so much that we like the *product* too.

5. *Plain Folks* The plain folks approach says, in effect, "Buy me or vote for me. I'm 16 just like you." Regular folks will surely like Bob Evans' Down on the Farm Country Sausage or good old-fashioned Countrytime Lemonade. Some ads emphasize the idea that "we're all in the same boat." We see people making long-distance calls for just the reasons we do—to put the baby on the phone to Grandma or to tell Mom we love her. And how do these folksy, warmhearted (usually saccharine) scenes affect us? They're supposed to make us feel that AT&T—the multinational corporate giant—has the same values we do. Similarly, we are introduced to the little people at Ford, the ordinary folks who work on the assembly line, not to bigwigs in their executive offices. What's the purpose of such an approach? To encourage us to buy a car built by these honest, hardworking "everyday Joes" who care about quality as much as we do.

Political advertisements make almost as much use of the "plain folks" appeal as they 17 do of transfer devices. Candidates wear hard hats, farmers' caps, and assembly-line coveralls. They jog around the block and carry their own luggage through the airport. The idea is to convince voters that the candidates are average people, not the elite—not wealthy lawyers or executives but the common citizen.

6. *Card Stacking* When people say that "the cards were stacked against me," they 18 mean that they were never given a fair chance. Applied to propaganda, card stacking means that one side may suppress or distort evidence, tell half-truths, oversimplify the facts, or set up a "straw man"—a false target—to divert attention from the issue at hand. Card stacking is a difficult form of propaganda both to detect and to combat. When a candidate claims that an opponent has "changed his mind five times on this important issue," we tend to accept the claim without investigating whether the candidate had good reasons for changing his mind. Many people are simply swayed by the distorted claim that the candidate is "waffling" on the issue.

Advertisers often stack the cards in favor of the products they are pushing. They 19 may, for instance, use what are called "weasel words." These are small words that usually slip right past us, but that make the difference between reality and illusion. The weasel words are underlined in the following claims:

"Helps control dandruff symptoms." (The audience usually interprets this as *stops* dandruff.)

"Most dentists surveyed recommend sugarless gum for their patients who chew gum." (We hear the "most dentists" and "for their patients," but we don't think about how many were surveyed or whether or not the dentists first recommended that the patients not chew gum at all.)

"Sticker price $1000 lower than most comparable cars." (How many is "most"? What car does the advertiser consider "comparable"?)

20 Advertisers also use a card stacking trick when they make an unfinished claim. For example, they will say that their product has "twice as much pain reliever." We are left with a favorable impression. We don't usually ask, "Twice as much pain reliever as what?" Or advertisers may make extremely vague claims that sound alluring but have no substance: Toyota's "Oh, what a feeling!"; Vantage cigarettes' "the taste of success"; "The spirit of Marlboro"; Coke's "the real thing." Another way to stack the cards in favor of a certain product is to use scientific-sounding claims that are not supported by sound research. When Ford claimed that its LTD model was "400% quieter," many people assumed that the LTD must be quieter than all other cars. When taken to court, however, Ford admitted that the phrase referred to the difference between the noise level inside and outside the LTD. Other scientific-sounding claims use mysterious ingredients that are never explained as selling points: "Retsyn," "special whitening agents," "the ingredient doctors recommend."

21 7. *Bandwagon* In the bandwagon technique, advertisers pressure, "Everyone's doing it. Why don't you?" This kind of propaganda often succeeds because many people have a deep desire not to be different. Political ads tell us to vote for the "winning candidate." The advertisers know we tend to feel comfortable doing what others do; we want to be on the winning team. Or ads show a series of people proclaiming, "I'm voting for the Senator. I don't know why anyone wouldn't." Again, the audience feels under pressure to conform.

22 In the marketplace, the bandwagon approach lures buyers. Ads tell us that "nobody doesn't like Sara Lee" (the message is that you must be weird if you don't). They tell us that "most people prefer Brand X two to one over other leading brands" (to be like the majority, we should buy Brand X). If we don't drink Pepsi, we're left out of "the Pepsi generation." To take part in "America's favorite health kick," the National Dairy Council asks us, "Got Milk?" And Honda motorcycle ads, praising the virtues of being a follower, tell us, "Follow the leader. He's on a Honda."

23 Why do these propaganda techniques work? Why do so many of us buy the products, viewpoints, and candidates urged on us by propaganda messages? They work because they appeal to our emotions, not to our minds. Often, in fact, they capitalize on our prejudices and biases. For example, if we are convinced that environmentalists are radicals who want to destroy America's record of industrial growth and progress, then we will applaud the candidate who refers to them as "treehuggers." Clear thinking requires hard work: analyzing a claim, researching the facts, examining both sides of an issue, using logic to see the flaws in an argument. Many of us would rather let the propagandists do our thinking for us.

24 Because propaganda is so effective, it is important to detect it and understand how it is used. We may conclude, after close examination, that some propaganda sends a truthful, worthwhile message. Some advertising, for instance, urges us not to drive

drunk, to become volunteers, to contribute to charity. Even so, we must be aware that propaganda is being used. Otherwise, we will have consented to handing over to others our independence of thought and action.

Questions for Close Reading

1. What is the selection's thesis? Locate the sentence(s) in which McClintock states her main idea. If she doesn't state the thesis explicitly, express it in your own words.

2. What is *propaganda?* What mistaken associations do people often have with this term?

3. What are "weasel words"? How do they trick listeners?

4. Why does McClintock believe we should be better informed about propaganda techniques?

5. Refer to your dictionary as needed to define the following words used in the selection: *seduced* (paragraph 1), *warmonger* (5), and *elite* (17).

Questions About the Writer's Craft

1. **The pattern and other patterns.** Before explaining the categories into which propaganda techniques can be grouped, McClintock provides a definition of propaganda. Is the definition purely informative, or does it have a larger objective? If you think the latter, what is the definition's broader purpose?

2. In her introduction, McClintock uses loaded words like *seduced* and *brain-washed.* What effect do these words have on the reader?

3. Locate places where McClintock uses questions. Which are rhetorical and which are genuine queries?

4. What kind of conclusion does McClintock provide for the essay?

Writing Assignments Using Division-Classification as a Pattern of Development

∞ 1. McClintock cautions us to be sensitive to propaganda in advertising. Young children, however, aren't capable of this kind of awareness. With pen or pencil in hand, watch some television commercials aimed at children, such as those for toys, cereals, and fast food. Then analyze the use of propaganda techniques in these commercials. Using division-classification, write an essay describing the main propaganda techniques you observed. Support your analysis with examples drawn from the commercials. Remember to provide a thesis that indicates your opinion of the advertising techniques used on television. To gain insight into television's powerful influence, read Ellen Goodman's "Family Counterculture" (page 7).

2. Like advertising techniques, television shows can be classified. Avoiding the obvious system of classifying according to game shows, detective shows, and situation comedies, come up with your own original division-classification principle. Possibilities include how family life is depicted, the way work is presented, how male-female relationships are portrayed. Using one such principle, write an essay in which you categorize popular TV shows into three types. Refer to specific shows to support your classification system. Your attitude toward the shows being discussed should be clear.

Writing Assignments Using Other Patterns of Development

∞ 3. McClintock says that card stacking "distort[s] evidence, tell[s] half-truths, over-simplif[ies] the facts" (18). Focusing on an editorial, a political campaign, a print ad, or a television commercial, analyze the extent to which card stacking is used as a persuasive strategy. Reading William Lutz's "Doublespeak" (page 295) will deepen your understanding of the extent to which the truth can be distorted.

4. To increase further your sensitivity to the moral dimensions of propaganda, write a proposal outlining an ad campaign for a real or imaginary product or elected official. The introduction to your proposal should identify who or what is to be promoted, and the thesis or plan of development should indicate the specific propaganda techniques you suggest. In the paper's supporting paragraphs, explain how these techniques would be used to promote your product or candidate.

Writing Assignment Using a Journal Entry as a Starting Point

5. Write an essay showing that, on the whole, you are fairly susceptible to *or* are fairly immune to advertising ploys. Drawing upon your pre-reading journal entry, illustrate your position with lively details of advertising campaigns that won you over—or that failed to sway you. Draw upon some of McClintock's terminology when describing advertisers' techniques. Your essay may have a serious or a playful tone.

DEBORAH TANNEN

Deborah Tannen (1945–) is a linguistics professor at Georgetown University and has been a Distinguished McGraw Lecturer at Princeton University. She has shared her research with the general public through appearances on the *Today* show and CNN, through pieces in *The New York Times* and *The Washington Post*, and in books, including *That's Not What I Meant: How Conversational Style Makes or Breaks Relationships* (1987), *You Just Don't Understand: Women and Men in Conversation* (1990), *The Argument Culture: Moving from Debate to Dialogue* (1998), and *I Only Say This Because I Love You* (2001). The following selection is from *Talking from 9 to 5: How Women's and Men's Conversational Styles Affect Who Gets Ahead, Who Gets Credit, and What Gets Done at Work* (1994).

Pre-Reading Journal Entry

It's been said that men and women communicate in different ways. Do you agree? Why or why not? Take a few moments to respond to this question in your journal, drawing upon your experiences and observations.

BUT WHAT DO YOU MEAN?

Conversation is a ritual. We say things that seem obviously the thing to say, with-   1
out thinking of the literal meaning of our words, any more than we expect the question "How are you?" to call forth a detailed account of aches and pains.

Unfortunately, women and men often have different ideas about what's appropriate,   2
different ways of speaking. Many of the conversational rituals common among women are designed to take the other person's feelings into account, while many of the conversational rituals common among men are designed to maintain the one-up position, or at least avoid appearing one-down. As a result, when men and women interact—especially at work—it's often women who are at the disadvantage. Because women are not trying to avoid the one-down position, that is unfortunately where they may end up.

Here, the biggest areas of miscommunication.   3

1. Apologies

Women are often told they apologize too much. The reason they're told to stop   4
doing it is that, to many men, apologizing seems synonymous with putting oneself down. But there are many times when "I'm sorry" isn't self-deprecating, or even an apology; it's an automatic way of keeping both speakers on an equal footing. For example, a well-known columnist once interviewed me and gave me her phone number in case I needed to call her back. I misplaced the number and had to go through the newspaper's main switchboard. When our conversation was winding down and we'd both made ending-type remarks, I added, "Oh, I almost forgot—I lost your direct number, can I get it again?" "Oh, I'm sorry," she came back instantly, even though she had done nothing wrong and *I* was the one who'd lost the number. But I understood she wasn't really apologizing; she was just automatically reassuring me she had no intention of denying me her number.

Even when "I'm sorry" *is* an apology, women often assume it will be the first step   5
in a two-step ritual: I say "I'm sorry" and take half the blame, then you take the other half. At work, it might go something like this:

A: When you typed this letter, you missed this phrase I inserted.

B: Oh, I'm sorry. I'll fix it.

A: Well, I wrote it so small it was easy to miss.

6   When both parties share blame, it's a mutual face-saving device. But if one person, usually the woman, utters frequent apologies and the other doesn't, she ends up looking as if she's taking the blame for mishaps that aren't her fault. When she's only partially to blame, she looks entirely in the wrong.

7   I recently sat in on a meeting at an insurance company where the sole woman, Helen, said "I'm sorry" or "I apologize" repeatedly. At one point she said, "I'm thinking out loud. I apologize." Yet the meeting was intended to be an informal brainstorming session, and *everyone* was thinking out loud.

8   The reason Helen's apologies stood out was that she was the only person in the room making so many. And the reason I was concerned was that Helen felt the annual bonus she had received was unfair. When I interviewed her colleagues, they said that Helen was one of the best and most productive workers—yet she got one of the smallest bonuses. Although the problem might have been outright sexism, I suspect her speech style, which differs from that of her male colleagues, masks her competence.

9   Unfortunately, not apologizing can have its price too. Since so many women use ritual apologies, those who don't may be seen as hard-edged. What's important is to be aware of how often you say you're sorry (and why), and to monitor your speech based on the reaction you get.

2. Criticism

10   A woman who cowrote a report with a male colleague was hurt when she read a rough draft to him and he leapt into a critical response—"Oh, that's too dry! You have to make it snappier!" She herself would have been more likely to say, "That's a really good start. Of course, you'll want to make it a little snappier when you revise."

11   Whether criticism is given straight or softened is often a matter of convention. In general, women use more softeners. I noticed this difference when talking to an editor about an essay I'd written. While going over changes she wanted to make, she said, "There's one more thing. I know you may not agree with me. The reason I noticed the problem is that your other points are so lucid and elegant." She went on hedging for several more sentences until I put her out of her misery: "Do you want to cut that part?" I asked—and of course she did. But I appreciated her tentativeness. In contrast, another editor (a man) I once called summarily rejected my idea for an article by barking, "Call me when you have something new to say."

12   Those who are used to ways of talking that soften the impact of criticism may find it hard to deal with the right-between-the-eyes style. It has its own logic, however, and neither style is intrinsically better. People who prefer criticism given straight are operating on an assumption that feelings aren't involved: "Here's the dope. I know you're good; you can take it."

3. Thank-Yous

13   A woman manager I know starts meetings by thanking everyone for coming, even though it's clearly their job to do so. Her "thank-you" is simply a ritual.

14   A novelist received a fax from an assistant in her publisher's office; it contained suggested catalog copy for her book. She immediately faxed him her suggested changes

and said, "Thanks for running this by me," even though her contract gave her the right to approve all copy. When she thanked the assistant, she fully expected him to reciprocate: "Thanks for giving me such a quick response." Instead, he said, "You're welcome." Suddenly, rather than an equal exchange of pleasantries, she found herself positioned as the recipient of a favor. This made her feel like responding, "Thanks for nothing!"

Many women use "thanks" as an automatic conversation starter and closer; there's 15 nothing literally to say thank you for. Like many rituals typical of women's conversation, it depends on the goodwill of the other to restore the balance. When the other speaker doesn't reciprocate, a woman may feel like someone on a seesaw whose partner abandoned his end. Instead of balancing in the air, she has plopped to the ground, wondering how she got there.

4. Fighting

Many men expect the discussion of ideas to be a ritual fight—explored through ver- 16 bal opposition. They state their ideas in the strongest possible terms, thinking that if there are weaknesses someone will point them out, and by trying to argue against those objections, they will see how well their ideas hold up.

Those who expect their own ideas to be challenged will respond to another's ideas 17 by trying to poke holes and find weak links—as a way of *helping.* The logic is that when you are challenged you will rise to the occasion: Adrenaline makes your mind sharper; you get ideas and insights you would not have thought of without the spur of battle.

But many women take this approach as a personal attack. Worse, they find it impos- 18 sible to do their best work in such a contentious environment. If you're not used to rit-ual fighting, you begin to hear criticism of your ideas as soon as they are formed. Rather than making you think more clearly, it makes you doubt what you know. When you state your ideas, you hedge in order to fend off potential attacks. Ironically, this is more likely to *invite* attack because it makes you look weak.

Although you may never enjoy verbal sparring, some women find it helpful to learn 19 how to do it. An engineer who was the only woman among four men in a small com-pany found that as soon as she learned to argue she was accepted and taken serious-ly. A doctor attending a hospital staff meeting made a similar discovery. She was becoming more and more angry with a male colleague who'd loudly disagreed with a point she'd made. Her better judgment told her to hold her tongue, to avoid making an enemy of this powerful senior colleague. But finally she couldn't hold it in any longer, and she rose to her feet and delivered an impassioned attack on his position. She sat down in a panic, certain she had permanently damaged her relationship with him. To her amazement, he came up to her afterward and said, "That was a great rebuttal. I'm really impressed. Let's go out for a beer after work and hash out our approaches to this problem."

5. Praise

A manager I'll call Lester had been on his new job six months when he heard that 20 the women reporting to him were deeply dissatisfied. When he talked to them about it, their feelings erupted; two said they were on the verge of quitting because he didn't appreciate their work, and they didn't want to wait to be fired. Lester was dumbfounded: He believed they were doing a fine job. Surely, he thought, he had said nothing to give them the impression he didn't like their work. And indeed he hadn't. That was the problem. He had said *nothing*—and the women assumed he was following the adage "If you can't say something nice, don't say anything." He thought he was showing confidence in them by leaving them alone.

21   Men and women have different habits in regard to giving praise. For example, Deirdre and her colleague William both gave presentations at a conference. Afterward, Deirdre told William, "That was a great talk!" He thanked her. Then she asked, "What did you think of mine?" and he gave her a lengthy and detailed critique. She found it uncomfortable to listen to his comments. But she assured herself that he meant well, and that his honesty was a signal that she, too, should be honest when he asked for a critique of his performance. As a matter of fact, she had noticed quite a few ways in which he could have improved his presentation. But she never got a chance to tell him because he never asked—and she felt put down. The worst part was that it seemed she had only herself to blame, since she *had* asked what he thought of her talk.

22   But had she really asked for his critique? The truth is, when she asked for his opinion, she was expecting a compliment, which she felt was more or less required following anyone's talk. When he responded with criticism, she figured, "Oh, he's playing 'Let's critique each other'"—not a game she'd initiated, but one which she was willing to play. Had she realized he was going to criticize her and not ask her to reciprocate, she would never have asked in the first place.

23   It would be easy to assume that Deirdre was insecure, whether she was fishing for a compliment or soliciting a critique. But she was simply talking automatically, performing one of the many conversational rituals that allow us to get through the day. William may have sincerely misunderstood Deirdre's intention—or may have been unable to pass up a chance to one-up her when given the opportunity.

6. Complaints

24   "Troubles talk" can be a way to establish rapport with a colleague. You complain about a problem (which shows that you are just folks) and the other person responds with a similar problem (which puts you on equal footing). But while such commiserating is common among women, men are likely to hear it as a request to *solve* the problem.

25   One woman told me she would frequently initiate what she thought would be pleasant complaint-airing sessions at work. She'd talk about situations that bothered her just to talk about them, maybe to understand them better. But her male office mate would quickly tell her how she could improve the situation. This left her feeling condescended to and frustrated. She was delighted to see this very impasse in a section in my book *You Just Don't Understand,* and showed it to him. "Oh," he said, "I see the problem. How can we solve it?" Then they both laughed, because it had happened again: He short-circuited the detailed discussion she'd hoped for and cut to the chase of finding a solution.

26   Sometimes the consequences of complaining are more serious: A man might take a woman's lighthearted griping literally, and she can get a reputation as a chronic malcontent. Furthermore, she may be seen as not up to solving the problems that arise on the job.

7. Jokes

I heard a man call in to a talk show and say, "I've worked for two women and nei- 27
ther one had a sense of humor. You know, when you work with men, there's a lot of
joking and teasing." The show's host and the guest (both women) took his comment
at face value and assumed the women this man worked for were humorless. The
guest said, "Isn't it sad that women don't feel comfortable enough with authority to
see the humor?" The host said, "Maybe when more women are in authority roles,
they'll be more comfortable with power." But although the women this man worked
for *may* have taken themselves too seriously, it's just as likely that they each had a
terrific sense of humor, but maybe the humor wasn't the type he was used to. They
may have been like the woman who wrote to me: "When I'm with men, my wit or
cleverness seems inappropriate (or lost!) so I don't bother. When I'm with my
women friends, however, there's no hold on puns or cracks and my humor is fully
appreciated."

The types of humor women and men tend to prefer differ. Research has shown that 28
the most common form of humor among men is razzing, teasing, and mock-hostile
attacks, while among women it's self-mocking. Women often mistake men's teasing as
genuinely hostile. Men often mistake women's mock self-deprecation as truly putting
themselves down.

Women have told me they were taken more seriously when they learned to joke the 29
way the guys did. For example, a teacher who went to a national conference with
seven other teachers (mostly women) and a group of administrators (mostly men) was
annoyed that the administrators always found reasons to leave boring seminars, while
the teachers felt they had to stay and take notes. One evening, when the group met at
a bar in the hotel, the principal asked her how one such seminar had turned out. She
retorted, "As soon as you left, it got much better." He laughed out loud at her response.
The playful insult appealed to the men—but there was a trade-off. The women seemed
to back off from her after this. (Perhaps they were put off by her using joking to align
herself with the bosses.)

There is no "right" way to talk. When problems arise, the culprit may be style 30
differences—and *all* styles will at times fail with others who don't share or understand them, just as English won't do you much good if you try to speak to someone who knows only French. If you want to get your message across, it's not a
question of being "right"; it's a question of using language that's shared—or at
least understood.

Questions for Close Reading

1. What is the selection's thesis? Locate the sentence(s) in which Tannen states her
   main idea. If she doesn't state the thesis explicitly, express it in your own
   words.

2. Describe the differences in the way men and women perceive women's use of
   apologies. According to Tannen, how does this difference in perception create
   a problem?

3. What is the difference between "straight" and "softened" criticism (11)? Does Tannen like one style more than the other? Why or why not?

4. What is a "ritual fight" (16)? How, according to Tannen, do men and women differ in their responses to ritual fighting?

5. Refer to your dictionary as needed to define the following words used in the selection: *synonymous* (paragraph 4), *self-deprecating* (4), *reciprocate* (14), *contentious* (18), *dumbfounded* (20), *soliciting* (23), *commiserating* (24), *malcontent* (26).

Questions About the Writer's Craft

1. **The pattern.**   Are Tannen's seven categories of male-female miscommunication mutually exclusive, or do they overlap? Cite specific examples to support your view. Why do you think she divided them as she did?

2. **Other patterns.**   Besides identifying the differences in men's and women's conversation rituals, Tannen often analyzes the causes and effects of these differences. Trace the causal chain in Tannen's discussion of apologies (paragraphs 7–9). How does this causal chain help Tannen reinforce her thesis?

3. Social scientists like Tannen often write impersonally, relying on statistics and a third-person point of view. Why do you suppose Tannen writes from the first-person point of view? What advantage does this point of view offer?

4. How would you characterize Tannen's tone in this selection? How does Tannen's attitude toward her subject and readers reinforce the essay's purpose?

Writing Assignments Using Division–Classification as a Pattern of Development

1. Tannen's essay shows how typical male-female conversational patterns may put women at a disadvantage. Focus on two other closely related groups whose relationship is imbalanced because the communication behaviors of one are at odds with the group's best self-interest. You might examine the relationship between parents and children, teachers and students, or employers and employees. Like Tannen, categorize the areas in which the imbalance is apparent, and be sure to explain the consequences as well as the origins of the counterproductive communication behavior. For more on miscommunication between people, you might read Dave Barry's "The Ugly Truth About Beauty" (page 367), a humorous take on gender-based behaviors.

2. Tannen's essay focuses on conversational patterns in the workplace. Select another setting you know well—perhaps a dormitory, classroom, subway, party, or sporting event. Focus on a specific type of speech (for example, gossip, compliments, or complaints) that occurs in this setting, and write an

essay investigating the component parts of that kind of speech. Reach some conclusion about the language behaviors you observe. Do you consider them funny, sad, frustrating, or something else? Be sure your tone is consistent with the conclusions you reach.

Writing Assignments Using Other Patterns of Development

3. Tannen discusses differences in men's and women's communication rituals. Extending her work, examine another area where you perceive significant gender differences. Possibilities include the way men and women eat, socialize, shop for clothes, furnish their rooms, or watch television. Write an essay comparing and contrasting the sexes' attitudes and behaviors in this area. Brainstorm with others to gather anecdotes that convincingly exemplify the behaviors you describe. Your essay may be serious, lighthearted, or both. Before writing, read at least two of the following essays for additional perspectives on gender issues: Susan Douglas's "Managing Mixed Messages" (page 251), Dave Barry's "The Ugly Truth About Beauty" (page 367), Camille Paglia's "Rape: A Bigger Danger Than Feminists Know" (page 489), and Susan Jacoby's "Common Decency" (page 494). You may also want to read relevant portions of Tannen's *You Just Don't Understand* or *Talking from 9 to 5*.

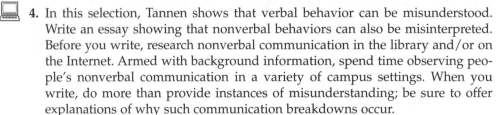

4. In this selection, Tannen shows that verbal behavior can be misunderstood. Write an essay showing that nonverbal behaviors can also be misinterpreted. Before you write, research nonverbal communication in the library and/or on the Internet. Armed with background information, spend time observing people's nonverbal communication in a variety of campus settings. When you write, do more than provide instances of misunderstanding; be sure to offer explanations of why such communication breakdowns occur.

Writing Assignment Using a Journal Entry as a Starting Point

5. Write an essay in which you agree *or* disagree with the claim that women and men have different styles of communication. To defend your contention, select and develop the most persuasive examples from your pre-reading journal entry. Brainstorming with friends, family, and classmates will help you generate additional supporting examples. Remember, too, to acknowledge the opposing argument, dismantling as much of it as you can. You might also consult two other essays that speculate about the nature of specific human behaviors: Stephen King's "Why We Crave Horror Movies" (page 398) and James Gleick's "Life As Type A" (page 433).

WILLIAM LUTZ

With a dash of humor, William Lutz (1941–), professor of English at Rutgers University, writes about a subject he takes very seriously: doublespeak—the use of language to evade, deceive, and mislead. And expert on language, Lutz has appeared on many national television programs, among them the *Today* show, the *Larry King Live Show*, and the *MacNeil-Lehrer News Hour.* Lutz has written over two dozen articles and is the author or coauthor of fourteen books, including the best-selling *Doublespeak: From Revenue Enhancement to Terminal Living* (1989) as well as its sequels, *The New Doublespeak: Why No One Knows What Anyone's Saying Anymore* (1996) and *Doublespeak Defined: Cut Through the Bull**** and Get to the Point* (1999). The following piece is from *Doublespeak.*

Pre-Reading Journal Entry

At one time or another, everyone twists language in order to avoid telling the full truth. In your journal, list several instances that demonstrate that indirect, partially true language ("doublespeak") is sometimes desirable, even necessary. In each case, why was this evasive language used?

DOUBLESPEAK

1   There are no potholes in the streets of Tucson, Arizona, just "pavement deficiencies." The Reagan Administration didn't propose any new taxes, just "revenue enhancement" through new "user's fees." Those aren't bums on the street, just "non-goal oriented members of society." There are no more poor people, just "fiscal underachievers." There was no robbery of an automatic teller machine, just an "unauthorized withdrawal." The patient didn't die because of medical malpractice, it was just a "diagnostic misadventure of a high magnitude." The U.S. Army doesn't kill the enemy anymore, it just "services the target." And the doublespeak goes on.

2   Doublespeak is language that pretends to communicate but really doesn't. It is language that makes the bad seem good, the negative appear positive, the unpleasant appear attractive or at least tolerable. Doublespeak is language that avoids or shifts responsibility, language that is at variance with its real or purported meaning. It is language that conceals or prevents thought; rather than extending thought, doublespeak limits it. . . .

How to Spot Doublespeak

3   How can you spot doublespeak? Most of the time you will recognize doublespeak when you see or hear it. But, if you have any doubts, you can identify doublespeak just by answering these questions: Who is saying what to whom, under what conditions and circumstances, with what intent, and with what results? Answering these questions will usually help you identify as doublespeak language that appears to be legitimate or that at first glance doesn't even appear to be doublespeak.

First Kind of Doublespeak

There are at least four kinds of doublespeak. The first is the euphemism, an inoffen-   4
sive or positive word or phrase used to avoid a harsh, unpleasant, or distasteful reality.
But a euphemism can also be a tactful word or phrase which avoids directly mentioning a painful reality, or it can be an expression used out of concern for the feelings of
someone else, or to avoid directly discussing a topic subject to a social or cultural taboo.

When you use a euphemism because of your sensitivity for someone's feelings or   5
out of concern for a recognized social or cultural taboo, it is not doublespeak. For example, you express your condolences that someone has "passed away" because you do
not want to say to a grieving person, "I'm sorry your father is dead." When you use
the euphemism "passed away," no one is misled. Moreover, the euphemism functions
here not just to protect the feelings of another person, but to communicate also your
concern for that person's feelings during a period of mourning. When you excuse yourself to go to the "restroom," or you mention that someone is "sleeping with" or
"involved with" someone else, you do not mislead anyone about your meaning, but
you do respect the social taboos about discussing bodily functions and sex in direct
terms. You also indicate your sensitivity to the feelings of your audience, which is usually considered a mark of courtesy and good manners.

However, when a euphemism is used to mislead or deceive, it becomes double-   6
speak. For example, in 1984 the U.S. State Department announced that it would no
longer use the word "killing" in its annual report on the status of human rights in
countries around the world. Instead, it would use the phrase "unlawful or arbitrary
deprivation of life," which the department claimed was more accurate. Its real purpose
for using this phrase was simply to avoid discussing the embarrassing situation of
government-sanctioned killings in countries that are supported by the United States
and have been certified by the United States as respecting the human rights of their
citizens. This use of a euphemism constitutes doublespeak, since it is designed to mislead, to cover up the unpleasant. Its real intent is at variance with its apparent intent.
It is language designed to alter our perception of reality.

The Pentagon, too, avoids discussing unpleasant realities when it refers to bombs   7
and artillery shells that fall on civilian targets as "incontinent ordnance." And in 1977
the Pentagon tried to slip funding for the neutron bomb unnoticed into an appropria-
tions bill by calling it a "radiation enhancement device."

Second Kind of Doublespeak

A second kind of doublespeak is jargon, the specialized language of a trade,   8
profession, or similar group, such as that used by doctors, lawyers, engineers,
educators, or car mechanics. Jargon can serve an important and useful function. Within
a group, jargon functions as a kind of verbal shorthand that allows members of the
group to communicate with each other clearly, efficiently, and quickly. Indeed, it is a
mark of membership in the group to be able to use and understand the group's jargon.

But jargon, like the euphemism, can also be doublespeak. It can be—and often is—   9
pretentious, obscure, and esoteric terminology used to give an air of profundity, authority, and prestige to speakers and their subject matter. Jargon as doublespeak often
makes the simple appear complex, the ordinary profound, the obvious insightful. In
this sense it is used not to express but impress. With such doublespeak, the act of
smelling something becomes "organoleptic analysis," glass becomes "fused silicate," a

crack in a metal support beam becomes a "discontinuity," conservative economic policies become "distributionally conservative notions."

10   Lawyers, for example, speak of an "involuntary conversion" of property when discussing the loss or destruction of property through theft, accident, or condemnation. If your house burns down or if your car is stolen, you have suffered an involuntary conversion of your property. When used by lawyers in a legal situation, such jargon is a legitimate use of language, since lawyers can be expected to understand the term.

11   However, when a member of a specialized group uses its jargon to communicate with a person outside the group, and uses it knowing that the nonmember does not understand such language, then there is doublespeak. For example, on May 9, 1978, a National Airlines 727 airplane crashed while attempting to land at the Pensacola, Florida airport. Three of the fifty-two passengers aboard the airplane were killed. As a result of the crash, National made an after-tax insurance benefit of $1.7 million, or an extra 18¢ a share dividend for its stockholders. Now National Airlines had two problems: It did not want to talk about one of its airplanes crashing, and it had to account for the $1.7 million when it issued its annual report to its stockholders. National solved the problem by inserting a footnote in its annual report which explained that the $1.7 million income was due to "the involuntary conversion of a 727." National thus acknowledged the crash of its airplane and the subsequent profit it made from the crash, without once mentioning the accident or the deaths. However, because airline officials knew that most stockholders in the company, and indeed most of the general public, were not familiar with legal jargon, the use of such jargon constituted doublespeak.

Third Kind of Doublespeak

12   A third kind of doublespeak is gobbledygook or bureaucratese. Basically, such doublespeak is simply a matter of piling on words, of overwhelming the audience with words, the bigger the words and the longer the sentences the better. Alan Greenspan, then chair of President Nixon's Council of Economic Advisors, was quoted in *The Philadelphia Inquirer* in 1974 as having testified before a Senate committee that "It is a tricky problem to find the particular calibration in timing that would be appropriate to stem the acceleration in risk premiums created by falling incomes without prematurely aborting the decline in the inflation-generated risk premiums."

13   Nor has Mr. Greenspan's language changed since then. Speaking to the meeting of the Economic Club of New York in 1988, Mr. Greenspan, now Federal Reserve chair, said, "I guess I should warn you, if I turn out to be particularly clear, you've probably misunderstood what I've said." Mr. Greenspan's doublespeak doesn't seem to have held back his career.

14   Sometimes gobbledygook may sound impressive, but when the quote is later examined in print it doesn't even make sense. During the 1988 presidential campaign, vice-presidential candidate Senator Dan Quayle explained the need for a strategic-defense initiative by saying, "Why wouldn't an enhanced deterrent, a more stable peace, a better prospect to denying the ones who enter conflict in the first place to have a reduction of offensive systems and an introduction to defense capability? I believe this is the route the country will eventually go."

15   The investigation into the *Challenger* disaster in 1986 revealed the doublespeak of gobbledygook and bureaucratese used by too many involved in the shuttle program. When Jesse Moore, NASA's associate administrator, was asked if the performance of the shuttle program had improved with each launch or if it had remained the same, he

answered, "I think our performance in terms of the liftoff performance and in terms of the orbital performance, we knew more about the envelope we were operating under, and we have been pretty accurately staying in that. And so I would say the performance has not by design drastically improved. I think we have been able to characterize the performance more as a function of our launch experience as opposed to it improving as a function of time." While this language may appear to be jargon, a close look will reveal that it is really just gobbledygook laced with jargon. But you really have to wonder if Mr. Moore had any idea what he was saying.

Fourth Kind of Doublespeak

The fourth kind of doublespeak is inflated language that is designed to make the ordinary seem extraordinary; to make everyday things seem impressive; to give an air of importance to people, situations, or things that would not normally be considered important; to make the simple seem complex. Often this kind of doublespeak isn't hard to spot, and it is usually pretty funny. While car mechanics may be called "automotive internists," elevator operators members of the "vertical transportation corps," used cars "pre-owned" or "experienced cars," and black-and-white television sets described as having "non-multicolor capability," you really aren't misled all that much by such language.   16

However, you may have trouble figuring out that, when Chrysler "initiates a career alternative enhancement program," it is really laying off five thousand workers; or that "negative patient care outcome" means the patient died; or that "rapid oxidation" means a fire in a nuclear power plant.   17

The doublespeak of inflated language can have serious consequences. In Pentagon doublespeak, "pre-emptive counterattack" means that American forces attacked first; "engaged the enemy on all sides" means American troops were ambushed; "backloading of augmentation personnel" means a retreat by American troops. In the doublespeak of the military, the 1983 invasion of Grenada was conducted not by the U.S. Army, Navy, Air Force, and Marines, but by the "Caribbean Peace Keeping Forces." But then, according to the Pentagon, it wasn't an invasion, it was a "predawn vertical insertion." . . .   18

The Dangers of Doublespeak

These . . . examples of doublespeak should make it clear that doublespeak is not the product of carelessness or sloppy thinking. Indeed, most doublespeak is the product of clear thinking and is carefully designed and constructed to appear to communicate when in fact it doesn't. It is language designed not to lead but mislead. It is language designed to distort reality and corrupt thought. . . . When a fire in a nuclear reactor building is called "rapid oxidation," an explosion in a nuclear power plant is called an "energetic disassembly," the illegal overthrow of a legitimate government is termed "destabilizing a government," and lies are seen as "inoperative statements," we are hearing doublespeak that attempts to avoid responsibility and make the bad seem good, the negative appear positive, something unpleasant appear attractive; and which seems to communicate but doesn't. It is language designed to alter our perception of reality and corrupt our thinking. Such language does not provide us with the tools we need   19 to develop, advance, and preserve our culture and our civilization. Such language breeds suspicion, cynicism, distrust, and, ultimately, hostility.

Questions for Close Reading

1. What is the selection's thesis? Locate the sentence(s) in which Lutz states his main idea. If he doesn't state the thesis explicitly, express it in your own words.

2. According to Lutz, four questions help people "spot" doublespeak. What are the questions? How do they help people distinguish between legitimate language and doublespeak?

3. Lutz's headings indicate simply "First Kind of Doublespeak," "Second Kind of Doublespeak," and so on. What terms does Lutz use to identify the four kinds of doublespeak? Cite one example of each kind.

4. What, according to Lutz, are the dangers of doublespeak?

5. Refer to your dictionary as needed to define the following words used in the selection: *variance* (paragraph 6), *esoteric* (9), *profundity* (9), *dividend* (11), and *initiative* (14).

Questions About the Writer's Craft

1. **The pattern.** Does Lutz make his four categories of doublespeak mutually exclusive, or does he let them overlap? Cite specific examples to support your answer. Why do you think Lutz took the approach he did?

2. **Other patterns.** What other patterns, besides division-classification, does Lutz use in this selection? Cite examples of at least two other patterns. Explain how each pattern reinforces Lutz's thesis.

3. Lutz quotes Alan Greenspan twice: first in paragraph 12 and again in paragraph 13. What is surprising about Greenspan's second comment (paragraph 13)? Why might Lutz have included this second quotation?

4. How would you characterize Lutz's tone in the essay? What key words indicate his attitude toward the material he discusses? Why do you suppose he chose this particular tone?

Writing Assignments Using Division-Classification as a Pattern of Development

∞ 1. According to Lutz, doublespeak "is language designed to alter our perception of reality." Using two of Lutz's categories (or any others you devise), analyze an advertisement or commercial that you think deliberately uses doublespeak to mislead consumers. Before writing your paper, read Ann McClintock's "Propaganda Techniques in Today's Advertising" (page 281). Feel free to include any of McClintock's interpretations in your paper.

2. Select *one* area of life that you know well. Possibilities include life in a college dormitory, the parent-child relationship, the dating scene, and sibling conflicts. Focus on a specific type of speech (for example, gossip, reprimands, flirtation, or criticism) that occurs in this area. Then identify the component parts of that type of speech. You might, for example, analyze dormitory gossip about individual students, couples, and professors. Reach some conclusions about the kinds of speech you discuss. Do you consider them funny, pathetic, or troubling? Your tone should be consistent with the conclusions you reach.

Writing Assignments Using Other Patterns of Development

3. Find a spoken or written example of doublespeak that disturbs you. Possibilities include a political advertisement, television commercial, newspaper article, or legal document. Write a letter of complaint to the appropriate person or office, using convincing examples to point out what is misleading about the communication.

∞ 4. In his essay, Lutz examines the relationship between language and perception. Identify two closely related terms, and contrast the different perceptions of reality represented by each term. For example, you might contrast "African-American" and "Negro," "Ms." and "Miss," "gay" and "homosexual," "dolls" and "action figures," or "pro-life" and "anti-abortion." Interviewing family, friends, and classmates will help you identify ideas to explore in the essay. For a discussion of the connection between language and perception, read Susan Douglas's "Managing Mixed Messages" (page 251) and Ann McClintock's "Propaganda Techniques in Today's Advertising" (page 281).

Writing Assignment Using a Journal Entry as a Starting Point

∞ 5. Select from your pre-reading journal entry two or three compelling instances of *beneficial* doublespeak. Use these examples in an essay arguing that doublespeak isn't always harmful. For each example cited, contrast the positive effects of doublespeak with the potentially negative consequences of *not* using it. Brainstorming with others will help you generate convincing examples. Before you begin writing, consider reading at least two of the following essays, all of which illustrate varying instances of doublespeak: Audre Lorde's "The Fourth of July" (page 216), Beth Johnson's "Bombs Bursting in Air" (page 245), and Ann McClintock's "Propaganda Techniques in Today's Advertising" (page 281).

ADDITIONAL
WRITING TOPICS:
DIVISION-
CLASSIFICATION

General Assignments

Choose one of the following subjects and write an essay developed wholly or in part through division-classification. Start by determining the purpose of the essay. Do you want to inform, compare and contrast, or persuade? Apply a single, significant principle of division or classification to your subject. Don't switch the principle midway through your analysis. Also, be sure that the types or categories you create are as complete and mutually exclusive as possible.

Division

1. A shopping mall
2. A video or stereo system
3. A particular kind of team
4. A school library
5. A playground, gym, or other recreational area
6. A significant event
7. A college campus
8. A television show or movie

Classification

1. People in a waiting room
2. Parents
3. Holidays
4. Students in a class
5. Summer movies
6. College courses
7. Television watchers
8. Commercials

Assignments with a Specific Purpose, Audience, and Point of View

On Campus

1. You're a dorm counselor. During orientation week, you'll be talking to students on your floor about the different kinds of problems they may have with room-mates. Write your talk, describing each kind of problem and explaining how to cope.

2. As your college newspaper's TV critic, you plan to write a review of the fall shows, most of which—in your opinion—lack originality. To show how stereo-typical the programs are, select one type (for example, situation comedies or crime dramas). Then use a specific division-classification principle to illustrate that the same stale formulas are trotted out from show to show.

3. Asked to write an editorial for the campus paper, you decide to do a half-serious piece on taking "mental health" days off from classes. Structure your essay around three kinds of occasions when "playing hooky" is essential for maintaining sanity.

At Home or in the Community

4. Your favorite magazine runs an editorial asking readers to send in what they think are the main challenges facing their particular gender group. Write a let-ter to the editor in which you identify at least three categories of problems that your sex faces. Be sure to provide lively, specific examples to illustrate each cat-egory. In your letter, you may adopt a serious or lighthearted tone, depending on your overall subject matter.

On the Job

5. As a driving instructor, you decide to prepare a lecture on the types of drivers that your students are likely to encounter on the road. In your lecture, catego-rize drivers according to a specific principle and show the behaviors of each type.

6. A seasoned camp counselor, you've been asked to prepare, for new coun-selors, an informational sheet on children's emotional needs. Categorizing those needs into types, explain what counselors can do to nurture youngsters emotionally.

15
PROCESS ANALYSIS

WHAT IS PROCESS ANALYSIS?

Perhaps you've noticed the dogged determination of small children when they're learning how to do something new. Whether trying to tie their shoelaces or tell time, little children struggle along, creating knotted tangles, confusing the hour with the minute hand. But they don't give up. Mastering such basic skills makes them feel less dependent on the adults of the world—all of whom seem to know how to do everything. Actually, none of us is born knowing how to do very much. We spend a good deal of our lives learning—everything from speaking our first word to balancing our first bank statement. Indeed, the milestones in our lives are often linked to the processes we have mastered: how to cross the street alone; how to drive a car; how to make a speech without being paralyzed by fear.

Process analysis, a technique that explains the steps or sequence involved in doing something, satisfies our need to learn as well as our curiosity about how the world works. All the self-help books flooding the market today (*Managing Stress, How to Make a Million in Real Estate, Ten Days to a Perfect Body*) are examples of process analysis. The instructions on the federal tax form and the recipes in a cookbook are also process analyses. Several television classics, now seen in reruns, capitalize on our desire to learn how things happen: *The Wild Kingdom* shows how animals survive in faraway lands, and *Mission: Impossible* has great fun detailing elaborate plans for preventing the triumph of evil. Process analysis can be more than merely interesting or entertaining, though; it can be of critical importance. Consider a waiter hurriedly skimming the "Choking Aid" instructions posted on a restaurant wall or an air-traffic controller following emergency procedures in an effort to prevent a midair collision. In these last examples, the consequences could be fatal if the process analyses are slipshod, inaccurate, or confusing.

Undoubtedly, all of us have experienced less dramatic effects of poorly written process analyses. Perhaps you've tried to assemble a bicycle and spent hours sorting through a stack of parts, only to end up with one or two extra pieces never mentioned in the instructions. Or maybe you were baffled when putting up a set of wall shelves because the instructions used unfamiliar terms like *mitered cleat*, *wing nut*, and *dowel pin*. No wonder many people stay clear of anything that actually admits "assembly required."

HOW PROCESS ANALYSIS FITS YOUR PURPOSE AND AUDIENCE

You will use process analysis in two types of writing situations: (1) when you want to give step-by-step instructions to readers showing how they can do something, or (2) when you want readers to understand how something happens even though they won't actually follow the steps outlined. The first kind of process analysis is **directional;** the second is **informational.**

When you look at the cooking instructions on a package of frozen vegetables or follow guidelines for completing a job application, you're reading directional process analysis. A serious essay explaining how to select a college and a humorous essay telling readers how to get on the good side of a professor are also examples of directional process analysis. Using a variety of tones, informational process analyses can range over equally diverse subjects; they can describe mechanical, scientific, historical, sociological, artistic, or psychological processes: for example, how the core of a nuclear power plant melts down; how television became so important in political campaigns; how abstract painters use color; how to survive a blind date.

Process analysis, both directional and informational, is often appropriate in *problem-solving situations.* In such cases, you say, "Here's the problem and here's what should be done to solve the problem." Indeed, college assignments frequently take the form of problem-solving process analyses. Consider these examples:

Because many colleges and universities have changed the eligibility requirements for financial aid, fewer students can depend on loans or scholarships. How can students cope with the increasing costs of obtaining a higher education?

Over the years, there have been many reports citing the abuse of small children in day-care centers. What can parents do to guard against the mistreatment of their children?

Community officials have been accused of mismanaging recent unrest over the public housing ordinance. Describe the steps the officials took, indicating why you think their strategy was unwise. Then explain how you think the situation should have been handled.

Note that the last assignment asks students to explain what's wrong with the current approach before they present their own step-by-step solution. Problem-solving process analyses are often organized in this way. You may also have noticed that none of the assignments explicitly requires an essay response using process analysis. However, the wording of the assignments—*"Describe the steps,"* *"What* can parents *do,"* *"How* can students *cope"*—indicates that process analysis would be an appropriate strategy for developing the responses.

Assignments don't always signal the use of process analysis so clearly. But during the prewriting stage, as you generate material to support your thesis, you'll often realize that you can best achieve your purpose by developing the essay—or part of it—using process analysis.

Sometimes process analysis will be the primary strategy for organizing an essay; other times it will be used to help make a point in an essay organized around another pattern of development. Let's take a look at process analysis as a supporting strategy.

Assume that you're writing a *causal analysis* examining the impact of television commercials on people's buying behavior. To help readers see that commercials create a need where none existed before, you might describe the various stages in an advertising campaign to pitch a new, completely frivolous product. In an essay *defining* a good boss, you could convey the point that effective managers must be skilled at settling disputes by explaining the steps your boss took to resolve a heated disagreement between two employees. If you write an *argumentation-persuasion* paper urging the funding of programs to ease the plight of the homeless, you would have to dramatize for readers the tragedy of these people's lives. To achieve your purpose, you could devote part of the paper to an explanation of how the typical street person goes about finding a place to sleep and getting food to eat.

PREWRITING STRATEGIES

The following checklist shows how you can apply to process analysis some of the prewriting strategies discussed in Chapter 2.

 PROCESS ANALYSIS: A PREWRITING CHECKLIST

Choose a Process to Analyze

☐ What processes do you know well and feel you can explain clearly (for example, how to jog without injury, how lobbyists influence legislators)?

□ What processes have you wondered about (how to meditate; how the greenhouse effect works)?

□ What process needs changing if a current problem is to be solved?

Determine Your Purpose, Audience, Tone, and Point of View

□ What is the central purpose of your process analysis? Do you want to inform readers so that they will acquire a new skill (how to buy a used car)? Do you want readers to gain a better understanding of a complex process (how young children develop a conscience)? Do you want to persuade readers to accept your point of view about a process, perhaps even urge them to adopt a particular course of action ("If you disagree with the proposed plan for reorganizing academic advisement, you should take the following steps to register your protest with college officials")?

□ What audience are you writing for? What will they need to know to understand the process? What will they not need to know?

□ What point of view will you adopt when addressing the audience?

□ What tone do you want to project? Do you want to come across as serious, humorous, sarcastic, ironic, objective, impassioned?

Use Prewriting to Generate the Stages of the Process

□ How could brainstorming or mapping help you identify primary and secondary steps in the process?

□ How could brainstorming or mapping help you identify the ingredients or materials that the reader will need?

STRATEGIES FOR USING PROCESS ANALYSIS IN AN ESSAY

After prewriting, you're ready to draft your essay. The following suggestions will be helpful whether you use process analysis as a dominant or supportive pattern of development.

1. Formulate a thesis that clarifies your attitude toward the process. Like the thesis in any other paper, the thesis in a process analysis should do more than announce your subject ("Here's how the college's work-study program operates"). It should also state or imply your attitude toward the process: "Enrolling in the college's work-study program has become unnecessarily complicated. The procedure could be simplified if the college adopted the helpful guidelines prepared by the Student Senate."

2. Keep your audience in mind when deciding what to cover. Only after you gauge how much your readers already know (or don't know) about the process can you determine how much explanation to provide. Suppose you've been asked to write an article informing students of the best way to use the university computer center. The article will be published in a newsletter for computer science majors. You would seriously misjudge your audience—and probably put them to sleep—if you explained in detail how to transfer material from disk to disk or how to delete information from a file. However, an article on the same topic prepared for a general audience—your composition class, for instance—would probably require such detailed instructions. The audience's level of knowledge also determines whether you should define technical terms. The computer science majors wouldn't need terms such as *modem, interface,* and *byte* defined, whereas students in your composition class would likely require easy-to-understand explanations. Indeed, with any general audience, you should use as little specialized language as possible.

To determine how much explanation is needed, put yourself in your readers' shoes. Don't assume readers will know something just because you do. Ask questions like these about your audience: "Will my readers need some background about the process before I describe it in depth?" and "If my essay is directional, should I specify near the beginning the ingredients, materials, and equipment needed to perform the process?" (For more help in analyzing your audience, see the checklist on page 23.)

3. Focusing on your purpose, thesis, and audience, explain the process—one step at a time.   After using prewriting techniques to identify primary and secondary steps and needed equipment, you're ready to organize your raw material into an easy-to-follow sequence. At times your purpose will be to explain a process with a *fairly fixed chronological sequence:* how to make a pizza, how to pot a plant, how to change a tire. In such cases, you should include all necessary steps in the correct chronological order. However, if a strict chronological ordering of steps means that a particularly important part of the sequence gets buried in the middle, the sequence probably should be juggled so that the crucial step receives the attention it deserves.

Other times your goal will be to describe a process having *no commonly accepted sequence.* For example, in an essay explaining how to discipline a child or how to pull yourself out of a blue mood, you will have to come up with your own definition of the key steps and then arrange those steps in some logical order. You may also use process analysis to *reject* or *reformulate* a traditional sequence. In this case, you would propose a more logical series of steps: "Our system for electing congressional representatives is inefficient and undemocratic; it should be reformed in the following ways."

Whether the essay describes a generally agreed-on process or one that is not commonly accepted, you must provide all the details needed to explain the process. Your readers should be able to understand, even visualize, the process. There should be no fuzzy patches or confusing cuts from one step to another. Don't, however, go into obsessive detail about minor stages or steps. If you dwell for several hundred words on how to butter the pan, your readers will never stay with you long enough to learn how to make the omelet.

It's not unusual, especially in less defined sequences, for some steps in a process to occur simultaneously and to overlap. When this happens, you should present the steps in the most logical order, being sure to tell your readers that several steps are not perfectly distinct and may merge. For example, in an essay explaining how a species becomes extinct, you would have to indicate that overpopulation of hardy strains and destruction of endangered breeds are often simultaneous events. You would also need to clarify that the depletion of food sources both precedes and follows the demise of a species.

4. Sort out the directional and informational aspects of the process analysis. As you may have discovered when prewriting, directional and informational process analyses are not always distinct. In fact, they may be complementary: You may need to provide background information about a process before outlining its steps. For example, in a paper describing a step-by-step approach for losing weight, you might first need to explain how the body burns calories. Or, in a paper on gardening, you could provide some theory about the way organic fertilizers work before detailing a plan for growing vegetables. Although both approaches may be appropriate in a paper, one generally predominates.

The kind of process analysis chosen has implications for the way you will relate to your reader. When the process analysis is *directional*, the reader is addressed in the *second person:* "You should first rinse the residue from the radiator by . . ." or "Wrap the injured person in a blanket and then. . . ." (In the second example, the pronoun *you* is implied.)

If the process analysis has an *informational* purpose, you won't address the reader directly but will choose from a number of other options. For example, you might use the *first person.* In a humorous essay explaining how not to prepare for finals, you could cite your own disastrous study habits: "Filled with good intentions, I sit on my bed, pick up a pencil, open my notebook, and promptly fall asleep." The *third-person singular or plural* can also be used in informational process essays: "The door-to-door salesperson walks up the front walk, heart pounding, more than a bit nervous, but also challenged by the prospect of striking a deal," or "The new recruits next underwent a series of important balance tests in what was called the 'horror chamber.'" Whether you use the first, second, or third person, avoid shifting point of view midstream.

You might have noticed that in the third-person examples, the present tense ("walks up") is used in one sentence, the past tense ("underwent") in the other. The past tense is appropriate for events already completed, whereas the present tense is used for habitual or ongoing actions. ("A dominant male goose usually flies at the head of the V-wedge during migration.") The present tense is also effective when you want to lend a sense of dramatic immediacy to a process, even if the steps were performed in the past. ("The surgeon gently separates the facial skin and muscle from the underlying bony skull.") As with point of view, be on guard against changing tenses in the middle of your explanation.

5. Provide readers with the help they need to follow the sequence. As you move through the steps of a process analysis, don't forget to *warn readers about* *difficulties* they might encounter. For example, in a paper on the artistry involved in butterflying a shrimp, you might write something like this:

```
Next, make a shallow cut with your sharpened knife along the
convex curve of the shrimp's intestinal tract. The tract, usually
a faint black line along the outside curve of the shrimp, is
faintly visible beneath the translucent flesh. But some shrimp
have a thick orange, blue, or gray line instead of a thin black
one. In all cases, be careful not to slice too deeply, or you will
end up with two shrimp halves instead of one butterflied shrimp.
```

You have told readers what to look for, citing the exceptions, and have warned them against making too deep a cut. Anticipating spots where communication might break down is a key part of writing an effective process analysis.

Transitional words and phrases are also critical in helping readers understand the order of the steps being described. Time signals like *first, next, now, while, after, before,* and *finally* provide readers with a clear sense of the sequence. Entire sentences can also be used to link parts of the process, reminding your audience of what has already been discussed and indicating what will now be explained: "Once the panel of experts finishes its evaluation of the exam questions, randomly selected items are field-tested in schools throughout the country."

6. Select and maintain an appropriate tone. When writing a process analysis essay, be sure your tone is consistent with your purpose, your attitude toward your subject, and the effect you want to have on readers. When explaining how fraternities and sororities recruit new members, do you want to use an objective, nonjudgmental tone, or do you want to project an angry, even accusatory tone? To decide, take into account readers' attitudes toward your subject. Does your audience have a financial or emotional investment in the process being described? Does your own interest in the process coincide or conflict with that of your audience? Awareness of your readers' stance can be crucial. Consider another example: Assume you're writing a letter to the director of the student health center proposing a new system to replace the currently chaotic one. You'd do well to be tactful in your criticisms. Offend your reader, and your cause is lost. If, however, the letter is slated for the college newspaper and directed primarily to other students, you could adopt a more pointed, even sarcastic tone. Readers, you would assume, will probably share your view and favor change.

Once you settle on the essay's tone, maintain it throughout. If you're writing a light piece on the way computers are taking over our lives, you wouldn't include a grim, step-by-step analysis of the way confidential computerized medical records may become public.

7. Open and close the process analysis effectively. A paper developed primarily through process analysis should have a strong beginning. The introduction should state the process to be described and imply whether the essay has an informational or directional intent.

If you suspect readers are indifferent to your subject, use the introduction to motivate them, telling them how important the subject is:

> Do you enjoy the salad bars found in many restaurants? If you do, you probably have noticed that the vegetables are always crisp and fresh--no matter how many hours they have been exposed to the air. What are the restaurants doing to make the vegetables look so inviting? There's a simple answer. Many restaurants dip and spray the vegetables with potent chemicals to make them look appetizing.

If you think your audience may be intimidated by your subject (perhaps because it's complex or relatively obscure), the introduction is the perfect spot to reassure them that the process being described is not beyond their grasp:

> Studies show that many people prefer to accept a defective product rather than deal with the uncomfortable process of making a complaint. But once a few easy-to-learn basics are mastered, anyone can register a complaint that gets results.

Most process analysis essays don't end as soon as the last step in the sequence is explained. Instead, they usually include some brief final comments that round out the piece and bring it to a satisfying close. This final section of the essay may summarize the main steps in the process—not by repeating the steps verbatim but by rephrasing and condensing them in several concise sentences. The conclusion can also be an effective spot to underscore the significance of the process, recalling what may have been said in the introduction about the subject's importance. Or the essay can end by echoing the note of reassurance that may have been included at the start.

REVISION STRATEGIES

Once you have a draft of the essay, you're ready to revise. The following checklist will help you and those giving you feedback apply to process analysis some of the revision techniques discussed in Chapters 7 and 8.

 PROCESS ANALYSIS: A REVISION/PEER REVIEW
    CHECKLIST

Revise Overall Meaning and Structure

☐ What purpose does the process analysis serve? To inform, to persuade, or to do both?

□ Where does the process seem confusing? Where have steps been left out? Which steps need simplifying?

□ What tone does the essay project? Is the tone appropriate for the essay's purpose and readers? Where are there distracting shifts in tone?

Revise Paragraph Development

□ Does the introduction specify the process to be described? Does it provide an overview? Should it? Does it mention ingredients or materials the reader needs to know about? Should it?

□ Which paragraphs are difficult to follow? Have any steps been explained in unnecessary detail? Have key steps been omitted? Which paragraphs should warn readers about potential trouble spots or overlapping steps?

□ Where do time signals (after, before, next) clarify the sequence within and between paragraphs? Where does overreliance on time signals make the sequence awkward and mechanical?

□ Which paragraph describes the most crucial step in the sequence? How has the step been highlighted?

□ What closing comments round out the piece? Would the conclusion be more effective if the main stages were summarized? Or would such a conclusion be too repetitive?

Revise Sentences and Words

□ What technical or specialized terms appear in the essay? Have they been sufficiently defined or explained? Where could simpler, less technical language be used?

□ Are there any places where the essay awkwardly switches from, say, second person to third person? How could this problem be corrected?

□ Does the essay use correct verb tenses—the past tense for completed events, the present tense for habitual or ongoing actions?

□ Where does the essay use the passive voice ("The earth is hoed")? Would the active voice ("You hoe the earth") be more effective?

STUDENT ESSAY: FROM PREWRITING THROUGH REVISION

The student essay that follows was written by Robert Barry in response to this assignment:

In "Watching the Animals," Richard Rhodes describes how the meat that Americans love to eat is processed. Think of something else that Americans enjoy and show, step-by-step, how it has worked its way into Americans' everyday lives. Your essay, either serious or light in tone, might focus on a form of entertainment, a pastime, an invention, or the like.

Before writing his essay, Robert used the prewriting strategy of *mapping* to generate material for the subject he decided to write on: VCR addiction. Then, with his map as a foundation, he prepared a topic outline that organized and developed his thoughts more fully. Both the map and the outline are reprinted here.

Mapping

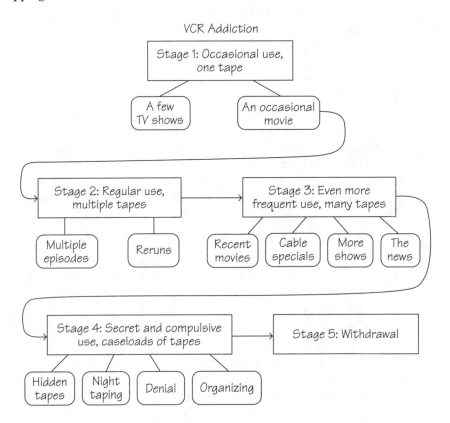

Outline

Thesis: Without realizing it, a person can turn into a compulsive videotaper. This movement from innocent hobby to full-blown addiction occurs in several stages.

   I. Stage One: Occasional use (only one tape)

      A. TV show reruns

         1. Star Trek

         2. Seinfeld

      B. An occasional movie

    II. Stage Two: More frequent use (more tapes)

         A. Many episodes of Star Trek

         B. Reruns of The Honeymooners and Mission: Impossible

   III. Stage Three: Much more frequent use (stockpile of tapes)

         A. Taping of news shows

         B. Taping of recent movies--add examples

         C. Not enough time to watch taped cable shows plus regularly
            taped shows

    IV. Stage Four: Secret and compulsive use (caseloads of tapes)

         A. Reaction to family's concern

            1. Denial

            2. Hiding tapes in suitcase

            3. Nighttime taping

         B. Obsessive organization of tapes

     V. Stage Five: Withdrawal

         A. Forced withdrawal at college

         B. Success at last

After looking at Robert's map and outline, read his paper, "Becoming a Videoholic," noting the similarities and differences among his map, outline, and final essay. You'll see that Robert dropped one idea (taping news shows), expanded other points (his obsessive organization of tapes into Westerns, comedies, and horror movies), and added some completely new details (his near backsliding during withdrawal). Note, too, that the analogy between VCR addiction and alcoholism doesn't appear in either the map or the outline. The analogy didn't occur to Robert until he began writing his first draft. Despite these differences, the map and outline depict essentially the same five stages in VCR addiction as the essay. Finally, as you read the essay, consider how well it applies the principles of process analysis discussed in this chapter. (The commentary that follows the paper will help you look at Robert's essay more closely and will give you some sense of how he went about revising.)

Becoming a Videoholic

by Robert Barry

1   In the last several years, videocassette recorders   Introduction
(VCRs) have become popular additions in many American
homes. A recent newspaper article notes that one in
three households has a VCR, with sales continuing to
climb every day. VCRs seem to be the most popular technological breakthrough since television itself. No consumer
warning labels are attached to these rapidly multiplying VCRs, but they should be. VCRs can be dangerous.

Start of two-sentence thesis → Barely aware of what is happening, a person can turn into a compulsive videotaper. The descent from innocent hobby to full-blown addiction takes place in several stages.

Topic sentence → In the first innocent stage, the unsuspecting person 2
buys a VCR for occasional use. I was at this stage when I asked my parents if they would buy me a VCR as a combined birthday and high school graduation gift. With the VCR, I

First stage in process (VCR addiction) could tape reruns of Star Trek and Seinfeld, shows I would otherwise miss on nights I was at work. The VCR was perfect. I hooked it up to the old TV in my bedroom, recorded the intergalactic adventures of Captain Kirk and the slapstick escapades of Kramer, then watched the tapes the next day. Occasionally, I taped a movie that my friends and I watched over the weekend. I had just one cassette, but that was all I needed since I watched every

Beginning of analogy to alcoholism show I recorded and simply taped over the preceding show when I recorded another. In these early days, my VCR was the equivalent of light social drinking.

Topic sentence → In the second phase on the road to videoholism, an 3

Second stage in process individual uses the VCR more frequently and begins to stockpile tapes rather than watch them. My troubles began in July when my family went to the shore for a week's vacation. I programmed the VCR to tape all five episodes of Star Trek while I was at the beach perfecting my tan. Since I used the VCR's long-play mode, I could get all five Star Treks on one cassette. But that ended up creating a problem. Even I, an avid Trekkie, didn't want to watch five shows in one sitting. I viewed two shows, but the three unwatched shows tied up my tape, making it impossible to record other shows. How did I resolve this dilemma? Very easily. I went out and bought several more cassettes. Once I had these additional tapes, I was free to record as many Star Treks as I wanted, plus I could tape reruns of classics like The Honeymooners and Mission: Impossible. Very quickly, I accumulated six Star Treks, four Honeymooners, and three Mission: Impossibles. Then a friend--who shall go nameless--told me that only eighty-two episodes of Star Trek were ever made. Excited by the thought that I

could acquire as impressive a collection of tapes as a
Hollywood executive, I continued recording Star Trek,
even taping shows while I watched them. Clearly, my once ──── Continuation of analogy
innocent hobby was getting out of control. I was now
using the VCR on a regular basis--the equivalent of
several stiff drinks a day.

4   In the third stage of videoholism, the amount of ←──── Topic sentence
taping increases significantly, leading to an even more
irrational stockpiling of cassettes. The catalyst that   Third stage in process
propelled me into this third stage was my parents'
decision to get cable TV. Selfless guy that I am, I
volunteered to move my VCR and hook it up to the TV in
the living room, where the cable outlet was located. Now
I could tape all the most recent movies and cable ──────── Continuation of analogy
specials. With that delightful possibility in mind, I
went out and bought two six-packs of blank tapes. Then,
in addition to my regulars, I began to record a couple
of other shows every day. I taped Rocky III, Lethal
Weapon 4, a James Bond movie, an HBO comedy special with
Chris Rock, and an MTV concert featuring Janet Jackson.
Where did I get time to watch all these tapes? I didn't.
Taping at this point was more satisfying than watching.
Reason and common sense were abandoned. Getting things
on tape had become an obsession, and I was taping all
the time.

5   In the fourth stage, videoholism creeps into other ←──── Topic sentence
parts of the addict's life, influencing behavior in
strange ways. Secrecy becomes commonplace. One day, my   Fourth stage in process
mother came into my room and saw my bookcase filled with
tapes--rather than with the paperbacks that used to be
there. "Robert," she exclaimed, "isn't this getting a ──────── Continuation of analogy
bit out of hand?" I assured her it was just a hobby, but
I started hiding my tapes, putting them in a suitcase
stored in my closet. I also taped at night, slipping
downstairs to turn on the VCR after my parents had gone
to bed and getting down first thing in the morning to
turn off the VCR and remove the cassette before my
parents noticed. Also, denial is not unusual during this
stage of VCR addiction. At the dinner table, when my
younger sister commented, "Robert tapes all the time," I

laughingly told everyone--including myself--that the taping was no big deal. I was getting bored with it and was going to stop any day, I assured my family.

Obsessive behavior also characterizes the fourth stage of videoholism. Each week, I pulled out the TV magazine from the Sunday paper and went through it carefully, circling in red all the shows I wanted to tape. Another sign of addiction was my compulsive organization of all the tapes I had stockpiled. Working more diligently than I ever had for any term paper, I typed up labels and attached them to each cassette. I also created an elaborate list that showed my tapes broken down into categories such as Westerns, horror movies, and comedies.

Topic sentence ⟶ In the final stage of an addiction, the individual   6

Continuation of analogy — either succumbs completely to the addiction or is able to break away from the habit. I broke my addiction, and I broke it cold turkey. This total withdrawal occurred when I went off to college. There was no point in taking my VCR to school because TVs were not allowed in the freshman dorms. Even though there were many things to occupy my time during the school week, cold sweats overcame me whenever I thought about everything on TV I

Final stage in process   was not taping. I even considered calling home and asking members of my family to tape things for me, but I knew they would think I was crazy. At the beginning of the semester, I also had to resist the overwhelming desire to travel the three hours home every weekend so I could get my fix. But after a while, the urgent need to tape subsided. Now, months later, as I write this, I feel detached and sober.

Conclusion   I have no illusions, though. I know that once a   7 videoholic, always a videoholic. Soon I will return home for the holidays, which, as everyone knows, can

Final references to
analogy   be a time for excess eating--and taping. But I will cope with the pressure. I will take each day one at a time. I will ask my little sister to hide my blank tapes. And if I feel myself succumbing to the temptations of taping, I will pick up the telephone and dial the videoholics' hot line: (800) VCR-TAPE. I will win the battle.

Commentary

Purpose, Thesis, and Tone

Robert's essay is an example of *informational process analysis;* his purpose is to describe—rather than teach—the process of becoming a "videoholic." The title, with its coined term *videoholic,* tips us off that the essay is going to be entertaining. And the introductory paragraph clearly establishes the essay's playful, mock-serious tone. The tone established, Robert briefly defines the term *videoholic* as a "compulsive videotaper" and then moves to the essay's *thesis:* "Barely aware of what is happening, a person can turn into a compulsive videotaper. The descent from innocent hobby to full-blown addiction takes place in several stages."

Throughout the essay, Robert sustains the introduction's humor by mocking his own motivations and poking fun at his quirks: "Selfless guy that I am, I volunteered to move my VCR" (paragraph 4), and "Working more diligently than I ever had for any term paper, I typed up labels" (5). Robert probably uses a bit of *dramatic license* when reporting some of his obsessive behavior, and we, as readers, understand that he's exaggerating for comic effect. Most likely he didn't break out in a cold sweat at the thought of the TV shows he was unable to tape, and he probably didn't hide his tapes in a suitcase. Nevertheless, this tinkering with the truth is legitimate because it allows Robert to create material that fits the essay's lightly satiric tone.

Organization and Topic Sentences

To meet the requirements of the assignment, Robert needed to provide a *step-by-step* explanation of a process. And because he invented the term *videoholism,* Robert also needed to invent the stages in the progression of his addiction. During his prewriting, Robert discovered five stages in his videoholism. Presented *chronologically,* these stages provide the organizing focus for his paper. Specifically, each supporting paragraph is devoted to one stage, with the *topic sentence* for each paragraph indicating the stage's distinctive characteristics.

Transitions

Although Robert's essay is playful, it is nonetheless a process analysis and so must have an easy-to-follow structure. Keeping this in mind, Robert wisely includes *transitions* to signal what happened at each stage of his videoholism: "*Once* I had these additional tapes, I was free to record" (paragraph 3); "*Then,* in addition to my regulars, I began to record" (4); "*One day,* my mother came into my room" (5); and "*But after a while,* the urgent need to tape subsided" (6). In addition to such transitions, Robert uses crisp questions to move from idea to idea within a paragraph: "How did I resolve this dilemma? Very easily. I . . . bought several more cassettes" (3), and "Where did I get time to watch all these tapes? I didn't" (4).

Other Patterns of Development

Even though Robert's essay is a process analysis, it contains elements of other patterns of development. For example, his paper is unified by an *analogy*—a sustained *comparison* between Robert's video addiction and the obviously more serious addiction to alcohol. Handled incorrectly, the analogy could have been offensive, but Robert makes the comparison work to his advantage. The analogy is stated specifically in several spots: "In these early days, my VCR was the equivalent of light social drinking" (2); "I was now using the VCR on a regular basis—the equivalent of several stiff drinks a day" (3). Another place where Robert touches wittily on the analogy occurs in the middle of the fourth paragraph: "I went out and bought two six-packs of blank tapes." To illustrate his progression toward videoholism, Robert depicts the *effects* of his addiction. Finally, he generates numerous lively details or *examples* to illustrate the different stages in his addiction.

Two Unnecessary Sentences

Perhaps you noticed that Robert runs into a minor problem at the end of the fourth paragraph. Starting with the sentence "Reason and common sense were abandoned," he begins to ramble and repeat himself. The paragraph's last two sentences fail to add anything substantial. Take a moment to read paragraph 4 aloud, omitting the last two sentences. Note how much sharper the new conclusion is: "Where did I get time to watch all these tapes? I didn't. Taping at this point was more satisfying than watching." This new ending says all that needs to be said.

Revising the First Draft

When it was time to revise, Robert—in spite of his apprehension—showed his paper to his roommate and asked him to read it out loud. Robert knew this strategy would provide a more objective point of view on his work. His roommate, at first an unwilling recruit, nonetheless laughed as he read the essay aloud. That was just the response Robert wanted. But when his roommate got to the conclusion, Robert heard that the closing paragraph was flat and anticlimactic. His roommate agreed, so the two of them brainstormed ways to make the conclusion livelier and more in spirit with the rest of the essay.

Reprinted here is Robert's original conclusion. The handwritten notes, numbered in order of importance, represent both Robert's ideas for revision and those of his roommate.

Original Version of the Conclusion

③ Shorten first sentence.

① Get back to analogy.

② Boring. Add humor.

> I have no illusions, though, that I am over my videoholism. Soon I will be returning home for the holidays, which can be a time for excess taping. All I can do is ask my little sister to hide my blank tapes. After that, I will hope for the best.

As you can see, Robert and his roommate decided that the best approach would be to reinforce the playful, mock-serious tone that characterized earlier parts of the essay. Robert thus made three major changes to his conclusion. First, he tightened the first sentence of the paragraph ("I have no illusions, though, that I am over my videoholism"), making it crisper and more dramatic: "I have no illusions, though." Second, he added a few sentences to sustain the light, self-deprecating tone he had used earlier: "I know that once a videoholic, always a videoholic"; "But I will cope with the pressure"; "I will win the battle." Third, and perhaps most important, he returned to the alcoholism analogy: "I will take each day one at a time. . . . And if I feel myself succumbing to the temptations of taping, I will pick up the telephone and dial the videoholics' hotline. . . ."

These weren't the only changes Robert made while reworking his paper, but they help illustrate how sensitive he was to the effect he wanted to achieve. Certainly, the recasting of the conclusion was critical to the overall success of this amusing essay.

ACTIVITIES: PROCESS ANALYSIS

Prewriting Activities

1. Imagine you're writing two essays: One defines the term *comparison shopping;* the other contrasts two different teaching styles. Jot down ways you might use process analysis in each essay.

2. Look at the essay topics that follow. Assuming that your readers will be students in your composition class, which topics would lend themselves to directional process analysis, informational process analysis, or a blend of both? Explain your responses.

   a. Going on a job interview
   b. Using a computer in the college library
   c. Cleaning up oil spills
   d. Negotiating personal conflicts
   e. Curing a cold
   f. Growing vegetables organically

3. For *one* of the following essay topics, decide—given the audience indicated in parentheses—what your purpose, tone, and point of view might be. Then use brainstorming, questioning, mapping, or another prewriting technique to identify the steps you'd include in a process analysis for that audience. After reviewing the material generated, delete, add, and combine points as needed. Then organize the material in the most logical sequence.

   a. How to write effective essays (*college students*)
   b. How to get along with parents (*high school students*)
   c. How the college administration handled a controversial campus issue (*alumni*)
   d. How to deal with a bully (*elementary school children*)
   e. How a specific ceremony is performed in your religion (*an adult unfamiliar with the practice*)
   f. How malls encourage spending sprees (*general public*)

4. Select *one* of the essay topics that follow and determine what your purpose, tone, and point of view would be for each audience indicated in parentheses. Then use prewriting to identify the points you'd cover for each audience. Finally, organize the raw material, noting the differences in emphasis and sequence for each group of readers.

   a. How to buy a car (*young people who have just gotten a driver's license; established professionals*)
   b. How children acquire their values (*first-time parents; elementary school teachers*)
   c. How to manage money (*grade-school children; college students*)
   d. How loans or scholarships are awarded to incoming students on your campus (*high school graduates applying for financial aid; high school guidance counselors*)
   e. How arguments can strengthen relationships (*preteen children; young adults*)
   f. How to relax (*college students; parents with young children*)

5. For *one* of the following process topics, identify an appropriate audience, purpose, tone, and point of view. Then use prewriting to generate raw material showing that there's a problem with the way the process is performed. After organizing that material, use prewriting once again—this time to identify how the process *should* be performed. Sequence this new material in a logical order.

   a. How students select a college or a major
   b. How local television news covers national events
   c. How a specific group of people mismanage their finances
   d. How your campus or your community is handling a difficult situation

Revising Activities

6. The following paragraph is from an essay making the point that over-the-phone sales can be a challenging career. The paragraph, written as a process analysis, describes the steps involved in making a sales call. Revise the paragraph, deleting any material that undermines the paragraph's unity, organizing the steps in a logical sequence, and supplying transitions where needed. Also be sure to correct any inappropriate shifts in person. Finally, do some brainstorming—individually or in a group—to generate details to bolster underdeveloped steps in the sequence.

   Establishing rapport with potential customers is the most challenging part of phone sales. The longer you can keep customers on the phone, the more you can get a sense of their needs. And the more you know about customers, the more successful the salesperson is bound to be. Your opening comments are critical. After setting the right tone, you gently introduce your product. There are a number of ways you can move gracefully from your opening remarks to the actual selling phase of the call. Remember: Don't try to sell the customer at the beginning. Instead, try in a friendly way to keep the prospective customer on the phone. Maintaining such a connection is easier than you think because many people have an almost desperate need to talk. Their lives are isolated and lonely--a sad fact of contemporary life. Once you shift to the distinctly selling phase of the call, you should present the advantages of the product, especially the advantages of price and convenience. Mentioning installment payments is often effective. If the customer says that he or she isn't interested, the salesperson should try to determine--in a genial way--why the person is reluctant to buy. Don't, however, push aggressively for reasons or try to steamroll the person into thinking his or her reservations are invalid. Once the person agrees to buy, try to encourage credit card payment, rather than check or money order. The salesperson can explain that credit card payment means the customer will receive the product sooner. End the call as you began--in an easy, personable way.

7. Reprinted here is a paragraph from the first draft of a humorous essay advising shy college students how to get through a typical day. Written as a process analysis, the paragraph outlines techniques for surviving class. Revise the paragraph, deleting digressions that disrupt the paragraph's unity, eliminating unnecessary repetition, and sequencing the steps in the proper order. Also correct inappropriate shifts in person and add transitions where needed. Feel free to add any telling details.

Simply attending class can be stressful for shy people. Several strategies, though, can lessen the trauma. Shy students should time their arrival to coincide with that of most other class members--about two minutes before the class is scheduled to begin. If you arrive too early, you may be seen sitting alone or, even worse, may actually be forced to talk with another early arrival. If you arrive late, all eyes will be upon you. Before heading to class, the shy student should dress in the least conspicuous manner possible--say, in the blue jeans, sweatshirt, and sneakers that 99.9 percent of your classmates wear. That way you won't stand out from everyone else. Take a seat near the back of the room. Don't, however, sit at the very back since professors often take sadistic pleasure in calling on students back there, assuming they chose those seats because they didn't want to be called on. A friend

of mine who is far from shy uses just the opposite ploy. In an
attempt to get in good with her professors, she sits in the
front row and, incredibly enough, volunteers to participate.
However, since shy people don't want to call attention to
themselves, they should stifle any urge to sneeze or cough. You
run the risk of having people look at you or offer you a tissue
or cough drop. And of course, never, ever volunteer to answer.
Such a display of intelligence is sure to focus all eyes on
you. In other words, make yourself as inconspicuous as
possible. How, you might wonder, can you be inconspicuous if
you're blessed (or cursed) with great looks? Well, . . . have
you ever considered earning your degree through the mail?

PROFESSIONAL SELECTIONS: PROCESS ANALYSIS

DIANE COLE

Diane Cole (1952–), a former contributing editor of *Psychology Today,* has written articles for numerous publications, including *The Wall Street Journal, Newsweek, Ms.,* and *Mademoiselle.* Cole has also written several books, among them *Hunting the Head Hunters: A Woman's Guide* (1988) and *After Great Pain: Coping with Loss and Change* (1996). The following selection, which first appeared in *The New York Times* in 1989, was underwritten by the Anti-Defamation League of B'nai B'rith as part of its ongoing campaign against prejudice.

Pre-Reading Journal Entry

Many of us—at some point—have encountered, either in jokes or more serious contexts, offensive language directed at a person or people solely because of their race, ethnicity, gender, sexual preference, or other such characteristic. In your journal, write about one or more such experiences. For each incident, answer the following: Who was involved? What happened? How did the parties, including yourself, respond?

DON'T JUST STAND THERE

It was my office farewell party, and colleagues at the job I was about to leave were   1
wishing me well. My mood was one of ebullience tinged with regret, and it was in this

spirit that I spoke to the office neighbor to whom I had waved hello every morning for the past two years. He smiled broadly as he launched into a long, rambling story, pausing only after he delivered the punch line. It was a very long pause because, although he laughed, I did not: This joke was unmistakably anti-Semitic.

2   I froze. Everyone in the office knew I was Jewish; what could he have possibly meant? Shaken and hurt, not knowing what else to do, I turned in stunned silence to the next well-wisher. Later, still angry, I wondered, what else should I—could I—have done?

3   Prejudice can make its presence felt in any setting, but hearing its nasty voice in this way can be particularly unnerving. We do not know what to do and often we feel another form of paralysis as well: We think, "Nothing I say or do will change this person's attitude, so why bother?"

4   But left unchecked, racial slurs and offensive ethnic jokes "can poison the atmosphere," says Michael McQuillan, adviser for racial/ethnic affairs for the Brooklyn borough president's office. "Hearing these remarks conditions us to accept them; and if we accept these, we can become accepting of other acts."

5   Speaking up may not magically change a biased attitude, but it can change a person's behavior by putting a strong message across. And the more messages there are, the more likely a person is to change that behavior, says Arnold Kahn, professor of psychology at James Madison University, Harrisonburg, Virginia, who makes this analogy: "You can't keep people from smoking in *their* house, but you can ask them not to smoke in *your* house."

6   At the same time, "Even if the other party ignores or discounts what you say, people always reflect on how others perceive them. Speaking up always counts," says LeNorman Strong, director of campus life at George Washington University, Washington, D.C.

7   Finally, learning to respond effectively also helps people feel better about themselves, asserts Cherie Brown, executive director of the National Coalition Building Institute, a Boston-based training organization. "We've found that, when people felt they could at least in this small way make a difference, that made them more eager to take on other activities on a larger scale," she says. Although there is no "cookbook approach" to confronting such remarks—every situation is different, experts stress—these are some effective strategies.

8   When the "joke" turns on who you are—as a member of an ethnic or religious group, a person of color, a woman, a gay or lesbian, an elderly person, or someone with a physical handicap—shocked paralysis is often the first response. Then, wounded and vulnerable, on some level you want to strike back.

9   Lashing out or responding in kind is seldom the most effective response, however. "That can give you momentary satisfaction, but you also feel as if you've lowered yourself to that other person's level," Mr. McQuillan explains. Such a response may further label you in the speaker's mind as thin-skinned, someone not to be taken seriously. Or it may up the ante, making the speaker, and then you, reach for new insults—or physical blows.

10   "If you don't laugh at the joke, or fight, or respond in kind to the slur," says Mr. McQuillan, "that will take the person by surprise, and that can give you more control over the situation." Therefore, in situations like the one in which I found myself—a private conversation in which I knew the person making the remark—he suggests voicing your anger calmly but pointedly: "I don't know if you realize what that sounded like to me. If that's what you meant, it really hurt me."

State how *you* feel, rather than making an abstract statement like, "Not everyone who   11
hears that joke might find it funny." Counsels Mr. Strong: "Personalize the sense of 'this
is how I feel when you say this.' That makes it very concrete"—and harder to dismiss.

Make sure you heard the words and their intent correctly by repeating or rephras-   12
ing the statement: "This is what I heard you say. Is that what you meant?" It's important to give the other person the benefit of the doubt because, in fact, he may *not* have
realized that the comment was offensive and, if you had not spoken up, would have
had no idea of its impact on you.

For instance, Professor Kahn relates that he used to include in his exams multiple-   13
choice questions that occasionally contained "incorrect funny answers." After one
exam, a student came up to him in private and said, "I don't think you intended this,
but I found a number of those jokes offensive to me as a woman." She explained why.
"What she said made immediate sense to me," he says. "I apologized at the next class,
and I never did it again."

But what if the speaker dismisses your objection, saying, "Oh, you're just being sen-   14
sitive. Can't you take a joke?" In that case, you might say, "I'm not so sure about that,
let's talk about that a little more." The key, Mr. Strong says, is to continue the dialogue,
hear the other person's concerns, and point out your own. "There are times when
you're just going to have to admit defeat and end it," he adds, "but I have to feel that
I did the best I could."

When the offending remark is made in the presence of others—at a staff meeting,   15
for example—it can be even more distressing than an insult made privately.

"You have two options," says William Newlin, director of field services for the   16
Community Relations division of the New York City Commission on Human Rights.
"You can respond immediately at the meeting, or you can delay your response until
afterward in private. But a response has to come."

Some remarks or actions may be so outrageous that they cannot go unnoted at the   17
moment, regardless of the speaker or the setting. But in general, psychologists say,
shaming a person in public may have the opposite effect of the one you want: The
speaker will deny his offense all the more strongly in order to save face. Further, few
people enjoy being put on the spot, and if the remark really was not intended to be
offensive, publicly embarrassing the person who made it may cause an unnecessary rift
or further misunderstanding. Finally, most people just don't react as well or thoughtfully under a public spotlight as they would in private.

Keeping that in mind, an excellent alternative is to take the offender aside after-   18
ward: "Could we talk for a minute in private?" Then use the strategies suggested above
for calmly stating how you feel, giving the speaker the benefit of the doubt, and proceeding from there.

At a large meeting or public talk, you might consider passing the speaker a note,   19
says David Wertheimer, executive director of the New York City Gay and Lesbian Anti-
Violence Project: You could write, "You may not realize it, but your remarks were
offensive because. . . ."

"Think of your role as that of an educator," suggests James M. Jones, Ph.D., execu-   20
tive director for public interest at the American Psychological Association. "You have
to be controlled."

Regardless of the setting or situation, speaking up always raises the risk of rocking   21
the boat. If the person who made the offending remark is your boss, there may be an

even bigger risk to consider: How will this affect my job? Several things can help minimize the risk, however. First, know what other resources you may have at work, suggests Caryl Stern, director of the A World of Difference—New York City campaign: Does your personnel office handle discrimination complaints? Are other grievance procedures in place?

22   You won't necessarily need to use any of these procedures, Ms. Stern stresses. In fact, she advises, "It's usually better to try a one-on-one approach first." But simply knowing a formal system exists can make you feel secure enough to set up that meeting.

23   You can also raise the issue with other colleagues who heard the remark: Did they feel the same way you did? The more support you have, the less alone you will feel. Your point will also carry more validity and be more difficult to shrug off. Finally, give your boss credit—and the benefit of the doubt: "I know you've worked hard for the company's affirmative action programs, so I'm sure you didn't realize what those remarks sounded like to me as well as the others at the meeting last week. . . ."

24   If, even after this discussion, the problem persists, go back for another meeting, Ms. Stern advises. And if that, too, fails, you'll know what other options are available to you.

25   It's a spirited dinner party, and everyone's having a good time, until one guest starts reciting a racist joke. Everyone at the table is white, including you. The others are still laughing, as you wonder what to say or do.

26   No one likes being seen as a party-pooper, but before deciding that you'd prefer not to take on this role, you might remember that the person who told the offensive joke has already ruined your good time.

27   If it's a group that you feel comfortable in—a family gathering, for instance—you will feel freer to speak up. Still, shaming the person by shouting "You're wrong!" or "That's not funny!" probably won't get your point across as effectively as other strategies. "If you interrupt people to condemn them, it just makes it harder," says Cherie Brown. She suggests trying instead to get at the resentments that lie beneath the joke by asking open-ended questions: "Grandpa, I know you always treat everyone with such respect. Why do people in our family talk that way about black people?" The key, Ms. Brown says, "is to listen to them first, so they will be more likely to listen to you."

28   If you don't know your fellow guests well, before speaking up you could turn discreetly to your neighbors (or excuse yourself to help the host or hostess in the kitchen) to get a reading on how they felt, and whether or not you'll find support for speaking up. The less alone you feel, the more comfortable you'll be speaking up: "I know you probably didn't mean anything by that joke, Jim, but it really offended me. . . ." It's important to say that *you* were offended—not state how the group that is the butt of the joke would feel. "Otherwise," LeNorman Strong says, "you risk coming off as a goody two-shoes."

29   If you yourself are the host, you can exercise more control; you are, after all, the one who sets the rules and the tone of behavior in your home. Once, when Professor Kahn's party guests began singing offensive, racist songs, for instance, he kicked them all out, saying, "You don't sing songs like that in my house!" And, he adds, "they never did again."

30   At school one day, a friend comes over and says, "Who do you think you are, hanging out with Joe? If you can be friends with those people, I'm through with you!"

Peer pressure can weigh heavily on kids. They feel vulnerable and, because they are   31
kids, they aren't as able to control the urge to fight. "But if you learn to handle these
situations as kids, you'll be better able to handle them as an adult," William Newlin
points out.

Begin by redefining to yourself what a friend is and examining what friendship   32
means, advises Amy Lee, a human relations specialist at Panel of Americans, an inter-
group-relations training and educational organization. If that person from a different
group fits your requirement for a friend, ask, "Why shouldn't I be friends with Joe? We
have a lot in common." Try to get more information about whatever stereotypes or
resentments lie beneath your friend's statement. Ms. Lee suggests: "What makes you
think they're so different from us? Where did you get that information?" She explains:
"People are learning these stereotypes from somewhere, and they cannot be blamed
for that. So examine where these ideas came from." Then talk about how your own
experience rebuts them.

Kids, like adults, should also be aware of other resources to back them up: Does the   33
school offer special programs for fighting prejudice? How supportive will the principal,
the teachers, or other students be? If the school atmosphere is volatile, experts warn,
make sure that taking a stand at that moment won't put you in physical danger. If that
is the case, it's better to look for other alternatives.

These can include programs or organizations that bring kids from different back-   34
grounds together. "When kids work together across race lines, that is how you break
down the barriers and see that the stereotypes are not true," says Laurie Meadoff, president of CityKids Foundation, a nonprofit group whose programs attempt to do just
that. Such programs can also provide what Cherie Brown calls a "safe place" to express
the anger and pain that slurs and other offenses cause, whether the bigotry is directed
against you or others.

In learning to speak up, everyone will develop a different style and a slightly differ-   35
ent message to get across, experts agree. But it would be hard to do better than these
two messages suggested by teenagers at CityKids: "Everyone on the face of the earth
has the same intestines," said one. Another added, "Cross over the bridge. There's a
lot of love on the streets."

Questions for Close Reading

1. What is the selection's thesis? Locate the sentence(s) in which Cole states her
   main idea. If she doesn't state the thesis explicitly, express it in your own
   words.

2. Why does Cole believe it is better to speak up against prejudice rather than to
   keep silent or ignore it?

3. Although Cole acknowledges that there is no "cookbook approach" for dealing
   with offensive comments, she nevertheless presents some general steps that
   can be followed. What are these general steps? Cole also describes more specific steps that can be taken in particular situations. What are the situations and
   the steps to be taken?

4. According to Cole's sources, what types of comments and responses are *not* useful in dealing with prejudicial jokes and remarks?

5. Refer to your dictionary as needed to define the following words used in the selection: *ebullience* (paragraph 1), *anti-Semitic* (1), *slurs* (4), *discounts* (6), *lashing* (9), *ante* (9), *abstract* (11), *personalize* (11), *rift* (17), *grievance* (21), and *volatile* (33).

Questions About the Writer's Craft

1. **The pattern.** Does Cole's process analysis have a primarily informative or persuasive purpose? How do you know? Where does the author suggest her purpose? How does her use of the second-person "you" reinforce that purpose?

2. **Other patterns.** What examples does Cole provide to illustrate the process she's explaining? Why do you think she provides so many examples?

3. Cole uses quotations extensively in the essay. Why do you suppose she quotes so many people? What effect do you think Cole hopes the quotations will have on her readers?

4. What purpose do the essay's three sections set off with smaller type serve? Why might Cole have chosen to set off these sections? Which one of the three sections seems to address a different audience than the other two? Taking into account why this essay was written and where it was published (see the biographical note), do you think Cole is justified in shifting her essay's focus in this way? Why or why not? Is the shift effective? Explain.

Writing Assignments Using Process Analysis as a Pattern of Development

∞ 1. Cole describes a process for handling offensive *comments*, but there are many times when we wonder whether to protest someone's objectionable *behavior*. Write an essay explaining a process for dealing with one such behavior. You might describe a process for confronting a friend who forgets to repay loans, a teacher who grades unfairly, or a boss who treats employees rudely. Like Cole, tell readers what they should do if a step in the process doesn't yield the hoped-for results. For additional accounts about how to deal with others' problematic behavior, read Brent Staples's "Black Men and Public Space" (page 407) and Susan Jacoby's "Common Decency" (page 494).

2. In paragraph 27, Cole describes a family gathering during which a grandchild confronts a grandfather as one adult to another. However, dealing with older relatives in such a forthright manner can be difficult, especially when the older adults don't perceive the grown-up child as a mature individual. Write an essay describing the process by which a grown child can confront such relatives

and request that they treat the "child" like an adult. Use examples from your own family and from friends' families when explaining how to deal—and not deal—with such relatives.

Writing Assignments Using Other Patterns of Development

3. Cole writes about one type of behavior that most of us find obnoxious. But, as we all know, there are many types of obnoxious or annoying people. Focusing on a specific setting (a library, a highway, a store, a classroom), write a light-spirited essay in which you categorize the kinds of obnoxious people you typically encounter there. Be sure to provide vivid descriptions of the behavior that makes these people so unpleasant.

∞ 4. When confronted by offensive language and behavior, people should—Cole argues—take a stand. Write an essay constructing your personal definition of *assertiveness*. Illustrate your definition by providing specific examples of what it is and what it isn't. To gain additional insight into assertiveness, read "Why People Don't Help in a Crisis" (page 401) by John M. Darley and Bibb Latané.

Writing Assignment Using a Journal Entry as a Starting Point

∞ 5. Cole conveys the short-term discomfort and long-term damage that offensive language can inflict on recipients. Write an essay narrating an incident—that you witnessed or participated in—of hurtful speech directed at an individual or group because of race, ethnicity, gender, or sexual preference. Review your pre-reading journal entry, selecting the *one* occasion that is the most compelling and/or thought-provoking. As you narrate the incident, be sure to use dialog and descriptive language to convey what was said and done and how people reacted. End your essay by reflecting on what you now, in retrospect, realize about the incident and whether you think it could have been handled differently by those involved. Also, consider reading Joseph H. Suina's "And Then I Went to School" (page 371) and Yuh Ji-Yeon's "Let's Tell the Story of All America's Cultures" (page 499) for two accounts about how painful racial misconceptions can be.

BILL BRYSON

Bill Bryson (1951–) has kept audiences on both sides of the Atlantic chuckling by exposing, in rollicking, down-to-earth fashion, the humor inherent in the world around him. A native of Iowa who resided in England for almost twenty years, Bryson earned fame as a columnist and best-selling author in England before returning to live with his wife and four children in Hanover, New Hampshire. Bryson's cross-cultural sensibility and talent for unearthing the absurd are apparent in his books on language, including *The Mother Tongue* (1990), and in his travel writing, including *In a Sunburned Country* (2000) and *A Walk in the Woods,* his best-selling 1998 account of a hike along the Appalachian trail. The following selection first appeared in *I'm a Stranger Here Myself: Notes on Returning to America After 20 Years Away* (1999).

Pre-Reading Journal Entry

Like most people, you've probably found that today's sophisticated technologies often complicate life, rather than making it easier. Take a moment to list in your journal some of the technologies that have added stress to your life. Under each technology, jot down some specifics about the problems you've experienced.

YOUR NEW COMPUTER

Congratulations. You have purchased an Edsel[1]/2000 Multimedia 615X Personal   1
Computer with Digital Doo-Dah Enhancer. It will give years of faithful service, if you ever get it up and running. Also included with your PC is a bonus pack of preinstalled software—Lawn Mowing Planner, Mr. Arty-Farty, Blank Screen Saver, and Antarctica Route Finder—which will provide hours of pointless diversion while using up most of your computer's spare memory.

So turn the page and let's get started!   2

Getting Ready

Congratulations. You have successfully turned the page and are ready to proceed.   3

Important meaningless note: The Edsel/2000 is configured to use 80386, 214J10,   4
or higher processors running at 2472 Herz on variable speed spin cycle. Check your electrical installations and insurance policies before proceeding. Do not machine wash.

To prevent internal heat buildup, select a cool, dry environment for your computer.   5
The bottom shelf of the refrigerator is ideal.

Unpack the box and examine its contents. (Warning: Do not open box if contents   6
are missing or faulty, as this will invalidate your warranty. Return all missing contents in their original packaging with a note explaining where they have gone and a replacement will be sent within twelve working months.)

The contents of the box should include some of the following: monitor with myste-   7
rious De Gauss[2] button; keyboard; computer unit; miscellaneous wires and cables not necessarily designed for this model; 2,000-page Owner's Manual; Short Guide to the Owner's Manual; Quick Guide to the Short Guide to the Owner's Manual; Laminated

---

[1]Short-lived automobile (produced for only three model years, from 1958 to 1960), built by Ford Motors and named after Henry Ford's son. Its demise owed to the general perception that it was poorly designed and engineered—essentially, a "lemon" (editors' note).

[2]Refers to neutralizing a magnetic field (something a computer owner would not want to happen to a hard drive) (editors' note).

Super-Kwik Set-Up Guide for People Who Are Exceptionally Impatient or Stupid; 1,167 pages of warranties, vouchers, notices in Spanish, and other loose pieces of paper; 292 cubic feet of Styrofoam packing material.

Something They Didn't Tell You at the Store

Because of the additional power needs of the preinstalled bonus software, you will need to acquire an Edsel/2000 auxiliary software upgrade pack, a 900-volt memory capacitator for the auxiliary software pack, a 50-megaherz oscillator unit for the memory capacitator, 2,500 mega-gigabytes of additional memory for the oscillator, and an electrical substation.   8

Setting Up

Congratulations. You are ready to set up. If you have not yet acquired a degree in electrical engineering, now is the time to do so.   9

Connect the monitor cable (A) to the portside outlet unit (D); attach power offload unit suborbiter (Xii) to the coaxial AC/DC servo channel (G); plug three-pin mouse cable into keyboard housing unit (make extra hole if necessary); connect modem (B2) to offside parallel audio/video lineout jack. Alternatively, plug the cables into the most likely looking holes, switch on, and see what happens.   10

Additional important meaningless note: The wires in the ampule modulator unit are marked as follows according to international convention: blue = neutral or live; yellow = live or blue; blue and live = neutral and green; black = instant death. (Except where prohibited by law.)   11

Switch the computer on. Your hard drive will automatically download. (Allow three to five days.) When downloading is complete, your screen will say: "Yeah, what?"   12

Now it is time to install your software. Insert Disc A (marked "Disk D" or "Disk G") into Drive Slot B or J, and type: "Hello! Anybody home?" At the DOS command prompt, enter your License Verification Number. Your License Verification Number can be found by entering your Certified User Number, which can be found by entering your License Verification Number. If you are unable to find your License Verification or Certified User numbers, call the Software Support Line for assistance. (Please have your License Verification and Certified User numbers handy as the support staff cannot otherwise assist you.)   13

If you have not yet committed suicide, then insert Installation Diskette 1 in drive slot 2 (or vice versa) and follow the instructions on your screen. (Note: Owing to a software modification, some instructions will appear in Turkish.) At each prompt, reconfigure the specified file path, double-click on the button launch icon, select a single equation default file from the macro selection register, insert the VGA graphics card in the rear aerofoil, and type "C:\." followed by the birthdates of all the people you have ever known.   14

Your screen will now say: "Invalid file path. Whoa! Abort or continue?" Warning: Selecting "Continue" may result in irreversible file compression and a default overload in the hard drive. Selecting "Abort," on the other hand, will require you to start the installation process all over again. Your choice.   15

When the smoke has cleared, insert disc A2 (marked "Disc A1") and repeat as directed with each of the 187 other discs.   16

17   When installation is complete, return to file path, and type your name, address, and credit card numbers and press "SEND." This will automatically register you for our free software prize, "Blank Screensaver IV: Nighttime in Deep Space," and allow us to pass your name to lots and lots of computer magazines, online services, and other commercial enterprises, who will be getting in touch shortly.

18   Congratulations. You are now ready to use your computer. Here are some simple exercises to get you off to a flying start.

Writing a Letter

19   Type "Dear ———" and follow it with a name of someone you know. Write a few lines about yourself, and then write, "Sincerely yours" followed by your own name. Congratulations.

Saving a File

20   To save your letter, select File Menu. Choose Retrieve from Sub-Directory A, enter a backup file number, and place an insertion point beside the macro dialogue button. Select secondary text box from the merge menu, and double-click on the supplementary cleared document window. Assign the tile cascade to a merge file and insert in a text equation box. Alternatively, write the letter out in longhand and put it in a drawer.

Advice on Using the Spreadsheet Facility

21   Don't.

Troubleshooting Section

22   You will have many, many problems with your computer. Here are some common problems and their solutions.

23   *Problem: My computer won't turn on.*
24   Solution: Check to make sure the computer is plugged in; check to make sure the power button is in the ON position; check the cables for damage; dig up underground cables in your yard and check for damage; drive out into the country and check electricity pylons of signs of fallen wires; call hotline.

25   *Problem: My keyboard doesn't seem to have any keys.*
26   Solution: Turn the keyboard the right way up.

27   *Problem: My mouse won't drink its water or go on the spinning wheel.*
28   Solution: Try a high-protein diet or call your pet shop support line.

29   *Problem: I keep getting a message saying: "Non-System General Protection Fault."*
30   Solution: This is probably because you are trying to use the computer. Switch the computer to OFF mode and any annoying messages will disappear.

Problem: My computer is a piece of useless junk.   31

Correct—and congratulations. You are now ready to upgrade to an Edsel/3000   32
Turbo model, or go back to pen and paper.

Questions for Close Reading

1. What is the selection's thesis? Locate the sentence(s) in which Bryson states his main idea. If he doesn't state the thesis explicitly, express it in your own words.

2. Paragraphs 6 and 13 target a similar flaw in computer manuals. What unfortunate tendency do the paragraphs ridicule?

3. Using humor to make a serious point, in paragraph 8 Bryson levels a not-so-funny charge against computer manufacturers. What accusation does he make? What support for this accusation does he provide?

4. Which Edsel model does Bryson cite at the beginning of the essay? Which does he refer to at the end? In what way do these two references reinforce Bryson's thesis?

5. Refer to your dictionary as needed to define the following words used in the selection: *diversion* (paragraph 1), *configured* (4), *invalidate* (6), *miscellaneous* (7), *auxiliary* (8), *convention* (11), and *pylons* (24).

Questions About the Writer's Craft

1. **The pattern.** Is Bryson's process analysis *directional* or *informational* (see pages 304–308)? How do you know? What *purpose* (see pages 307–308) do you think Bryson had in mind when writing the piece? Explain.

2. Although Bryson voices serious complaints about computers, their manufacturers, and computer manuals, he uses wry humor to do so. Why do you think Bryson uses humor rather than angry accusation to voice his grievances?

3. Bryson's essay is a *parody;* it mimics and mildly ridicules the instructional manuals that come with computers. How does Bryson's use of subheads contribute to the effectiveness of his parody?

4. Bryson repeats the word *Congratulations* several times in the essay. Identify each place the word appears. What effect do you think Bryson hoped this word would have each time he used it?

Writing Assignments Using Process Analysis as a Pattern of Development

1. With lightly barbed humor, Bryson shows how needlessly frustrating it can be to set up a computer. Write a humorous essay of your own explaining to the

uninitiated how to do something that is supposedly easy but in practice is unnecessarily complicated. You might explain how to correct an erroneous credit card charge, how to apply for a scholarship or loan, how to program a VCR, and so on. Like Bryson, devise several tongue-in-cheek headings that convey your attitude about the absurd complexities of the process.

2. In his essay, Bryson ironically suggests actions that in reality should *not* be done in order to get a computer functioning—for example, typing "the birthdates of all the people you have ever known" (paragraph 14). Taking a similarly ironic stance, write your own how-*not*-to guide to do something. You could, for example, explain how *not* to get a raise, how *not* to pass a college course, how *not* to pass a driver's test. Adopt whatever tone you wish, though a lighthearted one seems particularly appropriate for this essay.

Writing Assignments Using Other Patterns of Development

3. Write an essay exploring the impact that a relatively recent technological development has had on your life. You might focus on ATMs, answering machines, cell phones, beepers, or satellite television. To illustrate how this technology has affected you personally, contrast your life *before* and *after* the introduction of the innovation. Your essay may have a serious or a lighthearted tone. Before you begin writing, consider reading James Gleick's "Life As Type A" (page 433) and Clifford Stoll's "Why Computers Don't Belong in the Classroom" (page 484), two essays exploring technology's impact on daily life.

4. Bryson uses humor to express his frustration with computers. But some people don't regard computers with amusement; they are upset about threats posed by computer technology. Brainstorm with others to identify some of the concerns people have about computers. They may, for example, be disturbed about unauthorized access to computerized personal information or about children's exposure to Internet pornography. Review your brainstormed material and select *one* area of concern that seems especially compelling. Also consider doing some library and/or Internet research to gain further insight into the issue. Then write an essay in which you provide dramatic examples to illustrate the validity of people's concerns. End by briefly describing steps that could be taken to minimize these problems.

Writing Assignments Using a Journal Entry as a Starting Point

5. Write an essay showing how technologies that are supposed to make life easier actually create stress. Review your pre-reading journal entry, selecting one or two technologies to write about. Draw upon the material in your journal as

well as discussions with other people about their frustrating encounters with today's technologies. Your essay may have a serious or a lighthearted tone. Before writing, you might consider reading Clifford Stoll's "Why Computers Don't Belong in the Classroom" (page 484) for an exposition of specific short- and long-term problems caused by technology.

RICHARD RHODES

Following his graduation with honors from Yale University, Richard Rhodes (1937–) worked for Hallmark Cards before becoming a contributing editor for *Playboy* and *Harper's.* Rhodes's fascination with the step-by-step unfolding of a process is evident in many of his books, including *The Making of the Atomic Bomb* (1987), *Dark Sun: The Making of the Hydrogen Bomb* (1995), and *How to Write: Advice and Reflections* (1996). He is also the author of *Deadly Feasts: Tracking the Secrets of a Terrifying New Plague* (1997) and the editor of *Visions of Technology: A Century of Vital Debate About Machines, Systems, and the Human World* (1999). The excerpted selection reprinted here was first published in *Harper's* in 1970.

Pre-Reading Journal Entry

Animal-rights activists have traditionally protested a variety of activities, including hunting or fishing, the eating of meat, confining animals in zoos, the wearing of fur or leather, animal experimentation, and so on. Where do you stand on these issues? Pick the *two* animal-rights issues you feel most strongly about one way or the other, and use your journal to record your thoughts and feelings about them.

WATCHING THE ANIMALS

The loves of flint and iron are naturally a little rougher than those of the nightingale and the rose.

—Ralph Waldo Emerson

I remembered today about this country lake in Kansas where I live: that it is artificial, built at the turn of the century, when Upton Sinclair was writing *The Jungle,*[1] as an ice lake. The trains with their loads of meat from the Kansas City stockyards would stop by the Kaw River, across the road, and ice the cars. "You have just dined," Emerson once told what must have been a shocked Victorian audience, "and however scrupulously the slaughterhouse is concealed in the graceful distance of miles, there is complicity, expensive races—race living at the expense of race. . . ."

The I-D Packing Company of Des Moines, Iowa: a small outfit which subcontracts from Armour the production of fresh pork. It can handle about 450 pigs an hour on its

1

2

---

[1]Upton Sinclair (1878–1968) was an American writer and social reformer. His novel *The Jungle* (1906) is an exposé of the inhumane conditions found in Chicago's stockyards in the early 1900s (editor's note).

lines. No beef or mutton. No smoked hams or hot dogs. Plain fresh pork. A well-run outfit, with federal inspectors alert on all the lines.

3   The kind of slaughterhouse Upton Sinclair was talking about doesn't exist around here any more. The vast buildings still stand in Des Moines and Omaha and Kansas City, but the operations are gone. The big outfits used to operate on a profit margin of 1.5 per cent, which didn't give them much leeway, did it. Now they are defunct, and their buildings, which look like monolithic enlargements of concentration-camp barracks, sit empty, the hundreds of windows broken, dusty, jagged pieces of glass sticking out of the frames as if the animals heard the good news one day and leaped out the nearest exit. . . .

4   There are no stockyards inside the I-D Packing Company. The pigs arrive by trailer truck from Sioux City and other places. Sometimes a farmer brings in two or three in the back of his pickup. He unloads them into the holding pens, where they are weighed and inspected, goes into the office and picks up his check. . . .

5   Down goes the tail gate and out come the pigs, enthusiastic after their drive. Pigs are the most intelligent of all farm animals, by actual laboratory test. Learn the fastest, for example, to push a plunger with their foot to earn a reward of pelletized feed. And not as reliable in their instincts. You don't have to call cattle to dinner. They are waiting outside the fence at 4:30 sharp, having arrived as silently as the Vietcong.[2] But perhaps that is pig intelligence too: let you do the work, laze around until the last minute, and then charge over and knock you down before you can slop the garbage into the trough. Cattle will stroll one by one into a row of stalls and usually fill them in serial order. Not pigs. They squeal and nip and shove. Each one wants the entire meal for himself. They won't stick together in a herd, either. Shoot out all over the place, and you'd damned better have every gate closed or they'll be in your garden and on your lawn and even in your living room, nodding by the fire.

6   They talk a lot, to each other, to you if you care to listen. I am not romanticizing pigs. They always scared me a little on the farm, which is probably why I watched them more closely than the other animals. They do talk: low grunts, quick squeals, a kind of hum sometimes, angry shrieks, high screams of fear.

7   I have great respect for the I-D Packing Company. They do a dirty job and do it as cleanly and humanely as possible, and do it well. They were nice enough to let me in the door, which is more than I can say for the Wilson people in Omaha, where I first tried to arrange a tour. What are you hiding, Wilson people?

8   Once into the holding pen, the pigs mill around getting to know each other. The I-D holding pens are among the most modern in the nation, my spokesman told me. Tubular steel painted tinner's red to keep it from rusting. Smooth concrete floors with drains so that the floors can be washed down hygienically after each lot of pigs is run through.

9   The pigs come out of the first holding pen through a gate that allows only one to pass at a time. Just beside the gate is a wooden door, and behind the door is the first worker the pigs encounter. He has a wooden box beside him filled with metal numbers, the shape of each number picked out with sharp needles. For each lot of pigs he selects a new set of numbers—2473, say—and slots them into a device like a hammer and dips it in nontoxic purple dye. As a pig shoots out of the gate he hits the pig

---

[2]Vietnamese Communist rebels, noted for moving silently through the jungle (editor's note).

in the side with the numbers, making a tattoo.[3] The pig gives a grunt—it doesn't especially hurt, pigskin is thick, as you know—and moves on to one of several smaller
pens where each lot is held until curtain time. The tattoo, my spokesman told me,
will stay on the animal through all the killing and cleaning and cutting operations, to
the very end. Its purpose is to identify any animal or lot of animals which might be
diseased, so that the seller can be informed and the carcasses destroyed. Rather too
proud of his tattooing process, I thought, but then, you know the tattoos I am thinking about.[4]

It would be more dramatic, make a better story, if the killing came last, but it comes   10
first. We crossed a driveway with more red steel fencing. Lined up behind it, pressing
into it because they sensed by now that all was not well with them, were perhaps a
hundred pigs. But still curious, watching us go by in our long white canvas coats.
Everyone wore those, and hard plastic helmets, white helmets for the workers, yellow
helmets for the foremen. I got to be a foreman.

Before they reach their end, the pigs get a shower,[5] a real one. Water sprays from   11
every angle to wash the farm off of them. Then they begin to feel crowded. The pen
narrows like a funnel; the drivers behind urge the pigs forward, until one at a time
they climb onto a moving ramp. The ramp's sides move as well as its floor. The floor
is created to give the pigs footing. The sides are made of blocks of wood so that they
will not bruise, and they slant inward to wedge the pigs along. Now they scream,
never having been on such a ramp, smelling the smells they smell ahead. I do not
want to overdramatize, because you have read all this before. But it was a frightening experience, seeing their fear, seeing so many of them go by. It had to remind
me of things no one wants to be reminded of anymore, all mobs, all death marches, all mass murders and extinctions, the slaughter of the buffalo, the slaughter of
the Indian, the Inferno, Judgment Day, complicity, expensive races, race living at
the expense of race. That so gentle a religion as Christianity could end up in
Judgment Day. That we are the most expensive of races, able in our affluence to
hire others of our kind to do this terrible necessary work of killing another race of
creatures so that we may feed our oxygen-rich brains. Feed our children, for that
matter.

At the top of the ramp, one man. With rubber gloves on, holding two electrodes that   12
looked like enlarged curling irons except that they sported more of those needles. As
a pig reached the top, this man jabbed the electrodes into the pig's butt and shoulder,
and that was it. No more pain, no more fear, no more mudholes, no more sun in the
lazy afternoon. Knocked instantly unconscious, the pig shuddered in a long spasm and
fell onto a stainless steel table a foot below the end of the ramp. Up came another pig,
and the same result. And another, and another, 450 an hour, 3,600 a day, the belts
returning below to coax another ride.

The pigs are not dead, merely unconscious. The electrodes are humane, my   13
spokesman said, and relatively speaking, that is true. They used to gas the pigs—put
them on a conveyor belt that ran through a room filled with anesthetic gas. That was
humane too. The electrodes are more efficient. Anesthesia relaxes the body and

---

[3,4,5]Rhodes's description of the pigs' slaughter echoes Germany's extermination of Jews
and other minorities during World War II. Uprooted from their homes, the prisoners
were sent to death camps, where they were tattooed with identification numbers. Then,
having been told they were going to be allowed to shower, the unsuspecting prisoners
were herded into gas chambers, where they were put to death (editors' note).

loosens the bowels. The pigs must have been a mess. More efficient, then, to put their bodies in spasm.

14   They drop to the table, and here the endless chain begins. A worker takes the nearest dangling chain by its handle as it passes. The chain is attached at the top to a belt of links, like a large bicycle chain. At the bottom the dangling chain has a metal handle like the handle on a bike. The chain runs through the handle and then attaches to the end of the handle, so that by sliding the handle the worker forms a loop. Into the loop he hooks one of the pig's hind feet. Another worker does the same with the other foot. Each has his own special foot to grab, or the pig would go down the line backwards, which would not be convenient. Once hooked into the line, the pig will stay in place by the force of its own weight.

15   Now the line ascends, lifting the unconscious animal into the air. The pig proceeds a distance of ten feet, where a worker standing on a platform deftly inserts a butcher knife into its throat. They call it "sticking," which it is. Then all hell breaks loose, if blood merely is hell. It gushes out, at about a 45-degree angle downward, thick as a ship's hawser, pouring directly onto the floor. Nothing is so red as blood, an incandescent red and most beautiful. It is the brightest color we drab creatures possess. Down on the floor below, with a wide squeegee on a long handle, a worker spends his eight hours a day squeegeeing that blood, some of it clotted, jellied, now, into an open drain. It is cycled through a series of pipes into a dryer, later to be made into blood meal for animal feed.

16   The line swings around a corner, high above the man with the squeegee, around the drain floor, turns left at the next corner, and begins to ascend to the floor above. This interval—thirteen seconds, I think my spokesman said, or was it thirty?—so that the carcass may drain completely before further processing. Below the carcass on the ascent is a trough like those lowered from the rear of cement trucks, there to catch the last drainings of blood.

17   Pigs are not skinned, as cattle are, unless you are after the leather, and we are after the meat. But the hair must be taken off, and it must first be scalded loose. Courteously, the line lowers the carcass into a long trough filled with water heated to 180 degrees. The carcass will float if given a chance, fat being lighter than water, so wooden pushers on crankshafts spaced equally along the scalding tank immerse and roll the carcasses. Near the end of the trough, my spokesman easily pulls out a tuft of hair. The line ascends again, up and away, and the carcass goes into a chamber where revolving brushes as tall as a man whisk away the hair. We pass to the other side of the chamber and find two workers with wide knives scraping off the few patches of hair that remain. The carcasses then pass through great hellish jets of yellowish-blue gas flame to singe the skin and harden it. The last step is polishing: more brushes. Our pig has turned pink and clean as a baby.

18   One of the small mercies of a slaughterhouse: what begins as a live animal loses all similarity as the processing goes on, until you can actually face the packaged meat at the exit door and admire its obvious flavor.

19   The polished carcasses swing through a door closed with rubber flaps, and there, dear friends, the action begins. Saws. Long knives. Butcher knives. Drawknives. Boning knives. Wails from the saws, large and small, that are driven by air like a dentist's drill. Shouts back and forth from the men, jokes, announcements, challenges. The temperature down to 50 degrees, everyone keen. Men start slicing off little pieces of the head right inside the door, each man his special slice, throwing them onto one of several lines that will depart for special bins. A carcass passes me and I see a bare eyeball staring, stripped of its lids. Deft knives drop the head from the neck, leaving it

dangling by a two-inch strip of skin. Around a corner, up to a platform, and three men gut the carcasses, great tubs of guts, each man taking the third carcass as it goes by. One of them sees me with my tape recorder and begins shouting at us something like "I am the greatest!" A crazy man, grinning and roaring at us, turning around and slipping in the knife, and out comes everything in one great load flopped onto a stainless-steel trough. And here things divide, and so must our attention.

My spokesman is proud of his chitterling machine. "I call them chitlins, but they're really chitterlings." It is the newest addition to his line. A worker separates the intestines from the other internal organs and shoves them down a slide, gray and shiny. Another worker finds one end and feeds it onto a steel tube flushed with water. Others trim off connective tissue, webbings, fat. The intestines shimmer along the tube into a washing vat, shinny up to the top of the machine where they are cooled, shinny back down where they are cooled further, and come out the other side ready for the supermarket. A worker drops them into wax buckets, pops on a lid, and packs them into shipping boxes. That is today's chitlin machine. They used to have to cool the chitlins overnight before they could be packaged. Now five men do the work of sixteen, in less time. **20**

The remaining organs proceed down a waist-high conveyor; on the other side of the same walkway, the emptied carcasses pass; on a line next to the organ line the heads pass. By now all the meat has been trimmed off each head. A worker sockets them one at a time into a support like a footrest in a shoeshine parlor and a wedge neatly splits them in half. Out come the tongues, out come the brains, and at the end of the line, out come the pituitaries, each tiny gland being passed to a government inspector in white pants, white shirt, and a yellow hard hat, who looks it over and drops it into a wax bucket. All these pieces, the brain, the tongue, the oddments of sidemeat off the head and carcass, will become "by-products": hot dogs, baloney, sausage. You are what you eat. . . . **21**

And that is a tour of a slaughterhouse, as cheerful as I could make it. **22**

But the men there. Half of them blacks, some Mexicans, the rest whites. It gets harder and harder to hire men for this work, even though the pay is good. The production line keeps them hopping; they take their breaks when there is a break in the line, so that the killing floor breaks first, and their break leaves an empty space ten minutes long in the endless chain, which, arriving at the gutting operation, allows the men there to break, and so on. Monday morning absenteeism is a problem, I was told. Keeping the men under control can be a problem, too, I sensed: when the line broke down briefly during my tour, the men cheered as convicts might at a state license-plate factory when the stamping machine breaks down. It cannot be heartening to kill animals all day. . . . **23**

The technology at the I-D Packing Company is humane by present standards, at least so far as the animals are concerned. Where the workers are concerned, I'm not so sure. They looked to be in need of lulling. **24**

Beyond technology is the larger question of attitude. Butchering on the farm when I was a boy had the quality of a ceremony. We would select, say, a steer, and pen it separately overnight. The next morning several of us boys—this was a boys' home as well as a farm—would walk the steer to a large compound and leave it standing, trusting as **25** hell, near the concrete-floored area where we did the skinning and gutting. Then the farm manager, a man of great kindness and reserve, would take aim with a .22 rifle at the crosspoint of two imaginary lines drawn from the horns to the opposite eyes. And hold his bead until the steer was entirely calm, looking at him, a certain shot, because this man did not want to miss, did not want to hurt the animal he was about to kill. And we would stand in a spread-out circle, at a respectful distance, tense with the drama of it, because we didn't want him to miss either.

26   The shot cracked out, the bullet entered the brain, and the animal instantly collapsed. Then the farm manager handed back the rifle, took a knife, ran forward, and cut into the throat. Then we dragged the steer onto the concrete, hooked its back legs through the Achilles tendons to a cross tree, and laboriously winched it into the air with a differential pulley. Four boys usually did the work, two older, two younger. The younger boys were supposed to be learning this skill, and you held your stomach together as best you could at first while the older boys played little tricks like, when they got there in the skinning, cutting off the pizzle and whipping it around your neck, but even these crudities had their place: they accustomed you to contact with flesh and blood.

27   And while the older boys did their work of splitting the halves with a hacksaw, you got to take the guts, which on the farm we did not save except for the liver, the heart, and the sweetbreads, in a wheelbarrow down to the back lane where you built with wood you had probably cut yourself, a most funereal pyre. Then we doused the guts with gasoline, tossed in a match, and Whoosh! off they went. And back on the concrete, the sawing done, the older boys left the sides hanging overnight in the winter cold to firm the meat for cutting.

28   By now it was noon, time for lunch, and you went in with a sort of pride that you had done this important work, and there on the table was meat some other boys had killed on some other ceremonial day. It was bloody work, of course, and sometimes I have wondered how adults could ask children to do such work, but it was part of a coherent way of life, as important as plowing or seeding or mowing or baling hay. It had a context, and I was literary enough even then to understand that burning the guts had a sacrificial significance. We could always have limed them and dumped them into a ditch. Lord knows they didn't burn easily.

29   I never saw our farm manager more upset than the day we were getting ready to butcher five pigs. He shot one through the nose rather than through the brain. It ran screaming around the pen, and he almost cried. It took two more bullets to finish the animal off, and this good man was shaking when he had finished. "I hate that," he said to me. "I hate to have them in pain. Pigs are so damned hard to kill clean."

30   But we don't farm anymore. The coherence is gone. Our loves are no longer the loves of flint and iron, but of the nightingale and the rose, and so we delegate our killing. Our farm manager used to sleep in the sheep barn for nights on end to be sure he was there to help the ewes deliver their lambs, ewes being so absentminded they sometimes stop labor with the lamb only halfway out. You saw the beginning and the end on the farm, not merely the prepackaged middle. Flint and iron, friends, flint and iron. And humility, and sorrow that this act of killing must be done, which is why in those days good men bowed their heads before they picked up their forks.

Questions for Close Reading

1. What is the selection's thesis? Locate the sentence(s) in which Rhodes states his main idea. If he doesn't state the thesis explicitly, express it in your own words.

2. How are pigs slaughtered at the I-D Packing Company? What steps are involved? How do the plant workers react to the process?

3. According to Rhodes, what are pigs like? What is it about their personalities and reactions that makes them so compelling?

4. What is the difference between the way farm animals were killed in the past and the way they are killed at the I-D Packing House? How does Rhodes know about the way farm animals used to be killed?

5. Refer to your dictionary as needed to define the following words used in the selection: *defunct* (paragraph 3), *monolithic* (3), *hygienically* (8), *complicity* (11), *affluence* (11), *hawser* (15), *deft* (19), *chitterlings* (20), *lulling* (24), *winched* (26), *differential* (26), *pizzle* (26), *coherent* (28), *sacrificial* (28).

Questions About the Writer's Craft

1. **The pattern.**   Throughout this disturbing but riveting piece, Rhodes uses several techniques to help readers follow the sequence of steps in the butchering process. Identify some of these techniques and explain how each of them keeps readers focused on the part of the process being explained.

2. Why do you think Rhodes chose to preface his essay with the quotation from Ralph Waldo Emerson? How does this quotation and the subsequent references to Emerson (in paragraphs 1, 11, and 30) reinforce Rhodes's central point?

3. **Other patterns.**   Although Rhodes's description becomes especially graphic from paragraph 11 on, the descriptive elements in earlier paragraphs play a critical role in establishing Rhodes's thesis. How, for example, do the descriptive details in paragraphs 3–9 reinforce Rhodes's thesis?

4. Rhodes often uses a breezy colloquial style. Consider, for example, the fragment combined with a full sentence at the end of paragraph 5: "Shoot out all over the place, and you'd damned better have every gate closed. . . ." Locate other examples of this informal style. Why might Rhodes have chosen to express himself so informally at various points in the essay?

Writing Assignments Using Process Analysis as a Pattern of Development

1. Like Rhodes, write an essay describing a process you think is wrong or flawed in some way. You might, for example, describe how your college

determines competency in writing, how a particular business handles customer complaints, how a township approaches recycling. Describe the process so fully that readers will have no question about the need for reform.

∞ 2. Focus on a societal problem that concerns you. Perhaps you're upset that cheating is on the rise among elementary schoolchildren, that tensions between college students and townspeople have escalated in your community, that a local newspaper discourages debate by failing to publish views that differ from those of the editorial board. Write an essay explaining step-by-step what needs to be done to resolve the problem. To demonstrate the need for change, begin the paper with a brief yet dramatic description of the problem. Diane Cole's "Don't Just Stand There" (page 322), John Leo's "Absolutophobia" (page 438), Camille Paglia's "Rape: A Bigger Danger Than Feminists Know" (page 489), and Susan Jacoby's "Common Decency" (page 494) should provide some ideas for writing an essay that exposes a significant social problem.

Writing Assignments Using Other Patterns of Development

∞ 3. Rhodes implies that, at some level, we know about the suffering experienced by animals but choose to close our eyes to it. There are, of course, other kinds of suffering that people often push out of their minds. Write an essay narrating the story of a single representative of a group whose pain or difficulty tends to be ignored or disregarded. Possibilities include an adult who cannot read, a child with special learning needs, a family without medical insurance. Using vivid narrative details to dramatize what the person's life is like, make a strong case for treating the whole group more sympathetically. Before writing, read George Orwell's "Shooting an Elephant" (page 209) and John M. Darley and Bibb Latané's "Why People Don't Help in a Crisis" (page 401) for two powerful depictions of human insensitivity.

∞ 4. When Rhodes says, "Our loves are . . . of the nightingale and the rose, and so we delegate our killing," he points out the hypocrisy that people themselves don't want to kill animals but are willing to eat the meat of creatures slaughtered by others. Most of us have observed similar contradictions in our own life or in someone else's. For instance, we might believe in honesty but don't protest a friend's shoplifting, or perhaps a male relative preaches respect for women but treats his dates with a swaggering disregard. Write an essay about *one* such moral discrepancy, using vivid details to tell about its appearance in your life or in someone else's. Indicate whether the person was aware of the contradiction and whether it was resolved. Be sure, too, to state or imply your feelings about the discrepancy. Before writing, you might want to read George Orwell's "Shooting an Elephant" (page 209) and Diane Cole's "Don't Just Stand There" (page 322), essays that explore the issue of morality.

Writing Assignment Using a Journal Entry as a Starting Point

 5. Besides criticizing the methods used to kill animals, many animal-rights activists protest what they consider other kinds of animal abuse. Review your pre-reading journal entry and select *one* such issue. Consider doing some research in the library and/or on the Internet and discussing the topic with people holding diverse viewpoints. Then write an essay supporting your viewpoint with persuasive reasons and examples, remembering to refute opposing views whenever you can.

ADDITIONAL WRITING TOPICS: PROCESS ANALYSIS

General Assignments

Develop one of the following topics through process analysis. Explain the process one step at a time, organizing the steps chronologically. If there's no agreed-on sequence, design your own series of steps. Use transitions to ease the audience through the steps in the process. You may use any tone you wish, from serious to light.

Directional: How to Do Something

1. How to improve a course you have taken

2. How to drive defensively

3. How to get away with _____

4. How to improve the place where you work or study

5. How to relax

6. How to show appreciation to others

7. How to get through school despite personal problems

8. How to complain effectively

Informational: How Something Happens

1. How a student becomes burned out

2. How a library's card catalog or computerized catalog organizes books

3. How a dead thing decays (or some other natural process)

4. How the college registration process works

5. How *homo sapiens* choose a mate

6. How a VCR (or some other machine) works

7. How a bad habit develops

8. How people fall into debt

Assignments with a Specific Purpose, Audience, and Point of View

On Campus

1. As an experienced campus tour guide for prospective students, you've been asked by your school's Admissions Office to write a pamphlet explaining to new tour guides how to conduct a tour of your school's campus. When explaining the process, keep in mind that tour guides need to portray the school in its best light.

2. You write an "advice to the lovelorn" column for the campus newspaper. A correspondent writes saying that he or she wants to break up with a steady girlfriend/boyfriend but doesn't know how to do it without hurting the person. Give the writer guidance on how to end a meaningful relationship with a minimal amount of pain.

At Home or in the Community

3. To help a sixteen-year-old friend learn how to drive, explain a specific driving maneuver one step at a time. You might, for example, describe how to make a three-point turn, parallel park, or handle a skid. Remember, your friend lacks self-confidence and experience.

4. Your best friend plans to move into his or her own apartment but doesn't know the first thing about how to choose one. Explain the process of selecting an apartment—where to look, what to investigate, what questions to ask before signing a lease.

On the Job

5. As a staff writer for a consumer magazine, you've been asked to write an article on how to shop for a certain product. Give specific steps explaining how to save money, buy a quality product, and the like.

6. An author of books for elementary school children, you want to show children how to do something—take care of a pet, get along with siblings, keep a room clean. Explain the process in terms a child would understand yet not find condescending.

16
COMPARISON-CONTRAST

WHAT IS COMPARISON-CONTRAST?

We frequently try to make sense of the world by finding similarities and differences in our experiences. Seeing how things are alike (**comparing**) and seeing how they are different (**contrasting**) help us impose meaning on experiences that otherwise might remain fragmented and disconnected. Barely aware of the fact that we're comparing and contrasting, we may think to ourselves, "I woke up in a great mood this morning, but now I feel uneasy and anxious. I wonder why I feel so different." This inner questioning, which often occurs in a flash, is just one example of the way we use comparison and contrast to understand ourselves and our world.

Comparing and contrasting also helps us make choices. We compare and contrast everything—from two brands of soap we might buy to two colleges we might attend. We listen to a favorite radio station, watch a preferred nightly news show, select a particular dessert from a menu—all because we have done some degree of comparing and contrasting. We often weigh these alternatives in an unstudied, casual manner, as when we flip from one radio station to another. But when we have to make important decisions, we tend to think rigorously about how things are alike or different: Should I live in a dorm or rent an apartment? Should I accept the higher-paying job or the lower-paying one that offers more challenges? Such a deliberate approach to comparison-contrast may also provide us with needed insight into complex contemporary issues: Is television's coverage of political candidates more or less objective than it used to be? What are the merits of the various positions on abortion?

HOW COMPARISON-CONTRAST FITS YOUR PURPOSE AND AUDIENCE

When is it appropriate in writing to use the comparison-contrast pattern of development? Comparison-contrast works well if you want to demonstrate any of the following: (1) that one thing is better than another (the first example below); (2) that things that seem different are actually alike (the second example below); (3) that things that seem alike are actually different (the third example below).

> Compare and contrast the way male and female relationships are depicted in *Cosmopolitan, Ms., Playboy,* and *Esquire.* Which publication has the most limited view of men and women? Which has the broadest perspective?

> Football, basketball, and baseball differ in the ways they appeal to fans. Describe the unique drawing power of each sport, but also reach some conclusions about the appeals the three sports have in common.

> Studies show that both college students and their parents feel that post-secondary education should equip young people to succeed in the marketplace. Yet the same studies report that the two groups have a very different understanding of what it means to succeed. What differences do you think the studies identify?

Other assignments will, in less obvious ways, lend themselves to comparison-contrast. For instance, although words like *compare, contrast, differ,* and *have in common* don't appear in the following assignments, essay responses to the assignments could be organized around the comparison-contrast format:

> The emergence of the two-career family is one of the major phenomena of our culture. Discuss the advantages and disadvantages of having both parents work, showing how you feel about such two-career households.

> Some people believe that the 1950s, often called the golden age of television, produced several never-to-be equaled comedy classics. Do you agree that such shows as *I Love Lucy* and *The Honeymooners* are superior to the situation comedies aired on television today?

> There has been considerable criticism recently of the news coverage by the city's two leading newspapers, the *Herald* and the *Beacon.* Indicate whether you think the criticism is valid by discussing the similarities and differences in the two papers' news coverage.

Note: The last assignment shows that a comparison-contrast essay may cover similarities *and* differences, not just one or the other.

As you have seen, comparison-contrast can be the key strategy for achieving an essay's purpose. But comparison-contrast can also be a supplemental method used to help make a point in an essay organized chiefly around another pattern of development. A serious, informative essay intended for laypeople might *define* clinical depression by contrasting that state of mind with ordinary run-of-the-mill blues. Writing humorously about the exhausting *effects* of trying to get in shape, you might dramatize your plight for readers by contrasting the leisurely way you used to spend your day with your current rigidly compulsive exercise regimen. Or, in an urgent *argumentation-persuasion* essay on the need for stricter controls over drug abuse in the workplace, you might provide readers with background by comparing several companies' approaches to the problem.

PREWRITING STRATEGIES

The following checklist shows how you can apply to comparison-contrast some of the prewriting strategies discussed in Chapter 2.

☑ COMPARISON-CONTRAST: A PREWRITING CHECKLIST

Choose Subjects to Compare and Contrast

☐ What have you recently needed to compare and contrast (subjects to major in, events to attend, ways to resolve a disagreement) in order to make a choice? What would a comparison-contrast analysis disclose about the alternatives, your priorities, and the criteria by which you judge?

☐ Can you show a need for change by contrasting one way of doing something (say, the way your college awards athletic scholarships) with a better way (either imagined or actual)?

☐ Do any people you know show some striking similarities and differences? What would a comparison-contrast analysis reveal about their characters and the personal qualities you prize?

☐ How does your view on an issue (the legal drinking age, birth control, a new policy at your college) differ from that of other people (your parents, a friend, most students at your college)? What would a comparison-contrast analysis of these views indicate about your values?

Determine Your Purpose, Audience, Tone, and Point of View

☐ Is your purpose primarily to inform readers of similarities and differences? To evaluate your subjects' relative merits? To persuade readers to choose between alternative courses of action?

☐ What audience are you writing for? To what tone and point of view will they be most receptive?

Use Prewriting to Generate Points of Comparison-Contrast

☐ How could brainstorming, freewriting, mapping, or journal entries help you gather information about your subjects' most significant similarities and differences?

STRATEGIES FOR USING COMPARISON-CONTRAST IN AN ESSAY

After prewriting, you're ready to draft your essay. The following suggestions will be helpful whether you use comparison-contrast as a dominant or supportive pattern of development.

1. Be sure your subjects are at least somewhat alike. Unless you plan to develop an *analogy* (see the following numbered suggestion), the subjects you choose to compare or contrast should share some obvious characteristics or qualities. It makes sense to compare different parts of the country, two comedians, or several college teachers. But a reasonable paper wouldn't result from, let's say, a comparison of a television game show with a soap opera. Your subjects must belong to the same general group so that your comparison-contrast stays within logical bounds and doesn't veer off into pointlessness.

2. Stay focused on your purpose. When writing, remember that comparison-contrast isn't an end in itself. That is, your objective isn't to turn an essay into a mechanical list of "how *A* differs from *B*" or "how *A* is like *B*." As with the other patterns of development discussed in this book, comparison-contrast is a strategy for making a point or meeting a larger purpose.

Consider the assignment on page 345 about the two newspapers. Your purpose here might be simply to *inform*, to present information as objectively as possible: "This is what the *Herald*'s news coverage is like. This is what the *Beacon*'s news coverage is like."

More frequently, though, you'll use comparison-contrast to *evaluate* your subjects' pros and cons, your goal being to reach a conclusion or make a judgment: "Both the *Herald* and the *Beacon* spend too much time reporting local news," or "The *Herald*'s analysis of the recent hostage crisis was more insightful than the *Beacon*'s." Comparison-contrast can also be used to *persuade* readers to take action: "People interested in thorough coverage of international events should read the *Herald* rather than the *Beacon*." Persuasive essays may also propose a change, contrasting what now exists with a more ideal situation: "For the *Beacon* to compete with the *Herald*, it must assign more reporters to international stories."

Yet another purpose you might have in writing a comparison-contrast essay is to *clear up misconceptions* by revealing previously hidden similarities or differences. For example, perhaps your town's two newspapers are thought to be sharply different. However, a comparison-contrast analysis might reveal that— although one paper specializes in sensationalized stories while the other adopts a more muted approach—both resort to biased, emotionally charged analyses of local politics. Or the essay might illustrate that the tabloid's treatment of the local arts scene is surprisingly more comprehensive than that of its competitor.

Comparing and contrasting also make it possible to *draw an analogy* between two seemingly unrelated subjects. An analogy is an imaginative comparison that delves beneath the surface differences of subjects in order to expose their significant and often unsuspected similarities or differences. Your purpose may be to show that singles bars and zoos share a number of striking similarities. Or you may want to illustrate that wolves and humans raise their young in much the same way, but that wolves go about the process in a more civilized manner. The analogical approach can make a complex subject easier to understand—as, for example, when the national deficit is compared to a household budget gone awry. Analogies are often dramatic and instructive, challenging you and your audience to consider subjects in a new light. But analogies don't speak for themselves. You must make clear to the reader how the analogy demonstrates your purpose.

3. Formulate a strong thesis.   An essay that is developed primarily through comparison-contrast should be focused by a solid thesis. Besides revealing your attitude, the thesis will often do the following:

• Name the subjects being compared and contrasted
• Indicate whether the essay focuses on the subjects' similarities, differences, or both
• State the essay's main point of comparison or contrast

Not all comparison-contrast essays need thesis statements as structured as those that follow. Even so, these examples can serve as models of clarity. Note that the first thesis statement signals similarities, the second differences, and the last both similarities and differences:

> Middle-aged parents are often in a good position to empathize with adolescent children because the emotional upheavals experienced by the two age groups are much the same.

> The priorities of most retired people are more conducive to health and happiness than the priorities of most young professionals.

> College students in their thirties and forties face many of the same pressures as younger students, but they are better equipped to withstand these pressures.

4. Select the points to be discussed.   Once you have identified the essay's subject, purpose, and thesis, you need to decide which of the many points generated during prewriting you will discuss: You have to identify which aspects of the subjects to compare or contrast. College professors, for instance, could be compared and contrasted on the basis of their testing methods, ability to motivate students, confidence in front of a classroom, personalities, level of enthusiasm, and so forth.

When selecting points to cover, be sure to consider your audience. Ask your-self: "Will my readers be familiar with this item? Will I need it to get my message across? Will my audience find this item interesting or convincing?" What your readers know, what they don't know, and what you can project about their reac-tions should influence your choices. And, of course, you need to select points that support your thesis. If your essay explains the differences between healthy, sen-sible diets and dangerous crash diets, it wouldn't be appropriate to talk about aerobic exercise. Similarly, imagine you want to write an essay making the point that, despite their differences, hard rock of the 1960s and punk rock of the 1970s both reflected young people's disillusionment with society. It wouldn't make much sense to contrast the long, uncombed hairstyles of the 1960s with the short, spiky cuts of the 1970s. But contrasting song lyrics (protest versus nihilistic messages) would help support your thesis and lead to interesting insights.

5. Organize the points to be discussed.   After deciding which points to include, you should use a systematic, logical plan for presenting those ideas. If the points aren't organized, your essay will be little more than a confusing jumble of ideas. There are two common ways to organize an essay developed wholly or in part by comparison-contrast: the one-side-at-a-time method and the point-by-point method. Although both strategies may be used in a paper, one method usually predominates.

In the **one-side-at-a-time method** of organization, you discuss everything rele-vant about one subject before moving to another subject. For example, responding to the earlier assignment that asked you to analyze the news coverage in two local papers, you might first talk about the *Herald*'s coverage of international, national, and local news; then you would discuss the *Beacon*'s coverage of the same cate-gories. Note that the areas discussed should be the same for both newspapers. It wouldn't be logical to review the *Herald*'s coverage of international, national, and local news and then to detail the *Beacon*'s magazine supplements, modern living section, and comics page. Moreover, the areas compared and contrasted should be presented in the same order.

This is how you would organize the essay using the one-side-at-a-time method:

Everything about subject *A*   *Herald*'s news coverage:
- International
- National
- Local

Everything about subject *B*   *Beacon*'s news coverage:
- International
- National
- Local

In the **point-by-point method** of organization, you alternate from one aspect of the first subject to the same aspect of your other subject(s). For example, to use this method when comparing or contrasting the *Herald* and the *Beacon*, you would first discuss the *Herald*'s international coverage, then the *Beacon*'s international cover-age; next, the *Herald*'s national coverage, then the *Beacon*'s; and finally, the *Herald*'s local coverage, then the *Beacon*'s.

An essay using the point-by-point method would be organized like this:

First aspect of subjects *A* and *B*	*Beacon:* International coverage
	Herald: International coverage
Second aspect of subjects *A* and *B*	*Beacon:* National coverage
	Herald: National coverage
Third aspect of subjects *A* and *B*	*Beacon:* Local coverage
	Herald: Local coverage

Deciding which of these two methods of organization to use is largely a personal choice, though there are several factors to consider. The one-side-at-a-time method tends to convey a more unified feeling because it highlights broad similarities and differences. It is, therefore, an effective approach for subjects that are fairly uncomplicated. This strategy also works well when essays are brief; the reader won't find it difficult to remember what has been said about subject *A* when reading about subject *B*.

Because the point-by-point method permits more extensive coverage of similarities and differences, it is often a wise choice when subjects are complex. This pattern is also useful for lengthy essays since readers would probably find it difficult to remember, let's say, ten pages of information about subject *A* while reading the next ten pages about subject *B*. The point-by-point approach, however, may cause readers to lose sight of the broader picture, so remember to keep them focused on your central point.

6. Supply the reader with clear transitions. Although a well-organized comparison-contrast format is important, it doesn't guarantee that readers will be able to follow your line of thought easily. *Transitions*—especially those signaling similarities or differences—are needed to show readers where they have been and where they are going. Such cues are essential in all writing, but they're especially crucial in a paper using comparison-contrast. By indicating clearly when subjects are being compared or contrasted, the transitions help weave the discussion into a coherent whole.

The transitions (in boldface) in the following examples could be used to *signal similarities* in an essay discussing the news coverage in the *Herald* and the *Beacon*:

- The *Beacon* **also** allots only a small portion of the front page to global news.
- **In the same way,** the *Herald* tries to include at least three local stories on the first page.
- **Likewise,** the *Beacon* emphasizes the importance of up-to-date reporting of town meetings.
- The *Herald* is **similarly** committed to extensive coverage of high school and college sports.

The transitions (in boldface) in these examples could be used to *signal differences*:

- **By way of contrast,** the *Herald*'s editorial page deals with national matters on the average of three times a week.

- **On the other hand,** the *Beacon* does not share the *Herald*'s enthusiasm for interviews with national figures.
- The *Beacon,* **however,** does not encourage its reporters to tackle national stories the way the *Herald* does.
- **But** the *Herald*'s coverage of the Washington scene is much more comprehensive than its competitor's.

REVISION STRATEGIES

Once you have a draft of the essay, you're ready to revise. The following checklist will help you and those giving you feedback apply to comparison-contrast some of the revision techniques discussed in Chapters 7 and 8.

☑ COMPARISON-CONTRAST: A REVISION/PEER REVIEW CHECKLIST

Revise Overall Meaning and Structure

□ Are the subjects sufficiently alike for the comparison-contrast to be logical and meaningful?

□ What purpose does the essay serve? Does it inform? Evaluate? Persuade readers to accept a viewpoint and perhaps take action? Eliminate misconceptions or draw a surprising analogy?

□ What is the essay's thesis? How could the thesis be stated more effectively?

□ Is the overall essay organized primarily by the one-side-at-a-time method or by the point-by-point method? What is the advantage of that strategy for this essay?

□ Regardless of the method used to organize the essay, are the same features discussed for each subject? What are the features? Are they discussed in the same order?

□ Which points of comparison and/or contrast might be unfamiliar to readers? Do these need further development? Which points should be deleted because they're unconvincing or irrelevant? Where do significant points seem to be missing? How has the most important point of similarity or difference been emphasized?

Revise Paragraph Development

□ If the essay uses the one-side-at-a-time method, which paragraph marks the switch from one subject to another?

□ If the essay uses the point-by-point method, do paragraphs consistently alternate between subjects (one aspect of one subject, then the same aspect for another subject, and so on)? If this alternation

---

becomes too elaborate or predictable, what could be done to eliminate the problem?

☐ If the essay uses both the one-side-at-a-time and the point-by-point methods, which paragraph marks the switch from one method to the other? If the switch is confusing, how could it be made less so?

☐ Where would transitions signaling similarities or differences (*also, likewise, in contrast*) make it easier to follow the line of thought within and between paragraphs?

Revise Sentences and Words

☐ Where do too many transitions make sentences awkward and mechanical?

☐ Which sentences and words fail to convey the intended tone?

STUDENT ESSAY: FROM PREWRITING THROUGH REVISION

The student essay that follows was written by Carol Siskin in response to this assignment:

> In "And Then I Went to School," Joseph H. Suina contrasts his home and school environments, showing that one was much more favorable than the other. In an essay of your own, contrast two personality types, life-styles, or stages of life, demonstrating that one is superior to the other.

Having recently turned forty, Carol decided to write an essay taking issue with the idea that being young is better than being old. From time to time, Carol had used her *journal* to explore what it means to grow older. Rather than writing a new journal entry on the subject, she decided to look at earlier entries to see if they contained any helpful material for the assignment. One rather free-ranging entry, typewritten the evening of her birthday, proved especially valuable. The original entry starts below. The handwritten marks indicate Carol's later efforts to shape and develop this raw material. Note the way Carol added details, circled main ideas, and indicated a possible sequence. These annotations paved the way for her outline, which is presented after the journal entry.

Journal Entry

Forty years old today. At 20 I thought 40 would mean the end of everything, but that's not the case at all. I'm much happier now.

Mom and Dad made a dinner for the occasion.
Talking of happy, they look great. Mom said this is
the best part of their lives. They love retirement--
and obviously each other. I hope Mitch and I will be
that happy when we're in our sixties. And Dave and
Elaine seem as good as ever. They look right
together. What a pleasure it is to be a couple. I
remember how lonely I was before Mitch and how
lonely Dave was after his divorce. I sure don't envy
young singles.

Dave seems content now. He looks handsome and
robust, partly because he feels good about his life,
partly because he tries to run pretty regularly. I
remember how desperately he used to work out with
weights because he worried about his appearance. I'm
glad I don't have to be obsessed with my appearance the
way I used to be. Mitch loves me the way I am. And I'm
not obsessed anymore with being super stylish. Or
thin. In fact, tonight, with no qualms whatever, I ate
two healthy slices of birthday cake.

Dave says that Nancy (I can't believe she's 22) is
thinking of going to graduate school, but she's not sure
what to study. I can remember all the confusion I
felt about schools and majors. I don't miss those days
at all. Dave thinks Nancy is just plain confused
about who she is and what she wants. Her goals
change from day to day, especially because she's
trying to please everyone. One day she feels
confident; the next she's frightened. And she blames
her parents' unhappy marriage for her confusion. No
wonder she can't decide whether to marry and have kids.
What chaos!

Tonight, though, was anything but chaos and
confusion. It was an evening of quiet contentment.
All of us enjoyed each other and got along. Quite
different from the way it used to be. How I used to
fight with Mom and Dad. I remember slamming the door
and yelling, "It's your fault I was born." What
unhappy times those were.

Possible conclusion

I (Appearance)

My diets. Hated big
waist and legs.

blazers vs. leather
jackets

II (Decisions)

III (Sense of self)

II

Outline

Thesis: Being young is good, but being older is better.

I. Appearance

    A. Dave and I when young

        1. Dave's weight lifting to build himself up

        2. My constant dieting to change my body

        3. Both begging for "right" clothes

    B. Attitudes now

        1. My contentment with my rounded shape

        2. Dave's satisfaction with his thinness

        3. Our clothes fashionable but comfortable

II. Decisions

    A. My major decisions mostly in the past

        1. About education

        2. About marriage and children

    B. Nancy's major decisions mostly in the future

        1. About education

        2. About marriage and children

III. Sense of self

    A. Nancy's uncertainty

        1. Unclear values and goals

        2. Strong need to be liked

        3. Unresolved feelings about parents

    B. Older person's surer self-identity

        1. Have clearer values and goals

        2. Can stand being disliked

        3. Don't blame parents

Now read Carol's paper, "The Virtues of Growing Older," noting the similarities and differences among her journal entry, outline, and final essay. You'll see that the essay is more developed than either the journal entry or outline. In the essay, Carol added numerous specific details—like those about Dave gobbling vitamins and milk shakes when he was a teen. In contrast, she omitted from the essay some journal material because it would have required burdensome explanations. For instance, if she hadn't eliminated the reference to Nancy, it would have been necessary to explain that Nancy is the daughter of Dave's wife by his first marriage. Despite these differences, you'll note that the essay's basic plan is derived largely from the journal entry and outline. As you read the essay, also consider how well it applies the principles of comparison-contrast discussed in this chapter. (The commentary that follows the paper will help you look at Carol's essay more closely and will give you some sense of how she went about revising her first draft.)

The Virtues of Growing Older
by Carol Siskin

1   Our society worships youth. Advertisements convince us to buy Grecian Formula and Oil of Olay so we can hide the gray in our hair and smooth the lines on our face. Television shows feature attractive young stars with firm bodies, perfect complexions, and thick manes of hair. Middle-aged folks work out in gyms and jog down the street, trying to delay the effects of age.

The first of a two-paragraph introduction

2   Wouldn't any person over thirty gladly sign with the devil just to be young again? Isn't aging an experience to be dreaded? Perhaps it is un-American to say so, but I believe the answer is "No." Being young is often pleasant, but being older has distinct advantages.

The second introductory paragraph

Thesis

3   When young, you are apt to be obsessed with your appearance. When my brother Dave and I were teens, we worked feverishly to perfect the bodies we had. Dave lifted weights, took megadoses of vitamins, and drank a half-dozen milk shakes a day in order to turn his wiry adolescent frame into some muscular ideal. And as a teenager, I dieted constantly. No matter what I weighed, though, I was never satisfied with the way I looked. My legs were too heavy, my shoulders too broad, my waist too big. When Dave and I were young, we begged and pleaded for the "right" clothes. If our parents didn't get them for us, we felt our world would fall apart. How could we go to school wearing loose-fitting blazers when everyone else would be wearing smartly tailored leather jackets? We could be considered freaks. I often wonder how my parents, and parents in general, manage to tolerate their children during the adolescent years. Now, however, Dave and I are beyond such adolescent agonies. My rounded figure seems fine, and I don't deny myself a slice of pecan pie if I feel in the mood. Dave still works out, but he has actually become fond of his tall, lanky frame. The two of us enjoy wearing fashionable clothes, but we are no longer slaves to style. And women, I'm embarrassed to admit, even more than men,

First half of topic sentence for point 1: Appearance

Start of what it's like being young

Second half of topic sentence for point 1

Start of what it's like being older

have always seemed to be at the mercy of fashion. Now my clothes--and my brother's--are attractive yet easy to wear. We no longer feel anxious about what others will think. As long as we feel good about how we look, we are happy.

First half of topic sentence for point 2: Life choices — Being older is preferable to being younger in 4 another way. Obviously, I still have important choices to make about my life, but I have already made many of the critical decisions that confront

Start of what it's like being older — those just starting out. I chose the man I wanted to marry. I decided to have children. I elected to

Second half of topic sentence for point 2 — return to college to complete my education. But when you are young, major decisions await you at every

Start of what it's like being younger — turn. "What college should I attend? What career should I pursue? Should I get married? Should I have children?" These are just a few of the issues facing young people. It's no wonder that, despite their care-free facade, they are often confused, uncertain, and troubled by all the unknowns in their future.

Topic sentence for point 3: Self-concept — But the greatest benefit of being forty is knowing who 5 I am.

Start of what it's like being younger — The most unsettling aspect of youth is the uncertainty you feel about your values, goals, and dreams. Being young means wondering what is worth working for. Being young means feeling happy with yourself one day and wishing you were never born the next. It means trying on new selves by taking up with different crowds. It means resenting your parents and

Start of what it's like being older — their way of life one minute and then feeling you will never be as good or as accomplished as they are. By way of contrast, forty is sanity. I have a surer self-concept now. I don't laugh at jokes I don't think are funny. I can make a speech in front of a town meeting or complain in a store because I am no longer terrified that people will laugh at me; I am no longer anxious that everyone must like me. I no longer blame my parents for my every personality quirk or keep a running score of everything they did wrong raising me. Life has taught me that I, not they, am responsible for who I am. We are all human beings--neither saints nor devils.

Conclusion — Most Americans blindly accept the idea that newer is 6 automatically better. But a human life contradicts this

premise. There is a great deal of happiness to be found
as we grow older. My own parents, now in their sixties,
recently told me that they are happier now than they have
ever been. They would not want to be my age. Did this
surprise me? At first, yes. Then it gladdened me. Their
contentment holds out great promise for me as I move into
the next--perhaps even better--phase of my life.

Commentary

Purpose and Thesis

In her essay, Carol disproves the widespread belief that being young is preferable to being old. The *comparison-contrast* pattern allows her to analyze the drawbacks of one and the merits of the other, thus providing the essay with an *evaluative purpose*. Using the title to indicate her point of view, Carol places the *thesis* at the end of her two-paragraph introduction: "Being young is often pleasant, but being older has distinct advantages." Note that the thesis accomplishes several things. It names the two subjects to be discussed and clarifies Carol's point of view about her subjects. The thesis also implies that the essay will focus on the contrasts between these two periods of life.

Points of Support and Overall Organization

To support her assertion that older is better, Carol supplies examples from her own life and organizes the examples around three main points: attitudes about appearance, decisions about life choices, and questions of self-concept. Using the *point-by-point method* to organize the overall essay, she explores each of these key ideas in a separate paragraph. Each paragraph is further focused by one or two sentences that serve as a topic sentence.

Sequence of Points, Organizational Cues, and Paragraph Development

Let's look more closely at the way Carol presents her three central points in the essay. She obviously considers appearance the least important of a person's worries, life choices more important, and self-concept the most critical. So she uses *emphatic order* to sequence the supporting paragraphs, with the phrase "But the greatest benefit" signaling the special significance of the last issue. Carol is also careful to use *transitions* to help readers follow her line of thinking: "*Now, however,* Dave and I are beyond such adolescent agonies" (3); "*But* when you are young, major decisions await you at every turn" (4); and "*By way of contrast,* forty is sanity" (5).

Although Carol has worked hard to write a well-organized paper—and has on the whole been successful—she doesn't feel compelled to make the paper fit a rigid format. As you've seen, the essay as a whole uses the point-by-point method, but each supporting paragraph uses the *one-side-at-a-time method*—that is, everything about one age group is discussed before there is a shift to the other age group. Notice too that the third and fifth paragraphs start with young people and then move to adults, whereas the fourth paragraph reverses the sequence by starting with older people.

Other Patterns of Development

Carol uses the comparison-contrast format to organize her ideas, but other patterns of development also come into play. To illustrate her points, she makes extensive use of *illustration,* and her discussion also contains elements typical of *causal analysis.* Throughout the essay, for instance, she traces the effect of being a certain age on her brother, herself, and her parents.

A Problem with Unity

As you read the third paragraph, you might have noted that Carol's essay runs into a problem. Two sentences in the paragraph disrupt the *unity* of Carol's discussion: "I often wonder how my parents, and parents in general, manage to tolerate their children during the adolescent years," and "women, I'm embarrassed to admit . . . have always seemed to be at the mercy of fashion." These sentences should be deleted because they don't develop the idea that adolescents are overly concerned with appearance.

Conclusion

Carol's final paragraph brings the essay to a pleasing and interesting close. The conclusion recalls the point made in the introduction: Americans overvalue youth. Carol also uses the conclusion to broaden the scope of her discussion. Rather than continuing to focus on herself, she briefly mentions her parents and the pleasure they take in life. By bringing her parents into the essay, Carol is able to make a gently philosophical observation about the promise that awaits her as she grows older. The implication is that a similarly positive future awaits us, too.

Revising the First Draft

To help guide her revision, Carol asked her husband to read her first draft aloud. As he did, Carol took notes on what she sensed were the paper's strengths and weaknesses. She then jotted down her observations, as well as her husband's, onto the draft. Because Carol wasn't certain which observations were most valid, she didn't rank them. Carol made a number of changes when revising the essay. You'll get a good sense of how she proceeded if you compare the annotated original introduction reprinted here with the final version in the full essay.

Original Version of the Introduction

Boring paragraph
First sentence dull

Cut?

America is a land filled with people who worship youth. We admire dynamic young achievers; our middle-aged citizens work out in gyms; all of us wear tight tops and colorful sneakers--clothes that look fine on the young but ridiculous on aging bodies. Television shows revolve around perfect-looking young stars, while commercials entice us with products that will keep us young.

Make point about TV more specific

Make questions more vigorous

Wouldn't every older person want to be young again? Isn't aging to be avoided? It may be slightly unpatriotic to say so, but I believe the answer is "No." Being young

may be pleasant at times, but I would rather be my forty-
year-old self. I no longer have to agonize about my
physical appearance, I have already made many of my crucial
life decisions, and I am much less confused about who I am.

Maybe cut plan of development

After hearing her original two-paragraph introduction read aloud, Carol was dissatisfied with what she had written. Although she wasn't quite sure how to proceed,
she knew that the paragraphs were flat and that they failed to open the essay on a
strong note. She decided to start by whittling down the opening sentence, making it
crisper and more powerful: "Our society worships youth." That done, she eliminated
two bland statements ("We admire dynamic young achievers" and "all of us wear
tight tops and colorful sneakers") and made several vague references more concrete
and interesting. For example, "commercials entice us with products that will keep us
young" became "Grecian Formula and Oil of Olay . . . hide the gray in our hair and
smooth the lines on our face"; "perfect-looking young stars" became "attractive
young stars with firm bodies, perfect complexions, and thick manes of hair." With the
addition of these specifics, the first paragraph became more vigorous and interesting.

Carol next made some subtle changes in the two questions that opened the second paragraph of the original introduction. She replaced "Wouldn't every older
person want to be young again?" and "Isn't aging to be avoided?" with two more
emphatic questions: "Wouldn't any person over thirty gladly sign with the devil
just to be young again?" and "Isn't aging an experience to be dreaded?" Carol also
made some changes at the end of the original second paragraph. Because the
paper is relatively short and the subject matter easy to understand, she decided to
omit her somewhat awkward *plan of development* ("I no longer have to agonize
about my physical appearance, I have already made many of my crucial life decisions, and I am much less confused about who I am"). This deletion made it possible to end the introduction with a clear statement of the essay's thesis.

Once these revisions were made, Carol was confident that her essay got off to
a stronger start. Feeling reassured, she moved ahead and made changes in other
sections of her paper. Such work enabled her to prepare a solid piece of writing
that offers food for thought.

ACTIVITIES: COMPARISON- CONTRAST

Prewriting Activities

1. Imagine you're writing two essays: One explores the effects of holding a job
while in college; the other explains how to budget money wisely. Jot down
ways you might use comparison-contrast in each essay.

2. Suppose you plan to write a series of articles for your college newspaper. What purpose might you have for comparing and/or contrasting each of the following subject pairs?

   a. Videotapes and DVDs
   b. Paper or plastic bags at the supermarket
   c. Two courses—one taught by an inexperienced newcomer, the other by an old pro
   d. Cutting class and not showing up at work

3. Use the patterns of development or another prewriting technique to compare and/or contrast a current situation with the way you would like it to be. After reviewing your prewriting material, decide what your purpose, audience, tone, and point of view might be if you were to write an essay. Finally, write out your thesis and main supporting points.

4. Using your journal or freewriting, jot down the advantages and disadvantages of two ways of doing something (for example, watching movies in the theater versus watching them on a VCR at home; following trends versus ignoring them; dating one person versus playing the field; and so on). Reread your prewriting and determine what your thesis, purpose, audience, tone, and point of view might be if you were to write an essay. Make a scratch list of the main ideas you would cover. Would a point-by-point or a one-side-at-a-time method of organization work more effectively?

Revising Activities

5. Of the statements that follow, which would *not* make effective thesis statements for comparison-contrast essays? Identify the problem(s) in the faulty statements and revise them accordingly.

   a. Although their classroom duties often overlap, teacher aides are not as equipped as teachers to handle disciplinary problems.
   b. This college provides more assistance to its students than most schools.
   c. During the state's last congressional election, both candidates relied heavily on television to communicate their messages.
   d. There are many differences between American and foreign cars.

6. The following paragraph is from the draft of an essay detailing the qualities of a skillful manager. How effective is this comparison-contrast paragraph? What revisions would help focus the paragraph on the point made in the topic sentence? Where should details be added or deleted? Rewrite the paragraph, providing necessary transitions and details.

   A manager encourages creativity and treats employees courteously, while a boss discourages staff resourcefulness and views it as a threat. At the hardware store where I work, I got

my boss's approval to develop a system for organizing excess
stock in the storeroom. I shelved items in roughly the same
order as they were displayed in the store. The system was
helpful to all the salespeople, not just to me, since everyone
was stymied by the boss's helter-skelter system. What he did
was store overstocked items according to each wholesaler, even
though most of us weren't there long enough to know which items
came from which wholesaler. His supposed system created chaos.
When he saw what I had done, he was furious and insisted that
we continue to follow the old slap-dash system. I had assumed
he would welcome my ideas the way my manager did last summer
when I worked in a drugstore. But he didn't and I had to scrap
my work and go back to his eccentric system. He certainly could
learn something about employee relations from the drugstore
manager.

PROFESSIONAL SELECTIONS: COMPARISON-CONTRAST

TONI MORRISON

One of the most honored contemporary American writers, Nobel Prize-winner Toni
Morrison (1931—) also received the National Book Critics Circle Award for Fiction
for her novel *Song of Solomon* (1977) and the Pulitzer Prize for her novels *Tar Baby*
(1981) and *Beloved* (1986). Her other books include *Dancing Mind* (1967) and
Paradise (1997). In her capacity as an editor for Random House, she worked on autobiographies of boxer Muhammad Ali and civil rights activist Angela Davis, as well as
on *To Die for the People* (1995), an account of the Black Panther Party. The essay
reprinted here first appeared in *The New York Times Magazine* on July 4, 1976, the
date of the American bicentennial.

Pre-Reading Journal Entry

Though the members of a family often share some specific values and beliefs,
they are just as likely to differ in their opinions on other subjects. In your journal,

list the topics about which you and relatives of an older generation—your parents'
or grandparents', for example—hold different, possibly opposite views. Then, for
each topic on your list, go back and jot down what these differing beliefs are.

A SLOW WALK OF TREES

His name was John Solomon Willis, and when at age 5 he heard from the old folks   1
that "the Emancipation Proclamation was coming," he crawled under the bed. It was
his earliest recollection of what was to be his habitual response to the promise of white
people: horror and an instinctive yearning for safety. He was my grandfather, a musician who managed to hold on to his violin but not his land. He lost all 88 acres of his
Indian mother's inheritance to legal predators who built their fortunes on the likes of
him. He was an unreconstructed black pessimist who, in spite of or because of emancipation, was convinced for 85 years that there was no hope whatever for black people in this country. His rancor was legitimate, for he, John Solomon, was not only an
artist but a first-rate carpenter and farmer, reduced to sending home to his family
money he had made playing the violin because he was not able to find work. And this
during the years when almost half the black male population were skilled craftsmen
who lost their jobs to white ex-convicts and immigrant farmers.

His wife, however, was of a quite different frame of mind and believed that all things   2
could be improved by faith in Jesus and an effort of the will. So it was she, Ardelia
Willis, who sneaked her seven children out of the back window into the darkness,
rather than permit the patron of their sharecropper's existence to become their exe-
cutioner as well, and headed north in 1912, when 99.2 percent of all black people in
the U.S. were native-born and only 60 percent of white Americans were. And it was
Ardelia who told her husband that they could not stay in the Kentucky town they
ended up in because the teacher didn't know long division.

They have been dead now for 30 years and more and I still don't know which of   3
them came closer to the truth about the possibilities of life for black people in this
country. One of their grandchildren is a tenured professor at Princeton. Another, who
suffered from what the Peruvian poet called "anger that breaks a man into children,"
was picked up just as he entered his teens and emotionally lobotomized by the refor-
matories and mental institutions specifically designed to serve him. Neither John
Solomon nor Ardelia lived long enough to despair over one or swell with pride over
the other. But if they were alive today each would have selected and collected enough
evidence to support the accuracy of the other's original point of view. And it would be
difficult to convince either one that the other was right.

Some of the monstrous events that took place in John Solomon's America have been   4
duplicated in alarming detail in my own America. There was the public murder of a
President in a theater in 1865 and the public murder of another President on television in 1963. The Civil War of 1861 had its encore as the civil-rights movement of
1960. The torture and mutilation of a black West Point Cadet (Cadet Johnson
Whittaker) in 1880 had its rerun with the 1970's murders of students at Jackson State
College, Texas Southern and Southern University in Baton Rouge. And in 1976 we
watch for what must be the thousandth time a pitched battle between the children of
slaves and the children of immigrants—only this time, it is not the New York draft riots
of 1863, but the busing turmoil in Paul Revere's home town, Boston.

5   Hopeless, he'd said. Hopeless. For he was certain that white people of every political, religious, geographical and economic background would band together against
black people everywhere when they felt the threat of our progress. And a hundred
years after he sought safety from the white man's "promise," somebody put a bullet in
Martin Luther King's brain. And not long before that some excellent samples of the
master race demonstrated their courage and virility by dynamiting some little black
girls to death. If he were here now, my grandfather, he would shake his head, close his
eyes and pull out his violin—too polite to say, "I told you so." And his wife would pay
attention to the music but not to the sadness in her husband's eyes, for she would see
what she expected to see—not the occasional historical repetition, but, *like the slow
walk of certain species of trees from the flatlands up into the mountains,* she would
see the signs of irrevocable and permanent change. She, who pulled her girls out of an
inadequate school in the Cumberland Mountains, knew all along that the gentlemen
from Alabama who had killed the little girls would be rounded up. And it wouldn't surprise her in the least to know that the number of black college graduates jumped
12 percent in the last three years: 47 percent in 20 years. That there are 140 black
mayors in this country; 14 black judges in the District Circuit, 4 in the Courts of
Appeals and one on the Supreme Court. That there are 17 blacks in Congress, one in
the Senate; 276 in state legislatures—223 in state houses, 53 in state senates. That
there are 112 elected black police chiefs and sheriffs, 1 Pulitzer Prize winner; 1 winner of the Prix de Rome; a dozen or so winners of the Guggenheim; 4 deans of predominantly white colleges. . . . Oh, her list would go on and on. But so would John
Solomon's sweet sad music.

6   While my grandparents held opposite views on whether the fortunes of black people
were improving, my own parents struck similarly opposed postures, but from another
slant. They differed about whether the moral fiber of white people would ever improve.
Quite a different argument. The old folks argued about how and if black people could
improve themselves, who could be counted on to help us, who would hinder us and so
on. My parents took issue over the question of whether it was possible for white people
to improve. They assumed that black people were the humans of the globe, but had
serious doubts about the quality and existence of white humanity. Thus my father,
distrusting every word and every gesture of every white man on earth, assumed that the
white man who crept up the stairs one afternoon had come to molest his daughters and
threw him down the stairs and then our tricycle after him. (I think my father was wrong,
but considering what I have seen since, it may have been very healthy for me to have
witnessed that as my first black-white encounter.) My mother, however, *believed* in
them—their possibilities. So when the meal we got on relief was bug-ridden, she wrote
a long letter to Franklin Delano Roosevelt. And when white bill collectors came to our
door, it was she who received them civilly and explained in a sweet voice that we were
people of honor and that the debt would be taken care of. Her message to Roosevelt got
through—our meal improved. Her message to the bill collectors did not always get
through and there was occasional violence when my father (self-exiled to the bedroom
for fear he could not hold his temper) would hear that her reasonableness had failed. My
mother was always wounded by these scenes, for she thought the bill collector knew that
she loved good credit more than life and that being in arrears on a payment horrified her
probably more than it did him. So she thought he was rude because he was white. For
years she walked to utility companies and department stores to pay bills in person and
even now she does not seem convinced that checks are legal tender. My father loved

excellence, worked hard (he held three jobs at once for 17 years) and was so outraged by the suggestion of personal slackness that he could explain it to himself only in terms of racism. He was a fastidious worker who was frightened of one thing: unemployment. I can remember now the doomsday-*cum*-graveyard sound of "laid off" and how the minute school was out he asked us, "Where you workin'?" Both my parents believed that all succor and aid came from themselves and their neighborhood, since "they"—white people in charge and those not in charge but in obstructionist positions—were in some way fundamentally, genetically corrupt.

So I grew up in a basically racist household with more than a child's share of   7
contempt for white people. And for each white friend I acquired who made a small crack in that contempt, there was another who repaired it. For each one who related to me as a person, there was one who in my presence at least, became actively "white." And like most black people of my generation, I suffer from racial vertigo that can be cured only by taking what one needs from one's ancestors. John Solomon's cynicism and his deployment of his art as both weapon and solace, Ardelia's faith in the magic that can be wrought by sheer effort of the will; my mother's open-mindedness in each new encounter and her habit of trying reasonableness first; my father's temper, his impatience and his efforts to keep "them" (throw them) out of his life. And it is out of these learned and selected attitudes that I look at the quality of life for my people in this country now. These widely disparate and sometimes conflicting views, I suspect, were held not only by me, but by most black people. Some I know are clearer in their positions, have not sullied their anger with optimism or dirtied their hope with despair. But most of us are plagued by a sense of being worn shell-thin by constant repression and hostility as well as the impression of being buoyed by visible testimony of tremendous strides. There *is* repetition of the grotesque in our history. And there *is* the miraculous walk of trees. The question is whether our walk is progress or merely movement. O.J. Simpson leaning on a Hertz car[1] *is* better than the Gold Dust Twins on the back of a soap box. But is *Good Times*[2] better than Stepin Fetchit? Has the first order of business been taken care of? Does the law of the land work for us?

---

[1]Prior to his arrest and trial for the murder of his ex-wife, O. J. Simpson, a former football superstar, was the spokesperson for Hertz Rent-a-Car (editors' note).

[2]A popular 1970s television show featuring an African American family. Many critics felt that the show perpetuated harmful stereotypes (editors' note).

Questions for Close Reading

1. What is the selection's thesis? Locate the sentence(s) in which Morrison states her main idea. If she doesn't state the thesis explicitly, express it in your own words.

2. How did Morrison's grandfather and grandmother feel about opportunities for blacks? Why did they disagree?

3. Why does Morrison say she grew up in a "racist household"? To what extent does Morrison consider herself a racist?

4. What evidence is there, according to Morrison, that life for blacks in the United States has improved? What evidence does she cite to the contrary?

5. Refer to your dictionary as needed to define the following words used in the selection: *unreconstructed* (paragraph 1), *rancor* (1), *sharecropper* (2), *lobotomized* (3), *virility* (5), *irrevocable* (5), *hinder* (6), *arrears* (6), *fastidious* (6), *succor* (6), *vertigo* (7), and *deployment* (7).

Questions About the Writer's Craft

1. **The pattern.** Morrison builds her essay around the comparison-contrast between first, her grandparents, and then her parents. However, numerous other comparisons and contrasts appear in the essay. Identify some of these and explain how Morrison uses them to reinforce her thesis.

2. Look closely at paragraph 5. How does Morrison's sentence structure there underscore her central point?

3. Examine the lengthy analysis of the differences between Morrison's parents (paragraph 6). How does Morrison shift the focus from her grandparents to her parents, then from one parent to the other?

4. Reread the final seven sentences in paragraph 7, starting with "There *is* repetition. . . ." Why do you suppose Morrison italicized the word *is* in the first, second, and fourth sentences, but not in the third?

Writing Assignments Using Comparison-Contrast as a Pattern of Development

∞ 1. Morrison writes that when she was a child, occasionally "a white friend . . . made a small crack" in her distrust of whites. Who in your life has "made a crack" in your generalizations about an issue, about people, or about yourself? Perhaps an aging but energetic relative changed your opinion that the elderly are to be pitied, or a friend's passion for Bach and Chopin challenged your belief that those who like classical music are boringly highbrow, or a neighbor showed you that you had real athletic potential. Write an essay contrasting your "before" and "after" beliefs, remembering to provide vivid details to bring the contrast to life. You may want to read Maya Angelou's "Sister Flowers" (page 178) to gain insight into the way one person can alter another individual's entrenched views.

2. Write an essay contrasting the belief systems of two individuals whose views affected the way you think about a particular aspect of life—for example, academic success, tolerance for others, financial well-being. Like Morrison, begin by describing the differences in the individuals' beliefs.

Writing Assignments Using Other Patterns of Development

∞ **3.** Morrison writes that her grandfather's "rancor [toward whites] was legitimate." Write an essay in which you offer your personal definition of the phrase "legitimate rancor." Develop your definition by narrating a single event that shows the circumstances under which you believe rancor would be a valid response. Let the power of your details rather than inflamed language show that anger would be a justified reaction. For a narrative about situations that justify anger, read Brent Staples's "Black Men and Public Space" (page 407).

4. Despite the racism they encountered, Morrison's grandparents and parents believed in themselves and lived lives of great dignity. Focus on a specific group of individuals who, because of prejudice, often struggle to maintain their self-esteem. Possibilities include immigrants, the elderly, the overweight, the learning disabled, the physically challenged. Write an essay describing the specific steps that *one* group (for example, parents, schools, communities, or religious organizations) can take to encourage a healthy sense of optimism and possibility in these people.

Writing Assignment Using a Journal Entry as a Starting Point

5. Morrison reveals how members of the same family can hold different beliefs about the same issue. Write an essay in which you contrast your beliefs about *one* subject with the beliefs held by a family member of an older generation. Possible subjects include the status of women or men, the work ethic, racial relations, homosexuality, education, and so on. Before beginning to write, review the material you generated in your pre-reading journal entry, and try to come up with additional details and examples of these contesting viewpoints. At some point in the essay, indicate what you think has caused the shift in thinking between generations.

DAVE BARRY

Pulitzer Prize-winning humorist Dave Barry (1947–) began his writing career covering—as he puts it—"incredibly dull municipal meetings" for *The Daily Local News* of West Chester, Pennsylvania. In 1983, Barry joined the staff of *The Miami Herald,* where his rib-tickling commentary on the absurdities of everyday life quickly brought him a legion of devoted fans. Barry's column is now syndicated in more than 150 newspapers. A popular guest on television and radio, Barry has written many books, including *Dave Barry's Complete Guide to Guys* (1995), *Dave Barry in Cyberspace* (1996), *Big Trouble* (1999), and *Dave Barry Hits Below the Beltway* (2001). The essay on the following page first appeared in *The Miami Herald* in 1998.

Pre-Reading Journal Entry

To what extent would you say our images of personal attractiveness are influenced by TV commercials and magazine advertisements? Think of commercials and ads you've seen recently. What physical traits are typically identified as attractive in women? In men? List as many as you can. What assumptions does each trait suggest? Use your journal to respond to these questions.

THE UGLY TRUTH ABOUT BEAUTY

1   If you're a man, at some point a woman will ask you how she looks.

2   "How do I look?" she'll ask.

3   You must be careful how you answer this question. The best technique is to form an honest yet sensitive opinion, then collapse on the floor with some kind of fatal seizure. Trust me, this is the easiest way out. Because you will never come up with the right answer.

4   The problem is that women generally do not think of their looks in the same way that men do. Most men form an opinion of how they look in the seventh grade, and they stick to it for the rest of their lives. Some men form the opinion that they are irresistible stud muffins, and they do not change this opinion even when their faces sag and their noses bloat to the size of eggplants and their eyebrows grow together to form what appears to be a giant forehead-dwelling tropical caterpillar.

5   Most men, I believe, think of themselves as average-looking. Men will think this even if their faces cause heart failure in cattle at a range of 300 yards. Being average does not bother them; average is fine, for men. This is why men never ask anybody how they look. Their primary form of beauty care is to shave themselves, which is essentially the same form of beauty care that they give to their lawns. If, at the end of his four-minute daily beauty regimen, a man has managed to wipe most of the shaving cream out of his hair and is not bleeding too badly, he feels that he has done all he can, so he stops thinking about his appearance and devotes his mind to more critical issues, such as the Super Bowl.

6   Women do not look at themselves this way. If I had to express, in three words, what I believe most women think about their appearance, those words would be: "not good enough." No matter how attractive a woman may appear to be to others, when she looks at herself in the mirror, she thinks: woof. She thinks that at any moment a municipal–animal-control officer is going to throw a net over her and haul her off to the shelter.

7   Why do women have such low self-esteem? There are many complex psychological and societal reasons, by which I mean Barbie. Girls grow up playing with a doll proportioned such that, if it were human, it would be seven feet tall and weigh 81 pounds, of which 53 pounds would be bosoms. This is a difficult appearance standard to live up to, especially when you contrast it with the standard set for little boys by their dolls . . . excuse me, by their action figures. Most of the action figures that my son played with when he was little were hideous-looking. For example, he was very fond of an action figure (part of the He-Man series) called "Buzz-Off," who was part human, part flying insect. Buzz-Off was not a looker. But he was extremely self-confident. You could not imagine Buzz-Off saying to the other action figures: "Do you think these wings make my hips look big?"

8   But women grow up thinking they need to look like Barbie, which for most women is impossible, although there is a multibillion-dollar beauty industry devoted to

convincing women that they must try. I once saw an Oprah show wherein supermod-
el Cindy Crawford dispensed makeup tips to the studio audience. Cindy had all these
middle-aged women applying beauty products to their faces; she stressed how important it was to apply them in a certain way, using the tips of their fingers. All the women
dutifully did this, even though it was obvious to any sane observer that, no matter how
carefully they applied these products, they would never look remotely like Cindy
Crawford, who is some kind of genetic mutation.

I'm not saying that men are superior. I'm just saying that you're not going to get a   9
group of middle-aged men to sit in a room and apply cosmetics to themselves under
the instruction of Brad Pitt, in hopes of looking more like him. Men would realize that
this task was pointless and demeaning. They would find some way to bolster their self-
esteem that did not require looking like Brad Pitt. They would say to Brad: "Oh YEAH?
Well what do you know about LAWN CARE, pretty boy?"

Of course many women will argue that the reason they become obsessed with try-   10
ing to look like Cindy Crawford is that men, being as shallow as a drop of spit, WANT
women to look that way. To which I have two responses:

1. Hey, just because WE'RE idiots, that does not mean YOU have to be; and   11

2. Men don't even notice 97 percent of the beauty efforts you make anyway. Take   12
fingernails. The average woman spends 5,000 hours per year worrying about her fingernails; I have never once, in more than 40 years of listening to men talk about
women, heard a man say, "She has a nice set of fingernails!" Many men would not
notice if a woman had upward of four hands.

Anyway, to get back to my original point: If you're a man, and a woman asks you   13
how she looks, you're in big trouble. Obviously, you can't say she looks bad. But you
also can't say that she looks great, because she'll think you're lying, because she has
spent countless hours, with the help of the multibillion-dollar beauty industry, obsess-
ing about the differences between herself and Cindy Crawford. Also, she suspects that
you're not qualified to judge anybody's appearance. This is because you have shaving
cream in your hair.

Questions for Close Reading

1. What is the selection's thesis? Locate the sentence(s) in which Barry states his
   main idea. If he doesn't state the thesis explicitly, express it in your own words.

2. Barry tells us that most men consider themselves to be "average-looking"
   (paragraph 5). Why, according to Barry, do men feel this way?

3. When Barry writes that most women think of themselves as "not good
   enough" (6), what does he mean? What, according to Barry, causes women to
   develop low opinions of themselves?

4. Barry implies that women could have a more rational response to the "difficult
   appearance standard" that pervades society (7). What would that response be?

5. Refer to your dictionary as needed to define the following words used in the
   selection: *regimen* (paragraph 5), *municipal* (6), *societal* (7), *dispensed* (8), *genetic*
   (8), *mutation* (8), *demeaning* (9), and *bolster* (9).

Questions About the Writer's Craft

1. **The pattern.** Which comparison-contrast method of organization (point-by-point or one-side-at-a-time) does Barry use to develop his essay? Why might he have chosen this pattern?

2. Barry uses exaggeration, a strategy typically associated with humorous writing. Locate instances of exaggeration in the selection. Why do you think he uses this strategy?

3. **Other patterns.** Barry demonstrates a series of cause-effect chains in his essay. Locate some of the cause-effect series. How do they help Barry reinforce his thesis?

4. Barry's title involves an *oxymoron*—a contradiction in terms. What does this title imply about Barry's attitude toward his subject?

Writing Assignments Using Comparison-Contrast as a Pattern of Development

∞ 1. Examine the pitches made in magazines and on TV for the male and female versions of *one* kind of grooming product. Possibilities include deodorant, hair dye, soap, and so on. Then write an essay contrasting the persuasive appeals that the product makes to men with those it makes to women. (Don't forget to examine the assumptions behind the appeals.) To gain insight into advertising techniques, you'll find it helpful to read Ann McClintock's "Propaganda Techniques in Today's Advertising" (page 282). For useful perspectives on gender issues, consider reading Susan Douglas's "Managing Mixed Messages" (page 251) and Deborah Tannen's "But What Do You Mean?" (page 288).

2. Barry contrasts women's preoccupation with looking good to men's lack of concern about their appearance. Now consider the flip side—something men care about deeply that women virtually ignore. Write an essay contrasting men's stereotypical fascination with *one* area to women's indifference. You might, for example, examine male and female attitudes toward sports, cars, tools, even lawn care. Following Barry's example, adopt a playful tone in your essay, illustrating the absurdity of the obsession you discuss.

Writing Assignments Using Other Patterns of Development

3. Barry implies that most men, unaffected by the "multibillion-dollar beauty industry," are content to "think of themselves as average-looking." Do you agree? Conduct your own research into whether or not Barry's assertions about

men are true. Begin by interviewing several male friends, family members, and classmates to see how these men feel about their physical appearance. In addition, in the library or online, research magazines such as *People, Gentlemen's Quarterly,* or *Men's Health* for articles describing how everyday men as well as male celebrities view their looks. Then write an essay refuting or defending the view that being average-looking doesn't bother most men. Start by acknowledging the opposing view; then support your assertion with convincing evidence drawn from your research.

4. Barry blames Barbie dolls for setting up "a difficult appearance standard" for girls to emulate. Many would argue that the toys that *boys* play with also teach negative, ultimately damaging values. Write an essay exploring the values that are conveyed to boys through their toys. Brainstorm with others, especially males, about the toys of their youth or the toys that boys have today. Identify two to three key negative values to write about, illustrating each with several examples of toys.

Writing Assignment Using a Journal Entry as a Starting Point

∞ 5. Review your pre-reading journal entry. Focusing on the characteristics of male *or* female attractiveness conveyed by the mass media, identify two to three assumptions suggested by these standards. Illustrate each assumption with examples from TV commercials and/or magazine advertisements. Be sure to make clear how you feel about these assumptions. For additional insight into the possible consequences of mass media messages, read Joyce Garity's "Is Sex All That Matters?" (page 256).

JOSEPH H. SUINA

Still living on the Cochiti Pueblo Reservation in New Mexico where he grew up, Joseph H. Suina (1944–) teaches in the Multicultural Teacher Education Program at the University of New Mexico. Suina's work as an educator led to his coauthoring a book for teachers, *The Learning Environment: An Instructional Strategy* (1982). The following selection first appeared in *Linguistic and Cultural Influences on Learning Mathematics*, edited by Rodney Cocking and Jose Mestre (1988).

Pre-Reading Journal Entry

Bilingualism—instruction in a student's native language as well as in English—remains an important educational issue in many parts of the country. Do you think non-English-speaking students should be forced to speak only English when they start school, or should they for a time be taught in their native tongue as well? Why? Use your journal to reflect on your beliefs about this question.

AND THEN I WENT TO SCHOOL

1   I lived with my grandmother from the ages of 5 through 9. It was the early 1950s when electricity had not yet invaded the homes of the Cochiti Indians. The village day school and health clinic were first to have it and to the unsuspecting Cochitis this was the approach of a new era in their uncomplicated lives.

2   Transportation was simple then. Two good horses and a sturdy wagon met most needs of a villager. Only five or six individuals possessed an automobile in the Pueblo of 300. A flatbed truck fixed with wooden rails and a canvas top made a regular Saturday trip to Santa Fe. It was always loaded beyond capacity with Cochitis taking their wares to town for a few staples. With an escort of a dozen barking dogs, the straining truck made a noisy exit, northbound from the village.

3   During those years, Grandmother and I lived beside the plaza in a one-room house. It consisted of a traditional fireplace, a makeshift cabinet for our few tin cups and dishes, and a wooden crate that held our two buckets of all-purpose water. At the far end of the room were two rolls of bedding we used as comfortable sitting "couches." Consisting of thick quilts, sheepskin, and assorted blankets, these bed rolls were undone each night. A wooden pole the length of one side of the room was suspended about 10 inches from the ceiling beams. A modest collection of colorful shawls, blankets, and sashes was draped over the pole making this part of the room most interesting. In one corner was a bulky metal trunk for our ceremonial wear and a few valuables. A dresser, which was traded for some of my grandmother's well-known pottery, held the few articles of clothing we owned and the "goody bag." Grandmother always had a flour sack filled with candy, store bought cookies, and Fig Newtons. These were saturated with a sharp odor of moth balls. Nevertheless, they made a fine snack with coffee before we turned in for the night. Tucked securely in my blankets, I listened to one of her stories or accounts of how it was when she was a little girl. These accounts seemed so old fashioned compared to the way we lived. Sometimes she softly sang a song from a ceremony. In this way I fell asleep each night.

4   Earlier in the evening we would make our way to a relative's house if someone had not already come to visit us. I would play with the children while the adults caught up on all the latest. Ten-cent comic books were finding their way into the Pueblo homes. For us children, these were the first link to the world beyond the Pueblo. We enjoyed looking at them and role playing as one of the heroes rounding up the villains. Everyone preferred being a cowboy rather than an Indian because cowboys were always victorious. Sometimes, stories were related to both children and adults. These get-togethers were highlighted by refreshments of coffee and sweet bread or fruit pies baked in the outdoor oven. Winter months would most likely include roasted pinon nuts or dried deer meat for all to share. These evening gatherings and sense of closeness diminished as the radios and televisions increased over the following years. It was never to be the same again.

5   The winter months are among my fondest recollections. A warm fire crackled and danced brightly in the fireplace and the aroma of delicious stew filled our one-room house. To me the house was just right. The thick adobe walls wrapped around the two of us protectingly during the long freezing nights. Grandmother's affection completed the warmth and security I will always remember.

6   Being the only child at Grandmother's, I had lots of attention and plenty of reasons to feel good about myself. As a pre-schooler, I already had the chores of chopping

firewood and hauling in fresh water each day. After "heavy work," I would run to her and flex what I was certain were my gigantic biceps. Grandmother would state that at the rate I was going I would soon attain the status of a man like the adult males in the village. Her shower of praises made me feel like the Indian Superman of all times. At age 5, I suppose I was as close to that concept of myself as anyone.

In spite of her many years, Grandmother was still active in the village ceremonial 7 setting. She was a member of an important women's society and attended all the functions, taking me along to many of them. I would wear one of my colorful shirts she handmade for just such occasions. Grandmother taught me the appropriate behavior at these events. Through modeling she taught me to pray properly. Barefooted, I would greet the sun each morning with a handful of cornmeal. At night I would look to the stars in wonderment and let a prayer slip through my lips. I learned to appreciate cooperation in nature and my fellowmen early in life. About food and material things, Grandmother would say, "There is enough for everyone to share and it all comes from above, my child." I felt very much a part of the world and our way of life. I knew I had a place in it and I felt good about me.

At age 6, like the rest of the Cochiti 6-year-olds that year, I had to begin my school- 8 ing. It was a new and bewildering experience. One I will not forget. The strange surroundings, new concepts about time and expectations, and a foreign tongue were overwhelming to us beginners. It took some effort to return the second day and many times thereafter.

To begin with, unlike my grandmother, the teacher did not have pretty brown skin 9 and a colorful dress. She was not plump and friendly. Her clothes were one color and drab. Her pale and skinny form made me worry that she was very ill. I thought that explained why she did not have time just for me and the disappointed looks and orders she seemed to always direct my way. I didn't think she was so smart because she couldn't understand my language. "Surely that was why we had to leave our 'Indian' at home." But then I did not feel so bright either. All I could say in her language was "yes teacher," "my name is Joseph Henry," and "when is lunch time." The teacher's odor took some getting used to also. In fact, many times it made me sick right before lunch. Later, I learned from the girls that this odor was something she wore called perfume.

The classroom too had its odd characteristics. It was terribly huge and smelled of 10 medicine like the village clinic I feared so much. The walls and ceiling were artificial and uncaring. They were too far from me and I felt naked. The fluorescent light tubes were eerie and blinked suspiciously above me. This was quite a contrast to the fire and sunlight that my eyes were accustomed to. I thought maybe the lighting did not seem right because it was man-made, and it was not natural. Our confinement to rows of desks was another unnatural demand from our active little bodies. We had to sit at these hard things for what seemed like forever before relief (recess) came midway through the morning and afternoon. Running carefree in the village and fields was but a sweet memory of days gone by. We all went home for lunch because we lived within walking distance of the school. It took coaxing and sometimes bribing to get me to return and complete the remainder of the school day.

School was a painful experience during those early years. The English language and 11 the new set of values caused me much anxiety and embarrassment. I could not comprehend everything that was happening but yet I could understand very well when I messed up or was not doing so well. The negative aspect was communicated too effectively and I became unsure of myself more and more. How I wished I could understand other things just as well in school.

12   The value conflict was not only in school performance but in other areas of my life as well. For example, many of us students had a problem with head lice due to "the lack of sanitary conditions in our homes." Consequently, we received a severe shampooing that was rough on both the scalp and the ego. Cleanliness was crucial and a washing of this type indicated to the class how filthy a home setting we came from. I recall that after one such treatment I was humiliated before my peers with a statement that I had "She'na" (lice) so tough that I must have been born with them. Needless to say, my Super Indian self-image was no longer intact.

13   My language, too, was questionable from the beginning of my school career. "Leave your Indian (language) at home" was like a trademark of school. Speaking it accidentally or otherwise was a sure reprimand in the form of a dirty look or a whack with a ruler. This punishment was for speaking the language of my people which meant so much to me. It was the language of my grandmother and I spoke it well. With it, I sang beautiful songs and prayed from my heart. At that young and tender age, comprehending why I had to part with it was most difficult for me. And yet at home I was encouraged to attend school so that I might have a better life in the future. I knew I had a good village life already but this was communicated less and less each day I was in school. . . .

14   I had to leave my beloved village of Cochiti for my education beyond Grade 6. I left to attend a Bureau of Indian Affairs boarding school 30 miles from home. Shined shoes and pressed shirt and pants were the order of the day. I managed to adjust to this just as I had to most of the things the school shoved at me or took away from me. Adjusting to leaving home and the village was tough indeed. It seemed the older I got, the further away I became from the ways I was so much a part of. Because my parents did not own an automobile, I saw them only once a month when they came up in the community truck. They never failed to come supplied with "eats" for me. I enjoyed the outdoor oven bread, dried meat, and tamales they usually brought. It took a while to get accustomed to the diet of the school. I longed for my grandmother and my younger brothers and sisters. I longed for my house. I longed to take part in a Buffalo Dance. I longed to be free.

15   I came home for the 4-day Thanksgiving break. At first, home did not feel right anymore. It was much too small and stuffy. The lack of running water and bathroom facilities were too inconvenient. Everything got dusty so quickly and hardly anyone spoke English. I did not realize I was beginning to take on the white man's ways, the ways that belittled my own. However, it did not take long to "get back with it." Once I established my relationships with family, relatives, and friends I knew I was where I came from and where I belonged.

16   Leaving for the boarding school the following Sunday evening was one of the saddest events in my entire life. Although I enjoyed myself immensely the last few days, I realized then that life would never be the same again. I could not turn back the time just as I could not do away with school and the ways of the white man. They were here to stay and would creep more and more into my life. The effort to make sense of both worlds together was painful and I had no choice but to do so. The schools, television, automobiles, and other white man's ways and values had chipped away at the simple cooperative life I grew up in. The people of Cochiti were changing. The winter evening gatherings, exchanging of stories, and even the performing of certain ceremonies were

already only a memory that someone commented about now and then. Still the demands of both worlds were there. The white man's was flashy, less personal, but comfortable. The Indian was both attracted and pushed toward these new ways that he had little to say about. There was no choice left but to compete with the white man on his terms for survival. For that I knew I had to give up a part of my life.

Determined not to cry, I left for school that dreadfully lonely night. My right hand   17
clutched tightly the mound of cornmeal Grandmother placed there and my left hand brushed away a tear as I made my way back to school.

Questions for Close Reading

1. What is the selection's thesis? Locate the sentence(s) in which Suina states his main idea. If he doesn't state the thesis explicitly, express it in your own words.

2. How did the Cochiti instill their values and native culture in their children? How was the Cochiti approach different from the teaching methods used in the white school Suina attended?

3. What non-native influences appear in Suina's town and life before he starts attending school?

4. Why is Suina forced to attend a white school and learn about the whites' life-style and language? What does he find confusing about school? How does school change him?

5. Refer to your dictionary as needed to define the following words used in the selection: *adobe* (paragraph 5), *ego* (12), and *belittled* (15).

Questions About the Writer's Craft

1. **The pattern.** Comparison-contrast essays organize material according to the point-by-point or one-side-at-a-time method. Which method predominates in this essay? Why do you think Suina uses this method? Locate places where Suina uses the other method of organization.

2. **Other patterns.** Suina uses description to evoke the simple, emotional warmth of the Native American life-style as well as the sterile, stark coldness of the white school. Locate places in the essay where Suina provides sensory details to help readers understand the differences between the two cultures.

3. Consider Suina's word choice in the opening paragraph. How do the words *invade* and *unsuspecting* help establish the essay's overall tone? What do these terms reveal about Suina's attitude toward the transformation of Native American culture?

4. Where in paragraph 14 does Suina use repetition? What is the effect of the repetition?

Writing Assignments Using Comparison-Contrast as a Pattern of Development

∞ 1. As a Native American, Suina is made to feel like an outsider in the white school. But cultural differences aren't the only factors that cause children to feel uncomfortable in school. For example, they may have trouble fitting in because they have a learning disability, are shy, are extroverted, or need more (or less) structure than the school provides. Focusing on *one* such problem, write an essay comparing and contrasting present-day education with the way it should be. For a tragic account about one young "outsider," consider reading Sophronia Liu's "So Tsi-fai" (page 221).

2. After attending boarding school for a few months, Suina reappraises his home and earlier life-style. In a similar way, separation can cause the rest of us to view our home, our school, another institution, or an individual in a more positive or a more negative light. Write an essay comparing and contrasting the feelings you had for a person, place, or institution with your attitude after being separated for a while. Provide vigorous details to show why your attitude changed.

Writing Assignments Using Other Patterns of Development

∞ 3. Suina reports that his grandmother showered him with praise and made him feel like a "Superman." However, once he entered school, the constant scoldings, dirty looks, and ruler slaps eroded his self-esteem. Write an essay illustrating how a person affected your view of yourself, either by praising or by criticizing your efforts. Provide several dramatic examples or a single, richly detailed example to show how this person affected you. Before writing, read Maya Angelou's "Sister Flowers" (page 178), an essay that illustrates the influence of powerful individuals.

4. Everyone, at some level of their education, has felt anxious about the first day of school. Write an essay in which you explain steps that a student can take to reduce the nervousness associated with beginning his or her first semester in college. You may adopt a serious or a lighthearted tone in your essay.

Writing Assignment Using a Journal Entry as a Starting Point

5. In school, Suina is pressured to abandon his native language and to speak only English. Refer to your pre-reading journal essay, and conduct some research in the library and/or on the Internet on the subject of bilingualism in education.

Then write an essay arguing that schools either should *or* should not teach non-English-speaking students in their own language until they become sufficiently proficient in English to join regular classes. At some point, you should acknowledge and perhaps refute opposing views.

ADDITIONAL WRITING TOPICS: COMPARISON-CONTRAST

General Assignments

Using comparison-contrast, write an essay on one of the following topics. Your thesis should indicate whether the two subjects are being compared, contrasted, or both. Organize the paper by arranging the details in a one-side-at-a-time or point-by-point pattern. Remember to use organizational cues to help the audience follow your analysis.

1. Two-career family versus one-career family
2. Two approaches for dealing with problems
3. Children's pastimes today and yesterday
4. Two attitudes toward money
5. Watching a movie on television versus viewing it in a theater
6. Two approaches to parenting
7. Two approaches to studying
8. Marriage versus living together
9. Two views on a controversial issue
10. The coverage of an event on television versus its coverage in a newspaper

Assignments with a Specific Purpose, Audience, and Point of View

On Campus

1. You would like to change your campus living arrangements. Perhaps you want to move from a dormitory to an off-campus apartment or from home to a dorm. Before you do, though, you'll have to convince your parents (who are paying most of your college costs) that the move will be beneficial. Write out what you would say to your parents. Contrast your current situation with your proposed one, explaining why the new arrangement would be better.

2. Write a guide on "Passing Exams" for first-year college students, contrasting the right and wrong ways to prepare for and take exams. Although your purpose is basically serious, write the section on how *not* to approach exams with some humor.

At Home or in the Community

3. As president of your local Neighbors' Association, you're concerned about the way your local government is dealing with a particular situation (for example, an increase in robberies, muggings, graffiti, and so on). Write a letter to your mayor contrasting the way your local government handles the situation with another city or town's approach. In your conclusion, point out the advantages of adopting the other neighborhood's strategy.

4. Your old high school has invited you back to make a speech before an audience of seniors. The topic will be "how to choose the college that is right for you." Write your speech in the form of a comparison-contrast analysis. Focus on the choices available (two-year versus four-year schools, large versus small, local versus far-away, and so on), showing the advantages and/or disadvantages of each.

On the Job

5. As a store manager, you decide to write a memo to all sales personnel explaining how to keep customers happy. Compare and/or contrast the needs and shopping habits of several different consumer groups (by age, spending ability, or sex), and show how to make each group comfortable in your store.

6. You work as a volunteer for a mental health hot line. Many people call simply because they feel "stressed out." Prepare a brochure for these people, recommending a "Type B" approach to stressful situations. Focus the brochure on the contrast between "Type A" and "Type B" personalities: the former is nervous, hard-driving; competitive; the latter is relaxed and noncompetitive. Give specific examples of how each "type" tends to act in stressful situations.

17
CAUSE-EFFECT

WHAT IS CAUSE-EFFECT?

Superstition has it that curiosity killed the cat. Maybe so. Yet our science, technology, storytelling, and fascination with the past and future all spring from our determination to know "Why" and "What if." Seeking explanations, young children barrage adults with endless questions: "Why do trees grow tall?" "What would happen if the sun didn't shine?" But children aren't the only ones who wonder in this way. All of us think in terms of cause and effect, sometimes consciously, sometimes unconsciously: "Why did they give me such an odd look?" we wonder, or "How would I do at another college?" we speculate. This exploration of reasons and results is also at the heart of most professions: "What led to our involvement in Vietnam?" historians question; "What will happen if we administer this experimental drug?" scientists ask.

Cause-effect writing, often called **causal analysis,** is rooted in this elemental need to make connections. Because the drive to understand reasons and results is so fundamental, causal analysis is a common kind of writing. An article analyzing the unexpected outcome of an election, a report linking poor nutrition to low academic achievement, an editorial analyzing the impact of a proposed tax cut—all are examples of cause-effect writing.

Done well, cause-effect pieces uncover the subtle and often surprising connections between events or phenomena. By rooting out causes and projecting effects, causal analysis enables us to make sense of our experiences, revealing a world that is somewhat less arbitrary and chaotic.

How Cause-Effect Fits Your Purpose and Audience

Many assignments and exam questions in college involve writing essays that analyze causes, effects, or both. Sometimes, as in the following examples, you'll be asked to write an essay developed primarily through the cause-effect pattern:

Although divorces have leveled off in the last few years, the number of marriages ending in divorce is still greater than it was a generation ago. What do you think are the causes of this phenomenon?

Political commentators were surprised that so few people voted in the last election. Discuss the probable causes of this weak voter turnout.

Americans never seem to tire of gossip about the rich and famous. What effect has this fascination with celebrities had on American culture?

The federal government is expected to pass legislation that will significantly reduce the funding of student loans. Analyze the possible effects of such a cutback.

Other assignments and exam questions may not explicitly ask you to address causes and effects, but they may use words that suggest causal analysis would be appropriate. Consider these examples, paying special attention to the italicized words:

Cause

In contrast to the socially involved youth of the 1960s, many young people today tend to remove themselves from political issues. What do you think are the *sources* of the political apathy found among 18- to 25-year-olds?

Effect

A number of experts forecast that drug abuse will be the most significant factor affecting American productivity in the coming decade. Evaluate the validity of this observation by discussing the *impact* of drugs on the workplace.

Cause and Effect

According to school officials, a predictable percentage of entering students drop out of college at some point during their first year. What *motivates* students to drop out? What *happens* to them once they leave?

In addition to serving as the primary strategy for achieving an essay's purpose, causal analysis can also be a supplemental method used to help make a point in an essay developed chiefly through another pattern of development. Assume, for example, that you want to write an essay *defining* the term *the homeless.* To help readers see that unfavorable circumstances can result in nearly anyone becoming homeless, you might discuss some of the unavoidable, everyday factors causing people to live on streets and in subway stations. Similarly, in a *persuasive* proposal urging your college administration to institute an honors program, you would probably spend some time analyzing the positive effects of such a program on students and faculty.

PREWRITING STRATEGIES

The following checklist shows how you can apply to cause-effect some of the prewriting techniques discussed in Chapter 2.

✔ CAUSE-EFFECT: A PREWRITING CHECKLIST

Choose a Topic

☐ Do your journal entries reflect an ongoing interest in the causes of and/or effects of something? (What causes friends to drop out of school? What will be the effect of recent legislation regarding abortion?)

☐ Will you analyze a personal phenomenon (for example, your decision to stop smoking), a change at your college (new requirements for graduation), a nationwide trend (the growing popularity of "tabloid television"), or a historical event (the defeat of the Equal Rights Amendment)?

☐ Does your subject intrigue, anger, puzzle you? Is it likely to interest your readers as well?

Make Sure the Topic Is Manageable

☐ Can you tackle your subject—especially if it's a social trend or historical event—in the number of pages allotted?

☐ Can you gather enough information for your analysis? Does the topic require library research? Do you have time for such research?

☐ Will you examine causes (why your parents got divorced), effects (how their separation changed you), or both? Will your topic still be manageable if you discuss both causes and effects?

Identify Your Purpose, Audience, Tone, and Point of View

☐ Is the purpose of your causal analysis to inform (the reasons for a rock star's climb to fame)? To persuade (why the rock star merits his or her success)? To speculate about possibilities (whether the rock star will continue to grow as an artist)? Do you want to combine purposes?

□ Given your purpose and audience, what tone and point of view should you adopt?

Use Individual and Group Brainstorming, Mapping, and/or Freewriting to Explore Causes and Effects

□ *Causes:* What happened? What are the possible reasons? Which are most likely? Who was involved? Why?

□ *Effects:* What happened? Who was involved? What were the observable results? What are some possible future consequences? Which consequences are negative? Which are positive?

STRATEGIES FOR USING CAUSE-EFFECT IN AN ESSAY

After prewriting, you're ready to draft your essay. The following suggestions will be helpful whether you use causal analysis as a dominant or supportive pattern of development.

1. Stay focused on the purpose of your analysis.   When writing a causal analysis, don't lose sight of your overall purpose. Consider, for example, an essay on the causes of widespread child abuse. If you're concerned primarily with explaining the problem of child abuse to your readers, you might take a purely *informative* approach:

    Although parental stress is the immediate cause of child abuse,
    the more compelling reason for such behavior lies in the way
    parents were themselves mistreated as children.

Or you might want to *persuade* your audience about some point or idea concerning child abuse:

    The tragic consequences of child abuse provide strong support
    for more aggressive handling of such cases by social workers and
    judges.

Then again, you could choose a *speculative* approach, your main purpose being to suggest possibilities:

    Psychologists disagree about the potential effect on youngsters
    of all the media attention given to child abuse. Will children
    exposed to this media coverage grow up assertive, self-confident,
    and able to protect themselves? Or will they become fearful and
    distrustful?

These examples illustrate that an essay's causal analysis may have more than one purpose. For instance, although the last example points to a paper with a primarily speculative purpose, the essay would probably start by informing readers of experts' conflicting views. The paper would also have a persuasive slant if it ended by urging readers to complain to the media about their sensationalized treatment of the child-abuse issue.

2. Adapt content and tone to your purpose and readers.   Your purpose and audience determine what supporting material and what tone will be most effective in a cause-effect essay. Assume you want to direct your essay on child abuse to general readers who know little about the subject. To *inform* readers, you might use facts, statistics, and expert opinion to provide an objective discussion of the causes of child abuse. Your analysis might show the following: (1) adults who were themselves mistreated as children tend to abuse their own offspring; (2) marital stress contributes to the mistreatment of children; and (3) certain personality disorders increase the likelihood of child abuse. Sensitive to what your readers would and wouldn't understand, you would stay away from a technical or formal tone. Rather than writing "Pathological pre-abuse symptomatology predicts adult transference of high aggressivity," you would say "Psychologists can often predict, on the basis of family histories, who will abuse children."

Now imagine that your purpose is to *convince* future social workers that the failure of social service agencies to act authoritatively in child-abuse cases often has tragic consequences. Hoping to encourage more responsible behavior in the prospective social workers, you would adopt a more emotional tone in the essay, perhaps citing wrenching case histories that dramatize what happens when child abuse isn't taken seriously.

3. Think rigorously about causes and effects.   Cause-effect relationships are usually complex. To write a meaningful analysis, you should do some careful thinking about your subject. (The two sets of questions at the end of this chapter's Prewriting Checklist [page 381] will help you think creatively about causes and effects.)

If you look beyond the obvious, you'll discover that a cause may have many effects. Imagine you're writing a paper on the effects of cigarette smoking. A number of consequences might be discussed, some less obvious but perhaps more interesting than others: increased risk of lung cancer and heart disease, evidence of harm done by secondhand smoke, legal battles regarding the rights of smokers and nonsmokers, lower birth weights in babies of mothers who smoke, and developmental problems experienced by such underweight infants.

In the same way, an effect may have multiple causes. An essay analyzing the reasons for world hunger could discuss many causes, again some less evident but perhaps more thought-provoking than others: overpopulation, climatic changes, inefficient use of land, and poor management of international relief funds.

Your analysis may also uncover a **causal chain** in which one cause (or effect) brings about another, that, in turn, brings about another, and so on. Here's an example of a causal chain: Prohibition went into effect; bootleggers and organized crime stepped in to supply public demand for alcoholic beverages; ordinary citizens began breaking the law by buying illegal alcohol and patronizing speakeasies; disrespect for legal authority became widespread and acceptable. As you can see, a causal chain often leads to interesting points. In this case, the subject of Prohibition leads not just to the obvious (illegal consumption of alcohol) but also to the more complex issue of society's decreasing respect for legal authority.

Don't grapple with so complex a chain, however, that you become hopelessly entangled. If your subject involves multiple causes and effects, limit what you'll discuss. Identify which causes and effects are *primary* and which are *secondary.* How extensively you cover secondary factors will depend on your purpose and audience. In an essay intended to inform a general audience about the harmful effects of pesticides, you would most likely focus on everyday dangers—polluted drinking water, residues in food, and the like. You probably wouldn't include a discussion of more long-range consequences (evolution of resistant insects, disruption of the soil's acid-alkaline balance).

Similarly, decide whether to focus on *immediate,* more obvious causes and effects, or on less obvious, more *remote* ones. Or perhaps you need to focus on both. In an essay about a faculty strike at your college, should you attribute the strike simply to the faculty's failure to receive a salary increase? Or should you also examine other factors: the union's failure to accept a salary package that satisfied most professors; the administration's inability to coordinate its negotiating efforts? It may be more difficult to explore more remote causes and effects, but it can also lead to more original and revealing essays. Thoughtful analyses take these less obvious considerations into account.

When developing a causal analysis, be careful to avoid the ***post hoc* fallacy.** Named after the Latin phrase *post hoc, ergo propter hoc,* meaning "after this, therefore because of this," this kind of faulty thinking occurs when you assume that simply because one event *followed* another, the first event *caused* the second. For example, if the Republicans win a majority of seats in Congress and, several months later, the economy collapses, can you conclude that the Republicans caused the collapse? A quick assumption of "Yes" fails the test of logic, for the timing of events could be coincidental and not indicative of any cause-effect relationship. The collapse may have been triggered by uncontrolled inflation that began well before the congressional elections. (For more on *post hoc* thinking, see page 463 in Chapter 19.)

Also, be careful not to mistake *correlation* for *causation.* Two events correlate when they occur at about the same time. Such co-occurrence, however, doesn't guarantee a cause-effect relationship. For instance, while the number of ice cream cones eaten and the instances of heat prostration both increase during the summer months, this doesn't mean that eating ice cream causes heat prostration! A third factor—in this case, summer heat—is the actual cause. When writing causal analyses, then, use with caution words that imply a causal link (such as *therefore* and *because*). Words that express simply time of occurrence (*following* and *previously*) are safer and more objective.

Finally, keep in mind that a rigorous causal analysis involves more than loose generalizations about causes and effects. Creating plausible connections may require library research, interviewing, or both. Often you'll need to provide facts, statistics, details, personal observations, or other corroborative material if readers are going to accept the reasoning behind your analysis.

4. Write a thesis that focuses the paper on causes, effects, or both.   The thesis in an essay developed through causal analysis often indicates whether the essay will deal mostly with causes, effects, or both. Here, for example, are three thesis statements for causal analyses dealing with the public school system. You'll see that each thesis signals that essay's particular emphasis:

Causes

Our school system has been weakened by an overemphasis on trendy electives.

Effects

An ineffectual school system has led to crippling teachers' strikes and widespread disrespect for the teaching profession.

Causes and Effects

Bureaucratic inefficiency has created a school system unresponsive to children's emotional, physical, and intellectual needs.

Note that the thesis statement—in addition to signaling whether the paper will discuss causes or effects or both—may also point to the essay's plan of development. Consider the last thesis statement; it makes clear that the paper will discuss children's emotional needs first, their physical needs second, and their intellectual needs last.

The thesis statement in a causal analysis doesn't have to specify whether the essay will discuss causes, effects, or both. Nor does the thesis have to be worded in such a way that the essay's plan of development is apparent. But when first writing cause-effect essays, you may find that a highly focused thesis will help keep your analysis on track.

5. Choose an organizational pattern.   There are two basic ways to organize the points in a cause-effect essay: you may use a chronological or an emphatic sequence. If you select *chronological order,* you discuss causes and effects in the order in which they occur or will occur. Suppose you're writing an essay on the causes for the popularity of imported cars. These causes might be discussed in chronological sequence: American plant workers became frustrated and dissatisfied on the job; some workers got careless while others deliberately sabotaged the production of sound cars; a growing number of defective cars hit the market; consumers grew dissatisfied with American cars and switched to imports.

Chronology might also be used to organize a discussion about effects. Imagine you want to write an essay about the need to guard against disrupting delicate balances in the country's wildlife. You might start the essay by discussing what happened when the starling, a non-native bird, was introduced into the American environment. Because the starling had few natural predators, the starling population soared out of control; the starlings took over food sources and habitats of native species; the bluebird, a native species, declined and is now threatened with extinction.

Although a chronological pattern can be an effective way to organize material, a strict time sequence can present a problem if your primary cause or effect ends up buried in the middle of the sequence. In such a case, you might use *emphatic order*, reserving the most significant cause or effect for the end. For example, time order could be used to present the reasons behind a candidate's unexpected victory: Less than a month after the candidate's earlier defeat, a full-scale fund-raising campaign for the next election was started; the candidate spoke to many crucial power groups early in the campaign; the candidate did exceptionally well in the pre-election debates; good weather and large voter turnout on election day favored the candidate. However, if you believe that the candidate's appearance before influential groups was the key factor in the victory, it would be more effective to emphasize that point by saving it for the end. This is what is meant by emphatic order—saving the most important point for last.

Emphatic order is an especially effective way to sequence cause-effect points when readers hold what, in your opinion, are mistaken or narrow views about a subject. To encourage readers to look more closely at the issues, you present what you consider the erroneous or obvious views first, show why they are unsound or limited, then present what you feel to be the actual causes and effects. Such a sequence nudges the audience into giving further thought to the causes and effects you have discovered. Here are informal outlines for two causal analyses using this approach:

Subject: The causes of the riot at a rock concert

1. Some commentators blame the excessively hot weather.

2. Others cite drug use among the concertgoers.

3. Still others blame the liquor sold at the concessions.

4. But the real cause of the disaster was poor planning by the concert promoters.

Subject: The effects of campus crime

1. Immediate problems

   a. Students feel insecure and fearful.

   b. Many nighttime campus activities have been curtailed.

2. More significant long-term problems

   a. Unfavorable publicity about campus crime will affect future student enrollment.

   b. Unfavorable publicity about campus crime will make it difficult to recruit top-notch faculty.

When using emphatic order, you might want to word the thesis in such a way that it signals which point your essay will stress. Look at the following thesis statements:

Although many immigrants arrive in this country without marketable skills, their most pressing problem is learning how to make their way in a society whose language they don't know.

The space program has led to dramatic advances in computer technology and medical science. Even more importantly, though, the program has helped change many people's attitudes toward the planet we live on.

These thesis statements reflect an awareness of the complex nature of cause-effect relationships. While not dismissing secondary issues, the statements establish which points the writer considers most noteworthy. The second thesis, for instance, indicates that the paper will touch on the technological and medical advances made possible by the space program but will emphasize the way the program has changed people's attitudes toward the earth.

Whether you use a chronological or emphatic pattern to organize your essay, you'll need to provide clear *signals* to identify when you're discussing causes and when you're discussing effects. Expressions such as "Another reason" and "A final outcome" help readers follow your line of thought.

6. Use language that hints at the complexity of cause-effect relationships. Because it's difficult—if not impossible—to identify causes and effects with certainty, you should avoid such absolutes as "It must be obvious" and "There is no doubt." Instead, try phrases such as "Most likely" or "It is probable." Such language isn't indecisive; it's reasonable and reflects your understanding of the often tangled nature of causes and effects. Don't, however, go to the other extreme and be reluctant to take a stand on the issues. If you have thought carefully about causes and effects, you have a right to state your analysis with conviction.

REVISION STRATEGIES

Once you have a draft of the essay, you're ready to revise. The following checklist will help you and those giving you feedback apply to cause-effect writing some of the revision techniques discussed in Chapters 7 and 8.

 CAUSE-EFFECT: A REVISION/PEER REVIEW CHECKLIST

Revise Overall Meaning and Structure

☐ Is the essay's purpose informative, persuasive, speculative, or a combination of these?

☐ What is the essay's thesis? Is it stated specifically or implied? Where? Could it be made any clearer? How?

☐ Does the essay focus on causes, effects, or both? How do you know?

☐ Where has correlation been mistaken for causation? Where is the essay weakened by *post hoc* thinking?

☐ Where does the essay distinguish between primary and secondary causes and effects? How do the most critical causes and effects receive special attention?

☐ Where does the essay dwell on the obvious?

Revise Paragraph Development

☐ Which paragraphs fail to support the essay's thesis?

☐ Are the essay's paragraphs sequenced chronologically or emphatically? Was the decision to use that order a good one? Why or why not?

☐ Where would signal devices (such as *afterward, before, then,* and *next*) make it easier to follow the progression of thought within and between paragraphs?

☐ Which paragraphs would be strengthened by vivid examples, such as statistics, facts, anecdotes, or personal observations, that support the causal analysis?

Revise Sentences and Words

☐ Where do expressions like *as a result, because,* and *therefore* mislead the reader by implying a cause-effect relationship? Would words such as *following* and *previously* eliminate the problem?

☐ Do any words or phrases convey an arrogant or dogmatic tone (*there is no question, undoubtedly, always, never*)? What other expressions (*most likely, probably*) would improve credibility?

STUDENT ESSAY: FROM PREWRITING THROUGH REVISION

The student essay that follows was written by Carl Novack in response to this assignment:

> In "Black Men and Public Space," Brent Staples reminds us that, sadly, racist attitudes have not changed much over the years. There are, though, some areas in which people's attitudes *have* changed dramatically. Identify a significant shift in an activity, practice, or institution. Then write an essay in which you discuss the factors that you believe are responsible for the attitudinal change.

After deciding to write about Americans' changing food habits, Carl used the *mapping technique* to generate material on his subject. On the following page, his map is shown. The marks in color indicate Carl's later efforts to organize and elaborate the original map. Note that he added some branches, eliminated others, drew arrows indicating that some topics should be moved, and changed the wording of some key ideas. These annotations paved the way for Carl's topic outline, which is presented after the map.

Mapping

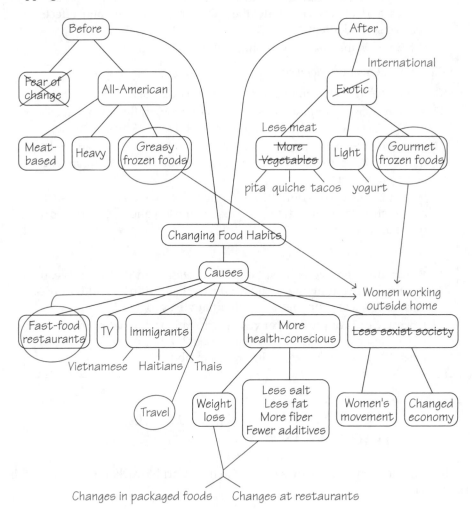

Outline

```
Thesis: America has changed and so has what we Americans eat and
how we eat.

   I. We used to eat "All-American" meals.
      A. Heavy
```

        B. Meat-based
   II. Now our tastes are more international.
        A. Lighter--yogurt
        B. Less meat--pita, quiche, tacos
  III. There are several reasons for our tastes becoming more
       international.
        A. Television
        B. Travel abroad
        C. Immigrants in this country
   IV. Two social trends have also changed how and what we eat.
        A. Health consciousness
            1. Concern about weight
            2. Concern about salt, fat, fiber, additives
                a. Changes in packaged foods (lunch meat, canned veg-
                   etables, soups)
                b. Changes in restaurants (salad bars)
        B. More women working outside the home because of the
           economy and the women's movement
            1. Increase in fast-food restaurants
            2. More frozen foods, some even gourmet

   Now read Carl's paper, "Americans and Food," noting the similarities and differences among his map, outline, and final essay. See, for example, how the diagram suggests a "before" and "after" contrast—a contrast the essay develops. Also
note Carl's decision to move "frozen foods" and "fast-food restaurants" to the
"women working outside home" section of the diagram. This decision is reflected
in the outline and in the final essay, where frozen foods and fast-food restaurants
are discussed in the same paragraph. As you read the essay, also consider how well
it applies the principles of causal analysis discussed in this chapter. (The commentary that follows the paper will help you look at Carl's essay more closely and will
give you some sense of how he went about revising his first draft.)

                        Americans and Food
                        by Carl Novack

1   An offbeat but timely cartoon recently appeared in the   Introduction
    local newspaper. The single panel showed a gravel-pit
    operation with piles of raw earth and large cranes. Next
    to one of the cranes stood the owner of the gravel pit--
    a grizzled, tough-looking character, hammer in hand,
    pointing proudly to the new sign he had just tacked up.

The sign read, "Fred's Fill Dirt and Croissants." The cartoon illustrates an interesting phenomenon: the changing food habits of Americans. Our meals used to consist of something like home-cooked pot roast, mashed potatoes laced with butter and salt, a thick slice of apple pie topped with a healthy scoop of vanilla ice cream--plain, heavy meals, cooked from scratch, and eaten leisurely at home. But America has changed, and because it has, so have what we Americans eat and how we eat it.

Thesis ————————

We used to have simple, unsophisticated tastes and looked with suspicion at anything more exotic than hamburger. Admittedly, we did adopt some foods from the various immigrant groups who flocked to our shores. We learned to eat Chinese food, pizza, and bagels. But in the last few years, the international character of our diet has grown tremendously. We can walk into any mall in Middle America and buy pita bread, quiche, and tacos. Such foods are often changed on their journey from exotic imports to ordinary "American" meals (no Pakistani, for example, eats frozen-on-a-stick boysenberry-flavored yogurt), but the imports are still a long way from hamburger on a bun.

Topic sentence: Background paragraph

Topic sentence: Three causes answer the question

First cause ————————

Why have we become more worldly in our tastes? For one thing, television blankets the country with information about new food products and trends. Viewers in rural Montana know that the latest craving in Washington, D.C., is Cajun cooking or that something called tofu is now available in the local supermarket. Another reason for the growing international flavor of our food is that many young Americans have traveled abroad and gotten hooked on new tastes and flavors. Backpacking students and young professionals vacationing in Europe come home with cravings for authentic French bread or German beer. Finally, continuing waves of immigrants settle in the cities where many of us live, causing significant changes in what we eat. Vietnamese, Haitians, and Thais, for instance, bring their native foods and cooking styles with them and eventually open small markets or restaurants. In time, the new food will become Americanized enough to take its place in our national diet.

Second Cause ————————

Third cause ————————

2

3

4   Our growing concern with health has also affected the _____   Topic sentence: Another
way we eat. For the last few years, the media have   cause
warned us about the dangers of our traditional diet,
high in salt and fat, low in fiber. The media also began
to educate us about the dangers of processed foods _____   Start of a causal chain
pumped full of chemical additives. As a result,
consumers began to demand healthier foods, and
manufacturers started to change some of their products.
Many foods, such as lunch meat, canned vegetables, and
soups, were made available in low-fat, low-sodium
versions. Whole-grain cereals and high-fiber breads also
began to appear on the grocery shelves. Moreover, the
food industry started to produce all-natural products--
everything from potato chips to ice cream--without
additives and preservatives. Not surprisingly, the
restaurant industry responded to this switch to
healthier foods, luring customers with salad bars,
broiled fish, and steamed vegetables. _____   Topic sentence: Another

5   Our food habits are being affected, too, by the rapid   cause
increase in the number of women working outside the
home. Sociologists and other experts believe that two
important factors triggered this phenomenon: the women's
movement and a changing economic climate. Women were
assured that it was acceptable, even rewarding, to work
outside the home; many women also discovered that they
had to work just to keep up with the cost of living. As
the traditional role of homemaker changed, so did the
way families ate. With Mom working, there wasn't time
for her to prepare the traditional three square meals a
day. Instead, families began looking for alternatives to _____   Start of a causal chain
provide quick meals. What was the result? For one thing,
there was a boom in fast-food restaurants. The suburban
or downtown strip that once contained a lone McDonald's
now features Wendy's, Roy Rogers, Taco Bell, Burger
King, and Pizza Hut. Families also began to depend on
frozen foods as another time-saving alternative. Once
again, though, demand changed the kind of frozen food
available. Frozen foods no longer consist of foil trays
divided into greasy fried chicken, watery corn niblets,
and lumpy mashed potatoes. Supermarkets now stock a

```
                          range of supposedly gourmet frozen dinners--from
                          fettucini in cream sauce to braised beef en brochette.
```

Conclusion
```
                              It may not be possible to pick up a ton of fill dirt      6
                          and a half-dozen croissants at the same place, but
                          America's food habits are definitely changing. If it is
                          true that "you are what you eat," then America's
                          identity is evolving along with its diet.
```

Commentary

Title and Introduction

Asked to prepare a paper analyzing the reasons behind a change in our lives, Carl decided to write about a shift he had noticed in Americans' eating habits. The title of the essay, "Americans and Food," identifies Carl's subject but could be livelier and more interesting.

Despite his rather uninspired title, Carl starts his *causal analysis* in an engaging way—with the vivid description of a cartoon. He then connects the cartoon to his subject with the following sentence: "The cartoon illustrates an interesting phenomenon: the changing food habits of Americans." To back up his belief that there has been a revolution in our eating habits, Carl uses the first paragraph to summarize the kind of meal that people used to eat. He then moves to his *thesis*: "But America has changed, and because it has, so have what we Americans eat and how we eat it." The thesis implies that Carl's paper will focus on both causes and effects.

Purpose

Carl's purpose was to write an *informative* causal analysis. But before he could present the causes of the change in eating habits, he needed to show that such a change had, in fact, taken place. He therefore uses the second paragraph to document one aspect of this change—the internationalization of our eating habits.

Topic Sentences

At the start of the third paragraph, Carl uses a question—"Why have we become more worldly in our tastes?"—to signal that his discussion of causes is about to begin. This question also serves as the paragraph's *topic sentence,* indicating that the paragraph will focus on reasons for the increasingly international flavor of our food. The next two paragraphs, also focused by topic sentences, identify two other major reasons for the change in eating habits: "Our growing concern with health has also affected the way we eat" (paragraph 4), and "Our food habits are being affected, too, by the rapid increase in the number of women working outside the home" (5).

Other Patterns of Development

Carl draws on two patterns of development—*comparison-contrast* and *illustration*—to develop his causal analysis. At the heart of the essay is a basic *contrast* between the way we used to eat and the way we eat now. And throughout his essay, Carl provides convincing *examples* to demonstrate the validity of his points. Consider for a moment the third paragraph. Here Carl asserts that one reason for our new eating habits is our growing exposure to international foods. He then presents concrete evidence to show that we have indeed become more familiar with international cuisine: Television exposes rural Montana to Cajun cooking; students traveling abroad take a liking to French bread; urban dwellers enjoy the exotic fare served by numerous immigrant groups. The fourth and fifth paragraphs use similarly specific evidence (for example, "low-fat, low-sodium versions" of "lunch meat, canned vegetables, and soups") to illustrate the soundness of key ideas.

Causal Chains

Let's look more closely at the evidence in the essay. Not satisfied with obvious explanations, Carl thought through his ideas carefully and even brainstormed with friends to arrive at as comprehensive an analysis as possible. Not surprisingly, much of the evidence Carl uncovered took the form of *causal chains.* In the fourth paragraph, Carl writes, "The media also began to educate us about the dangers of processed foods pumped full of chemical additives. As a result, consumers began to demand healthier foods, and manufacturers started to change some of their products." And the next paragraph shows how the changing role of American women caused families to look for alternative ways of eating. This shift, in turn, caused the restaurant and food industries to respond with a wide range of food alternatives.

Making the Paper Easy to Follow

Although Carl's analysis digs beneath the surface and reveals complex cause-effect relationships, he wisely limits his pursuit of causal chains to *primary* causes and effects. He doesn't let the complexities distract him from his main purpose: to show why and how the American diet is changing. Carl is also careful to provide his essay with abundant *connecting devices,* making it easy for readers to see the links between points. Consider the use of *transitions* (signaled by italics) in the following sentences: "*Another* reason for the growing international flavor of our food is that many young Americans have traveled abroad" (paragraph 3); "*As a result,* consumers began to demand healthier foods" (4); and "*As* the traditional role of homemaker changed, so did the way families ate" (5).

A Problem with the Essay's Close

As you read the essay, you probably noticed that Carl's conclusion is a bit weak. Although his reference to the cartoon works well, the rest of the paragraph limps to a tired close. Ending an otherwise vigorous essay with such a slight conclusion undercuts the effectiveness of the whole paper. Carl spent so much energy developing the body of his essay that he ran out of the stamina needed to conclude the piece more forcefully. Careful budgeting of his time would have allowed him to prepare a stronger concluding paragraph.

Revising the First Draft

When Carl was ready to revise, he showed the first draft of his essay to several classmates who used the revision checklist on pages 386–387 to focus their feed-back. Listening carefully, Carl jotted down their most helpful comments and eventually transferred them, numbered in order of importance, to his draft. Comparing Carl's original version of his fourth paragraph (shown below) with his final version in the essay will show you how he went about revising.

Original Version of the Fourth Paragraph

② First sentence cluttered, too long

(A growing concern with health has also affected the way we eat, especially because the media has sent us warnings the last few years about the dangers of salt, sugar, food additives, and high-fat and low-fiber diets.) We have started to worry that our traditional meals may have been shortening our lives. As a result, consumers demanded healthier foods and manufacturers started taking some of the salt and sugar out of canned foods. "All-natural" became an effective selling point, leading to many preservative-free products. Restaurants, too, adapted their menus, luring customers with light meals. Because we now know about the link between overweight and a variety of health problems, including heart attacks, we are counting calories. In turn, food companies made fortunes on diet beer and diet cola. Sometimes, though, we seem a bit confused about the health issue; we drink soda that is sugar-free but loaded with chemical sweeteners. Still, we believe we are lengthening our lives through changing our diets.

③ Add specifics

① Doesn't fit point being made

On the advice of his classmates, Carl decided to omit all references to the way our concern with weight has affected our eating habits. It's true, of course, that calorie-counting has changed how we eat. But as soon as Carl started to discuss this point, he got involved in a causal chain that undercut the paragraph's unity. He ended up describing the paradoxical situation in which we find ourselves: In an attempt to eat healthy, we stay away from sugar and turn to possibly harmful artificial sweeteners. This is an interesting issue, but it detracts from Carl's main point—that our concern with health has affected our eating habits in a *positive* way.

Carl's editing team also pointed out that the fourth paragraph's first sentence contained too much material to be an effective topic sentence. Carl corrected the problem by breaking the overlong sentence into two short ones: "Our growing concern with health has also affected the way we eat. For the last few years, the media have warned us about the dangers of our traditional diet, high in salt and fat, low in fiber." The first of these sentences serves as a crisp topic sentence that focuses the rest of the paragraph.

Finally, when Carl heard the essay read aloud, he realized the fourth paragraph lacked convincing specifics. When revising, he changed "manufacturers started taking some of the salt and sugar out of canned foods" to the more specific "Many foods, such as lunch meat, canned vegetables, and soups, were made available in low-fat, low-sodium versions." Similarly, generalizations about "light meals" and "all-natural" products gained life through the addition of concrete examples: restaurants lured "customers with salad bars, broiled fish, and steamed vegetables," and the food industry produced "everything from potato chips to ice cream—without additives and preservatives."

Carl did an equally good job revising other sections of his paper. With the exception of the weak spots already discussed, he made the changes needed to craft a well-reasoned essay, one that demonstrates his ability to analyze a complex phenomenon.

ACTIVITIES: CAUSE-EFFECT

Prewriting Activities

1. Imagine you're writing two essays: One proposes the need for high school courses in personal finance (how to budget money, balance a checkbook, and the like); the other explains how to show appreciation. Jot down ways you might use cause-effect in each essay.

2. Use mapping, collaborative brainstorming, or another prewriting technique to generate possible causes and/or effects for *one* of the following topics. Then organize your raw material into a brief outline, with related causes and effects grouped in the same section.

   a. Pressure on students to do well

   b. Children's access to soft-core pornography on cable television

   c. Being physically fit

   d. Spiraling costs of a college education

3. For the topic you selected in activity 2, note the two potential audiences indicated below in parentheses. For each audience, devise a thesis and decide whether your essay's purpose would be informative, persuasive, speculative, or some combination of these. Then, with your thesis statements and purposes in mind, review the outline you prepared for the preceding activity. How

would you change it to fit each audience? What points should be added? What points would be primary causes and effects for one audience but secondary for the other? Which organizational pattern—chronological, spatial, or emphatic— would be most effective for each audience?

a. Pressure on students to do well (*college students, parents of elementary school children*)

b. Children's access to soft-core pornography on cable television (*cable executives, parents of young children*)

c. Being physically fit (*those who show a reasonable degree of concern, those who are obsessed with being fit*)

d. Spiraling costs of a college education (*college officials, high school students planning to attend college*)

Revising Activities

4. Explain how the following statements demonstrate *post hoc* thinking and confuse correlation and cause-effect.

a. Our city now has many immigrants from Latin American countries. The crime rate in our city has increased. Latin American immigrants are the cause of the crime wave.

b. The divorce rate has skyrocketed. More women are working outside the home than ever before. Working outside the home destroys marriages.

c. A high percentage of people in Dixville have developed cancer. The landfill, used by XYZ Industries, has been located in Dixville for twenty years. The XYZ landfill has caused cancer in Dixville residents.

5. The following paragraph is from the first draft of an essay arguing that technological advances can diminish the quality of life. How solid is the paragraph's causal analysis? Which causes and/or effects should be eliminated? Where is the analysis simplistic? Where does the writer make absolute claims even though cause-effect relationships are no more than a possibility? Keeping these questions in mind, revise the paragraph.

```
    How did the banking industry respond to inflation? It simply
introduced a new technology--the automated teller machine
(ATM). By making money more available to the average person,
the ATM gives people the cash to buy inflated goods--whether or
not they can afford them. Not surprisingly, automated teller
machines have had a number of negative consequences for the
average individual. Since people know they can get cash at any
time, they use their lunch hours for something other than going
to the bank. How do they spend this newfound time? They go
```

shopping, and machine-vended money means more impulse buying, even more than with a credit card. Also, because people don't need their checkbooks to withdraw money, they can't keep track of their accounts and therefore develop a casual attitude toward financial matters. It's no wonder children don't appreciate the value of money. Another problem is that people who would never dream of robbing a bank try to trick the machine into dispensing money "for free." There's no doubt that this kind of fraud contributes to the immoral climate in the country.

PROFESSIONAL SELECTIONS: CAUSE-EFFECT

STEPHEN KING

Probably the best-known living horror writer, Stephen King (1947–) is the author of more than thirty books. Before earning fame through his vastly popular books, including *Carrie* (1974), *The Shining* (1977), *Cujo* (1981), and *Tommyknockers* (1987), King worked as a high school English teacher and an industrial laundry worker. Much of King's prolific output has been adapted for the screen; movies based on King's work include *Misery* (1990), *Stand by Me* (1986), and *The Green Mile* (1999). And in *On Writing: A Memoir of the Craft* (2000), King offers insight into the writing process and examines the role that writing has played in his own life—especially following a near-fatal accident in 1999. King lives with his family in Bangor, Maine. The following essay first appeared in *Playboy* in 1982.

Pre-Reading Journal Entry

Several forms of entertainment, besides horror movies, are highly popular despite what many consider a low level of quality. In your journal, list as many "lowbrow" forms of entertainment as you can. Possibilities include professional wrestling, aggressive video games, Internet chat rooms, and so on. Review your list, and respond to the following question in your journal: What is it about each form of entertainment that attracts such popularity—and inspires such criticism?

WHY WE CRAVE HORROR MOVIES

I think that we're all mentally ill: those of us outside the asylums only hide it a lit- 1
tle better—and maybe not all that much better, after all. We've all known people who
talk to themselves, people who sometimes squinch their faces into horrible grimaces
when they believe no one is watching, people who have some hysterical fear—of
snakes, the dark, the tight place, the long drop . . . and, of course, those final worms
and grubs that are waiting so patiently underground.

When we pay our four or five bucks and seat ourselves at tenth-row center in a 2
theater showing a horror movie, we are daring the nightmare.

Why? Some of the reasons are simple and obvious. To show that we can, that we 3
are not afraid, that we can ride this roller coaster. Which is not to say that a really good
horror movie may not surprise a scream out of us at some point, the way we may
scream when the roller coaster twists through a complete 360 or plows through a lake
at the bottom of the drop. And horror movies, like roller coasters, have always been
the special province of the young; by the time one turns 40 or 50, one's appetite for
double twists or 360-degree loops may be considerably depleted.

We also go to re-establish our feelings of essential normality; the horror movie is innate- 4
ly conservative, even reactionary. Freda Jackson as the horrible melting woman in *Die,
Monster, Die!* confirms for us that no matter how far we may be removed from the beauty of a Robert Redford or a Diana Ross, we are still light-years from true ugliness.

And we go to have fun. 5

Ah, but this is where the ground starts to slope away, isn't it? Because this is a very 6
peculiar sort of fun indeed. The fun comes from seeing others menaced—sometimes
killed. One critic has suggested that if pro football has become the voyeur's version of combat, then the horror film has become the modern version of the public lynching.

It is true that the mythic, "fairytale" horror film intends to take away the shades of 7
gray. . . . It urges us to put away our more civilized and adult penchant for analysis and
to become children again, seeing things in pure blacks and whites. It may be that horror movies provide psychic relief on this level because this invitation to lapse into simplicity, irrationality and even outright madness is extended so rarely. We are told we
may allow our emotions a free rein . . . or no rein at all.

If we are all insane, then sanity becomes a matter of degree. If your insanity leads 8
you to carve up women like Jack the Ripper or the Cleveland Torso Murderer, we clap
you away in the funny farm (but neither of those two amateur-night surgeons was ever
caught, heh-heh-heh); if, on the other hand your insanity leads you only to talk to yourself when you're under stress or to pick your nose on the morning bus, then you are
left alone to go about your business . . . though it is doubtful that you will ever be
invited to the best parties.

The potential lyncher is in almost all of us (excluding saints, past and present; but then, 9
most saints have been crazy in their own ways), and every now and then, he has to be let
loose to scream and roll around in the grass. Our emotions and our fears form their own
body, and we recognize that it demands its own exercise to maintain proper muscle tone.
Certain of these emotional muscles are accepted—even exalted—in civilized society; they
are, of course, the emotions that tend to maintain the status quo of civilization itself. Love,
friendship, loyalty, kindness—these are all the emotions that we applaud, emotions that
have been immortalized in the couplets of Hallmark cards. . . .

10   When we exhibit these emotions, society showers us with positive reinforcement; we learn this even before we get out of diapers. When, as children, we hug our rotten little puke of a sister and give her a kiss, all the aunts and uncles smile and twit and cry, "Isn't he the sweetest little thing?" Such coveted treats as chocolate-covered graham crackers often follow. But if we deliberately slam the rotten little puke of a sister's fingers in the door, sanctions follow—angry remonstrance from parents, aunts and uncles; instead of a chocolate-covered graham cracker, a spanking.

11   But anticivilization emotions don't go away, and they demand periodic exercise. We have such "sick" jokes as, "What's the difference between a truckload of bowling balls and a truckload of dead babies?" (You can't unload a truckload of bowling balls with a pitchfork . . . a joke, by the way, that I heard originally from a ten-year-old.) Such a joke may surprise a laugh or a grin out of us even as we recoil, a possibility that confirms the thesis: If we share a brotherhood of man, then we also share an insanity of man. None of which is intended as a defense of either the sick joke or insanity but merely as an explanation of why the best horror films, like the best fairy tales, manage to be reactionary, anarchistic, and revolutionary all at the same time.

12   The mythic horror movie, like the sick joke, has a dirty job to do. It deliberately appeals to all that is worst in us. It is morbidity unchained, our most base instincts let free, our nastiest fantasies realized . . . and it all happens, fittingly enough, in the dark. For those reasons, good liberals often shy away from horror films. For myself, I like to see the most aggressive of them—*Dawn of the Dead*, for instance—as lifting a trap door in the civilized forebrain and throwing a basket of raw meat to the hungry alligators swimming around in that subterranean river beneath.

13   Why bother? Because it keeps them from getting out, man. It keeps them down there and me up here. It was Lennon and McCartney who said that all you need is love, and I would agree with that.

14   As long as you keep the gators fed.

Questions for Close Reading

1. What is the selection's thesis? Locate the sentence(s) in which King states his main idea. If he doesn't state the thesis explicitly, express it in your own words.

2. In what ways do King's references to "Jack the Ripper" and the "Cleveland Torso Murderer" (paragraph 8) support his thesis?

3. What does King mean in paragraph 4 when he says that horror movies are "innately conservative, even reactionary"? What does he mean in paragraph 11 when he calls them "anarchistic, and revolutionary"?

4. In paragraphs 12 and 14, King refers to "alligators" and "gators." What does the alligator represent? What does King mean when he says that all the world needs is love—"[a]s long as you keep the gators fed"?

5. Refer to your dictionary as needed to define the following words used in the selection: *hysterical* (paragraph 1), *reactionary* (4), *voyeur's* (6), *lynching* (6), *penchant* (7), *immortalized* (9), *anarchistic* (11), and *morbidity* (12).

Questions About the Writer's Craft

1. **The pattern.** Does King's causal analysis have an essentially informative, speculative, or persuasive (see page 449) purpose? What makes you think so? How might King's profession as a horror writer have influenced his purpose?

2. **Other patterns.** King compares and contrasts horror movies to roller coasters (3), public lynchings (6), and sick jokes (11–12). How do these comparisons and contrasts reinforce King's thesis about horror movies?

3. **Other patterns.** Throughout the essay, King uses several examples involving children. Identify these instances. How do these examples help King develop his thesis?

4. What is unusual about paragraphs 2, 5, and 14? Why do you think King might have designed these paragraphs in this way?

Writing Assignments Using Cause-Effect as a Pattern of Development

1. King argues that horror movies have "a dirty job to do": they feed the hungry monsters in our psyche. Write an essay in which you put King's thesis to the test. Briefly describe the first horror movie you ever saw; then explain its effect on you. Like King, speculate about the nature of your response—your feelings and fantasies—while watching the movie.

∞ 2. Many movie critics claim that horror movies nowadays are more violent and bloody than they used to be. Write an essay about *one* other medium of popular culture that you think has changed for the worse. You might consider action movies, televised coverage of sports, men's or women's magazines, radio talk shows, TV sitcoms, and so on. Briefly describe key differences between the medium's past and present forms. Analyze the reasons for the change, and, at the end of the essay, examine the effects of the change. Ellen Goodman's "Family Counterculture" (page 7) and Susan Douglas's "Managing Mixed Messages" (page 251) present additional perspectives on this issue.

Writing Assignments Using Other Patterns of Development

3. King advocates the horror movie precisely because "It deliberately appeals to all that is worst in us." Write an essay in which you rebut King. Argue instead that horror movies should be avoided precisely *because* they satisfy monstrous feelings in us. To refute King, provide strong examples drawn from your own and other people's experience. Consider supplementing your informal research with material gathered in the library and/or on the Internet.

4. Write an essay in which you illustrate, contrary to King, that humans are by nature essentially benevolent and kind. Brainstorm with others to generate vivid examples in support of your thesis.

Writing Assignment Using a Journal Entry as a Starting Point

5. King believes that horror movies involve "a very peculiar sort of fun." Review your pre-reading journal entry, and select *one* other form of popular entertainment that you think provides its own strange kind of enjoyment. Like King, write an essay in which you analyze the causes of people's enjoyment of this type of entertainment. Brainstorm with others to identify convincing examples. You may, like King, endorse the phenomenon you examine—or you may condemn it.

JOHN M. DARLEY
BIBB LATANÉ

John M. Darley (1938–), professor of psychology at Princeton University, studies the principles of moral judgment in children and adults. Bibb Latané (1937–), the former director of the Behavioral Sciences Laboratory at Ohio State University, is professor of psychology at Florida Atlantic University. Darley and Latané are coauthors of *The Unresponsive Bystander: Why Doesn't He Help* (1970) and *Help in a Crisis: Bystander Response to an Emergency* (1976). Based on their research into the origins of noninvolvement, "Why People Don't Help in a Crisis" (1968) was awarded an essay prize from the American Association for the Advancement of Science.

Pre-Reading Journal Entry

Faced with a challenging or difficult situation, people sometimes choose *not* to get involved—and then later regret this decision. Such situations might include, for example, helping an injured stranger, standing up for someone being bullied, and letting in a stray animal on a cold day. In your journal, write about one or more times when you faced a difficult situation and failed to respond in a way that you now believe you should have.

WHY PEOPLE DON'T HELP IN A CRISIS

1 Kitty Genovese is set upon by a maniac as she returns home from work at 3 A.M. Thirty-eight of her neighbors in Kew Gardens, N.Y., come to their windows when she cries out in terror; not one comes to her assistance, even though her assailant takes half an hour to murder her. No one so much as calls the police. She dies.

2 Andrew Mormille is stabbed in the head and neck as he rides in a New York City subway train. Eleven other riders flee to another car as the 17-year-old boy bleeds to death; not one comes to his assistance, even though his attackers have left the car. He dies.

Eleanor Bradley trips and breaks her leg while shopping on New York City's Fifth   3
Avenue. Dazed and in shock, she calls for help, but the hurrying stream of people simply parts and flows past. Finally, after 40 minutes, a taxi driver stops and helps her to
a doctor.

How can so many people watch another human being in distress and do nothing?   4
Why don't they help?

Since we started research on bystander responses to emergencies, we have heard   5
many explanations for the lack of intervention in such cases. "The megalopolis in
which we live makes closeness difficult and leads to the alienation of the individual
from the group," says the psychoanalyst. "This sort of disaster," says the sociologist,
"shakes the sense of safety and sureness of the individuals involved and causes psychological withdrawal." "Apathy," say others. "Indifference."

All of these analyses share one characteristic: they set the indifferent witness apart   6
from the rest of us. Certainly not one of us who reads about these incidents in horror
is apathetic, alienated or depersonalized. Certainly these terrifying cases have no personal implications for us. We needn't feel guilty, or re-examine ourselves, or anything
like that. Or should we?

If we look closely at the behavior of witnesses to these incidents, the people   7
involved begin to seem less inhuman and a lot more like the rest of us. They were not
indifferent. The 38 witnesses of Kitty Genovese's murder, for example, did not merely look at the scene once and then ignore it. They continued to stare out of their windows, caught, fascinated, distressed, unwilling to act but unable to turn away.

Why, then, didn't they act?   8

There are three things the bystander must do if he is to intervene in an emergency: 9
notice that something is happening; *interpret* that event as an emergency; and decide
that he has *personal responsibility* for intervention. As we shall show, the presence of
other bystanders may at each stage inhibit his action.

The Unseeing Eye

Suppose that a man has a heart attack. He clutches his chest, staggers to the near-   10
est building and slumps sitting to the sidewalk. Will a passerby come to his
assistance? First, the bystander has to notice that something is happening. He must
tear himself away from his private thoughts and pay attention. But Americans consider it bad manners to look closely at other people in public. We are taught to
respect the privacy of others, and when among strangers we close our ears and
avoid staring. In a crowd, then, each person is less likely to notice a potential emergency than when alone.

Experimental evidence corroborates this. We asked college students to an interview   11
about their reactions to urban living. As the students waited to see the interviewer,
either by themselves or with two other students, they filled out a questionnaire.
Solitary students often glanced idly about while filling out their questionnaires: those
in groups kept their eyes on their own papers.

As part of the study, we staged an emergency: smoke was released into the waiting   12
room through a vent. Two thirds of the subjects who were alone noticed the smoke
immediately, but only 25 percent of those waiting in groups saw it as quickly. Although
eventually all the subjects did become aware of the smoke—when the atmosphere
grew so smoky as to make them cough and rub their eyes—this study indicates that

the more people present, the slower an individual may be to perceive an emergency and the more likely he is not to see it at all.

Seeing Is Not Necessarily Believing

13   Once an event is noticed, an onlooker must decide if it is truly an emergency. Emergencies are not always clearly labeled as such; "smoke" pouring into a waiting room may be caused by fire, or it may merely indicate a leak in a steam pipe. Screams in the street may signal an assault or a family quarrel. A man lying in a doorway may be having a coronary—or he may simply be sleeping off a drunk.

14   A person trying to interpret a situation often looks at those around him to see how he should react. If everyone else is calm and indifferent, he will tend to remain so; if everyone else is reacting strongly, he is likely to become aroused. This tendency is not merely slavish conformity; ordinarily we derive much valuable information about new situations from how others around us behave. It's a rare traveler who, in picking a roadside restaurant, chooses to stop at one where no other cars appear in the parking lot.

15   But occasionally the reactions of others provide false information. The studied nonchalance of patients in a dentist's waiting room is a poor indication of their inner anxiety. It is considered embarrassing to "lose your cool" in public. In a potentially acute situation, then, everyone present will appear more unconcerned than he is in fact. A crowd can thus force inaction on its members by implying, through its passivity, that an event is not an emergency. Any individual in such a crowd fears that he may appear a fool if he behaves as though it were.

16   To determine how the presence of other people affects a person's interpretation of an emergency, Latané and Judith Rodin set up another experiment. Subjects were paid $2 to participate in a survey of game and puzzle preferences conducted at Columbia University by the Consumer Testing Bureau. An attractive young market researcher met them at the door and took them to the testing room, where they were given questionnaires to fill out. Before leaving, she told them that she would be working next door in her office, which was separated from the room by a folding room-divider. She then entered her office, where she shuffled papers, opened drawers and made enough noise to remind the subjects of her presence. After four minutes she turned on a high-fidelity tape recorder.

17   On it, the subjects heard the researcher climb up on a chair, perhaps to reach for a stack of papers on the bookcase. They heard a loud crash and a scream as the chair collapsed and she fell, and they heard her moan, "Oh, my foot . . . I . . . I . . . can't move it. Oh, I . . . can't get this . . . thing off me." Her cries gradually got more subdued and controlled.

18   Twenty-six people were alone in the waiting room when the "accident" occurred. Seventy percent of them offered to help the victim. Many pushed back the divider to offer their assistance; others called out to offer their help.

19   Among those waiting in pairs, only 20 percent—8 out of 40—offered to help. The other 32 remained unresponsive. In defining the situation as a nonemergency, they explained to themselves why the other member of the pair did not leave the room; they also removed any reason for action themselves. Whatever had happened, it was believed to be not serious. "A mild sprain," some said. "I didn't want to embarrass her." In a "real" emergency, they assured us, they would be among the first to help.

The Lonely Crowd

Even if a person defines an event as an emergency, the presence of other bystanders   20
may still make him less likely to intervene. He feels that his responsibility is diffused
and diluted. Thus, if your car breaks down on a busy highway, hundreds of drivers
whiz by without anyone's stopping to help—but if you are stuck on a nearly deserted
country road, whoever passes you first is likely to stop.

To test this diffusion-of-responsibility theory, we simulated an emergency in which   21
people overheard a victim calling for help. Some thought they were the only person to
hear the cries; the rest believed that others heard them, too. As with the witnesses to
Kitty Genovese's murder, the subjects could not *see* one another or know what others
were doing. The kind of direct group inhibition found in the other two studies could
not operate.

For the simulation, we recruited 72 students at New York University to participate   22
in what was referred to as a "group discussion" of personal problems in an urban university. Each student was put in an individual room equipped with a set of headphones
and a microphone. It was explained that this precaution had been taken because participants might feel embarrassed about discussing their problems publicly. Also, the
experimenter said that he would not listen to the initial discussion, but would only ask
for reactions later. Each person was to talk in turn.

The first to talk reported that he found it difficult to adjust to New York and his stud-   23
ies. Then, hesitantly and with obvious embarrassment, he mentioned that he was
prone to nervous seizures when he was under stress. Other students then talked about
their own problems in turn. The number of people in the "discussion" varied. But
whatever the apparent size of the group—two, three or six people—only the subject
was actually present; the others, as well as the instructions and the speeches of the
victim-to-be, were present only on a pre-recorded tape.

When it was the first person's turn to talk again, he launched into the following per-   24
formance, becoming louder and having increasing speech difficulties: "I can see a lot of
er of er how other people's problems are similar to mine because er I mean er they're
not er e-easy to handle sometimes and er I er um I think I I need er if if could er er somebody er er er give me give me a little er give me a little help here because er I er *uh*
I've got a a one of the er seiz-er er things coming *on* and and er uh uh (choking
sounds) . . ."

Eighty-five percent of the people who believed themselves to be alone with the vic-   25
tim came out of their room to help. Sixty-two percent of the people who believed there
was *one* other bystander did so. Of those who believed there were four other
bystanders, only 31 percent reported the fit. The responsibility-diluting effect of other
people was so strong that single individuals were more than twice as likely to report
the emergency as those who thought other people also knew about it.

The Lesson Learned

People who failed to report the emergency showed few signs of the apathy and indif-   26
ference thought to characterize "unresponsive bystanders." When the experimenter
entered the room to end the situation, the subject often asked if the victim was "all
right." Many of them showed physical signs of nervousness; they often had trembling
hands and sweating palms. If anything, they seemed more emotionally aroused than

did those who reported the emergency. Their emotional behavior was a sign of their continuing conflict concerning whether to respond or not.

27   Thus, the stereotype of the unconcerned, depersonalized *homo urbanus,* blandly watching the misfortunes of others, proves inaccurate. Instead, we find that a bystander to an emergency is an anguished individual in genuine doubt, wanting to do the right thing but compelled to make complex decisions under pressure of stress and fear. His reactions are shaped by the actions of others—all too frequently by their inaction.

28   And we are that bystander. Caught up by the apparent indifference of others, we may pass by an emergency without helping or even realizing that help is needed. Once we are aware of the influence of those around us, however, we can resist it. We can choose to see distress and step forward to relieve it.

Questions for Close Reading

1. What is the selection's thesis? Locate the sentence(s) in which Darley and Latané state their main idea. If they don't state the thesis explicitly, express it in your own words.

2. According to the authors, what three factors prevent people in a crowd from helping victims during an emergency?

3. Why did Darley and Latané isolate the subjects in separate rooms during the staged emergency described in paragraphs 21–26?

4. What kind of person, according to the authors, would tend to ignore or bypass a person experiencing a problem? What might encourage this person to act more responsibly?

5. Refer to your dictionary as needed to define the following words used in the selection: *megalopolis* (paragraph 5), *apathy* (5), *indifference* (5), *alienated* (6), *depersonalized* (6), *inhibit* (9), *corroborates* (11), *coronary* (13), *slavish* (14), *nonchalance* (15), *diffused* (20), and *blandly* (27).

Questions About the Writer's Craft

1. **The pattern.** What techniques do Darley and Latané use to help readers focus on the causes of people's inaction during an emergency?

2. **Other patterns.** The three brief narratives that open the essay depict events that happened well before Darley and Latané wrote their essay. Why might the authors have chosen to recount these events in the present tense rather than in the past tense?

3. Locate places where Darley and Latané describe the experiments investigating bystander behavior. How do the authors show readers the steps—and the implications—of each experiment?

4. What purpose do you think the authors had in mind when writing the selection? How do you know?

Writing Assignments Using Cause-Effect as a Pattern of Development

∞ **1.** Write an essay showing the "responsibility-diluting effect" that can occur when several people witness a critical event. Brainstorm with others to gather examples of this effect; then select two or three dramatic situations as the basis of your essay. Be sure to acknowledge other factors that may have played a role in inhibiting people's ability to act responsibly. To gain additional insight into the pressures that can compel group conformity, read George Orwell's "Shooting an Elephant" (page 209), Sophronia Liu's "So Tsi-fai" (page 221), and Diane Cole's "Don't Just Stand There" (page 322).

2. Although Darley and Latané focus on times when individuals fail to act responsibly, people often respond with moral heroism during difficult situations. Brainstorm with others to identify occasions in which people have taken the initiative to avert a crisis. Focusing on two or three compelling instances, write an essay in which you analyze the possible motives for people's responsible behavior. Also show how their actions affected the other individuals involved.

Writing Assignments Using Other Patterns of Development

3. How could families or schools or communities or religious organizations encourage children to act rather than withdraw when confronted by someone in difficulty? Focusing on *one* of these institutions, talk with friends, classmates, and family members to gather their experiences and recommendations. Then consider doing some research on this subject in the library and/or on the Internet. Select the most provocative ideas, and write an essay explaining the steps that this particular institution could take to help develop children's sense of responsibility to others. Develop your points with specific examples of what has been done and what could be done.

∞ **4.** Darley and Latané cite social critics who believe that the United States has become a nation of strangers, alienated and withdrawn from one another. Write an essay refuting this claim by presenting several vivid instances of small acts of everyday kindness—examples in which people demonstrate their sense of connectedness to those around them. Generate examples by drawing on your own and other people's experiences. Before writing, you might want to read Maya Angelou's "Sister Flowers" (page 178) for a portrait of an individual who shows—in small, quiet ways—that she cares for others.

Writing Assignment Using a Journal Entry as a Starting Point

∞ **5.** Though the authors don't state so directly, they suggest that unresponsive bystanders often may regret their inaction later on. Reviewing the material you generated in your journal entry, select the most compelling or profound of the incidents you described. Then write an essay in which you narrate *one* situation in which you chose not to get involved, but now realize you should have. Be sure to provide dialog and vivid descriptive details to bring the incident to life for your readers. Conclude your easy with a brief reflection on what you wish you had done and how your failure to respond properly has affected you. You might also begin by reading Gordon Parks's "Flavio's Home" (page 184), which conveys the author's impulse to get involved when he witnesses the desperate circumstances of another.

BRENT STAPLES

After earning a Ph.D. in psychology from the University of Chicago, Brent Staples (1951–) soon became a nationally recognized essayist. He has worked on numerous newspapers and is now an Editorial Board member of *The New York Times.* Staples's autobiography, *Parallel Time: Growing Up in Black and White,* was published in 1995. He is currently working on a history of the Negro Press and lives in Brooklyn, New York, with his wife. This selection first appeared in slightly different form in *Ms.* magazine (1986) and then in *Harper's* (1987).

Pre-Reading Journal Entry

In recent years, racial profiling—targeting people for investigation based on their race or ethnicity—has become a controversial issue. What is your opinion of this practice? Is racial profiling ever acceptable? Freewrite on these questions in your journal.

BLACK MEN AND PUBLIC SPACE

1   My first victim was a woman—white, well dressed, probably in her early twenties. I came upon her late one evening on a deserted street in Hyde Park, a relatively affluent neighborhood in an otherwise mean, impoverished section of Chicago. As I swung onto the avenue behind her, there seemed to be a discreet, uninflammatory distance between us. Not so. She cast back a worried glance. To her, the youngish black man—a broad six feet two inches with a beard and billowing hair, both hands shoved into the pockets of a bulky military jacket—seemed menacingly close. After a few more quick glimpses, she picked up her pace and was soon running in earnest. Within seconds she disappeared into a cross street.

2   That was more than a decade ago. I was twenty-two years old, a graduate student newly arrived at the University of Chicago. It was in the echo of that terrified woman's footfalls that I first began to know the unwieldy inheritance I'd come into—the ability to alter public space in ugly ways. It was clear that she thought herself the quarry of a mugger, a rapist, or worse. Suffering a bout of insomnia, however, I was stalking sleep, not defenseless wayfarers. As a softy who is scarcely able to take a knife to a raw chicken—let alone hold one to a person's throat—I was surprised, embarrassed, and dismayed all at once. Her flight made me feel like an accomplice in tyranny. It also made it clear that I was indistinguishable from the muggers who occasionally seeped into the

area from the surrounding ghetto. That first encounter, and those that followed, signified that a vast, unnerving gulf lay between nighttime pedestrians—particularly women—and me. And I soon gathered that being perceived as dangerous is a hazard in itself. I only needed to turn a corner into a dicey situation, or crowd some frightened, armed person in a foyer somewhere, or make an errant move after being pulled over by a policeman. Where fear and weapons meet—and they often do in urban America—there is always the possibility of death.

In that first year, my first away from my hometown, I was to become thoroughly   3
familiar with the language of fear. At dark, shadowy intersections, I could cross in front of a car stopped at a traffic light and elicit the *thunk, thunk, thunk, thunk* of the driver—black, white, male, or female—hammering down the door locks. On less traveled streets after dark, I grew accustomed to but never comfortable with people crossing to the other side of the street rather than pass me. Then there were the standard unpleasantries with policemen, doormen, bouncers, cabdrivers, and others whose business it is to screen out troublesome individuals *before* there is any nastiness.

I moved to New York nearly two years ago and I have remained an avid night walk-   4
er. In central Manhattan, the near-constant crowd cover minimizes tense one-on-one street encounters. Elsewhere—in SoHo, for example, where sidewalks are narrow and tightly spaced buildings shut out the sky—things can get very taut indeed.

After dark, on the warrenlike streets of Brooklyn where I live, I often see women   5
who fear the worst from me. They seem to have set their faces on neutral, and with their purse straps strung across their chests bandolier-style, they forge ahead as though bracing themselves against being tackled. I understand, of course, that the danger they perceive is not a hallucination. Women are particularly vulnerable to street violence, and young black males are drastically overrepresented among the perpetrators of that violence. Yet these truths are no solace against the kind of alienation that comes of being ever the suspect, a fearsome entity with whom pedestrians avoid making eye contact.

It is not altogether clear to me how I reached the ripe old age of twenty-two with-   6
out being conscious of the lethality nighttime pedestrians attributed to me. Perhaps it was because in Chester, Pennsylvania, the small, angry industrial town where I came of age in the 1960s, I was scarcely noticeable against a backdrop of gang warfare, street knifings, and murders. I grew up one of the good boys, had perhaps a half-dozen fist-fights. In retrospect, my shyness of combat has clear sources.

As a boy, I saw countless tough guys locked away; I have since buried several, too.   7
They were babies, really—a teenage cousin, a brother of twenty-two, a childhood friend in his mid-twenties—all gone down in episodes of bravado played out in the streets. I came to doubt the virtues of intimidation early on. I chose, perhaps unconsciously, to remain a shadow—timid, but a survivor.

The fearsomeness mistakenly attributed to me in public places often has a perilous   8
flavor. The most frightening of these confusions occurred in the late 1970s and early 1980s, when I worked as a journalist in Chicago. One day, rushing into the office of a magazine I was writing for with a deadline story in hand, I was mistaken for a burglar. The office manager called security and, with an ad hoc posse, pursued me through the labyrinthine halls, nearly to my editor's door. I had no way of proving who I was. I could only move briskly toward the company of someone who knew me.

Another time I was on assignment for a local paper and killing time before an inter-   9
view. I entered a jewelry store on the city's affluent Near North Side. The proprietor excused herself and returned with an enormous red Doberman pinscher straining at

the end of a leash. She stood, the dog extended toward me, silent to my questions, her eyes bulging nearly out of her head. I took a cursory look around, nodded, and bade her good night.

10   Relatively speaking, however, I never fared as badly as another black male journalist. He went to nearby Waukegan, Illinois, a couple of summers ago to work on a story about a murderer who was born there. Mistaking the reporter for the killer, police officers hauled him from his car at gunpoint and but for his press credentials would probably have tried to book him. Such episodes are not uncommon. Black men trade tales like this all the time.

11   Over the years, I learned to smother the rage I felt at so often being taken for a criminal. Not to do so would surely have led to madness. I now take precautions to make myself less threatening. I move about with care, particularly late in the evening. I give a wide berth to nervous people on subway platforms during the wee hours, particularly when I have exchanged business clothes for jeans. If I happen to be entering a building behind some people who appear skittish, I may walk by, letting them clear the lobby before I return, so as not to seem to be following them. I have been calm and extremely congenial on those rare occasions when I've been pulled over by the police.

12   And on late-evening constitutionals I employ what has proved to be an excellent tension-reducing measure: I whistle melodies from Beethoven and Vivaldi and the more popular classical composers. Even steely New Yorkers hunching toward nighttime destinations seem to relax, and occasionally they even join in the tune. Virtually everybody seems to sense that a mugger wouldn't be warbling bright, sunny selections from Vivaldi's *Four Seasons.* It is my equivalent of the cowbell that hikers wear when they know they are in bear country.

Questions for Close Reading

1. What is the selection's thesis? Locate the sentence(s) in which Staples states his main idea. If he doesn't state the thesis explicitly, express it in your own words.

2. How did Staples first learn that he was considered a threat by many people? How did this discovery make him feel?

3. What are some of the dangers that Staples has encountered because of his race? How has he handled each dangerous situation?

4. What "precautions" does Staples take to appear nonthreatening to others? Why do these precautions work?

5. Refer to your dictionary as needed to define the following words used in the selection: *uninflammatory* (paragraph 1), *dicey* (2), *bandolier* (5), *lethality* (6), *bravado* (7), *berth* (11), and *constitutionals* (12).

Questions About the Writer's Craft

1. **The pattern.** Brent Staples reveals both causes and effects of people's reacting with fear to a black male. Does the essay end with a discussion of causes or of effects? Why do you suppose Staples concludes the essay as he does?

2. **Other patterns.** Why do you think Staples opens the piece with such a dramatic, yet intentionally misleading narrative? What effect does he achieve?

3. Is Staples writing primarily for whites, blacks, or both? How do you know?

4. What is Staples's tone? Why do you think he chose this tone?

Writing Assignments Using Cause-Effect as a Pattern of Development

1. Write an essay showing how your or someone else's entry into a specific public space (for example, a bus, party, elevator, or table at the library) influenced other people's behavior. Identify the possible reasons that others reacted as they did, and explain how their reactions, in turn, affected the newcomer. Use your analysis to reach some conclusions about human nature.

2. Staples describes circumstances that often result in fear. Focusing on a more positive emotion, like admiration or contentment, illustrate the situations that tend to elicit that emotion in you. Discuss why these circumstances have the effect they do.

Writing Assignments Using Other Patterns of Development

∞ 3. Staples describes how others' expectations oblige him to alter his behavior. Narrate an event during which you felt forced to conform to what others expected. What did you learn from the experience? George Orwell's "Shooting an Elephant" (page 209), Sophronia Liu's "So Tsi-fai" (page 221), Diane Cole's "Don't Just Stand There" (page 322), and Joseph H. Suina's "And Then I Went to School" (page 371) may prompt some interesting thoughts on the issue of conformity.

4. When he encounters a startled pedestrian, Staples feels some fear but manages to control it. Write an essay showing the steps you took one time when you felt afraid but, like Staples, remained in control and got through safely. Convey your initial fear, your later relief, and any self-discovery that resulted from the experience.

Writing Assignment Using a Journal Entry as a Starting Point

5. Though he doesn't say so explicitly, Staples has been the target of racial profiling. Review your pre-reading journal entry, and then research the topic of racial profiling in the library and/or on the Internet. Write an essay in which you argue that racial profiling is *or* is not a justifiable practice. In the course of your essay, be sure to cite examples of hypothetical or actual situations in order to

reinforce your position. You should also acknowledge and, where appropriate, refute opposing points of view.

ADDITIONAL WRITING TOPICS: CAUSE-EFFECT

General Assignments

Write an essay that analyzes the causes and/or effects of one of the following topics. Determine your purpose before beginning to write: Will the essay be informative, persuasive, or speculative? As you prewrite, think rigorously about causes and effects; try to identify causal chains. Provide solid evidence for the thesis, and use either chronological or emphatic order to organize your supporting points.

1. Sleep deprivation

2. Having the parents you have

3. Lack of communication in a relationship

4. Overexercising or not exercising

5. A particular TV or rock star's popularity

6. Skill or ineptitude in sports

7. A major life decision

8. Changing attitudes toward the environment

9. Voter apathy

10. An act of violence or cruelty

Assignments with a Specific Purpose, Audience, and Point of View

On Campus

1. A debate about the prominence of athletics at colleges and universities is going to be broadcast on the local cable station. For this debate, prepare a speech

pointing out either the harmful or the beneficial effects of "big-time" college athletic programs.

2. Why do students "flunk out" of college? Write an article for the campus newspaper outlining the main causes of failure. Your goal is to steer students away from dangerous habits and situations that lead to poor grades or dropping out.

At Home or in the Community

3. Write a letter to the editor of your favorite newspaper, analyzing the causes of the country's current "trash crisis." Be sure to mention the nationwide love affair with disposable items and the general disregard of the idea of thrift. Conclude by offering brief suggestions for how people in your community can begin to remedy this problem.

4. Write a letter to the mayor of your town or city suggesting a "Turn Off the TV" public relations effort, convincing residents to stop watching television for a month. Cite the positive effects that "no TV" would have on parents, children, and the community in general.

On the Job

5. As the manager of a store or office, you've noticed that a number of employees have negative workplace habits and/or attitudes. Write a memo for your employees in which you identify these negative behaviors and show how they affect the workplace environment. Be sure to adopt a tone that will sound neither patronizing nor overly harsh.

6. Why do you think teenage suicide is on the rise? You're a respected psychologist. Write a fact sheet for parents of teenagers and for high school guidance counselors, describing the factors that could make a young person desperate enough to attempt suicide. At the end, suggest what parents and counselors can do to help confused, unhappy young people.

18
DEFINITION

WHAT IS DEFINITION?

In Lewis Carroll's wise and whimsical tale *Through the Looking Glass*, Humpty Dumpty proclaims, "When I use a word . . . it means just what I choose it to mean—neither more nor less." If the world were filled with characters like Humpty Dumpty, all of them bending the meanings of words to their own purposes and accepting no challenges to their personal definitions, communication would creak to a halt.

For language to communicate, words must have accepted definitions. Dictionaries, the sourcebooks for definitions, are compilations of current word meanings, enabling speakers of a language to understand one another. But as you might suspect, things are not as simple as they first appear. We all know that a word like *discipline* has a standard dictionary definition. We also know that parents argue every day over the meaning of *discipline,* as do teachers and school administrators. Moreover, many of the wrenching moral debates of our time are attempts to resolve questions of definition. Much of the controversy over abortion, for instance, centers on what is meant by "life" and when it "begins."

Words can, in short, be slippery. Each of us has unique experiences, attitudes, and values that influence the way we use words and the way we interpret the words of others. Lewis Carroll may have been exaggerating, but to some degree Humpty Dumpty's attitude exists in all of us.

In addition to the idiosyncratic interpretations we may attach to words, some words shift in meaning over time. The word *pedagogue,* for instance, originally meant "a teacher or leader of children." However, with the passage of time, *pedagogue* has come to mean "a dogmatic, pedantic teacher." And, of course, we invent new words as the need arises. For example, *modem* and *byte* are just two of many new words created in response to recent breakthroughs in computer technology.

Writing a **definition,** then, is no simple task. Primarily, the writer tries to answer basic questions: "What does _____ mean?" and "What is the special or true nature of _____?" The word to be defined may be an object, a concept, a type of person, a place, or a phenomenon. Potential subjects might be the "user-friendly" computer, animal rights, a model teacher, cabin fever. As you will see, there are various strategies for expanding definitions far beyond the single-word synonyms or brief phrases that dictionaries provide.

HOW DEFINITION FITS YOUR PURPOSE AND AUDIENCE

Many times, short-answer exam questions call for definitions. Consider the following examples:

Define the term *mob psychology.*

What is the difference between a metaphor and a simile?

How would you explain what a religious cult is?

In such cases, a good response might involve a definition of several sentences or several paragraphs.

Other times, definition may be used in an essay organized mainly around another pattern of development. In this situation, all that's needed is a brief formal definition or a short definition given in your own words. For instance, a *process analysis* showing readers how computers have revolutionized the typical business office might start with a textbook definition of the term *artificial intelligence.* In an *argumentation-persuasion* paper urging students to support recent efforts to abolish fraternities and sororities, you could refer to the definitions of *blackballing* and *hazing* found in the university handbook. Or your personal definition of *hero* could be the starting point for a *causal analysis* that explains to readers why there are few real heroes in today's world.

But the most complex use of definition, and the one we focus on in this chapter, involves exploring a subject through an **extended definition.** Extended definition allows you to apply a personal interpretation to a word, to propose a revisionist view of a commonly accepted meaning, to analyze words representing complex or controversial issues. *Pornography, gun control, secular humanism,* and *right to privacy* would be good subjects for extended definition; each is multifaceted, often misunderstood, and fraught with emotion. *Junk food, anger, leadership,* and *anxiety* could also make interesting subjects, especially if the extended definition helped readers develop a new understanding of the word. You might, for example, define *anxiety* not as a negative state but as a positive force that propels us to take action.

An extended definition may run several paragraphs or a few pages. Keep in mind, however, that some definitions require a chapter or even an entire book to develop. Theologians, philosophers, and pop psychologists have devoted entire texts to concepts like *evil* and *love.*

PREWRITING STRATEGIES

The following checklist shows how you can apply to definition some of the prewriting techniques discussed in Chapter 2.

☑ DEFINITION: A PREWRITING CHECKLIST

Choose Something to Define

☐ Is there something you're especially qualified to define? What about that thing do you hope to convey?

☐ Do any of your journal entries reflect an attempt to pinpoint something's essence: courage, pornography, a well-rounded education?

☐ Will you define a concept (energy), an object (the microchip), a type of person (the bigot), a place (the desert), a phenomenon (the rise in volunteerism), a complex or controversial issue (euthanasia)?

☐ Can your topic be meaningfully defined within the space and time allotted?

Identify Your Purpose, Audience, Tone, and Point of View

☐ Do you want simply to inform and explain—that is, to make meaning clear? Or do you want to persuade readers to accept your understanding of a term? Do you want to do both?

☐ Will you offer a personal interpretation? Propose a revised meaning? Explain an obscure or technical term? Discuss shifts in meaning over time? Distinguish one term from another, closely related term? Show conflicts in definition?

☐ Are your readers apt to be open to your interpretation of a term? What information will they need to understand your definition and to feel that it is correct and insightful?

☐ What tone and point of view will make your readers receptive to your definition?

Use Prewriting to Develop the Definition

☐ How might mapping, brainstorming, freewriting, and speaking with others generate material that develops your definition?
☐ Which of the prewriting questions below would generate the most details and, therefore, suggest patterns for developing your definition?

Question	Pattern
How does X look, taste, smell, feel, and sound?	Description
What does X do? When? Where?	Narration
What are some typical instances of X?	Illustration
What are X's component parts? What different forms can X take?	Division-classification
How does X work?	Process analysis
What is X like or unlike?	Comparison-contrast
What leads to X? What are X's consequences?	Cause-effect

STRATEGIES FOR USING DEFINITION IN AN ESSAY

After prewriting, you're ready to draft your essay. The following suggestions will be helpful whether you use definition as a dominant or supportive pattern of development.

1. Stay focused on the essay's purpose, audience, and tone. Since your purpose for writing an extended definition shapes the entire paper, you need to keep that objective in mind when developing your definition. Suppose you decide to write an essay defining *jazz*. The essay could be purely *informative* and discuss the origins of jazz, its characteristic tonal patterns, and some of the great jazz musicians of the past. Or the essay could move beyond pure information and take on a *persuasive* edge. It might, for example, argue that jazz is the only contemporary form of music worth considering seriously.

Just as your purpose in writing will vary, so will your tone. A strictly informative definition will generally assume a detached, objective tone ("Apathy is an emotional state characterized by listlessness and indifference"). By way of contrast, a definition essay with a persuasive slant might be urgent in tone ("To combat student apathy, we must design programs that engage students in campus life"), or it might take a satiric approach ("An apathetic stance is a wise choice for any thinking student").

As you write, keep thinking about your audience as well. Not only do your readers determine what terms need to be defined (and in how much detail), but they also keep you focused on the essay's purpose and tone. For instance, you probably wouldn't write a serious, informative piece for the college newspaper about the "mystery meat" served in the campus cafeteria. Instead, you would adopt a light tone as you defined the culinary horror and might even make a persuasive pitch about improving the food prepared on campus.

2. Formulate an effective definition. A definition essay sometimes begins with a brief **formal definition**—the dictionary's, a textbook's, or the writer's— and then expands that initial definition with supporting details. Formal definitions are traditionally worded as three-part statements, including (1) the **term,** (2) the **class** to which the term belongs, and (3) the **characteristics** that distinguish the term from other members of its class. Consider these examples of formal definition:

Term	Class	Characteristics
The peregrine falcon,	an endangered bird,	is the world's fastest flyer.
A bodice-ripper	is a paperback book	that deals with highly charged romance in exotic places and faraway times.
Back to basics	is a trend in education	that emphasizes skill mastery through rote learning.

A definition that meets these three guidelines—term, class, and characteristics—will clarify what your subject *is* and what it *is not*. These guidelines also establish the boundaries or scope of your definition. For example, defining *back to basics* as "a trend that emphasizes rote . . . learning" signals a certain boundary; it lets readers know that other educational trends (such as those that emphasize children's social or emotional development) won't be part of the essay's definition.

Because they are formulaic, formal definitions tend to be dull. For this reason, it's best to reserve them for clarifying potentially confusing words—perhaps words with multiple meanings. For example, the term *the West* can refer to the western section of the United States, to the United States and its non-Communist allies (as in the "Western world"), or to the entire Western Hemisphere. Before discussing the West, then, you would need to provide a formal definition that clarifies your use of the term. Highly specialized or technical terms may also require clarification. Few readers are likely to feel confident about their understanding of the term *cognitive dissonance* unless you supply them with a formal definition: "a conflict of thoughts arising when two or more ideas do not go together."

If you decide to include a formal definition in your essay, avoid tired openings like "the dictionary says" or "according to *Webster's*." Such weak starts lack imagination. You should also keep in mind that a strict dictionary definition may actually confuse readers. Suppose you're writing a paper on the way people tend to absorb their ideas and values from the media. Likening this automatic response to the process of osmosis, you decide to open the paper with a dictionary definition. If you write "Osmosis is the tendency of a solvent to disperse through a semipermeable membrane into a more concentrated medium," readers are apt to be baffled. *Remember:* The purpose of a definition is to clarify meaning, not obscure it.

You should also stay clear of ungrammatical "is when" definitions: "Blind ambition is when you want to get ahead, no matter how much other people are hurt." Instead, write "Blind ambition is wanting to get ahead, no matter how much other people are hurt." A final pitfall to avoid in writing formal definitions is **circularity,** saying the same thing twice and therefore defining nothing: "A campus tribunal is a tribunal composed of various members of the university community." Circular definitions like this often repeat the term being defined (*tribunal*) or use words having the same meaning (*campus; university community*). In this case, we learn nothing about what a campus tribunal is; the writer says only that "*X* is *X*."

3. Develop the extended definition.   You can use the patterns of development when formulating an extended definition. Description, narration, process analysis, comparison-contrast, or any of the other patterns discussed in this book may be drawn upon—alone or in combination. Imagine you're planning to write an extended definition of *robotics*. You might develop the term by providing *examples* of the way robots are currently being used in scientific research; by *comparing* and *contrasting* human and robot capabilities; or by *classifying* robots, starting with the most basic and moving to the most advanced or futuristic models. (To deepen your understanding of which patterns to use when developing a particular extended definition, take a moment to review the last item in this chapter's Prewriting Checklist.)

4. Organize the material that develops the definition.   If you use a single pattern to develop the extended definition, apply the principles of organization suited to that pattern, as described in the appropriate chapter of this book. Assume that you're defining *fad* by means of *process analysis*. You might organize your paragraphs according to the steps in the process: a fad's slow start as something avant-garde or eccentric; its wildfire acceptance by the general public; the fad's demise as it becomes familiar or tiresome. If you want to define *character* by means of a single *narration*, you would probably organize paragraphs chronologically. In a definition essay using several methods of development, you should devote separate paragraphs to each pattern. A definition of *relaxation*, for instance, might start with a paragraph that *narrates* a particularly relaxing day; then it might move to a paragraph that presents several *examples* of people who find it difficult to unwind; finally, it might end with a paragraph that explains a *process* for relaxing the mind and body.

5. Write an effective introduction.   It can be helpful to provide—near the beginning of a definition essay—a brief formal definition of the term you're going to develop in the rest of the paper. Beyond this basic element, the introduction might include a number of other features. You may explain the *origin* of the term being defined: "*Acid* rock is a term first coined in the 1960s to describe music that was written or listened to under the influence of the drug LSD." Similarly, you could explain the *etymology*, or linguistic origin, of the key word that focuses the paper: "The term *vigilantism* is derived from a Latin word meaning 'to watch and be awake.'"

You may also use the introduction to clarify what your subject is *not*. Such **definition by negation** can be an effective strategy at a paper's beginning, especially if readers don't share your view of the subject. In such a case, you might write something like this: "The gorilla, far from being the vicious killer of jungle movies and popular imagination, is a sedentary, gentle creature living in a closely knit family group." Such a statement provides the special focus for your essay and signals some of the misconceptions or fallacies soon to be discussed.

In addition, you may include in the introduction a **stipulative definition,** one that puts special restrictions on a term: "Strictly defined, a mall refers to a one- or two-story enclosed building containing a variety of retail shops and at least two large anchor stores. Highway-strip shopping centers or downtown centers cannot be considered true malls." When a term has multiple meanings, or when its meaning has become fuzzy through misuse, a stipulative definition sets the record straight right at the start, so that readers know exactly what is, and is not, being defined.

Finally, the introduction may end with a *plan of development* that indicates how the essay will unfold. A student who returned to school after having raised a family decided to write a paper defining the mid-life crisis that had led to her enrollment in college. After providing a brief formal definition of *mid-life crisis,* the student rounded off her introduction with this sentence: "Such a mid-life crisis often starts with vague misgivings, turns into depression, and ends with a significant change in life-style."

REVISION STRATEGIES

Once you have a draft of the essay, you're ready to revise. The following checklist will help you and those giving you feedback apply to definition some of the revision techniques discussed in Chapters 7 and 8.

✔ DEFINITION: A REVISION/PEER REVIEW CHECKLIST

Revise Overall Meaning and Structure

☐ Is your essay's purpose informative, persuasive, or both?

☐ Is the term being defined clearly distinguished from similar terms?

☐ Where does a circular definition cloud meaning?

☐ Where would a word's historical or linguistic origin clarify meaning? Where would a formal definition, stipulative definition, or definition by negation help?

☐ Where are technical, nonstandard, or ambiguous terms a source of confusion?

☐ Which patterns of development are used to develop the definition? How do these help the essay achieve its purpose?

☐ If the essay uses only one pattern, is the essay's method of organization characteristic of that pattern (step by step for process analysis, chronological for narration, and so on)?

☐ Where could a dry formal definition be deleted without sacrificing overall clarity?

Revise Paragraph Development

☐ If the essay uses several patterns of development, where would separate paragraphs for different patterns be appropriate?

☐ Which paragraphs (or passages) are flat or unconvincing? How could they be made more compelling?

Revise Sentences and Words

☐ Which sentences and words are inconsistent with the essay's tone?

☐ Where should overused phrases like, "the dictionary says" and "according to Webster's" be replaced by more original wording?

☐ Have "is when" definitions been avoided?

STUDENT ESSAY: FROM PREWRITING THROUGH REVISION

The student essay that follows was written by Laura Chen in response to this assignment:

> In "Entropy," K. C. Cole takes a scientific term from physics and gives it a broader definition and a wider application. Choose another specialized term and define it in such a way that you reveal something significant about contemporary life.

Before writing her essay, Laura sat down at a computer and *brainstormed* material on the subject she decided to write about: inertia in everyday life. Later on, when she started shaping this material, she jotted down notes in the margin, starred important ideas, crossed out an item, added other ideas, drew connecting arrows, and used numbers and letters to sequence points. In the process, the essay's underlying structure began to emerge so clearly that an outline seemed unnecessary; Laura felt she could move directly from her brainstormed material to a first draft. Laura's original brainstormed list is reprinted on page 421. The handwritten marks indicate her later efforts to organize the preliminary material.

Now read Laura's paper, "Physics in Everyday Life," noting the similarities and differences between her prewriting and final essay. You'll see, for example, that Laura's decision to discuss national inertia *after* individual inertia makes the essay's sequence of points more emphatic. Similarly, by moving the mention of gravity to the essay's end, Laura creates a satisfying symmetry: The paper now opens and closes with principles of physics. As you read the essay, also consider how well it applies the principles of definition discussed in this chapter. (The commentary that follows the paper will help you look at Laura's essay more closely and will give you some sense of how she went about revising her first draft.)

Brainstorming

Entropy--an imp. term in physics. (Put in _conclusion_? Just like gravity.)

Formal definition
Boulder sitting or rolling
*③ National inertia (save broadest for last)

3b We accept pollution

3a Accept shoddy products

Accept growing homelessness
3c Go ahead with genetic engineering even though uncomfortable
3d Keep producing nuclear arms

3e Watch too much TV, despite all the reports

1c Racial discrimination remains a problem Move to section on the individual

① Individual inertia, too

We resist change

1a Vote the same way all the time

1b Need jolts to change (a perfect teenage daughter becomes pregnant) Add example here

② But on TV--no inertia

2a Soap operas, commercials--everyone changes easily give specifics

2b In real life--wear same hairstyle, use same products, wars and national problems drag on

Physics in Everyday Life
by Laura Chen

1   A boulder sits on a mountainside for a thousand years.   Introduction
The boulder will remain there forever unless an outside

force intervenes. Suppose a force does affect the
boulder--an earthquake, for instance. Once the boulder
begins to thunder down the mountain, it will remain in
motion and head in one direction only--downhill--until
another force interrupts its progress. If the boulder
tumbles into a gorge, it will finally come to rest as
gravity anchors it to the earth once more. In both cases,
Formal definition the boulder is exhibiting the physical principle of
inertia: the tendency of matter to remain at rest or, if
Thesis moving, to keep moving in one direction unless affected
by an outside force. Inertia, an important factor in the
Plan of development world of physics, also plays a crucial role in the human
world. Inertia affects our individual lives as well as
the direction taken by society as a whole.

Topic sentence Inertia often influences our value systems and   2
personal growth. Inertia is at work, for example, when
people cling to certain behaviors and views. Like the
boulder firmly fixed to the mountain, most people are
set in their ways. Without thinking, they vote
Republican or Democratic because they have always voted
that way. They regard with suspicion a couple having no
Start of a series of children, simply because everyone else in the
causes and effects neighborhood has a large family. It is only when an
outside force--a jolt of some sort--occurs that people
change their views. A white American couple may think
little about racial discrimination, for instance, until
they adopt an Asian child and must comfort her when
classmates tease her because she looks different. Parents
may consider promiscuous any unmarried girl who has a
baby until their 17-year-old honors student confesses
that she is pregnant. Personal jolts like these force
people to think, perhaps for the first time, about
issues that now affect them directly.

Topic sentence To illustrate how inertia governs our lives, it is   3
helpful to compare the world of television with real
life. On TV, inertia does not exist. Television shows
Start of a series of and commercials show people making all kinds of drastic
contrasts changes. They switch brands of coffee or try a new hair
color with no hesitation. In one car commercial, an
ambitious young accountant abandons her career with a

flourish and is seen driving off into the sunset as she
heads for a small cabin by the sea to write poetry. In a
soap opera, a character may progress from homemaker to
hooker to nun in a single year. But in real life,
inertia rules. People tend to stay where they are, to
keep their jobs, to be loyal to products. A second major
difference between television and real life is that, on
television, everyone takes prompt and dramatic action to
solve problems. The construction worker with a thudding
headache is pain-free at the end of the sixty-second
commercial; the police catch the murderer within an
hour; the family learns to cope with their son's life-
threatening drug addiction by the time the made-for-TV
movie ends at eleven. But in the real world, inertia
persists, so that few problems are solved neatly or
quickly. Illnesses drag on, few crimes are solved, and
family conflicts last for years. ———————————————— Topic sentence

4   Inertia is, most importantly, a force at work in the
life of our nation. Again, inertia is two-sided. It
keeps us from moving and, once we move, it keeps us
pointed in one direction. We find ourselves mired in a
certain path, accepting the inferior, even the dangerous.
We settle for toys that break, winter coats with no ———————————————— Start of a series
warmth, and rivers clogged with pollution. Inertia also   of examples
compels our nation to keep moving in one direction--
despite the uncomfortable suspicion that it is the wrong
direction. We are not sure if manipulating genes is a
good idea, yet we continue to fund scientific projects
in genetic engineering. More than fifty years ago, we
were shaken when we saw the devastation caused by an
atomic bomb. But we went on to develop weapons hundreds
of times more destructive. Although warned that excessive
television viewing may be harmful, we continue to watch
hours of television each day.

5   We have learned to defy gravity, one of the basic   Conclusion
laws of physics; we fly high above the earth, even float
in outer space. But most of us have not learned to defy
inertia. Those special individuals who are able to act
when everyone else seems paralyzed are rare. But the
fact that such people do exist means that *inertia* is not

```
all-powerful. If we use our reasoning ability and our
creativity, we can conquer inertia, just as we have
conquered gravity.
```

Commentary

Introduction

As the title of her essay suggests, Laura has taken a scientific term (*inertia*) from a specialized field and drawn on the term to help explain some everyday phenomena. Using the *simple-to-complex* approach to structure the introduction, she opens with a vivid *descriptive* example of inertia. This description is then followed by a *formal definition* of inertia: "the tendency of matter to remain at rest or, if moving, to keep moving in one direction unless affected by an outside force." Laura wisely begins the paper with the easy-to-understand description rather than with the more-difficult-to-grasp scientific definition. Had the order been reversed, the essay would not have gotten off to nearly as effective a start. She then ends her introductory paragraph with a *thesis*, "Inertia, an important factor in the world of physics, also plays a crucial role in the human world," and with a *plan of development*, "Inertia affects our individual lives as well as the direction taken by society as a whole."

Organization

To support her definition of inertia and her belief that it can rule our lives, Laura generates a number of compelling examples. She organizes these examples by grouping them into three major points, each point signaled by a *topic sentence* that opens each of the essay's three supporting paragraphs (2–4).

A definite organizational strategy determines the sequence of Laura's three central points. The essay moves from the way inertia affects the individual to the way it affects the nation. The phrase "most importantly" at the beginning of the fourth paragraph indicates that Laura has arranged her points emphatically, believing that inertia's impact on society is most critical.

A Problem with Organization and a Weak Example

When reading the fourth paragraph, you might have noticed that Laura's examples aren't sequenced as effectively as they could be. To show that we, as a nation, tend to keep moving in the same direction, Laura discusses our ongoing uneasiness about genetic engineering, nuclear arms, and excessive television viewing. The point about nuclear weapons is most significant, yet it gets lost in the middle. The paragraph would be stronger if it ended with the point about nuclear arms. Moreover, the example about excessive television viewing doesn't belong in this paragraph since, at best, it has limited bearing on the issue being discussed.

Other Patterns of Development

In addition to using numerous *examples* to illustrate her points, Laura draws on several other patterns of development to show that inertia can be a powerful force. In the second and fourth paragraphs, she uses *causal analysis* to explain how inertia can paralyze people and nations. The second paragraph indicates that only "an outside force—a jolt of some sort—" can motivate inert people to change. To support this view, Laura provides two examples of parents who experience such jolts. Similarly, in the fourth paragraph, she contends that inertia causes the persistence of specific national problems: shoddy consumer goods and environmental pollution.

Another pattern, *comparison-contrast*, is used in the third paragraph to highlight the differences between television and real life: on television, people zoom into action, but in everyday life, people tend to stay put and muddle through. The essay also contains a distinct element of *argumentation-persuasion* since Laura clearly wants readers to accept her definition of inertia and her view that it often governs human behavior.

Conclusion

Laura's *conclusion* rounds off the essay nicely and brings it to a satisfying close. Laura refers to another law of physics, one with which we are all familiar—gravity. By creating an *analogy* between gravity and inertia, she suggests that our ability to defy gravity should encourage us to defy inertia. The analogy enlarges the scope of the essay; it allows Laura to reach out to her readers by challenging them to action. Such a challenge is, of course, appropriate in a definition essay having a persuasive bent.

Revising the First Draft

When it was time to rework her essay, Laura began by reading her paper out loud. Then, referring to the revision checklist on pages 419–420, she noted in the margin of her draft the problems she detected, numbering them in order of importance. After reviewing her notes, she started to revise in earnest, paying special attention to her third paragraph. The first draft of that paragraph, together with her annotations, is reprinted here:

Original Version of the Third Paragraph

The ordinary actions of daily life are, in part, determined by inertia. To understand this, it is helpful to compare the world of television with real life, for, in the TV-land of ads and entertainment, inertia does not exist. For example, on television, people are often shown making all kinds of drastic changes. They switch brands of coffee or try a new hair color with no hesitation. In one car commercial, <u>a young accountant leaves her career</u> and sets off for a cabin by the sea to write poetry. In a soap opera, a character may progress from homemaker to hooker to nun in a single year. In contrast, inertia rules in real life. People tend to stay where they are, to keep their jobs, to be loyal to products (wives get annoyed if a husband brings home the wrong brand or color

① Paragraph rambles
④ First two sentences awkward

⑦ Make more specific

③ Delete part about annoyed wives and hairstyles

⑤ Trite—replace

⑥ Point about life-
   style not clear

② Last two sentences
   don't belong

of bathroom tissue from the market). Middle-aged people
wear the hairstyles or makeup that suited them in high
school. A second major difference between television and
real life is that, on TV, everyone takes prompt and
dramatic action to solve problems. (A woman finds the
solution to dull clothes) at the end of a commercial; the
police catch the murderer within an hour; the family
learns to cope with a son's disturbing life-style by the
time the movie is over. In contrast, the law of real-life
inertia means that few problems are solved neatly or
quickly. Things, once started, tend to stay as they are.
Few crimes are actually solved. Medical problems are not
easily diagnosed. Messy wars in foreign countries seem
endless. National problems are identified, but Congress
does not pass legislation to solve them.

   After rereading her draft, Laura realized that her third paragraph rambled. To
give it more focus, she removed the last two sentences ("Messy wars in foreign
countries seem endless" and "National problems are identified, but Congress
does not pass legislation. . . .") because they referred to national affairs but were
located in a section focusing on the individual. Further, she eliminated two flat,
unconvincing examples: wives who get annoyed when their husbands bring
home the wrong brand of bathroom tissue and middle-aged people whose hairstyles and makeup are outdated. Condensing the two disjointed sentences that
originally opened the paragraph also helped tighten this section of the essay. Note
how much crisper the revised sentences are: "To illustrate how inertia governs our
lives, it is helpful to compare the world of television with real life. On TV, inertia
does not exist."

   Laura also worked to make the details and the language in the paragraph more
specific and vigorous. The vague sentence "A woman finds the solution to dull
clothes at the end of the commercial" is replaced by the more dramatic "The construction worker with a thudding headache is pain-free at the end of the sixty-
second commercial." Similarly, Laura changed a "son's disturbing life-style" to a
"son's life-threatening drug addiction"; "by the time the movie is over" became "by
the time the made-for-TV movie ends at eleven"; and "a young accountant leaves
her career and sets off for a cabin by the sea to write poetry" was changed to "an
ambitious young accountant abandons her career with a flourish and is seen driving
off into the sunset as she heads for a small cabin by the sea to write poetry."

   After making these changes, Laura decided to round off the paragraph with a
powerful summary statement highlighting how real life differs from television:
"Illnesses drag on, few crimes are solved, and family conflicts last for years."

   These third-paragraph revisions are similar to those that Laura made elsewhere
in her first draft. Her astute changes enabled her to turn an already effective paper
into an especially thoughtful analysis of human behavior.

Prewriting Activities

1. Imagine you're writing two essays: One explains an effective strategy for registering a complaint; the other contrasts the styles of two stand-up comics. Jot down ways you might use definition in each essay.

2. Use the prewriting questions for the patterns of development on pages 415–416 to generate material for an extended definition of *one* of the terms that follow. Then answer these questions about your prewriting material: What thesis does the prewriting suggest? Which pattern(s) yielded the most supporting material? In what order would you present this support when writing an essay?

   a. popularity
   b. cruelty
   c. "dork"
   d. self-esteem
   e. "wimp"
   f. loneliness

3. Select a term whose meaning varies from person to person or one for which you have a personal definition. Some possibilities include:

success	femininity	a liberal
patriotism	affirmative action	a housewife
individuality	pornography	intelligence

   Brainstorm with others to identify variations in the term's meaning. Then examine your prewriting material. What thesis comes to mind? If you were writing an essay, would your purpose be informative, persuasive, or both? Finally, prepare a scratch list of the points you might cover.

Revising Activities

4. Explain why each of the following is an effective or ineffective definition. Rewrite those you consider ineffective.

   a. *Passive aggression* is when people show their aggression passively.
   b. A *terrorist* tries to terrorize people.

    c. Being *assertive* means knowing how to express your wishes and goals in a positive, noncombative way.

    d. *Pop music* refers to music that is popular.

    e. *Loyalty* is when someone stays by another person during difficult times.

5. The following introductory paragraph is from the first draft of an essay contrasting walking and running as techniques for reducing tension. Although intended to be a definition paragraph, it actually doesn't tell us anything we don't already know. It also relies on the old-hat *"Webster's* says." Rewrite the paragraph so it is more imaginative. You might use a series of anecdotes or one extended example to define *tension* and introduce the essay's thesis more gracefully.

> According to <u>Webster's</u>, <u>tension</u> is "mental or nervous strain, often accompanied by muscular tightness or tautness." Everyone feels tense at one time or another. It may occur when there's a deadline to meet. Or it could be caused by the stress of trying to fulfill academic, athletic, or social goals. Sometimes it comes from criticism by family, bosses, or teachers. Such tension puts wear and tear on our bodies and on our emotional well-being. Although some people run to relieve tension, research has found that walking is a more effective tension reducer.

PROFESSIONAL SELECTIONS: DEFINITION

K. C. COLE

K. C. Cole (1946–   ) has contributed articles on science to numerous national publications and has written a regular column for *Discovery* magazine. Her essays are collected in *Sympathetic Vibrations: Reflections on Physics as a Way of Life* (1985). She has written several books, including *Facets of Light: Color Images and Things That Glow in the Dark* (1980), *Order in the Universe: The Shape of Relative Motion* (1986), *The Universe and the Teacup* (1998), and *The Hole in the Universe* (2000). The selection that follows first appeared as a "Hers" column in *The New York Times* (1982).

Pre-Reading Journal Entry

Do you consider yourself an orderly or a disorderly person? What about those around you? What are the benefits and the drawbacks of being orderly? Of being disorderly? Use your journal to reflect on these questions.

ENTROPY

1   It was about two months ago when I realized that entropy was getting the better of me. On the same day my car broke down (again), my refrigerator conked out and I learned that I needed root-canal work in my right rear tooth. The windows in the bedroom were still leaking every time it rained and my son's baby sitter was still failing to show up every time I really needed her. My hair was turning gray and my typewriter was wearing out. The house needed paint and I needed glasses. My son's sneakers were developing holes and I was developing a deep sense of futility.

2   After all, what was the point of spending half of Saturday at the Laundromat if the clothes were dirty all over again the following Friday?

3   Disorder, alas, is the natural order of things in the universe. There is even a precise measure of the amount of disorder, called entropy. Unlike almost every other physical property (motion, gravity, energy), entropy does not work both ways. It can only increase. Once it's created it can never be destroyed. The road to disorder is a one-way street.

4   Because of its unnerving irreversibility, entropy has been called the arrow of time. We all understand this instinctively. Children's rooms, left on their own, tend to get messy, not neat. Wood rots, metal rusts, people wrinkle and flowers wither. Even mountains wear down; even the nuclei of atoms decay. In the city we see entropy in the rundown subways and worn-out sidewalks and torn-down buildings, in the increasing disorder of our lives. We know, without asking, what is old. If we were suddenly to see the paint jump back on an old building, we would know that something was wrong. If we saw an egg unscramble itself and jump back into its shell, we would laugh in the same way we laugh at a movie run backward.

5   Entropy is no laughing matter, however, because with every increase in entropy energy is wasted and opportunity is lost. Water flowing down a mountainside can be made to do some useful work on its way. But once all the water is at the same level it can work no more. That is entropy. When my refrigerator was working, it kept all the cold air ordered in one part of the kitchen and warmer air in another. Once it broke down the warm and cold mixed into a lukewarm mess that allowed my butter to melt, my milk to rot and my frozen vegetables to decay.

6   Of course the energy is not really lost, but it has defused and dissipated into a chaotic caldron of randomness that can do us no possible good. Entropy is chaos. It is loss of purpose.

7   People are often upset by the entropy they seem to see in the haphazardness of their own lives. Buffeted about like so many molecules in my tepid kitchen, they feel that they have lost their sense of direction, that they are wasting youth and opportunity at every turn. It is easy to see entropy in marriages, when the partners are too preoccupied to patch small things up, almost guaranteeing that they will fall apart. There is much entropy in the state of our country, in the relationships between

nations—lost opportunities to stop the avalanche of disorders that seems ready to swallow us all.

Entropy is not inevitable everywhere, however. Crystals and snowflakes and galax- 8
ies are islands of incredibly ordered beauty in the midst of random events. If it was not for exceptions to entropy, the sky would be black and we would be able to see where the stars spend their days; it is only because air molecules in the atmosphere cluster in ordered groups that the sky is blue.

The most profound exception to entropy is the creation of life. A seed soaks up some 9
soil and some carbon and some sunshine and some water and arranges it into a rose. A seed in the womb takes some oxygen and pizza and milk and transforms it into a baby.

The catch is that it takes a lot of energy to produce a baby. It also takes energy to 10
make a tree. The road to disorder is all downhill but the road to creation takes work. Though combating entropy is possible, it also has its price. That's why it seems so hard to get ourselves together, so easy to let ourselves fall apart.

Worse, creating order in one corner of the universe always creates more disorder 11
somewhere else. We create ordered energy from oil and coal at the price of the entropy of smog.

I recently took up playing the flute again after an absence of several months. As the 12
uneven vibrations screeched through the house, my son covered his ears and said, "Mom, what's wrong with your flute?" Nothing was wrong with my flute, of course. It was my ability to play it that had atrophied, or entropied, as the case may be. The only way to stop that process was to practice every day, and sure enough my tone improved, though only at the price of constant work. Like anything else, abilities deteriorate when we stop applying our energies to them.

That's why entropy is depressing. It seems as if just breaking even is an uphill fight. 13
There's a good reason that this should be so. The mechanics of entropy are a matter of chance. Take any ice-cold air molecule milling around my kitchen. The chances that it will wander in the direction of my refrigerator at any point are exactly 50-50. The chances that it will wander away from my refrigerator are also 50-50. But take billions of warm and cold molecules mixed together, and the chances that all the cold ones will wander toward the refrigerator and all the warm ones will wander away from it are virtually nil.

Entropy wins not because order is impossible but because there are always so many 14
more paths toward disorder than toward order. There are so many more different ways to do a sloppy job than a good one, so many more ways to make a mess than to clean it up. The obstacles and accidents in our lives almost guarantee that constant collisions will bounce us on to random paths, get us off the track. Disorder is the path of least resistance, the easy but not the inevitable road.

Like so many others, I am distressed by the entropy I see around me today. I am 15
afraid of the randomness of international events, of the lack of common purpose in the world; I am terrified that it will lead into the ultimate entropy of nuclear war. I am upset that I could not in the city where I live send my child to a public school; that people are unemployed and inflation is out of control; that tensions between sexes and races seem to be increasing again; that relationships everywhere seem to be falling apart.

Social institutions—like atoms and stars—decay if energy is not added to keep them 16
ordered. Friendships and families and economies all fall apart unless we constantly make an effort to keep them working and well oiled. And far too few people, it seems to me, are willing to contribute consistently to those efforts.

Of course, the more complex things are, the harder it is. If there were only a dozen 17
or so air molecules in my kitchen, it would be likely—if I waited a year or so—that at

some point the six coldest ones would congregate inside the freezer. But the more factors in the equation—the more players in the game—the less likely it is that their paths will coincide in an orderly way. The more pieces in the puzzle, the harder it is to put back together once order is disturbed. "Irreversibility," said a physicist, "is the price we pay for complexity."

Questions for Close Reading

1. What is the selection's thesis? Locate the sentence(s) in which Cole states her main idea. If she doesn't state the thesis explicitly, express it in your own words.

2. How does entropy differ from the other properties of the physical world? Is the image "the arrow of time" helpful in establishing this difference?

3. Why is the creation of life an exception to entropy? What is the relationship between entropy and energy?

4. Why does Cole say that entropy "is no laughing matter"? What is so depressing about the entropy she describes?

5. Refer to your dictionary as needed to define the following words used in the selection: *futility* (paragraph 1), *dissipated* (6), *buffeted* (7), *tepid* (7), and *atrophied* (12).

Questions About the Writer's Craft

1. **The pattern.** What is Cole's underlying purpose in defining the scientific term *entropy*? What gives the essay its persuasive edge?

2. What tone does Cole adopt to make reading about a scientific concept more interesting? Identify places in the essay where her tone is especially prominent.

3. Cole uses such words as *futility, loss,* and *depressing.* How do these words affect you? Why do you suppose she chose such terms? Find similar words in the essay.

4. **Other patterns.** Many of Cole's sentences follow a two-part pattern involving a contrast: "The road to disorder is all downhill but the road to creation takes work" (paragraph 10). Find other examples of this pattern in the essay. Why do you think Cole uses it so often?

Writing Assignments Using Definition as a Pattern of Development

1. Define *order* or *disorder* by applying the term to a system that you know well— for example, your school, dorm, family, or workplace. Develop your definition through any combination of writing patterns: by supplying examples, by showing contrasts, by analyzing the process underlying the system, and so on.

2. Choose, as Cole does, a technical term that you think will be unfamiliar to most readers. In a humorous or serious paper, define the term as it is used technically; then show how the term can shed light on some aspect of your life. For example, the concept in astronomy of a *supernova* could be used to explain your sudden emergence as a new star on the athletic field, in your schoolwork, or on the social scene. Here are a few suggested terms:

symbiosis	volatility	resonance
velocity	erosion	catalyst
neutralization	equilibrium	malleability

Writing Assignments Using Other Patterns of Development

∞ 3. Can one person make much difference in the amount of entropy—disorder and chaos—in the world? Share your view in an essay. Use examples of people who have tried to overcome the tendency of things to "fall apart." Make clear whether you think these people succeeded or failed in their attempts. To inform your perspective before writing, read James Gleick's "Life As Type A" (page 433), an evaluation of the factors that influence people's compulsion for order.

∞ 4. Cole claims that our lives contain a distressing amount of "haphazardness" (paragraph 7). Write an essay arguing that people either do or do not control their own fates. Support your point with a series of specific examples. For one author's reflections on life's unpredictability, read Beth Johnson's "Bombs Bursting in Air" (page 245).

Writing Assignment Using a Journal Entry as a Starting Point

5. Write an essay arguing that disorder can be liberating *or* that it can be stifling. Review your pre-reading journal entry, and select strong, compelling examples that support your position. Aim to refute as many opposing arguments as possible. Your essay may have a serious or a humorous tone.

JAMES GLEICK

After graduating from Harvard College in 1976, James Gleick helped found *Metropolis,* an alternative newspaper in Minneapolis. He then spent ten years as a reporter and editor with *The New York Times,* where he wrote a column about the impact of science and technology on modern life. His earlier books, *Chaos: Making a New Science* (1987) and *Genius: The Life and Science of Richard Feynman* (1992), were both finalists for the National Book Award and Pulitzer Prize. Formerly McGraw Distinguished Lecturer at Princeton University, Gleick lives with his wife, writer Cynthia Crossen, in New York. The following piece is taken from Gleick's most recent book, *Faster: The Acceleration of Just About Everything* (1999).

Pre-Reading Journal Entry

Like many people, you may feel harried and under pressure at least some of the time. Use your journal to reflect on the sources of stress in your everyday life. List several examples. For each, consider the factors leading to this frenzied feeling.

LIFE AS TYPE A

1   Everyone knows about Type A. This magnificently bland coinage, put forward by a pair of California cardiologists in 1959, struck a collective nerve and entered the language. It is a token of our confusion: are we victims or perpetrators of the crime of haste? Are we living at high speed with athleticism and vigor, or are we stricken by hurry sickness?

2   The cardiologists, Meyer Friedman and Ray Rosenman, listed a set of personality traits which, they claimed, tend to go hand in hand with one another and also with heart disease. They described these traits rather unappealingly, as characteristics about and around the theme of impatience. Excessive competitiveness. Aggressiveness. "A harrying sense of time urgency." The Type A idea emerged in technical papers and then formed the basis of a popular book and made its way into dictionaries. The canonical Type A, as these doctors portrayed him, was "Paul":

> A very disproportionate amount of his emotional energy is consumed in struggling against the normal constraints of time. "How can I move faster, and do more and more things in less and less time?" is the question that never ceases to torment him.
>
> Paul hurries his thinking, his speech and his movements. He also strives to hurry the thinking, speech, and movements of those about him; they must communicate rapidly and relevantly if they wish to avoid creating impatience in him. Planes must arrive and depart precisely on time for Paul, cars ahead of him on the highway must maintain a speed he approves of, and there must never be a queue of persons standing between him and a bank clerk, a restaurant table, or the interior of a theater. In fact, he is infuriated whenever people talk slowly or circuitously, when planes are late, cars dawdle on the highway, and queues form.

Let's think. . . Do we know anyone like "Paul"?

3   This was the first clear declaration of *hurry sickness*—another coinage of Friedman's. It inspired new businesses: mind-body workshops; videotapes demonstrating deep breathing; anxiety-management retreats; seminars on and even institutes of stress medicine. "I drove all the way in the right-hand lane," a Pacific Gas and Electric Company executive said proudly one morning in 1987 to a group of self-confessed hurriers, led by Friedman himself, by then seventy-six years old. In the battle against Type A jitters, patients tried anything and everything—the slow lane,

yoga, meditation, visualization: "Direct your attention to your feet on the floor. . . . Be aware of the air going in your nostrils cool and going out warm. . . . Visualize a place you like to be. . . . Experience it and see the objects there, the forms and shadows. Take another deep breath and experience the sounds, the surf, the wind, leaves, a babbling brook." Some hospital television systems now feature a "relaxation channel," with hour after hour of surf, wind, leaves, and babbling brooks.

We believe in Type A—a triumph for a notion with no particular scientific validity. The Friedman-Rosenman claim has turned out to be both obvious and false. Clearly some heart ailments do result from, or at least go along with, stress (itself an ill-defined term), both chronic and acute. Behavior surely affects physiology, at least once in a while. Sudden dashes for the train, laptop computer in one hand and takeout coffee in the other, can accelerate heartbeats and raise blood pressure. That haste makes coronaries was already a kind of folk wisdom—that is, standard medical knowledge untainted by research. "Hurry has a clearly debilitating effect upon the tissues and may in time injure the heart," admonished Dr. Cecil Webb-Johnson in *Nerve Troubles,* an English monograph of the early 1900s. "The great men of the centuries past were never in a hurry," he added sanctimoniously, "and that is why the world will never forget them in a hurry." It might be natural—even appealing—to expect certain less-great people to receive their cardiovascular comeuppance. But in reality, three decades of attention from cardiologists and psychologists have failed to produce any carefully specified and measurable set of character traits that predict heart disease—or to demonstrate that people who change their Type A behavior will actually lower their risk of heart disease.

Indeed, the study that started it all—Friedman and Rosenman's "Association of Specific Overt Behavior Pattern with Blood and Cardiovascular Findings"—appears to have been a wildly flawed piece of research. It used a small sample—eighty-three people (all men) in what was then called "Group A." The selection process was neither random nor blind. White-collar male employees of large businesses were rounded up by acquaintances of Friedman and Rosenman on a subjective basis—they fit the type. The doctors further sorted the subjects by interviewing them personally and observing their appearance and behavior. Did a man gesture rapidly, clench his teeth, or exhibit a "general air of impatience"? If so, he was chosen. It seems never to have occurred to these experienced cardiologists that they might have been consciously or unconsciously selecting people whose physique indicated excess weight or other markers for incipient heart disease. The doctors' own data show that the final Group A drank more, smoked more, and weighed more than Group B. But the authors dismissed these factors, asserting, astonishingly, that there was no association between heart disease and cigarette smoking.

In the years since, researchers have never settled on a reliable method for identifying Type A people, though not for want of trying. Humans are not reliable witnesses to their own impatience. Researchers have employed questionnaires like the Jenkins Activity Survey, and they have used catalogues of grimaces and frowns—Ekman and Friesen's Facial Action Coding System, for example, or the Cook-Medley Hostility Inventory. In the end, nothing conclusive emerges. Some studies have found Type A people to have *lower* blood pressure. The sedentary and obese have cardiac difficulties of their own.

The notion of Type A has expanded, shifted, and flexed to suit the varying needs of different researchers. V.A. Price adds *hypervigilance* to the list of traits. Some doctors lose patience with the inconclusive results and shift their focus to anger and hostility—mere subsets of the original Type A grab-bag. Cynthia Perry finds that Type A people have fewer daydreams. How does she know? She asks them to monitor lines flashing across a computer screen for forty painfully boring minutes and finds that, when interrupted by a beep (1000 hertz at 53 decibels), they are less likely to press a black button to confess that irrelevant thoughts had strayed into their minds. Studies have labeled as Type A not only children (those with a tendency to interrupt and to play competitively at games) but even babies (those who cry more). Meanwhile, researchers interested in pets link the Type A personality to petlessness; a National Institutes of Health panel reports: "The description of a 'coronary-prone behavior pattern,' or Type A behavior, and its link to the probability of developing overt disease provided hope that, with careful training, individuals could exercise additional control over somatic illness by altering their lifestyle. . . . Relaxation, meditation, and stress management have become recognized therapies. . . . It therefore seems reasonable that pets, who provide faithful companionship to many people, also might promote greater psychosocial stability for their owners, and thus a measure of protection from heart disease." This is sweet, but it is not science.

8   Typically a Type A study will begin with researchers who assume that there are some correlations to be found, look for a wide variety of associations, fail to find some and succeed in finding others. For example, a few dozen preschool children are sorted according to their game-playing styles and tested for blood pressure. No correlation is found. Later, however, when performing a certain "memory game," the supposed Type A children rank somewhat higher in, specifically, systolic pressure. Interesting? The authors of various published papers evidently think so, but they are wrong, because if their technique is to keep looking until they find some correlation, somewhere, they are bound to succeed. Such results are meaningless.

9   The categorizations are too variable and the prophecies too self-fulfilling. It is never quite clear which traits *define* Type A and which are fellow travelers. The "free-floating, but well-rationalized form of hostility"? The "deep-seated insecurity"? "Their restlessness, their tense facial muscles, their tics, or their strident-staccato manner of speaking"? If you are hard-driving yet friendly, chafing yet self-assured—if you race for the airport gate and then settle *happily* into your seat—are you Type A or not? If you are driven to walk briskly, briskly, all the time, isn't that good for your heart?

10   Most forget that there is also supposed to be a Type B, defined not by the personality traits its members possess but by the traits they lack. Type B people are the shadowy opposites of Type A people. They are those who are not so very Type A. They do *not* wear out their fingers punching that elevator button. They do *not* allow a slow car in the fast lane to drive their hearts to fatal distraction; in fact, they are at the wheel of that slow car. Type B played no real part in that mass societal gasp of recognition in the 1970's. Type B-ness was just a foil. Doctors Friedman and Rosenman actually claimed to have had trouble finding eighty men in all San Francisco who were not under any time pressure. They finally came up with a few, they wrote solemnly, "in the municipal clerks' and the embalmers' unions."

11   Even more bizarrely, that first Friedman-Rosenman study also included a Group C, comprising forty-six unemployed blind men. Not much haste in Group C. "The primary reason men of Group C exhibited little ambition, drive, or desire to compete," the doctors wrote, "was the presence of total blindness for ten or more years and the

lack of occupational deadlines because none was gainfully employed." No wonder they omitted Type C from the subsequent publicity.

If the Type A phenomenon made for poor medical research, it stands nonetheless   12 as a triumph of social criticism. Some of us yield more willingly to impatience than others, but on the whole Type A is who we are—not just the coronary-prone among us, but all of us, as a society and as an age. No wonder the concept has proven too rich a cultural totem to be dismissed.

Questions for Close Reading

1. What is the selection's thesis? Locate the sentence(s) in which Gleick states his main idea. If he doesn't state the thesis explicitly, express it in your own words.

2. What is Gleick's opinion of the study Friedman and Rosenman conducted? List at least two elements of the study that Gleick uses to support his assessment.

3. In paragraph 7, Gleick observes that the concept of Type A has changed since Friedman and Rosenman's study first chronicled it. How has it changed? What accounts for this change?

4. According to Gleick, how do Friedman and Rosenman define the Type B personality? Why does Gleick find fault with their definition of this personality type?

5. Refer to your dictionary as needed to define the following words used in the selection: *coinage* (paragraph 1), *harrying* (2), *canonical* (2), *circuitously* (2), *sanctimoniously* (4), *overt* (5), *incipient* (5), *sedentary* (6), *hypervigilance* (7), *correlations* (8), *strident* (9), *staccato* (9), *foil* (10), and *totem* (12).

Questions About the Writer's Craft

1. **The pattern.** In their work, Friedman and Rosenman use a description of Paul to define "canonical Type A" behavior (paragraph 2). Why do you suppose that Gleick, who criticizes Friedman and Rosenman's research, quotes their portrait of Paul at such length?

2. **The pattern.** Gleick uses a sequence of three fragments when discussing (in paragraph 2) how Type A has been defined. Identify these fragments. What effect do you think Gleick wanted the fragments to have?

3. Locate places where Gleick uses the first-person pronouns *we, us,* and *our.* What do you think Gleick's purpose is in using these pronouns?

4. In paragraph 1, Gleick sarcastically refers to the phrase *Type A* as "magnificently bland." Find other places in the essay where he uses sarcasm. Why might he have chosen to employ such language?

Writing Assignments Using Definition
as a Pattern of Development

1. Write an essay offering a fuller definition of the Type B personality than Gleick's essay provides. Rather than defining Type B through negation, as Friedman and Rosenman do, marshal convincing evidence that illustrates the validity of the Type B phenomenon. Brainstorming with friends, family, and classmates will help you generate strong examples of this personality type. At some point in the essay, you might offer a brief personality sketch of the "canonical" Type B as well as discuss the factors that shape the Type B personality as you define it. You might find that K. C. Cole's "Entropy" (page 428) offers some useful insights into why people might be better off as Type B.

2. Gleick notes that, like *Type A, stress* is an ill-defined term. Brainstorm with others to identify as many examples of different kinds of stress as you can. Review the brainstormed material, and select a specific type of stress to focus on. Then write an essay providing a *clear* definition of that particular stress. Possibilities include "dating stress," "workplace stress," "online stress," "fitness stress." Near the end of the essay, you might provide concise hints for managing the stress you define. Your essay may have a humorous or a serious tone—whichever seems appropriate to your subject.

Writing Assignments Using Other
Patterns of Development

3. Write an essay contrasting situations in which being Type A would be beneficial with situations in which it would be counterproductive. Under what circumstances would Type A characteristics be desirable? Under what circumstances would they be undesirable? Drawing upon your own experiences and observations, reach some conclusions about the advantages and/or limitations of the Type A personality. Before writing, consider reading K. C. Cole's "Entropy" (page 428), a commentary on the difficulty of controlling life's disorder.

4. Gleick observes that "hurry sickness" is a trait induced by society at large. Identify a trait of yours that you think is also a reflection of the society in which you live. You might discuss your tendency to be aggressive or non-assertive, materialistic or idealistic, studious or fun-loving. Write an essay illustrating this character trait at work in your everyday behavior. Explain whether you think this trait works to your advantage or disadvantage.

Writing Assignment Using a Journal Entry
as a Starting Point

5. Gleick claims that the Type A phenomenon is pervasive in our society. Write an essay of your own illustrating the extent to which your life reflects this

phenomenon. Draw upon the most dramatic examples in your pre-reading journal entry. At the end of the essay, describe steps that you or anyone with similar pressures could take to slow down the frenetic pace of everyday life. Gathering information in the library and/or on the Internet might be helpful when you develop the final section of your paper.

JOHN LEO

Syndicated columnist John Leo (1935–   ) writes a controversial, widely read column in *U.S. News & World Report.* A former writer for *The New York Times* and *Time* magazine, Leo also began the "Press Clips" column of media criticism for *The Village Voice.* He is the author of *How the Russians Invented Baseball and Other Essays of Enlightenment* (1989) and two collections of columns, *Two Steps Ahead of the Thought Police* (1994) and *Incorrect Thoughts: Notes on Our Wayward Culture* (2000). "Absolutophobia" (originally titled "A No-Fault Holocaust") first appeared in *U.S. News* in July 1997.

Pre-Reading Journal Entry

One lively argument in the current debate over education is whether schools should be required to provide "character education"—the instruction of students in proper values and morals (as well as traditional academics). Do you think schools should become more responsible for providing students with ethical instruction? Use your journal to freewrite about the pros and cons of including "character education" in the classroom.

ABSOLUTOPHOBIA

In 20 years of college teaching, Prof. Robert Simon has never met a student who   1
denied that the Holocaust happened. What he sees quite often, though, is worse: students who acknowledge the fact of the Holocaust but can't bring themselves to say that killing millions of people is wrong. Simon reports that 10 to 20 percent of his students think this way. Usually they deplore what the Nazis did, but their disapproval is expressed as a matter of taste or personal preference, not moral judgment. "Of course I dislike the Nazis," one student told Simon, "but who is to say they are morally wrong?"

Overdosing on nonjudgmentalism is a growing problem in the schools. Two dis-   2
turbing articles in the *Chronicle of Higher Education* say that some students are unwilling to oppose large moral horrors, including human sacrifice, ethnic cleansing, and slavery, because they think that no one has the right to criticize the moral views of another group or culture.

One of the articles is by Simon, who teaches philosophy at Hamilton College in   3
Clinton, N.Y. The other is by Kay Haugaard, a freelance writer who teaches creative writing at Pasadena City College in California. Haugaard writes that her current students have a lot of trouble expressing any moral reservations or objections about human sacrifice. The subject came up when she taught her class Shirley Jackson's "The

Lottery," a short story about a small American farm town where one person is killed each year to make the crops grow. In the tale, a woman is ritually stoned to death by her husband, her 12-year-old daughter, and her 4-year-old son.

4   Haugaard has been teaching since 1970. Until recently, she says, "Jackson's message about blind conformity always spoke to my students' sense of right and wrong." No longer, apparently. A class discussion of human sacrifice yielded no moral comments, even under Haugaard's persistent questioning. One male said the ritual killing in "The Lottery" "almost seems a need." Asked if she believed in human sacrifice, a woman said, "I really don't know. If it was a religion of long standing. . . ." Haugaard writes: "I was stunned. This was the woman who wrote so passionately of saving the whales, of concern for the rain forests, of her rescue and tender care of a stray dog."

5   **The Aztecs did it.** Both writers believe multiculturalism has played a role in spreading the vapors of nonjudgmentalism. Haugaard quotes a woman in her class, a "50-something red-headed nurse," who says, "I teach a course for our hospital personnel in multicultural understanding, and if it is part of a person's culture, we are taught not to judge. . . ." Simon says we should "welcome diversity rather than fear it" but says his students often think they are so locked into their own group perspectives of ethnicity, race, and gender that moral judgment is impossible, even in the face of great evils.

6   In the new multicultural canon, human sacrifice is hard to condemn, because the Aztecs practiced it. In fact, however, this nonjudgmental stance is not held consistently. Japanese whaling and the genital cutting of girls in Africa are criticized all the time by white multiculturalists. Christina Hoff Sommers, author and professor of philosophy at Clark University in Massachusetts, says that students who can't bring themselves to condemn the Holocaust will often say flatly that treating humans as superior to dogs and rodents is immoral. Moral shrugging may be on the rise, but old-fashioned and rigorous moral criticism is alive and well on certain selected issues: smoking, environmentalism, women's rights, animal rights.

7   Sommers points beyond multiculturalism to a general problem of so many students coming to college "dogmatically committed to a moral relativism that offers them no grounds to think" about cheating, stealing, and other moral issues. Simon calls this "absolutophobia"—the unwillingness to say that some behavior is just plain wrong. Many trends feed this fashionable phobia. Postmodern theory on campuses denies the existence of any objective truth: All we can have are clashing perspectives, not true moral knowledge. The pop-therapeutic culture has pushed nonjudgmentalism very hard. Intellectual laziness and the simple fear of unpleasantness are also factors. By saying that one opinion or moral stance is as good as another, we can draw attention to our own tolerance, avoid antagonizing others, and get on with our careers.

8   The "values clarification" programs in the schools surely should come in for some lumps, too. Based on the principle that teachers should not indoctrinate other people's children, they leave the creation of values up to each student. Values emerge as personal preferences, equally as unsuited for criticism or argument as personal decisions on pop music or clothes.

9   But the wheel is turning now, and "values clarification" is giving way to "character education," and the paralyzing fear of indoctrinating children is gradually fading. The search is on for a teachable consensus rooted in simple decency and respect. As a spur to shaping it, we might discuss a culture so morally confused that students are showing up at colleges reluctant to say anything negative about mass slaughter.

Questions for Close Reading

1. What is the selection's thesis? Locate the sentence(s) in which Leo states his main idea. If he doesn't state the thesis explicitly, express it in your own words.

2. Leo discusses Kay Haugaard's experience in teaching Shirley Jackson's "The Lottery." Why are both Leo and Haugaard troubled by students' responses to this short story?

3. According to Leo, how does multiculturalism spread "the vapors of nonjudgmentalism" (5)?

4. According to Leo, what current trends encourage "absolutophobia"?

5. Refer to your dictionary as needed to define the following words used in the selection: *conformity* (paragraph 4), *perspective* (5), *rigorous* (6), *dogmatically* (7), *relativism* (7), *phobia* (7), *antagonizing* (7), and *indoctrinate* (8).

Questions About the Writer's Craft

1. **The pattern.**   Leo provides a definition of "absolutophobia" in paragraph 7. Why do you suppose he waits until nearly the end of the essay to offer his definition?

2. **Other patterns.**   Where does Leo use the cause-effect pattern in his essay? How does this pattern contribute to Leo's overall purpose?

3. **Other patterns.**   At the end of his essay, Leo contrasts "values clarification" and "character education." Why do you think Leo concludes his essay with this contrast?

4. How does Leo's language reveal his attitude toward "absolutophobia"?

Writing Assignments Using Definition
as a Pattern of Development

1. In his essay, Leo presents the term "absolutophobia" and proceeds to define what he means by this term. In an essay of your own, coin a "phobia" and define what you mean by it. You might, for instance, discuss "shoppingmallophobia" (fear of being dragged to crowded shopping centers) or "SuperBowlophobia" (fear of TV football-watching) or "examcramophobia" (fear of learning a semester's worth of material in one night). Be sure to provide specific examples to illustrate the meaning of your "phobia." You may adopt whatever tone you wish, though a humorous tone seems especially appropriate for this kind of essay.

∞ 2. In his essay, Leo discusses a new term, "absolutophobia." In an essay of your own, focus on an already existing term or definition that you think is misused or misunderstood. Possibilities include "feminism," "new age," "senior citizen," "adolescence," "illiteracy," "homeless," "addiction," "liberal," "family," or "the disabled." Provide several examples showing how the word is commonly misused. Then offer your own definition, using clear examples to convey why your understanding of the word is more accurate. For another author's critique of a misused term, read James Gleick's "Life As Type A" (page 433).

Writing Assignments Using Other Patterns of Development

∞ 3. Leo explains the phenomenon of "absolutophobia" in terms of students' unwillingness to make moral judgments in the classroom. Brainstorm with others to identify additional areas of life where there is evidence of this reluctance to make judgments. Focusing on *one* such area, write an essay in which you provide compelling examples of moral paralysis in that setting. The following essays will provide insight into the complexities of morality: George Orwell's "Shooting an Elephant" (page 209), Joyce Garity's "Is Sex All That Matters?" (page 256), Diane Cole's "Don't Just Stand There" (page 322), Richard Rhodes's "Watching the Animals" (page 334), and Susan Jacoby's "Common Decency" (page 495).

4. Leo suggests that the moral fiber of young people has deteriorated. Ask several people of varying ages to read Leo's essay. Do they think his view is valid? Why or why not? Encourage each person to provide one personal experience that explains why he or she agrees or disagrees with Leo. Review all the material you gather, and write an essay arguing your own position. Use convincing examples from the interviews and your own experience to support your viewpoint. Near the beginning of your essay, acknowledge and, when possible, refute opposing viewpoints.

Writing Assignment Using a Journal Entry as a Starting Point

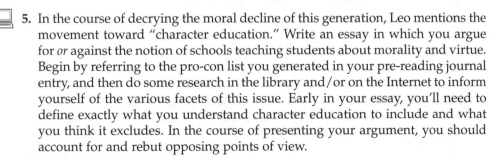

5. In the course of decrying the moral decline of this generation, Leo mentions the movement toward "character education." Write an essay in which you argue for *or* against the notion of schools teaching students about morality and virtue. Begin by referring to the pro-con list you generated in your pre-reading journal entry, and then do some research in the library and/or on the Internet to inform yourself of the various facets of this issue. Early in your essay, you'll need to define exactly what you understand character education to include and what you think it excludes. In the course of presenting your argument, you should account for and rebut opposing points of view.

ADDITIONAL
WRITING
TOPICS:
DEFINITION

General Assignments

Using definition, write an essay on one of the following topics. Once you fix on a limited subject, decide if the essay has an informative or a persuasive purpose. The paper might begin with the etymology of the term, a stipulative definition, or a definition by negation. You may want to use a number of writing patterns—such as description, comparison, narration, process analysis—to develop the definition. Remember, too, that the paper doesn't have to be scholarly and serious. There is no reason it can't be a lighthearted discussion of the meaning of a term.

1. Fads
2. Helplessness
3. An epiphany
4. Empowerment
5. A Yiddish term such as *mensch, klutz, chutzpah,* or *dreck,* or a commonly used term imported from some other language
6. Idiomatic expressions
7. Hypocrisy
8. Inner peace
9. Exploitation
10. A double bind

Assignments with a Specific Purpose, Audience, and Point of View

On Campus

1. You've been asked to write part of a pamphlet for students who come to the college health clinic. For this pamphlet, define *one* of the following conditions and its symptoms: *depression, stress, burnout, test anxiety, addiction* (to alcohol, drugs, or TV), *workaholism.* Part of the pamphlet should describe ways to cope with the condition described.

2. One of your responsibilities as a peer counselor in the student counseling center involves helping students communicate more effectively. To assist students,

write a definition of some term that you think represents an essential component of a strong interpersonal relationship. You might, for example, define *respect, sharing, equality,* or *trust.* Part of the definition should employ definition by negation, a discussion of what the term is *not.*

At Home or in the Community

3. *Newsweek* magazine runs a popular column called "My Turn," consisting of readers' opinions on subjects of general interest. Write a piece for this column defining *today's college students.* Use the piece to dispel some negative stereotypes (for example, that college students are apathetic, ill-informed, self-centered, and materialistic).

4. In your apartment building, several residents have complained about their neighbors' inconsiderate and rude behavior. You're president of the Residents' Association, and it's your responsibility to address this problem at your next meeting. Prepare a talk in which you define *courtesy,* the quality you consider most essential to neighborly relations. Use specific examples of what courtesy is and isn't to illustrate your definition.

On the Job

5. You're an attorney arguing a case of sexual harassment—a charge your client has leveled against an employer. To win the case, you must present to the jury a clear definition of exactly what *sexual harassment* is and isn't. Write such a definition for your opening remarks in court.

6. A new position has opened in your company. Write a job description to be sent to employment agencies that will screen candidates. Your description should define the job's purpose, state the duties involved, and outline essential qualifications.

19
ARGUMENTATION-PERSUASION

WHAT IS ARGUMENTATION-PERSUASION?

"You can't possibly believe what you're saying."

"Look, I know what I'm talking about, and that's that."

Does this heated exchange sound familiar? Probably. When we hear the word *argument*, most of us think of a verbal battle propelled by stubbornness and irrational thought, with one person pitted against the other.

Argumentation in writing, though, is a different matter. Using clear thinking and logic, the writer tries to convince readers of the soundness of a particular opinion on a controversial issue. If, while trying to convince, the writer uses emotional language and dramatic appeals to readers' concerns, beliefs, and values, then the piece is called **persuasion.** Besides encouraging acceptance of an opinion, persuasion often urges readers (or another group) to commit themselves to a course of action. Assume you're writing an essay protesting the federal government's policy of offering aid to those suffering from hunger in other countries while many Americans go hungry. If your purpose is to document, coolly and objectively, the presence of hunger in the United States, you would prepare an argumentation essay. Such an essay would be filled with statistics, report findings, and expert opinion to demonstrate how widespread hunger is nationwide. If, however, your purpose is to shake up readers, even motivate them to write letters to their congressional representatives and push for a change in policy, you would write a persuasive essay. In this case, your essay might contain emotional accounts of undernourished children, ill-fed pregnant women, and nearly starving elderly people.

Because people respond rationally *and* emotionally to situations, argumentation and persuasion are usually *combined*. Suppose you decide to write an article for the campus newspaper advocating a pre-Labor Day start for the school year. Your audience includes the college administration, students, and faculty. The article might begin by *arguing* that several schools starting the academic year earlier were able to close for the month of January and thus reduce heating and other maintenance expenses. Such an argument, supported by documented facts and figures, would help convince the administration. Realizing that you also have to gain student and faculty support for your idea, you might argue further that the proposed change would mean that students and faculty could leave for winter break with the semester behind them—papers written, exams taken, grades calculated and recorded. To make this part of your argument especially compelling, you could adopt a *persuasive* strategy by using emotional appeals and positively charged language: "Think how pleasant it would be to sleep late, spend time with family and friends, toast the New Year—without having to worry about work awaiting you back on campus."

When argumentation and persuasion blend in this way, emotion *supports* rather than *replaces* logic and sound reasoning. Although some writers resort to emotional appeals to the exclusion of rational thought, when you prepare argumentation-persuasion essays, you should advance your position through a balanced appeal to reason and emotion.

How ARGUMENTATION-PERSUASION FITS YOUR PURPOSE AND AUDIENCE

You probably realize that argumentation, persuasion, or a combination of the two is everywhere: an editorial urging the overhaul of an ill-managed literacy program; a commercial for a new shampoo; a scientific report advocating increased funding for AIDS research. Your own writing involves argumentation-persuasion as well. When you prepare a *causal analysis, descriptive piece, narrative,* or *definition essay,* you advance a specific point of view: MTV has a negative influence on teens' view of sex; Cape Cod in winter is imbued with a special kind of magic; a disillusioning experience can teach people much about themselves; *character* can be defined as the willingness to take unpopular positions on difficult issues. Indeed, an essay organized around any of the patterns of development described in this book may have a persuasive intent. You might, for example, encourage readers to try out a *process* you've explained, or to see one of the two movies you've *compared*.

Argumentation-persuasion, however, involves more than presenting a point of view and providing evidence. Unlike other forms of writing, it assumes controversy and addresses opposing viewpoints. Consider the following assignments, all of which require the writer to take a position on a controversial issue:

> In parts of the country, communities established for older citizens or childless couples have refused to rent to families with children. How do you feel about this situation? What do you think are the rights of the parties involved?

> Citing the fact that the highest percentage of automobile accidents involve young men, insurance companies consistently charge their highest rates to young males. Is this practice fair? Why or why not?

> Some colleges and universities have instituted a "no pass, no play" policy for athletes. Explain why this policy is or is not appropriate.

It's impossible to predict with absolute certainty what will make readers accept the view you advance or take the action you propose. But the ancient Greeks, who formulated our basic concepts of logic, isolated three factors crucial to the effectiveness of argumentation-persuasion: *logos, pathos,* and *ethos.*

Your main concern in an argumentation-persuasion essay should be with the *logos,* or **soundness,** of your argument: the facts, statistics, examples, and authoritative statements you gather to support your viewpoint. This supporting evidence must be unified, specific, sufficient, accurate, and representative (see pages 48–51 and 68–73). Imagine, for instance, you want to convince people that a popular charity misappropriates the money it receives from the public. Your readers, inclined to believe in the good works of the charity, will probably dismiss your argument unless you can substantiate your claim with valid, well-documented evidence that enhances the *logos* of your position.

Sensitivity to the *pathos,* or the **emotional power of language,** is another key consideration for writers of argumentation-persuasion essays. *Pathos* appeals to readers' needs, values, and attitudes, encouraging them to commit themselves to a viewpoint or course of action. The *pathos* of a piece derives partly from the writer's language. *Connotative* language—words with strong emotional overtones—can move readers to accept a point of view and may even spur them to act.

Advertising and propaganda generally rely on *pathos* to the exclusion of logic, using emotion to influence and manipulate. Consider the following pitches for a man's cologne and a woman's perfume. The language—and the attitudes to which it appeals—are different in each case:

> Brawn: Experience the power. Bold. Yet subtle. Clean. Masculine. The scent for the man who's in charge.

> Black Lace is for you—the woman who dresses for success but who dares to be provocative, slightly naughty. Black Lace. Perfect with pearls by day and with diamonds by night.

The appeal to men plays on the impact that the words *Brawn, bold, power,* and *in charge* may have for some males. Similarly, the charged words *Black Lace, provocative, naughty,* and *diamonds* are intended to appeal to business women who—in the advertiser's mind, at least—may be looking for ways to reconcile sensuality and professionalism. (For more on slanted language, read Ann McClintock's "Propaganda Techniques in Today's Advertising," page 282.)

Like an advertising copywriter, you must select language that reinforces your message. In a paper supporting an expanded immigration policy, you might use evocative phrases like "land of liberty," "a nation of immigrants," and "America's open-door policy." However, if you were arguing for strict immigration quotas, you might use language like "save jobs for unemployed Americans," "flood of unskilled labor," and "illegal aliens." Remember, though: Such language should *support, not supplant,* clear thinking. (See pages 452–453 for additional information on persuasive language.)

Finally, whenever you write an argumentation-persuasion essay, you should establish your *ethos,* or **credibility** and **reliability.** You cannot expect readers to accept or act on your viewpoint unless you convince them that you know what you're talking about and that you're worth listening to. You will come across as knowledgeable and trustworthy if you present a logical, reasoned argument that takes opposing views into account. Make sure, too, that your appeals to emotion aren't excessive. Overwrought emotionalism undercuts credibility.

Writing an effective argumentation-persuasion essay involves an interplay of *logos, pathos,* and *ethos.* The exact balance among these factors is determined by your audience and purpose (that is, whether you want the audience simply to agree with your view or whether you also want them to take action). More than any other kind of writing, argumentation-persuasion requires that you *analyze your readers* and tailor your approach to them. You need to determine how much they know about the issue, how they feel about you and your position, what their values and attitudes are, what motivates them.

In general, most readers will fall into one of three broad categories: supportive, wavering, or hostile. Each type of audience requires a different blend of *logos, pathos,* and *ethos* in an argumentation-persuasion essay.

1. A supportive audience.   If your audience agrees with your position and trusts your credibility, you don't need a highly reasoned argument dense with facts, examples, and statistics. Although you may want to solidify support by providing additional information (*logos*), you can rely primarily on *pathos*—a strong emotional appeal—to reinforce readers' commitment to your shared viewpoint. Assume that you belong to a local fishing club and have volunteered to write an article encouraging members to support threatened fishing rights in state parks. You might begin by stating that fishing strengthens the fish population by thinning out overcrowded streams. Since your audience would certainly be familiar with this idea, you wouldn't need to devote much discussion to it. Instead, you would attempt to move them emotionally. You might evoke the camaraderie in the sport, the pleasure of a perfect cast, the beauty of the outdoors, and perhaps conclude with "If you want these enjoyments to continue, please make a generous contribution to our fund."

2. A wavering audience.   At times, readers may be interested in what you have to say but may not be committed fully to your viewpoint. Or perhaps they're not as informed about the subject as they should be. In either case, because your readers need to be encouraged to give their complete support, you don't want to risk alienating them with a heavy-handed emotional appeal. Concentrate instead on *ethos* and *logos*, bolstering your image as a reliable source and providing the evidence needed to advance your position. If you want to convince an audience of high school seniors to take a year off to work between high school and college, you might establish your credibility by recounting the year you spent working and by showing the positive effects it had on your life (*ethos*). In addition, you could cite studies indicating that delayed entry into college is related to higher grade point averages. A year's savings, you would explain, allow students to study when they might otherwise need to hold down a job to earn money for tuition (*logos*).

3. A hostile audience. An apathetic, skeptical, or hostile audience is obviously most difficult to convince. With such an audience you should avoid emotional appeals because they might seem irrational, sentimental, or even comical. Instead, weigh the essay heavily in favor of logical reasoning and hard-to-dispute facts (*logos*). Assume your college administration is working to ban liquor from the student pub. You plan to submit to the campus newspaper an open letter supporting this generally unpopular effort. To sway other students, you cite the positive experiences of schools that have gone dry. Many colleges, you explain, have found their tavern revenues actually increase because all students—not just those of drinking age—can now support the pub. With the greater revenues, some schools have upgraded the food served in the pubs and have hired disc jockeys or musical groups to provide entertainment. Many schools have also seen a sharp reduction in alcohol-related vandalism. Readers may not be won over to your side, but your sound, logical argument may encourage them to be more tolerant of your viewpoint. Indeed, such increased receptivity may be all you can reasonably expect from a hostile audience. (*Note:* The checklists on pages 23 and 447–448 provide additional guidelines for analyzing your audience.)

PREWRITING STRATEGIES

The following checklist shows how you can apply to argumentation-persuasion some of the prewriting techniques discussed in Chapter 2.

 ARGUMENTATION-PERSUASION: A PREWRITING
CHECKLIST

Choose a Controversial Issue

☐ What issue (academic, social, political, moral, economic) do you feel strongly about? With what issues are your journal entries concerned? What issues discussed in recent newspaper, television, or magazine reports have piqued your interest?

□ What is your view on the issue?

Determine Your Purpose, Audience, Tone, and Point of View

□ Is your purpose limited to convincing readers to adopt your view-point, or do you also hope to spur them to action?

□ Who is your audience? How much do your readers already know about the issue? Are they best characterized as supportive, waver-ing, or hostile? What values and needs may motivate readers to be responsive to your position?

□ What tone is most likely to increase readers' commitment to your point of view? Should you convey strong emotion or cool objectivity?

□ What point of view is most likely to enhance your credibility?

Use Prewriting to Generate Supporting Evidence

□ How might brainstorming, journal entries, freewriting, or mapping help you identify personal experiences, observations, and examples to support your viewpoint?

□ How might the various patterns of development help you generate supporting material? What about the issue can you describe? Narrate? Illustrate? Compare and contrast? Analyze in terms of process or cause-effect? Define or categorize in some especially revealing way?

□ How might interviews or library research help you uncover relevant examples, facts, statistics, expert opinion?

STRATEGIES FOR USING ARGUMENTATION-PERSUASION IN AN ESSAY

After prewriting, you're ready to draft your essay. The following suggestions will help you prepare a convincing and logical argument.

1. At the beginning of the paper, identify the controversy surrounding the issue and state your position. Your introduction should clarify the controversy about the issue. In addition, it should provide as much background information as your readers are likely to need.

The thesis of an argumentation-persuasion paper is often called the **assertion** or **proposition.** Occasionally, the proposition appears at the paper's end, but it is usually stated at the beginning. If you state the thesis right away, your audience knows where you stand and is better able to evaluate the evidence presented.

Remember: Argumentation-persuasion assumes conflicting viewpoints. Be sure your proposition focuses on a controversial issue and indicates your view. Avoid a proposition that is merely factual; what is demonstrably true allows little room for debate. To see the difference between a factual statement and an effective thesis, examine the two statements that follow.

Fact

In the last few years, the nation's small farmers have suffered financial hardships.

Thesis

Inefficient management, rather than competition from agricultural conglomerates, is responsible for the financial plight of the nation's small farmers.

The first statement is certainly true. It would be difficult to find anyone who believes that these are easy times for small farmers. Because the statement invites little opposition, it can't serve as the focus of an argumentation-persuasion essay. The second statement, though, takes a controversial stance on a complex issue. Such a proposition is a valid starting point for a paper intended to argue and persuade. However, don't assume that this advice means that you should take a highly opinionated position in your thesis. A dogmatic, overstated proposition ("Campus security is staffed by overpaid, badge-flashing incompetents") is bound to alienate some readers.

Remember also to keep the proposition narrow and specific, so you can focus your thoughts in a purposeful way. Consider the following statements:

Broad Thesis

The welfare system has been abused over the years.

Narrowed Thesis

Welfare payments should be denied to unmarried mothers under the age of eighteen.

If you tried to write a paper based on the first statement, you would face an unmanageable task—showing all the ways that welfare has been abused. Your readers would also be confused about what to expect in the paper: Will it discuss unscrupulous bureaucrats, fraudulent bookkeeping, dishonest recipients? In contrast, the revised thesis is limited and specific. It signals that the paper will propose severe restrictions. Such a proposal will surely have opponents and is thus appropriate for argumentation-persuasion.

The thesis in an argumentation-persuasion essay can simply state your opinion about an issue, or it can go a step further and call for some action:

Opinion

The lack of affordable day-care centers discriminates against low-income families.

Call for Action

The federal government should support the creation of more day-care centers in low-income neighborhoods.

In either case, your stand on the issue must be clear to your readers.

2. Offer readers strong support for your thesis.   Finding evidence that relates to your readers' needs, values, and experience (see pages 23 and 447–448) is a crucial part of writing an argumentation-persuasion essay. Readers will be responsive to evidence that is *unified, adequate, specific, accurate, dramatic,* and *representative* (see pages 48–51 and 68–73). The evidence might consist of personal experiences or observations. Or it could be gathered from outside sources—statistics; facts; examples; or expert opinion taken from books, articles, reports, interviews, and documentaries. A paper arguing that elderly Americans are better off than they used to be might incorporate the following kinds of evidence:

- *Personal observation or experience:* A description of the writer's grandparents who are living comfortably on Social Security and pensions.
- *Statistics from a report:* A statement that the per-capita after-tax income of older Americans is $335 greater than the national average.
- *Fact from a newspaper article:* The point that the majority of elderly Americans do not live in nursing homes or on the streets; rather, they have their own houses or apartments.
- *Examples from interviews:* Accounts of several elderly couples living comfortably in well-managed retirement villages in Florida.
- *Expert opinion cited in a documentary:* A statement by Dr. Marie Sanchez, a specialist in geriatrics: "An over-sixty-five American today is likely to be healthier, and have a longer life expectancy, than a fifty-year-old living only a decade ago."

You may wonder whether to use the *first-person (I)* or *third-person (he, she, they)* point of view when presenting evidence based on personal observation, experience, or interviews. The subjective immediacy typical of the first person often delivers a jolt of persuasive power; however, many writers arguing a point prefer to present personal evidence in an objective way, using the third person to keep the focus on the issue rather than on themselves. When you write an argumentation-persuasion essay, your purpose, audience, and tone will help you decide which point of view will be most effective. If you're not sure which point of view to use, check with your instructor. Some encourage a first-person approach; others expect a more objective stance.

As you seek outside evidence, you may—perhaps to your dismay—come across information that undercuts your argument. Resist the temptation to ignore such material; instead, use the evidence to arrive at a more balanced, perhaps somewhat qualified viewpoint. Conversely, don't blindly accept or disregard flaws in the arguments made by sources agreeing with you. Retain a healthy skepticism, analyzing the material as rigorously as if it were advanced by the opposing side.

Also, keep in mind that outside sources aren't infallible. They may have biases that cause them to skew evidence. So be sure to evaluate your sources. If you're writing an essay supporting a woman's right to abortion, the National Abortion Rights Action League (NARAL) can supply abundant statistics, case studies, and reports. But realize that NARAL won't give you the complete picture; it will probably present evidence that supports its "pro-choice" position only. To counteract such bias, you should review what those with differing opinions have to say. You should, for example, examine material published by such "pro-life" organizations as the National Right-to-Life Committee—keeping in mind, of course, that this material is also bound to present support for its viewpoint only. Remember, too, that there are more than two sides to a complex issue. To get as broad a perspective as possible, you should track down sources that have no axe to grind—that is, sources that make a deliberate effort to examine all sides of the issue. For example, published proceedings from a debate on abortion or an in-depth article that aims to synthesize various views on abortion would broaden your understanding of this controversial subject.

Whatever sources you use, be sure to *document* (give credit to) that material. Otherwise, readers may dismiss your evidence as nothing more than your subjective opinion, or they may conclude that you have *plagiarized*—tried to pass off someone else's ideas as your own. (Documentation isn't necessary when material is commonly known or is a matter of historical or scientific record.) In brief informal papers, documentation may consist of simple citations like "Psychologist Aaron Beck believes depression is the result of distorted thoughts" or "*Newsweek* (December 10, 2001) observes that teens have embraced new technologies in their everyday lives." (For information about documenting sources in longer, more formal papers, see Chapters 20 and 21.)

3. Seek to create goodwill. Since your goal is to convince others of your position's soundness, you need to be careful about alienating readers—especially those who don't agree with you. Be careful, then, about using close-minded, morally superior language ("*Anyone* can see that . . ."). Exaggerated, overly emotional language can also antagonize readers. Consider an essay in which you argue that the speed limit shouldn't be raised from 55 m.p.h. to 65 m.p.h. Some readers may tune you out if you write "Truckers, the beer-bellied bullies of the highways, have no respect for other drivers or for the speed limit. They roar along the highway, tailgating and driving at least 20 m.p.h. over the speed limit. Now, with the new 65 m.p.h. speed limit, they're racing up on our bumpers at 80 m.p.h.—with disastrous consequences." Readers will probably be more receptive if you use less charged language: "The majority of truck drivers have more driving experience than anyone else on the road, and they handle their rigs responsibly. But when delivery deadlines encourage truckers to drive above the speed limit, an accident at 65 m.p.h. rather than at 55 m.p.h. will almost certainly be fatal." Last, guard against using confrontational language: "*My opponents* find the existing laws more effective than the proposed legislation" sounds adversarial, whereas "*Opponents* of the proposed legislation . . . ," "*Those opposed* to the proposed legislation . . . ," and "*Supporters* of the existing laws . . ." seem more even-handed and respectful. The last three statements also focus—as they should—on the issue, not on the people involved in the debate.

Goodwill can also be established by finding a *common ground*—some points on which all sides can agree, despite their differences. Assume a township council has voted to raise property taxes. The additional revenues will be used to preserve, as parkland, a wooded area that would otherwise be sold to developers. Before introducing its tax-hike proposal, the council would do well to remind homeowners of everyone's shared goals: maintaining the town's beauty and preventing the community's overdevelopment. This reminder of the common values shared by the town council and homeowners will probably make residents more receptive to the tax hike.

4. Organize the supporting evidence. The support for an argumentation-persuasion paper can be organized in a variety of ways. Any of the patterns of development described in this book (description, narration, definition, cause-effect, and so on) may be used—singly or in combination—to develop the essay's proposition. Imagine you're writing a paper arguing that car racing should be banned from television. Your essay might contain a *description* of a horrifying accident that was televised in graphic detail; you might devote part of the paper to a *causal analysis* showing that the broadcast of such races encourages teens to drive carelessly; you could include a *process analysis* to explain how young drivers "soup up" their cars in a dangerous attempt to imitate the racers seen on television. If your essay includes several patterns, you may need a separate paragraph for each.

When presenting evidence, arrange it so you create the strongest possible effect. In general, you should end with your most compelling point, leaving readers with dramatic evidence that underscores your proposition's validity.

5. Use Rogerian strategy to acknowledge differing viewpoints. If your essay has a clear thesis and strong, logical support, you've taken important steps toward winning readers over. However, because argumentation-persuasion focuses on controversial issues, you should also take opposing views into account. As you think about and perhaps research your subject, seek out conflicting viewpoints. As journalist Walter Lippman argued more than sixty years ago in an essay aptly titled "The Indispensable Opposition," it is through the "confrontation of opinion in debate" that we test our views. A good argument seeks out contrary viewpoints, acknowledges them, perhaps even admits they have some merit. Such a strategy strengthens your argument in several ways. It helps you anticipate objections, alerts you to flaws in your own position, and makes you more aware of the other sides' weaknesses. Further, by acknowledging the dissenting views, you come across as reasonable and thorough—qualities that may disarm readers and leave them more receptive to your argument. You may not convince them to surrender their views, but you can enlarge their perspectives and encourage them to think about your position.

Psychologist Carl Rogers took the idea of acknowledging contrary viewpoints a step further. He believed that argumentation's goal should be to *reduce conflict*, rather than to produce a "winner" and a "loser." But he recognized that people identify so strongly with their opinions that they experience any challenge to those opinions as highly threatening. Such a challenge feels like an attack on their very identity. And what's the characteristic response to such a perceived attack? People become defensive; they dig in their heels and become more adamant than ever about their position. Indeed, when confronted with solid information that calls their opinion into question, they devalue that evidence rather than allow themselves to be persuaded. The old maxim about the power of first impressions demonstrates this point. Experiments show that after people form a first impression of another person, they are unlikely to let future conflicting information affect that impression. If, for example, they initially perceive someone to be unpleasant and disagreeable, they tend to reject subsequent evidence that casts the person in a more favorable light.

Taking into account this tendency to cling tenaciously to opinions in the face of a challenge, Rogerian strategy rejects the adversarial approach that often characterizes argumentation. It adopts, instead, a respectful, conciliatory posture—one that demonstrates a real understanding of opposing views, one that emphasizes shared interests and values. Such an approach makes it easier to negotiate differences and arrive at—ideally—a synthesis: a new position that both parties find at least as acceptable as their original positions.

How can you apply Rogerian strategy in your writing? Simply follow these steps:

- Begin by making a conscientious effort to *understand* the viewpoints of those with whom you disagree. As you listen to or read about their opinions, try to put yourself in their shoes; focus on *what they believe* and *why they believe it,* rather than on how you will challenge their beliefs.

- Open your essay with an unbiased, even-handed *restatement of opposing points of view.* Such an objective summary shows that you're fair and open-minded—and not so blinded by the righteousness of your own position that you can't consider any other. Typically, people respond to such a respectful approach by lowering their defenses. Because they appreciate your ability to understand what they have to say, they become more open to your point of view.

- When appropriate, *acknowledge the validity* of some of the arguments raised by those with differing views. What should you do if they make a well-founded point? You'll enhance your credibility if you concede that point while continuing to maintain that, overall, your position is stronger.

- Point out areas of *common ground* (see pages 452–453) by focusing on interests, values, and beliefs that you and those with opposing views share. When you say to them, "Look at the beliefs we share. Look at our common concerns," you communicate that you're not as unlike them as they first believed.

- Finally, *present evidence* for your position. Since those not agreeing with you have been "softened up" by your noncombative stance and disarmed by the realization that you and they share some values and beliefs, they're more ready to consider your point of view.

Let's consider, more specifically, how you might draw upon essentially Rogerian strategy when writing an argumentation-persuasion essay. In the following paragraphs, we discuss three basic strategies. As you read about each strategy, keep in mind this key point: The earlier you acknowledge alternate viewpoints, the more effective you will be. Establishing—right at the outset—your awareness of opposing positions shows you to be fair-minded and helps reduce resistance to what you have to say.

First, you may acknowledge the opposing viewpoint in a two-part proposition consisting of a subordinate clause followed by a main clause. The *first part of the proposition* (the subordinate clause) *acknowledges opposing opinions;* the *second part* (the main clause) *states your opinion* and implies that your view stands on more solid ground. (When using this kind of proposition, you may, but don't have to, discuss opposing opinions.) The following thesis illustrates this strategy (the opposing viewpoint is underlined once; the writer's position is underlined twice):

> Although some instructors think that standardized finals restrict academic freedom, such exams are preferable to those prepared by individual professors.

Second, *in the introduction,* you may provide—separate from the proposition— a *one- or two-sentence summary of the opposing viewpoint.* Suppose you're writing an essay advocating a ten-day waiting period before an individual can purchase a handgun. Before presenting your proposition at the end of the introductory paragraph, you might include sentences like these: "Opponents of the waiting period argue that the ten-day delay is worthless without a nationwide computer network that can perform background checks. Those opposed also point out that only a percentage of states with a waiting period have seen a reduction in gun-related crime."

Third, you can take *one or two body paragraphs* near the beginning of the essay to *present in greater detail arguments raised by opposing viewpoints.* After that, you *grant* (when appropriate) the validity of some of those points ("It may be true that . . . ," "Granted, . . ."). Then you go on to *present evidence* for your position ("Even so . . . ," "Nevertheless . . ."). Imagine you're preparing an editorial for your student newspaper arguing that fraternities and sororities on your campus should be banned. Realizing that many students don't agree with you, you "research" the opposing viewpoint by seeking out supporters of Greek organizations and listening respectfully to the points they raise. When it comes time to write the editorial, you decide not to begin with arguments for your position; instead, you start by summarizing the points made by those supporting fraternities and sororities. You might, for example, mention their argument that Greek organizations build college spirit, contribute to worthy community causes, and provide valuable contacts for entry into the business world. Following this summary of the opposing viewpoint, you might concede that the point about the Greeks' contributions to community causes is especially valid; you could then reinforce this conciliatory stance by stressing some common ground you share— perhaps you acknowledge that you share your detractors' belief that enjoyable social activities with like-minded people are an important part of campus life. Having done all that, you would be in a good position to present arguments why you nevertheless think fraternities and sororities should be banned. Because you prepared readers to listen to your opinion, they would tend to be more open to your argument.

6. Refute differing viewpoints.   There will be times, though, that acknowledging opposing viewpoints and presenting your own case won't be enough. Particularly when an issue is complex and when readers strongly disagree with your position, you may have to *refute* all or part of the *dissenting views*. Refutation means pointing out the problems with opposing viewpoints, thereby highlighting your own position's superiority. You may focus on the opposing sides' inaccurate or inadequate evidence; or you may point to their faulty logic. (Some common types of illogical thinking are discussed on pages 458–461 and 463–464.)

Let's consider how you could refute a competing position in an essay you're writing that supports sex education in public schools. Adapting the Rogerian approach to suit your purposes, you might start by acknowledging the opposing viewpoint's key argument: "Sex education should be the prerogative of parents." After granting the validity of this view in an ideal world, you might show that many parents don't provide such education. You could present statistics on the number of parents who avoid discussing sex with their children because the subject makes them uncomfortable; you could cite studies revealing that children in single-parent homes are apt to receive even less parental guidance about sex; and you could give examples of young people whose parents provided sketchy, even misleading information.

There are various ways to develop a paper's refutation section. The best method to use depends on the paper's length and the complexity of the issue. Two possible sequences are outlined here:

First Strategy

- State your proposition.
- Cite opposing viewpoints and the evidence for those views.
- Refute opposing viewpoints by presenting counterarguments.

Second Strategy

- State your proposition.
- Cite opposing viewpoints and the evidence for those views.
- Refute opposing viewpoints by presenting counterarguments.
- Present additional evidence for your proposition.

In the first strategy, you simply refute all or part of the opposing positions' arguments. The second strategy takes the first one a step further by presenting *additional evidence* to support your proposition. In such a case, the additional evidence *must be different* from the points made in the refutation. The additional evidence may appear at the essay's end (as in the preceding outline), or it may be given near the beginning (after the proposition); it may also be divided between the beginning and end.

No matter which strategy you select, you may refute opposing views *one side at a time* or *one point at a time*. When using the one-side-at-a-time approach, you cite all the points raised by the opposing side and then present your counterargument to each point. When using the one-point-at-a-time strategy, you mention the first point made by the opposing side, refute that point, then move on to the second point and refute that, and so on. (For more on comparing and contrasting the sides of an issue, see pages 349–350.) No matter which strategy you use, be sure to provide clear signals so that readers can distinguish your arguments from the other side's: "Despite the claims of those opposed to the plan, many think that . . ." and "Those not in agreement think that. . . ."

7. Use induction or deduction to think logically about your argument. The line of reasoning used to develop an argument is the surest indicator of how rigorously you have thought through your position. There are two basic ways to think about a subject: inductively and deductively. Though the following discussion treats induction and deduction as separate processes, the two often overlap and complement each other.

Inductive reasoning involves examination of specific cases, facts, or examples. Based on these specifics, you then draw a conclusion or make a generalization. This is the kind of thinking scientists use when they examine evidence (the results of experiments, for example) and then draw a *conclusion:* "Smoking increases the risk of cancer." All of us use inductive reasoning in everyday life. We might think the following: "My head is aching" (evidence); "My nose is stuffy" (evidence); "I'm coming down with a cold" (conclusion). Based on the conclusion, we might go a step further and take some action: "I'll take an aspirin."

With inductive reasoning, the conclusion reached can serve as the proposition for an argumentation-persuasion essay. If the paper advances a course of action, the proposition often mentions the action, signaling an essay with a distinctly persuasive purpose.

Let's suppose that you're writing a paper about a crime wave in the small town where you live. You might use inductive thinking to structure the essay's argument:

Several people were mugged last month while shopping in the center of town. (*evidence*)

Several homes and apartments were burglarized in the past few weeks. (*evidence*)

Several cars were stolen from people's driveways over the weekend. (*evidence*)

The police force hasn't adequately protected town residents. (*conclusion, or proposition, for an argumentation essay with probable elements of persuasion*)

The police force should take steps to upgrade its protection of town residents. (*conclusion, or proposition, for an argumentation essay with a clearly persuasive intent*)

This inductive sequence highlights a possible structure for the essay. After providing a clear statement of your proposition, you might detail recent muggings, burglaries, and car thefts. Then you could move to the opposing viewpoint: a description of the steps the police say they have taken to protect town residents. At that point, you would refute the police's claim, citing additional evidence that shows the measures taken have not been sufficient. Finally, if you wanted your essay to have a decidedly persuasive purpose, you could end by recommending specific action the police should take to improve its protection of the community.

As in all essays, your evidence should be *unified, specific, accurate, dramatic, sufficient,* and *representative* (see pages 48–51 and 68–73). These last two characteristics are critical when you think inductively; they guarantee that your conclusion would be equally valid even if other evidence were presented. Insufficient or atypical evidence often leads to **hasty generalizations** that mar the essay's logic. For example, you might think the following: "Some elderly people are very wealthy and do not need Social Security checks" (evidence), and "Some Social Security recipients illegally collect several checks" (evidence). If you then conclude, "Social Security is a waste of taxpayers' money," your conclusion is invalid and hasty because it's based on only a few atypical examples. Millions of Social Security recipients aren't wealthy and don't abuse the system. If you've failed to consider the full range of evidence, any action you propose ("The Social Security system should be disbanded") will probably be considered suspect by thoughtful readers. It's possible, of course, that Social Security should be disbanded, but the evidence leading to such a conclusion must be sufficient and representative.

When reasoning inductively, you should also be careful that the evidence you collect is *recent* and *accurate.* No valid conclusion can result from dated or erroneous evidence. To ensure that your evidence is sound, you also need to evaluate the reliability of your sources. When a person who is legally drunk claims to have seen a flying saucer, the evidence is shaky, to say the least. But if two respected scientists, both with 20-20 vision, saw the saucer, their evidence is worth considering.

Finally, it's important to realize that there's always an element of uncertainty in inductive reasoning. The conclusion can never be more than an *inference,* involving what logicians call an **inductive leap.** There could be other explanations for the evidence cited and thus other positions to take and actions to advocate. For example, given a small town's crime wave, you might conclude not that the police force has been remiss but that residents are careless about protecting themselves and their property. In turn, you might call for a different kind of action—perhaps that the police conduct public workshops in self-defense and home security. In an inductive argument, your task is to weigh the evidence, consider alternative explanations, then choose the conclusion and course of action that seem most valid.

Unlike inductive reasoning, which starts with a specific case and moves toward a generalization or conclusion, **deductive reasoning** begins with a generalization that is then applied to a specific case. This movement from general to specific involves a three-step form of reasoning called a **syllogism.** The first part of a syllogism is called the **major premise,** a general statement about an entire group. The second part is the **minor premise,** a statement about an individual within that group. The syllogism ends with a **conclusion** about that individual.

Just as you use inductive thinking in everyday life, you use deductive thinking—often without being aware of it—to sort out your experiences. When trying to decide which car to buy, you might think as follows:

Major Premise	In an accident, large cars are safer than small cars.
Minor Premise	The Turbo Titan is a large car.
Conclusion	In an accident, the Turbo Titan will be safer than a small car.

Based on your conclusion, you might decide to take a specific action, buying the Turbo Titan rather than the smaller car you had first considered.

To create a valid syllogism and thus arrive at a sound conclusion, you need to avoid two major pitfalls of deductive reasoning. First, be sure not to start with a *sweeping* or *hasty generalization* (see page 233 in Chapter 13) as your *major premise*. Second, don't accept as truth a *faulty conclusion*. Let's look at each problem.

Sweeping major premise. Perhaps you're concerned about a trash-to-steam incinerator scheduled to open near your home. Your thinking about the situation might follow these lines:

Major Premise	Trash-to-steam incinerators have had serious problems and posed significant threats to the well-being of people living near the plants.
Minor Premise	The proposed incinerator in my neighborhood will be a trash-to-steam plant.
Conclusion	The proposed trash-to-steam incinerator in my neighborhood will have serious problems and pose significant threats to the well-being of people living near the plant.

Having arrived at this conclusion, you might decide to join organized protests against the opening of the incinerator. But your thinking is somewhat illogical. Your *major premise* is a *sweeping* one because it indiscriminately groups all trash-to-steam plants into a single category. It's unlikely that you're familiar with all the trash-to-steam incinerators in this country and abroad; it's probably not true that *all* such plants have had serious difficulties that endangered the public. For your argument to reach a valid conclusion, the major premise must be based on repeated observations or verifiable facts. You would have a better argument, and thus reach a more valid conclusion, if you restricted or qualified the major premise, applying it to some, not all, of the group:

Major Premise	A *number* of trash-to-steam incinerators have had serious problems and posed significant threats to the well-being of people living near the plants.
Minor Premise	The proposed incinerator in my neighborhood will be a trash-to-steam plant.
Conclusion	*It's possible* that the proposed trash-to-steam incinerator in my neighborhood will run into serious problems and pose significant threats to the well-being of people living near the plant.

This new conclusion, the result of more careful reasoning, would probably encourage you to learn more about trash-to-steam incinerators in general and about the proposed plant in particular. If further research still left you feeling uncomfortable about the plant, you would probably decide to join the protest. On the other hand, your research might convince you that the plant has incorporated into its design a number of safeguards that have been successful at other plants. This added information could reassure you that your original fears were unfounded. In either case, the revised deductive process would lead to a more informed conclusion and course of action.

   Faulty conclusion.   Your syllogism—and thus your reasoning—would also be invalid if your *conclusion reverses the "if . . . then" relationship implied in the major premise.* Assume you plan to write a letter to the college newspaper urging the resignation of the student government president. Perhaps you pursue a line of reasoning that goes like this:

Major Premise	Students who plagiarize papers must appear before the Faculty Committee on Academic Policies and Procedures.
Minor Premise	Yesterday Jennifer Kramer, president of the student government, appeared before the Faculty Committee on Academic Policies and Procedures.
Conclusion	Jennifer must have plagiarized a paper.
Action	Jennifer should resign her position as student government president.

Such a chain of reasoning is illogical and unfair. Here's why. *If* students plagiarize their term papers and are caught, *then* they must appear before the committee. However, the converse isn't necessarily true—that *if* students appear before the committee, *then* they must have plagiarized. In other words, not *all* students appearing before the Faculty Committee have been called up on plagiarism charges. For instance, Jennifer could have been speaking on behalf of another student; she could have been protesting some action taken by the committee; she could have been seeking the committee's help on an article she plans to write about academic honesty. The conclusion doesn't allow for these other possible explanations.

   Now that you're aware of the problems associated with deductive reasoning, let's look at the way you can use a syllogism to structure an argumentation-persuasion essay. Suppose you decide to write a paper advocating support for a projected space mission. You know that controversy surrounds the space program, especially since seven astronauts died in a 1986 launch. Confident that the tragedy has led to more rigorous controls, you want to argue that the benefits of an upcoming mission outweigh its risks. A deductive pattern could be used to develop your argument. In fact, outlining your thinking as a syllogism might help you formulate a proposition, organize your evidence, deal with the opposing viewpoint, and—if appropriate—propose a course of action:

Major Premise	Space programs in the past have led to important developments in technology, especially in medical science.
Minor Premise	The *Cosmos* Mission is the newest space program.
Proposition *(essay might be persuasive)*	The *Cosmos* Mission will most likely lead to important developments in technology, especially in medical science.
Proposition *(essay is clearly persuasive)*	Congress should continue its funding of the *Cosmos* Mission.

Having outlined the deductive pattern of your thinking, you might begin by stating your proposition and then discuss some new procedures developed to protect the astronauts and the rocket system's structural integrity. With that background established, you could detail the opposing claim that little of value has been produced by the space program so far. You could then move to your refutation, citing significant medical advances derived from former space missions. Finally, the paper might conclude on a persuasive note, with a plea to Congress to continue funding the latest space mission.

8. Use Toulmin logic to establish a strong connection between your evidence and thesis. Whether you use an essentially inductive or deductive approach, your argument depends on strong evidence. In *The Uses of Argument*, Stephen Toulmin describes a useful approach for strengthening the connection between evidence and thesis. Toulmin divides a typical argument into three parts:

- **Claim**—the thesis, proposition, or conclusion
- **Data**—the evidence (facts, statistics, examples, observations, expert opinion) used to convince readers of the claim's validity
- **Warrant**—the underlying assumption that justifies moving from evidence to claim.

Here's a sample argument using Toulmin's terminology:

The train engineer was under the influence of drugs when the train crashed.

(Data)

Transportation employees entrusted with the public's safety should be tested for drug use.

(Claim)

Transportation employees entrusted with the public's safety should not be allowed on the job if they use drugs.

(Warrant)

As Toulmin explains in his book, readers are more apt to consider your argument valid if they know what your warrant is. Sometimes your warrant will be so obvious that you won't need to state it explicitly; an *implicit warrant* will be sufficient. Assume you want to argue that the use of live animals to test product toxicity should be outlawed. To support your claim, you cite the following evidence: first, current animal tests are painful and usually result in the animal's death; second, human cell cultures frequently offer more reliable information on how harmful a product may be to human tissue; and third, computer simulations often can more accurately rate a substance's toxicity. Your warrant, although not explicit, is nonetheless clear: "It is wrong to continue product testing on animals when more humane and valid test methods are available."

Other times, you'll do best to make your *warrant explicit*. Suppose you plan to argue that students should be involved in deciding which faculty members are granted tenure. To develop your claim, you present some evidence. You begin by noting that, currently, only faculty members and administrators review candidates for tenure. Next, you call attention to the controversy surrounding two professors, widely known by students to be poor teachers, who were nonetheless granted tenure. Finally, you cite a decision, made several years ago, to discontinue using student evaluations as part of the tenure process; you emphasize that since that time complaints about teachers' incompetence have risen dramatically. Some readers, though, still might wonder how you got from your evidence to your claim. In this case, your argument could be made stronger by stating your warrant explicitly: "Since students are as knowledgeable as the faculty and administrators about which professors are competent, they should be involved in the tenure process."

The more widely accepted your warrant, Toulmin explains, the more likely it is that readers will accept your argument. If there's no consensus about the warrant, you'll probably need to *back it up*. For the preceding example, you might mention several reports that found students evaluate faculty fairly (most students don't, for example, use the ratings to get back at professors against whom they have a personal grudge); further, students' ratings correlate strongly with those given by administrators and other faculty.

Toulmin describes another way to increase receptivity to an argument: *qualify the claim*—that is, explain under what circumstances it might be invalid or restricted. For instance, you might grant that most students know little about their instructors' research activities, scholarly publications, or participation in professional committees. You could, then, qualify your claim this way: "Because students don't have a comprehensive view of their instructors' professional activities, they should be involved in the tenure process but play a less prominent role than faculty and administrators."

As you can see, Toulmin's approach provides strategies for strengthening an argument. So, when prewriting or revising, take a few minutes to ask yourself the following questions:

- What data (*evidence*) should I provide to support my claim (*thesis*)?
- Is my warrant clear? Should I state it explicitly? What back-up can I provide to justify my warrant?
- Would qualifying my claim make my argument more convincing?

Your responses to these questions will help you structure a convincing and logical argument.

9. Recognize logical fallacies. When writing an argumentation-persuasion essay, you need to recognize **logical fallacies** both in your own argument and in points raised by the opposing side. Work to eliminate such gaps in logic from your own writing and, when they appear in the opposing argument, try to expose them in your refutation. Logicians have identified many logical fallacies—including the sweeping or hasty generalization and the faulty conclusion discussed earlier in this chapter. Other logical fallacies are described in Ann McClintock's "Propaganda Techniques in Today's Advertising" (page 282) and in the paragraphs that follow.

The *post hoc* **fallacy** (short for a Latin phrase meaning "after this, therefore because of this") occurs when you conclude that a cause-effect relationship exists simply because one event preceded another. Let's say you note the growing number of immigrants settling in a nearby city, observe the city's economic decline, and conclude that the immigrants' arrival caused the decline. Such a chain of thinking is faulty because it assumes a cause-effect relationship based purely on co-occurrence. Perhaps the immigrants' arrival was a factor in the economic slump, but there could also be other reasons: the lack of financial incentives to attract business to the city, restrictions on the size of the city's manufacturing facilities, citywide labor disputes that make companies leery of settling in the area. Your argument should also consider these possibilities. (For more on the *post hoc* fallacy, see page 383 in Chapter 17.)

The *non sequitur* **fallacy** (Latin for "it does not follow") is an even more blatant muddying of cause-effect relationships. In this case, a conclusion is drawn that has no logical connection to the evidence cited: "Millions of Americans own cars, so there is no need to fund public transportation." The faulty conclusion disregards the millions of Americans who don't own cars; it also ignores pollution and road congestion, both of which could be reduced if people had access to safe, reliable public transportation.

An *ad hominem* **argument** (from the Latin meaning "to the man") occurs when someone attacks a person rather than a point of view. Suppose your college plans to sponsor a physicians' symposium on the abortion controversy. You decide to write a letter to the school paper opposing the symposium. Taking swipes at two of the invited doctors who disapprove of abortion, you mention that one was recently involved in a messy divorce and that the other is alleged to have a drinking problem. By hurling personal invective, you avoid discussing the issue. Mudslinging is a poor substitute for reasoned argument. And as politician Adlai Stevenson once said, "He who slings mud generally loses ground."

Appeals to questionable or faulty authority also weaken an argument. Most of us have developed a healthy suspicion of phrases like *sources close to, an unidentified spokesperson states, experts claim,* and *studies show.* If these people and reports are so reliable, they should be clearly identified.

Begging the question involves failure to establish proof for a debatable point. The writer expects readers to accept as given a premise that's actually controversial. For instance, you would have trouble convincing readers that prayer should be banned from public schools if you based your argument on the premise that school prayer violates the U.S. Constitution. If the Constitution does, either explicitly or implicitly, prohibit prayer in public education, your essay must demonstrate that fact. You can't build a strong argument if you pretend there's no controversy surrounding your premise.

A **false analogy** disregards significant dissimilarities and wrongly implies that because two things share *some* characteristics, they are therefore *alike in all respects.* You might, for example, compare nicotine and marijuana. Both, you could mention, involve health risks and have addictive properties. If, however, you go on to conclude, "Driving while smoking a cigarette isn't illegal, so driving while smoking marijuana shouldn't be illegal either," you're employing a false analogy. You've overlooked a major difference between tobacco and marijuana: Marijuana impairs perception and coordination—important aspects of driving—while there's no evidence that tobacco does the same.

The *either/or* **fallacy** occurs when you assume that a particular viewpoint or course of action can have only one of two diametrically opposed outcomes— either totally this or totally that. Say you argue as follows: "Unless colleges continue to offer scholarships based solely on financial need, no one who is underprivileged will be able to attend college." Such a statement ignores the fact that bright, underprivileged students could receive scholarships based on their potential or their demonstrated academic excellence.

Finally, a **red herring** argument is an intentional digression from the issue—a ploy to deflect attention from the matter being discussed. Imagine you're arguing that condoms shouldn't be dispensed to high school students. You would introduce a red herring if you began to rail against parents who fail to provide their children with any information about sex. Most people would agree that parents *should* provide such information. However, the issue being discussed is not parents' irresponsibility but the pros and cons of schools' distributing condoms to students.

Revision Strategies

Once you have a draft of the essay, you're ready to revise. The following checklist will help you and those giving you feedback apply to argumentation-persuasion some of the revision techniques discussed in Chapters 7 and 8.

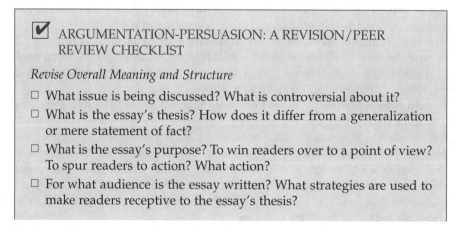

☑ ARGUMENTATION-PERSUASION: A REVISION/PEER
   REVIEW CHECKLIST

Revise Overall Meaning and Structure

☐ What issue is being discussed? What is controversial about it?

☐ What is the essay's thesis? How does it differ from a generalization or mere statement of fact?

☐ What is the essay's purpose? To win readers over to a point of view? To spur readers to action? What action?

☐ For what audience is the essay written? What strategies are used to make readers receptive to the essay's thesis?

- ☐ What tone does the essay project? Is the tone likely to win readers over? Why or why not?

- ☐ If the essay's argument is essentially deductive, is the major premise sufficiently restricted? What repeated observations or verifiable facts is the premise based on? Are the minor premise and conclusion valid? If not, how could these problems be corrected?

- ☐ Where is the essay weakened by hasty generalizations, a failure to weigh evidence honestly, or a failure to draw the most valid conclusion?

- ☐ Where does the essay commit any of the following logical fallacies: Concluding that a cause-effect relationship exists simply because one event preceded another? Attacking a person rather than an issue? Drawing a conclusion that isn't logically related to the evidence? Failing to establish proof for a debatable point? Relying on questionable or vaguely specified authority? Drawing a false analogy? Resorting to *either/or* thinking?

Revise Paragraph Development

- ☐ How apparent is the link between the evidence (data) and the thesis (claim)? How could an explicit warrant clarify the connection? How would supporting the warrant or qualifying the claim strengthen the argument?

- ☐ Which paragraphs lack sufficient evidence (facts, examples, statistics, and expert opinion)?

- ☐ Which paragraphs lack unity? How could they be made more focused? In which paragraph does the evidence seem bland, overly general, unrepresentative, or inaccurate?

- ☐ Which paragraphs take opposing views into account? Are these views refuted? If so, are they refuted *in toto* or one point at a time? Which counterarguments are ineffective? Why?

- ☐ Where do outside sources require documentation?

Revise Sentences and Words

- ☐ What words and phrases ("Contrary to what opponents claim . . ." or "Those opposed feel . . .") help readers distinguish the essay's arguments from those advanced by the opposing side?

- ☐ Which words carry strong emotional overtones? Is this connotative language excessive? Where does emotional language replace rather than reinforce clear thinking?

- ☐ Where might dogmatic language ("Anyone can see that . . ." and "Obviously, . . .") alienate readers?

STUDENT ESSAY: FROM PREWRITING THROUGH REVISION

The student essay that follows was written by Mark Simmons in response to this assignment:

> In "Rape: A Bigger Danger Than Feminists Know," Camille Paglia invites controversy by accusing feminism of having misled women regarding the subject of rape. Select another controversial issue, one that you feel strongly about. Using logic and solid evidence, convince readers that your viewpoint is valid.

Before writing his essay, Mark used the prewriting strategy of *group brainstorming* to generate material on the subject he decided to write about: compulsory national service. In a lively give-and-take with friends, Mark jotted down, as they occurred, ideas that seemed especially promising. Later on, he typed up his jottings so he could review them more easily. At that point, he began to organize the material.

Mark's typed version of the brainstormed list is below and on the next page. The handwritten marks indicate his later efforts to organize the material. As you can see, he started organizing the list by crossing out one item (the possibility of low morale) and adding several others (for example, that compulsory national service would be a relatively inexpensive way to repair bridges and roads). Then he labeled points raised by the opposing side and his counter-arguments. In the process, the essay's underlying structure began to emerge so clearly that he had no trouble preparing an outline, which is presented on pages 467–468.

Brainstorming

Compulsory service--ages 17-25	
Two years--military or public service	Definition
Serve after high school or college	
Israel has it, and it works well	Example. Where to use?
Nazi Germany had it, too	Opposing position: Point 3 (potentially fascist)
Too authoritarian	
Start of a dictatorship	
Can choose what kind of service	
No uniforms	Refutation of point 3 (not fascist)
U.S. not a fascist country	

Americans very lucky--economic opportunity, right to vote, etc.

Take without giving

Should have to give--program provides that chance

Introduction

Program too expensive

Pay--at least minimum wage

Have to provide housing, too

Opposing position: Point 1 (too expensive)

Can live at home
Payments from participating towns, cities, states

Could be like AmeriCorps's small budget

Refutation of point 1 (not expensive)

Less costly way to repair bridges and roads and help elderly and homeless

~~Low morale because forced? (Unlike Volunteer Peace Corps)~~

Demoralizing

Interfere with careers

Opposing position: Point 2 (demoralizing)

Learn skills

Time to think about goals

Make real contribution to society
Feel good and worthwhile

Refutation of point 2 (not demoralizing)

Outline

Thesis: Compulsory national service would be good for both young people and the country.

    I. Definition of compulsory national service

  II. Cost of compulsory national service

       A. Would be expensive

           1. Would have high administrative costs

           2. Would have high salary and housing costs

       B. Wouldn't be expensive

           1. Could follow AmeriCorps model

           2. Would require the towns, cities, and states using the
             corps to pay salary and housing costs

       3. Would cut costs by having young people live at home
       4. Would provide a cost-efficient way to repair deterio-
          rating bridges, roads, and neighborhoods
       5. Would provide a cost-efficient way to help the elderly
          and homeless
 III. Effect of compulsory national service on young people
    A. Would be demoralizing
       1. Would interrupt career plans
       2. Would waste young people's time by making them do work
          that isn't personally meaningful
    B. Wouldn't be demoralizing
       1. Would give young people time to evaluate life and
          career goals
       2. Would equip young people with marketable skills
       3. Would make young people from different backgrounds feel
          good about coming together to contribute to society
 IV. Effect of compulsory national service on American democracy
    A. Could encourage fascism, as it did in Germany
    B. Wouldn't encourage fascism
       1. Wouldn't undermine our present system of checks and
          balances
       2. Would offer young people choices about when they would
          serve and in which branch they would serve
       3. Wouldn't require uniforms or confinement in a barracks
       4. Wouldn't be that different from a regular nine-to-five job

Now read Mark's paper, "Compulsory National Service," noting the similarities and differences between his prewriting, outline, and final essay. One difference is especially striking: During prewriting, Mark and his friends tended to
identify an objection to compulsory service, brainstorm an appropriate counterargument, then move to the next objection and its counterargument. Mark used
the same *point-by-point* format in his outline. When drafting his paper, though,
Mark decided to use the *one-side-at-a-time* format. He summarized all reservations
first, then devoted the rest of the essay to a detailed refutation. This change in
organization strengthened Mark's argument because his rebuttals acquired
greater force when gathered together, instead of remaining scattered throughout
the paper. As you read the essay, also consider how well it applies the principles
of argumentation-persuasion discussed in this chapter. (The commentary that follows the paper will help you look at Mark's essay more closely and will give you
some sense of how he went about revising his first draft.)

Compulsory National Service

by Mark Simmons

1   Our high school history class spent several weeks   Introduction
studying the events of the 1960s. The most intriguing
thing about that decade was the spirit of service and
social commitment among young people. In the '60s, young
people thought about issues beyond themselves; they
joined the Peace Corps, worked in poverty-stricken
Appalachian communities, and participated in freedom
marches against segregation. Most young people today,
despite their obvious concern with careers and getting
ahead, would also like an opportunity to make a worthwhile contribution to society. Convinced that many young
adults are indeed eager for such an opportunity, the   Common knowledge:
Clinton administration implemented in 1994 a pilot pro-   No need to document
gram of voluntary national service. The following year,
the program was formalized and given the name
AmeriCorps. Such voluntary national service has also been
endorsed by President George W. Bush. Following the devastating terrorist attacks on September 11, 2001,
President Bush urged Americans to volunteer as a way of
assisting in the nation's recovery and of demonstrating
a spirit of national unity. He issued an executive order
in early 2002 establishing USA Freedom Corps, an organization seeking to persuade Americans to perform 4,000
hours of volunteer service over a lifetime. In general,
programs such as USA Freedom Corps and the more established AmeriCorps hold out so much promise that it seems
only natural to go one step further and make participa-   Start of two-sentence
tion for young people required. By instituting a program   thesis
of compulsory national service, our country could tap
youth's idealistic desire to contribute. Such a system
would yield significant benefits.

2   Compulsory national service means that everyone   Definition paragraph
between the ages of 17 and 25 would serve the country
for two years. Young people could choose between two
major options: military service or a public-service
corps. They could serve their time at any point within

the eight-year span. The unemployed or the uncertain
could join immediately after high school; college-bound
students could complete their education before joining
the national service.

The idea of compulsory national service has been   3
discussed for many years, and some nations such as
Topic sentence ———— Israel have embraced it wholeheartedly. The idea could
also be workable in this country. Unfortunately,
Beginning of summary detractors have prevented the idea from taking hold.
of three points raised by ⟶ Opponents contend, first of all, that the program would
opposing viewpoint
cost too much; they argue that a great deal of money
would have to be spent administering the program. In
addition, young people would have to receive at least a
minimum wage for their work, and some of them would need
housing--both costly items. Another argument against
compulsory national service is that it would demoralize
young people; the plan would prevent the young from
getting on with their careers and would make them feel
as though they were engaged in work that had no personal
reward. A final argument is that compulsory service
would lay the groundwork for a military state. The
picture is painted of an army of young robots totally at
the mercy of the government, like the Hitler Youth of
the Second World War.

Topic sentence: ———— ⟶ Despite opponents' claims that compulsory national   4
Refutation of first point
service would involve exorbitant costs, the program would
not have to be that expensive to run. AmeriCorps has
already provided an excellent model for achieving
substantial benefits at reasonable cost. Also, the sums
required for wages and housing could be reduced
considerably through payments made by the towns, cities,
and states using the corps' services. And the economic
benefits of the program could be significant. The
public-service corps could repair deteriorating bridges,
highways, public buildings, and inner-city neighborhoods.
The corps could organize recycling projects; it could
staff public health clinics, day-care centers, legal aid
centers, and homeless shelters. The corps could also
monitor pollution, clean up litter, and help care for
the country's growing elderly population. All of these

projects would help solve many of the problems that
plague our nation, and they would probably cost much
less than if they were handled by traditional government
bureaucracies or the private sector. ————————————— Topic sentence:
Refutation of second
point

5   Also, rather than undermining the spirit of young
people, as opponents contend, the program would probably
boost their morale. Many young people feel enormous
pressure and uncertainty. They are not sure what they
want to do, or they have trouble finding a way to begin
their careers. Compulsory national service could give
young people a much-needed breathing space and could
even equip them with the skills needed to start a
career. Moreover, participating in compulsory national
service could provide an emotional boost for the young;
all of them would experience the pride that comes from
working hard, reaching goals, acquiring skills, and
handling responsibilities. A positive mind-set would also
result from the sense of community that would be created
by serving in the national service. All young people--
rich or poor, educated or not, regardless of sex or
social class--would come together during this time. Young
people would grow to understand one another and learn
that every person has an ability to aid the welfare of
the whole group. Each young person would have the
satisfaction of knowing that he or she has made a real
contribution to the nation. ————————————————— Topic sentence:
Refutation of third point

6   Finally, contrary to what opponents claim, compulsory
national service would not signal the start of a
dictatorship. Although the service would be required,
young people would have complete freedom to choose any
two years between the ages of 17 and 25. They would
also have complete freedom to choose the branch of the
military or public-service corps that suits them best.
And the corps would not need to be outfitted in
military uniforms or to live in barracks-like camps. It
could be set up like a regular job, with young people
living at home as much as possible, following a nine-
to-five schedule, enjoying all the personal freedoms
that would ordinarily be theirs. Also, a dictatorship
would no more likely emerge from a program of

compulsory national service than it has from our present
military system. We would still have a series of checks
and balances to prohibit the taking of power by one group
or individual. We should also keep in mind that our
system is different from that of fascist regimes; our long
tradition of personal liberty makes improbable the seizing
of absolute power by one person or faction. A related but
even more important point to remember is that freedom does
not mean people are guaranteed the right to pursue only
their individual needs. That is mistaking selfishness for
freedom. And, as everyone knows, selfishness leads only to
misery. It cannot lead to a happy life. The national
service would not take away freedom. On the contrary, it
would help young people grasp this larger concept of
freedom, a concept that is badly needed to counteract the
deadly "look out for number one" attitude that is
spreading like a poison across the nation.

Conclusion: Echoes
material in introduction

Perhaps there will never be a time like the 1960s   7
when so many young people were concerned with remaking
the world. Still, a good many of today's young people
want meaningful work. They want to feel that what they
do makes a difference. A program of compulsory national
service would tap this willingness in young people,
helping them realize the best in themselves. Such a
program would also allow us as a nation to make
substantial headway against the social problems that
haunt the country. AmeriCorps, an efficient and
successful program of voluntary service, has paved the
way. Now seems the perfect time to expand the concept
and make compulsory national service a reality.

Commentary

Blend of Argumentation and Persuasion

In his essay, Mark tackles a controversial issue: He takes the position that compulsory national service would benefit both the country as a whole and its young
people in particular. Mark's essay is a good example of the way argumentation
and persuasion often mix; although the paper presents Mark's position in a logical, well-reasoned manner (argumentation), it also appeals to readers' personal
values and suggests a course of action (persuasion).

Audience Analysis

When planning the essay, Mark realized that his audience—his composition class—would consist largely of two kinds of readers. Some, not sure of their views, would be inclined to agree with him if he presented his case well. Others would probably be reluctant to accept his view. Because of this mixed audience, Mark knew he couldn't depend on *pathos* (an appeal to emotion) to convince readers. Rather, his argument had to rely mainly on *logos* (reason) and *ethos* (credibility). So Mark organized his essay around a series of logical arguments and evoked his own authority, drawing on his knowledge of history and his "inside" knowledge of young people.

Introduction and Thesis

Mark introduces his subject by discussing an earlier decade when large numbers of young people worked for social change. Mark's references to the Peace Corps, community work, and freedom marches reinforce his image as a knowledgeable source and establish a context for his position. These historical references, combined with the comments about President Clinton's and President Bush's support of voluntary national service, lead into the two-sentence thesis at the end of the introduction: "By instituting a system of compulsory national service, our country could tap youth's idealistic desire to contribute. Such a system would yield significant benefits."

Background Paragraph

The next paragraph is developed around a *definition* of compulsory national service. The definition guarantees that Mark's readers will share his understanding of the essay's central concept.

Acknowledging the Opposing Viewpoint

Mark is now in a good position to move into the body of his essay. Even though the assignment didn't call for research, Mark wisely decided to get together with some friends to brainstorm some issues that might be raised by the dissenting view. Using the *one-side-at-a-time* format, he acknowledges this position in the *topic sentence* of the essay's third paragraph: "Unfortunately, detractors have prevented the idea from taking hold." Next he summarizes the main points the dissenting opinion might advance: compulsory national service would be expensive, demoralizing to young people, and dangerously authoritarian. Mark uses the rest of the essay to counter these criticisms.

Refutation

The next three paragraphs (4–6) *refute* the opposing stance and present Mark's evidence for his position. Adapting material he brainstormed with friends, Mark structures the essay so that readers can follow his *counter-argument* with ease. Each paragraph argues against one opposing point and begins with a *topic sentence* that serves as Mark's response to the dissenting view. Note the way the italicized portion of each topic sentence recalls a dissenting point cited earlier: "Despite opponents' claims that *compulsory national service would involve exorbitant costs,* the program would not have to be that expensive to run" (paragraph 4); "Also, rather than *undermining the spirit of young people,* as opponents contend, the program would probably boost their morale" (5); "Finally, contrary to what opponents claim, *compulsory national service would not signal the start of a dictatorship*" (6). Mark also guides the reader through the various points in the refutation by using *transitions* within paragraphs: "*And* the economic benefits . . . could be significant" (4); "*Moreover,* participating in compulsory national service could provide an emotional boost . . ." (5); "*Also,* a dictatorship would no more likely emerge . . ." (6).

Some Problems with the Refutation

Overall, Mark's three-paragraph refutation is strong, but it would have been even more effective if the paragraphs had been resequenced. As it now stands, the last paragraph (6) seems anticlimactic. The refutation would have been more persuasive if Mark had placed the final paragraph in the refutation in a less emphatic position. He could, for example, have put it first or second in the sequence, saving for last either of the other two more convincing paragraphs.

You may also have felt that there's another problem with the third paragraph in the refutation. Here, Mark seems to lose control of his counterargument. Beginning with "And, as everyone knows . . . ," Mark falls into the *logical fallacy* called *begging the question.* He shouldn't assume that everyone agrees that a selfish life inevitably brings misery. He also indulges in charged emotionalism when he refers—somewhat melodramatically—to the "deadly 'look out for number one' attitude that is spreading like a poison across the nation."

Inductive Reasoning

Mark arrived at his position *inductively*—through an *inference* or *inductive leap.* He started with a number of specific observations about the nation and its young people. To support those observations, he added his friends' comments and insights. Combined, this material led him to the general *conclusion* that compulsory national service would be both workable and beneficial. In other words, Mark's evidence, as thoughtful and convincing as it may be, consists not of researched fact but of reasonable speculation.

Other Patterns of Development

To develop his argument, Mark draws on several patterns of development. The second paragraph relies on *definition* to clarify what is meant by compulsory national service. The introduction and conclusion *compare* and *contrast* young people of the 1960s with those of today. Finally, to support his position, Mark uses a kind of *causal analysis* that speculates on the likely consequences of compulsory national service.

Conclusion

Despite some minor problems along the way, Mark closes the essay effectively. He echoes the point made in the introduction about the 1960s and restates his thesis. The essay then ends with a crisp assertion that suggests a course of action.

Revising the First Draft

Mark revised his first draft with the help of two classmates, who used the checklist on pages 464–465 to focus their comments. After jotting his classmates' suggestions on a separate sheet, Mark transferred those he found most helpful to the margin of his paper. He then numbered the comments in order of importance. As Mark reviewed these notes, he realized that his introduction needed special attention.

A comparison of the introduction's original and final versions reveals the way Mark proceeded when revising. The annotations on the original (reprinted here) signal the problems that Mark and his partners saw in the first version.

Original Introduction

"There's no free lunch." "You can't get something for nothing." "You have to earn your way." In America, these sayings are not really true. In America, we gladly take but give back little. In America, we receive economic opportunity, legal protection, the right to vote, and, most of all, a personal freedom unequaled throughout the world. How do we repay our country for such gifts? In most cases, we don't. This unfair relationship must be changed. The best way to make a start is to institute a system of national compulsory service for young people. This system would be of real benefit to the country and its citizens.

③ Choppy

① Focus right from start on young people—maybe mention youth of the 1960s

② Need stronger link between early part of paragraph and thesis

Following his classmates' suggestion, Mark deleted the introduction's references to Americans in general. He made this change because the paper focuses not on all Americans but on American youth. To reinforce this emphasis, he also added the point about the social commitment of young people who joined the Peace Corps in the 1960s and AmeriCorps in the 1990s. Besides providing a logical lead-in to the thesis, these references gave the discussion an important historical perspective and lent a note of authority to Mark's argument. Mark was also pleased to see that adding this new material helped unify and smooth out the paragraph.

These are just a few of the many changes Mark made while reworking his essay. Because he budgeted his time carefully, he was able to revise thoroughly. With the exception of some weak spots in the sixth paragraph, Mark's essay is well reasoned and convincing.

ACTIVITIES: ARGUMENTATION-PERSUASION

Prewriting Activities

1. Imagine you're writing two essays: One defines hypocrisy; the other contrasts license and freedom. Identify an audience for each essay (college students, professors, teenagers, parents, employers, employees, or some other group). Then jot down how each essay might argue the merits of certain ways of behaving.

2. Following are several thesis statements for argumentation-persuasion essays. For each thesis, determine whether the three audiences indicated in parentheses are apt to be supportive, wavering, or hostile. Then select *one* thesis and use group brainstorming to identify, for each audience, general concerns on which you might successfully base your persuasive appeal (for example, the concern for approval, for financial well-being, for self-respect, for the welfare of others).

   a. The minimum wage should be raised every two years (*low-income employees, employers, congressional representatives*).

   b. Students should not graduate from college until they have passed a comprehensive exam in their majors (*college students, their parents, college officials*).

   c. Abandoned homes owned by the city should be sold to low-income residents for a nominal fee (*city officials, low-income residents, general citizens*).

   d. The town should pass a law prohibiting residents near the reservoir from using pesticides on their lawns (*environmentalists, homeowners, members of the town council*).

   e. Faculty advisers to college newspapers should have the authority to prohibit the publication of articles that reflect negatively on the school (*alumni, college officials, student journalists*).

3. Using the thesis you selected in activity 2, focus—for each group indicated in parentheses—on one or two of the general concerns you identified. Then brainstorm with others to determine the specific points you'd make to persuade each group. How would Rogerian argument (pages 453–455) and other techniques (page 448) help you disarm the most hostile audience?

4. Clip an effective advertisement from a magazine or newspaper. Through brainstorming, determine to what extent the ad depends on *logos, ethos,* and *pathos.* Consider the persuasive approaches described in Ann McClintock's

"Propaganda Techniques in Today's Advertising" (page 282) as well as the logical fallacies discussed in this chapter. After reviewing your brainstorming, devise a thesis that expresses your feelings about the ad's persuasive strategies. Are they responsible? Why or why not?

5. In a campus, local, or major newspaper, find an editorial with which you disagree. Using the patterns of development, freewriting, or another prewriting technique, generate points that refute the editorial. You may, for example, identify any logical fallacies in the editorial. Then, following one of the refutation strategies discussed in this chapter, organize your rebuttal, keeping in mind the power of Rogerian argument.

Revising Activities

6. Examine the following sets, each containing *data* (evidence) and a *claim* (thesis), For each set, identify the implied *warrant*. Which sets would benefit from an explicit warrant? Why? How might the warrant be expressed? In which sets would it be helpful to support the warrant or qualify the claim? Why? How might the warrant be supported or the claim qualified?

   a. *Data:* An increasing number of Americans are buying Japanese cars. The reason, they report, is that Japanese cars tend to have superior fuel efficiency and longevity. Japanese cars are currently manufactured under stricter quality control than American models.
   Claim: Implementing stricter quality controls is one way for the American auto industry to compete with Japanese imports.

   b. *Data:* Although laws guarantee learning-impaired children an education suitable to their needs, no laws safeguard the special needs of intellectually gifted children. There are, proportionately, far more programs that assist the slow learner than there are those that challenge the fast learner.
   Claim: Our educational system is unfair to gifted children.

   c. *Data:* To date, no woman or nonwhite and only one non-Protestant (John F. Kennedy) has ever been elected president of the United States.
   Claim: Until prejudicial attitudes change, American voters will not elect a president who is a female, a member of a racial minority, or a non-Protestant.

   d. *Data:* Minors aren't permitted to vote, marry without parental consent, or sign contracts. Nevertheless, the Supreme Court has ruled that a minor can receive the full penalty of the law—in some cases, even be executed—for a crime.
   Claim: Minors who engage in criminal acts should be treated with greater leniency than adults.

7. Examine the faulty chains of reasoning that follow. Which use essentially inductive logic? Which use essentially deductive logic? In each set, determine,

in general terms, why the conclusion is invalid. (The next activity offers practice
in identifying specific logical fallacies that render conclusions invalid.)

   a. Whenever I work in the college's computer lab, something goes wrong.
      The program crashes, the cursor freezes, the margins unset themselves.
      Conclusion: The college needs to allocate additional funds to repair and
      upgrade the computers in the lab.
   b. Many cars in the student parking lot are dented and look as though they
      have been in accidents.
      Conclusion: Students are careless drivers.
   c. Many researchers believe that children in families where both parents
      work develop confidence and independence. In a nearby community, the
      number of two-career families increased 15 percent over a two-year period.
      Conclusion: Children in the nearby community will develop confidence and
      independence.
   d. The local Chamber of Commerce elected a woman as president. The all-
      male Metropolitan Business Club approved a woman for membership.
      Conclusion: Traditionally conservative male groups are starting to accept
      women's role in business.
   e. Anyone found guilty of sexual harassment will be fired by XYZ
      Corporation. Curt A. was fired by XYZ Corporation.
      Conclusion: Curt A. is guilty of sexual harassment.

8. Each set of statements that follows contains at least one of the logical fallacies
   described earlier in the chapter and in Ann McClintock's essay "Propaganda
   Techniques in Today's Advertising" (page 282). Identify the fallacy or fallacies
   in each set and explain why the statements are invalid.

   a. Grades are irrelevant to learning. Students are in college to get an
      education, not good grades. The university should eliminate grading
      altogether.
   b. The best policy is to put juvenile offenders in jail so that they can get a
      taste of reality. Otherwise, they will repeat their crimes again and again.
   c. Legal experts say that this bill will weaken consumers' rights. Based on
      their views, we should petition legislators not to sign the bill.
   d. So-called sex education programs do nothing to decrease the rate of teenage
      pregnancy. Further expenditures on these programs should be curtailed.
   e. This country should research environmentally sound ways to use coal as
      an energy source. If we don't, we will become enslaved to the oil-rich
      Middle East nations.
   f. If we allow abortion, people will think it's acceptable to kill the homeless
      or pull the plug on sick people—two groups that are also weak and frail.
   g. The curfews that some towns impose on teenagers are as repressive as the
      curfews in totalitarian countries.

    h. Each day, Americans throw out ton after ton of edible food; it isn't true that some Americans suffer from hunger.

    i. Two members of the state legislature have introduced gun-control legislation. Both have led sheltered, pampered lives that prevent them from seeing how ordinary people need guns to protect themselves.

    j. Some say that auto insurance rates need to be more strictly regulated, but how strict are regulations on health insurance?

    k. Last year, a few students managed to avoid paying for their parking decals. This year's increased student parking fees unfairly penalize everyone for the dishonesty of a few.

9. Following is the introduction from the first draft of an essay advocating the elimination of mandatory dress codes in public schools. Revise the paragraph, being sure to consider these questions: How effectively does the writer deal with the opposing viewpoint? Does the paragraph encourage those who might disagree with the writer to read on? Why or why not? Do you see any logical fallacies in the writer's thinking? Where? Does the writer introduce anything that veers away from the point being discussed? Where? Before revising, you may find it helpful to do some brainstorming—individually or in a group—to find ways to strengthen the paragraph.

    After reworking the paragraph, take a few minutes to consider how the rest of the essay might unfold. What persuasive strategies could be used? How could Rogerian argument win over readers? What points could be made? What action could be urged in the effort to build a convincing argument?

      In three nearby towns recently, high school administrators joined forces to take an outrageously strong stand against students' constitutional rights. Acting like Fascists, they issued an edict in the form of a preposterous dress code that prohibits students from wearing expensive jewelry, designer jeans, leather jackets--anything that the administrators, in their supposed wisdom, consider ostentatious. Perhaps the next thing they'll want to do is forbid students to play rock music at school dances. What prompted the administrators' dictatorial prohibition against certain kinds of clothing? Somehow or other, they got it into their heads that having no restrictions on the way students dress creates an unhealthy environment, where students vie with each other for the flashiest attire. Students and parents alike should protest this and any other dress code. If such codes go into effect, we might as well throw out the Constitution.

PROFESSIONAL
SELECTIONS:
ARGUMENTATION-
PERSUASION

MARY SHERRY

Following her graduation from Dominican University in 1962 with a degree in English, Mary Sherry (1940–) wrote freelance articles and advertising copy while raising her family. Over the years, a love of writing and an interest in education have been integral to all that Sherry does professionally. Founder and owner of a small research and publishing firm in Minnesota, she has taught creative and remedial writing to adults for more than sixteen years. The following selection first appeared as a 1991 "My Turn" column in *Newsweek.*

Pre-Reading Journal Entry

Imagine you had a son or daughter who didn't take school seriously. How would you go about motivating the child to value academic success? Would your strategies differ depending on the age and gender of the child? If so, how and why? What other factors might influence your approach? Use your journal to respond to these questions.

IN PRAISE OF THE "F" WORD

Tens of thousands of 18-year-olds will graduate this year and be handed meaningless diplomas. These diplomas won't look any different from those awarded their luckier classmates. Their validity will be questioned only when their employers discover that these graduates are semiliterate.   1

Eventually a fortunate few will find their way into educational repair shops—adult-literacy programs, such as the one where I teach basic grammar and writing. There, high-school graduates and high-school dropouts pursuing graduate-equivalency certificates will learn the skills they should have learned in school. They will also discover they have been cheated by our educational system.   2

As I teach, I learn a lot about our schools. Early in each session I ask my students to write about an unpleasant experience they had in school. No writers' block here! "I wish someone would have made me stop doing drugs and made me study." "I liked to party and no one seemed to care." "I was a good kid and didn't cause any trouble, so they just passed me along even though I didn't read well and couldn't write." And so on.   3

I am your basic do-gooder, and prior to teaching this class I blamed the poor academic skills our kids have today on drugs, divorce and other impediments to   4 concentration necessary for doing well in school. But, as I rediscover each time I walk into the classroom, before a teacher can expect students to concentrate, he has to get their attention, no matter what distractions may be at hand. There are many ways to do this, and they have much to do with teaching style. However, if style alone won't do it, there is another way to show who holds the winning hand in the classroom. That is to reveal the trump card[1] of failure.

5   I will never forget a teacher who played that card to get the attention of one of my children. Our youngest, a world-class charmer, did little to develop his intellectual talents but always got by. Until Mrs. Stifter.

6   Our son was a high-school senior when he had her for English. "He sits in the back of the room talking to his friends," she told me. "Why don't you move him to the front row?" I urged, believing the embarrassment would get him to settle down. Mrs. Stifter looked at me steely-eyed over her glasses. "I don't move seniors," she said. "I flunk them." I was flustered. Our son's academic life flashed before my eyes. No teacher had ever threatened him with that before. I regained my composure and managed to say that I thought she was right. By the time I got home I was feeling pretty good about this. It was a radical approach for these times, but, well, why not? "She's going to flunk you," I told my son. I did not discuss it any further. Suddenly English became a priority in his life. He finished out the semester with an A.

7   I know one example doesn't make a case, but at night I see a parade of students who are angry and resentful for having been passed along until they could no longer even pretend to keep up. Of average intelligence or better, they eventually quit school, concluding they were too dumb to finish. "I should have been held back" is a comment I hear frequently. Even sadder are those students who are high-school graduates who say to me after a few weeks of class, "I don't know how I ever got a high-school diploma."

8   Passing students who have not mastered the work cheats them and the employers who expect graduates to have basic skills. We excuse this dishonest behavior by saying kids can't learn if they come from terrible environments. No one seems to stop to think that—no matter what environments they come from—most kids don't put school first on their list unless they perceive something is at stake. They'd rather be sailing.

9   Many students I see at night could give expert testimony on unemployment, chemical dependency, abusive relationships. In spite of these difficulties, they have decided to make education a priority. They are motivated by the desire for a better job or the need to hang on to the one they've got. They have a healthy fear of failure.

10   People of all ages can rise above their problems, but they need to have a reason to do so. Young people generally don't have the maturity to value education in the same way my adult students value it. But fear of failure, whether economic or academic, can motivate both.

11   Flunking as a regular policy has just as much merit today as it did two generations ago. We must review the threat of flunking and see it as it really is—a positive teaching tool. It is an expression of confidence by both teachers and parents that the students have the ability to learn the material presented to them. However, making it work again would take a dedicated, caring conspiracy between teachers and parents. It would mean facing the tough reality that passing kids who haven't learned the material—while it might save them grief for the short term—dooms them to long-term

---

[1]In cards, an advantage held in reserve until it's needed (editors' note).

illiteracy. It would mean that teachers would have to follow through on their threats, and parents would have to stand behind them, knowing their children's best interests are indeed at stake. This means no more doing Scott's assignments for him because he might fail. No more passing Jodi because she's such a nice kid.

This is a policy that worked in the past and can work today. A wise teacher, with the support of his parents, gave our son the opportunity to succeed—or fail. It's time we return this choice to all students.   12

Questions for Close Reading

1. What is the selection's thesis? Locate the sentence(s) in which Sherry states her main idea. If she doesn't state the thesis explicitly, express it in your own words.

2. Sherry opens her essay with these words: "Tens of thousands of 18-year-olds will graduate this year and be handed meaningless diplomas." Why does Sherry consider these diplomas meaningless?

3. According to Sherry, what justification do many teachers give for "passing students who have not mastered the work" (paragraph 8)? Why does Sherry think that it is wrong to pass such students?

4. What does Sherry think teachers should do to motivate students to focus on school despite the many "distractions . . . at hand" (4)?

5. Refer to your dictionary as needed to define the following words used in the selection: *validity* (paragraph 1), *semiliterate* (1), *equivalency* (2), *impediments* (4), *composure* (6), *radical* (6), *priority* (6), *resentful* (7), *testimony* (9), *motivate* (10), *merit* (11), *conspiracy* (11), and *illiteracy* (11).

Questions About the Writer's Craft

1. **The pattern.** To write an effective argumentation-persuasion essay, writers need to establish their credibility. How does Sherry convince readers that she is qualified to write about her subject? What does this attempt to establish credibility say about Sherry's perception of her audience's point of view?

2. Sherry's title is deliberately misleading. What does her title lead you to believe the essay will be about? Why do you think Sherry chose this title?

3. Why do you suppose Sherry quotes her students rather than summarizing what they had to say? What effect do you think Sherry hopes the quotations will have on readers?

4. **Other patterns.** What example does Sherry provide to show that the threat of failure can work? How does this example reinforce her case?

Writing Assignments Using Argumentation-Persuasion as a Pattern of Development

∞ 1. Like Sherry, write an essay arguing your position on a controversial school-related issue. Possibilities include but need not be limited to the following: College students should *or* should not have to fulfill a physical education requirement; high school students should *or* should not have to demonstrate computer proficiency before graduating; elementary school students should *or* should not be grouped according to ability; a course in parenting should *or* should not be a required part of the high school curriculum. Once you select a topic, brainstorm with others to gather insight into varying points of view. When you write, restrict your argument to one level of education, and refute as many opposing arguments as you can. The following essays will help you identify educational issues worth writing about: Sophronia Liu's "So Tsi-fai" (page 221), Joseph H. Suina's "And Then I Went to School" (page 371), Clifford Stoll's "Why Computers Don't Belong in the Classroom" (page 485), Yuh Ji-Yeon's "Let's Tell the Story of All America's Cultures" (page 500), and Arthur Schlesinger, Jr.'s "The Cult of Ethnicity: Good and Bad" (page 504).

2. Sherry acknowledges that she used to blame students' poor academic skills on "drugs, divorce and other impediments." To what extent should teachers take these and similar "impediments" into account when grading students? Are there certain situations that call for leniency, or should out-of-school forces affecting students not be considered? To gain perspective on this issue, interview several friends, classmates, and instructors. Then write an essay in which you argue your position. Provide specific examples to support your argument, being sure to acknowledge and—when possible—to refute opposing viewpoints.

Writing Assignments Using Other Patterns of Development

∞ 3. You probably feel, as Sherry does, that Mrs. Stifter is a strong, committed professional. Write an essay illustrating the qualities you think a teacher needs to have to be effective. Ask friends, classmates, family members, and instructors for their opinions; however, in your paper, focus on only those attributes you believe are most critical. To highlight the importance of these qualities, begin with a dramatic example of an ineffective teacher—someone who lacks the attributes you consider most important. To gain insight into some of the factors that make teachers effective or ineffective, read Sophronia Liu's "So Tsi-fai" (page 221) and Joseph H. Suina's "And Then I Went to School" (page 371).

∞ 4. Where else, besides in the classroom, do you see people acting irresponsibly, expending little effort, and taking the easy way out? You might consider the workplace, a school-related club or activity, family life, or interpersonal relationships. Select *one* area and write an essay illustrating the effects of this behavior on everyone concerned. For a broader perspective on the issue of personal responsibility, read Diane Cole's "Don't Just Stand There" (page 322), Richard Rhodes's "Watching the Animals" (page 334), and John M. Darley & Bibb Latané's "Why People Don't Help in a Crisis" (page 401).

Writing Assignment Using a Journal Entry as a Starting Point

5. Write the text for a brochure presenting parents with a step-by-step guide for dealing with academically unmotivated students. Focus your discussion on a specific level of schooling. From your pre-reading journal entry, select those strategies you consider most realistic and productive. When presenting your ideas, take into account children's likely resistance to the strategies described, and instruct parents how to deal with this resistance. Interviewing others (especially parents) and doing some research in the library and/or on the Internet will broaden your understanding of the issues involved.

CLIFFORD STOLL

An astronomer at the University of California at Berkeley, Clifford Stoll (1950–) is also a lecturer, commentator on MSNBC, and occasional visiting teacher of astronomy in elementary, middle, and high schools. He is the best-selling author of *The Cuckoo's Egg: Tracking a Spy Through the Maze of Computer Espionage* (1990) and of *Silicon Snake Oil: Second Thoughts on the Information Superhighway* (1995), both of which address the complications of the computer age. As he reveals in the preface of *High-Tech Heretic: Reflections of a Computer Contrarian* (1999), despite having programmed and used computers "since the mid-sixties," Stoll seeks to inject "a few notes of skepticism into the utopian dreams of a digital wonderland." According to his website, he is a "stay-at-home daddy" who lives with his family in the San Francisco Bay area. The following essay appears as a chapter in *High-Tech Heretic*.

Pre-Reading Journal Entry

Over the past several years, the Internet has become more popular as an educational resource. What do you think are the merits and the drawbacks of including the Internet as part of academic assignments in school curricula? Does your response depend on the age of the students in question? Record in your journal the pros and cons of having students—in elementary, high school, and college levels, respectively—access the Net as part of their studies.

WHY COMPUTERS DON'T BELONG
IN THE CLASSROOM

1   Technology promises shortcuts to higher grades and painless learning. Today's edu-tainment[1] software comes shrink-wrapped in computing's magic mantra: "Makes Learning Fun."

2   You'll hear it from IBM: "The latest Aptivas have a superior selection of top-rated educational software titles like Kid's Room, an Aptiva exclusive that gives your kids a fun place to learn." The fluff goes on about "extreme multimedia delivers full-screen action, blazing graphics and front-row-center-seat sound, resulting in maximum impact in any application."

3   Public schools agree. Here's a press release pushing software developed by the Texas Agricultural Extension Service, and aimed at 4-H clubs: "It may sound fishy, but Texas 4th graders now have the opportunity to go fishing for facts on the computer, improve their academic skills, learn how they can conserve water and maintain its quality in the state's lakes and streams and have fun at the same time."

4   The phrase shows up in promotions for college classes, too: The School of Journalism at University of North Carolina at Chapel Hill teaches a core course in Electronic Information Sources. The class motto: Learning Is Fun.

5   An Oregon high school student who's spent plenty of time online wrote: "I mean if I had a choice to learn in a fun matter or a traditial [sic] book manner I would choice [sic] the fun way of learning."

6   Read the promotion for Western Michigan University software to learn about groundwater: It "uses animation, so learning about Calhoun County is more of a video game than a dry lesson or research project. . . ."

7   Learn on your own. Blazing graphics and maximum impact. Go fishing for facts. Learning will be more of a video game than a lesson. Technology makes learning fun. Just one problem.

8   It's a lie.

9   Most learning isn't fun. Learning takes work. Discipline. Commitment, from both teacher and student. Responsibility—you have to do your homework. There's no shortcut to a quality education. And the payoff isn't an adrenaline rush, but a deep satisfaction arriving weeks, months, or years later. Equating learning with fun says that if you don't enjoy yourself, you're not learning.

10   What good are glitzy gadgets to a child who can't pay attention in class, won't read more than a paragraph, and is unable to write analytically? If we want our children to read books, why direct them to computer screens, where it's painful to read more than a few pages? If kids watch too much TV, why bring multimedia video systems into schools?

11   These teaching machines direct students away from reading, away from writing, away from scholarship. They dull questioning minds with graphical games where quick answers take the place of understanding, and the trivial is promoted as educational. They substitute quick answers and fast action for reflection and critical thinking. Thinking, after all, involves originality, concentration, and intention.

12   Computing's instant gratification—built into the learning-is-fun mind-set—encourages intellectual passivity, driven mainly by conditioned amusement. Fed a diet of

---

[1]A combination of the words "education" and "entertainment" (editors' note).

interactive insta-grat, students develop a distaste for persistence, trial and error, attentiveness, or patience.

This obsession with turning the classroom into a funhouse isn't new. Eighty years 13 ago, Austrian educator Rudolf Steiner wrote, "I've often heard that there must be an education which makes learning a game for children; school must become all joy. The children should laugh all the time and learning will be play. This is the best educational principle to ensure that nothing at all is learned."[2]

Yep, kids love computers. Indeed, it's mainly adults who are uncomfortable around 14 keyboards and monitors. But just what do children learn from computers?

Turning learning into fun denigrates the most important things we can do in life: to 15 learn and to teach. It cheapens both process and product: Dedicated teachers try to entertain, students expect to learn without working, and scholarship becomes a computer game. When in doubt, turn to the electronic mind-crutch.

Is the main problem of today's children that they haven't enough fun? Are kids really 16 deprived of excitement? Are schoolchildren exposed to too few media messages— so that we must bring them the Internet with still more? Must every classroom lesson be sugarcoated by dancing animatrons and singing cartoon characters? Is the job of our schools to provide additional screen time for students who watch three or four hours of television a night? . . .

Along with a small group of parents, I visited a kindergarten class near San 17 Francisco. The other visitors were immediately taken by the display of computer graphic printouts hung on the wall . . . clipart, designed by professionals and printed out by the children. The teacher, busy showing several children how to run the computer, didn't notice one frustrated child working at the crafts table.

While the visitors chatted about the computers, I watched that six-year-old clumsily fold 18 construction paper into the shape of a house. Struggling with round-nosed scissors, he cut a door, drew windows with a crayon, and pasted the paper onto a base. Near the end of our visit, he completed his project—he called it a firehouse—and proudly showed it to the adults in the room. The teacher gave him a "Go away, I'm busy" nod; none of the other visitors so much as glanced at the boy. You could see his face drop. . . .

New teachers, fresh out of college, seem to be most affected with the connection 19 between gizmos, classrooms, and fun in learning. Ms. Jennifer Donovan, a student teacher from Stetson University, wrote to me, repeating the standard party line: Lessons must be fun in order to compete with television and to motivate students. "In the 1950s, the job market did not call for computer education. But in a changing world, students are hard pressed to find well-paying jobs that do not involve computer technology."

These fit together: Jobs go to those who know computers. Computers motivate stu- 20 dents. Students won't learn unless it's fun.

Well, many subjects aren't fun.[3] I wonder how the fun-to-learn teacher handles the 21 Holocaust, Rape of Nanking,[4] or American slavery. Perhaps her class creates websites

---

[2]"The Younger Generation" in *Thirteen Lectures* by Rudolf Steiner, 1922.
[3]Plenty of jobs aren't fun, either.
[4]Following their December 13, 1937, takeover of the Chinese city of Nanking, Japanese troops committed widespread atrocities against Nanking's citizens. Anywhere between 260,000 and 350,000 people were killed, and tens of thousands of women were raped. Some historians argue that the "Rape of Nanking"—as this campaign has come to be known—is generally underacknowledged, "a forgotten holocaust" (editors' note).

about these subjects—and the students concentrate on graphic design instead of history. But scholarship isn't about browsing the Internet—it's about understanding events, appreciating history, and interpreting our world.

22   "But you don't understand," say my techie friends. "Computers are wonderful motivators for students. In this age of television, they won't write or do their homework without one."

23   And so we happily provide computers to students and expect them to suddenly become interested in academic topics. We encourage them to play with the machine . . . any scholastic connection is secondary.

24   Kids do seem to be motivated by computers. But doesn't that multimedia machine mainly motivate kids to play with the computer, in the same way that television motivates kids to watch more videos? . . .

25   The old saw still rings true: What requires the least effort is least cherished. Yet somehow we expect a simple, easy, fun digital education to be both lasting and valuable. . . .

26   Learning isn't about acquiring information, maximizing efficiency, or enjoyment. Learning is about developing human capacity. To turn learning into fun is to denigrate the two most important things we can do as humans: To teach. To learn.

Questions for Close Reading

1. What is the selection's thesis? Locate the sentence(s) in which Stoll states his main idea. If he doesn't state the thesis explicitly, express it in your own words.

2. What does Stoll assert are the two most important activities we human beings can perform? How does this claim fit in with his overarching argument in the essay?

3. In paragraphs 17 and 18, Stoll narrates a personal anecdote about visiting a kindergarten class. What did he observe there? What do you think he inferred from the behavior of each of the involved parties?

4. What specific segment of educators does Stoll identify as being especially enamored of using computers in the classroom? According to Stoll, what justification do these educators give for using computers to teach children?

5. Refer to your dictionary as needed to define the following words used in the selection: *mantra* (paragraph 1), *adrenaline* (9), *scholarship* (11), *conditioned* (12), *denigrates* (15), *animatrons* (16), *gizmos* (19), *maximizing* (26), and *capacity* (26).

Questions About the Writer's Craft

1. **The pattern.** To write an effective argumentation-persuasion essay, writers need to establish their credibility, appealing to *ethos* (see page 447). Based on what you learned about Stoll in his biography (page 484) and in his essay, what makes him appear qualified to write about his subject?

2. **The pattern.** Focusing on his word choice, describe Stoll's tone when he addresses conflicting viewpoints. How does the attitude he conveys help reinforce his thesis?

3. Why do you suppose Stoll directly quotes advertisements in paragraph 2, 3, and 6 rather than summarizing what they say? Why does he quote the student in paragraph 5? What effect do you think Stoll hopes the quotations will have on readers?

4. What is unusual about how paragraphs 10 and 16 are written? Why do you suppose Stoll might have designed these paragraphs in this way?

5. **Other patterns.** In paragraphs 11 and 12, Stoll identifies a cause-effect relationship between classroom computer use and children's attitudes toward learning. What are some of these effects? How does this causal connection reinforce Stoll's thesis?

Writing Assignments Using Argumentation-Persuasion as a Pattern of Development

1. Write an essay in which you argue, contrary to Stoll, that computers in fact significantly *benefit* students and therefore *should* be used in the classroom. Brainstorm on your own or with others to generate points in support of your thesis. To gather additional information supporting your position, you might also consider visiting the library and/or going online.

2. Increasingly, colleges are turning to "distance learning"—including videotaped lectures, chat-room discussions, and e-mailed homework—as a method of reaching more students and doing so in the comfort of the students' own homes. What do you think of this movement toward non-classroom-based education? Write an essay in which you argue in favor of *or* against distance learning in colleges. Before you begin, consider researching this subject in the library and/or on the Internet to gather information that will help bolster your position and assist you in formulating supporting arguments.

Writing Assignments Using Other Patterns of Development

3. According to Stoll, computers serve as a distraction to students rather than as a legitimate learning tool. What are other kinds of distractions students face? Write an essay in which you classify the different types of distractions students encounter that can make learning difficult. You may adopt a serious tone and address categories such as problems at home and pressure from peers. Or you might adopt a humorous tone and discuss distractions that include interest in the opposite sex and the temptation of video games. Provide vivid examples to illustrate each of the categories you create. For additional viewpoints about the pressures to which students are subject, read Sophronia Liu's "So Tsi-fai" (page 221) and Mary Sherry's "In Praise of the 'F' Word" (page 480).

4. With the increasing popularity of the Internet, the future of traditional printed materials—such as books, magazines, and newspapers—has come into question. Write an essay in which you compare and contrast using printed materials with using the Internet in order to perform research. Your best source of information might be a "hands-on" approach: to attempt to use each of the methods of researching and see for yourself what the differences are. By the end of your essay, make clear to your reader which of the two methods you find preferable, and why.

Writing Assignment Using a Journal Entry as a Starting Point

5. Stoll vehemently argues against the overemphasis on computers in the classroom because of the frivolous brand of "edutainment" they purvey. Write an essay in which you argue that the Internet in specific should *or* should not play a significant role in the education of *one* particular school-level of students (elementary, high school, or college). In formulating your argument, refer to the material you generated in your pre-reading journal entry. For additional perspectives on this issue, you might consider doing some research on this topic in the library and/or on the Internet. In writing your essay, you should account for and dispute opposing points of view.

Debating the Issues: Date Rape

CAMILLE PAGLIA

Before 1990, Camille Paglia, professor of humanities at Philadelphia's University of the Arts, was known primarily for her electrifying performance in the classroom. Then came the publication of Paglia's *Sexual Personae: Art and Decadence from Nefertiti to Emily Dickinson,* a sweeping book that moves with dizzying speed from the days of cave art to the nineteenth century. *Sexual Personae* makes the case that man creates art as a defensive response to woman's terrifying cosmic power. Suddenly Paglia became an international celebrity and had many opportunities to express her controversial views. Born in 1947, Paglia earned her doctorate from Yale University, where her Ph.D. thesis was an early version of *Sexual Personae. Sex, Art, and American Culture: Essays* (1992), *Vamps and Tramps: New Essays* (1994), and *Alfred Hitchcock's "The Birds"* (1998) are Paglia's latest works. She is also a regular columnist for *Salon* online magazine. The following selection first appeared in *New York Newsday* in 1991.

Pre-Reading Journal Entry

How would you define "date rape"? Use your journal to formulate a preliminary definition. Working as quickly as you can, jot down your preliminary thoughts about what it is and what it isn't.

RAPE: A BIGGER DANGER THAN
FEMINISTS KNOW

Rape is an outrage that cannot be tolerated in civilized society. Yet feminism, which   1
has waged a crusade for rape to be taken more seriously, has put young women in danger by hiding the truth about sex from them.

In dramatizing the pervasiveness of rape, feminists have told young women that   2
before they have sex with a man, they must give consent as explicit as a legal contract's. In this way, young women have been convinced that they have been the victims of rape. On elite campuses in the Northeast and on the West Coast, they have
held consciousness-raising sessions, petitioned administrations, demanded inquests.
At Brown University, outraged, panicky "victims" have scrawled the names of alleged
attackers on the walls of women's rest rooms. What marital rape was to the '70s, "date
rape" is to the '90s.

The incidence and seriousness of rape do not require this kind of exaggeration. Real   3
acquaintance rape is nothing new. It has been a horrible problem for women for all or
recorded history. Once, father and brothers protected women from rape. Once, the
penalty for rape was death. I come from a fierce Italian tradition where, not so long
ago in the motherland, a rapist would end up knifed, castrated, and hung out to dry.

But the old clans and small rural communities have broken down. In our cities, on   4
our campuses far from home, young women are vulnerable and defenseless. Feminism
has not prepared them for this. Feminism keeps saying the sexes are the same. It keeps
telling women they can do anything, go anywhere, say anything, wear anything. No,
they can't. Women will always be in sexual danger.

One of my male students recently slept overnight with a friend in a passageway of   5
the Great Pyramid in Egypt. He described the moon and sand, the ancient silence and
eerie echoes. I am a woman. I will never experience that. I am not stupid enough to
believe I could ever be safe there. There is a world of solitary adventure I will never
have. Women have always known these somber truths. But feminism, with its pie-in-
the-sky fantasies about the perfect world, keeps young women from seeing life as it is.

We must remedy social injustice whenever we can. But there are some things we   6
cannot change. There are sexual differences that are based in biology. Academic feminism is lost in a fog of social constructionism. It believes we are totally the product of
our environment. This idea was invented by Rousseau.[1] He was wrong. Emboldened
by dumb French language theory, academic feminists repeat the same hollow slogans
over and over to each other. Their view of sex is naive and prudish. Leaving sex to the
feminists is like letting your dog vacation at the taxidermist's.

The sexes are at war. Men must struggle for identity against the overwhelming   7
power of their mothers. Women have menstruation to tell them they are women. Men
must do or risk something to be men. Men become masculine only when other men
say they are. Having sex with a woman is one way a boy becomes a man.

College men are at their hormonal peak. They have just left their mothers and are   8
questing for their male identity. In groups, they are dangerous. A woman going to a fraternity party is walking into Testosterone Flats, full of prickly cacti and blazing guns. If
she goes, she should be armed with resolute alertness. She should arrive with girlfriends and leave with them. A girl who lets herself get dead drunk at a fraternity party

---

[1]A French political writer and philosopher (1712–78) (editors' note).

is a fool. A girl who goes upstairs alone with a brother at a fraternity party is an idiot. Feminists call this "blaming the victim." I call it common sense.

9   For a decade, feminists have drilled their disciples to say, "Rape is a crime of violence but not of sex." This sugar-coated Shirley Temple nonsense has exposed young women to disaster. Misled by feminism, they do not expect rape from the nice boys from good homes who sit next to them in class.

10   Aggression and eroticism, in fact, are deeply intertwined. Hunt, pursuit and capture are biologically programmed into male sexuality. Generation after generation, men must be educated, refined, and ethically persuaded away from their tendency toward anarchy and brutishness. Society is not the enemy, as feminism ignorantly claims. Society is woman's protection against rape. Feminism, with its solemn Carry Nation[2] repressiveness, does not see what is for men the eroticism or fun element in rape, especially the wild, infectious delirium of gang rape. Women who do not understand rape cannot defend themselves against it.

11   The date-rape controversy shows feminism hitting the wall of its own broken promises. The women of my '60s generation were the first respectable girls in history to swear like sailors, get drunk, stay out all night—in short, to act like men. We sought total sexual freedom and equality. But as time passed, we woke up to cold reality. The old double standard protected women. When anything goes, it's women who lose.

12   Today's young women don't know what they want. They see that feminism has not brought sexual happiness. The theatrics of public rage over date rape are their way of restoring the old sexual rules that were shattered by my generation. Yet nothing about the sexes has really changed. The comic film *Where the Boys Are* (1960), the ultimate expression of '50s man-chasing, still speaks directly to our time. It shows smart, lively women skillfully anticipating and fending off the dozens of strategies with which horny men try to get them into bed. The agonizing date-rape subplot and climax are brilliantly done. The victim, Yvette Mimieux, makes mistake after mistake, obvious to the other girls. She allows herself to be lured away from her girlfriends and into isolation with boys whose character and intentions she misreads. *Where the Boys Are* tells the truth. It shows courtship as a dangerous game in which the signals are not verbal but subliminal.

13   Neither militant feminism, which is obsessed with politically correct language, nor academic feminism, which believes that knowledge and experience are "constituted by" language, can understand preverbal or nonverbal communication. Feminism, focusing on sexual politics, cannot see that sex exists in and through the body. Sexual desire and arousal cannot be fully translated into verbal terms. This is why men and women misunderstand each other.

14   Trying to remake the future, feminism cut itself off from sexual history. It discarded and suppressed the sexual myths of literature, art and religion. Those myths show us the turbulence, the mysteries and passions of sex. In mythology we see men's sexual anxiety, their fear of woman's dominance. Much sexual violence is rooted in men's sense of psychological weakness toward women. It takes many men to deal with one woman. Woman's voracity is a persistent motif. Clara Bow,[3] it was rumored, took on the USC[4] football team on weekends. Marilyn Monroe, singing "Diamonds Are a Girl's Best Friend," rules a conga line of men in tuxes. Half-clad Cher, in the video for "If I Could Turn Back Time," deranges a battleship of screaming sailors and straddles a pink-lit

---

[2]A nineteenth-century reformer who advocated the abolition of alcohol (editors' note).

[3]A movie star from the Roaring Twenties era (editors' note).

[4]University of Southern California (editors' note).

cannon. Feminism, coveting social power, is blind to woman's cosmic sexual power.

To understand rape, you must study the past. There never was and never will be   15
sexual harmony. Every woman must be prudent and cautious about where she goes
and with whom. When she makes a mistake, she must accept the consequences and,
through self-criticism, resolve never to make that mistake again. Running to mommy
and daddy on the campus grievance committee is unworthy of strong women. Posting
lists of guilty men in the toilet is cowardly, infantile stuff.

The Italian philosophy of life espouses high-energy confrontation. A male student   16
makes a vulgar remark about your breasts? Don't slink off to whimper with the campus shrinking violets. Deal with it. On the spot. Say, "Shut up, you jerk! And crawl
back to the barnyard where you belong!" In general, women who project this take-
charge attitude toward life get harassed less often. I see too many dopey, immature,
self-pitying women walking around like melting sticks of butter. It's the Yvette
Mimieux syndrome: make me happy. And listen to me weep when I'm not.

The date-rape debate is already smothering in propaganda churned out by the   17
expensive Northeastern colleges and universities, with their overconcentration of boring, uptight academic feminists and spoiled, affluent students. Beware of the deep
manipulativeness of rich students who were neglected by their parents. They love to
turn the campus into hysterical psychodramas of sexual transgression, followed by
assertions of parental authority and concern. And don't look for sexual enlightenment
from academe, which spews out mountains of books but never looks at life directly.

As a fan of football and rock music, I see in the simple, swaggering masculinity of   18
the jock and in the noisy posturing of the heavy-metal guitarist certain fundamental,
unchanging truths about sex. Masculinity is aggressive, unstable, combustible. It is also
the most creative cultural force in history. Women must reorient themselves toward
the elemental powers of sex, which can strengthen or destroy.

The only solution to date rape is female self-awareness and self-control. A woman's   19
number-one line of defense against rape is herself. When a real rape occurs, she
should report it to the police. Complaining to college committees because the courts
"take too long" is ridiculous. College administrations are not a branch of the judiciary. They are not equipped or trained for legal inquiry. Colleges must alert incoming
students to the problems and dangers of adulthood. Then colleges must stand back
and get out of the sex game.

Questions for Close Reading

1. What is the selection's thesis? Locate the sentence(s) in which Paglia states her
   main idea. If she doesn't state the thesis explicitly, express it in your own words.

2. In Paglia's opinion, why are women more "vulnerable and defenseless" now
   than in the past?

3. According to Paglia, what "truth about sex" has feminism hidden from young
   women?

4. What does Paglia believe is "the only solution to date rape"?

5. Refer to your dictionary as needed to define the following words used in the selection: *inquests* (paragraph 2), *testosterone* (8), *constituted* (13), *grievance* (15), and *judiciary* (19).

Questions About the Writer's Craft

1. **The pattern.** Examine the way Paglia develops her argument in paragraphs 6 and 8. Which of her assertions in these paragraphs can be assumed to be true without further proof? Why do you think Paglia includes these essentially incontestable statements? Conversely, which of her assertions in paragraphs 6 and 8 require further proof before their truth can be demonstrated? Does Paglia provide such support? Explain.

2. **Other patterns.** How does Paglia use the comparison-contrast pattern to develop her argument?

3. Paglia's style is frequently characterized by short sentences strung together with few transitions. Locate some examples of this style. Why might Paglia have chosen this style? What is its effect?

4. Where does Paglia use emotional, highly connotative language? Where does she employ strongly worded absolute statements? Do you think that this use of pathos makes Paglia's argument more or less convincing? Explain.

Writing Assignments Using Argumentation-Persuasion as a Pattern of Development

∞ 1. Read Susan Jacoby's "Common Decency" (page 495), an essay that takes exception to Paglia's view of date rape. Decide which writer presents her case more convincingly. Then write an essay arguing that the *other writer* has trouble making a strong case for her position. Consider the merits and flaws (including any logical fallacies) in the argument, plus such issues as the writer's credibility, strategies for dealing with the opposing view, and use of emotional appeals. Throughout, support your opinion with specific examples drawn from the selection. Keep in mind that you're critiquing the effectiveness of the writer's argument. It's not appropriate, then, simply to explain why you agree or disagree with the writer's position or merely to summarize what the writer says.

∞ 2. Paglia criticizes those who claim that the environment, or social climate, is primarily responsible for shaping gender differences. She believes that such differences "are based in biology." Write an essay arguing your own position about the role that environment and biology play in determining sex-role attitudes and behavior. Remembering to acknowledge opposing views, defend your own viewpoint with plentiful examples based on your experiences and observations. You may also need to conduct some library research to gather support for your position. The following essays will provide insights that you may want to draw upon in your paper: Susan Douglas's "Managing Mixed Messages" (page 251), Joyce Garity's "Is Sex All That Matters?" (page 256), Deborah Tannen's "But What Do You Mean?" (page 288), and Dave Barry's "The Ugly Truth About Beauty" (page 367).

Writing Assignments Using Other Patterns of Development

3. Paglia writes in paragraph 7 that "men become masculine only when other men say they are. Having sex with a woman is one way a boy becomes a man." Write an essay constructing your own definition of masculinity. Comment on the extent to which you feel being sexually active is an important criterion, but also include other hallmarks of masculinity.

4. Date rape seems to be on the rise. Brainstorm with others to identify what may be leading to its growing occurrence. Focusing on several related factors, write an essay showing how these factors contribute to the problem. Possible factors include the following: the way males and females are depicted in the media (advertisements, movies, television, rock videos); young people's use of alcohol; the emergence of co-ed college dorms. At the end of the essay, offer some recommendations about what can be done to create a safer climate for dating. You should consider supporting your speculations with information about date rape gathered in the library and/or on the Internet.

Writing Assignment Using a Journal Entry as a Starting Point

5. Drawing upon the material in your pre-reading journal entry, write an essay in which you present a carefully considered definition of the term *date rape*. Explain clearly what constitutes date rape and what doesn't. To deepen your understanding of this thorny issue, consider brainstorming with others as well as conducting research in the library and/or on the Internet. One issue to consider: Do males and females define the term differently? If so, how do they define it, and why might their definitions differ?

SUSAN JACOBY

In the first job as a newspaper reporter, Susan Jacoby (1945–) carefully avoided doing "women's stories," believing that such features weren't worthy of a serious journalist. However, Jacoby's opinion changed with the times, especially as women's issues began to gain increasing attention. Indeed, many of her essays—including those in *The*

New York Times and *McCall's*—have dealt with women's concerns. Several of Jacoby's essays have been collected in *The Possible She* (1979) and *Money, Manners, and Morals* (1993). In 1994, she coauthored the biography *Soul to Soul: A Black Russian American Family 1865–1992*. Jacoby's most recent books include *Body* and *Geotrivia Sports*, both published in 1996, and *Half-Jew: A Daughter's Search for Her Family's Buried Past* (2000). The following selection, published in *The New York Times* in April 1991, was written in response to the book *Sexual Personae* by Camille Paglia (see page 489).

Pre-Reading Journal Entry

The phrase "boys will be boys" is often cited to explain certain types of male behavior. What kinds of actions typically fall into this category? List a few of these in your journal. Which behaviors are positive? Why? Which are negative? Why?

COMMON DECENCY

1   She was deeply in love with a man who was treating her badly. To assuage her wounded ego (and to prove to herself that she could get along nicely without him), she invited another man, an old boyfriend, to a dinner *à deux* in her apartment. They were on their way to the bedroom when, having realized that she wanted only the man who wasn't there, she changed her mind. Her ex-boyfriend was understandably angry. He left her apartment with a not-so-politely phrased request that she leave him out of any future plans.

2   And that is the end of the story—except for the fact that he was eventually kind enough to accept her apology for what was surely a classic case of "mixed signals."

3   I often recall this incident, in which I was the embarrassed female participant, as the controversy over "date rape"—intensified by the assault that William Kennedy Smith[1] has been accused of—heats up across the nation. What seems clear to me is that those who place acquaintance rape in a different category from "stranger rape"—those who excuse friendly social rapists on grounds that they are too dumb to understand when "no" means no—are being even more insulting to men than to women.

4   These apologists for date rape—and some of them are women—are really saying that the average man cannot be trusted to exercise any impulse control. Men are nasty and men are brutes—and a woman must be constantly on her guard to avoid giving a man any excuse to give way to his baser instincts.

5   If this view were accurate, few women would manage to get through life without being raped, and few men would fail to commit rape. For the reality is that all of us, men as well as women, send and receive innumerable mixed signals in the course of our sexual lives—and that is as true in marital beds at age fifty as in the back seats of cars at age fifteen.

6   Most men somehow manage to decode these signals without using superior physical strength to force themselves on their partners. And most women manage to handle

---

[1]William Kennedy Smith, the nephew of John, Robert, and Edward Kennedy, was accused of raping a woman in 1991. Kennedy was acquitted, but the trial, broadcast on television, created a national furor and generated heated debate on the issue of date rape (editors' note).

conflicting male signals without, say, picking up carving knives to demonstrate their displeasure at sexual rejection. This is called civilization.

Civilized is exactly what my old boyfriend was being when he didn't use my muddleheaded emotional distress as an excuse to rape me. But I don't owe him excessive gratitude for his decent behavior—any more than he would have owed me special thanks for not stabbing him through the heart if our situations had been reversed. Most date rapes do not happen because a man honestly mistakes a woman's "no" for a "yes" or a "maybe." They occur because a minority of men—an ugly minority, to be sure—can't stand to take "no" for an answer.

This minority behavior—and a culture that excuses it on grounds that boys will be boys—is the target of the movement against date rape that has surfaced on many campuses during the past year.

It's not surprising that date rape is an issue of particular importance to college-age women. The campus concentration of large numbers of young people, in an unsupervised environment that encourages drinking and partying, tends to promote sexual aggression and discourage inhibition. Drunken young men who rape a woman at a party can always claim they didn't know what they were doing—and a great many people will blame the victim for having been there in the first place.

That is the line adopted by antifeminists like Camille Paglia,[2] author of the controversial *Sexual Personae: Art and Decadence from Nefertiti to Emily Dickinson.* Paglia, whose views strongly resemble those expounded twenty years ago by Norman Mailer[3] in *The Prisoner of Sex,* argues that feminists have deluded women by telling them they can go anywhere and do anything without fear of rape. Feminism, in this view, is both naïve and antisexual because it ignores the power of women to incite uncontrollable male passions.

Just to make sure there is no doubt about a woman's place, Paglia also links the male sexual aggression that leads to rape with the creative energy of art. "There is no female Mozart," she has declared, "because there is no female Jack the Ripper." According to this "logic," one might expect to discover the next generation of composers in fraternity houses and dorms that have been singled out as sites of brutal gang rapes.

This type of unsubtle analysis makes no distinction between sex as an expression of the will to power and sex as a source of pleasure. When domination is seen as an inevitable component of sex, the act of rape is defined not by a man's actions but by a woman's signals.

It is true, of course, that some women (especially the young) initially resist sex not out of real conviction but as part of the elaborate persuasion and seduction rituals accompanying what was once called courtship. And it is true that many men (again, especially the young) take pride in the ability to coax a woman a step further than she intended to go.

But these mating rituals do not justify or even explain date rape. Even the most callow youth is capable of understanding the difference between resistance and

7

8

9

10

11

12

13

14

---

[2]For information on Camille Paglia, see page 489 (editors' note).

[3]An American essayist and novelist (editors' note)

genuine fear; between a halfhearted "no, we shouldn't" and tears or screams; between a woman who is physically free to leave a room and one who is being physically restrained.

15   The immorality and absurdity of using mixed signals as an excuse for rape is cast in high relief when the assault involves one woman and a group of men. In cases of gang rape in a social setting (usually during or after a party), the defendants and their lawyers frequently claim that group sex took place but no force was involved. These upright young men, so the defense invariably contends, were confused because the girl had voluntarily gone to a party with them. Why, she may have even displayed sexual interest in *one* of them. How could they have been expected to understand that she didn't wish to have sex with the whole group?

16   The very existence of the term "date rape" attests to a slow change in women's consciousness that began with the feminist movement of the late 1960s. Implicit in this consciousness is the conviction that a woman has the right to say no at any point in the process leading to sexual intercourse—and that a man who fails to respect her wishes should incur serious legal and social consequences.

17   The other, equally important half of the equation is respect for men. If mixed signals are the real cause of sexual assault, it behooves every woman to regard every man as a potential rapist.

18   In such a benighted universe, it would be impossible for a woman (and, let us not forget, for a man) to engage in the tentative emotional and physical exploration that eventually produces a mature erotic life. She would have to make up her mind right from the start in order to prevent a rampaging male from misreading her intentions.

19   Fortunately for everyone, neither the character of men nor the general quality of relations between the sexes is that crude. By censuring the minority of men who use ordinary socializing as an excuse for rape, feminists insist on sex as a source of pure pleasure rather than as a means of social control. Real men want an eager sexual partner—not a woman who is quaking with fear or even one who is ambivalent. Real men don't rape.

Questions for Close Reading

1. What is the selection's thesis? Locate the sentence(s) in which Jacoby states her main idea. If she doesn't state the thesis explicitly, express it in your own words.

2. Why does Jacoby feel that she doesn't owe her old boyfriend a great deal of gratitude, even though she sent mixed signals about what type of relationship she wanted?

3. What does Jacoby mean in paragraph 6 by her comment, "This is called civilization"? How does this comment support her thesis?

4. Why does Jacoby think that it's insulting to men to accept Paglia's notion that men are ruled by uncontrollable passions?

5. Refer to your dictionary as needed to define the following words used in the selection: *apologists* (paragraph 4), *deluded* (10), *unsubtle* (12), *implicit* (16), *benighted* (18), *erotic* (18), *rampaging* (18), and *ambivalent* (19).

Questions About the Writer's Craft

1. **The pattern.**   One way to refute an idea is to carry it to its logical extreme, thus revealing its inherent falsity or absurdity. This technique is called *reduction ad absurdum.* Examine paragraphs 4–5 and 15 and explain how Jacoby uses this technique to refute Paglia's position on date rape.

2. **Other patterns.**   Locate places in the essay where Jacoby compares and contrasts male and female behavior or the behavior of rapists and nonrapists. How does her use of comparison-contrast help her build her argument?

3. What introduction technique (see pages 76–79) does Jacoby use to begin the essay? How does this type of introduction help her achieve her persuasive goal?

4. How would you characterize Jacoby's tone? Identify specific sentences and words that convey this tone. What effect might Jacoby have hoped this tone would have on readers?

Writing Assignments Using Argumentation- Persuasion as a Pattern of Development

∞ 1. Jacoby feels that Camille Paglia and others "excuse . . . rapists." If you haven't already done so, read "Rape: A Bigger Danger Than Feminists Know" (page 490) to see what Paglia says about who bears primary responsibility for preventing rape. Then decide to what degree you feel men who commit date rape should be held accountable for their actions. Argue your position in an essay, making reference to both Jacoby's and Paglia's ideas to support your case. Also include reasons and evidence of your own.

2. Determine what your campus is doing about date rape. Does it have a formal policy defining date rape, a hearing process, ongoing workshops, discussions during orientation for incoming students? Write a paper explaining how your college deals with date rape. Then argue either that more attention should be devoted to this issue or that your college has adopted fair and comprehensive measures to deal with the problem. If you feel the college should do more, indicate what additional steps should be taken.

Writing Assignments Using Other Patterns of Development

∞ 3. Jacoby acknowledges that males and females often send "mixed signals" and cause each other confusion. Select one time that you found "mixed signals" with a person of the opposite sex to be a problem. For example, you might have conflicted because of different ways of expressing anger or because of dissimilar styles in asking for support. Describe what happened and explain why you think such mixed signals occurred. Before writing the paper, you may want to read "But What Do You Mean?" (page 288) by Deborah Tannen and "The Ugly Truth About Beauty" (page 367) by Dave Barry to see what these authors have to say about some basic differences between men and women.

4. Interview some people, both males and females, to determine their definition of date rape. In an essay, discuss any differences between the two sexes' perspectives. That done, present your own definition of date rape, explaining what it is and what it isn't.

Writing Assignment Using a Journal Entry as a Starting Point

5. Some people believe that "boys-will-be-boys" behavior is potentially dangerous and therefore not acceptable. Others argue that it is perfectly innocent and therefore permissible. What do you think? Drawing upon your pre-reading journal entry, write an essay taking a position on this issue. Provide persuasive examples to support your viewpoint, refuting as much of the opposing argument as you can. Discussing the topic with others and doing some research in the library and/or on the Internet will broaden your understanding of this complex issue.

Debating the Issues: Multiculturalism

YUH JI-YEON

Yuh Ji-Yeon was born in Seoul, Korea, in 1965. Her family immigrated to the United States and settled in Chicago when Yuh was five years old. A 1987 graduate of Stanford University, she worked as a reporter for the *Omaha World-Herald* and *New York Newsday* and is currently pursuing a doctorate at the University of Pennsylvania. The essay reprinted here originally appeared in *The Philadelphia Inquirer* in 1991.

Pre-Reading Journal Entry

Which events in American history do you consider shameful? List these events in your journal. For each, jot down what your teachers taught you about the event when you were a child. Does what you were taught as a child differ from what you know now? In what way? If you did later on learn harsher truths about these events, how did you feel? Do you believe that you should have been told the truth from the beginning? Why or why not?

LET'S TELL THE STORY OF ALL
AMERICA'S CULTURES

I grew up hearing, seeing and almost believing that America was white—albeit with   1
a little black tinge here and there—and that white was best.

The white people were everywhere in my 1970s Chicago childhood: Founding   2
Fathers, Lewis and Clark, Lincoln, Daniel Boone, Carnegie, presidents, explorers and
industrialists galore. The only black people were slaves. The only Indians were scalpers.

I never heard one word about how Benjamin Franklin was so impressed by the   3
Iroquois federation of nations that he adapted that model into our system of state and
federal government. Or that the Indian tribes were systematically betrayed and mas-
sacred by a greedy young nation that stole their land and called it the United States.

I never heard one word about how Asian immigrants were among the first to turn   4
California's desert into fields of plenty. Or about Chinese immigrant Ah Bing, who bred
the cherry now on sale in groceries across the nation. Or that plantation owners in
Hawaii imported labor from China, Japan, Korea and the Philippines to work the sugar
cane fields. I never learned that Asian immigrants were the only immigrants denied
U.S. citizenship, even though they served honorably in World War I. All the
immigrants in my textbook were white.

I never learned about Frederick Douglass, the runaway slave who became a leading   5
abolitionist and statesman, or about black scholar W. E. B. Du Bois. I never learned that
black people rose up in arms against slavery. Nat Turner wasn't one of the heroes in
my childhood history class.

I never learned that the American Southwest and California were already settled by   6
Mexicans when they were annexed after the Mexican-American War. I never learned
that Mexico once had a problem keeping land-hungry white men on the U.S. side of
the border.

So when other children called me a slant-eyed chink and told me to go back where I   7
came from, I was ready to believe that I wasn't really an American because I wasn't white.

America's bittersweet legacy of struggling and failing and getting another step clos-   8
er to democratic ideals of liberty and equality and justice for all wasn't for the likes of
me, an immigrant child from Korea. The history books said so.

Well, the history books were wrong.   9

Educators around the country are finally realizing what I realized as a teenager in the   10
library, looking up the history I wasn't getting in school. America is a multicultural
nation, composed of many people with varying histories and varying traditions who have
little in common except their humanity, a belief in democracy and a desire for freedom.

America changed them, but they changed America too.   11

A committee of scholars and teachers gathered by the New York State Department   12
of Education recognizes this in their recent report, "One Nation, Many Peoples: A
Declaration of Cultural Interdependence."

They recommend that public schools provide a "multicultural education, anchored   13
to the shared principles of a liberal democracy."

What that means, according to the report, is recognizing that America was shaped   14
and continues to be shaped by people of diverse backgrounds. It calls for students to
be taught that history is an ongoing process of discovery and interpretation of the past,
and that there is more than one way of viewing the world.

15   Thus, the westward migration of white Americans is not just a heroic settling of an untamed wild, but also the conquest of indigenous peoples. Immigrants were not just white, but Asian as well. Blacks were not merely passive slaves freed by northern whites, but active fighters for their own liberation.

16   In particular, according to the report, the curriculum should help children "to assess critically the reasons for the inconsistencies between the ideals of the U.S. and social realities. It should provide information and intellectual tools that can permit them to contribute to bringing reality closer to the ideals."

17   In other words, show children the good with the bad, and give them the skills to help improve their country. What could be more patriotic?

18   Several dissenting members of the New York committee publicly worry that America will splinter into ethnic fragments if this multicultural curriculum is adopted. They argue that the committee's report puts the focus on ethnicity at the expense of national unity.

19   But downplaying ethnicity will not bolster national unity. The history of America is the story of how and why people from all over the world came to the United States, and how in struggling to make a better life for themselves, they changed each other, they changed the country, and they all came to call themselves Americans.

20   *E pluribus unum.* Out of many, one.

21   This is why I, with my Korean background, and my childhood tormentors, with their lost-in-the-mist-of-time European backgrounds, are all Americans.

22   It is the unique beauty of this country. It is high time we let all our children gaze upon it.

Questions for Close Reading

1. What is the selection's thesis? Locate the sentence(s) in which Yuh states her main idea. If she doesn't state the thesis explicitly, express it in your own words.

2. Yuh makes the rather shocking claim that "the history books were wrong" (paragraph 9). Why does she make this statement? What evidence does she offer to support it?

3. According to Yuh, what changes are needed in American history courses?

4. Why does Yuh feel it is critical that American students receive more than the traditional whites-only version of our nation's history? Who will be served by making history books more multicultural?

5. Refer to your dictionary as needed to define the following words used in the selection: *albeit* (paragraph 1), *tinge* (1), *galore* (2), *multicultural* (10, 13, 18), *interdependence* (12), *indigenous* (15), *dissenting* (18), *ethnicity* (18), and *bolster* (19).

Questions About the Writer's Craft

1. **The pattern.**   Where in her argument does Yuh present the opposing viewpoint? Why do you suppose she waits so long to deal with the dissenting opinion? What effect does this delay have on her argument's effectiveness?

2. **Other patterns.**   Why might Yuh have decided to use so many examples in paragraphs 2 through 6? How do these examples contribute to the persuasiveness of her position? Why might she have placed these examples before her thesis statement?

3. Yuh mixes the subjective and the objective in her argument. Where does she use specifics from her own life? How do these personal details help persuade readers to accept her viewpoint?

4. Yuh often uses parallelism and repetition of phrases, particularly in paragraphs 1 through 6 and paragraph 15. What effect do you think she intended these two stylistic devices to have on her readers?

Writing Assignments Using Argumentation-Persuasion as a Pattern of Development

1. Using the resources of the library and/or Internet, read several articles about the ongoing debate over multiculturalism's role in contemporary education. You should find coverage of the 1991 New York State Department of Education Study (cited by Yuh in paragraph 12) and historian Arthur Schlesinger, Jr.'s *Time* essay "The Cult of Ethnicity: Good and Bad" (July 8, 1991) especially helpful. Review your research, and decide whether or not you support the idea of a multicultural curriculum. Then write an essay in which you argue your position, refuting as many of the opposing views as possible. Draw upon your own experiences as well as your research when developing your point of view.

2. Yuh cites a problem she encountered in her education. Brainstorm the problems or insufficiencies you found in your own education. Then select a single problem at one level of education, and meet with others to discuss their experiences with the problem. Drawing upon the most compelling examples, write a persuasive essay directed at those who think all is well in our educational system. For additional perspectives on educational problems, consider reading Sophronia Liu's "So Tsi-fai" (page 221), Joseph H. Suina's "And Then I Went to School" (page 371), and Mary Sherry's "In Praise of the 'F' Word" (page 480).

Writing Assignments Using Other Patterns of Development

3. Because the mainstream culture they lived in didn't recognize the presence of minorities, the author's classmates considered Yuh almost a nonbeing. To what extent, in your opinion, does television contribute to the dehumanization of minorities? For several days, watch a variety of television shows, noting how a particular ethnic or minority group (such as African Americans, Hispanic Americans, or the elderly) is portrayed. Then write an essay showing that television's depiction of this group is either accurate *or* distorted. Support your main

idea with plentiful references to specific television shows, including newscasts, situation comedies, talk shows, and so forth. In addition, Brent Staples's "Black Men and Public Space" (page 407) might shed further light on this issue.

4. The New York State Department of Education report (paragraphs 12–16) argues that curriculum should encourage young people to examine "the reasons for the inconsistencies between the ideals of the U.S. and social realities." Like most people, you probably detected such disparities when you were growing up. Perhaps you heard an admired neighbor brag about padding an expense account or learned that an esteemed high school coach took kickbacks from college recruiters. Focus on one such clash between the ethical ideal and the everyday reality, and write about the incident's effect on you. At the end of the essay, reach some conclusions about the way children can be helped to deal with such collisions between ideals and reality.

Writing Assignment Using a Journal Entry as a Starting Point

5. Write an essay in which you argue for *or* against schools' revealing harsh historical realities to children. Review your pre-reading journal entry, and select *one* historical event to focus on. Provide plentiful reasons to support your position, whenever possible pointing out weaknesses in opposing viewpoints. To deepen your understanding of the issue, consider reading Audre Lorde's "The Fourth of July" (page 216), Beth Johnson's "Bombs Bursting in Air" (page 245), and Arthur Schlesinger, Jr.'s "The Cult of Ethnicity: Good and Bad" (page 504), essays exploring parents' quandary between protecting their children and educating them about life's painful realities.

ARTHUR SCHLESINGER, JR.

Special adviser to the Kennedy administration from 1961–64, Arthur Schlesinger, Jr., won a Pulitzer Prize for *A Thousand Days* (1965), his book on John F. Kennedy. A professor at the graduate school of the City University of New York, Schlesinger is a widely regarded author of American history. His many publications include *The Politics of Upheaval* (1974), *The Imperial Presidency* (1973), *Robert Kennedy and His Times* (1980), *The Age of Jackson* (1988), *The Disunity of America* (1992), and *The History of U.S. Political Parties* (2001). "The Cult of Ethnicity: Good and Bad" was first published in *Time* in 1991.

Pre-Reading Journal Entry

If you were asked to explain to someone from another country what it's like to be an American, how would you respond? In your journal, freewrite on what you think it means to be American—what characteristics, in your opinion, generally distinguish citizens of the United States as a whole from citizens of other nations.

THE CULT OF ETHNICITY: GOOD AND BAD

The history of the world has been in great part the history of the mixing of peoples.   1
Modern communication and transport accelerate mass migrations from one continent
to another. Ethnic and racial diversity is more than ever a salient fact of the age.

But what happens when people of different origins, speaking different languages   2
and professing different religions, inhabit the same locality and live under the same
political sovereignty? Ethnic and racial conflict—far more than ideological conflict—is
the explosive problem of our times.

On every side today ethnicity is breaking up nations. The Soviet Union,[1] India,   3
Yugoslavia,[2] Ethiopia, are all in crisis. Ethnic tensions disturb and divide Sri Lanka,
Burma, Indonesia, Iraq, Cyprus, Nigeria, Angola, Lebanon, Guyana, Trinidad—you
name it. Even nations as stable and civilized as Britain and France, Belgium and
Spain, face growing ethnic troubles. Is there any large multiethnic state that can be
made to work?

The answer to that question has been, until recently, the United States. "No other   4
nation," Margaret Thatcher has said, "has so successfully combined people of different
races and nations within a single culture." How have Americans succeeded in pulling
off this almost unprecedented trick?

We have always been a multiethnic country. Hector St. John de Crèvecoeur, who   5
came from France in the 18th century, marveled at the astonishing diversity of the settlers—"a mixture of English, Scotch, Irish, French, Dutch, Germans and Swedes . . .
this promiscuous breed." He propounded a famous question: "What then is the
American, this new man?" And he gave a famous answer: "Here individuals of all
nations are melted into a new race of men." *E pluribus unum.*[3]

The U.S. escaped the divisiveness of a multiethnic society by a brilliant solution: the   6
creation of a brand-new national identity. The point of America was not to preserve old
cultures but to forge a new, *American* culture. "By an intermixture with our people,"
President George Washington told Vice President John Adams, immigrants will "get assimilated to our customs, measures and laws: in a word, soon become one people." This was
the ideal that a century later Israel Zangwill crystallized in the title of his popular 1908
play *The Melting Pot.* And no institution was more potent in molding Crèvecoeur's
"promiscuous breed" into Washington's "one people" than the American public school.

The new American nationality was inescapably English in language, ideas and insti-   7
tutions. The pot did not melt everybody, not even all the white immigrants; deeply
bred racism put black Americans, yellow Americans, red Americans and brown
Americans well outside the pale. Still, the infusion of other stocks, even of nonwhite
stocks, and the experience of the New World reconfigured the British legacy and made
the U.S., as we all know, a very different country from Britain.

In the 20th century, new immigration laws altered the composition of the American   8
people, and a cult of ethnicity erupted both among non-Anglo whites and among nonwhite minorities. This had many healthy consequences. The American culture at last

---

[1]In 1991, the Soviet Union was dissolved into fifteen separate nations, partly because of the
very ethnic conflicts Schlesinger describes (editors' note).

[2]In 1991, Yugoslavia also split into six nations because of ethnic rivalries (editors' note).

[3]A reference to the official motto of the United States, *E pluribus unum*, a Latin phrase meaning "Out of many, one." Schlesinger suggests that the emphasis is shifting from one (*unum*)
single American nationality to many (*pluribus*) separate ethnic groups (editors' note).

began to give shamefully overdue recognition to the achievement of groups subordinated and spurned during the high noon of Anglo dominance, and it began to acknowledge the great swirling world beyond Europe. Americans acquired a more complex and invigorating sense of their world—and of themselves.

9   But, pressed too far, the cult of ethnicity has unhealthy consequences. It gives rise, for example, to the conception of the U.S. as a nation composed not of individuals making their own choices but of inviolable ethnic and racial groups. It rejects the historic American goals of assimilation and integration. And, in an excess of zeal, well-intentioned people seek to transform our system of education from a means of creating "one people" into a means of promoting, celebrating and perpetuating separate ethnic origins and identities. The balance is shifting from *unum* to *pluribus.*

10   That is the issue that lies behind the hullabaloo over "multiculturalism" and "political correctness," the attack on the "Eurocentric" curriculum and the rise of the notion that history and literature should be taught not as disciplines but as therapies whose function is to raise minority self-esteem. Group separatism crystallizes the differences, magnifies tensions, intensifies hostilities. Europe—the unique source of the liberating ideas of democracy, civil liberties and human rights—is portrayed as the root of all evil, and non-European cultures, their own many crimes deleted, are presented as the means of redemption.

11   I don't want to sound apocalyptic about these developments. Education is always in ferment, and a good thing too. The situation in our universities, I am confident, will soon right itself. But the impact of separatist pressures on our public schools is more troubling. If a Kleagle[4] of the Ku Klux Klan wanted to use the schools to disable and handicap black Americans, he could hardly come up with anything more effective than the "Afrocentric" curriculum. And if separatist tendencies go unchecked, the result can only be the fragmentation, resegregation and tribalization of American life.

12   I remain optimistic. My impression is that the historic forces driving toward "one people" have not lost their power. The eruption of ethnicity is, I believe, a rather superficial enthusiasm stirred by romantic ideologues on the one hand and by unscrupulous con men on the other: self-appointed spokesmen whose claim to represent their minority groups is carelessly accepted by the media. Most American-born members of minority groups, white or nonwhite, see themselves primarily as Americans rather than primarily as members of one or another ethnic group. A notable indicator today is the rate of intermarriage across ethnic lines, across religious lines, even (increasingly) across racial lines. "We Americans," said Theodore Roosevelt, "are children of the crucible."

13   The growing diversity of the American population makes the quest for unifying ideals and a common culture all the more urgent. In a world savagely rent by ethnic and racial antagonisms, the U.S. must continue as an example of how a highly differentiated society holds itself together.

---

[4]An official of the Ku Klux Klan (editors' note).

Questions for Close Reading

1. What is the selection's thesis? Locate the sentence(s) in which Schlesinger states his main idea. If he doesn't state the thesis explicitly, express it in your own words.

2. According to Schlesinger, how has the United States, despite its ethnic diversity, managed to forge a unified national identity?

3. What, in Schlesinger's opinion, are the possible benefits of a "cult of ethnicity"? What are its drawbacks?

4. Why is Schlesinger optimistic about America's future as a unified, undivided nation?

5. Refer to your dictionary as needed to define the following words used in the selection: *salient* (paragraph 1), *sovereignty* (2), *ideological* (2), *unprecedented* (4), *promiscuous* (5), *assimilated* (6), *crystallized* (6), *potent* (6), *infusion* (7), *reconfigured* (7), *spurned* (8), *Anglo* (8), *inviolable* (9), *zeal* (9), *apocalyptic* (11), *ferment* (11), *crucible* (12), and *rent* (13).

Questions About the Writer's Craft

1. **The pattern.**   Where in the essay does Schlesinger cite the opposing viewpoint? How does his characterization of this viewpoint help him achieve his purpose?

2. Schlesinger poses a series of questions in paragraphs 2–4. How do these questions help him convey his ideas to an audience of mainstream readers?

3. **Other patterns.**   Throughout his essay, Schlesinger uses terms that have become "buzzwords"—words with specialized, often emotional connotations. Two examples are *Anglo* (paragraph 8) and *Eurocentric* (10). Locate other instances. Why do you think Schlesinger decided not to define these terms? How do these undefined terms help Schlesinger reinforce his argument?

4. Schlesinger includes a number of quotations in his essay. Locate several of them. Why might he have decided to quote these particular sources?

Writing Assignments Using Argumentation-Persuasion as a Pattern of Development

∞ 1. Write an essay defending *or* challenging Schlesinger's point that heightened ethnic awareness may have "unhealthy consequences." To gather material on both sides of the issue, speak to individuals with varying viewpoints, drawing on their experiences as well as your own to support your position. For additional insights on multicultural perspectives, read Joseph H. Suina's "And Then I Went to School" (page 371), Brent Staples's "Black Men and Public Space" (page 407), and Yuh Ji-Yeon's "Let's Tell the Story of All America's Cultures" (page 500).

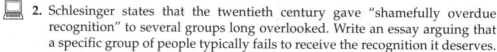 2. Schlesinger states that the twentieth century gave "shamefully overdue recognition" to several groups long overlooked. Write an essay arguing that a specific group of people typically fails to receive the recognition it deserves.

You might focus on the accomplishments of a particular ethnic, racial, or religious group, or on the achievements of a group distinguished in some other way—for example, single parents or caregivers of the elderly. Assume that some of your readers are apathetic about the group you're writing, so be sure to provide compelling examples that challenge their indifference. Consider supplementing your ideas with research performed in the library and/or on the Internet.

Writing Assignments Using Other Patterns of Development

3. Schlesinger implies that Americans are more similar than they are different. Write an essay about a racial, ethnic, generational, gender, or other tension that you have observed—perhaps at your college, in your community, in your home, or on the job. Begin the paper with a vivid example that demonstrates the nature of the conflict. Then explain what steps *one* group—for example, students, administrators, townspeople, the clergy, parents, and so on—could take to improve the situation. How might they defuse hostilities by highlighting the similarities between the groups at odds?

∞ 4. As Schlesinger points out, public education has functioned as a strong unifying national force. However, it has also tended, perhaps in the service of that unity, to ignore some of the less heroic, more shameful events in American history: for example, the massacre of Native Americans in the West and the internment of Japanese Americans during World War II. Write an essay in which you show how children are affected by the withholding of this information. Then discuss how they might be affected if they were taught some of these harsh truths. To deepen your understanding of the issue, be sure to read Yuh Ji-Yeon's "Let's Tell the Story of All America's Cultures" (page 499). Talking with others and conducting some library research will also help you sort out the issue's complexities.

Writing Assignment Using a Journal Entry as a Starting Point

5. In offering his theory about what constitutes "Americanness," Schlesinger quotes Crèvecoeur, who asked "What then is the American?" In an essay of your own, offer your definition of *American*. Begin by reviewing your initial thoughts on this topic as recorded in your pre-reading journal entry. Then interview friends and family for their impressions. In your essay, feel free to consider positive as well as negative values and characteristics of being American. Be sure to provide examples throughout to illustrate the features of your definition. Alternatively, write an essay arguing that *American* cannot be easily defined, giving specific examples of American traits and behaviors to prove your case.

ADDITIONAL WRITING TOPICS: ARGUMENTATION-PERSUASION

General Assignments

Using argumentation-persuasion, develop one of the following topics in an essay. After choosing a topic, think about your purpose and audience. Remember that the paper's thesis should state the issue under discussion as well as your position on the issue. As you work on developing evidence, you might want to do some outside research. Keep in mind that effective argumentation-persuasion usually means that some time should be spent acknowledging and perhaps refuting opposing points of view. Be careful not to sabotage your argument by basing your case on a logical fallacy.

1. Hiring quotas
2. Giving birth-control devices to teenagers
3. Prayer in the schools
4. Spouses sharing housework equally
5. Big-time sports in college
6. Music videos
7. Drugs and alcohol on campus
8. Requiring college students to pass a comprehensive exam in their majors before graduating
9. Putting elderly parents in nursing homes
10. Financial aid for college students

Assignments with a Specific Purpose, Audience, and Point of View

On Campus

1. Your college's Financial Aid Department has decided not to renew your scholarship for next year, citing a drop in your grades last semester and an unenthusiastic recommendation from one of your instructors. Write a letter to the Director of Financial Aid arguing for the renewal of your scholarship.

2. You strongly believe that a particular policy or regulation on campus is unreasonable or unjust. Write a letter to the Dean of Students (or other appropriate administrator) arguing that the policy needs to be, if not completely revoked, amended in some way. Support your contention with specific examples showing how the regulation has gone wrong. End by providing constructive suggestions for how the policy problem can be solved.

At Home or in the Community

3. You and one or more family members don't agree on some aspect of your romantic life (you want to live with your boyfriend/girlfriend and they don't approve; you want to get married and they want you to wait; they simply don't like your partner). Write a letter explaining why your preference is reasonable. Try hard to win your family member(s) over to your side.

4. Assume you're a member of a racial, ethnic, religious, or social minority. You might, for example, be a Native American, an elderly person, a female executive. On a recent television show or in a TV commercial, you saw something that depicts your group in an offensive way. Write a letter (to the network or the advertiser) expressing your feelings and explaining why you feel the material should be taken off the air.

On the Job

5. As a staff writer for an online pop-culture magazine, you've been asked to nominate the "Most Memorable TV Moment of the Last 50 Years" to be featured as the magazine's lead article. Write a letter to your supervising editor in support of your nominee.

6. As a high school teacher, you support some additional restriction on students. The restriction might be "no radios in school," "no T-shirts," "no food in class," "no smoking on school grounds." Write an article for the school newspaper, justifying this new rule to the student body.

THE
RESEARCH
PAPER

PART IV

20
SELECTING A SUBJECT, USING THE LIBRARY AND THE INTERNET, AND TAKING NOTES

SOME GENERAL COMMENTS ABOUT THE RESEARCH PAPER

If you're like many of the students we know, **research papers** probably make you nervous. Why, you may wonder, do instructors assign them? Such projects take time, and the payoff, you may feel, doesn't seem worth the effort. If this *is* how you feel, we hope to show you that conducting research and writing up your findings can be rewarding, even fun.

Think of library research as a treasure hunt. The deeper you dig, the more you unearth material that's new to you. Besides experiencing the pleasure of such discovery, you become an expert of sorts in your subject and grow more comfortable with research methods. Most important, writing a research paper enlarges your perspective. As you test your own views against existing evidence, evaluate conflicting opinions, and learn how to detect other people's biases, you acquire analytic skills that will benefit you throughout life. These skills enable you to move beyond casual, off-the-top-of-the-head opinions to those that are well reasoned and thoughtful. In everyday conversation, most of us feel free to voice all kinds of opinions, even if they're based on nothing more than emotion and secondhand information. Researched opinions, though, are sounder and more logical. They're based on authoritative evidence rather than on limited personal experience, on fact rather than on hearsay. Instead of being rooted in unexamined personal belief, researched opinions emerge from a careful consideration of the evidence.

All of this may sound intimidating, but keep in mind that writing a research paper expands what you already know about writing essays; many of the steps are the same. The two major differences are the greater length of the research paper—usually five or more pages—and the kind of support you offer for your thesis. Rather than relying on your own experience or that of friends or family, you use published information and expert opinion to support your thesis. Even so, writing a research paper *can* be a challenge. One way to make the project more manageable is to view it as a process consisting of two major phases: (1) the **research stage,** when you find out all you can about your subject and identify a working thesis, and (2) the **writing stage,** when you present in an accepted format what you've discovered. This chapter focuses on the first stage; the next, Chapter 21, examines the second stage. Although we discuss the research process as a series of steps, we encourage you to modify the sequence to suit your subject, your personal approach to writing, and the requirements of a particular assignment.

During the first stage of the research process, you do the following:

- Plan the research
- Find sources in the library
- Prepare a working bibliography
- Take notes to support the thesis with evidence

PLAN THE RESEARCH

Understand the Paper's Boundaries

Your first step in planning the research is to *clarify the project's requirements.* How long is the paper supposed to be? How extensively should you deal with opposing viewpoints? Are there any restrictions about the number and type of sources? Are popular magazines and books acceptable, or should you use only scholarly sources? Has the instructor limited your subject choices?

Also, be sure you *understand the paper's overall purpose.* Unless you've been assigned a purely informative report ("explain several psychologists' theories of hostility"), your research paper shouldn't simply display all the information you have gathered. Instead of merely patching together ideas from a variety of sources, you should develop your own position, using outside sources to arrive at a balanced but definitive conclusion.

One more point: You should be aware that most instructors expect students to use the third-person point of view in research papers. If you plan to include any personal experiences, observations, or interviews (see the following page and page 577) along with your outside research, ask your instructor whether the use of the first-person point of view would be appropriate.

Understand Primary Versus Secondary Research

You should determine whether your instructor expects you to conduct any **primary research**—information gathered from firsthand observations, personal interviews, and the like. Most college research papers involve **library** or **secondary research**—information gathered secondhand from the Internet (see pages 534–544) or from published print sources. Such material includes information gathered from published accounts, including statistics, facts, case studies, expert opinion, critical interpretations, and experimental results. Occasionally, though, you may want or be asked to conduct primary research. You may, for example, run an experiment, visit an organization, observe a situation, schedule an interview, or conduct a survey. In such cases of primary research, you'll need to prepare carefully and establish a strict deadline schedule for yourself. (See page 577 for hints on incorporating primary research into a paper.)

Conducting Interviews in Person, by Phone, and Through E-Mail

If you plan to go on an information-gathering interview, put some careful thought into how you will proceed. If you use a letter rather than a telephone call to request an interview, get feedback on the letter's overall effectiveness before mailing it. When you set up your appointment, request enough time (30–60 minutes) to discuss your topic in depth; keep in mind, however, that the person may not be able to set aside as much time as you'd like. If you hope to tape-record the interview, you must obtain permission to do so beforehand. (Some organizations don't permit employees to be recorded during interviews.) Also, when making the appointment, ask if you may quote the person directly; he or she is entitled to know that all comments will be "on the record."

Most important, plan the interview carefully. First, determine what you want to accomplish: Do you want to gather general background material or do you want to clear up confusion about a specific point? Then, well in advance of the interview, prepare a list of questions geared toward that goal. During the interview, though, remain flexible—follow up on interesting remarks even if they diverge somewhat from your original plan. (If you discover that your interviewee isn't as informed as you had hoped, graciously request the names of other people who might help you further.) Throughout the interview, take accurate and complete notes (unless, of course, you're taping). If certain remarks seem especially quotable, make sure you get the statements down correctly. Finally, soon after the interview ends, be sure to fill in any gaps in your notes.

If a face-to-face interview isn't feasible, a phone interview often will provide the information you need. Don't, however, call the person and expect a phone interview on the spot. Instead, call, explain the kind of help you would like, and see if the person is willing to schedule time to talk at a later date. If so, follow the guidelines above for conducting a focused interview.

Another way to conduct an interview is through the Internet. Perhaps you read an article and have questions about several of the author's points. Or maybe you want to see if the author can direct you to additional material on your topic. You note that the author's e-mail address is provided, so you decide to connect with the author electronically. Your e-mail correspondence should describe the topic you're researching, explain your reasons for establishing contact, and list clearly and concisely the information you would like the author to provide. It's also a good idea to give the date by which you hope the author can get back to you. If the author's e-mail address isn't provided, the following search directory can help you track down the address:

SMARTpages.com at <http://www.smartpages.com>

(For additional information about the Internet and e-mail interviews, see pages 534–544).

Conducting Surveys

A survey helps you gather a good deal of information from many people (called "respondents")—and in a much shorter period of time than would be needed to interview each person individually. If you believe that citing the opinions of a group of people will strengthen your paper, you might want to conduct a survey. Bear in mind, though, that designing, administering, and interpreting a survey questionnaire are time-consuming tasks that demand considerable skill. Be sure, then, to have someone knowledgeable about surveys evaluate both your questionnaire and the responses it evokes.

When you write your survey questions, make them as clear and precise as possible. For example, if your goal is to determine the frequency with which something occurs, do not ask for vague responses such as "seldom," "often," and "occasionally." Instead, ask the respondents to identify more specific time periods: "weekly," "1–3 times a week," "4–6 times a week," and "daily." Also, steer away from questions that favor one side of an issue or that restrict the range of responses. Consider the following survey questions:

Should already overburdened college students be required to participate in a community-service activity before they can graduate?

Yes _____   No _____   Maybe _____

In your opinion, how knowledgeable are college students about jobs in their majors?

Knowledgeable _____   Not knowledgeable _____

Both of the preceding questions need to be revised but for different reasons. The first, by assuming that students are "already overburdened," biases respondents to reply negatively. To make the question more neutral, you would have to eliminate the prejudicial words. The second question asks respondents to answer in terms of a simple contrast: "Knowledgeable" or "Not knowledgeable." It ignores the likelihood that some respondents may wish to reply "Very knowledgeable," "Somewhat knowledgeable," and so on.

You should include in your survey only those items that will yield useful information. For example, if administering a survey to students on your campus, you would ask respondents some questions about their age, college year, major, and so forth—as long as you planned to break responses into subgroups. But these questions would be unnecessary if you didn't intend to analyze responses in such a manner. In any case, be sure to limit the number of questions you ask. If you don't, you'll regret it later on when you sort out the responses.

When you conduct a survey, it's unlikely that you'll be able to poll every member of the group whose opinions you seek. Instead, you must poll a *representative subgroup* of the whole. By *representative*, we mean "having characteristics similar to the group as a whole." Imagine you're writing a research paper on unfair employment practices. As part of your data collection, you decide to poll students on campus about their job experiences. If you, a first-year student, give the questionnaire only to students in your introductory courses, your sample won't be representative of the student body as a whole. Upper-level students might have significantly different work experiences and thus quite different opinions about employer fairness. So, to gauge students' attitudes at your college with accuracy, you'll have to hand out your survey in numerous places and on varied occasions on the campus. That way, your responses will be drawn from the whole spectrum of undergraduate backgrounds, majors, ages, and so forth.

This method of collecting student responses still wouldn't amount to what is called a *random sample*. To achieve a random sample, you must choose respondents by a scientific method—one that would, theoretically, give each person in the group to be studied the chance to respond. For example, to survey undergraduates on your campus, you would have to obtain a comprehensive list of all enrolled students. From this list, you would pick names at a regular interval, perhaps every tenth; to each tenth person, you would deliver (or mail or e-mail) a survey, or you would telephone to ask the questions orally. With this method, every enrolled student has the potential of being chosen as a respondent.

Since there's so much time and, possibly, cost involved in doing a random sample, you'll most likely use an informal method of collecting responses. Using the "street corner" approach, you might hand your survey to passersby or to people seated in classes, in student lounges, and so on. Or, if you're collecting information about the service provided at a particular facility, you might (with permission) place a short questionnaire where respondents can pick it up, quickly fill it out, and return it. Because of your informal methods, your results would be an *approximate* portrait of the group polled; however, the more people you survey, the more accurate your profile of the larger population is likely to be. (See page 577 for hints on incorporating survey results into a research paper.)

Once you're sure of the paper's boundaries and understand your instructor's expectations regarding primary and secondary research, it's time for you to move on. At this point, you'll need to (1) choose a general subject, (2) limit that subject, (3) conduct preliminary research, (4) identify a working thesis, and (5) make a schedule.

Choose a General Subject

Your instructor may provide a list of acceptable topics for a research paper, or you may be free to select a topic on your own. In the latter case, your second step in planning the research is to *choose a general subject*. If you have an area of interest—say, Native American culture or animal rights—the subject might be suitable for a research paper. If you don't immediately know what you'd like to research, consider current events, journal entries, the courses you're taking, the reading you've done on your own, or some of the selections in this book. A sociology course may have piqued your interest in child abuse or the elderly. Current events might suggest research on water pollution or business ethics. Several of your journal entries may focus on an issue that concerns you—maybe, for example, use of drugs in college athletics. Perhaps you've come across a provocative article on nuclear power or the nation's health-care crisis. Maybe you find yourself disagreeing with what Clifford Stoll says about classroom computer use in "Why Computers Don't Belong in the Classroom" on page 484 of this book. (In the activities at the end of this chapter, you'll find a list of suggested research topics derived from the readings in this text.)

If you're still not sure of what subject to research, go to the library and do some background reading on several possible general subjects. Also try using one or more prewriting techniques to identify areas that interest or puzzle you. Brainstorming, questioning, freewriting, and mapping (see pages 26–31) should help you generate ideas worth exploring. As soon as you have a list of possible topics, use the following checklist to help you determine which of these subjects would or would not be appropriate for a research paper.

☑ SELECTING AN APPROPRIATE SUBJECT TO RESEARCH:
   A CHECKLIST

☐ Will you enjoy learning about the subject for the substantial period of time you'll be working on the research paper? If you think you might get bored, select another subject.

☐ Can you obtain enough information on the subject? Recent developments (an ongoing government scandal or a controversial new program to help the homeless) can be investigated only through mass-circulation newspapers and magazines. Books as well as specialized or scholarly journal articles on recent events may not be available for some time.

☐ Has the topic been researched so often (the legalization of marijuana, violence in sports) that there's nothing new or interesting left to say about it?

☐ Is the topic surrounded by unreliable testimony (ESP, UFOs, the Bermuda Triangle), making it unsuitable for a research paper?

□ Is the topic (a rock star's conflict with the recording industry, for example) too trivial for an academic project?

□ Does the subject lend itself to or call for research? If it doesn't, think about selecting another topic. For example, the dangers of smoking are now almost universally acknowledged and so probably wouldn't make an appropriate topic for a research paper.

□ Has the topic been written about by only one major source? If so, your research will be one-sided.

□ Can you be objective about your topic? Researching both sides of an issue about which you feel strongly usually deepens your understanding of the issue's complexity. But if you feel so committed to a point of view that you'll have trouble considering opposing opinions, it's best to avoid that subject altogether.

Once you have a general topic in mind, you may want to clear it with your instructor. Or you can wait until the next stage to do so—after you've narrowed the topic further.

Prewrite to Limit the General Subject

The next step in planning your research is to *limit* or *narrow your topic.* "Pollution" is too broad a topic, but "The Effect of Acid Rain on Urban Structures" poses a realistic challenge. Similarly, "Cable Television" is way too general, but "Trends in Cable Comedy" is manageable. Remember, you aren't writing a book but a paper of probably five to fifteen pages.

Sometimes you'll know the particular aspect of a subject you want to explore. Usually, though, you'll have to do some work to restrict your subject. In such cases, try using the prewriting techniques of questioning, mapping, freewriting, and brainstorming described in Chapter 2. Discussing the topic with other people and doing some background reading on your subject can also help focus your thinking. (For more on limiting general subjects, see pages 25–28.)

Conduct Preliminary Research

Frequently, you won't be able to narrow your topic until you learn more about it. When that's the case, background reading, often called **preliminary research,** is necessary. Just as prewriting precedes a first draft, preliminary research precedes the in-depth research you conduct further along in the process.

At this point, you don't have to track down highly specialized material. Instead, you simply browse the Internet (see pages 534–544) and skim books and mass-market or newspaper articles on your topic to get an overview and to identify possible slants on your subject. If your broad subject is inspired by a class, you can check out the topic in your textbook. And, of course, you can consult library sources—the *computerized* or *card catalog,* the *reference section,* and *periodical indexes* such as the *Readers' Guide to Periodical Literature.* All of these sources break broad subjects into subtopics, thus helping you focus your research. These and other library resources, discussed in greater detail later in the chapter, are among the most valuable tools available to researchers.

After you locate several promising books or articles on your general subject, glance through the material rapidly to get a sense of issues and themes. Do the sources suggest a particular angle of inquiry? If you don't find much material on your subject, think about selecting another topic, one about which more has been written.

While conducting preliminary research, there's no need to take notes, unless you want to jot down possible limited topics. However, you should keep an informal record of the books and articles you skim. Using a sheet of paper or preferably an index card for each source, note the following information: For each book, record the author, title, and call number; for each article, record the date and the page numbers. Such basic information will help you relocate material later on, when you'll need to look at your sources more closely. Also, it's a good idea to jot down the authors and titles of other works mentioned in the sources you skim. You may decide to consult them at another point.

Once you arrive at your limited topic—or several possibilities—ask your instructor for feedback, listening carefully to any reservations he or she may have about your idea. Moreover, even though you've identified a limited subject, don't be surprised if it continues to shift and narrow further as you go along. Such reshaping is part of the research process.

Identify a Working Thesis

Once you have done some preliminary research on your limited topic and have determined there's sufficient material available, your next step is to form a **working thesis**—an idea of your own that is in some way original.

Having a tentative thesis guides your research and helps you determine which sources will be appropriate. However, general statements like "Congress should not make further cuts in social programs," "Prayer in public schools should not be allowed," and "Higher education is male-dominated" are so broad that they fail to restrict the scope of research. Whole books have been written on welfare, just one of many social programs. Be sure, then, that your working thesis focuses on a *limited subject.* The thesis should also take a stand by *expressing your point of view,* or *attitude, about the subject.* Note the difference between the broad statements above and the effective limited thesis statements that follow (the limited subjects are underlined once, the attitudes twice):

> The Congressional decision to reduce funding of school lunch
> programs has had unfortunate consequences for disadvantaged
> children.
>
> A moment of silence in public schools does not violate the
> constitutional separation of church and state.

<u>The funding of college athletics</u> <u>discriminates against</u> women.

It's important for you to view your working thesis as tentative; you probably won't have a thesis until your research is almost complete and all the facts are in. Indeed, if your thesis *doesn't* shift as you investigate your topic, you may not be tapping a wide enough range of sources, or you may be resisting challenges to your original point of view. *Remember:* Gathering information with a closed mind undermines the purpose of a research project.

In its *final* form, your thesis should accomplish at least one of three things. First, it may offer your personal synthesis of multiple findings, your own interpretation of "what it all means." Second, it may refine or extend other people's theories or interpretations. Third, it may offer a perspective that differs from or opposes the one you find expressed in most of your sources. (For more on thesis statements, see pages 38–42.)

Make a Schedule

Having identified your working thesis, you're nearly ready to begin the research stage of your project. Before you begin, though, *make a schedule.* First, list what you need to do. Then, working back from your paper's due date, set rough time limits for the different phases of the project: locating and reading relevant periodicals and books; taking notes; interviewing an expert or sending away for information; drafting, revising, and editing the paper.

FIND SOURCES IN THE LIBRARY

Now is the time to start your research in earnest. Always keep in mind that you're looking for material to support your working thesis. What should you do if you come across material that contradicts your thesis? Resist the temptation to disregard such material. Instead, evaluate it as objectively as you can, and use it to arrive at a more valid statement of your thesis.

Even if your paper contains some primary research, most of your information-gathering will take place in your college library or its equivalent. If the college library is new to you, look for informative handouts near the main desk, and sign up for a library tour if one is offered. Most college libraries contain several floors of bookshelves (often called *stacks*), with fiction and nonfiction arranged according to the Dewey Decimal or Library of Congress system of classification (see page 525). You'll also find sections for periodicals, microfilm and microfiche files, reference works, reserved books, government documents, rare books, and the like. Special collections may be housed in the main library or elsewhere; for example, an extensive music library may be located in the music department. In any case, the main library catalog lists all the material contained in such special collections.

The pages ahead provide detailed information about using library resources—the computerized or card catalog, the reference section, and periodicals.

The Computerized Catalog

Most college libraries now have **computerized catalogs** of their book holdings, some of which can even be accessed online. If computer technology makes you nervous, you'll be pleased to learn that most computerized systems are equipped with on-screen prompts that make it easy to search for sources. Even so, don't wait until your paper is due to familiarize yourself with your college's online catalog system. It can be overwhelming to learn the system *and* conduct research at the same time. Instead, early in the academic year, spend an hour or so at the library. Take an orientation tour, read any handouts that are provided, speak to the librarian, experiment with the system. The confidence you gain will make all the difference when you begin researching in earnest.

In a typical online search, you'll be asked by the computer whether you want to search by *author, title,* or *subject.* If you're searching by author or title, you type into the search box the author's first and last names or the title, respectively. If you're searching by subject, you type in a key word or phrase that summarizes your topic. You may have to try several key terms to discover under which term(s) the computer lists sources on your topic. Assume you're conducting research to identify classroom strategies that undermine student success. You might start by keying in the word *Education.* But that word would probably yield so many possibilities that you wouldn't know where to start. You might narrow your search by keying in "teaching techniques," "classroom practices," or "academic failure." For help in identifying appropriate key terms, speak with your college librarian. He or she will probably have you consult the *Library of Congress Subject Headings* or a bound or on-screen thesaurus of headings used in your library's database.

One other point: When you search for a book by subject, the screen will usually indicate narrower subheadings under that topic. As soon as one of those subheads is clicked, the screen provides a list of books on that subject. To get complete bibliographic information about a specific book, follow the computer's instructions. The book's publisher, publication date, call number, and so on will then appear on the screen. Most computerized catalogs also indicate the status of a book— whether it is out on loan, overdue, lost, or available on loan. Figure 20.1 shows one college's computerized card catalog display for a book on education in the inner city.

Once the computer identifies books on your subject, you can copy down the authors, titles, and call numbers (see pages 523–526) of promising books; or, in many libraries, you can direct the computer to print out a list. By mastering your library's computerized catalog, you'll find that it will take only minutes to identify sources that in the past might have taken you several hours to track down. One caution, however, about computerized catalogs: Few libraries have their entire collections online. Special collections and older books may not be included. If the database isn't posted near the terminals, check with the librarian. You'll have to use the traditional card catalog to track down those sources not covered by the computerized catalog.

Other subject headings to look under to find additional relevant books. The underlining indicates that these are links to related subjects in the computerized catalog.

AUTHOR:	**Rathbone, Cristina.**
TITLE:	**On the Outside Looking In: A Year at an Inner-City High School**
PUBLICATION INFO:	**New York: Atlantic Monthly Press, 1998.**
PAGING AND SIZE:	**387p.; 24 cm.**
SUBJECTS:	**Education, Urban, Case Studies—United States.**
	Economically Disadvantaged Youth, Education (Secondary)—United States.
	New York City High Schools.

1. CALL NUMBER: LC5131.R38 1998—STACKS—Checked Out

2. CALL NUMBER: LC5131.R38 1998—STACKS—Available

Indicates the book's call number, location, and availability in the library. In this case, the library owns two copies, one checked out, the other available.

Figure 20.1

The Card Catalog

If your library isn't computerized, you'll need to use the traditional **card catalog,** a file of cards listing all the books in the library. The catalog is arranged alphabetically by word rather than letter by letter: *music* would come before *musicians; social reformers* before *socialism.* If you're not sure with what word or term to start your search, consult a reference book that lists (alphabetically) the card catalog's subject headings. For libraries using the Dewey Decimal system, this book is the *Sears List of Subject Headings;* for libraries using the more common Library of Congress system, it is the *Library of Congress Subject Headings.*

Subject, Title, and Author Cards

To locate books on your topic, look under the appropriate subject headings; that is, use the catalog's **subject cards.** You'll find a card for each book the library owns on that subject. Again, suppose you're researching the classroom factors that inhibit student success. You could start by looking under the subject heading *Education,* jotting down the titles and call numbers (see below) of promising books. One might be the classic work *Hope Fulfilled for At-Risk and Violent Youth* by Robert D. Barr and William H. Parrett. If you don't find appropriate books under the first subject heading (or if that heading yields a daunting number of prospects), try alternative headings. They are often listed on a separate card at the front of each catalog section devoted to a major subject heading. The *Education* card, for example, might list *Learning, styles of* and *Teaching strategies.* If you don't find such a cross-reference card, consult the *Library of Congress Subject Headings* or brainstorm words related to your topic. You could, for instance, look under *Instruction* or *Schools.*

The catalog also indexes books by *title* and by *author.* Imagine you already know about Barr and Parrett's book and want to start your research by reading it. To see if your library has the book, you would look under the title or under the authors. **Title cards** are arranged alphabetically according to the first word in the title, or according to the second word if the first is *A, An,* or *The.* **Author cards** are arranged alphabetically according to the author's last name. If a book has more than one author, there's a card for each.

Some libraries file author, title, and subject cards in a single catalog; others maintain one catalog for subject cards and a second for author and title cards.

Subject, title, and author cards contain the same information. The only difference is that subject cards have subject headings at the top, while title and author cards have, respectively, titles and authors' names at the top. Look carefully at the subject card in Figure 20.2, paying special attention to the information it provides.

Call number indicating the book's location in the library

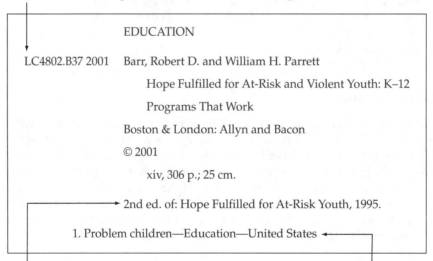

EDUCATION

LC4802.B37 2001   Barr, Robert D. and William H. Parrett

Hope Fulfilled for At-Risk and Violent Youth: K–12

Programs That Work

Boston & London: Allyn and Bacon

© 2001

xiv, 306 p.; 25 cm.

2nd ed. of: Hope Fulfilled for At-Risk Youth, 1995.

1. Problem children—Education—United States

Publication date of the original edition.
If the catalog has cards for the original and
revised editions of a book, refer to the most
recent edition for updated information.
Figure 20.2

Other subject headings
to look under to find
additional relevant books

How to Find a Book

To locate a book on the shelves, use its **call number.** Besides appearing in the upper-left corner of the catalog card, the call number is printed on the spine of the book. There are two systems of call numbers in use in the United States—the **Dewey Decimal** and the **Library of Congress.** Most college libraries use the latter system, though some still reference older books by the Dewey Decimal system and more recent acquisitions by the Library of Congress. Check with the librarian to see which system(s) your library uses. Listed here are both systems' call numbers and the subjects they represent:

Dewey Decimal System

000–099 General Works

100–199 Philosophy and Psychology

200–299 Religion

300–399 Social Science

400–499 Language

500–599 Pure Science

600–699 Technology (Applied Sciences)

700–799 The Arts

800–899 Literature

900–999 History

Library of Congress System

A	General works—Polygraphy
B	Philosophy—Religion
C	History—Auxiliary Sciences
D	History and Topography (except America)
E–F	America
G	Geography—Anthropology
H	Social Sciences
J	Political Science
K	Law
L	Education
M	Music
N	Fine Arts
P	Language and Literature
Q	Science
R	Medicine
S	Agriculture—Plant and Animal Industry
T	Technology
U	Military Science
V	Naval Science
Z	Bibliography and Library Science

Once you have a book's call number, consult a map or list posted near the card catalog to determine the book's location in the stacks. If you don't see a list, ask the librarian. In libraries with closed stacks, make out a call slip so that a member of the staff can get the book for you.

If you can't find a book in the stacks, don't assume that it's been checked out. Perhaps it's tossed on a table close by, or it may have been replaced carelessly; take a look at books tucked at the ends of the shelves and placed sideways. If you still can't locate the book, consult the person at the circulation desk. If the book has been checked out, you can usually fill out a form to have the current borrower notified that you're waiting for the book, which will be held for you as soon as it is returned. You might also check with a librarian to see if the book has been put on reserve or moved to a special collection, or if it is available through an inter-library loan system. In libraries with computerized circulation systems, all you need to do is type in the book's call number, and the computer screen will tell you whether the book has been checked out, moved to a special location, or lost.

The Reference Section

As you already know, **reference works** can help you conduct preliminary research on a topic. Though they have limitations, reference volumes can also be useful at this point. Some reference works (*Encyclopaedia Britannica* and the *World Almanac and Book of Facts*) cover a wide range of subjects. Others (*Mathematics Dictionary* and *Dance Encyclopedia*) are more specialized and provide information about specific fields. Despite these differences, all reference volumes present significantly condensed information. They provide basic facts but not much interpretation. Explanations are brief. Most reference works are, then, unsuitable as sources for in-depth research. In fact, they're usually omitted from the list of Works Cited at the end of a paper.

How do you track down reference works that might be helpful? Start by looking up your subject in your library's card catalog or in its computerized catalog—or, if your library has one, in the separate card catalog for reference books. Record the call numbers and titles of those books marked "Ref" (Reference). The Library of Congress call number for reference is "Z," but a library may keep only some of its "Z" books in the reference section and the rest in the stacks. Most libraries arrange reference shelves alphabetically by subject ("Art," "Economics," "History"), making it easy to browse for other useful references once you've identified one on a subject. Keep in mind that reference materials don't circulate; that is, they cannot be checked out, so you must consult them while in the library.

Listed here are some of the common reference books found in most college libraries:

Biography

International Who's Who
Who's Who in America

Business/Economics

Dictionary of Banking and Finance
Encyclopedia of Economics

Ethnic/Feminist Studies

Encyclopedia of Feminism
Harvard Encyclopedia of American Ethnic Groups

Fine Arts

New Grove Dictionary of American Music
The New Harvard Dictionary of Music
The Oxford Companion to Art
The Thames and Hudson Dictionary of Art Terms

History/Political Science

Editorials on File
Encyclopedia of American Political History
Facts on File
A Political Handbook of the World

Literature/Film

The Oxford Companion to American Literature
The Oxford Companion to English Literature
World Encyclopedia of the Film

Philosophy/Religion

A Dictionary of Non-Christian Religions
The Encyclopedia of American Religions
An Encyclopedia of Philosophy

Psychology/Education

Encyclopedia of Education
Encyclopedia of Psychology
Encyclopedia of Special Education

Science/Technology/Mathematics

A Dictionary of Mathematics
Encyclopedia of Medical History
McGraw-Hill Encyclopedia of Science and Technology
The Merck Index of Chemicals and Drugs

Social Sciences

Dictionary of Anthropology
Encyclopedia of Crime and Justice
International Encyclopedia of the Social Sciences

Periodicals

Periodicals are publications issued at periodic (regular or intermittent) intervals throughout the year. There are three broad types of periodicals: general, scholarly, and serious.

General periodicals (daily newspapers and magazines such as *Time, Newsweek,* and *Psychology Today*) are designed for the average person. Such publications often adopt a personal or anecdotal writing style and offer easy-to-read overviews of subjects. Usually written by generalists rather than experts, the articles in such mass-market publications provide background information, but their lack of comprehensive coverage limits their usefulness for in-depth research. Moreover, since general circulation periodicals usually give only the briefest credit to the writers whose ideas they mention, readers have difficulty tracking down sources and being assured that information is reliable.

Intended for readers with specialized knowledge, **scholarly periodicals** (*Journal of Experimental Child Psychology, Renaissance Drama,* and *Veterinary Medicine*) provide objective, in-depth analyses written by authorities in the field. Such publications develop ideas with facts, studies, and well-reasoned commentary; they document fully the ideas they borrow.

Serious periodicals (*National Geographic, Scientific American,* and *Smithsonian*) are designed for well-educated laypeople rather than experts. These publications develop subjects with less depth than scholarly periodicals but provide a broader perspective. Like scholarly publications, they use a generally objective tone and back up their ideas with information and logic. Documentation is provided but often isn't as complete as it is in scholarly publications.

Periodical Indexes, Abstracts, and Bibliographies

Periodical indexes, issued anywhere from every two weeks to once a year, are cumulative directories that list articles published in certain journals, newspapers, and magazines. In addition, major newspapers, including *The New York Times,* publish annual subject directories. Most periodical indexes arrange listed articles under subject headings. Beneath the headings, individual articles are organized alphabetically by authors' last names.

To locate periodical indexes, you must learn how your library is organized. If there's a periodicals room, you'll probably find the periodical indexes located there, arranged alphabetically by title. In such a case, simply scan the shelves to find the index you want. Sometimes, periodical indexes are located in a separate, alphabetically arranged section in the reference room, or, less helpfully, are shelved with reference volumes according to call number. Occasionally, you may find the periodical index to a highly specialized field shelved in the stacks near books in the same field of study. If you can't find the index you want in any of these locations, check with the librarian. You may have to use the computerized card catalog to find the index you want.

You're probably familiar with one index—the *Readers' Guide to Periodical Literature.* It lists general-interest articles published by popular newsstand magazines, such as *U.S. News & World Report* and *Sports Illustrated.* When you were in high school, you probably used the *Readers' Guide* because it indexes accessible, nontechnical publications. To locate articles appropriate for college-level research, you'll need to consult indexes that list articles from more academic, professional, and specialized publications. The college equivalents of the *Readers' Guide* are the *Humanities Index* and the *Social Sciences Index* (below). You should become familiar with these indexes as well as with the major indexes for the field in which you plan to major (see below).

Some specialized indexes provide brief descriptions of the articles they list. These indexes are usually called **abstracts.** Examples are *Abstracts of Folklore Studies, Criminal Justice Abstracts,* and *Psychological Abstracts.* Abstracts usually contain fewer listings than other types of indexes and are restricted to a limited field. In contrast to indexes that list only articles, **bibliographies** like the *Modern Language Association International Bibliography* list books as well as articles.

Listed here are representative indexes, abstracts, and bibliographies found in most college libraries. To save time, check with the librarian to see which of these sources can be accessed electronically at your library. (For information on indexes, abstracts, and bibliographies that are available in electronic form, see page 531.)

General

Biography Index
Humanities Index
The New York Times Index
Readers' Guide to Periodical Literature
Social Sciences Index
Speech Index

Arts/Literature

Art Index
Book Review Index
Film Literature Index
Modern Language Association International Bibliography
Music Index
The New York Times Book Review Index
Play Index

Business/Economics

Business Periodicals Index
International Bibliography of Economics
Wall Street Journal Index

Education

Education Abstracts
Education Index
ERIC (Educational Resources Information Center)

History, Political Science, Government

> *Historical Abstracts*
> *Monthly Index to United States Government Publications*
> *Political Science Bibliographies*
> *Public Affairs Information Service*
> *Vertical File Index*

Philosophy/Religion

> *Philosopher's Index*
> *Religion Index*

Psychology/Sociology

> *Psychological Abstracts*
> *Sociological Abstracts*

Sciences

> *Applied Science and Technology Index*
> *Biological Abstracts*
> *Botanical Bibliographies*
> *Chemical Abstracts*
> *Engineering Index Annual*
> *Environment Index*
> *International Computer Bibliography*

Women's and Ethnic Studies

> *Bibliography on Women*
> *Ethnic Newswatch*
> *Hispanic American Periodicals Index*
> *Index to Periodical Articles by and About Blacks*
> *Women's Resources International*

Computerized Indexes, Abstracts, and Bibliographies

A growing number of college libraries now offer computerized searches of many of the major indexes, abstracts, and bibliographies listed on page 531. In some libraries, a database that groups directories alphabetically by subject is maintained in the same system as the computerized catalog for books (see pages 522–524). In other libraries, there may be a separate bank of terminals for searching periodical directories. These terminals are usually hooked up to a **CD-ROM** (compact disc read-only memory) player containing compact discs on which periodical indexes are stored. The CDs are usually updated monthly so that the information is more current than that found in the bound versions of the directories.

Here is a list of some of the most popular CD-ROM indexes. There are many others. Check to see which your library subscribes to.

- *Academic Search FullTEXT* (provides complete text of many articles, plus an index to *The New York Times*)
- *Art Index*
- *Business Periodicals Index*
- *Education Index*
- *Government Publications Index*
- *Health Index*
- *Humanities Index*
- *InfoTrac Academic Index* (includes the previous six months of *The New York Times*)
- *InfoTrac Magazine Index* (provides full text for many articles)
- *InfoTrac National Newspaper Index*
- *Magazine Index Plus*
- *Modern Language Association International Bibliography*
- *National Newspaper Index* (covers *The New York Times* and other important national newspapers like *The Atlanta Journal-Constitution* and the *Los Angeles Times*)
- *News Bank*
- *ProQuest General Periodicals Ondisc*
- *Readers' Guide to Periodical Literature*
- *Social Sciences Index*

More and more libraries offer Internet access to databases located off campus. These Internet-access databases not only list the titles of specific journal articles but also print out the articles themselves. Some major online databases are Dialog, Wilsonline, LexisNexis, and EBSCOhost.

As you no doubt realize, library technology is changing rapidly. Book catalogues, major reference works, as well as periodical indexes, abstracts, and bibliographies are available at some colleges not just on the library's computer terminals but also campus-wide through a complex computer network. At such technically sophisticated schools, students can conduct much of their research from their dorms at any time of the day or night. Other colleges have just begun to computerize their library operations. (For more information on accessing electronic information, see pages 534–544.)

Using Computerized and Printed Indexes

Besides saving time, computerized directories have the advantage of being current. Most are updated monthly (unlike print volumes, which are generally updated quarterly or annually). Plus, in many libraries the computer terminals at which you view database listings are hooked up to printers, enabling you to print out the listings rather than record them from the screen. Some online and CD-ROM databases offer access to the full text of selected articles or books. These texts may be read on screen, e-mailed to you, or, if the computer terminal connects to a printer, printed out. Even when full text isn't available, you may have the option of accessing the *abstract* of a work that seems promising. Remember, though, an abstract is simply a summary. Although it can help you decide whether you should track down the original complete text, an abstract can't be cited as a source in your paper.

Being able to print out computerized text of work that originally appeared in print form is, of course, a real time-saver. However, computerized text has its drawbacks. Most online and CD-ROM databases don't indicate where page breaks occurred in the original. So, if you read computerized text of an article that originally appeared on, say, pages 22, 23, and 26 of a magazine, you'll have no way of knowing where one page ended and another began. Since you won't be able to provide exact page numbers, your readers may have difficulty locating, in the original, specific passages cited in your paper. The lack of page breaks under-scores the fact that computerized text often works best for accessing texts that are unavailable or difficult to obtain in print; otherwise, it's usually preferable to read and take notes on texts in their original print form.

Many computerized databases catalog only recent material, from the past few years or decades. When researching a topic with a historical component, you may find computerized indexes inadequate. For instance, to discover how J. D. Salinger's novel *The Catcher in the Rye* was received when it first appeared in 1951, you would need to identify articles and reviews written in that year. Bound volumes of the *Modern Language Association International Bibliography, Book Review Index,* and *The New York Times Book Review Index* would provide you with the needed information.

Whether a periodicals directory is in computerized or print form, you can search by subject (or keywords) to uncover titles of relevant articles. If you don't find your subject listed in a printed index, or if a computerized database yields no titles when you type in keywords, try alternate terms for your topic. Suppose you're researching the subject of business ethics. In addition to using "Business ethics" as your subject heading or keywords, you might try "Bribery" or "Fraud" to find relevant articles. Both computerized and print indexes also show cross-references. By looking under "Business ethics," you might see suggested search terms such as "Advertising ethics," "Banking, ethical aspects," and "Commercial crime."

Periodicals directories in print form list articles alphabetically, both by subject and by author. Under each subject, articles are listed alphabetically by title. When using a computerized guide to articles in periodicals, type in either an author's name or your subject. The database will then list appropriate articles, usually in reverse chronological order (most recent first). The precise procedures for searching computerized databases vary; libraries usually post instructions for the particular databases they offer.

Figure 20.3 shows an entry from the computerized database EBSCOhost. The entry gives all the information you need to track down the article in the library.

EBSCOhost

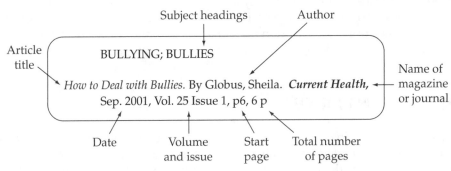

Figure 20.3

In the event of any puzzling abbreviations or symbols in computerized guides, ask your librarian either to explain their meaning or to direct you to a printed key for an explanation.

Be sure not to end your search for appropriate material until you've consulted the most pertinent indexes and bibliographies. For a paper on the psychology of child abuse, you might start with *The New York Times Index* and then move to more specialized volumes, such as *Psychological Abstracts, Child Development Abstracts,* and *Mental Health Book Review Index.* To ensure that you don't miss current developments in your subject area, always start with the most recent years and work your way back.

Locating Specific Issues of Periodicals

If you can't print out computerized text of relevant articles, you'll need to obtain the original text. To do so, you first have to determine whether your library owns the specific periodicals and the issues you want. If your library catalogs its periodicals online, search for a periodical by typing in its name. Does that particular name appear on screen? If it does, your library owns issues of that publication. With a few additional keystrokes, you can obtain more detailed information—such as the specific volumes held by your library and the periodical's call number and location in the library.

If your library doesn't catalog its periodicals online, look for a card catalog of holdings. Some libraries list the periodicals they own in the general card catalog. Other libraries have a separate periodicals card catalog, usually located in the periodicals or reference room. Whether the card catalog you use is general or restricted to periodicals, look up periodicals by name. A periodical card will usually tell you the issues owned by the library, their call number, and their location. Issue numbers and dates given at the top of the card usually refer to the first issues published, not to the first issues owned by the library. Information about issues owned by the library generally appears at the bottom of the card.

If your library maintains neither an online catalog nor a card catalog that references periodicals, check with your librarian. He or she will direct you to a computer printout, a spiral-bound volume, or some other source that lists the library's periodicals.

Recent issues of magazines, newspapers, and journals are kept in the library's current periodicals section, where they are arranged alphabetically by name. Less current issues can be found in the periodicals room, in the stacks, or on microfilm. Bound volumes of periodicals don't circulate. Back issues of major newspapers are usually stored on microfilm filed in cabinets in a separate location.

USE THE INTERNET

Computer technology—in one form or another—is part of nearly everyone's life nowadays. Nothing demonstrates the staggering impact of the computer revolution more powerfully than the growth of the **Internet,** also called the **Net.** This global network of interlinked computer systems puts a massive storehouse of information within the reach of anyone with access to a personal computer and a **modem,** a device that transmits electronic data over a telephone or cable line.

Such a wealth of material presents obvious research benefits to you as a student. However, when faced with the task of using the Internet, you may feel overwhelmed and unsure of how to proceed. The following pages will help; they'll introduce you to the Internet, show you how to access its resources, and offer pointers on evaluating the material you find there.

The Internet and the World Wide Web

The Internet is the catch-all term for the global network that links individual computer networks at tens of thousands of educational, scientific, state, federal, and commercial agencies in more than 63 countries. While the **World Wide Web** exists *on* the Internet, the two are not synonymous. The Internet is the nuts-and-bolts of the network: the cables and computers. The World Wide Web refers to a global information system existing *within* the Internet. The Web consists of uncounted millions of **websites.** Some websites feature text only; others contain graphics; still others contain audio and video components. Although there's great variation in the content and design of websites, all contain a *home page* (generally modeled after the contents page of a book) that provides the site's title, introductory descriptive material about the site, and a menu consisting of **links** to the information that can be accessed from the site. A link is a stepping stone to other pages on the site or to a related website. You can jump from the first location to the next just by clicking on the link. (For more on links, see pages 538–540.)

What the Web Offers

While often compared to a library, the Web is more accurately thought of as an enormous storage shed, piled to the ceiling with boxes and crates and items of every description. Because it's not subject to a central system of organization, and because anyone—from Nobel Prize winners to representatives of the most extreme fringe groups—can post material on it at any time, the Web is in a state of constant flux. The quality of information found on the Web ranges from authoritative to speculative to fraudulent. It's impossible to say with certainty even how large the Web is. Anywhere from 20 to 50 million pages of data may be represented by the millions of websites in operation.

What can be stated with confidence is that the World Wide Web offers a collection of data that surpasses anything the world has ever seen. With the click of a mouse, you can read electronic versions of *The Washington Post* or *The London Times;* you can search the holdings of the Library of Congress, check the temperature in Moscow, or get up-to-the-minute stock quotes; you can scan breaking news from the Associated Press or learn the latest information on alternative treatments for arthritis.

The Advantages and Limitations of the Library and the Web

The availability of the Web makes doing research over the computer an attractive option. But that doesn't mean that libraries have become obsolete. Both the library and the Web have strengths and weaknesses. Depending upon your topic and its focus, one may be a better starting point than the other. Here are some issues to consider:

- The library is *consistently organized.* With some guidance from the catalog system and the reference librarian, you can quickly locate materials that are relevant to your topic.
- Because the Web *doesn't have a centralized organizational structure,* you are automatically—and somewhat haphazardly—exposed to a staggering array of material. If you're not sure how to focus your topic, browsing the Web may help you narrow your topic by identifying directions you wouldn't have thought of on your own. Conversely, the sheer volume of material on your subject may leave you stunned and glassy-eyed, the information overload making you feel all the more confused about how to proceed.
- Some sources in the library may be dated or even no longer accurate. By contrast, online material is almost always up-to-date because it can be posted on the Web as soon as it's created. (See page 543 for hints on evaluating the currency of electronic data.)
- The instantaneous nature of Web postings can create problems, though. Library materials certainly aren't infallible, but most have gone through a process of editorial review before being published. This is often *not* the case with material on the Web. Most of us realize that the claim "I saw it in the newspaper!" doesn't ensure that information is accurate or valid. "I saw it on the Web!" is even less of a guarantee. Given this basic limitation, it's a good idea not to rely solely on the Web when you research your topic. Consider using it as a supplement to, rather than a substitute for, library research. (For more about evaluating the validity of material on the Web, see page 543.)

Accessing the Web

Access to the Web ("going online") is provided through a software program called a **web browser.** Netscape and Internet Explorer are several widely used browsers. If you're a student at one of the many colleges or universities providing Web access to students, you'll probably use one of these browsers. Commercial online services, such as America Online and Earthlink, have their own browsers.

If you don't have access to a college-provided browser, you'll probably want to subscribe to a commercial online service and use its browser. (Most commercial services offer two options: You pay only for the time you're online—which is best if you use the service only occasionally and for brief periods—or you pay a flat monthly fee that allows you all the online time you want.) An online service, along with your modem and a printer, makes it possible for you to conduct a good deal of your research at home.

Using Online Time Efficiently

Whether you access the Web through a university-provided service or a commercial provider, you need to learn how to make efficient use of your online time. The Internet is known as the "information superhighway," and the analogy is a good one. Like any superhighway, the Internet has its rush hours and even its periods of gridlock. Here are some suggestions to keep you cruising in the express lane:

- Experiment with logging on at different times of day and evening. Typically, evening hours (approximately 6 p.m. to 10 p.m.) are times of peak Internet traffic. If you have trouble getting through to particular sites, you may have more success earlier in the day or later at night.

- If it takes more than a couple of minutes to retrieve files from a website, hit the "Stop" or "Cancel" button and try again later.

- If you don't need to see the graphics (illustrations, photographs, charts, and so on) included in a website, check if your browser offers a "text only" option. If it does, activate that option. Waiting for graphics to download can increase your online time substantially.

- Just as you do when conducting library research, be sure to record sufficient information about your online source so you can provide full documentation when it comes time to write your paper. Specifically, when you print information from the Web, make sure your browser is set so that the material's title, date, and page as well as the date of your retrieval appear on the printed copy. You also need to check that the **URL** (*uniform resource locator*), or Internet **address,** appears clearly on the copy. Having the address makes it possible for you to return to the site in the future.

Here is the address—broken down into elements—for the weekly edition of the news magazine *U.S. News & World Report:*

http://www.usnews.com/usnews/home.htm

You'll note that *http:* ("hypertext transfer protocol") is the first element in the Web address. It tells the sending and receiving computers how to transfer the information. Next is *www.usnews.com,* with *www.* indicating that the site is located on the World Wide Web. After *www.* comes the Internet address of the institution, agency, corporation, or organization (in this case *U.S. News & World Report,* represented by *usnews*). The *.com* portion indicates that the site is a commercial one.[1] Following the slash, the *usnews/home.htm* tells where the site's files are stored, the path to those files, and the name of the particular file being retrieved. (The *.htm*—often written as *html*—stands for *hypertext mark-up language,* the language in which these particular Web pages are written.)

It's critical that you key in an address exactly as it appears on the website's home page. Don't capitalize something that originally was in lowercase letters, and don't leave extra space between elements in the address. Keying in even slight changes in the address usually makes it impossible to access the site.

- When you find a website that you like and may want to visit again, use your browser's **Bookmark** or **Favorite Places** option. (Typically, you will find the bookmark option on your browser's pull-down menu.) After you "bookmark" a site, its address is saved in your personal file, so you can click on its name and instantly return to the site, without having to remember (and key in) its address.

Using the Net to Find Books on Your Topic

Assume that you've used your college's computerized catalog to track down several books on your subject. Now you'd like to go online to see if there are additional books you might find helpful. In such a case, you access one or both of the following national booksellers:

Barnes and Noble Books at http://www.bn.com
Amazon Books at http://www.amazon.com

At either site, you would use the "Browse Subjects" box on the bookseller's home page to identify relevant books. Let's say you want to investigate the way the experience of childhood poverty affected the politics of specific American presidents. Using the "Browse Subjects" box, you note that one of the subject listings is "Biography." Clicking on "Biography," you see that one of the subcategories is "Presidents." Click on "Presidents," and a list of books on American presidents

---

[1]The **domain name** is that portion of the address indicating the type of organization at a specific address. The domain name consists of the organization's name (in the case above, *usnews*), followed by a period (called a **dot**) and one of several domain abbreviations (in the example above, *.com* for *U.S. News & World Report*). The primary domains are as follows:

.com—commercial   .mil—military
.net—Internet service providers   .org—non-profit organizations
.edu—educational institutions   .gov—government

For example, tusk.edu is the domain name for Tuskegee University.

appears. By clicking on specific titles from the list, you obtain information about each book, including reviewer and reader comments. With this information, you can usually determine which books are appropriate for your purpose. At that point, you might purchase the relevant books online or, more likely, check the availability of the books at a library other than the one at your college.

Online booksellers can also help you narrow your topic. Perhaps you want to research the topic of illiteracy. As soon as you type the word *illiteracy* in the "Keywords" box on the bookseller's home page, you receive a long list of books on the subject. Simply looking at the range of titles can help you narrow your research. You might, for example, decide to focus on illiteracy in the workplace, teenagers' declining reading scores, or programs that teach marginally literate parents how to read to their children.

Using the Net to Find Articles and Other Materials on Your Topic

What do you do if you want to go online to track down articles, speeches, legislation, TV transcripts, and so on about your subject? How, given the overwhelming array of online material, can you identify sources that will be pertinent? Search directories and search engines will help.

Search Directories

A **search directory,** a service that organizes websites by categories, will begin pointing you in the right direction. If you're not sure how to narrow your topic, seeing the search directory's categories may help you by identifying directions you wouldn't have thought of on your own. New search directories crop up regularly, but one of the most popular and user-friendly is Yahoo! The address of Yahoo! is http://www.yahoo.com.[2] Figure 20.4 is an approximation of what you'll see when you go to Yahoo!'s home page. (Bear in mind that websites change constantly. What appears on your computer screen may not be identical to what is presented here.)

Making Use of Links on the Web.   As you see, Yahoo! divides websites into 14 categories: Arts & Humanities, Business & Economy, and so on. Each category is presented as a **link** (see page 534). Typically, a link shows up as an underlined word or phrase that is a different color from the type elsewhere on the page. When you click on a link, you're automatically transported to a more detailed list of websites to choose from. As you move from link to link, you move from the general topic to more specific aspects of the topic. For example, say you are researching the legal rights of the disabled. You notice that there's a section titled "Law" under the category "Government." Click on "Law" and you're presented with a screen that lists several dozen law-related links, from "arbitration and mediation" to "trade." (There's even a link for "lawyer jokes.") When you see the link

---

[2]Addresses are subject to change. Addresses given in the chapter are current as of April 2002.

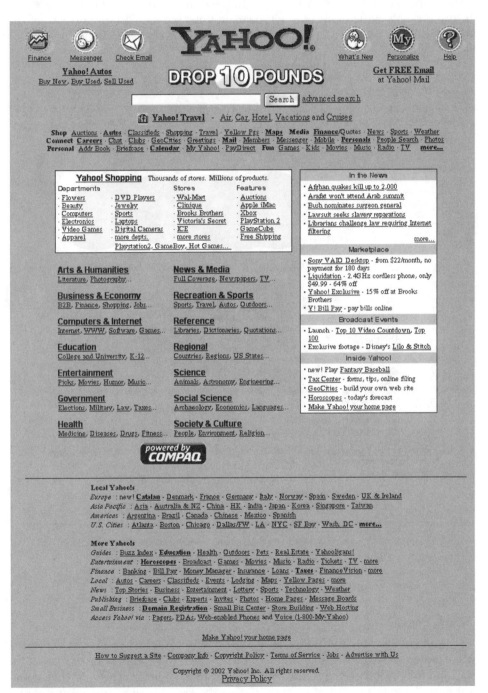

Figure 20.4 Yahoo! home page

"disability," you know you're on the right track. You click on that link; Figure 20.5 below presents what would then appear on your screen. Clicking on any of the displayed links provides access to that website as well as related ones.

YAHOO!   Help - Check Email

Yahoo! Directory   [   ] [Search]   Advanced Search
Law > Disability   ⦿ all of Yahoo! ○ just this category   Help

Home > Government > Law > **Disability**

Categories

- Abuse@
- **Americans with Disabilities Act (ADA)** *(12)*
- **Universal Design@**

Site Listings

- Commission on Mental and Physical Disability Law, The NEW! - news on disability legislation and concerns from the American Bar Association (ABA).

- Air Carrier Access Act - Make It Work for You - information on the 1986 act, which insures that people with disabilities receive consistent and nondiscriminatory treatment when traveling by air.
- Carolina Disability - attorney answers questions and provides forum about the laws of social security disability benefits, worker's compensation, and supplemental security income (SSI) for lawyers and the disabled.
- Council for Disability Rights - advancing rights and enhancing lives of people with disabilities.
- Disability Discrimination Act - contains a full list of publications available to order online.
- Disability Etiquette Handbook - guide for employers of people with disabilities. Includes ADA information.
- Disability Law Update - resource for recent cases dealing with disability issues.
- Disability Laws - from FedLaw.
- Disability Rights Advocates - provides disability rights litigation that has successfuly challenged discriminatory practices in all aspects of society.
- Disability Rights Education & Defense Fund, Inc. - DREDF is a national law and policy center dedicated to furthering the civil rights of people with disabilities.
- Guide to Disability Rights Laws - includes Fair Housing Act, Air Carrier Access Act, ADA, and more.
- Legal & Advocacy Resources
- Personal Advocacy; Accessibility Issues - web author who lives with the symptoms of Multiple Sclerosis shares a letter to his state representative.
- Rights of People with Disabilities

⬤ **Add this Category to My Yahoo!**   📑 **Email this Category to a Friend**

Figure 20.5   Disability legal issues page from Yahoo!

Search Engines

Search directories, like Yahoo!, are wonderful tools when you begin exploring your topic. But when you're refining your investigation, you'll want to use another kind of resource—the **search engine.** Search engines are tools that comb through the vast amount of information on the Web for sites or documents that match your research needs. You activate a search engine by typing in key words or phrases that tell the engine what to look for.

Increasingly, search engines and search directories are combined, making it possible to access both from one site's home page. (Yahoo! is one such combined search tool.) See Figure 20.6 for a list of some popular search engines, search directories, and their Web addresses.

AltaVista at www.altavista.com

Galaxy at www.einet.net

Google at www.google.com

GoTo at www.goto.com

HotBot at www.hotbot.com

LookSmart at www.looksmart.com

Lycos at www.lycos.com

Northern Light at www.northernlight.com

Webcrawler at www.webcrawler.com

Yahoo! at www.yahoo.com

Figure 20.6   Some popular search directories and search engines

Tips for Using Search Engines.   When you reach the home page of a search engine, it's a good idea to click on the "Help" or "Tips" button. When you do, you'll receive specific guidelines for using that particular search engine efficiently. As you proceed, don't forget to "bookmark" (see page 537) the search engines you use so you can return to them easily at a later date.

Return to Figure 20.4, the example of a Yahoo! home page. Note that at the top, there's an empty box beside "Search." That's where you type in the keyword(s) describing your research topic. After you click on "Search" (or whatever your search engine calls its "search" command), the engine scans the Web for your keyword(s). It then provides you with a list of "hits," or links, to websites where your keyword is found. Most search engines also provide a brief description of each site.

How to Limit Your Search.   The success of your search depends on how carefully you follow your search engine's guidelines and on how specific and descriptive your search terms are. For example, say you're doing research on animal-rights activism. Depending upon your search engine, if you simply enter the words *animal rights activism* in the search box, the engine may provide a list of *every* document that contains the word *animal* or *rights* or *activism*—hundreds of thousands of hits. Again, the most efficient way to limit the number of hits you get is to follow with great care your search engine's specific guidelines. If no guidelines are provided or if the guidelines are confusing, try these suggestions:

- Put quotation marks around the phrase you are searching for—in this case, "animal rights activism." Many search engines interpret the quotation marks to mean you want only those documents that include the words *animal rights activism* next to each other. If you don't include the quotation marks, you may receive listings for each word.

- To focus your search further, use the plus (+) and minus (−) signs, leaving no space before or after the signs. Say you're interested in animal-rights activism as it applies to protests against the wearing of fur. Try typing this in the search box:

  "animal rights activism"+fur

  The + sign between *animal rights activism* and *fur* instructs the search engine to locate items that contain both sets of keywords. A minus (−) sign has the opposite effect. If you want information about animal-rights activism, *excluding* information about fur, you would type your search phrase like this:

  "animal rights activism"−fur

- Use the Boolean[3] operative words AND, OR, and NOT to limit your search. When you investigate a topic via a search engine that recognizes Boolean logic (the search tips will indicate if it does, or you can experiment on your own as you type in search phrases), using these operatives between key terms broadens or narrows the range of your search. For example, assume you typed the following: reggae music AND Rastafarians AND Jamaica. Using the operative *AND* instructs the search engine to return only those documents containing all three search terms.

Using Discussion Groups and Newsgroups

Thousands of discussion groups and newsgroups operate on the Web, focusing on every topic imaginable. You can find addresses for these groups in various ways: in computer publications and special-interest magazines, or by conducting a search through a search engine.

An online **discussion group** (also known as a **listserv**) consists of individuals who share a similar interest, with members of the group communicating with one another through e-mail. Each e-mail message is automatically distributed to everyone on the discussion group's membership list. A **newsgroup** operates in a similar fashion, except that no membership is required. Instead of communicating through e-mail, people post messages on a central "bulletin board," where anyone can read and respond to a message. In a moderated newsgroup, contributions are reviewed by a group facilitator before being posted to the group at

---

[3]Named for George Boole, a nineteenth-century mathematician, Boolean logic modifies search items through the use of the "operators" AND, OR, and NOT.

large. In unmoderated newsgroups, there is no such review. Not surprisingly, unmoderated newsgroups tend to have a high ratio of junk mail.

Keep in mind that anyone—scholar, fraud, con artist, or saint—can voice an opinion in a discussion group. Also, be careful not to assume that a talkative member of a group is necessarily an expert: any self-styled "authority" can access an online group. Despite these problems, newsgroups and discussion groups *can* be helpful sources of information and provide valuable leads as you do your research. They may also put you in e-mail touch with respected authorities in your field of research.

Evaluating Internet Materials

As noted in the preceding section and on pages 534–535, you need to take special care to evaluate the worth of material you find on the Web. Electronic documents may appear seemingly out of nowhere and can disappear without a trace. And anyone with access to a computer and modem can create a webpage or state a position in a discussion group. How, then, do you know if a source found on the Net is credible? Here are some questions to ask when you work with online material:

- Who is the author of the material? Does the author offer his or her credentials in the form of a résumé or biographical information? Do these credentials qualify the author to provide information on the topic? Does the author provide an e-mail address so you can request more information? The less you know about an author, the more suspicious you should be about using the data.

- Can you verify the accuracy of the information presented? Does the author refer to studies or to other authors you can investigate? If the author doesn't cite other works or other points of view, that may suggest the document is opinionated and one-sided. In such a case, it's important to track down material addressing alternative points of view.

- Who is sponsoring the website? Many sites are published by organizations—businesses, agencies, lobby groups—as well as by individuals. If a sponsor pushes a single point of view, you should use the material with great caution. And once again, make an extra effort to locate material addressing other sides of the issue.

- Is the information cited recent and up-to-date? Being on the Internet doesn't guarantee that information is current. To assess the timeliness of Internet materials, check at the top or bottom of the document for copyright date, publication date, and/or revision date. Having those dates will help you determine whether the material is recent enough for your purposes.

Using Other Internet Tools

The World Wide Web is not the only portion of the Internet that you'll find interesting or useful. Other aspects of the Net include Telnet, a software networking tool that allows you to log onto another computer and access its files; FTPs (File Transfer Protocols), through which you download files from remote computers and upload files to computers to which you have access; and Gopher, a comprehensive menu-based program developed at the University of Minnesota. If you become interested in the workings of the Net beyond the World Wide Web and want to investigate further, your favorite search engine—and your college librarian—should provide the help you need. Finally, don't be shy about asking any Net-savvy folks you know for advice. Most computer buffs are more than willing to share their knowledge. With very little prodding from you, they'll be happy to explain the ins and outs of the Net and provide valuable assistance for accessing its wealth of information.

PREPARE A WORKING BIBLIOGRAPHY

As you gather promising books, reference volumes, print articles, and online material about your subject, prepare a **working bibliography**—a master list of potential sources. Having such a list means you won't have to waste time later tracking down a source whose title you remember only vaguely.

Since you want to read as much as you can about your subject, the working bibliography will contain more sources than your instructor requires for the final paper. In the long run, you probably won't use all the sources in your working bibliography. Some will turn out to be less helpful than you thought they would be; others may focus on an aspect of your topic you decide not to cover after all.

The working bibliography may be compiled on standard notebook paper or, preferably, on index cards, one card for each source. We recommend 4×6-inch cards rather than 3×5-inch ones or sheets of paper. Unlike sheets of paper, index cards can be arranged in alphabetical order quickly, making it easy to prepare your Works Cited list (see page 567). And the larger index cards give you room to comment on a source's value ("Good discussion of landfill regulations") or availability ("See if book is on reserve").

Whether you use notebook paper or index cards to prepare your working bibliography, take time to record the following information (to see sample bibliography cards, turn to pages 548–550):

- If the source is a book, write down its title, author, and call number.
- If the source is an article in a reference volume, note the titles of both the article and the reference work, the article's author, and the reference work's call number.
- If the source is an article in a periodical, note the titles of both the article and periodical, the article's author, and the article's date and pages.
- If you obtain an article title by using a CD-ROM or going online, write down the same information you would if you were using a print directory. If you don't expect to locate the article in print form (because a print version is either nonexistent or difficult to obtain), then also note any information essential for accessing the article electronically. For example, if later on you want to locate the article's text on the same CD-ROM you are using as an index, write down "CD-ROM" and the database (for example, *ERIC*). For an online source, note the database (for example, *Magazine Database Plus*); the computer network or

service through which you access the database (for example, Earthlink), and any keyboard commands you need to access the material, especially the online address).

Recording this basic information helps you locate these potentially useful sources later on. In the next stage, as you start taking notes, you'll refine the information in your working bibliography.

TAKE NOTES TO SUPPORT THE THESIS WITH EVIDENCE

Why Take Notes?

Now that you've formed a working thesis, identified promising sources, and compiled a working bibliography, it's almost time to take notes. Your goal at this point is to find support for your preliminary thesis—*and* to pay close attention to material suggesting alternative viewpoints. Sifting through this conflicting information will enable you to refine your working thesis with more precision. (For more about evaluating contrasting positions, see page 546). At this point you may be wondering why you should take notes at all. Why not simply read the sources and then draft the research paper, referring to the sources when you need to check a fact or quote something?

Such an approach is bound to create problems. For one thing, you may have to return a source to the library before you're ready to start writing. Taking the time to go back to the library to retrieve the source later on can slow you down considerably—and, in fact, someone else could have checked out the only copy of the source. With note cards, though, you'll have all the necessary information at hand without having to return to the original source.

Moreover, if you have your sources in front of you as you write, you'll be tempted to move large chunks of material directly from your sources to your paper, without first evaluating and distilling the material. Writing directly from your sources also aggravates any tendency you may have to string together one quotation after another, without providing many ideas of your own. Worst of all, such an approach often leads to *plagiarism:* passing off someone else's work as your own. (For more on plagiarism, see pages 553–554, 558–559, and 577–586.)

Note-taking can eliminate such problems. When done well, it encourages you to assess, synthesize, and react to your sources. Keeping your working thesis firmly in mind, you examine what others have to say about your subject. Some authors will support your working thesis; others will serve as "devil's advocates," prodding you to consider opposing viewpoints. In either case, note-taking helps you refine your position and develop a sound basis for your conclusions.

Before Note-Taking: Evaluate Sources

You shouldn't take notes on a source until after you've evaluated its *relevance, timeliness, seriousness of approach,* and *objectivity.* Titles can be misleading. If a source turns out to be irrelevant, skip note-taking; just indicate on your working bibliography that you consulted the source and found it didn't relate to your topic. Next, consider the source's age. To some extent, the topic and kind of research you're doing determine whether a work is outdated. If you're researching a historical topic such as the internment of Japanese Americans during World War II, you would most likely consult sources published in the 1940s and 1950s, as well as more up-to-date sources. In contrast, if you're investigating a recent scientific development—*in vitro* fertilization, for example—it would make sense to restrict your search to current material. For most college research, a source older than ten years is considered outdated unless it was the first to present key concepts in a field.

You should also ask yourself if each source is serious and scholarly enough for your purpose and your instructor's requirements. Finally, examine your sources for possible bias, keeping in mind that a strong conclusion or opinion is *not in itself* a sign of bias. As long as a writer doesn't ignore opposing positions or distort evidence, a source can't be considered biased. A biased source presents only those facts that fit the writer's predetermined conclusions. Such a source is often marked by emotionally charged language (see pages 23–24). Publications sponsored by special interest groups—a particular industry, religious association, or political party—are usually biased. Reading such materials *does* familiarize you with a specific point of view, but remember that contrary evidence has probably been ignored or skewed.

A special problem occurs when you find a source that takes a position contrary to the one that you had previously considered credible. When you come across such conflicting material, you can be sure you've identified a pivotal issue within your topic. To decide which position is more valid, you need to take good notes from both sources (see pages 550–560) or carefully annotate your photocopies (see page 553). Then evaluate each source for bias. On this basis alone, you might discover serious flaws in one or both sources. Also compare the key points and supporting evidence in the two sources. Where do they agree? Where do they disagree? Does one source argue against the other's position, perhaps even discrediting some of the opposing view's evidence? The answers to these questions may very well cause you to question the quality, completeness, or fairness of one or both sources. To resolve such a conflict of sources, you can also research your subject more fully. For example, if your conflicting sources are at the general or serious level (see page 528), you should probably turn to more scholarly sources. By referring to more authoritative material, you may be able to determine which of the conflicting sources is more valid.

When you try to resolve discrepancies between sources, be sure not to let your own bias come into play. Try not to favor one position over the other simply because it supports your working thesis. Remember, your goal is to arrive at the most well-founded position you can. In fact, researching a topic may lead you to change your original viewpoint. In this case, you shouldn't hesitate to revise your working thesis to accord with the evidence you gather.

Before Note-Taking: Refine Your Working Bibliography

After determining the sources from which you will take notes, spend some time refining the relevant entries in your working bibliography. With the sources in front of you, use the following guidelines to fill in any missing information. (At times, the guidelines include a bit more information than MLA requires. This precision will often be helpful if you use a format other than MLA.)

- Take down the *authors' names* exactly as they appear on the title pages of the original works and in the order shown there. The author listed first is considered the primary author, so don't rearrange the names alphabetically. Occasionally, a work will be attributed to an organization, university, or institute rather than to a person. If so, consider that organization the author.

- For a *book,* record from the title page the full title (including any subtitle) and the publisher's name. Also, record the publisher's location. If the publisher is international, use the publishing location in your country, if there is one. If several locations within your country are listed, use as the city of publication the one that's listed first on the title page. Also record the copyright year, the most recent year in which the text was registered, as well as the volume number for multivolume books. If you have doubts whether your edition is the most recent, check the computerized online or card catalog to see if the library has a later one. Remember, the number of editions in which a book has appeared is not the same as the number of printings the book has gone through. A book may say "ninth printing," yet be only the second edition. Finally, don't forget to note the book's call number.

- For a *mass-publication magazine,* note the author's name (if any), the article title, the magazine title, the date (usually month and year), and the pages on which the article appears.

- For a *newspaper article,* take down the author's name (if any), the article title, the newspaper title, the date (month, day, and year), the edition, and the section and pages where the article appears.

- For an *article in a book-length collection,* record the authors of the article, the article title, the book title, the book's editor, the publisher and its location, the copyright date, and the specific book pages on which the article appears.

- For an *article in a scholarly or serious journal,* note the article's author(s), the article title, the journal title, the date (including month and year), the volume and issue (if any), and the pages on which the article appears. Also indicate whether the journal is paginated continuously from issue to issue throughout a given year or whether each issue is paginated separately.

- For all periodicals, note the library location of relevant issues.

- For *text obtained on CD-ROM or online,* note the identical information you would for a printed source in the same category (for example, a magazine article), with the possible exception of page numbers. If the database doesn't specify an article's precise page numbers (see pages 573–574), write down the page number (if available) on which the article began in the original, plus the number of pages or number of paragraphs in the article. In addition, for CD-ROM text, note the database (for instance, *The New York Times Ondisc*), CD-ROM publisher (for example, UMI-ProQuest), and CD-ROM publication date. For text accessed online, note the database (for instance, *The New York Times Online*), the computer service or network (for example, LexisNexis), your date of access, and any other information someone would need to retrieve the text (such as the online address).

We suggest that you display bibliographic information as it appears in the sample cards in Figures 20.7(*a*) to (*g*). Be sure to include any information you might need for your paper's Works Cited or References page. If your working bibliography is accurate and complete, you won't need to refer to your sources later on when preparing your paper's final reference list.

Before Note-Taking: Read Your Sources

At this point, you should spend some time analyzing each source for its *central ideas, main supporting points,* and *key details.* As you read, keep asking yourself how the source's content meshes with your working thesis and with what you know about your subject. Does the source repeat what you already know? If so, you may not need any notes. But if a source provides detailed support for important ideas, plan to take full notes.

> TP248.23
> .P75
> 2001
>
>
> Priest, Susanna Hornig. A Grain of Truth: The
>   Media, the Public, and Biotechnology.
>   Oxford: Rowman, 2001.

Figure 20.7(*a*)   Bibliography card: Book

> Current Periodicals
>
>
> Benham, Barbara. "Securing the Skies." Travel and
>   Leisure Dec. 2001: 88–97.

Figure 20.7(*b*)   Bibliography card: Article in a general-interest magazine

Microfilm

Johnston, Chris. "High-Tech Alone Will Not Catch Out Cheats." Times Higher Education Supplement 10 Aug. 2001: 15+.

Figure 20.7(c)   Bibliography card: Newspaper article

Bound Periodicals

Travis, Jon E. "Censorship in Higher Education: Is the Public Forum at Risk?" Community College Journal of Research and Practice 24 (2001): 809–821.

Figure 20.7(d)   Bibliography card: Article in a scholarly journal that is paginated continuously

Bound Periodicals

Laird, Ellen. "We All Pay for Internet Plagiarism." Education Digest 67.3 (2001): 56–60.

Figure 20.7(e)   Bibliography card: Article in a scholarly journal that paginates each issue separately

```
                                              CD-ROM

   Johnson, David W., and Roger Johnson. "Peer
       Mediation in an Inner-City Elementary
       School." Urban Education 36.2 (2001):
       165–79 (31 pars.). ERIC. CD-ROM.
       U.S. Department of Education. 1 Oct.
       2001.
```

Figure 20.7(*f*)   Bibliography card: Periodical article on CD-ROM

```
                                              Online

   Nielsen, Amanda. "Life on the Verge of a Dot-com
       Breakdown." Salon.com 25 Jan. 2001: 8
       pars. 6 Feb. 2002 <http://www.salon.com/
       tech/feature/2001/01/25/lay_off_sidebar/
       index.html>.
```

Figure 20.7(*g*)   Bibliography card: Periodical article obtained online

When Note-Taking: What to Select

What, specifically, should you take notes on? Your notes might include any of the following: facts, statistics, anecdotal accounts, expert opinion, case studies, surveys, reports, results of experiments. If a source suggests a new angle on your subject, thoughtful and extensive notes are in order. As you begin taking notes, you may not be able to judge how helpful a source will be. In that case, you probably should take fairly detailed notes. After a while, you'll become more selective.

As you go along, you may come across material that challenges your working thesis and forces you to think differently about your subject. Indeed, the more you learn, the more difficult it may be to state anything conclusively. This is a sign that you're synthesizing and weighing all the evidence. In time, the confusion will lessen, and you'll emerge with a clearer understanding of your subject.

When Note-Taking: How to Record Statistics

As you read your sources, you'll probably come across statistics that reinforce points you want to make. Follow these guidelines when taking notes on statistics:

- Check that you record the figures accurately. Also note how and by whom the statistics were gathered as well as where and when they were first reported.

- Take down your source's interpretation of the statistics, but be sure to scrutinize the interpretation. Although the source's figures may be correct, they could have been given a "spin" that distorts them. For example, if 80 percent of Americans think violent crime is our number one national problem, that doesn't mean that violent crime *is* our main problem; it simply means that 80 percent of the people polled *think* it is. And if a "majority" of people think that homelessness should be among our top national priorities, it may be that a mere 51 percent—a bare majority—feels that way. In short, make sure the statistics mean what your sources say they mean.

- Examine each source for possible bias. If a source takes a highly impassioned stance, you should regard its statistics with healthy skepticism. Indeed, it's a good idea to corroborate such figures elsewhere; tracking down the original source of a statistic is the best way to ensure that numbers are being reported fairly.

- Be suspicious of statistics that fail to indicate the number of respondents or that are based on a small, nonrepresentative sample (see pages 516–517). For instance, assume the claim is made that 90 percent of the people sampled wouldn't vote for a candidate who had an extramarital affair. However, if only ten people were polled one Sunday as they left church, then the 90 percent statistic is meaningless. (For hints on using statistics in a paper, see pages 585–586.)

When Note-Taking: Use Index Cards

With your sources and bibliography cards close at hand, you're ready to begin taking notes on a second set of index cards. Your instructor will probably ask you to take notes on 4 × 6-inch (or larger) cards. On each card, record notes from only *one source* and on only *one subtopic* of your subject.

Note cards have several advantages over sheets of paper. First, cards help you break information into small, easy-to-manage chunks. Second, they allow you to rearrange information since they can be piled and sorted, unlike information on pages, which must be cut and taped. You can also delete information easily by simply removing a card. Last, note cards save time once you begin writing; you can, for example, staple a quotation on a card right onto your first draft.

For every note card, do the following:

- *Key* each card *to the appropriate source* in your working bibliography by writing the author's last name on each note card. If you have more than one source by the same author, also record the source's title.

- Record the *page* or *pages* in the source that the note refers to. If the note card material is drawn from several pages, indicate clearly where the page breaks occur in the source. That way, if you use only a portion of the material later, you will know its exact page number.

- Write a key word or phrase at the top of each note card, indicating the gist of the note and the aspect of your topic the card focuses on. Often your key terms will themselves develop subtopics. For example, a paper on erosion may have two major stacks of cards: "Beach erosion" and "Mountain erosion," with beach erosion being divided into "Dune" and "Shoreline" erosion.

- Finally, write down the actual note. Pages 553–560 describe specific kinds of notes to take. In the meantime, here's some general advice. Some cards will have only a line or two; others will be quite full. If you run out of space on a card, don't use the other side; this makes it hard to see at a glance what the note is about. Instead, use a second card, being sure to record the source, page, and so on. Also label successive cards carefully (1 of 2, 2 of 2) and clip them to the first card in the series.

It's up to you where on the note card you place identifying information. The sample card in Figure 20.8 illustrates one way. Whichever way you set up your note cards, be consistent. When you scan your cards before finishing with a source, you'll be more inclined to notice any missing information if you've prepared them in some consistent style. You'll also find it easier to retrieve information later on from well-organized note cards.

Note cards may also include your comments about a source. Enclosing your observations in square brackets ["helpful summary," "controversial interpretation"] keeps these interpretive remarks separate from your notes on a source. If taking notes sparks new ways of looking at your subject, get down such thoughts, carefully separating them from your source material. Write "Me" or "My idea" on the card, or enclose your observations in a box. If your own comments become extensive, use separate note cards, clearly labeling them as your own ideas.

Unethical business behavior: causes   Etzioni, p. 22
    Economists suggest that people's desire for profit causes them to cheat—cheat to stay ahead.
    But recent studies by social scientists show otherwise—"social ties" and other non-economic factors cause ethical or noneth. behav.
    Most important "social ties"—family mores and the culture of one's business peers.

Figure 20.8   Note-taking index card

Two Other Note-Taking Approaches

Although index cards are the most efficient way to take notes, there are other methods available. If you can't get the hang of the note-card system, try using **sheets of paper.** To minimize the problems you may encounter later when you start organizing the paper, head each sheet with a key to the source. Then enter all notes from that source, along with page numbers, on the same sheet. If you run out of space, don't take notes on the other side. Instead, start a new sheet, entering on each a key to the source, and continue to keep track of the pages in the source from which you're taking notes. Mark each sheet in the sequence clearly (1 of 3, 2 of 3, and so on). Using key phrases to signal subtopics will also make it easier to organize your notes later.

Photocopying material is another way to gather information. You have the right to duplicate published work as long as you use it for your own research and give credit for borrowed material. Photocopying *does* have advantages. It allows unhurried analysis and reconsideration of research material at home. It can also be a way of ensuring accuracy since sources can be checked so easily. Duplicating can be especially useful if you need to retrieve a detail that initially seemed unimportant.

However, photocopying is not without dangers, especially if you're an inexperienced researcher. You may get a false sense of security if you convince yourself that once you've photocopied material, you've done most of the work. *Remember:* You still have to evaluate and synthesize your source material, figuring out what evidence supports your working thesis. That means you should dig into the photocopied material, underlining or boxing sections you might use, jotting subtopics in the margins, recording your reaction to the material.

There's one more pitfall to consider: Working with duplicated material can encourage *plagiarism.* Instead of recasting material in your own words, you may be tempted to copy others' language and ideas. If that is the case, you'd be better off steering clear of duplicating altogether. (For more on plagiarism, see pages 553–554, 558–559, and 577–586.)

If you do photocopy, don't forget to include the duplicated sources in your working bibliography and to write complete source information on the photocopy itself.

Kinds of Notes

There are four broad kinds of notes: direct quotations, summaries, paraphrases, and combined notes. Knowing how and when to use each type is an important part of the research process.

Direct Quotations

A **quotation note** reproduces, word for word, that which is stated in a source. Although quoting can demonstrate the thoroughness with which you reviewed relevant sources, don't take one direct quote note card after another; such a string of quotations means you haven't evaluated and synthesized your sources sufficiently.

When should you quote? If a source's ideas are unusual or controversial, record a representative quotation in your notes so you can include it in your paper to show you have accurately conveyed the source's viewpoint. Also record a quotation if a source's wording is so eloquent or convincing that it would lose its power if you restated the material in your own words. And, of course, you should take down a quotation if a source's ideas reinforce your own conclusions. If the source is a respected authority, such a quotation will lend authority to your own ideas. When taking notes, you might aim for one to three quotations from each major source. More than that can create a problem when you write the paper.

A card containing a direct quotation from a source should be clearly indicated by quotation marks, perhaps even a handwritten note like "Direct Quotation" or "DQ." Whenever your source quotes someone else (a secondary source) and you want to take notes on what that other person said, put the statement in quotes and indicate its original source. (See page 585 for more on quoting secondary sources.)

When copying a quotation, you must record the author's statement *exactly* as it appears in the original work, right down to the punctuation. As long as you don't change the meaning of the original, you may delete a phrase or sentence from a quotation if it's not pertinent to the point you're making. In such cases, insert three periods, called an **ellipsis** (. . .), in place of the deleted words. Leave a space before the second and the third period but not before the first or after the third. To make it clear that the ellipsis stands for material that you rather than your source deleted, place brackets around the ellipsis points.[4]

Original Passage

The plot, with one exciting event after another, was representative of the usual historical novel. But *Gone with the Wind* placed its emphasis as much on the private individual as on the panorama.

Ellipsis Used to Show Material Omitted

When omitting material *in or near the middle* of the original sentence, proceed as follows: Leave a space before the first bracket, provide the ellipsis, and leave a space after the final bracket before continuing with the quoted matter:

```
"The plot [. . .] was representative of the usual historical
novel. But Gone with the Wind placed its emphasis as much on the
private individual as on the panorama."
```

---

[4]The 1999 edition of the *MLA Handbook for Writers of Research Papers* was the first edition calling for the use of brackets with ellipsis points. Earlier editions required only the ellipsis. To be consistent with the most recent guidelines, the examples here and on page 555 use brackets with the ellipsis. Check with your instructor to see which guidelines they want you to follow.

Ellipsis at the End

When deleting material *at the end* of the original sentence, proceed as above, but follow the last bracket with the period that ends the sentence; then provide the closing quotation mark:

```
"The plot, with one exciting event after another, was representa-
tive of the usual historical novel [. . .]."
```

You don't need an ellipsis if you omit material at the start of a quotation. Simply place the quotation marks where you begin quoting directly. Also, don't capitalize the first word in the quotation unless it ordinarily requires capitalization:

No Ellipsis Needed

```
Gone with the Wind's piling up of "one exciting event after
another" was typical of the historical potboiler.
```

This example also illustrates that you can omit the ellipsis if all you quote is a key term or short phrase. In such cases, just enclose the borrowed material in quotation marks. (For more examples of the ellipsis, see page 579.)

If, for clarity's sake, you need to add a word or short phrase to a quotation (for example, by changing a verb tense or replacing a vague pronoun with a noun), enclose your insertion in **brackets:**

```
"Not only did it [Gone with the Wind] for a short time become
America's speediest-selling novel, but over the long haul, it
became the nation's largest-selling novel."
```

When a source you're quoting quotes another source, place single quotation marks around the words of the secondary source:

```
"Despite its massive scope, Gone with the Wind sustained, accord-
ing to one reviewer, 'remarkable continuity in its plot and char-
acter development.'"
```

Summaries

By **summaries,** we mean *condensing* someone else's ideas and restating them *in your own words.* Skim the source; then, using your own language, condense the material to its central idea, main supporting points, and key details. Summary note cards may be written as lists, brief paragraphs, or both. You may use abbreviations and phrases as well as complete sentences. *A caution:* When summarizing, don't use the ellipsis and brackets to signal that you have omitted some ideas. The ellipsis and brackets are used only when quoting.

The length of the summary depends on your topic and purpose. Read the following excerpt from page 8 of Julian Stamp's book *The Homeless and History.* Then look at the subsequent summary note cards.

> The key to any successful homeless policy requires a clear understanding of just who are the homeless. Since fifty percent of shelter residents have drug and alcohol addictions, programs need to provide not only a place to sleep but also comprehensive treatment for addicts and their families. Since roughly one-third of the homeless population is mentally ill, programs need to offer psychiatric care, perhaps even institutionalization, and not just housing subsidies. Since the typical head of a homeless family (a young woman with fewer than six months' working experience) usually lacks the know-how needed to maintain a job and a home, programs need to supply employment and life skills training; low-cost housing alone will not ensure the family's stability.
>
> However, if we switch our focus from the single person to the larger *economic* issues, we begin to see that homelessness cannot be resolved solely at the level of individual treatment. Beginning in the 1980s and through the 1990s, the gap between the rich and the poor has widened, buying power has stagnated, industrial jobs have fled overseas, and federal funding for low-cost housing has been almost eliminated. Given these developments, homelessness begins to look like a product of history, our recent history, and only by addressing shifts in the American economy can we begin to find effective solutions for people lacking homes. Moreover, these solutions—ranging from renewed federal spending to tax laws favoring job-creating companies—will require a sustained national commitment that transcends partisan politics.

The summary notes shown in Figures 20.9(*a*) and (*b*) were taken by two students writing on related but different topics. Although both students eventually used more scholarly and detailed sources in their papers, they found—in the early stages of their research—that Stamp's book provided helpful background and perspective. The first student, planning to write on the causes of homelessness, prepared an in-depth summary card labeled "Personal and Economic Causes of Homelessness." The second student, planning to write on the day-to-day experience of homeless families, took a much shorter note under the heading "Profile: Heads of Homeless Families."

Summarizing Problems. The sample note cards in Figure 20.9 were prepared by students who were careful about translating ideas into their own language. The note cards shown in Figures 20.10(*a*) and (*b*), however, were prepared by students who had difficulty recasting ideas from the Stamp passage. In the first example, the student was so determined to put things her way that she added her own ideas and ended up *distorting* Stamp's meaning. For instance, note the way she emphasizes personal problems over economic issues, making the former the cause of the latter. Stamp does just the opposite and highlights economic solutions rather than individual treatment. In the second example, the student worked so hard to compress material that he prepared an *overly condensed* note card. His excessively terse statement, lacking detail and explanation, renders the summary almost meaningless.

Personal and Economic Causes   Stamp, p. 8
of Homelessness

Point: As individuals, homeless have personal problems.

    50% in shelters are substance abusers.

    33% of all homeless suffer mental illnesses.

    Head of homeless family usually has little or no job
    experience.

    Treatment program needed to solve these problems.

Stamp, p. 8 cont.

Point: As a nation, homelessness is an economic
problem. Since 1980:

    Growing gulf between rich and poor.
    Decline in industrial jobs.
    Loss of federal money for housing.

    Only economic treatment—from government
    spending to new tax laws—can permanently
    solve the homeless problem.

Figure 20.9(*a*) First student's summary cards

Profile: Heads of Homeless Families   Stamp, p. 8

Most homeless families are led by young women who
haven't held a job for longer than six months. Without
training in work skills and household management,
these women can't maintain their families or any
housing that might be available.

Figure 20.9(*b*) Second student's summary card

Who Are the Homeless?   Stamp, p. 8

The homeless are people with big problems like addiction, mental illness, and poor job skills. Because they haven't been provided with proper treatment and training, the homeless haven't been able to adapt to a changing economy. So their numbers soared in the 1990s.

Figure 20.10(*a*)   Summary: Distorting the original

Effective Homeless Programs   Stamp, p. 8

Homeless need economic—not psychiatric— treatment and solutions.

Figure 20.10(*b*)   Summary: Overly condensed

Paraphrases

You may have heard of another kind of note prepared in your own words: **paraphrase notes.** Unlike a summary, which condenses the original, a paraphrase recasts material by using roughly the same number of words, retaining the same level of detail, and adopting the same style as the original. Since the research process requires you to distill information, you'll probably find summary note cards much more helpful than paraphrases.

Plagiarism

One problem with paraphrases is that they can lead to **plagiarism**—which occurs when a writer borrows someone else's ideas, facts, or language but doesn't properly credit that source. Look, for example, at the first note card in Figure 20.11. When preparing his paraphrase, the student stayed too close to the source and borrowed much of Stamp's language *word for word*. Note, for example, the underlined words, which are taken directly from Stamp. If the student transferred this phrasing to his paper without supplying quotation marks, he'd be guilty of plagiarism. Indeed, even if this student acknowledged Stamp in the paper, he'd still be plagiarizing—the lack of quotation marks implies that the language is the student's when, in fact, it is Stamp's.

As the second sample card in Figure 20.11 shows, another student believed, erroneously, that if she changed a word here and omitted a word there, she'd be preparing an effective paraphrase. Note that the language is all Stamp's except for the underlined words, which signal the student's slight rephrasings of Stamp. Notice, too, that the student occasionally deleted a word from Stamp, thinking that such changes would constitute a legitimate paraphrase. For instance, Stamp's "only by addressing shifts in the American economy can we begin to find effective solutions" became "only by addressing shifts in the economy can we find solutions." The student couldn't place quotation marks around these *near-quotes* because her wording isn't identical to that of the source. Yet to place the near-quotes in a paper without quotation marks would be deceptive; the lack of quotation marks would suggest that the language is the student's when actually

> Homelessness: An Economic Problem   Stamp, p. 8
>
> <u>Only by</u> addressing changes <u>in the American economy</u>—from <u>the</u> gap between <u>the</u> wealthy <u>and the poor to the</u> loss of industrial jobs to overseas markets—can we begin to find solutions for the homeless. And <u>these solutions, ranging from renewed federal spending to tax laws favoring job-creating companies,</u> will not be easy to find or implement.

Figure 20.11(*a*)   Plagiarized paraphrase: Word-for-word

> Homelessness: An Economic Problem   Stamp, p. 8
>
> Only by addressing shifts in the economy can we find solutions <u>for the homeless</u>. These solutions will require a sustained <u>federal</u> commitment <u>avoids</u> partisan politics.

Figure 20.11(*b*)   Plagiarized paraphrase: Near-quotes

it's substantially (but not exactly) Stamp's. Such near-quotes are also considered plagiarism, even if, when writing the paper, the student supplied a note citing the source. (For hints on steering clear of plagiarism when you actually write a research paper, see the discussion of documentation on pages 577–586.)

Combined Notes

When taking notes, you may summarize someone else's ideas in your own words but also include some of the source's exact wording. The result, a **combined note,** is legitimate as long as you put quotation marks around the source's language. The combined note cards in Figure 20.12 are based on the same passage from Stamp's book.

Combination note cards are effective. They allow you to retain key phrases as well as eloquent or controversial statements from your source; you don't have to spend time recasting material that resists translation into your own words. At the same time, combined notes indicate that you're actively involved with your research material, that you're continually asking yourself, "What should I state in my own words? What is so informative, so interesting, so provocative that I want to use it exactly as it is, word for word?" Such questions prompt discipline and careful thought, two qualities that will serve you well as you move ahead to the next phase of your research—organizing and writing the paper, our focus in Chapter 21.

Homelessness: An Economic Problem   Stamp, p. 8

Beyond the individual problems of homeless people, homelessness is a matter of "larger <u>economic</u> issues."
During the 1980s and 1990s:

Growing gulf between rich and poor
Flat growth in "buying power"
Decline in industrial jobs and federal money
    for housing

Stamp, p. 8 cont.

Only "by addressing shifts in the American economy"—through government spending and new tax laws—can we permanently solve the homeless problem.

Figure 20.12   One student's combined note cards

ACTIVITIES: SELECTING A SUBJECT, USING THE LIBRARY AND THE INTERNET, AND TAKING NOTES

1. Use the card or computer catalog to answer the following questions:

   a. What are three books dealing with the subject of adoption? Of the Internet? Of urban violence? Of genetic research?

   b. What is the title of a book by Betty Friedan? By John Kenneth Galbraith?

   c. Who is the author of *The Invisible Man?* Of *A Swiftly Tilting Planet?*

2. Examine this entry from a computerized catalog and then use it to answer the questions that follow.

   a. Which catalog system does this library use?

   b. What is the title of the book?

   c. How many authors does the book have? What are their names?

   d. Under what subjects is this book listed in the catalog?

   e. When was the book published?

   f. Assume you're writing a paper about the ways computers are being used in the education of deaf preschoolers. Considering the information on the card, would you try to locate this book? Why or why not?

AUTHOR:	**Palloff, Rena M.; Keith Pratt**
TITLE:	**Lessons from the Cyberspace Classroom: The Realities of Online Teaching**
PUBLICATION INFO:	**San Francisco, CA: Jossey-Bass, 2001.**
PAGING AND SIZE:	**204 p.; 24 cm.**
SUBJECTS:	**Adult education.** **Teaching—Computer network resources.** **Computer-assisted instruction—Higher education.** **Distance education.**

1. CALL NUMBER: LB1044.87.P34 2001—STACKS—Checked Out

2. CALL NUMBER: LB1044.87.P34 2001—STACKS—Available

3. Prepare a bibliography card for each of the following books. Gather all the information necessary at the library so that you can write accurate and complete bibliography cards:

   a. Barbara Tuchman, *Practicing History*
   b. L. Jacobs, *The Documentary Tradition*
   c. Margaret Mead, *Coming of Age in Samoa*
   d. Stephen Bank, *The Sibling Bond*
   e. Ronald Gross, *The New Old*
   f. Matthew Arnold, *Culture and Anarchy*

4. Using reference works available in your library, find the answers to the following questions:

   a. When was the Persian Gulf War fought?
   b. Who invented Kodachrome film, and when?
   c. What is the medical condition *rosacea?*
   d. What television show won the Emmy in 2000 for Outstanding Comedy Series?
   e. What was artist John Sartain known for?
   f. When was an African American first elected to Congress?
   g. In economics, what is Pareto's Law?
   h. In art, what is *écorché?*
   i. Give two other names for a *mbira*, a musical instrument.
   j. In the religion of the Hopi Native Americans, what are *kachinas?*

5. Select *one* of the following limited topics. Then, using the appropriate periodical indexes and bibliographies (see pages 528–534), locate three periodicals that would be helpful in researching the topic. Examine each periodical to determine whether it is aimed at a general, serious, or scholarly audience.

   a. Drug abuse among health-care professionals
   b. Ethical considerations in organ-transplant surgery
   c. Women in prison
   d. Deforestation of the Amazon rain forest
   e. The difference between *Sense and Sensibility* as a novel and as a film

6. Select *one* of the following limited topics. Then, using the Internet, locate at least three relevant articles on the topic: one from a general-interest magazine, one from a newspaper, one from a serious or scholarly journal. Make a bibliography card for each article.

   a. Ordaining women in American churches
   b. Attempts to regulate Internet pornography
   c. The popularity of novelist and essayist Isak Dinesen

    d. The growing interest in painter David Hockney

    e. AIDS education programs

    f. The global economy

7. Listed here are some of this book's professional essays, along with broad research topics that they suggest. Choose *one* of these general subjects and, using the Internet and/or the library's resources, do some background reading. (You should find helpful some of the sources listed on pages 526–527 and 529–531.) On either index cards or notebook paper, keep an informal record of the works you consult. As you read, jot down potential limited topics. After doing some further reading on *one* of the limited topics, devise a working thesis. (Don't, by the way, feel constrained by the point of view expressed in the essay[s] that initially prompted your research.)

    a. "Sister Flowers" (page 178); "The Fourth of July" (page 216); "So Tsi-Fai" (page 221); "A Slow Walk of Trees" (page 362); "And Then I Went to School" (page 371); "Black Men and Public Space" (page 407); "Let's Tell the Story of All America's Cultures" (page 500); "The Cult of Ethnicity Good and Bad" (page 503)
       Preservation of cultural differences
       Teaching about diversity
       Relations between different racial or ethnic groups

    b. "Family Counterculture" (page 7); "Shooting an Elephant" (page 209); "The Fourth of July" (page 216); "Is Sex All That Matters?" (page 256); "Doublespeak" (page 295); "Don't Just Stand There" (page 322); "Absolutophobia" (page 438)
       Teaching morality to children
       Morality in the mass media
       Morality in the workplace
       Sexual morality

    c. "Managing Mixed Messages" (page 251); "Is Sex All That Matters?" (page 256); "But What Do You Mean?" (page 288); "The Ugly Truth About Beauty" (page 367); "Rape: A Bigger Danger Than Feminists Know" (page 489); "Common Decency" (page 494)
       Raising non-sexist children
       The mass-media depiction of gender roles
       Sexism on the college campus

8. Referring to paragraphs 1–5 in Ann McClintock's "Propaganda Techniques in Today's Advertising" (page 282), prepare three note cards: a direct quotation, a summary, and a combined note. Assume you're using the McClintock essay to research advertisers' use of emotional appeals to sell products.

21
WRITING THE RESEARCH PAPER

After you complete your note-taking, you're ready to begin the writing phase of the research project. When writing the paper, you'll probably find it helpful to follow these steps:

- Refine your working thesis.
- Sort the note cards.
- Organize the evidence by outlining.
- Prepare the Works Cited list.
- Write the first draft.
- Document borrowed material.
- Revise, edit, and proofread.

REFINE YOUR WORKING THESIS

This is a good time to *reexamine your working thesis*; it's undoubtedly evolved since you first started your research. Indeed, now that you're more informed about the topic, you may feel that your original thesis oversimplifies the issue. To clarify your position, begin by sifting through your note cards; your goal is to formulate a position that makes the most sense in light of the research you've done and the information you've gathered. Then, revise your working thesis, keeping in mind the evidence on your note cards. This refined version of your thesis will serve as the starting point for your first draft. Remember, though—as you write the paper, new thoughts may emerge that will cause you to modify your thesis even further. (For more on thesis statements, see Chapter 3.)

SORT THE NOTE CARDS

Keeping your refined thesis in mind, *sort your note cards* into piles *by topic*. If, for example, your thesis is "Lotteries are an inefficient means of raising money for state programs," you might form one pile of note cards on administrative costs, another on types of state programs, a third on the way money is allocated, and so on. Although you can sort by the key terms or headings you previously placed at the tops of cards, it's a good idea to reread the cards. You may find, for example, that a heading needs to be changed because its information better suits some other category. If some cards don't fit into any pile—and this is likely—put them aside. You don't need to use every note card. At this point, though, you should consider which organizational approach (see pages 55–57) will help you sequence your material. Arrange your topic piles to reflect this order.

Once you've arranged your note cards according to the topic headings at the top, sort each topic pile by *subtopic*. For example, the pile of cards about types of state programs might be divided into these three subtopic piles: programs for the elderly, programs for preschool children, programs for the physically disabled. Next, using the patterns of development and organizational approaches discussed, respectively, on pages 47–48 and 55–57, order each set of subtopic cards to match the sequence in which you think you'll discuss those subtopics in your paper. This sorting will make your next step—preparing an outline—much easier.

ORGANIZE THE EVIDENCE BY OUTLINING

Whether or not your instructor requires an *outline*, it's a good idea to prepare one before you begin writing the paper. Because an outline groups and sequences points, it provides a blueprint you can follow when writing. Outlining clarifies what your main ideas are, what your supporting evidence is, and how everything fits together. It reveals where your argument is well supported and where it is weak.

To design your outline, focus first on the paper's body. How can you best explain and support your thesis? For now, don't worry about your introduction or conclusion. General guidelines on outlining are discussed in Chapter 5 (pages

57–58). To apply those guidelines to a research paper, keep the following points in mind:

- Base your outline on your organized piles of note cards.
- Label your *main topic* headings (those on your main pile of cards) with roman numerals (I, II, III, and so on) to indicate the order in which you plan to discuss each topic in the paper.
- Label the *subtopics* grouped under each main topic heading with capital letters (A, B, C). Indent the subtopic entries under their respective main topics, listing them in the order you plan to discuss them.
- Label *supporting points* (ideas noted on your cards) with arabic numerals (1, 2, 3) and indent them under the appropriate subtopics.
- Label *specific details* (facts, quotations, statistics, examples, expert opinion) with lowercase letters (a, b, c) and indent them under the appropriate supporting points. Use shorthand for details. For example, write "Bitner quote here" instead of copying the entire quotation into your outline.
- Where appropriate, map out sections of the paper that will provide background information or define key terms.

Here's how the various outline elements look when they're properly labeled and indented:

```
I. Main topic
    A. Subtopic
        1. Supporting point
        2. Supporting point
            a. Specific detail
            b. Specific detail
    B. Subtopic
        1. Supporting point
        2. Supporting point
II. Main topic
    A. Subtopic
        1. Supporting point
        2. Supporting point
            a. Specific detail
            b. Specific detail
    B. Subtopic
```

Your first outline probably won't be a formal full-sentence one; rather, it's more likely to be a *topic* (or phrase) *outline*, like those on pages 312–313, 354, and 467–468. A topic outline helps you clarify a paper's overall structure. A *full-sentence outline* (see pages 237 and 595–597) or a *combined topic and sentence outline* (see pages 388–389) is better suited to mapping out in detail the development of a paper's ideas. If you're preparing an outline that will be submitted with the paper, find out in advance which kind your instructor prefers.

Before you go any further, it's a good idea to get some feedback on your outline—from an instructor or a critical friend—to make sure others agree that your meaning and organization are logical and clear. Then, based on your readers' reactions, make whatever changes seem necessary.

Finally, key your note cards to your outline. Label each card according to the section of the paper in which the card will be used: "IA," "IIB2," and so on. Using a different color ink for each main-topic section makes it easier to locate appropriate card stacks when you write the paper later on.

Prepare the Works Cited List: MLA Format

At this point, you should draft a tentative **Works Cited list** (or bibliography) before you write the paper. That way, each time you include borrowed material in your paper, you can easily key that material to the appropriate item on the Works Cited list.

The following discussion focuses on the MLA—Modern Language Association—format for preparing the Works Cited list. The **MLA format,** based on the *MLA Handbook for Writers of Research Papers,* is used widely in the liberal arts. (The system used in the social sciences—that of the American Psychological Association [APA]—is described on pages 588–592. On page 592, you'll also find a description of the format commonly used in the hard sciences and in technical fields.) For a sample paper that uses MLA documentation, turn to the student essay on pages 598–607.

As a first step in preparing your Works Cited list, pull out the bibliography cards (or working bibliography) for the sources you think you'll actually refer to in your paper. Alphabetize them by the authors' last names. For now, put any anonymous works at the end.

The Works Cited list, which will appear at the end of your final paper, should include only those works you actually quote, summarize, or otherwise directly refer to in your paper. Don't list other sources, no matter how many you may have read. Placed on its own page, the Works Cited list provides readers with full bibliographic information about the sources you cite in the paper.

Double-space the entries on the Works Cited list, and *don't* add extra space between entries. The first line of each new entry should start at the left margin; if an entry extends beyond one line of type, all subsequent lines should be indented five spaces. The major items in a bibliographic entry (the author's full name, the title, all the information on publication) are separated with periods. (See the sample Works Cited list on pages 606–607.)

The following sample entries will help you prepare an accurate Works Cited list.

Citing Book Sources

Here is the basic format for listing a book in Works Cited:

- Start with the author's name, last name first, then first name and any initial, with a comma between the first and last names. Put a period after the first name or initial. Leave one space between the period and the next item.
- Give the complete book title. If the book has a subtitle, separate it from the title with a colon. Leave a space after the colon. Underline the full title and follow it with a period. Leave one space between the period and the next item. (*Important note:* According to MLA guidelines, underlining titles is generally preferred to italicizing them because of the greater visibility of underlines; if you'd like to use italics instead, check with your instructor.)
- Next, give the city of publication, followed by a colon. Leave a space between the colon and the next item. If the publisher has more than one location, use the city listed first on the book's title page. If the book is published in the United States, give only the city. If it is published in a foreign city that may be unfamiliar to readers, give the city as well as an abbreviation of the country, separating them with a comma.
- Supply the publisher's name, giving only key words and omitting the words *Company, Press, Publishers, Inc.,* and the like. (For example, write *Rodale* for Rodale Press and *Norton* for W. W. Norton and Company). In addition, use *UP* to abbreviate the names of university presses (as in *Columbia UP* and *U of California P*). Place a comma and a space after the publisher's name.
- End with the publication date and a period. Supply the most recent year of copyright. Don't use the year of the most recent printing.

Here is a sample entry for a book in the MLA format:

Book by One Author

Cott, Nancy F. <u>Public Vows: A History of Marriage and the Nation</u>.
    Cambridge: Harvard UP, 2001.

For books varying from this basic entry, consult the examples that follow. If you don't spot a sample entry for the type of source you need to document, consult the latest edition of the *MLA Handbook for Writers of Research Papers* for more comprehensive examples.

Two or More Works by the Same Author

Sommers, Christina Hoff. <u>The War Against Boys: How Misguided</u>
    <u>Feminism Is Harming Our Young Men</u>. New York: Simon, 2000.

---. <u>Who Stole Feminism? How Women Have Betrayed Women</u>. New York:
    Simon, 1995.

If you use more than one work by the same author, list each book separately. Give the author's name in the first entry only; begin the entries for other books by that author with three hyphens followed by a period. Arrange the works alphabetically by title. The words *A, An,* and *The* are ignored when alphabetizing by title.

Book by Two or Three Authors

Rockquemore, Kerry Ann, and David L. Brunsma. <u>Beyond Black:</u>
    <u>Biracial Identity in America</u>. Thousand Oaks: Sage, 2002.

Wallerstein, Judith S., Julia M. Lewis, and Sandra Blakeslee. <u>The</u>
    <u>Unexpected Legacy of Divorce: A 25 Year Landmark Study</u>. New
    York: Hyperion, 2000.

For a book with two or three authors, give all the authors' names but reverse only the first name. List the names in the order shown on the title page.

Book by Four or More Authors

Frye, Northrop, et al. <u>The Harper Handbook to Literature</u>. New
    York: Longman, 1997.

For a work with four or more authors, give only the first author's name followed by a comma and *et al.* (Latin for "and others").

Revised Edition

Weiss, Thomas G., David P. Forsythe, and Roger A. Coate. <u>The</u>
    <u>United Nations and Changing World Politics</u>. 3rd ed. Boulder:
    Westview, 2001.

Kobliner, Beth. <u>Get a Financial Life: Personal Finance in Your</u>
    <u>Twenties and Thirties</u>. Rev. ed. New York: Simon, 2000.

Follow the title with the edition, identified either by number (for example, *2nd*) or by the abbreviation *Rev.* (for *Revised*), depending on how the book itself indicates edition.

Book with an Editor or Translator

Jacobs, Harriet. <u>Incidents in the Life of a Slave Girl, Written by</u>
    <u>Herself</u>. Ed. Jean Fagan Yellin. Cambridge: Harvard UP, 2000.

Place the editor's or translator's name after the title, with the identifying abbreviation *Ed.* or *Trans.* before the person's name. Don't reverse the first and last name of the editor or translator.

Anthology or Compilation of Works by Different Authors

Brown, Wesley, and Amy Ling, eds. <u>Visions of America: Personal</u>
    <u>Narratives from the Promised Land</u>. New York: Persea 2002.

If you refer in general to an edited book—rather than to the individual authors whose work it contains—give the editor's name in the author position, followed by a comma and the abbreviation *ed.*

Section of an Anthology or Compilation

Cofer, Judith Ortiz. "Silent Dancing." <u>Visions of America:</u>
    <u>Personal Narratives from the Promised Land</u>. Ed. Wesley Brown
    and Amy Ling. New York: Persea, 2002. 179-86.

If you use only a section from an anthology, list first the author of that particular selection or chapter. The remaining information should be presented in this order: selection title (in quotation marks), book title (underlined), editor's name (preceded by the abbreviation *Ed.*), publication data, and the selection's page numbers. Don't use *p.* or *page.*

Section or Chapter in a Book by One Author

Cortada, James W. "A Digital Democracy." <u>Making the Information</u>
    <u>Society: Experience, Consequences, and Possibilities</u>.
    London: Financial Times, 2002. 393-417.

If you use only one named section or chapter of a book, give the section's title in quotation marks before the title of the book. At the end, give the section's page numbers. Don't use *p.* or *page.* If you use several sections, don't name each of them; just put the page numbers for all the sections at the end of the entry.

Reference Work

"Temperance Movements." <u>Columbia Encyclopedia</u>. 6th ed. New York:
    Columbia UP, 2000.

Book by an Institution or Corporation

United Nations Commission on Women. <u>The World's Women, 2000:</u>
    <u>Trends and Statistics</u>. New York: United Nations, 2000.

Give the name of the institution or corporation in the author position, even if the same institution is the publisher.

Citing Periodical Sources

Here is the basic format for listing periodical articles in Works Cited:

- Start with the author's last name, following the guidelines for a book author. If the article is unsigned, begin with its title.
- Give the article's complete title followed by a period, all of which is enclosed in quotation marks. Leave one space between the terminal quotation mark and the next item in the entry.
- Supply the periodical's name, underlining it. Don't place any punctuation after it.
- Give the date of publication. For newspapers and weekly magazines, include the day, month, and year—in that order. Abbreviate the month (using the first three to four letters) if it is five letters or longer. For scholarly journals, give the volume number, issue number (if appropriate), and year. In both cases, follow the date with a colon. Leave a space between the colon and the next item.
- Provide page number(s) without using *p., pp., page,* or *pages* before the numbers. If the pages in an article are continuous, give the page range (for example, 67–72 or 427–432). If the pages in an article aren't continuous (for example, 67–68, 70, 72), write the first page number and a plus sign (67+). Place a period after the page-number information.

The following sample entries for articles in periodicals are formatted in the MLA style. If you don't spot an entry for the type of source you need to document, consult the *MLA Handbook* (see page 567) for more comprehensive examples.

Article in a Weekly or Biweekly Magazine

Gorman, Christine. "How Safe Are Your Prescription Pills?" Time 3
     Sept. 2001: 50-51.

Article in a Monthly or Bimonthly Magazine

Solovitch, Sara. "The Citizen Scientists." Wired Sept. 2001: 144-
     51.

Article in a Daily Newspaper

Schmitt, Eric. "For 7 Million People in Census, One Race
     Category Isn't Enough." New York Times 13 Mar. 2001,
     nat'l. ed.: A1+.

Eisner, Jane. "More Than Ever, National Service Merits
     Attention." Philadelphia Inquirer 11 Nov. 2001, sec. D: 1+.

Use the newspaper's name as it appears on the masthead, but delete any initial *The*. If the title doesn't specify the paper's location and the paper lacks nationwide recognition, put the town or city and (if necessary) the state in brackets after the title: *Today's Sunbeam* [Salem, NJ]. If the paper is a large daily, indicate the particular edition (late, early, national, and so on) after the date, abbreviating longer words such as national (*natl.*) and edition (*ed.*).

For a newspaper with sections, if the section letter is part of each page number (see the first example above), provide the page and section designation exactly as they appear (for example, *A15* or *10C*). However, if the section designation isn't part of the page number (see the second example above), use the abbreviation *sec.* followed by the section number or letter, a colon, and then the page number (for example, *sec. 3: 5* or *sec. C: 2+*). For a newspaper without sections, simply provide the page number. If the article is printed on multiple, nonconsecutive pages, simply list the first page (including both section and page numbers or letters) followed by a plus sign ("+").

Editorial, Letter to the Editor, or Reply to a Letter

```
"Immigrants Deserve Due Process." Editorial. Chicago Tribune 17
      Aug. 2001: A18.
```

List as you would any signed or unsigned article, but indicate the nature of the piece by adding *Editorial, Letter,* or *Reply to letter of [letter writer's name]* after the article's title.

Article in a Scholarly Journal

```
Goldscheider, Frances K., Arland Thornton, and Li-Shou Yang.
      "Helping Out the Kids: Expectations About Parental
      Support in Young Adulthood." Journal of Marriage & Family
      63 (2001): 727-41.

Matheson, Gordon O. "The Dark Side of Kids' Sports." Physician &
      Sports Medicine 29.9 (2001): 2-4.
```

Some journals are paged continuously (the first example); the first issue of each year starts with page 1, and each subsequent issue picks up where the previous one left off. For such journals, use numerals to indicate the volume number after the title, and then indicate the year in parentheses. Note that neither *volume* nor *vol.* is used. The article's page or pages appear at the end, separated from the year by a colon. For a journal that pages each issue separately (the second example), use numerals to indicate the volume *and issue* numbers; separate the two with a period, leaving no space after the period.

Citing Computerized Sources

Article in an Online Periodical

Weaver, Jane. "Pop Goes the Music Industry's Profit." Newsweek
Online 21 Nov. 2001: 25 pars. 19 May 2002 <http://
www.msnbc.com/news/661412.asp#BODY>.

"To Clone or Not to Clone?" Salon.com 15 Mar. 2001: 12 pars. 19
May 2002 <http://www.salon.com/news/feature/2001/03/15/
bullying/index.html>.

For an article obtained online, supply the same information you would for
printed text: author's name, selection's title, source, and (when available) publication date and number of pages or paragraphs. When the number of pages or
paragraphs is provided, list it after the date of publication (using *pp.* for "pages"
or *pars.* for "paragraphs.") Complete your listing with the date on which you
accessed the material, followed by the exact address of the website (in angle
brackets) and then a final period. (Since online material can be revised at any time,
it's critical that you provide your date of access to identify the version you
retrieved.) Note that URLs should be broken only after slashes.

Article in a Full-Text Online Periodicals Index

Bennett, Geoffrey. "Hip-Hop: A Roadblock or Pathway to Black
Entertainment?" Black Collegian 32.1 (2001): 94-96.
EBSCOhost. MasterFILE Premier. Camden County Lib., Voorhees.
6 June 2002 <http://ehostvg.wl.epnet.com>.

For full-text articles accessed through an online index (generally only available
to libraries by subscription), begin with the same information as for online periodicals. After the publication information (issue, date, and page numbers), list the
title of the index (underlined), its vendor, and the library through which you
gained access to it. Complete the entry with the date you accessed the index and
the index's Web address. (*Note:* Unlike material stored on CD-ROM, online material can be revised or updated at any time. Providing the date on which you
accessed the material is critical since that date is the only way to identify the version you retrieved.)

Article on CD-ROM

Leland, John. "Zero Tolerance Changes Life at One School." New
York Times 8 Apr. 2001, eastern ed., sec. 9:1+. New York
Times Ondisc. CD-ROM. UMI-ProQuest. Dec. 2002.

For text on CD-ROM, give the same information you would for printed text of the same kind (for example, a newspaper article), with the possible exception of page numbers. If the CD-ROM doesn't indicate an article's page numbers, give the page number (if available) on which the article begins and the article's length in pages or paragraphs (for example, *4 pp*, or *14 pars.*). Then give the database title (underlined), publication medium (*CD-ROM*), CD-ROM publisher, and CD-ROM publication date. (*Note:* When citing an article stored on CD-ROM, don't provide the date you accessed the material. Unlike online material, which can be revised or updated at any time, material stored on CD-ROM is unchangeable and will stay the same no matter when it is accessed.)

Online Book

Franklin, Benjamin. The Autobiography of Benjamin Franklin.
    London, 1793. Electronic Text Center. Ed. David Seaman.
    1998. Alderman Lib., U. of Virginia. 16 Aug. 2002 <http://
    etext.lib.virginia.edu/toc/modeng/public/Fra2Aut.html>.

When it's available, include the book's original publication information between the book's title and the underlined database name. Also include (when available) the name of the site's editor, its electronic publication data, its sponsoring organization, your date of access, and the Web address.

Online Reference Work

"Salem Witch Trials." Britannica.com. Apr. 2000. Encyclopedia
    Britannica. 29 Sept. 2002 <http://britannica.com/bcom/eb/
    article/html?/query=salem%20witch%20trials>.

Professional or Personal Website

Harriet Beecher Stowe and Uncle Tom's Cabin. 9 Oct. 2001. U. of
    Wisconsin-Milwaukee Golda Meir Lib.; U. of Wisconsin-
    Milwaukee. 30 May 2002 <http://www.uwm.edu/Dept/Library/
    special/exhibits/clastext/clspg149.htm>.

Mallen, Enrique. Online Picasso Project. 27 Mar. 2002 <http://
    www.tamu.edu/moc1/picasso>.

Note that in the first entry, *Uncle Tom's Cabin* is *not* underlined. It's a title that would ordinarily be underlined, but since the rest of the website title *is* underlined, the book title is set off by a *lack* of underlining.

Computer Software

World Book Encyclopedia 2002 Premiere Edition. CD-ROM. 2002 ed.
    Renton: Topics Entertainment, 2002.

Cite the following information (when available): author of the software, title (underlined), medium (CD-ROM or disk), version, publication city, publisher, and year of publication.

E-Mail Message

Bernard, Lynn. "New Developments in Early Childhood Education."
     E-mail to Ronnie Hotis. 30 Aug. 2002.

To cite e-mail, provide the name of the writer; the title of the message (if any), taken from the subject line of the posting and enclosed in quotation marks; a description of the message that includes the recipient (for example, "E-mail to the author"); and the date of the message.

Citing Other Nonprint Sources

Television or Radio Program

"Underground Culture Hits Main Street." Nightline. Narr. Robert
     Krulwich. Part 1 of 3. ABC. WPVI-TV, Philadelphia. 6 Sept.
     2000.

List, at a minimum, the program's title (underlined), the network that carried the program, the local station on which the program was seen or heard, and the city and date of the broadcast. If, as in the example above, the program is an episode in a continuing series, give the episode title first (in quotation marks), then the program title (underlined), then the series title, if any (neither underlined nor in quotation marks). You might also include additional information such as the director or narrator before the series title.

Movie, Recording, Videotape, DVD, Filmstrip, or Slide Program

Traffic. Dir. Steven Soderbergh. DVD. USA Films, 2001.

Neeson, Liam, narr. The Greeks: Crucible of Civilization. Dir.
     Cassian Harrison. Videotape. PBS Home Video, 2000.

List the title (underlined), director, distribution company, and year. The writer, main performers, or producers may be listed after the director and before the company. If the work is a videotape, filmstrip, or slide program, indicate the original release date (if applicable) and the medium (for example, *videotape, filmstrip,* etc.). If you use the source to discuss the work of a particular individual, begin with that person's name followed by his or her position (as in the second example above).

Personal or Phone Interview

Langdon, Paul. Personal interview. 26 Jan. 2002.

Como, Anna. Telephone interview. 1 Oct. 2002.

Lecture

```
Blacksmith, James. "Urban Design in the New Millennium."
    Cityscapes Lecture Series. Urban Studies Institute.
    Metropolitan College, Washington. 18 Apr. 2002.

Papa, Andrea. "Reforming the Nation's Tax Structure." Lecture.
    Accounting 302, Cypress College. Astoria, New York. 3 Dec.
    2001.
```

Start with the speaker's name, followed by the lecture's title (in quotation marks) if there is one. If not, identify the lecture with an appropriate label such as *Keynote address* or *Lecture.* Then provide the sponsoring organization's name, the site of the lecture, and the date.

WRITE THE FIRST DRAFT

Once you've refined your working thesis, sorted your note cards, constructed an outline, and prepared a preliminary Works Cited page, you're ready to write your first draft. As with the early versions of an essay, don't worry at this stage about grammar, spelling, or style. Just try to get down as much of the paper's basic content and structure as you can.

Chapter 6 offers general guidelines for writing a first draft (pages 64–65). When applying those guidelines to a research paper, keep the following points in mind:

- As you write, refer to your note cards and outline. Don't rely on your memory for the information you've gathered.
- Feel free to deviate from your outline if, as you write, you discover a more effective sequence, realize some material doesn't fit, or see new merit in previously discarded information.
- Include any quotations and summaries in the draft. Rather than recopy, you may tape or staple the appropriate note cards to the page.
- Provide rough documentation (see pages 577–586) for all material borrowed from your sources.
- Use the present tense when quoting or summarizing a source ("Stamp *reports* that . . . " rather than "Stamp *reported* that . . .").
- Use the third-person point of view throughout, unless your instructor has indicated that you may use the first person when presenting primary research (see pages 514–515).

There are two contrasting strategies for generating a first draft. One is to *overwrite*, explaining each point as fully as possible, even including alternative explanations and wordings. The other strategy is to *underwrite*. In this approach, you jot down your ideas quickly, leaving gaps where points need to be expanded, making notations like "Insert a quote here." The disadvantage of this strategy is that it simply defers filling in the gaps until a later time, when it might be difficult to recapture your original train of thought. The advantage is that generating material quickly can make a long piece of writing more manageable and less forbidding. Some writers combine the two strategies—writing out parts of the paper fully but only sketching out those sections where getting down all the details would interrupt the flow of thought.

Whichever strategy you use, keep in mind that your draft shouldn't merely string together other people's words and ideas. Rather than simply presenting fact after fact or quotation after quotation, you must *analyze* and *comment on* your research, clearly showing how it supports your thesis. Similarly, when drafting the paper, be sure your language doesn't stay too close to that of your sources. To avoid overreliance on your sources' language, refer to your note cards as you write, not to the sources themselves. Remember, too, that taking source material and merely changing a word here and there still constitutes *plagiarism*—passing off someone else's thoughts or language as your own. Such a charge isn't valid even if you acknowledge your source. (For more pointers on steering clear of plagiarism, see pages 545–546, 553–554, 558–559, and 577–586.)

Presenting the Results of Primary Research

If your instructor requires you to conduct primary research (see pages 515–516), you might be tempted to include in the draft every bit of information you gathered through any surveys, experiments, or interviews you conducted. Remember, though, your primary purpose is to provide evidence for your thesis, so include only that material that furthers your goal. To preserve the draft's overall unity, you should also avoid the temptation to mass, without commentary, all your primary research in one section of the paper. Instead, insert the material at those places where it supports the points you want to make. Sometimes instructors will ask you to devote one part of the paper to a detailed discussion of the process you used to conduct primary research—everything from your methodology to a detailed interpretation of your results. In such a case, before writing your draft, ask your instructor where you should cover that information. Perhaps it should be placed in a separate introductory section or in an appendix.

DOCUMENT BORROWED MATERIAL USING MLA FORMAT—HOW TO AVOID PLAGIARISM

Copyright law and the ethics of research require that you give credit to those whose words and ideas you borrow; that is, you must provide full and accurate **documentation.** A lack of such documentation results in *plagiarism*—borrowing someone's ideas, facts, and words without properly crediting your source. Faulty documentation undermines your credibility. For one thing, readers may suspect that you're hiding something if you fail to identify your sources clearly. Further, readers planning follow-up research of their own will be perturbed if they have trouble locating your sources. Finally, weak documentation makes it difficult for readers to distinguish your ideas from those of your sources.

To avoid plagiarizing, you must provide documentation in the following situations:

- When you include a *word-for-word quotation* from a source
- When you *summarize or restate in your own words* ideas or information from a source, *unless* that material is *commonly known* and *accepted* (whether or not you yourself were previously aware of it) *or* is a *matter* of historical or scientific *record*
- When you *combine* a *summary* and a *quotation*

One exception to formal documentation occurs in writing for the general public. For example, you may have noticed that the authors of this book's essays don't use full documentation when they borrow ideas. *Academic writers*, though, *must provide full documentation* for all borrowed information. The next section explains how to do this.

Indicate Author and Page

Both the MLA documentation system described here and the APA system described later in the chapter use the **parenthetic reference,** a brief note in parentheses inserted into the text after borrowed material. The parenthetic reference doesn't provide full bibliographic information, but it provides enough so that readers can turn to the Works Cited list for complete information. If the method of documentation you learned in high school involved footnotes or endnotes, you'll be happy to know that parenthetic documentation, which is currently preferred, is much easier to use and is accepted by most professors. To be on the safe side, though, check with your professors to determine their documentation preferences.

Whenever you use borrowed material, you must, within your paper's text, do two things. First, you must *identify the author.* (Since the Works Cited page is arranged according to authors' last names, readers can refer to that listing for title, publisher, and so on.) Second, you must *specify the page(s)* in your source on which the material appears.

Using Only Parentheses

The simplest way to provide documentation involves the use of *parentheses* for both *author* and *page* references. The examples that follow, based on references to Julian Stamp's *The Homeless and History,* illustrate this method. (If you like, turn to pages 553–554 for the extract from Stamp's book and compare the original there with the documentation here. And turn to pages 554–555 if you would like to review the use of ellipsis and brackets when deleting material from a source.)

Counseling and other support services are not enough to solve the problem of homelessness; proposed solutions must address the complex economic issues at the heart of homelessness (Stamp 8).

It is no coincidence that as "the gap between the rich and the poor has widened [. . .]" (Stamp 8), homelessness has emerged as a social ill.

If we look beyond the problems of homeless people "to larger <u>economic</u> issues, we [. . .] see that homelessness cannot be resolved solely at the level of individual treatment" (Stamp 8).

Because half of those taking refuge in shelters have substance-abuse problems, "programs need to provide not only a place to sleep but also comprehensive treatment for addicts [. . .]" (Stamp 8).

Take a moment to look again at the preceding examples. Note the following:

What to Provide Within the Parentheses

- Give the author's last name only, even when the author is cited for the first time.
- Write the page number immediately after the author's last name, with no punctuation between. (If the source is only one page, only the author's name is needed.) Provide a full page range of the summary or quotation if it spans more than one page. Don't use the designation *p.* or *page.*

Where to Place the Parentheses

- Immediately *after* the borrowed material, at a natural pause in the sentence, or at the end of the sentence
- Before any internal punctuation (comma, semicolon) or terminal punctuation (period, question mark)
- After an ellipsis and bracket at the end of a quotation but before the final period

Using Parentheses and Attributions

Skilled writers indicate clearly where their ideas stop and those of their sources begin. So, besides providing careful parenthetic documentation, writers often provide **attributions**—nonparenthetical source identifiers like those (underlined) in the following two *summary* statements:

<u>Julian Stamp argues that</u> homelessness must be addressed in terms of economics--and not simply in terms of individual counseling, addiction therapy, or job training (8).

According to statistics, one-half of the homeless individuals in shelters are substance abusers (Stamp 8).

A *quotation* should also be inserted smoothly with an attribution. Don't just drop a quotation into your text, as in this example:

Incorrect

"The key to any successful homeless policy requires a clear understanding of just who are the homeless" (Stamp 8).

Instead, provide an attribution for the quoted statement:

Correct

As Stamp states, "The key to any successful homeless policy requires a clear understanding of just who are the homeless" (8).

One social scientist points out that "the key to any successful homeless policy requires a clear understanding of just who are the homeless" (Stamp 8).

Glance back at the examples on this page and note the following:

- An attribution may specify the author's name (*Julian Stamp argues that; As Stamp states*), or it may refer to a source more generally (*According to statistics; One social scientist points out*). If you want to call attention to a specific author, use an attribution indicating the author's name. Otherwise, use a more general attribution—or a parenthetic citation that includes the name along with the page number.
- The first time an author is referred to in the text, the author's full name is provided; afterward, only the last name is given.
- When the author's name is provided in the text, the name is *not* repeated in the parentheses. (Later nonparenthetic references to the same author give only the last name.)

Sometimes, to inform readers of an author's area of expertise, you may identify that person by profession (*Social scientist Julian Stamp*). Don't, however, use such personal titles as *Mr.* or *Ms.* Finally, as part of an attribution, you may mention your source's title (In *The Homeless and History*, Stamp maintains that . . .). No matter what information you include, try to vary your attributions. In addition to those already mentioned, you might try the following lead-ins, placing them wherever they fit best—at the beginning, middle, or end of the sentence:

As _____ states, . . .

The information compiled by _____ shows . . .

In _____ 's opinion, . . .

_____ contends that . . .

_____ 's study reveals that . . .

Also, aim for smooth, graceful attributions, avoiding such awkward constructions as these: "According to Julian Stamp, he says that . . ." and "In the book by
Julian Stamp, he argues that. . . ."

Special Cases of Authorship

In some situations, providing authorship in the attribution or in the parenthetic citation becomes slightly more complicated. The guidelines that follow will help
you deal with special types of authorship.

More Than One Source by the Same Author.   When your paper includes references to more than one work by the same author, you must specify the particular
work being cited. You do this by providing the *title*, as well as the author's name
and the page(s). As with the author's name, the title may be given in *either* the
attribution *or* the parenthetic citation. Here are some examples:

In The Language and Thought of the Child, Jean Piaget states that
"discussion forms the basis for a logical point of view" (240).

Piaget considers dialog essential to the development of logical
thinking (Language and Thought 240).

The Child's Conception of the World shows that young children
think that the name of something can never change (Piaget 81).

Young children assume that everything has only one name and that
no others are possible (Piaget, Child's Conception 81).

Notice that when a work is named in the attribution, the full title appears; when
a title is given in the parenthetic citation, only the first few significant words
appear. (However, don't use the ellipsis to indicate that some words have been
omitted from a title; the ellipsis is used only when quoting a source.) In the preceding examples, the work is a book, so its title is underlined. If the source is
an article or a selection from a compilation, the title is placed in quotation
marks.

Two or Three Authors.   Supply all the authors' last names in either the
attribution or parentheses.

More Than Three Authors.   In either the attribution or parentheses, give the last name of the first author followed by *et al.* (which means "and others").

Two or More Authors with the Same Last Names.   When you use two or more sources written by authors with the same last names, you must include (in either the attribution or parentheses) each author's first name or initial(s).

A Source with No Author.   For a source without a named author, use, in your attribution or parenthetic reference, the title of the work *or* the name of the issuing organization—whichever you used to alphabetize the source on the Works Cited list.

Information Found in Two or More Sources.   During your research, you may come across several sources who cite the same *general* information or who share the same *widely accepted* opinion. Such material is considered *common knowledge* and *doesn't* need to be documented. However, when you come across several sources who cite the same *highly specialized* information or who share the same *controversial* opinion, that material *does* need to be documented. In such a case, state the material in your own words. Then present in the parenthetic citation each source, listed in the order in which it appears on the Works Cited list. Here's an example:

```
A number of educators agree that an overall feeling of
competence--rather than innate intelligence--is a key factor in
determining which students do well the first year in college
(Smith 465; Jones 72; Greene 208).
```

If you use a quotation to express an idea that occurs in several sources, provide an attribution for the quoted source and, in the parentheses, give the source's page number followed by a note that other sources make the same point:

```
Educator Henry Schneider argues that "students with low self-
esteem tend to disregard the academic success they achieve" (23;
also pointed out in Rabb 401).
```

Special Cases of Pagination

Occasionally, a source will have unusual pagination. Here's how to deal with such situations.

A Source with No Page Numbers.   The parenthetic citation simply lacks a page number and the Works Cited list indicates "unpaged" with the abbreviation *N. pag.*

Each Volume of a Multivolume Source Paged Separately.   Indicate the volume number, then the page number, with a colon between the two (Kahn 3: 246). Do not use *vol.* or *v.*

A Nonprint Source (Television Show, Lecture, Interview).   In a parenthetic citation, give only the item (title, speaker, person interviewed) you used to alphabetize the source on your Works Cited list. Or provide the identifying information in the attribution, thus eliminating the need for parenthetic information:

```
In the documentary Financing a College Education, Cheryl Snyder
states that . . .
```

Blending Quotations into Your Text

On the whole, you should try to state borrowed material in your own words. A string of quotations signals that you haven't sufficiently evaluated and distilled your sources. Use quotations sparingly; draw upon them only when they dramatically illustrate key points you want to make or when they lend authority to your own conclusions. Also, keep in mind that supplying the appropriate citation may not be enough to blend the quotation smoothly into your own writing; additional wording may be needed to achieve a smooth transition. Finally, don't forget that a quotation, by itself, won't always make your case for you; it may be necessary to interpret the quotation, showing why it's significant and explaining how it supports your central points. Indeed, such commentary is often precisely what's needed to blend quoted material gracefully into your discussion.

Consider the following examples, noting how the first quotation is dropped awkwardly into the text, without any transition or commentary. In contrast, brief interpretive remarks in the second example provide a transition that allows the quotation to merge easily with the surrounding material:

Original

Recent studies of parenting styles are designed to control researcher bias. "Recent studies screen out researchers whose strongly held attitudes make objectivity difficult" (Layden 10).

Revised

Recent studies of parenting styles are designed to control researcher bias. Psychologist Marsha Layden, a harsh critic of earlier studies, acknowledges that nowadays most investigations "screen out researchers whose strongly held beliefs make objectivity difficult" (10).

Besides following the guidelines on pages 554–555 for using ellipsis and brackets, you should be familiar with the following capitalization and punctuation conventions when quoting.

Capitalization and Punctuation of Short Quotations

The way a short quotation is used in a sentence determines whether it begins or doesn't begin with a capital letter and whether it is or isn't preceded by a comma.

1. When an attribution introduces a short quotation that can stand alone as a sentence, *do capitalize* the quotation's *first word*. Also, *precede the quotation with a comma*:

```
According to Stamp, "Beginning in the 1980s and through the 1990s,
the gap between the rich and the poor has widened, buying power
has stagnated, industrial jobs have fled overseas, and federal
funding for low-cost housing has been almost eliminated" (8).

Stamp observes, "Beginning in the 1980s and through the 1990s,
the gap between the rich and the poor has widened, buying power
has stagnated, industrial jobs have fled overseas, and federal
funding for low-cost housing has been almost eliminated" (8).
```

2. When blending a short quotation into the structure of your own sentence, *don't capitalize* the quotation's *first word* and *don't precede it with a comma*:

```
Stamp observes that "beginning in the 1980s and through the 1990s,
the gap between the rich and the poor has widened, buying power
has stagnated, industrial jobs have fled overseas, and federal
funding for low-cost housing has been almost eliminated" (8).
```

Even if—as in this case—the material being quoted originally started with a capital letter, you still use lowercase when incorporating the quotation into your own sentence. Quotations often merge with your own words in this way when they are introduced, as in the preceding example, by a pronoun (*that, which, who*)—either stated or implied.

3. If, for variety, you *interrupt a full-sentence quotation* with an attribution, *place commas on both sides of the attribution*, and *resume* the quotation with a *lowercase* letter:

```
"The key to any successful homeless policy," Stamp comments,
"requires a clear understanding of just who are the homeless" (8).
```

Long Quotations

A quotation longer than four lines starts on a new line and is indented, throughout, ten spaces from the left margin. Since this **block format** indicates a quotation, quotation marks are unnecessary. Double-space the block quotation, as you do the rest of your paper. Don't leave extra space above or below the quotation. Long quotations, always used sparingly, require a lead-in. A lead-in that *isn't* a full sentence is followed by a comma; a lead-in that *is* a full sentence (see below) is followed by a colon:

Stamp cites changing economic conditions as the key to a national
homeless policy:

> Beginning in the 1980s and through the 1990s, the gap
> between the rich and the poor has widened, buying power
> has stagnated, industrial jobs have fled overseas, and
> federal funding for low-cost housing has been almost
> eliminated. Given these developments, homelessness begins
> to look like a product of history, our recent history,
> and only by addressing shifts in the American economy can
> we begin to find effective solutions for people lacking
> homes. Moreover, these solutions--ranging from renewed
> federal spending to tax laws favoring job-creating
> companies--will require a sustained national commitment
> that transcends partisan politics. (8)

Notice that the page number in parentheses appears *after* the period, not before
as it would with a short quotation.

Quoting or Summarizing a Source Within a Source

If you quote or summarize a *secondary source* (someone whose ideas come to
you only through another source), you need to make this clear. The parenthetic
documentation should indicate "as quoted in" with the abbreviation *qtd. in:*

According to Sherman, "Recycling has, in several communities,
created unanticipated expenses" (qtd. in Pratt 3).

Sherman explains that recycling can be surprisingly costly (qtd.
in Pratt 3).

If the material you're quoting includes a quotation, place single quotation
marks around the secondary quotation:

Pratt believes that "recycling efforts will be successful if, as
Sherman argues, 'communities launch effective public-education
campaigns'" (2).

Note: Your Works Cited list should include the source you actually read (Pratt),
rather than the source you refer to secondhand (Sherman).

Presenting Statistics

Citing statistics can—if done well—be an effective strategy for supporting
your ideas. In your enthusiasm to make your points, though, be careful not to

misinterpret the data or twist its significance. When presenting statistics in your paper, remember to provide an attribution indicating their source. Also, be sure not to overwhelm readers with too many statistics; include only those that support your central points in compelling ways. Keep in mind, too, that statistics won't speak for themselves. You need to interpret them for readers, showing how the figures cited reinforce your key ideas. Suppose you're writing a paper showing that Medicare reform is needed to control increasing costs. It wouldn't be effective if you simply provided an attribution, then presented one statistic after the other, without explanatory commentary:

Incorrect

> The Centers for Medicaid and Medicare Services reports that 1992 revenues ($185 billion) exceeded spending ($120 billion). But in 1997, revenues ($204 billion) and spending ($208 billion) were almost the same. It is projected that by the year 2010, revenues will be $310 billion and spending $410 billion (Mohr 14).

Instead, after providing an attribution, present only the most telling statistics, being sure to explain their significance:

Correct

> The Centers for Medicaid and Medicare Services reports that in 1992, Medicare revenues actually exceeded spending by about $65 billion. But five years later, costs had increased so much that they exceeded revenues by about $4 billion. This trend toward escalated costs is expected to continue. It's projected that by the year 2010, revenues will be only $310 billion, whereas spending—if not controlled—will climb to at least $410 billion (Mohr 14).

(For more on statistics, see page 551.)

REVISE, EDIT, AND PROOFREAD THE FIRST DRAFT

After completing your first draft, reward yourself with a break. Set the paper aside for a while, as least for a few hours. When you pick up the draft later, you'll have a fresh, more objective point of view on it. Then, referring to the checklist on pages 98–99 and the first section of the revision checklist that follows, reread your entire draft to get a general sense of how well the paper works. Outlining the draft (see page 98)—*without* referring to the outline that guided the draft's preparation—is a good way to evaluate the paper's overall meaning and structure.

Despite all the work you've done, you may find when you reread the paper that a main point in support of your thesis seems weak. Sometimes a review of your note cards—including those you didn't use for your draft—will uncover appropriate material that you can add to the paper. Other times, though, you may need another trip to the library to gather additional information. Once you're confident that the paper's overall meaning and structure are strong, go ahead and write your introduction and conclusion—if you haven't already done so.

That done, move ahead and evaluate your paper's paragraph development. To focus your revision, use the checklist on pages 100–101, as well as the second section of the revision checklist that follows. As you work, it's a good idea to pay special attention to the way you present evidence in the paragraphs. Does your evidence consist of one quotation after another, or do you express borrowed ideas in your own words? Do you simply insert borrowed material without commentary, or do you interpret the material and show its relevance to the points you want to make?

Before moving to the next stage in the revision process, look closely at the way you introduce borrowed material. If you prepared the draft without providing many attributions, now is the time to supply them. Then, consulting the checklists on pages 118 and 128, as well as the third section of the revision checklist that follows, go ahead and refine your draft's words and sentences.

Finally, when you start editing and proofreading, allow enough time to verify the accuracy of quoted and summarized material. Check such material against your note cards, and check your documentation against both your bibliography cards and Works Cited list, making sure everything matches. When preparing the final copy of your paper, follow the format guidelines on pages 134–135, using the sample research paper (pages 594–607) as a model. Note that the research paper, when accompanied by an outline, has a separate title page. For a research paper without an outline, the title and other identifying information are usually placed at the top of the paper's first page.

Chapters 7, 8, and 9 discuss techniques for revising and editing an essay draft. The following checklist will help you and those giving you feedback apply those techniques to the research paper.

✔ REVISING THE RESEARCH PAPER: A CHECKLIST

Revise Overall Meaning and Structure

☐ What is the thesis of the research paper? Where is it stated? How could the thesis be expressed more clearly?

☐ Where would background material or a definition of terms clarify overall meaning?

☐ Where does research evidence (facts, statistics, expert opinion, surveys, and experimental results) seem irrelevant or contradict the thesis? What can be done to correct these problems?

☐ What principle of organization (chronological, spatial, emphatic, simple-to-complex) does the paper use? How does this organizing principle reinforce the paper's thesis and make it easy for readers to follow the paper's line of reasoning?

Revise Paragraph Development

☐ In which paragraphs is evidence solid and compelling? Where is it confusing, insufficient, irrelevant, too abstract, inaccurate, nonrepresentative, or predictable? How can these problems be remedied?

☐ Which paragraphs merely present research, without analyzing and relating it to the thesis? How can the research material be better incorporated into the paper's point of view?

☐ Which paragraphs simply string together quotations, without interpretive commentary? Where is commentary needed? Which quotations could be eliminated?

Revise Sentences and Words

☐ Where is more documentation needed to avoid plagiarism? Where do another author's words appear but without quotation marks? Where is a source's language only slightly modified? Which borrowed ideas are summarized but not credited?

☐ Where would attributions help signal more clearly where a source's ideas begin and stop?

☐ How could attributions be made more graceful and varied?

Edit and Proofread

☐ Where is parenthetic documentation lacking required information? Where must an author's name, a title, publication data, or page numbers be added?

☐ Which parenthetic citations contain punctuation errors? Where should a title be underlined or placed in quotation marks? Where should a comma be added or deleted?

☐ Where are quotations punctuated incorrectly? Which should start with a capital letter? Which should begin in lowercase? Which should be preceded by a comma? Which should not? Where should a capital letter be deleted? Where is a comma needed to connect the quotation to the text? Where should a comma be deleted?

☐ Where is the format for long quotations incorrect? How can it be corrected?

☐ Where is the format for the Works Cited list incorrect? Which entries are out of alphabetical order? Which titles should be underlined or placed in quotation marks? Where should commas or periods be added or deleted? Where should page numbers be added?

APA DOCUMENTATION FORMAT

MLA documentation style is appropriate for research papers written for courses in the humanities, such as your composition course. Researchers in the social sciences and in education use a different citation format, one developed by the American Psychological Association (APA) and explained in the *Publication Manual of the American Psychological Association*. If you're writing a paper for a course in sociology, psychology, anthropology, economics, or political science, your professor will probably expect **APA-style documentation.** History, philosophy, and religion are sometimes considered humanities, sometimes social sciences, depending on your approach to the topic.

Parenthetic Citations

As in the MLA format, APA citations are enclosed in parentheses within the text and provide the author's last name. The main difference between the two formats is that the APA parenthetic note *always includes the year* of publication but *may not include the page number.* Specifically, the page number is *required* when a source is *quoted* or when *specific parts* of a source are *paraphrased* or *summarized.* (A paraphrased or summarized citation without a page number refers to the source as a whole.) Also, APA citations are punctuated with commas between the author's name and the year and between the year and the page. Finally, *p.* or *pp.* appears before the page number(s).

Here are some examples of APA parenthetic citations:

APA Format

Experts have argued that, once cases of bullying have been identified in the school environment, it is "imperative that parents and teachers meet so that supervision and sanctions can be arranged" (Weir, 2001, p. 1249).

Parents and teachers need to work together in order to develop appropriate means of monitoring and intervening in school bullying (Weir, 2001, p. 1249).

Here are the same citations in MLA style:

MLA Format

Experts have argued that, once cases of bullying have been identified in the school environment, it is "imperative that parents and teachers meet so that supervision and sanctions can be arranged" (Weir 1249).

Parents and teachers need to work together in order to develop appropriate means of monitoring and intervening in school bullying (Weir 1249).

In APA format, if you lead into a quotation, paraphrase, or summary with an attribution that gives the author's name, the publication year follows the author's name in parentheses, and the page number appears at the end:

In arguing for free trade, Grant Aldanas (2001) asserts that "the real nexus between trade, labor, and the environment is that trade contributes to rising standards of living" (p. 35).

Grant Aldanas (2001) believes that free trade policies must be adopted because they will raise the standard of living of the nation's citizens (p. 35).

If a work has two authors, cite both. Join their names by *and* within the attribution and by an ampersand (&) within a parenthetic reference:

Ronald Kotulak and Jon Van (2001) observe that "[w]hen it comes to helping children weather adolescence, parents may play a more important role than they think" (p. D5).

Parents should not underestimate the role they can play in helping children cope with the difficulties and challenges of adolescence (Kotulak & Van, 2001, p. D5).

If a work has three to five authors, name all authors in the first citation. In subsequent citations, name only the first author followed by *et al.* If there are six or more authors, cite the first author followed by *et al.*

References List

As in the MLA style, a double-spaced alphabetical list of sources appears at the end of a research paper using APA documentation style. However, whereas the MLA titles this list "Works Cited," the APA gives it the heading *References.*

The MLA and APA formats for listing sources include the same basic information, but they present it in different ways. Here are some of the distinguishing features of APA-style entries:

- The first line of each entry should start at the left margin; subsequent lines are indented on the same margin as your paper's paragraphs.
- The publication date is placed in parentheses directly after the author's name and is followed by a period.
- Two or more works by the same author are arranged according to publication date, with the earliest appearing first.
- Two or more works written by the same author and published in the same year are differentiated by lowercase letters—(1996a), (1996b)—and are alphabetized by title.
- All authors' names, numbering up to five, are given in the reference. When there are six or more authors, use the ampersand instead of *and.* When there are one or more authors, write the name of the first, followed by *et al.*

- All authors' names are inverted. In addition, an author's first and middle names are represented by initials only.
- Only the first letter of a book or article title (and subtitle) and any proper names contained within it are capitalized.
- All titles appear *with* any initial *A, An,* or *The.*

Here's a sample APA-style reference for a *book with a single author*:[1]

Cott, N. F. (2001). *Public vows: A history of marriage and the nation*. Cambridge: Harvard University Press.

What about articles listed on the References page? Unlike the MLA, the APA uses no quotation marks around article titles. And, as noted, only the first word of an article's title and subtitle is capitalized. In addition, a periodical's name is italicized and all major words within it are capitalized. (*Important note*: According to APA guidelines, italicizing titles is now preferable to underlining them. However, if you're using a typewriter that doesn't allow for italics, underlining is the proper alternative.) Include any initial *A* or *An* in a periodical's name but drop any initial *The*. A journal title is immediately followed by a comma, a space, and the volume number (also italicized). Finally, precise and inclusive page numbers are required for all types of articles, even when the pages are not consecutive. In citations for a newspaper source, encyclopedia entry, or article or chapter in an edited book, *p.* or *pp.* precedes the page number(s). Otherwise, only the numbers themselves are given.

Following are sample APA listings for articles in print sources.

Magazine Article

Gorman, C. (2001, September 3). How safe are your prescription pills? *Time, 158*, 50-51.

Journal Article (Paginated by Issue)

Matheson, G. O. (2001). The dark side of kids' sports. *Physician & Sports Medicine, 29*(9), 2-4.

Article in an Anthology

Cofer, J. O. (2002). Silent dancing. In W. Brown & A. Ling (Eds.), *Visions of America: Personal narratives from the promised land* (pp. 179-186). New York: Persea Books.

---

[1]In order to illustrate the differences between MLA and APA formats, we have included here many of the same sources cited in the MLA documentation section (pages 567-576) but formatted them according to APA style.

Computerized Sources

Article Obtained Online

```
Weaver, J. (2001, November 21). Pop goes the music industry's
     profit. Newsweek Online. Retrieved May 19, 2002, from
     http://www.msnbc.com/news/661412.asp#BODY
```

For an article accessed online, provide the information for the print equivalent. Then type the word *Retrieved*, followed by the date of access and the word *from*, followed by the Web address and *no* final period. Please note that if the online source exactly duplicates the print version, you should insert the phrase "Electronic version" in brackets right after the title of the article and you don't need to include the retrieval date or Web address.

Article on CD-ROM

```
Leland, J. (2001, April 8). Zero tolerance changes life at one
     school. The New York Times, sec. 9:01. Retrieved July 7,
     2002, from The New York Times Ondisc database.
```

In general, to list an article on CD-ROM, provide the information for the print equivalent. Then type the word *Retrieved*, the date of access, the word *from*, and the name of the database.

More information about APA documentation format can be found in the latest edition of the *Publication Manual of the American Psychological Association*.

E-Mail Messages

According to the APA style, personal correspondence, including e-mail, doesn't need to be documented in your reference list. Instead, cite the person's name in your essay and in parentheses write *personal communication* and the date.

A NOTE ABOUT OTHER DOCUMENTATION SYSTEMS

Generally, professionals in the hard sciences (biology, chemistry, medicine, physics) and technical fields (computer science and electrical engineering) use neither the MLA nor the APA system of documentation. Rather, using bracketed or superscripted (raised) reference numbers, they key each item of borrowed material to an entry on the References page. The References list, therefore, isn't alphabetized; instead, the numbered sources simply appear in the order in which they are mentioned in the paper.

When you write a paper for a science course, ask your professor whether you should use MLA style, APA style, or the system found in most science and technical journals. If your instructor prefers the last, find out which publication can serve as your model. That way, you won't be unpleasantly surprised by any criticism that you've used an inappropriate system of documentation.

STUDENT RESEARCH PAPER: MLA-STYLE DOCUMENTATION

The sample outline and research paper that follow were written by Brian Courtney for a composition class. In his paper, Brian uses the MLA documentation system. To help you spot various types of sources, quotations, and attributions, we've annotated the paper. Our marginal comments also flag key elements, such as the paper's thesis statement, plan of development, and concluding summary.

Note that the main headings in Brian's outline parallel, to a large degree, the topic sentences of the paper's paragraphs; subheadings generally represent the points that develop those paragraphs. The outline contains no sections corresponding to Brian's introduction and conclusion because he wrote those only after completing the body of his paper. As you read the paper, pay special attention to the way Brian incorporates source material and uses it to support his own ideas.

As you'll see, Brian provided a title page because his paper was preceded by an outline. For a paper submitted without an outline, use a top heading rather than a title page. Here is the format for a first page with a top heading:

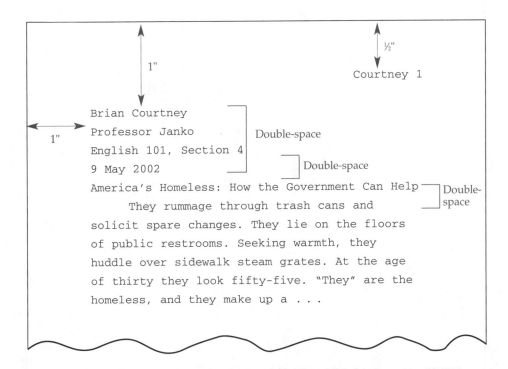

Although a title page isn't necessary, you may be asked to provide one.

A paper *with* an outline often has a separate title page.

Title begins about one-third of the way down the page.

Center the title. Double-space between lines of the title and your name.

Course and section, instructor's name, and date, on separate lines, are double-spaced and centered.

America's Homeless:

How the Government Can Help

by

Brian Courtney

English 101, Section 4

Professor Janko

9 May 2002

½"

1"

Courtney 1

Outline

Thesis: The federal government should do more to help the homeless toward independence.

   I. Homelessness is a major problem in the United States.

      A. Experts disagree about the number of Americans who are homeless.

      B. Experts agree that the number of homeless, particularly homeless families, is growing.

  II. Finding ways to help the homeless is difficult.

      A. Even if the homeless find shelter, they still often wander the street.

         1. Some homeless people are addicted to alcohol or drugs.

         2. Some have serious psychiatric problems.

         3. Others lack basic survival skills.

      B. Comprehensive programs are needed to address the complex problems that many homeless people have.

 III. Some programs offer exactly this kind of broad assistance to the homeless.

      A. Project Renewal and Pine Street Inn offer substance-abuse programs.

      B. Lenox Hill Neighborhood House and CANP also offer psychological-support programs for the homeless.

         1. Counseling sessions are attended by those with substance-abuse problems.

         2. Counseling sessions are attended by runaway teens.

1"

1"

After the title page, number all pages in upper-right corner—a half-inch from the top. Place your name before the page number. Use small roman numerals on outline pages. Use Arabic numbers on pages following the outline.

The word *Outline* (without underlining or quotation marks) is centered one inch from the top. Double-space to first line of outline.

Double-space both outline and text. Leave one-inch margins at top, bottom, and sides.

Courtney ii

   3. Counseling sessions are attended by
      those overwhelmed by personal difficul-
      ties.
IV. Some broad-assistance programs provide train-
     ing in everyday survival skills.
     A. Homes for the Homeless offers workshops on
        everything from nutrition to interview
        techniques.
     B. Project Hope shows clients how to apply
        for food stamps and other benefits to
        which they are entitled.
     C. House of Hope provides instruction in
        household budgeting and home maintenance.
  V. Some broad-assistance programs help the home-
     less get a job.
     A. Many of the homeless have no jobs or have
        never worked more than six months.
     B. CANP provides training in résumé writing
        and interviewing.
     C. CANP's job training has a high success
        rate.
 VI. The federal government should help such
     broad-assistance programs.
     A. CANP'S funding has slipped.
     B. Project Hope doesn't have the resources
        needed to meet the growing demands on its
        services.
VII. The government should also raise the minimum
     wage.
     A. Some of the homeless have jobs, but their
        low incomes put most housing out of their
        reach.

Courtney iii

      B. The last two decades have seen a dramatic
         drop in minimum-wage buying power.
VIII. A lack of affordable housing is at the center
        of the homeless problem.
      A. One magazine argues that people's deep
         disturbance--in addition to the unavail-
         ability of inexpensive housing--are another
         source of the homeless problem.
      B. Numerous studies and many experts refute
         this viewpoint and show that recent trends
         in housing are the real culprit.
  IX. The federal government should finance more
        low-cost housing.
      A. Affordable private housing is almost non-
         existent.
         1. Gentrification increases the price of
           previously low-cost housing units,
           putting them beyond the reach of poor
           people.
         2. Even rundown SRO hotels charge more than
           the poor can afford.
      B. Public housing can accommodate only a
         small percentage of those seeking relief
         from high costs in the private housing
         market.
         1. The federal government has cut funding
           of public housing and housing subsidies.
         2. Cities have slashed funding for the con-
           struction of public housing and shelters.

Courtney 1

For a paper with an outline, you may repeat the paper's title, centered, on the first page of the text. Double space between the title and text.

Introduction

America's Homeless: How the Government Can Help

They rummage through trash cans and solicit
spare change. They lie on the floors of public   1
restrooms. Seeking warmth, they huddle over sidewalk
steam grates. At the age of thirty, they look fifty-
five. "They" are the homeless, and they make up a
growing percentage of America's population. Indeed,
homelessness has reached such proportions that the
private sector and local governments can't possibly
cope. To help homeless people toward independence,

Thesis, with plan of development

the federal government must support rehabilitation
and job training programs, raise the minimum wage,
and fund more low-cost housing.

Not everyone agrees on the number of Americans
who are homeless. Estimates range anywhere from   2
600,000 to two million at any given time (Link et al.

Parenthetic citation for information that appears in two sources. Sources given in order they appear on Works Cited list. First citation indicates a work with more than three authors; page number *and* first author's name given since author is not cited earlier in the sentence. No author or page number given for the second source since it is an anonymous online article.

353; "Facts"). According to The Economist, a study in
the mid 1990s estimated that twelve million Americans
"have been homeless at some point in their lives"
("Out of Sight"). Although the figures may vary, analysts agree on another matter: that the number of
homeless, particularly of homeless families, is
increasing. According to the National Alliance to End
Homelessness, families with children are the "fastest
growing group of homeless people," comprising about
36% of the homeless population ("Facts"). A U.S.
Conference of Mayors survey in 2000 found that in the
past several years, requests for shelter access
increased in three-quarters of the country's top
twenty-five cities, while 72% of those cities
reported increases in families requesting such aid
("Facts").

Common knowledge is not documented.

Finding ways to assist this growing and chang-   3
ing homeless population has become increasingly difficult. Even when homeless individuals or families
manage to find a shelter that will give them three

Courtney 2

meals a day and a place to sleep at night, a good
number have trouble moving beyond the shelter system
and securing a more stable life-style. Part of the
problem, explains sociologist Christopher Jencks in
his now classic study, is that many homeless adults
are addicted to alcohol and drugs (41-42). And psychiatrist E. Fuller Torrey adds that nearly one-
third of the homeless have serious psychiatric disorders (17). Individuals suffering from such
disorders and from addiction often lack the ability
to seek and obtain jobs and homes, and therefore
remain homeless for a longer period of time
("Mental Illness"). While not addicted or mentally
ill, many others simply lack the everyday survival
skills needed to turn their lives around. Reporter
Lynette Holloway notes that New York City officials
believe the situation will improve only when shelters provide comprehensive programs that address
the many needs of the homeless (B1). As Catherine
Howard, director of the Bronx-based Paradise
Transitional Housing Program, wrote in a letter to
The New York Times, "Identifying the needs of the
homeless and linking them with services in the community is as important as finding suitable housing.
Many homeless people return to the [. . .] shelter
system and eventually to the street because of the
lack of such support services" (A26).

4   Luckily, a number of agencies are beginning
to act on the belief that the homeless need "more
than a key and a lease" if they are to acquire the
attitudes, skills, and behaviors needed to stay off
the street (Howard A26). Besides providing shelter,
nonprofit agencies such as New York City's Project
Renewal and Boston's Pine Street Inn offer substance-abuse programs and intensive follow-ups to
ensure that clients remain sober and drug-free

Attribution gives
author's name and
area of expertise.
Parenthetical
reference at end of
sentence gives just
the page number
since the author is
cited in the
attribution.

Parenthetic reference
gives page but not
author since author
is cited in the paper.

Full-sentence
quotation is preceded
by a comma and
begins with a capital
letter.

Ellipsis enclosed
in brackets
indicate that some
material has been
deleted from the
middle of the
original sentence.

Quotation blends
into rest of the
sentence (no
comma; quotation's
first word is not
capitalized).

Courtney 3

Second source is
a government
publication.

(Holloway B1; United States 29). To help the homeless cope with psychological problems, New York
City's Lenox Hill Neighborhood House and Boston's

No page number
given for second
source in parenthetic
citation because
source is an e-mail
interview.

Community Action Now Program (CANP) provide in-
house social workers and psychiatric care (Holloway
B1; Van Meder). Joan Van Meder, CANP's cofounder

E-mail interview
source is identified.

and director, explained in an e-mail interview that
her organization offers one-on-one and group sessions
helping not only recovering substance abusers but
also runaway teenagers (some of whom are pregnant)
as well as individuals overwhelmed by personal
traumas like divorce, death of a family member, or
loss of a job. Staff counselors refer individuals
with more severe psychological disturbances to community health agencies.

    In addition to providing psychological sup-   5
port, many organizations instruct the homeless in
basic survival skills. Adapting the principles of
"Continuum of Care," a project sponsored by the
Department of Housing and Urban Development, such
agencies provide training in the everyday skills
that clients need to live independently (Halper

Parenthetic citation
for a work with
two authors

and McCrummen 26). New York City's Homes for the
Homeless has established facilities called
"American Family Inns." Functioning as "residen-
tial, literacy, employment, and training centers
for entire families," these centers emphasize
good nutrition, effective parenting, education,
household-management skills, and job-search and

Parenthetic citation
for a single-author
source. Page
number and author
are given since the
author is not cited
earlier in the
sentence.

interview techniques (Nunez 72). Boston's Project
Hope also works to guide the homeless toward
self-sufficiency, showing them how to apply for
jobs and how to obtain disability compensation
and veterans' benefits (Leonard 12-13). At St.
Martin de Porres House of Hope, a Chicago shelter, homeless women and their children are assigned

Courtney 4

household jobs upon their arrival and learn the basics of domestic budgeting and home maintenance (Driscoll 46). Such increased responsibility teaches the homeless how to cope with life's everyday challenges--and prepares them for the demands of working life.

6   Since many of the homeless have little work experience, it is not surprising that vocational training is a key service provided by broad-based agencies. According to Jencks's often-cited survey, 94% of the homeless lack steady work (50). The same survey shows that most heads of homeless families have never worked longer than six months (Nunez 28). Through challenging instruction that includes practice in writing a résumé and interviewing for a position, CANP and other agencies coach the homeless in getting and keeping a job. As a result of such intensive training, CANP has an outstanding job placement rate, with 75% of those completing its job-training program moving on to self-sufficiency (Van Meder). ←——————————— E-mail interview source provided in parentheses since no attribution given in the sentence.

7   Unfortunately, organizations like CANP are struggling to survive on dwindling allocations. Boston's Project Hope, for example, served as a short-term way-station for homeless families through the late 1980s, until the recession of the early '90s. Then welfare and public-assistance policies of the mid 1990s reduced the program's operating budget. Fewer families now meet the tighter eligibility requirements to stay at the shelter, and those who do are forced to stay longer because so few housing subsidies are available (Leonard 11-12). It's apparent that government aid is necessary if suppliers of comprehensive assistance--like CANP and Project Hope--are to meet the needs of a growing population.

Courtney 5

Besides funding local programs for the home- 8
less, the government also needs to raise the minimum wage. Some homeless people are employed, but
their limited education locks them into minimum-
wage positions that make it nearly impossible for
them to afford available housing. Dennis Culhane,
professor of Social Welfare Policy at the
University of Pennsylvania, explains that employed
homeless individuals--who typically receive the
minimum-wage--pay such a high percentage of their
salary on housing that "their income doesn't cover
their housing costs" (qtd. in United States 12).
For instance, researchers studying the economics of
Baltimore, MD, determined that, per hour, the actual living wage is approximately $2.50 more than the
minimum wage earned by workers in that city (Hess).
Patrick Markee also points to this disastrous
decline in minimum-wage buying power:

> Indeed, the causes of modern mass home-
> lessness are a matter of little debate,
> and reside in what many academics and
> advocates call the affordability gap: the
> distance between the affordability (and
> availability) of secure, stable housing
> and the income levels of poor Americans
> [. . .]. The other side of the affordabil-
> ity gap has two elements, one of which is
> by now familiar to most Americans: the
> steep decline in real wages since the
> mid-seventies; the steady erosion of the
> minimum wage; the widening gulf between
> rich and poor during the past two
> decades; and the growing severity of
> poverty. (27)

The Economist concurs that this escalating 9
affordability gap makes it difficult for poor people

Where a secondary source is quoted—in a government publication

Attribution leading to a long quotation. Attribution is followed by a colon since the lead-in is a full sentence. If the lead-in isn't a full sentence, use a comma after the attribution.

Long quotation indented ten spaces. Double-space the quotation, as you do the rest of the paper. Don't leave extra space above or below the quotation.

The word *Americans* is followed by an ellipsis enclosed in brackets plus a period, indicating that some material has been deleted from the end of the original sentence.

Attribution naming periodical source for the article cited in parentheses later in the paragraph.

Courtney 6

to find suitable housing. Even so, the magazine
argues, eroding incomes and a lack of affordable
housing aren't the only culprits in the homeless
problem. For The Economist, homelessness owes to a
variety of social problems, including single-parent-
ing, substance abuse, and mental illness--and a
combination thereof ("Out of Sight"). Numerous
studies dispute such an interpretation; they conclude, as does one urban researcher, that a lack of
affordable housing--not "an enduring internal
state" like addiction or mental illness--plays the
critical role in putting people on the street
(Shinn). In Making Room: The Economics of
Homelessness, Brendan O'Flaherty points out that
large-scale deinstitutionalization of the mentally
ill occurred between 1960 and 1975; however, it wasn't
until the 1980s--a period marked by sharp cuts in
subsidized housing--that large numbers of the mentally ill wound up living on the streets (235).
Shinn cites a study that supports the view that a
lack of affordable housing is at the center of the
homelessness problem. She conducted a longitudinal
study of homeless families who received subsidized
housing in New York City and found that "whatever
other problems families may have had, an average of
5 years after entering shelter, 61% were stably
housed in their own apartments for at least a year
and an average of 3 years. Only 4% were in shelter."
Shinn concludes, "Receipt of subsidized housing was
both a necessity and a sufficient condition for
achieving stability." Even Jencks, whose views are
similar to those of The Economist, believes that
more affordable "housing is still the first step in
dealing with the homeless problem. Regardless of why
people are on the streets, giving them a place
to live [. . .] is usually the most important thing

No author or page number is given since source is an anonymous one-page article.

Parenthetic citation for article obtained online; author provided but no page given since electronic text does not follow the pagination of the original

Attribution naming book and its author

Quotation preceded by *that* blends into the rest of the sentence (no comma; quotation's first word is not capitalized).

No parenthetic citation is needed because author's name appears in text and because electronic text does not follow pagination of the original.

Part IV • The Research Paper

Courtney 7

we can do to improve their lives" (qtd. in United
States 7).

    Clearly, the federal government must increase   10
its funding of low-cost housing. Such a commitment
is essential given recent developments in both the
private and public housing markets. As Markee
explains, affordable private housing has become
increasingly scarce in the last several decades
(27). The major problem affecting the private market is gentrification, a process by which low-cost
units are transformed into high-cost housing for
affluent professionals. Following the economic boom
of the late 1990s, rents have risen across America,
tempting landlords to gentrify their low-income
housing ("Out of Sight"). As neighborhoods gentrify, housing that formerly trickled down to the poor
is taken off the low-cost market, increasing homelessness (O'Flaherty 117). Also, in gentrified
areas, many of the tenements and SRO (single-room
occupancy) hotels in which the desperately poor
used to live have been gutted and replaced by high-
priced condominiums. And the tenements and SROs
that remain generally demand more rent than the
poor can pay (Halper and McCrummen 29).

    Where can people turn to seek relief from   11
these inflated costs in the private housing market?
What remains of public housing can hardly answer
the problem. As Markee notes, the 1980s saw the
federal government cut spending on public housing
and housing subsidies by 75%. In 1980, for example,
federal agencies helped build 183,000 housing
units. By the mid-1980s, that number had fallen to
20,000 (27). To counteract these reductions, many
cities invested heavily in new housing in the
late1980s. In the 1990s, though, city budgets slashed such

Courtney 8

investments in half (Halper and McCrummen 28).
Municipal money now goes to constructing temporary
shelters that can house only 2% of the cities'
homeless population (Halper and McCrummen 27).

12   In light of all these problems, one conclusion seems inevitable: the federal government must
take a more active role in helping America's homeless. While debate may continue about the extent
and the causes of homelessness, we know which
approaches work and which do not. The government
must increase its support of programs that make a
demonstrable difference. Such programs do more than
provide food and shelter; they also offer substance-abuse counseling, psychological support,
instruction in basic survival skills, and job
training. Finally, unless the government guarantees
a decent minimum wage and affordable housing, even
skilled, well-adjusted individuals may be forced to
live on the street. The government can't continue
to walk past the homeless, face averted. In doing
so, it walks past millions in need.

Conclusion provides
a summary and
restates the thesis.

Courtney 9

Works Cited

Interview published ——→ Driscoll, Connie. "Responsibility 101: A Chat with
in a weekly maga-
zine—interview's   Sister Connie Driscoll." Interview with Bruce
pages are consecutive
                            Upbin. Forbes 19 May 1997: 46-47.

Anonymous material —— "Facts About Homelessness." National Alliance to
obtained on the
Internet. Name of   End Homelessness. 11 Dec. 2000. 22 Oct. 2001
website, publication,
and access date   <http://www.naeh.org/back/factsus.htm>.
appear. Web address
always required.   —→ Halper, Evan, and Stephanie McCrummen. "Out of

                            Sight, Out of Mind: New York City's New

                            Homeless Policy." Washington Monthly Apr.
Article by two ——
authors, in a month-   1998: 26-29.
ly magazine; pages
are consecutive   —→ Hess, Robert V. "Helping People Off the Streets:

                            Real Solutions to Urban Homelessness." USA
Article in a full-text ——
online periodicals   Today Magazine Jan. 2000: 18-20. EBSCOhost.
index. The title of
the index, its vendor,   MasterFILE Premier. Camden County Lib.,
the library, and the
access date are listed   Voorhees. 6 Feb. 2002 <http://
after the publication
information.   ehostvg.wl.epnet.com>.

                        Holloway, Lynette. "Shelters Improve Under Private

                            Groups, Raising a New Worry." New York Times

                            12 Nov. 1997, late ed.: B1+.
Article in a daily ——
newspaper—section   Howard, Catherine. Letter. New York Times. 18 Nov.
indicated along
with pages; pages   1997, late ed.: A26. New York Times Ondisc.
are not consecutive
                            CD-ROM. UMI-ProQuest. Oct. 1998.

                        Jencks, Christopher. The Homeless. Cambridge:
Letter to a daily ——
newspaper, obtained   Harvard UP, 1994.
from a CD-ROM
                        Leonard, Margaret A. "Project Hope: An Interview

                            with Margaret A. Leonard." Interview with
Book by one ——
author—publisher's   George Anderson. America 2 Nov. 1996: 10-14.
name is abbreviated
                        Link, Bruce, et al. "Lifetime and Five-Year

                            Prevalence of Homelessness in the United

                            States: New Evidence on an Old Debate."
Article, by more than ——
three authors, in a   American Journal of Orthopsychiatry 65
scholarly journal
with continuous   (1995): 347-54.
pagination

Courtney 10

Markee, Patrick. "The New Poverty: Homeless

     Families in America." Rev. of The New   ←——— Book review in a

     Poverty, by Ralph Nunez. The Nation 14 Oct.   monthly magazine

     1996: 27-28.

"Mental Illness and Homelessness." National

     Coalition for the Homeless. 18 Apr. 2001. 30

     Nov. 2001 <http://

     www.nationalhomeless.org/mental.html>.

Nunez, Ralph da Costa. The New Poverty: Homeless

     Families in America. New York: Insight, 1996.

O'Flaherty, Brendan. Making Room: The Economics of

     Homelessness. Cambridge: Harvard UP, 1998.   ┌— Anonymous

"Out of Sight, Out of Mind." Editorial. Economist ← editorial in a weekly

     20 May 2000: 27-29. EBSCOhost. MasterFILE   magazine obtained
                                       through an online

     Premier. Camden County Lib., Voorhees. 27   database

     Mar. 2002 <http://ehostvg.wl.epnet.com>.

Shinn, Marybeth. "Family Homelessness: State or ←——— Article in a scholarly

     Trait?" American Journal of Community   journal obtained
                                       through an online

     Psychology 25.6 (1997): 27 pars. Expanded   database. Electronic
                                       text does not

     Academic Index ASAP. On-line. InfoTrac Search   duplicate original
                                       pagination; text is 27

     Bank. 30 Oct. 1998.   paragraphs long.

Torrey, E. Fuller. Out of the Shadows: Confronting

     America's Mental Illness Crisis. New York:

     Wiley, 1997.

United States. Cong. House. Subcommittee on Housing ←— Government

     and Community Opportunity of the Committee on   publication

     Banking and Financial Services. Hearing on

     Homeless Housing Programs Consolidation and

     Flexibility Act. 105th Cong., 1st sess.

     Washington: GPO, 1997.

Van Meder, Joan. E-mail to the author. 18 Apr. ←——— E-mail interview

     2001.

Commentary

Brian begins his introduction with an evocative description of a typical street person's struggle to survive. These descriptive passages prepare readers for a general statement of the problem of homelessness. This two-sentence statement, starting with "'They' are the homeless" and ending with "the private sector and local governments can't possibly cope," leads the way to Brian's *thesis:* "To help homeless people toward independence, the federal government must support rehabilitation and job training programs, raise the minimum wage, and fund more low-cost housing."

By researching his subject thoroughly, Brian was able to marshal many compelling facts and opinions. He sorted through this complex web of material and arrived at a logical structure that reinforces his thesis. He describes the extent of the problem (paragraph 2), analyzes some of the causes of the problem (3, 4, 8–11), and points to solutions (4–6, 8, 10–11). He draws upon *statistics* to establish the severity of the problem and quotes *expert opinion* to demonstrate the need for particular types of programs. Note, too, that Brian writes in the *present tense* and uses the *third-person point of view.*

Beyond being clearly organized and maintaining a consistent point of view, the paper is *unified* and *coherent.* For one thing, Brian makes it easy for readers to follow his line of thought. He often uses *transitions:* "And" (3), "In addition" (5), "Besides" (8), and so forth. In other places, he asks a *question* (for example, at the beginning of the eleventh paragraph), or he uses a *bridging sentence* (for instance, at the beginning of the fifth, sixth, and eighth paragraphs). Moreover, he always provides clear attributions and parenthetic references so that readers know at every point along the way whose idea is being presented. Brian has, in short, prepared a well-written, carefully documented paper.

ACTIVITIES: WRITING THE RESEARCH PAPER

1. Imagine that you've just written a research paper exploring how parents can ease their children's passage through adolescence. Prepare a Works Cited list for the following sources, putting all information in the correct MLA format.

    a. "Distress, Depression, and Danger: This Is Not a Test," a chapter in Joseph DiPrisco and Michael Riena's *Field Guide to the American Teenager: A Parent's Companion.* The chapter runs from page 257 to 276. The book was published by Perseus Books (Cambridge, MA) in 2000.

b. One radio broadcast within a series called *Voices in the Family,* hosted by Dr. Daniel Gottlieb and produced by Laura Jackson. The broadcast, titled "Adolescents and Sexuality," aired on 2 October 2000, on WHYY-FM of Philadelphia, PA.

c. An article titled "The Relationship Between Early Maltreatment and Teenage Parenthood," by Ellen C. Herrenkohl and three coauthors. The article appeared in volume 21, issue 3 (1998) of the *Journal of Adolescence* and ran from pages 291 to 303. The article, which has twenty paragraphs, was found on the *ProQuest* database on December 19, 1998. The URL of *ProQuest* is http://proquest.umi.com.

d. A book and an article by Laurence Steinberg. The book, *You and Your Adolescent: A Parent's Guide for Ages 10–20,* was published in 1997 by HarperCollins Publishing (PA). The article, "Ethnicity and Adolescent Achievement," appeared on pages 28 to 35 and 44 to 48 in the Summer 1996 issue of *American Educator.*

e. An unpaginated article, titled "Normal Adolescent Development," on the website *Adolescence Directory On-Line,* published by the Center for Adolescent Studies at Indiana University. The article appeared on 29 September 1998 and was accessed on 27 March 2002. The URL is <http://education.indiana.edu/cas/adol/development.html>.

f. An article from pages 1 and 4, section B, of the July 21, 2001, issue of *The Wall Street Journal.* Written by Tara Parker-Pope, the article is titled "Rise in Early Puberty Causes Parents to Ask, 'When Is It Too Soon?'" and has nine paragraphs. The article was found on the *ERIC Database* CD-ROM, published by the U.S. Department of Education in 2001.

2. Assume you're writing a research paper on "type A" personalities. You decide to incorporate into your paper points made by James Gleick in "Life As Type A" (page 433). To practice using attributions, parenthetic citations, and correct punctuation with quoted material, do the following:

a. Choose a statement from the essay to quote. Then write one or more sentences that include the quotation, a specific attribution, and the appropriate parenthetic citation.

b. Choose an idea to summarize from the essay. Then write one or more sentences that include the summary and the appropriate parenthetic documentation.

c. Find a place in the essay where the author quotes an expert or experts. Use this quotation to write one or more sentences in which you:

   • first, quote the expert(s) quoted by Gleick

   • second, summarize the ideas of the expert(s) quoted by Gleick

Each of the above should include the appropriate attribution and parenthetic citation.

THE LITERARY PAPER AND EXAM ESSAY

PART V

22
WRITING
ABOUT
LITERATURE

Does the idea of writing a **literary analysis** make you anxious? If it does, we'd like to reassure you that in some ways writing a literary analysis is easier than writing other kinds of essays. For one thing, you don't have to root around, trying to figure out what you want to accomplish: Your purpose in any literary analysis is simply to share with readers some insights about an aspect of a poem, play, story, or novel.[1] Second, in a literary analysis, your thesis and supporting evidence grow directly out of your reading of the text. All you have to do is select the textual evidence that supports your thesis.

By examining both *what* the author says and *how* he or she expresses it, you increase your readers' understanding and appreciation of the work. And, of course, literary analysis rewards you as well. Close textual analysis develops your ability to think critically and independently. Studying literature also strengthens your own writing. As you examine literary works, you become familiar with the strategies that skilled writers use to convey meaning with eloquence and power. Finally, since literature deals with the largest, most timeless issues, literary analysis is one way to learn more about yourself, others, and life in general.

---

[1]For the sake of simplifying a complex subject, we discuss literary analysis as though it focuses on a single work. In practice, though, a literary analysis often examines two or more works.

ELEMENTS OF LITERARY WORKS

Before you can analyze a literary text, you need to become familiar with literature's key elements. The following list of literary terms will help you understand what to look for when reading and writing about literature.

List of Literary Terms

Theme: a work's controlling idea, the main issue the work addresses (for example, loyalty to an individual versus loyalty to a cause; the destructive power of a lie). Most literary analyses deal with theme, even if the analysis focuses on the methods by which that theme is conveyed.

Plot: the series of events that occurs within the work. Typically, plays and stories hinge on plot much more heavily than poetry, which is often constructed around images and ideas rather than actions.

Structure: a work's form, as determined by plot construction, act and scene divisions, stanza and line breaks, repeated images, patterns of meter and rhyme, and other elements that create discernible patterns. (See also *image, meter, rhyme,* and *stanza.*)

Setting: the time and place in which events unfold (the present, on a hot New York City subway car; a nineteenth-century sailing vessel in the South Pacific).

Character: an individual within a poem, play, story, or novel (Tom Sawyer, Ophelia, Oliver Twist, Bigger Thomas).

Characterization: the way in which the author develops an individual within the work.

Conflict: a struggle between individuals, between an individual and some social or environmental force, or within an individual.

Climax: the most dramatic point in the action, usually near the end of a work and usually involving the resolution of conflict.

Foreshadowing: hints, within the work, of events to come.

Narrator or **speaker:** the individual in the work who relates the story. It's important to remember that the narrator is not the same as the author. The opening of Mark Twain's *Huckleberry Finn* makes this distinction especially clear: "You don't know me, without you have read a book by the name of *The Adventures of Tom Sawyer,* but that ain't no matter. That book was made by Mr. Mark Twain, and he told the truth, mainly." A poorly educated boy named Huck Finn is the narrator; it is *his* captivating but ungrammatical voice that we hear. In contrast, Twain, the author, was a sophisticated middle-aged man whose command of the language was impeccable.

Point of view: the perspective from which a story is told. In the **first-person** (*I*) point of view, the narrator tells the story as he or she experienced it ("*I* saw the bird flap its wings"). The first-person narrator either participates in or observes the action. In the **third-person** point of view, the narrator tells the story the way someone else experienced it ("*Dave* saw the bird flap its wings"). The third-person narrator is not involved in the action. He or she may simply report outwardly observable behavior or events, enter the mind of only one character, or enter the minds of several characters. Such a third-person narrator may be *omniscient* (all-knowing) or have only *limited knowledge* of characters and events.

Irony: a discrepancy or incongruity of some kind. *Verbal irony,* which is often tongue-in-cheek, involves a discrepancy between the literal words and what is actually meant ("Here's some news that will make you sad. You received the highest grade in the course"). If the ironic comment is designed to be hurtful or insulting, it qualifies as *sarcasm* ("Congratulations! You failed the final exam"). In *dramatic irony,* the discrepancy is between what the speaker says and what the author means or what the audience knows. The wider the gap between the speaker's words and what can be inferred about the author's attitudes and values, the more ironic the point of view.

Satire: ridicule (either harsh or gentle) of vice or folly, with the purpose of developing awareness—even bringing about reform. Besides using wit, satire often employs irony to attack absurdity, injustice, and evil.

Figure of speech: a non-literal comparison of dissimilar things. The most common figures of speech are **similes,** which use the word *like* or *as* ("*Like* a lightning bolt, the hawk streaked across the sky"); **metaphors,** which state or imply that one thing *is* another ("All the world's a stage"); and **personification,** which gives human attributes to something nonhuman ("The angry clouds unleashed their fury").

Image: a short, vivid description that creates a strong sensory impression ("A black flag writhed in the wind").

Imagery: a combination of images.

Symbol: an object, place, characteristic, or phenomenon that suggests one or more things (usually abstract) in addition to itself (rain as mourning; a lost wedding ring as betrayal). Usually, though, symbols don't convey meaning in pat, unambiguous ways. Rain, for example, may suggest purification as well as mourning; a lost wedding ring may suggest a life-affirming break from a destructive marriage as well as betrayal.

Motif: a recurring word, phrase, image, figure of speech, or symbol that has particular significance.

Meter: a basic, fixed rhythm of accented and unaccented syllables that the lines of a particular poem follow.

Rhyme: a match between two or more words' final sounds (*Cupid, stupid; mark, park*).

Stanza: two or more lines of a poem that are grouped together. A stanza is preceded and followed by some blank space.

Alliteration: repetition of initial consonant sounds (such as the "b" sounds in "A *b*utterfly *b*looms on a *b*uttercup").

Assonance: repetition of vowel sounds (like the "a" sounds in "m*a*d *a*s *a* h*a*tter").

Sonnet: a fourteen-line, single-stanza poem following a strict pattern of meter and rhyme. The Italian, or *Petrarchan,* sonnet consists of two main parts: eight lines in the rhyme pattern *a b b a, a b b a,* followed by six lines in the pattern *c d c, c d c* or *c d e, c d e.* The English, or *Shakespearean,* sonnet consists of twelve lines in the rhyme scheme *a b a b, c d c d, e f e f,* followed by two rhymed lines *g g* (called a *couplet*). Traditionally, sonnets are love poems that involve some change in tone or outlook near the end.

HOW TO READ A LITERARY WORK

Read to Form a General Impression

The first step in analyzing a literary work is to read it through for an overall impression. Do you like the work? What does the writer seem to be saying? Do you have a strong reaction to the work? Why or why not?

Ask Questions About the Work

One way to focus your initial impressions is to ask yourself questions about the literary work. You could, for example, select from the following checklist those items that interest you the most or those that seem most relevant to the work you're analyzing.

✔ ANALYZING A LITERARY WORK: A CHECKLIST

☐ What *themes* appear in the work? How do *structure, plot, characterization, imagery,* and other literary strategies reinforce theme?

☐ What gives the work its *structure* or shape? Why might the author have chosen this form? If the work is a poem, how do *meter, rhyme, alliteration, assonance,* and *line breaks* emphasize key ideas? Where does the work divide into parts? What words and images are repeated? What patterns do they form?

☐ How is the *plot* developed? Where is there any *foreshadowing*? What are the points of greatest suspense? Which *conflicts* add tension? How are they resolved? Where does the *climax* occur? What does the *resolution* accomplish?

☐ What do the various *characters* represent? What motivates them? How is character revealed through dialog, action, commentary, and physical description? In what ways do major characters change? What events and interactions bring about the changes?

☐ What is the relationship between *setting* and *action?* To what extent does setting mirror the characters' psychological states?

□ Who is the *narrator?* Is the story told in the *first* or the *third person?* Is the narrator omniscient or limited in his or her knowledge of characters and events? Is the narrator recalling the past or reporting events as they happen?

□ What is the author's own *point of view?* What are the author's implied *values* and *attitudes?* Does the author show any religious, racial, sexual, or other biases? Is there any discrepancy between the author's values and attitudes and those of the narrator? To whom in the work does the author grant the most status and consideration? Who is presented as less worthy of consideration?

□ What about the work is *ironic* or surprising? Where is there a discrepancy between what is said and what is meant?

□ What role do *figures of speech* play? What *metaphors,* if any, are sustained and developed? Why might the author have used these metaphors?

□ What functions as a *symbol?* How can you tell?

□ What *flaws* do you find in the work? Which elements fail to contribute to thematic development? Where does the work lose impact because ideas are stated directly rather than implied? Do any of the characters seem lifeless or inconsistent? Are any of them unnecessary to the work's key events and themes?

Reread and Annotate

Focusing on what you consider the most critical questions from the preceding checklist, begin a second, closer reading of the literary work. With pen or pencil in hand, look for answers to your questions, being sure to note telling details and patterns. Underline striking words, images, and ideas. Draw connecting lines between related items. Jot down questions, answers, and comments in the margins. Of course, if you don't own the work, then you can't write in it. In this case, make notes on a sheet of paper or on index cards.

We've marked the accompanying poem to give you an idea of just what annotation involves. The poem is Shakespeare's Sonnet 29, first published in 1609. Notice that the annotations reveal patterns crucial to an interpretation. For example, jotting down the *rhyme scheme* (*a b a b, c d c d,* and so on) leads to the discovery that one change in rhyme corresponds to a turning point in the narrator's thoughts (see line 9). Similarly, the circling or underlining of repeated or contrasting words highlights ideas developed throughout the poem. The words, *I, my,* and *state,* for instance, are emphasized by repetition. The marginal comments also capture possible *themes,* such as love's healing, redemptive power and the futility of self-absorption and envy.

Contrast between
unhappy self-absorption   When, in disgrace with Fortune and men's eyes,   a
("beweep") and joyous   (I) all alone beweep (my) outcast state,   b
love ("haply"), between   useless
"outcast state" and   And trouble deaf heaven with (my) bootless cries,   a
"scorn to change my   And look upon (myself) and curse (my) fate,   b
state."   Wishing (me) like to one more rich in hope,   c
                        Envy ⎰ good looks
                             ⎱ Featur'd like him, like him with friends possess'd,   d
                                             talent   knowledge
                             Desiring this man's art, and that man's scope,   c

                             With what (I) most enjoy contented least;   d

Changes to increasing →   Yet in these thoughts (myself) almost despising   e
joy. Turns away from   (First time lover is mentioned.)
self-absorption.   Haply I think on thee, and then my state,   b
                             Like to the lark at break of day arising   e
                             From sullen earth, sings hymns at heaven's gate;   b
Joyous images. New
beginning. Healing power   For thy sweet love rememb'red such wealth brings   f
of love.   don't want to trade places
                             That then I scorn to change my state with kings.   f

Modify Your Annotations

Your annotations will help you begin to clarify your thoughts about the work. With these ideas in mind, try to read the work again; make further annotations on anything that seems relevant and modify earlier annotations in light of your greater understanding of the work. At this point, you're ready to move on to the actual analysis.

WRITE THE LITERARY ANALYSIS

When you prepare a literary analysis, the steps you follow are the same as those for writing an essay. You start with prewriting; next, you identify your thesis, gather evidence, write the draft, and revise; finally, you edit and proofread your paper.

Prewrite

Early in the prewriting stage, you should take a moment to think about your purpose, audience, point of view, and tone. Your **purpose** in writing a literary analysis is to share your insights about the work. Even if your paper criticizes some aspect of the work (perhaps it finds fault with the author's insensitive depiction of the poor), your primary purpose is still to convey your interpretation of the work's meaning and methods. When writing literary analysis, you customarily assume that your **audience** is composed of readers already familiar with the work. This makes your task easier. In the case of a play or story, for example, there's no need to rehash the plot.

As you write, you should adopt an objective, **third-person point of view.** Even though you're expressing your own interpretation of the work, guard against veering off into first-person statements like "In my opinion" and "I feel that." The **tone** of a literary analysis is generally serious and straightforward. However, if your aim is to point out that an author's perspective is narrow or biased or that a work is artistically unworthy of high regard, your tone may also have a critical edge. Be careful, though, to concentrate on the textual evidence in support of your view; don't simply state your objections.

Prewriting actually begins when you annotate the work in light of several key questions you pose about it (see pages 616–617). After refining your initial annotations (see page 618), try to impose a tentative order on your annotations. Ask yourself, "What points do my annotations suggest?" List the most promising of these points on a separate sheet; then link these points to your annotations. There are a number of ways to proceed. You could, for instance, simply list the annotations under the points they support. Or you can number each point and give relevant annotations the same number as that point. Another possibility is to color-code your annotations: Give each point a color; then underline or circle in the same color any annotation related to that point. Finally, prepare a scratch outline of the main points you plan to cover, inserting your annotations in the appropriate spots. (For more on scratch outlines, see pages 33–35 in Chapter 2.)

If you have trouble generating and focusing ideas in this way, experiment with other prewriting strategies. You might, for example, *freewrite* a page or two on what you have highlighted in the literary text, *brainstorm* a list of ideas, or *map out* the work's overall structure (see pages 27–31 in Chapter 2). Mapping is especially helpful when analyzing a poem.

If the work still puzzles you, it may be helpful to consult outside sources. Encyclopedias, biographies of the author, and history books can clarify the context in which the work was written. Such reference books as *The Oxford Companion to American Literature* and *The Oxford Companion to English Literature* offer brief biographies of authors and summaries of their major works. In addition, *Twentieth-Century Short Story Explication: Interpretations, 1900–1975, of Short Fiction* lists books and articles on particular stories; and *Poetry Explication: A Checklist of Interpretation Since 1925 of British and American Poems Past and Present* does the same for individual poems.

Identify Your Thesis

Looking over your scratch list and any supplementary prewriting material or research notes you've collected, try to formulate a **working thesis.** As in other kinds of writing, your thesis statement for a literary analysis should include both your *limited subject* (the literary work you'll analyze and what aspect of the work you'll focus on), as well as your *attitude* toward that subject (the claim you'll make about the work's themes, the author's methods, the author's attitudes, and so on).

Here are some effective thesis statements for literary analysis:

In the poem "The Garden of Love," William Blake uses sound and imagery to depict what he considers the deadening effect of organized religion.

The characters in the novel Judgment Day illustrate James Farrell's belief that psychology, not sociology, determines fate.

```
The figurative language in Marge Piercy's poem "The Longings of
Women" reveals much about women's feelings and their struggle for
power.
```

If your instructor asks you to include commentary from professional critics, or if you explore such sources at your own initiative, proceed with caution. To avoid merely adopting others' ideas, try to formulate your thesis about the work *before* you read anyone else's interpretation. Then use others' opinions as added evidence in support of your thesis or as opposing viewpoints that you can counter. (For more on thesis statements, see pages 38–42 in Chapter 3.)

Thesis Statements to Avoid

Guard against a *simplistic* thesis. A statement like "The author shows that people are often hypocritical" doesn't say anything surprising and fails to get at a work's complexity. More likely, the author shares insights about the *nature* of hypocrisy, the *reasons* underlying it, the *forms* it can take, or its immediate and long-term *effects*.

An *overly narrow* thesis is equally misguided. Don't limit your thesis to the time and place in which the work is set. You shouldn't, for example, sum up the theme of Hawthorne's *The Scarlet Letter* with the thesis "Hawthorne examines the intolerance of seventeenth-century Puritan New England." Hawthorne's novel probes the general, or universal, nature of communal intolerance. Puritan New England is simply the setting in which the work's themes are dramatized.

Also, make sure your thesis is *about the work*. Discussion of a particular *social* or *political issue* is relevant only if it sheds light on the work. If you feel a work has a strong feminist theme, it's fine to say so. It's a mistake, however, to stray to a non-literary thesis such as "Feminism liberates both men and women."

A *biographical thesis* is just as inappropriate as a sociopolitical one. By all means, point out the way a particular work embodies an author's prejudices or beliefs ("Through a series of striking symbols, Yeats pays tribute in 'Easter, 1916' to the valiant struggle for Irish independence"). Don't, however, devise a thesis that passes judgment on the author's personal or psychological shortcomings ("Poe's neurotic attraction to inappropriate women is reflected in the poem 'To Helen'"). It's usually impossible to infer such personal flaws from the text alone. Perhaps the author had a mother fixation, but that determination belongs in the domain of psychoanalysis, not literary analysis.

Support the Thesis with Evidence

Once you've identified a working thesis, return to the text to make sure that nothing in the text contradicts your theory. Also, keeping your thesis in mind, search for previously overlooked **evidence** (*quotations* and *examples*) that develops your thesis. Consider, too, how *summaries* of portions of the work might support your interpretation.

If you don't find solid textual evidence for your thesis, either drop or modify it. Don't—in an effort to support your thesis—cook up possible relationships among characters, twist metaphors out of shape, or concoct elaborate patterns of symbol-ism. As Sigmund Freud once remarked, "Sometimes a cigar is just a cigar." Be sure there's plentiful evidence in the work to support your interpretation. The text of Shakespeare's *Romeo and Juliet,* for instance, doesn't support the view that the feud between the lovers' two families represents a power struggle between right-wing and left-wing politics.

Organize the Evidence

When it comes time to **organize your evidence,** look over your scratch list and evaluate the main points, textual evidence, and outside research it contains. Focusing on your thesis, decide which points should be deleted and which new ones should be added. Then identify an effective sequence for your points. That done, check to see if you've placed textual evidence and outside research under the appropriate points. If you plan to refute what others have said about the work, the discussion on pages 456–457 will help you block out the outline's refutation sec-tion. What you're aiming for is a solid, well-developed outline that will guide your writing of the first draft. (For more on outlining, see pages 57–60 in Chapter 5.)

When preparing your outline, remember that the patterns of development can help you sequence material. If you're writing in response to an assignment, the assignment itself may suggest certain patterns. Consider these examples:

Comparison-Contrast

In Mark Twain's *Huckleberry Finn,* what traits do the Duke and the Dauphin have in common? In what ways do the two characters differ?

Definition

How does Ralph Waldo Emerson define "forbearance" in his poem of that name?

Process Analysis

Discuss the stages by which Morgan Evans is transformed into a scholar in Emlyn Williams's play *The Corn Is Green.*

Notice that, in these assignments, certain words and phrases (*have in common; in what ways . . . differ; define;* and *discuss the stages*) signal which pattern would be particularly appropriate. Often, though, you'll write on a topic of your own choice. For help in deciding which pattern(s) of development you might use in such circumstances, turn to pages 67–68 in Chapter 6.

Write the First Draft

At this point, you're all set to write. As you rough out your first draft, try to include textual evidence (quotations, examples, summaries), as well as any out-side commentary you may have gathered. However, if you get bogged down either incorporating all the evidence or making it blend smoothly with your own points, move on. You can go back and smooth out any rough spots later. In general, proceed as you would in a research paper when blending quotations and summaries with your own words (see pages 583–585 in Chapter 21).

When preparing the draft, you should also take into account the following four conventions of literary analysis.

Use the Present Tense

Literary analysis is written in the **present,** not the past, tense:

```
In "Arrangement in Black and White," Dorothy Parker depicts the
self-deception of a racist who is not conscious of her own
racism.
```

The present tense is used because the literary work continues to exist after its completion. Use of the past tense is appropriate only when you refer to a time earlier than that in which the narrator speaks.

Identify Your Text

Even if your only source is the literary work itself, some instructors may want you to identify it by author, title, and publication data in a formal bibliographic note. In such a case, the first time you refer to the work in the paper, place an asterisk after its title. Then, at the bottom of the page, type an asterisk, and, after it, provide full bibliographic information. Here's an example of such a bibliographic footnote:

```
¹Marianne Moore, "To a Steam Roller," The Voice That Is Great
Within Us: American Poetry of the Twentieth Century, ed. Hayden
Carruth (New York: Bantam, 1985) 126.
```

(For more about bibliographic footnotes, consult the most recent edition of the *MLA Handbook for Writers of Research Papers.*)

Use Parenthetic References

If you're writing about a very short literary work, your instructor may not require documentation. Usually, however, documentation is expected.

Fiction quotations are followed by the page number(s) in parentheses (89); poetry quotations, by the line number(s) (12–14); and drama quotations, by act, scene, and line numbers (2.1.34–37). The parenthetic reference goes right after the quotation, even if your own sentence continues. When your sentence concludes with the quotation, the final period belongs *after* the parenthetic reference. If you use sources other than the literary text itself, document these as you would quotations or borrowed ideas in a research paper, and provide a Works Cited page. In this case, the literary work you're writing about should also be listed on the Works Cited page, rather than in a bibliographic footnote. (For more on parenthetic documentation and Works Cited listings, see Chapter 21.)

Quote Poetry Appropriately

If you're writing about a short poem, it's a good idea to include the poem's entire text in your paper. When you need to quote fewer than four lines from a poem, you can enclose them in quotation marks and indicate each line break with a slash (/): "But at my back I always hear / Time's winged chariot hurrying near." (Notice that space appears before and after the slash.) Verse quotations of four or more lines should be indented ten spaces from the left margin of your paper and should appear line for line, as in the original source—without slashes to indicate line breaks.

Revise Overall Meaning, Structure, and Paragraph Development

After completing your first draft, you'll gain helpful advice by showing it to others. The checklist that follows will help you and your readers apply to literary analysis some of the revision techniques discussed in Chapters 7 and 8.

☑ REVISING A LITERARY ANALYSIS: A CHECKLIST

Revise Overall Meaning and Structure

☐ What is the thesis of the analysis? According to the thesis, which elements of the work (such as theme and structure) will be discussed? In what ways, if any, is the thesis simplistic or too narrow? In what ways, if any, does it introduce extraneous social, political, or biographical issues?

☐ What main points support the thesis? If any points stray from or contradict the thesis, what changes should be made?

☐ How well supported by textual evidence is the essay's thesis? What evidence, crucial to the thesis, needs more attention? What other interpretation, if any, seems better supported by the evidence?

☐ Which patterns of development (comparison-contrast, process analysis, and so on) help shape the analysis? How do these patterns support the thesis?

☐ What purpose does the analysis fulfill? Does it simply present a straightforward interpretation of some aspect of the work? Does it point out some flaw in the work? Does it try to convince readers to accept an unconventional interpretation?

☐ How well does the analysis suit an audience already familiar with the work? How well does it suit an audience that may or may not share the interpretation expressed?

- ☐ What tone does the analysis project? Is it too critical or too admiring? Where does the tone come across as insufficiently serious?

Revise Paragraph Development

- ☐ What method of organization underlies the sequence of paragraphs? How effective is the sequence?
- ☐ Which paragraphs lack sufficient or sufficiently developed textual evidence? Where does textual evidence fail to develop a paragraph's central point? What important evidence, if any, has been overlooked?
- ☐ Which paragraphs contain too much textual evidence? Which quotations are longer than necessary?
- ☐ Where could textual evidence in a paragraph be more smoothly incorporated into the analysis?
- ☐ If any of the paragraphs include outside research (expert commentary, biographical data, historical information), how does this material strengthen the analysis? If any of the paragraphs consider alternative interpretations, are these opposing views refuted? Should they be?

Revise Sentences and Words

- ☐ Which words and phrases wrongly suggest that there is only one correct interpretation of the work ("Everyone must agree..." "Obviously...")?
- ☐ What words give the false impression that it is possible to read an author's mind ("Clearly, Dickinson intends us to see the flowers as..." "With Willy Loman's suicide, Miller wants to show that...")
- ☐ Where does the analysis fail to maintain the present tense? Which uses of past tense aren't justified—that is, which don't refer to something that occurred earlier than the narrator's present?
- ☐ Where is there inadequate or incorrect documentation?
- ☐ Where does language lapse into needless literary jargon?
- ☐ If poetry is quoted, where should slash marks indicate line breaks? Where should lines be indented?

Edit and Proofread

When editing and proofreading your literary analysis, you should proceed as you would with any other type of essay (see pages 133–136 in Chapter 9). Be sure, though, to check textual quotations with special care. Make sure you quote correctly, use ellipses appropriately, and follow punctuation and capitalization conventions.

PULLING IT ALL TOGETHER

Read to Form a General Impression

By this time, you're familiar with the steps involved in writing a literary analysis, so you're probably ready to apply what you've learned. The following short story was written by Langston Hughes (1902–67), a poet and fiction writer who emerged as a major literary figure during the Harlem Renaissance of the 1920s. Published in 1963, the story first appeared in *Something in Common,* a collection of Hughes's work. Read the story and gather your first impressions. Then follow the suggestions after the story.

LANGSTON HUGHES

EARLY AUTUMN

1   When Bill was very young, they had been in love. Many nights they had spent walking, talking together. Then something not very important had come between them, and they didn't speak. Impulsively, she had married a man she thought she loved. Bill went away, bitter about women.

Yesterday, walking across Washington Square, she saw him for the first time in years.

"Bill Walker," she said.

He stopped. At first he did not recognize her, to him she looked so old.

5   "Mary! Where did you come from?"

Unconsciously, she lifted her face as though wanting a kiss, but he held out his hand. She took it.

"I live in New York now," she said.

"Oh"—smiling politely. Then a little frown came quickly between his eyes.

"Always wondered what happened to you, Bill."

10   "I'm a lawyer. Nice firm, way downtown."

"Married yet?"

"Sure. Two kids."

"Oh," she said.

A great many people went past them through the park. People they didn't know. It was late afternoon. Nearly sunset. Cold.

15   "And your husband?" he asked her.

"We have three children. I work in the bursar's office at Columbia."

"You're looking very . . ." (he wanted to say *old*) ". . . well," he said.

She understood. Under the trees in Washington Square, she found herself desperately reaching back into the past. She had been older than he then in Ohio. Now she was not young at all. Bill was still young.

"We live on Central Park West," she said. "Come and see us sometime."

20   "Sure," he replied. "You and your husband must have dinner with my family some night. Any night. Lucille and I'd love to have you."

The leaves fell slowly from the trees in the Square. Fell without wind. Autumn dusk.

She felt a little sick.

"We'd love it," she answered.

"You ought to see my kids." He grinned.

Suddenly the lights came on up the whole length of Fifth Avenue, chains of misty brilliance in the blue air.

"There's my bus," she said.

He held out his hand, "Good-by."

"When . . ." she wanted to say, but the bus was ready to pull off. The lights on the avenue blurred, twinkled, blurred. And she was afraid to open her mouth as she entered the bus. Afraid it would be impossible to utter a word.

Suddenly she shrieked very loudly, "Good-by!" But the bus door had closed.

The bus started. People came between them outside, people crossing the street, people they didn't know. Space and people. She lost sight of Bill. Then she remembered she had forgotten to give him her address—or to ask him for his—or tell him that her youngest boy was named Bill, too.

Ask Questions About the Work

Now that you've read Hughes's story, consult the questions on pages 616–617 so you can devise your own set of questions to solidify your first impressions. Here are some questions you might consider:

1. How does *setting* help bring out the theme?

   Answer: Both the time of year, "early autumn," and the time of day, "nearly sunset" suggest that time is running out. The place, a crowded walkway in a big city, highlights the idea of all the people with whom we never make contact—that is, of life's missed connections.

2. From what *point of view* is the story told? How does this relate to the story's meaning?

   Answer: The point of view is the third-person omniscient. This enables the author to show the discrepancy between what characters are thinking and what they are willing or able to communicate.

3. What *words* and *images* are repeated in the course of the story? How do these *motifs* reflect the story's theme?

   Answer: The words *young* and *old* appear a number of times. This repetition helps bring out the theme of aging, of time running out. *Walking* is another repeated word that gives the reader the sense of people's uninterrupted movement through life. The repeated phrase *people they don't know* emphasizes how hard it is for people to genuinely communicate and connect with one another. *Love,* another repeated word, underscores the tragedy of love lost or unfulfilled.

Reread and Annotate

In light of the questions you develop, reread and annotate Hughes's story. Then consider the writing assignments that follow.

1. Analyze how Hughes develops the theme that it is urgently important for people to "take time out" to communicate with one another.

2. Discuss some strategies that Hughes uses to achieve universality. You might, for example, call attention to the story's impersonal point of view, the lack of descriptive detail about the characters' appearances, and the generality of the information about the characters' lives.

3. Explain how Hughes uses setting to reveal the characters' psychological states and to convey their sense of loss.

STUDENT ESSAY

Which of the preceding assignments appeals to you most? Student Karen Vais decided to write in response to the first assignment. After using questions to focus her initial impressions and guide her annotations, Karen organized her prewriting and began to draft her literary analysis. The final version of her analysis follows. As you read the essay, consider how well Karen addresses both *what* Hughes expresses and *how* he expresses it. What literary devices does Karen discuss? How are these related to the story's theme? Also note that Karen doesn't identify "Early Autumn" with a bibliographic footnote. Because the story was assigned in class and everyone used the same text, she didn't need to provide such a footnote. Similarly, her instructor didn't require parenthetic documentation of quoted material because the story is so brief.

Stopping to Talk

by Karen Vais

1   In his short story "Early Autumn," Langston Hughes
dramatizes the idea that hurried movement through life
prevents people from forming or maintaining meaningful
relationships. Hughes develops his theme of "walking"
versus "talking" through such devices as setting, plot
construction, and dialog.

2   The story's setting continually reminds the reader
that time is running out; it is urgent for people to
stop and communicate before it is too late. The meeting
between the two characters takes place on a busy
walkway, where strangers hurry past one another. The
season is autumn, the time is "late afternoon," the
temperature is "cold." The end of the renewed connection
between Mary and Bill coincides with the blurring of the
streetlights. The chilly, dark setting suggests the
coming of winter, of night, even of death.

Introduction

Thesis with plan of development

First supporting paragraph: focus on setting

Second supporting para-
graph: focus on plot

In keeping with the setting, the plot is a series   3
of lost chances for intimacy. When they were young and
in love, Bill and Mary used to "walk . . . [and] talk
. . . together," but that was years ago. Then "something
not very important . . . [came] between them, and they
didn't speak." When she says Bill's name, Mary halts
Bill's movement through the park, and, for a short time,
Bill "Walker" stops walking. But when Mary hurries onto
the bus, the renewed connection snaps. Moreover, even
their brief meeting in the park is already a thing of
the past, having taken place "yesterday."

Third supporting para-
graph: focus on dialog

Like their actions, the characters' words   4
illustrate a reluctance to communicate openly. The dialog
consists of little more than platitudes: "I live in New
York now. . . . We have three kids. . . . You and your
husband must have dinner with my family some night." The
narrator's telling comments about what remains unspoken
("he wanted to say . . . ," "she wanted to say . . .")
underscore Bill and Mary's separateness. Indeed, Mary
fails to share the one piece of information that would
have revealed her feelings for Bill Walker--that her
youngest son is also named Bill.

Conclusion

The theme of walking vs. talking runs throughout   5
"Early Autumn." "Space and people," Hughes writes,
once again come between Bill and Mary, and, as in the
past, they go their separate ways. Through the two
characters, Hughes seems to be urging each of us to
speak--to slow our steps long enough to make emotional
contact.

Commentary

Note that Karen states her *thesis* in the opening paragraph; this first sentence
addresses the *what* of the story: "the idea that hurried movement through life prevents . . . meaningful relationships." The next sentence addresses the *how:*
"Hughes develops his theme . . . through such devices as setting, plot construction, and dialog." This second sentence also announces the essay's *plan of development.* Karen will discuss setting, then plot, then dialog, with one paragraph
devoted to each of these literary elements. In the body of the analysis, Karen
backs up her thesis with *textual evidence* in the form of summaries and quotations.
The quotations are no longer than is necessary to support her points. In the

concluding paragraph, Karen repeats her thesis, reinforcing it with Hughes's own words. She ends by pointing out the relevance of the story's theme to the reader's own life.

Writing Assignment on "Early Autumn"

Having seen what one student did with "Early Autumn," look back at the second and third writing assignments on page 627 and select one for your own analysis of Hughes's story. Then, in light of the assignment you select, read the story again, making any adjustments in your annotations. Next, organize your prewriting annotations into a scratch list, identify a working thesis, and organize your ideas into an outline. That done, write your first draft. Before submitting your analysis, take time to revise, edit, and proofread it carefully.

ADDITIONAL SELECTIONS AND WRITING ASSIGNMENTS

The two selections that follow—a poem by Robert Frost and a short story by Kate Chopin—will give you further practice in analyzing literary texts. No matter which selection you decide to write on, the following guidelines should help you approach the literary analysis with confidence.

Start by reading the text once to gain an overall impression. Then, draw on any of the questions on pages 616–617 to help you focus your first impressions and guide your annotations. When deciding what to write about, you may select a topic of your own, a subject proposed by your instructor, or one of the assignments suggested after the readings. With your topic in mind, reread the selection and evaluate the appropriateness of your earlier annotations. Make whatever changes are needed before moving your annotations into an informal scratch list. Next, review the scratch list so you can formulate a working thesis and prepare an outline of your ideas. Then go ahead and write your first draft, making sure you revise, edit, and proofread thoroughly before handing in your analysis.

ROBERT FROST

Best known for his poetry about New England life, Robert Frost (1874–1963) was born in San Francisco and moved to Massachusetts in 1885. After briefly attending

Dartmouth and Harvard Universities, Frost worked several jobs, including farming for five years. His first two collections of poetry, *A Boy's Will* (1913) and *North of Boston* (1914), were published in England, where he went after failing to be published in the United States. These collections—and the distinctly American voice shaping them—eventually won Frost recognition back home, where he returned to publish *Mountain Interval* (1916), a volume containing some of his most recognized poems. The recipient of numerous awards and honors, Frost received four Pulitzer Prizes and presented the poem "The Gift Outright" at President John F. Kennedy's inauguration in 1961. The following poem first appeared in *Mountain Interval*.

"OUT, OUT—"[1]

The buzz-saw snarled and rattled in the yard
And made dust and dropped stove-length sticks of wood,
Sweet-scented stuff when the breeze drew across it.
And from there those that lifted eyes could count
Five mountain ranges one behind the other   5
Under the sunset far into Vermont.
And the saw snarled and rattled, snarled and rattled,
As it ran light, or had to bear a load.
And nothing happened: day was all but done.
Call it a day, I wish they might have said   10
To please the boy by giving him the half hour
That a boy counts so much when saved from work.
His sister stood beside them in her apron
To tell them "Supper." At the word, the saw,
As if to prove saws knew what supper meant,   15
Leaped out at the boy's hand, or seemed to leap—
He must have given the hand. However it was,
Neither refused the meeting. But the hand!
The boy's first outcry was a rueful laugh,
As he swung toward them holding up the hand   20
Half in appeal, but half as if to keep
The life from spilling. Then the boy saw all—
Since he was old enough to know, big boy
Doing a man's work, though a child at heart—
He saw all spoiled. "Don't let him cut my hand off—   25
The doctor, when he comes. Don't let him, sister!"
So. But the hand was gone already.
The doctor put him in the dark of ether.
He lay and puffed his lips out with his breath.
And then—the watcher at his pulse took fright.   30

---

[1]This title alludes to the words of Shakespeare's Macbeth on receiving news that his queen is dead: "Out, out, brief candle!/Life's but a walking shadow, a poor player/That struts and frets his hour upon the stage/And then is heard no more. It is a tale/Told by an idiot, full of sound and fury,/Signifying nothing" (*Macbeth* 5.5.23–28).

No one believed. They listened at his heart.
Little—less—nothing—and that ended it.
No more to build on there. And they, since they
Were not the one dead, turned to their affairs.

Writing Assignments on "Out, Out—"

1. Because it tells a story, "Out, Out—" can be described as a narrative poem. Discuss the poem's various narrative elements, including its setting, plot, characters, conflict, climax, and resolution. Analyze how these narrative elements work to convey what you think is the poem's main theme.

2. Despite the concise language of the poem, Frost manages to provide clear descriptions of the boy and the men in the timber mill and of what each of them represents. Looking closely at how Frost depicts the boy and the men—known as *they* in the poem—write a paper analyzing the different views of human nature Frost conveys.

3. The buzz-saw plays a central role in Frost's poem—to such an extent that it can be considered a character in its own right. Analyze the ways in which the buzz-saw is characterized in the poem. Be sure to discuss what commentary Frost might be making about the relationship between people and their objects of labor in his depiction of the buzz-saw.

KATE CHOPIN

Fiction writer Kate Chopin (1851–1904) is best known for her novel *The Awakening* (1899). When first published, the novel shocked readers with its frank sensuality and the independent spirit of its female protagonist. The story that follows, first published in *Vogue* in 1894, shows a similar defiance of socially prescribed expectations and norms.

THE STORY OF AN HOUR

1   Knowing that Mrs. Mallard was afflicted with heart trouble, great care was taken to break to her as gently as possible the news of her husband's death.

2   It was her sister Josephine who told her, in broken sentences, veiled hints that revealed in half concealing. Her husband's friend Richards was there, too, near her. It was he who had been in the newspaper office when intelligence of the railroad disaster was received, with Brently Mallard's name leading the list of "killed." He had only taken the time to assure himself of its truth by a second telegram, and had hastened to forestall any less careful, less tender friend in bearing the sad message.

3   She did not hear the story as many women have heard the same, with a paralyzed inability to accept its significance. She wept at once, with sudden, wild abandonment,

in her sister's arms. When the storm of grief had spent itself she went away to her room alone. She would have no one follow her.

There stood, facing the open window, a comfortable, roomy armchair. Into this she 4 sank, pressed down by a physical exhaustion that haunted her body and seemed to reach into her soul.

She could see in the open square before her house the tops of trees that were all 5 aquiver with the new spring life. The delicious breath of rain was in the air. In the street below a peddler was crying his wares. The notes of a distant song which someone was singing reached her faintly, and countless sparrows were twittering in the eaves.

There were patches of blue sky showing here and there through the clouds that had 6 met and piled one above the other in the west facing her window.

She sat with her head thrown back upon the cushion of the chair, quite motionless, 7 except when a sob came up into her throat and shook her, as a child who has cried itself to sleep continues to sob in its dreams.

She was young, with a fair, calm face, whose lines bespoke repression and even a 8 certain strength. But now there was a dull stare in her eyes, whose gaze was fixed away off yonder on one of those patches of blue sky. It was not a glance of reflection, but rather indicated a suspension of intelligent thought.

There was something coming to her and she was waiting for it, fearfully. What was 9 it? She did not know, it was too subtle and elusive to name. But she felt it, creeping out of the sky, reaching toward her through the sounds, the scents, the color that filled the air.

Now her bosom rose and fell tumultuously. She was beginning to recognize this 10 thing that was approaching to possess her, and she was striving to beat it back with her will—as powerless as her two white slender hands would have been.

When she abandoned herself a little whispered word escaped her slightly parted 11 lips. She said it over and over under her breath: "Free, free, free!" The vacant stare and the look of terror that had followed it went from her eyes. They stayed keen and bright. Her pulses beat fast, and the coursing blood warmed and relaxed every inch of her body.

She did not stop to ask if it were not a monstrous joy that held her. A clear and exalt- 12 ed perception enabled her to dismiss the suggestion as trivial.

She knew that she would weep again when she saw the kind, tender hands folded 13 in death; the face that had never looked save with love upon her, fixed and gray and dead. But she saw beyond that bitter moment a long procession of years to come that would belong to her absolutely. And she opened and spread her arms out to them in welcome.

There would be no one to live for during those coming years; she would live for her- 14 self. There would be no powerful will bending her in that blind persistence with which men and women believe they have a right to impose a private will upon a fellow crea- ture. A kind intention or a cruel intention made the act seem no less a crime as she looked upon it in that brief moment of illumination.

And yet she had loved him—sometimes. Often she had not. What did it matter! 15 What could love, the unsolved mystery, count for in face of this possession of self-asser- tion which she suddenly recognized as the strongest impulse of her being.

"Free! Body and soul free!" she kept whispering.   16

Josephine was kneeling before the closed door with her lips to the keyhole, 17 imploring for admission. "Louise, open the door! I beg; open the door—you will make yourself ill. What are you doing, Louise? For heaven's sake open the door."

18   "Go away. I am not making myself ill." No; she was drinking in a very elixir of life through that open window.

19   Her fancy was running riot along those days ahead of her. Spring days, and summer days, and all sorts of days that would be her own. She breathed a quick prayer that life might be long. It was only yesterday she had thought with a shudder that life might be long.

20   She arose at length and opened the door to her sister's importunities. There was a feverish triumph in her eyes, and she carried herself unwittingly like a goddess of Victory. She clasped her sister's waist, and together they descended the stairs. Richards stood waiting for them at the bottom.

21   Some one was opening the front door with a latchkey. It was Brently Mallard who entered, a little travel-stained, composedly carrying his gripsack and umbrella. He had been far from the scene of the accident, and did not even know there had been one. He stood amazed at Josephine's piercing cry; at Richards' quick motion to screen him from the view of his wife.

22   But Richards was too late.

23   When the doctors came they said she had died of heart disease—of joy that kills.

Writing Assignments on "The Story of an Hour"

1. Show how Chopin uses imagery and descriptive detail to contrast the rich possibilities for which Mrs. Mallard yearns with the drab reality of her everyday life.

2. Argue that "The Story of an Hour" dramatizes the theme that domesticity saps a woman's spirit and physical strength.

3. Does Chopin's characterization of Mrs. Mallard justify the story's unexpected and ironic climax? Explain your response.

23
WRITING
EXAM
ESSAYS

You may never consider **exam essays** fun, but once you develop the knack, writing an essay as part of an exam can be as much of a learning experience as writing an essay or report out of class. There are differences, of course. At home, you can "hatch" your essay over several hours, days, or even weeks; you can write and rewrite; you can produce an impressively typed final copy.

Exam essays, though, are different. Time pressure is the name of the game. If you have trouble writing essays at home, the idea of preparing one in a test situation may throw you into a kind of panic. How, you may wonder, can you show what you know in such a short time? Indeed, you may feel that such tests are designed to show you at your worst.

Befuddling students and causing anxiety are not, however, the goals that instructors have in mind when they prepare essay exams. Instructors intend such exams to reveal your understanding of the subject—and to stimulate you to interpret course material in perceptive, new ways. They realize that the writing done under time pressure won't result in a masterpiece; such writing may include misspellings and awkward sentences. However, they *do* expect reasonably complete essay answers: no brief outlines, no rambling lists of unconnected points. Focused, developed, coherent responses are what instructors are looking for. Such expectations are not as unrealistic as they may first seem when you realize that all the writing techniques discussed in this book are applicable to taking essay tests.

THREE FORMS OF WRITTEN ANSWERS

There are three general types of questions that require written answers—some as short as one or two sentences, others as long as a full, several-paragraph essay.

Short Answers

One kind of question calls for a **short answer** of only a few sentences. Always read the instructions carefully to determine exactly what's expected. Such questions often ask you to identify (or define) a term *and* explain its importance. An instructor may give full credit only if you answer *both* parts of the question. Also, unless the directions indicate that fragmentary responses are acceptable, be prepared to write one to three full sentences.

Here are several examples of short answers for an exam in modern art history.

Directions: Identify and explain the significance of the following:

1. *Composition with Red, Yellow, and Blue,* 1921: Like most of Piet Mondrian's "compositions," this painting consists of horizontal and vertical lines and the primary colors, red, yellow, and blue. The painting also shows Matisse's influence on Mondrian since Matisse believed that art should express a person's spirit through pure form and color rather than depict real objects or scenes.

2. "Concerning the Spiritual in Art": This is an essay written by Wassily Kandinsky in 1912 to justify the abstract painting style he used. Showing Matisse's influence, the essay maintains that pure forms and basic colors convey reality more accurately than true-to-life depictions.

3. The Eiffel Tower Series: Done around 1910 by Robert Delaunay, this is a series of paintings having the Eiffel Tower as subject. Delaunay used a cubist approach, analyzing surface, space, and interesting planes.

Paragraph-Length Answers

Questions requiring a **paragraph-length answer** may signal—directly or indirectly—the length of response expected. For example, such questions may indicate "answer in a few sentences," or they may be followed by a paragraph-sized space on the answer sheet. In any case, a successful answer should address the question as completely yet as concisely as possible. Beginning with a strong topic sentence will help you focus your response.

Following is a paragraph-length answer to a question on a political science exam:

Directions: Discuss the meaning of the term *interest group* and comment briefly on the role such groups play in the governing of democratic societies.

```
       An interest group is an "informal" type of political
organization; its goal is to influence government policy and see
legislation enacted that favors its members. An interest group
differs from a political party; the interest group doesn't want
to control the government or have an actual share in governing
(the whole purpose of a political party). Interest groups are
considered "informal" because they are not officially part of the
governing process. Still, they exert tremendous power. Democratic
governments constantly respond to interest groups by passing new
laws and policies. Some examples of interest groups are institu-
tions (the military, the Catholic Church), associations (the
American Medical Association, Mothers Against Drunk Driving), and
nonassociational groups (car owners, television viewers).
```

Essay-Length Answers

You will frequently be asked to write an **essay-length answer** as part of a longer examination. Occasionally, an exam may consist of a single essay, as in a "test-out" exam at the end of a writing course.

Here is a typical essay question from an exam in an introductory course in linguistics. A response to this question can be found on pages 642–643.

Account for the differences in American and British English by describing at least *three* major influences that affected the way this country's settlers spoke English. Give as many examples as you can of words derived from these influences.

The rest of this chapter discusses the features of a strong essay response and shows how the writing process can be adapted to a test-taking situation.

HOW TO PREPARE FOR EXAM ESSAYS

Being able to write a good exam essay is the result of a certain type of studying. There are times when cramming is probably unavoidable, but you should try to avoid this last-minute crunch whenever possible. It prevents you from gaining a clear overview of a course and a real understanding of a course's main issues. In contrast, spaced study throughout the semester gives you a sense of the *whys* of the subject, not just the *who, what, where,* and *when.*

As you prepare for an exam essay, you should try to follow these steps:

- In light of the main concepts covered in the course, identify key issues that the exam might logically address.
- With these issues in mind, design several exam essay questions.
- Draft an answer for each anticipated question.
- Commit to memory any facts, quotations, data, lists of reasons, and so forth that you would include in your answers.

Although you may not anticipate the exam's actual questions, preparing some questions and answers can give you practice analyzing and working with the course material. In the process, you'll probably allay some pre-exam jitters as well.

At the Examination

Survey the Entire Test

Look over the entire written-answer section of a test before working on any part of it. Note which sections are worth the highest point value and plan to spend the longest time on those sections. Follow any guidelines that the directions may provide about the length of the response. When "a brief paragraph" is all that is required, don't launch into a full-scale essay.

If you're given a choice about which exam questions to answer, read them all before choosing. Of course, select those you feel best equipped to answer. If it's a toss-up between two, you might quickly sketch out answers to both (see page 639) before deciding which to do. To avoid mistakes, circle questions you plan to answer and cross out those you'll skip. Then give yourself a time limit for writing each response and, within reason, stick with your plan.

Understand the Essay Question

Once you've selected the question on which you're going to write, you need to make sure you know what the question is looking for. Examine the question carefully to determine its slant or emphasis. Most essay questions ask you to focus on a specific issue or to bring together material from different parts of a course.

Many questions use **key directional words** that suggest an answer developed according to a particular pattern of development. Here are some key directional words and the patterns they suggest:

Key Directional Words	Pattern of Development
Provide details about . . .	} Description
Give the history of . . . Trace the development of . . .	} Narration

Key Directional Words	Pattern of Development
Explain . . . List . . . Provide examples of . . .	Illustration
Analyze the parts of . . . Discuss the types of . . .	Division-classification
Analyze . . . Explain how . . . Show how . . .	Process analysis
Discuss advantages and disadvantages of . . . Show similarities and differences between . . .	Comparison-contrast
Account for . . . Analyze . . . Discuss the consequences of . . . Explain the reasons for . . . Explain why . . . Show the influence of . . .	Cause effect
Clarify . . . Explain the meaning of . . . Identify . . .	Definition
Argue . . . Defend . . . Evaluate . . . Justify . . . Show the failings or merits of . . . Support . . .	Argumentation-persuasion

The following sample questions show the way key directional words imply the approach to take. In each example, the key words are italicized. Note that some essay questions call for two or more patterns of development. The key terms could, for example, indicate that you should *contrast* two things before *arguing* the merits of one.

1. Galileo, now recognized as having made valuable contributions to our understanding of the universe, was twice tried by the Vatican. *Explain the factors* that *caused* the church and the astronomer to fall into what one historian has termed a "fatal collision of opposite philosophies." [Cause-effect]

2. *Define* the superego and *explain how,* according to Freud, the superego develops. [Definition; process analysis]

3. *Explain the difference* between "educational objectives" and "instructional objectives." *Provide specific examples* of each, focusing on the distinction between students' immediate and long-term needs. [Comparison-contrast; illustration]

WRITE THE ESSAY

The steps in the writing process are the same, whether you compose an essay at home or prepare an essay response in a classroom test situation. The main difference is that during a test the process is streamlined. Following are some helpful guidelines for handling each writing stage when you prepare an essay as part of an exam.

Prewrite

Prewriting begins when you analyze the essay question and determine your essay's basic approach (see pages 637–638). We suggest that you do your analysis of the question on the exam sheet: Underline key directional terms, circle other crucial words, and put numbers next to points that the question indicates you should cover.

Then, still using your exam page or a piece of scratch paper, make notes for an answer. (Writing on the exam sheet means you won't have several pieces of paper to keep track of.) Jot down main points as well as facts and examples. If you feel blocked, try brainstorming, freewriting, mapping, or another prewriting technique (see pages 28–31) to get yourself going.

What to Avoid.   Don't get overinvolved in the prewriting stage; you won't have time to generate pages of notes. Try using words and phrases, not full sentences or paragraphs. Also, don't spend time analyzing your audience (you know it's your instructor) or choosing a tone (exams obviously require a serious, analytic approach).

Identify Your Thesis

Like essays written at home, exam essays should have a **thesis.** Often, the thesis is a statement answering the exam question. For example, in response to a question asking you to "Discuss the origins of apartheid," your thesis might begin, "The South African law of 'separateness,' or apartheid, originated in 1948, a result of a series of factors that. . . ." Similarly, the essay answer to a question asking you to "Discuss the process by which nations are admitted to the European Community . . ." might start, "Nations are admitted to the European Community through the process of. . . ." Note that these thesis statements are somewhat informal. They state the *subject* of the essay but *not* the writer's *attitude* toward the subject. In a test-taking situation, these less-structured thesis statements are perfectly acceptable. (For more on thesis statements, see Chapter 3.)

Support the Thesis with Evidence

In the prewriting stage, you jotted down material needed to answer the question. At this point, you should review the **evidence** quickly to make sure it's *adequate.* Does it provide sufficient support for your thesis? If not, make some additional quick notes. Also, check that support for your thesis is *unified, specific, accurate,* and *representative* (see pages 48–51 and 68–72).

Organize the Evidence

Before you start writing, devise some kind of **outline.** You may simply sequence your prewriting jottings by placing numbers or letters beside them. Or you can quickly translate the jottings into a brief, informal outline.

However you proceed, go back and review the essay question one more time. If the question has two or three parts, your outline should tackle each one in turn. Suppose a question asks you to "Consider the effects of oil spills on wildlife, ocean ecology, and oil reserves." Your answer should address each of these three areas, with separate paragraphs for each area.

Also, focus again on the question's *key directional words.* If the question asks you to discuss similarities and differences, your outline should draw on one of the two basic *comparison-contrast* formats (see pages 349–350). Since many exam questions call for more than one task (for example, you may be asked both to *define* a theory and to *argue* its merits), you should make sure your outline reflects the appropriate patterns of development.

Many outlines use an *emphatic* approach to organize material ("Discuss which factors are most critical in determining whether a wildlife species will become extinct"). However, when discussing historical or developmental issues (for example, in psychology), you often structure material *chronologically.* In some fields (art history is one) you may choose a *spatial* approach—for instance, if you describe a work of art. Quickly assess the situation to determine which approach would work best, and keep it in mind as you sequence the points in your outline. (Turn to pages 57–60 and 55–57 for more on, respectively, outlining and emphatic, chronological, spatial, and simple-to-complex plans.)

What to Avoid. Don't prepare a formal or many-leveled outline; you'll waste valuable time. A phrase outline with two levels of support should be sufficient in most cases.

Write the Draft

Generally, you won't have time to write a formal introduction, so it's fine to begin the essay with your thesis, perhaps followed by a plan of development (see pages 40–41). Write as many paragraphs as you need to show you have command of the concepts and facts taught in the course. Refer to your outline as you write, but, if inspiration strikes, feel free to add material or deal with a point in a different order.

As you draft your response, you may want to write on every other line or leave several blank spaces at the bottom of the page. That way, you can easily slot in any changes you need to make along the way. Indeed, you shouldn't feel hesitant about crossing out material—a quotation you didn't get quite right, a sentence that reads awkwardly, a fact that should be placed elsewhere. *Do* make these changes, but make them neatly.

When preparing the draft, remember that you'll be graded in part on how *specific, accurate,* and *representative* your evidence is (see pages 49–51 and 69–72). Provide concrete, correct, true-to-type evidence. Make sure, too, that your response is *unified* (see pages 48–49 and 68–69). Don't include interesting but basically irrelevant information. Stay focused on the question. Using topic sentences to structure your paragraphs will help you stay on track.

Your instructor will need transitions and other markers to understand fully how your points connect to one another. Try to show how your ideas relate by using *signal devices,* such as *first, second, however, for instance,* and *most important* (see pages 74–75).

As you near the end of the essay, check the original question. Have you covered everything? Does the question call for a final judgment or evaluative comment? If so, provide it. Also, if you have time, you may want to close with a brief, one- or two-sentence summary.

What to Avoid. Don't write your essay on scrap paper and plan to recopy. You probably won't have enough time. Even if you do, you may, in your haste, leave out words, phrases, or whole sentences. Your first and only draft should be the one written on the exam booklet or paper. Also, unless your instructor specifically requests it, don't waste time recopying the question in your exam booklet.

Instructors find it easier to evaluate what you know if you've used paragraphs. Don't, then, cast your answer as one long paragraph spanning three pages. If you've outlined your ideas, you'll have a clear idea where paragraph breaks should occur. Finally, don't cram your response with everything you know about the subject. Most instructors can detect padded answers in a second. Give focused, intelligent responses, not one rambling paragraph after another.

Revise, Edit, and Proofread

If you've budgeted your time, you should have a few minutes left to review your essay answer. (Don't skip rereading it just so you can leave the room a few minutes early.) Above all, read your response to be sure it answers the question fully. Make any changes that will improve the answer—perhaps add a fact, correct a quotation, tighten a sentence. If you want to add a whole sentence or more, write the material in some nearby blank space and use an arrow to show where it goes. If something is in the wrong place, use an arrow and a brief note to indicate where it should go.

Instructors will accept insertions and deletions—as long as such changes are made with consideration for their sanity. Use a few bold strokes, not wild spidery scribbles, to cross out text. Use the standard editing marks such as the caret (see page 136) to indicate additions and other changes.

As you reread, check grammar and spelling. Obvious grammatical errors and spelling mistakes—especially if they involve the subject's key terms—may affect your grade. If spelling is a problem for you, request permission to have your dictionary at hand.

① Maritime pidgin
(Portug. influ.)
② African pidgin
(Slaves comm.
with each other
and with owners)
③ Native American
pidgin (words for
native plants
and animals)

Sample Essay Answer

The essay that follows was written by Andrew Kahan in response to this exam question:

Account for the <u>differences</u> in <u>American</u> and <u>British English</u> by describing at least <u>three major influences</u> that affected the way this country's settlers spoke English. Give as many <u>examples</u> as you can of <u>words derived</u> from these <u>influences</u>.

Andrew started by underlining the question's key words. Then he listed in the margin the main points and some of the supporting evidence he planned to include in his answer. That done, he formulated a thesis and began writing his essay. The handwritten annotations reflect the changes Andrew made when he refined his answer before handing in his exam.

American English diverged from British English because those who settled the New World had contact with people that those back in England generally did not. As a result of this contact, several pidgin languages developed. A pidgin language, which has its own grammar and vocabulary, comes about when the speakers of two or more unrelated languages communicate ~~for a while~~ over a period of time. Maritime pidgin, African pidgin, and Indian pidgin were three influences that helped shape American English.

By the time the New World began to be settled, sailors and sea merchants of all the European nations had traveled widely. A maritime pidgin thus ~~immerged~~ emerged that enabled diverse groups to communicate.* Since Portugal controlled the seas around the time the colonies were settled, maritime pidgin was largely influenced by the Portuguese. Such Portuguese-derived words as "cavort," "palaver," and "savvy" first entered American English in this way.

The New World's trade with Africa also ~~effec~~ affected American English. The slave trade, in particular, took American sailors and merchants all over the African continent. Since the traders mixed up slaves of many tribes to prevent them from becoming unified, the Africans had to rely on their own pidgin to communicate with each other. Moreover, slave owners relied on this African-based pidgin to communicate with their slaves.** Since slaves tended to be settled in the heavily populated American

*and trade with each other   **until they mastered English.

coastal areas, elements of the African pidgin readily worked
their way into the language of the New World. Words and phrases
derived from African pidgins include "caboodle" and "kick the
bucket." Other African-based words include "buckaroo" and
"goobers," plus words known only in the Deep South, like "cooter"
for turtle. African-based slang terms and constructions
("uptight," "put-on," and "hip," meaning "cool" or "in") continue
to enter mainstream English from black English even today.

Another important influence on American English, in the nation's early
days, was contact with Native American culture. As settlers moved
inland from coastal areas, they confronted Native Americans, and
new pidgins grew up, melding English and Native American terms.
Native American words like "squaw," "tomahawk," and "papoose"
entered English. Also, many words for Native American plants and
animals have Native American roots: "squash," "raccoon," and
"skunk" are just a few. Another possible effect of Native
American languages on American English may be the tendency to
form noun-noun compounds ("apple butter" and "shade tree"). While
such constructions do occur in British English, they are much more
frequent in American English.

British and American English differ because the latter has
been shaped by contact with European languages like Portuguese,
as well as by contact with non-European languages--especially
those spoken by Africans and Native Americans.

Commentary

Alert to such phrases as *account for* and *influences that affected* in the question, Andrew wrote an essay that describes three *causes* for the divergence of American from British English. The three causes are organized roughly chronologically, beginning with the influence of maritime exploration, moving to the effect of contact with African culture, and concluding with the influence of Native Americans.

Although the essay is developed mainly through a decision of causes, other patterns of development come into play. The first paragraph *defines* the term *pidgin*, while the second, third, and fourth paragraphs draw on *process analysis;* they describe how pidgins developed, as well as how they affected the language spoken by early settlers. Finally, the essay includes numerous *examples,* as the exam question requested. Andrew's response shows a solid knowledge of the material taught in the course and demonstrates his ability to organize the material into a clear, coherent statement.

ACTIVITY:
WRITING
EXAM ESSAYS

In preparation for an exam with essay questions, devise four possible essay questions on the material in one of your courses. For each, do some quick prewriting, determine a thesis, and jot down an outline. Then, for one of the questions, write a full essay answer, giving yourself a time limit of fifteen to twenty-five minutes, whatever is appropriate for the question. Don't forget to edit and proofread your answer.

A CONCISE HANDBOOK

PART VI

OPENING COMMENTS

Many students consider grammar a nuisance. Taking the easy way out, they cross their fingers and hope they haven't made too many mistakes. They assume that their meaning will come across, even if their writing contains some errors—perhaps a misplaced comma here or a dangling modifier there. Not so. Surface errors annoy readers and may confuse meaning. Such errors also weaken a writer's credibility because they defy language conventions—customs that readers expect writers to honor. By mastering grammar, punctuation, and spelling conventions, you increase your power and versatility as a writer. When you know the rules, you have the option of breaking them, occasionally, for *stylistic* effect. Sentence fragments serve as a good example. Used well, fragments can add dramatic emphasis. (Consider "Not so" a few sentences back.) If, however, fragments appear frequently in your writing because you can't distinguish them from full sentences, they'll only detract from your message.

This concise Handbook will help you brush up on the rules and conventions of writing. It's organized according to the broad skill areas that give writers the most trouble. (The areas are identified in the list on the next two pages.) Throughout the Handbook, grammatical terminology is kept to a minimum. Although we assume you know the major parts of speech (noun, verb, pronoun, and so on), we *do,* when appropriate, provide on-the-spot definitions of more technical grammatical terms.

Consult the Handbook whenever your instructor points out that you're on shaky ground about some aspect of grammar or punctuation. Certainly, use it also whenever you feel unsure about the correctness of what you've written. Most instructors won't devote much class time to grammar and punctuation, so it's your responsibility to take the steps needed to sharpen your skills.

Here's how the Handbook is arranged:

There are a few other things you should know about the Handbook:

- Each problem area is treated separately. This means that you don't have to study earlier skills before reviewing one that comes later.
- In the margin beside each problem area is a symbol or abbreviation that your instructor may use in marking your papers. A list of these symbols and the page locations where the corresponding skills are discussed in the Handbook can be found on the inside front cover of this book.
- On the whole, we've adopted a "do this—don't do this" approach. However, because things aren't always so simple, we also explain when you may break grammatical convention to achieve a specific effect.

Once you get used to looking up items in the Handbook, you'll find it's like any other tool—the more you use it, the more proficient you become. If you refer to the Handbook often, you can uncross your fingers and feel confident that your work is polished and correct.

SENTENCE FAULTS

FRAGMENTS

A full **sentence** satisfies two conditions: (1) it has a subject and a verb, and (2) it can stand alone as a complete thought. Although a **fragment** is punctuated like a full sentence—with a capital letter at the beginning and a period at the end—it doesn't satisfy these two requirements.[1] There are two kinds of fragments: phrase fragments and dependent clause fragments.

Phrase Fragments

A group of words missing either a subject or a verb is only a phrase, not a complete sentence. If you punctuate a phrase as if it were a sentence, the result is a **phrase fragment.** We illustrate here five kinds of phrase fragments (identified by italics in the examples). Then we present ways to correct such fragments.

---

[1]For information on the way an occasional fragment may be used for emphasis, see pages 116–117 in Chapter 8.

Noun Phrase Fragment

I was afraid of my wrestling coach. *A harsh and sarcastic man.* He was never satisfied with my performance.

Added-Detail Phrase Fragment

Many people have difficulty getting up in the morning. *Especially on Mondays after a hectic weekend.* They wish they had one more day to relax.

Prepositional Phrase Fragment

After a long day at work. I drove to the bank that opened last week. *On the corner of Holly Avenue and Red Oak Lane. Next to the discount supermarket.*

Every summer millions of Americans burn themselves to a crisp. *Despite warnings about the sun's dangers.* They spend hours at the beach, often without applying any protective lotion.

Present Participle, Past Participle, or Infinitive Phrase Fragment

Waiting [present participle] *to buy tickets for the concert.* The crowd stood quietly in line. No one cared that the box office would be closed until the morning.

The children presented the social worker with a present. *Wrapped* [past participle] *in gold aluminum foil.*

After years of negotiating, several nations signed a treaty. *To ban* [infinitive] *the sale of ivory in their countries.*

Missing-Subject Phrase Fragment

Every weekend, the fraternities sponsored a joint open-house party. *And blared music all night long.* Not surprisingly, neighbors became furious.

How to Correct Phrase Fragments

There are four strategies for eliminating phrase fragments from your writing. When using these strategies, you may need to reword sentences slightly to maintain smoothness.

1. Attach the fragment to the preceding or following sentence, changing punctuation and capitalization as needed.   When attaching a phrase fragment to the *beginning of a preceding sentence,* place a comma between the fragment and the start of the original sentence:

Fragment	Environmentalists predict a drought this summer. *In spite of heavy spring rains.* Everyone hopes the predictions are wrong.
Correct	In spite of heavy spring rains, environmentalists predict a drought this summer. Everyone hopes the predictions are wrong.

To attach a phrase fragment to the *end of a preceding sentence,* change the period at the end of the preceding sentence to a comma and change the first letter of the fragment to lowercase:

Fragment   I spent several hours in the college's Career Services Office. *Trying to find an interesting summer job.* Nothing looked promising.

Correct   I spent several hours in the college's Career Services Office, trying to find an interesting summer job. Nothing looked promising.

To attach a phrase fragment to the *beginning of a full sentence that follows it,* change the period at the end of the fragment to a comma and make the capital letter at the start of the full sentence lowercase:

Fragment   *Overwhelmed by school pressures and family demands.* She decided to postpone her education. That was a mistake.

Correct   Overwhelmed by school pressures and family demands, she decided to postpone her education. That was a mistake.

2. Insert the fragment into the preceding or following sentence, adding commas as needed:

Fragment   The tests were easy. *Especially the essay questions.* We felt confident that we had done well.

Correct   The tests, especially the essay questions, were easy. We felt confident that we had done well. [fragment inserted into preceding sentence]

Fragment   *A robust girl who loved physical activity from the time she was a baby.* My sister qualified for the Olympics when she was seventeen.

Correct   My sister, a robust girl who loved physical activity from the time she was a baby, qualified for the Olympics when she was seventeen. [fragment inserted into following sentence]

3. Attach the fragment to a newly created sentence:

Fragment   Although I proudly call it mine, my apartment does have some problems. *For example, very little heat in the winter.*

Correct   Although I proudly call it mine, my apartment does have some problems. For example, *it has* very little heat in the winter.

4. Supply the missing subject:

Fragment   Although they argued frequently, my grandparents doted on each other. *And held hands wherever they went.*

Correct   Although they argued frequently, my grandparents doted on each other. *They* held hands wherever they went.

or

Correct   Although they argued frequently, my grandparents doted on each other *and* held hands wherever they went.

Dependent Clause Fragments

Unlike phrases, which lack either a subject or a full verb, **clauses** contain both a subject and a full verb. Clauses may be **independent** (expressing a complete thought and able to stand alone as a sentence) or **dependent** (not expressing a complete thought and, therefore, not able to stand alone). A dependent clause (often called a **subordinate clause**) begins with a word that signals the clause's reliance on something more for completion. Such introductory words may take the form of **subordinating conjunctions** or **relative pronouns:**[2]

Subordinating Conjunctions		Relative Pronouns
after	once	that
although	since	what
as	so that	which
because	unless	who
even though	until	whoever
if	when	whom
in order that	while	whose

If you punctuate a dependent clause as though it were a complete sentence, the result is a **dependent clause fragment** (identified by italics in the examples):

Fragment	*Because my parents wanted to be with their children at bedtime.* They arranged to leave their late-shift jobs a few minutes early.
Fragment	The mayor, after months of deliberation, proposed a housing ordinance. *Which antagonized almost everyone in town.*

How to Correct Dependent Clause Fragments

There are two main ways to correct dependent clause fragments. When using the strategies, you may need to reword sentences slightly to maintain smoothness.

1. Connect the fragment to the preceding or following full sentence, adding a comma if needed:

Fragment	I thought both my car and I would be demolished. *When the motorcycle hit me from behind.*
Correct	When the motorcycle hit me from behind, I thought both my car and I would be demolished. [fragment attached, with a comma, to beginning of preceding sentence]

or

Correct	I thought both my car and I would be demolished when the motorcycle hit me from behind. [fragment attached, without a comma, to end of preceding sentence]

Fragment	*Although the clean-up crews tried to scrub the oil-coated rocks thoroughly.* Many birds nesting on the rocky shore are bound to die.

---

[2]Dependent clauses introduced by relative pronouns are often referred to as *relative clauses.*

Correct   Although the clean-up crews tried to scrub the oil-coated rocks thoroughly, many birds nesting on the rocky shore are bound to die. [fragment attached, with a comma, to beginning of following sentence]

or

Correct   Many birds nesting on the rocky shore are bound to die, although the clean-up crews tried to scrub the oil-coated rocks thoroughly. [fragment attached, with a comma, to end of following sentence]

When you connect a dependent clause to a full sentence, you need to decide whether to insert a comma. Consider the following:

Guidelines for Using Commas with Dependent Clauses

- If a dependent clause with a subordinating conjunction (like *when* or *although*) precedes the full sentence, the dependent clause is followed by a comma (as in the first corrected sentence on page 653 and the first corrected sentence above).
- If a dependent clause follows the full sentence, it isn't preceded by a comma (as in the second corrected sentence on page 653).
- The exception is dependent clauses beginning with such words as *although* and *though*—words that show contrast. When such clauses follow a full sentence, they are preceded by a comma (as in the second corrected sentence above).

When connecting a relative clause to a full sentence, you set *off* the *relative clause* with a comma if the clause is **nonrestrictive** (that is, if it is *not essential* to the sentence's meaning):

Fragment   As a child, I went to the mountains with my parents. *Who never relaxed long enough to enjoy the lazy times there.*
Correct   As a child, I went to the mountains with my parents, who never relaxed long enough to enjoy the lazy times there.

Note that in the corrected version there's a comma between the independent and relative clauses because the relative clause (*who never relaxed long enough to enjoy the lazy times there*) is nonrestrictive. In other words, it isn't needed to identify the writer's parents.

Take a look, though, at the following:

Fragment   As a child, I went to the mountains with the family. *Who lived next door.*
Correct   As a child, I went to the mountains with the family who lived next door.

In this case, the relative clause (*who lived next door*) is needed to identify which family is being referred to; that is, the clause is **restrictive** (*essential*) and, therefore, is *not* set off with a comma. (For information on punctuating restrictive and nonrestrictive phrases, see pages 682–683.)

When a relative clause beginning with *that* is attached to a nearby sentence, no comma is used between the relative and independent clauses:

Fragment   My uncle got down on his hands and knees to rake away the dry leaves. *That he felt spoiled the beauty of his flower beds.*

Correct   My uncle got down on his hands and knees to rake away the dry leaves that he felt spoiled the beauty of his flower beds.

2. Remove or replace the dependent clause's first word:

Fragment   The typical family-run farm is up for sale these days. *Because few small farmers can compete with agricultural conglomerates.*

Correct   The typical family-run farm is up for sale these days. Few small farmers can compete with agricultural conglomerates.

PRACTICE: CORRECTING SENTENCE FRAGMENTS

Correct any phrase and dependent clause fragments that you find in the following sentences. Be careful, though; some of the sentences may not contain fragments, and others may contain more than one.

1. Even though there must be millions of pigeons in the city. You never see a baby pigeon. It makes you wonder where they're hiding.

2. Children between the ages of eight and twelve often follow teenagers' trends. And look up to teens as role models. Mimicking their behavior in frequently disconcerting ways.

3. The least expensive remote-control toy car costs over fifty dollars. Which is more than many budget-conscious parents want to pay. Such high costs are typical in the toy industry.

4. The student's dorm room looked like a disaster area. Heaps of dirty clothes, crumpled papers, and half-eaten snacks were strewn everywhere. Keeping the room neat was obviously not a priority.

5. Because they feel urban schools are second-rate. Many parents hope to move their families to the suburbs. Even though they plan to continue working in the city.

6. Pulling the too-short hospital gown around his wasted body, the patient wandered down the hospital corridor. Unaware of the stares of the healthy people streaming by.

7. Last year, the student government overhauled its charter and created chaos. A confusing set of guidelines that muddled already contradictory policies. This year's senate has to find a way to remedy the situation.

8. Out of all the listed apartments we looked at that dreary week. Only one was affordable. And suitable for human habitation.

9. My grandfather likes to send off-beat greeting cards. Like the one with a picture of a lion holding on to a parachute. The card reads, "Just wanted to drop you a lion."

10. About a year ago, my mother was unexpectedly laid off by the restaurant. Where she had been hired five years earlier as head chef. The experience made her realize that she wanted to go into business for herself.

11. Occasionally looking up to see if anyone interesting had entered the room, the students sat hunched over their desks in the study carrels. Cramming for final exams. Scheduled to start the next day.

12. As prices have come down, compact-disc players have gained great popularity. With the development of these sophisticated sound systems, listening to concert music is more enjoyable than ever. Indeed, nearly as pleasurable as being at the concert itself.

13. Through the local adult education program, my parents took a course in electrical wiring last spring. They plan to enroll in a plumbing course this winter. Their goal is to save money on household repairs. Which cost them hundreds of dollars last year.

14. For breakfast, my health-conscious roommate drinks a strange concoction. That consists of soybean extract, wheat germ, and sunflower meal. It doesn't look very appealing.

15. Last night, I went to the hospital to visit my uncle. Who had been hospitalized four days earlier with a heart attack. I was relieved to see how healthy he looked.

16. The BB gun has changed dramatically. Over the last few years. Today's top-of-the-line gun can fire BBs or pellets 800 feet per second. Almost as fast as some handguns.

17. The hyacinths and daffodils in the garden were blooming beautifully. Until a freakish spring storm blasted their growth. Within hours, they shriveled up. And lay flat on the ground.

18. During last week's heated town meeting, several municipal officials urged the town council to adopt a controversial zoning ordinance. A proposal that had already been rejected by the town residents.

19. Strategically placed pine trees concealed the junkyard from nearby residents. Who otherwise would have protested its presence in the neighborhood. Well known for its lush lawns and colorful gardens.

20. In an effort to cover his bald spot. Al combs long strands of hair over the top of his head. Unfortunately, no one is fooled by his strategy. Especially not his wife. Who wishes her husband would accept the fact that he's getting older.

CS
r-o

COMMA SPLICES AND RUN-ON SENTENCES

Consider the following faulty sentences:

Almost everyone in the office smokes, cigarette breaks are more important than coffee breaks.

My grades are good too bad my social life isn't.

The first example is a **comma splice:** A comma is used to join, or splice together, two complete thoughts, even though a comma alone is not strong enough to connect the two independent clauses. The second example is a **run-on,** or **fused, sentence:** Two sentences are connected, or run together, without any punctuation at all to indicate where the first sentence ends and the second begins.

Three Common Pitfalls

Here we describe three situations that often lead to comma splices or run-on sentences. Then we present ways to correct these sentence errors.

1. When the second sentence starts with a personal or demonstrative pronoun
The following are **personal pronouns:** *I, you, he, she, it, we,* and *they. This, that, these,* and *those* are **demonstrative pronouns.**

Comma Splice	The college's computerized billing system needs to be overhauled, *it billed more than a dozen students twice for tuition.*
Run-on	Lobsters are cannibalistic and will feed on each other *this is one reason they are difficult to raise in captivity.*

2. When the second sentence starts with a transition Some common **transitions** include the words *finally, next, second,* and *then.*

Comma Splice	You start by buttering the baking dish, *next you pour in milk and mix it well with the butter.*
Run-on	The dentist studied my X rays *then she let out an ominous sigh.*

3. When two sentences are connected by a transitional adverb Here are some of the most common **transitional adverbs:**

Transitional Adverbs

accordingly	furthermore	meanwhile	still
also	however	moreover	therefore
anyway	indeed	nevertheless	thus
besides	instead	nonetheless	
consequently	likewise	otherwise	

Comma Splice	We figured the movie tickets would cost about five dollars, *however, we forgot to calculate the cost of all the junk food we would eat.*
Run-on	Fish in a backyard pond will thrive simply by eating the bugs, larvae, and algae in the pond *nevertheless, many people enjoy feeding fish by hand.*

How to Correct Comma Splices and Run-on Sentences

There are four strategies for eliminating comma splices and run-on sentences from your writing.

1. Place a period, question mark, or exclamation point at the end of the first sentence and capitalize the first letter of the second sentence:

Comma Splice	Our team played badly, *we deserved to lose by the wide margin we did.*
Correct	Our team played badly. We deserved to lose by the wide margin we did.
Run-on	Which computer do experts recommend for the average college student *which system do experts consider most all-purpose?* They seldom agree.
Correct	Which computer do experts recommend for the average college student? Which system do experts consider most all-purpose? They seldom agree.

2. Use a semicolon (;) to mark where the first sentence ends and the second begins:

Comma Splice	In the eighteenth century, beauty marks were considered fashionable, *people even glued black paper dots to their faces.*
Correct	In the eighteenth century, beauty marks were considered fashionable; people even glued black paper dots to their faces.
Run-on	Many men use hairstyling products, facial scrubs, and cologne *however, most draw the line at powder and eye makeup.*
Correct	Many men use hairstyling products, facial scrubs, and cologne; however, most draw the line at powder and eye makeup.

Note that when the second sentence starts with a transitional adverb (such as *however* in the last corrected sentence above), a *comma* is placed *after* the transition.[3]

3. Turn one of the sentences into a dependent clause:[4]

Comma Splice	The camping grounds have no electricity, *however, people flock there anyway.*
Correct	*Although* the camping grounds have no electricity, people flock there anyway.
Run-on	The highway was impassable *it had snowed all night and most of the morning.*
Correct	The highway was impassable *because* it had snowed all night and most of the morning.

When using this strategy, refer to the list of guidelines on page 663 to help you decide whether you should (as in the first corrected example) or shouldn't (as in the second corrected example) use a comma between the independent and dependent clauses.

4. Keep or add a comma at the end of the first sentence, but follow the comma with a coordinating conjunction. The following words are **coordinating conjunctions:** *and, but, for, nor, or, so, yet.*

---

[3]For information on punctuating transitional adverbs when they appear midsentence, see page 683.

[4]See page 653 for a list of words that introduce dependent clauses.

Comma Splice	Well-prepared and confident, I expected the exam to be easy, *it turned out to be a harrowing experience.*
Correct	Well-prepared and confident, I expected the exam to be easy, but it turned out to be a harrowing experience.
Run-on	Last election we campaigned enthusiastically *this year we expect to be equally involved.*
Correct	Last election we campaigned enthusiastically, *and* this year we expect to be equally involved.

PRACTICE: CORRECTING COMMA SPLICES AND RUN-ON SENTENCES

Correct any comma splices and run-ons that you find in the following sentences. Be careful, though; some commas belong just where they are.

1. Since the town appeared to be nearby, they left the car on the side of the road and started walking toward the village, they soon regretted their decision.

2. As we rounded the bend, we saw hundreds of crushed cars piled in neat stacks, the rusted hulks resembled flattened tin cans.

3. With unexpected intensity, the rain hit the pavement, plumes of heat rose from the blacktop, making it difficult to drive safely.

4. According to all reports, the day after Thanksgiving is the worst day of the year to shop, the stores are jammed with people, all looking for bargains.

5. Plants should be treated regularly with an organic insecticide, otherwise, spider mites and mealy bugs can destroy new growth.

6. Have you ever looked closely at a penny, do you know whether Lincoln faces right or left?

7. As we set up the tent, flies swarmed around our heads, we felt like day-old garbage.

8. If the phone rings when my parents are eating dinner, they don't answer it, they assume that, if the person wants to reach them, he or she will call back.

9. The library's security system needs improving, it allows too many people to sneak away, with books and magazines hidden in their pockets, purses, or briefcases.

10. Ocean air is always bracing, it makes everyone feel relaxed and carefree, as though the world of work is far away.

11. In the last few years, many prestigious art museums have developed plans to add on to buildings designed by such legendary architects as Frank Lloyd Wright and Louis Kahn, however, many irate museum-goers want the buildings to stay just as they are.

12. The salesperson stapled my bag in six places I must have looked like a shoplifter.

13. Throughout the last decade, publishing companies doled out huge advances to lure big-time authors, now many publishers, struggling with massive losses, regret the strategy.

14. Several communities in the country sponsor odd food festivals, in fact, one of the strangest takes place in Vineland, New Jersey, this small rural community celebrates spring with a dandelion-eating contest.

15. Only the female mosquito drinks blood the males live on plant juices.

16. Every Friday evening, my parents go out to eat, by themselves, at the local diner, then they do their marketing for the week.

17. Television commercials are valuable they give everyone a chance to stretch, visit the bathroom, and get a snack.

18. I start by wetting my feet in the lake's cold water then I wade up to my knees before plunging in, shivering all the while.

19. In this country, roughly three hundred new pizza parlors open every week, this shows that pizza has become a staple in the American diet, exceeding even hamburgers and hot dogs in popularity.

20. The first wave of crack babies is approaching school age, and health and social workers are discovering a whole new set of drug-related problems.

// FAULTY PARALLELISM

Words in a pair or in a series should be placed in parallel (matching) grammatical structures. If they're not, the result is **faulty parallelism:**

Faulty Parallelism   After the exam, we were *exhausted, hungry,* and *experienced depression.*

In the preceding sentence, three items make up the series. However, the first two items are adjectives (*exhausted* and *hungry*), while the last one is a verb plus a noun (*experienced depression*).

Words that follow correlative conjunctions (*either . . . or, neither . . . nor, both . . . and, not only . . . but also*) should also be parallel:

Faulty Parallelism   Every road into the city is either *jammed* or *is closed* for repairs.

Here, *either* is followed by an adjective (*jammed*), but *or* is followed by a verb (*is*).

How to Correct Faulty Parallelism

To correct faulty parallelism, *place words in a pair or in a series in the same grammatical structure:*

Faulty Parallelism   *After the car baked in the sun for hours, the steering wheel was hot, the seats were sticky, and there was stuffiness in the air.*

Correct   After the car baked in the sun for hours, the steering wheel was hot, the seats were sticky, and the air was stuffy.

or

Correct   After the car baked in the sun for hours, the steering wheel was hot, the seats sticky, and the air stuffy.

| **Faulty Parallelism** | *Parents are either too permissive or they are too strict.* |
| **Correct** | Parents are either too permissive or too strict. |

or

| **Correct** | Parents either are too permissive or are too strict. |

or

| **Correct** | Either parents are too permissive, or they are too strict. |

(For more on parallelism, see pages 115–116 in Chapter 8.)

PRACTICE: CORRECTING FAULTY PARALLELISM

Correct any faulty parallelism that you find in the following sentences. Be careful, though; not every sentence contains an error.

1. The professor's tests were long, difficult, and produced anxiety.

2. Medical tests showed that neither being allergic to dust nor seasonal hay fever caused the child's coughing fits.

3. One option that employees had was to accept a pay cut; the other was working longer hours.

4. The hairstylist warned her customers, "I'm a beautician, not a magician. This is a comb; it's not a wand."

5. The renovated concert hall is both beautiful and it is spacious.

6. My roommates and I are not only learning Japanese but also Russian.

7. The game-show contestants were told they had to be quick-witted, friendly, and demonstrate enthusiasm.

8. Having good rapport, being open to ideas, and believing strongly in a common goal can help group members complete a project.

9. While waiting in line at the supermarket, people often flip through the tabloids to read about celebrities, the latest scandals, and how to lose weight.

10. Smoking either will be eventually made illegal or people will give it up on their own.

VERBS

PROBLEMS WITH SUBJECT-VERB AGREEMENT

A **verb** should *match its subject in number.* If the subject is singular (one person, place, or thing), the verb should have a singular form. If the subject is plural (two or more persons, places, or things), the verb should have a plural form.

How to Correct Faulty Subject-Verb Agreement

The six situations described here often lead to problems with subject-verb agreement. To deal with each of these problems, you must determine the *verb's subject* and make sure the *verb agrees with it,* rather than with some other word in the sentence.

1. When there are two or more subjects   When the word *and* joins two or more subjects in a sentence, use a plural verb:

Correct   A beautiful maple *and* a straggly oak *flank* [not *flanks*] the building.

662

However, when the word *or* joins the subjects, use a singular verb:

Correct   A maple *or* an oak *offers* [not *offer*] good shade in the summer.

2. When the subject and verb are separated by a prepositional phrase   Be sure to match the verb to its subject—not to a word in a prepositional phrase that comes between the subject and the verb:

Correct

> *One* of the desserts *was* [not *were*] too sweet even for me.

> To pass inspection, the *plumbing* in all the apartments *needs* [not *need*] to be repaired.

3. When the words *either . . . or* or *neither . . . nor* connect subjects   When *either . . . or* or *neither . . . nor* link two subjects, use the verb form (singular or plural) that agrees with the subject *closer* to the verb:

Correct

> *Neither* the students *nor* the *professor likes* [not *like*] the textbook.

> *Neither* the professor *nor* the *students like* [not *likes*] the textbook.

4. When the subject is an indefinite pronoun   Some **indefinite pronouns** (such as *anyone, anything, each, either, every, everyone, everybody, everything, neither,* and *nobody*) take a *singular verb*—whether they act as a pronoun subject (as in the first sentence that follows) or as an adjective in front of a noun subject (as in the second sentence):

Correct

> *Neither* of the libraries *was* [not *were*] open.

> *Neither* library *was* [not *were*] open.

Other indefinite pronouns (such as *all, any, most, none,* and *some*) take a *singular or a plural verb,* depending on whether they refer to one thing or to a number of things. In the following sentence, *some* refers to a single tutoring session, so the verb is singular:

Correct   The student reported that only *some* of her tutoring *session was* helpful.

In this next sentence, however, *some* refers to multiple sessions, so the verb is plural:

Correct   The student reported that only *some* of her tutoring *sessions were* helpful.

5. When there is a group subject   When the subject of a sentence refers to a group acting in unison, or as a unit, use a singular verb:

Correct   The debate *club* is [not *are*] on a winning streak.

However, when the subject is a group whose members are acting individually, rather than as a unit, use a plural verb:

Correct   The *debate club argue* [not *argues*] among themselves constantly.

If, in this case, the plural verb sounds awkward, reword the sentence so that the group's individual members are referred to directly:

Correct   The debate club *members argue* among themselves constantly.

6. When the verb comes before the subject   Words such as *here, there, how, what, when, where, which, who,* and *why,* as well as *prepositional phrases,* are apt to invert normal sentence order, causing the verb to precede the subject. In such cases, look ahead for the subject and make sure it and the verb agree in number:

Correct

There *is* [not *are*] always a long *line* of students at the library's duplicating machine.

What *are* [not *is*] the *reasons* for consumers' complaints about the car?

Near the lifeguard station, looking for us everywhere, *were* [not *was*] our *parents.*

PRACTICE: CORRECTING PROBLEMS WITH SUBJECT-VERB AGREEMENT

Correct any errors in subject-verb agreement that you find in the following sentences. Be careful, though; some sentences may not contain any errors.

1. There is many secretaries who do their bosses' jobs, as well as their own.
2. At the back of the closet, behind all the clothes, are some old records.
3. Each of the children wear a name tag when the play group takes a field trip.
4. Next week, the faculty committee on academic standards plans to pass a controversial resolution, one that the student body have rejected in the past.
5. In the garage, leaning against the back wall, are a rusty sled and a broken tricycle.
6. Neither the sales representative nor the customers were happy with the price increase, which is scheduled to go into effect next month.
7. The human spinal column, with its circular discs, resemble a stack of wobbly poker chips.
8. Both the students and the instructor dislikes experimental music.
9. In most schools, either the college president or the provost is responsible for presenting the budget to the board of trustees. The board of trustees, in turn, are responsible for cutting costs whenever possible.
10. Nobody in the two classes think that the exam, which lasted three hours, was fair.
11. Chipped ceramic pots and half-empty bags of fertilizer lines the shelves of my grandparents' storage shed.

12. In the middle of the campus, near the two new dorms, are a row of spindly elms. The trees, especially the one at the end, were badly damaged in last week's storm.

13. A strong, secure bond between parent and child are formed when parents responds quickly and consistently to their babies' needs.

14. The crowd, consisting of irate teachers and parents, were quiet, but the police were alerted anyway.

15. The guidelines issued by the supervisor states that personal calls made during the business day violate company policy.

PROBLEMS WITH VERB TENSE

vt

A verb's tense indicates the time—*past, present,* or *future*—of an event. Here we show how to correct two common problems with verb tense: (1) inappropriate shifts in tense, and (2) faulty use of past tense.

How to Correct Inappropriate Shifts in Verb Tense

The first sentence that follows switches from the past tense (*bought*) to the present (*breaks*), even though both events took place in the same (past) period of time. The second sentence switches from the present tense (*is*) to the past (*was*). To avoid such inappropriate shifts, *use the same verb tense to relate all events occurring in the same time period:*

Inappropriate Tense Shift	The township *bought* a powerful new lawn mower, which *breaks* down after two weeks.
Correct	The township *bought* a powerful new lawn mower, which *broke* down after two weeks.
Inappropriate Tense Shift	The restaurant's homemade bread *is* thick and crunchy. It *was* a meal in itself.
Correct	The restaurant's homemade bread *was* thick and crunchy. It *was* a meal in itself.

When writing, decide which verb tense will be most effective; then use that tense throughout—unless you need to change tenses to indicate a different time period.

Much of the writing you do in college will use the past tense:

Changes in the tax law *created* chaos for accounting firms.

However, when writing about literature, you generally use the present tense:

Twain *examines* the conflict between humane impulses and society's prejudices.

How to Correct Faulty Use of Past Tense

The following sentence uses the **simple past tense** (*finished, burst*) for both verbs, even though one event ("the plane finished rolling down the runway") *preceded* the other (the plane "burst into flames"). To distinguish one past event from an earlier one, use the **past perfect tense** ("*had* washed," "*had* gone," "*had* finished") for the earlier event:

Faulty Past Tense	The plane already *finished* rolling down the runway when it *burst* into flames.
Correct	The plane *had* already *finished* [past perfect] rolling down the runway when it *burst* [simple past] into flames.

PRACTICE: CORRECTING PROBLEMS WITH VERB TENSE

Correct any errors in verb tense that you find in the following sentences. Be careful, though; some tenses shouldn't be changed.

1. I parked illegally, so my car is towed and gets dented in the process.

2. We had already ordered a truckload of lumber when we decided not to build a deck after all.

3. Although the union leaders called a strike, the union members voted not to stop working.

4. Dr. Alice Chase wrote a number of books on healthy eating. In 1974, she dies of malnutrition.

5. By the time we hiked back to the campsite, the rest of the group collected their gear to go home.

6. In her poetry, Marge Piercy often pays tribute to women's strength and resilience.

7. As a boy, Thomas Edison was told he will never succeed at anything.

8. The Museum of Modern Art once hung a painting upside down. The mistake goes unnoticed for more than a month.

9. When doctors in Los Angeles went on strike in 1976, the death rate drops 18 percent.

10. John Steinbeck's *The Grapes of Wrath* conveyed the horrors of poverty.

11. The championship players slapped each other's backs, hooted and hollered, and poured champagne all over the coach.

12. The aspiring comic walked to the front of the small stage. As he looked out at the audience, a wave of nausea sweeps over him.

PRONOUNS

PROBLEMS WITH PRONOUN USE

Pronouns are words that take the place of nouns (persons, places, things, and concepts). Indeed, the word *pronoun* means "for a noun." As the following sentences show, pronouns keep you from repeating words unnecessarily:

> After I fertilized the plant, *it* began to flourish. [it takes the place of *plant*]

> When the students went to register *their* complaint, *they* were told to come back later. [*their* and *they* replace *students*]

When using pronouns, you need to be careful not to run into problems with case, agreement, and reference.

Pronoun Case

A pronoun's correct form, or **case,** depends on the way the pronoun is used in the sentence. A pronoun acting as a *subject* requires the **nominative case.** One acting as a *direct object* (receiving a verb's action), an *indirect object* (indicating to or for whom the action is performed), or an *object of a preposition* (following a preposition such as *at, near,* or *to*) requires the **objective case.** And a pronoun

667

indicating *possession* takes the **possessive case.** The list below classifies pronouns by case:

Nominative Case	Objective Case	Possessive Case	
I	me	my	mine
we	us	our	ours
you	you	your	yours
he	him	his	his
she	her	her	hers
it	it	its	its
they	them	their	theirs
who	whom	whose	

How to Correct Faulty Pronoun Case

The five situations described here often lead to errors in pronoun case. To correct any of these problems, *determine whether the pronoun is used as object or subject; then put the pronoun in the appropriate case.*

1. Pronoun pairs or a pronoun and a noun   Use the nominative case when two pronouns act as subjects:

Correct   *He* and *I* [not *Him* and *me*] are different ages, but we have several traits in common.

Also use the nominative case when a pronoun and noun serve as subjects:

Correct   *She* [not *Her*] and *several transfer students* enrolled in the new course.

Conversely, use the objective case when a pronoun pair acts as direct object, indirect object, or object of a preposition:

Correct (Direct Objects)   My parents sent *her* [not *she*] and *me* [not *I*] to the store to buy decorations for the holiday.
Correct (Indirect Objects)   The committee presented *him* [not *he*] and *me* [not *I*] with the award.

Similarly, use the objective case when a pronoun and noun function as direct object, indirect object, or object of a preposition:

Correct (Object of Preposition)   The doctor gave the pills to the three other patients and *me* [not *I*].

A hint: When a pronoun is paired with another pronoun or with a noun, and you're not sure which case to use, imagine the sentence with only one pronoun. For example, perhaps you wonder whether it's correct to write "The student senate commended my roommates and *I* for our actions." "The student senate commended *I*" doesn't sound right, so you know *me* is the correct form.

2. A pronoun-noun pair acting together as subject or object   If a pronoun-noun pair acts as the subject, use the nominative case:

Correct   *We* [not *Us*] *dorm residents* plan to protest the ruling.

If the pronoun-noun pair serves as an object, use the objective case:

Correct   The dropout rate among *us* [not *we*] *commuting students* is high.

3. Pronouns following forms of the verb *to be*   In formal English, use the nominative case in constructions like the following:

Correct
It is *I* [not *me*].
This is *she* [not *her*].

In such constructions, the objective case (*me* and *her*, for example) is so common that the formally correct nominative case may sound strange. However, before using the more colloquial objective case, check with your instructor to make sure such informality will be acceptable.

4. Pronouns following the comparative *than*   Comparisons using the word *than* tend to imply, rather than state directly, the sentence's final word (placed in brackets in the following sentence):

The other employees are more willing to negotiate *than we* [are].

To determine the appropriate case for the pronoun in a sentence with a *than* comparison, simply add the implied word. For example, maybe you're not sure whether *we* or *us* is correct in the preceding sentence. As soon as you supply the implied word (*are*), it becomes clear that *we*, not *us*, is correct.

5. *Who* and *whom*   When, as in the first example that follows, a pronoun acts as the subject of a sentence or clause, use *who* (the nominative case). When, as in the second example, the pronoun acts as the object of a verb or preposition, use *whom* (the objective case). You can test whether *who* or *whom* is correct by answering the question stated or implied in the *who/whom* portion of the sentence. The pronoun that answers *who/whom* will reveal which case to use:

"*Who/Whom* did you meet at the jazz festival"? → "I met *him* at the festival." → Since *him* is the objective case, use *whom*.

"The employees want to know *who/whom* will supervise the project." → "*She* will supervise the project." → Since *she* is the nominative case, use *who*.

Correct any problems with pronoun case that you find in the following sentences. Be careful, though; some pronouns are used correctly.

1. At this college, neither the president nor the dean automatically assumes that, on every issue, the faculty is better informed than us students.

2. Between you and I, each of the dorms should have their security systems replaced.

3. The theater critic, whom slipped into her seat right before the curtain went up, gave him and the other actors favorable reviews.

4. Neither of the boys impressed she or me with their musical ability.

5. The salesperson explained to my husband and I that each of the videocassette recorders had its drawbacks.

6. My grandfather, who found knitting relaxing, made me and my brother beautiful scarves and sweaters.

7. After enjoying prosperity through most of the 1980s, she and him were unprepared for the rigors of the next decade.

8. To whom did the theater manager give the free passes?

9. Many of us baby boomers came of age in an era of social activism.

10. The people who lived next door, me and my roommates concluded, had no intention of being neighborly.

11. The director of housing, whom we had contacted two months ago, finally asked us dorm residents to itemize our complaints.

12. The plot twisted and turned so much it was difficult for my sister and I to keep track of who cheated on who.

pro agr

Pronoun Agreement

A pronoun must **agree in number** with its **antecedent**—the noun or pronoun it replaces or refers to. If the antecedent is singular, the pronoun must be singular. If the antecedent is plural, the pronoun must be plural.

How to Correct Faulty Pronoun Agreement

The four situations described here often lead to problems with pronoun agreement. To deal with these problems, either *change the pronoun so it agrees in number and person with its antecedent* or *change the noun to agree with the pronoun you have used.*

1. Compound subject   A compound subject (two or more nouns joined by *and*) requires plural pronouns:

Correct   Both the oak *tree* and the rose *bush* had trouble regaining *their* strength after the storm.

However, when the nouns are joined by *or* or *nor*, whichever noun is closer to the verb determines whether the pronoun should be singular or plural:

Faulty Pronoun Agreement	Neither the oak tree nor the rose *bushes* regained *its* strength after the storm.
Correct	Neither the oak tree nor the rose *bushes* regained *their* strength after the storm.
Correct	Neither the rose bushes nor the oak *tree* regained *its* strength after the storm.

2. Collective nouns   Collective nouns represent a collection of people or things. Some examples are *company, university, team,* and *committee.* If the collective noun refers to a group or entity that acts as one unit, use the singular pronoun:

Faulty Pronoun Agreement	The *band* showed *their* appreciation by playing several encores.
Correct	The *band* showed *its* appreciation by playing several encores.

If, in this case, the singular pronoun form sounds awkward, simply make the antecedent plural. Then use the plural pronoun:

Correct   The band *members* showed *their* appreciation by playing several encores.

When the collective noun refers to members of a group who act individually, use a plural pronoun:

Correct   *The band* disagreed among *themselves* about the songs to be played.

3. Indefinite pronouns   Here is a list of singular indefinite pronouns:

Indefinite Pronoun	Possessive Form		Reflexive Form
anybody	his, her	his, hers	himself, herself
everybody	his, her	his, hers	himself, herself
nobody	his, her	his, hers	himself, herself
somebody	his, her	his, hers	himself, herself
anyone	his, her	his, hers	himself, herself
everyone	his, her	his, hers	himself, herself
no one	his, her	his, hers	himself, herself
someone	his, her	his, hers	himself, herself
either	his, her	his, hers	himself, herself
neither	his, her	his, hers	himself, herself
each	his, her	his, hers	himself, herself
one	one's		oneself

In everyday speech, we often use plural pronouns (*their* and *themselves*) because such pronouns cause us to picture more than one person. For example, we may say

"*Everyone* should bring *their* own computer disks." In formal writing, though, these indefinite pronouns are considered singular and thus take singular pronouns:

Correct

Each of the buildings had *its* [not *their*] lobby redecorated.

Neither of the ballerinas was pleased with *her* [not *their*] performance.

Using the singular form with indefinite pronouns may mean that you find yourself in the awkward situation of having to choose between *his* or *her* or between *himself* and *herself*. As a result, you may end up writing sentences that exclude either males or females: "Everybody in the mall seemed lost in *his* own thoughts." (Surely some of the shoppers were female.) To avoid this problem, you may make the antecedent plural and use the plural pronoun:

The *shoppers* in the mall seemed lost in *their* own thoughts.

(See pages 126–128 in Chapter 8 for other ways to avoid language that excludes one sex or the other.)

4. A shift in person   Within a sentence, pronouns shouldn't—as in the following sentences—disrupt pronoun-antecedent agreement by shifting person (point of view):

Faulty Pronoun Agreement

To drop a course, *students* [third person] should go to the registrar's office, where *you* [second person] obtain a course-change card.

Most of *us* [first person] enjoy eating out, but *you* [second person] can never be sure that a favorite restaurant won't lower its standards.

Such shifts are most often from the third or first person to the second person (*you*). In the first example, *you* should be *they*; in the second example, *you* should be *we*.

PRACTICE: CORRECTING PROBLEMS WITH PRONOUN AGREEMENT

Correct any problems with pronoun agreement that you find in the following sentences. Be careful, though; some pronouns are used correctly.

1. We proponents of the recycling plan challenged everyone on the town council to express their objections.

2. Officials have asked every man competing in the weight-lifting event to sign a statement saying that he has never used steroids.

3. All job applicants must call for an appointment, so that the personnel office can interview you.

4. The committee passed their resolution that each of the apartments was to be free of asbestos before occupancy.

5. Typically, one of the girls loses their schedule of upcoming games, so the coach always reminds the team of its next event at the start of each competition.

6. I like living in a small town because there's always someone who remembers you as a child.

7. The instructor reminded everyone in class to pick up their term papers before they left for the semester break.

8. Neither the bank manager nor the bank officers admitted to their error in approving the risky loan.

9. Despite poor attendance last year, the library staff decided once again to hold their annual party at the Elmhurst Inn.

10. Many amateur photographers like to use one-step cameras that you don't have to focus.

Pronoun Reference

pro ref

Besides agreeing with its antecedent in number and person, a pronoun must have a *clear antecedent*. A sentence that lacks clear **pronoun reference** is vague and ambiguous.

How to Correct Unclear Pronoun Reference

To make sure that each pronoun has an unmistakable antecedent, use the four strategies described here.

1. Leave no ambiguity about the noun to which a pronoun refers:

Unclear Antecedent   The newcomer battled the longtime champion for the tennis prize. In the end, she won. [Who won? The newcomer or the longtime champion?]

Correct   The newcomer battled the longtime champion for the tennis prize. In the end, *the newcomer* won.

2. Replace a pronoun that lacks an antecedent with the appropriate noun:

Omitted Antecedent   In his talk on child abuse, the caseworker pointed out the number of *them* mistreated by day-care employees. [*Them* is meant to refer to *children*, but this word doesn't appear in the sentence.]

Correct   In his talk on child abuse, the caseworker pointed out the number of *children* mistreated by day-care employees.

3. Make sure a pronoun doesn't refer to the possessive form of a noun or to an adjective:

Omitted Antecedent   In *journalists' articles, they* often quote unidentified sources. [*They* refers to *journalists*, which is in the possessive case.]

Correct   *Journalists* often quote unidentified sources in *their* articles.

4. Place pronouns near their antecedents:

Unclear Antecedent   The *dancers*, performing almost daily, traveled by bus and train.
                      The trip spanned several states. *They* returned exhausted and out
                      of debt.

Correct   Performing almost daily, traveling by bus and train on a trip that
                      spanned several states, the *dancers* returned exhausted. *They* were
                      also out of debt.

PRACTICE: CORRECTING PROBLEMS WITH PRONOUN REFERENCE

Correct any problems with pronoun reference that you find in the following sentences. Be careful, though; some pronouns are used correctly.

1. In Anne Tyler's novels, she gives us a picture of family life—at its best and at its worst.

2. To keep children away from dangerous chemicals, lock them in a storage closet.

3. The student sat down glumly as soon as the professor began to criticize his research paper. After a few moments, though, he turned away in frustration, trying to collect his thoughts.

4. Many patients' lawsuits against doctors end when they receive an out-of-court settlement.

5. All too often, arguments between a big and a little sister are ended by the younger one, when she threatens to blackmail her sister with some violation of household rules.

6. In Ibsen's *A Doll's House,* he dramatizes the story of a woman treated as a plaything.

7. The swirling of the magician's cape distracted the audience as he opened the trap door slowly.

8. Since the old man's morning was planned around reading the newspaper, he became upset when it was delivered late.

9. The supervisor explained to the employee that he would be transferred soon.

10. Although the school board members talked far into the night, they couldn't reach an agreement. Opinions on the principal's performance were mixed, with some highly positive and others sharply critical. They decided to continue the discussion the following week.

MODIFIERS

PROBLEMS WITH MODIFICATION

Misplaced and Ambiguous Modifiers

A **modifier** is a word or group of words that describes something else. Sometimes sentences are written in such a way that modifiers are **misplaced** or **ambiguous.** Here are examples of misplaced and ambiguous modifiers:

Misplaced Modifier   Television stations carried the story of the disastrous fire *in every part of the nation.* [The fire was in every part of the nation?]

Ambiguous Modifier   Singers who don't warm up *gradually* lose their voices. [What does the sentence mean: that singers who don't warm up will lose their voices gradually or that singers who don't gradually warm up will lose their voices?]

How to Correct Misplaced or Ambiguous Modifiers

We describe here two strategies for correcting misplaced or ambiguous modifiers.

1. Place the modifier next to the word(s) it describes:

Misplaced Modifier	We scanned the menu *with hungry eyes.* [The menu had hungry eyes?]
Correct	With hungry eyes, we scanned the menu.
Misplaced Modifier	The paramedics covered the boy's forehead with a cold compress, *which was bruised and swollen.* [The cold compress was bruised and swollen?]
Correct	The paramedics covered the boy's forehead, which was bruised and swollen, with a cold compress.
Misplaced Modifier	They *only* studied a few minutes for the exam. [Doesn't the word *only* describe a few minutes, not *studied*?]
Correct	They studied *only* a few minutes for the exam.

2. Rewrite the sentence to eliminate ambiguity:

Ambiguous Modifier   Giving money *frequently* relieves people's guilt about living well.

Writing the sentence this way could mean *either* that the frequent giving of money relieves guilt or that giving money relieves guilt frequently. Moving the modifier to the front of the sentence conveys the first meaning.

Frequently, giving money relieves people's guilt about living well.

The second meaning, however, can be conveyed only by rewriting the sentence:

Giving money *on a frequent basis* relieves people's guilt about living well.

dgl   Dangling Modifiers

An introductory modifier must modify the subject of the sentence. If it doesn't, the result is a **dangling modifier.** Here's an example of a dangling modifier:

Dangling Modifier   *Driving along the highway,* the blinding sun obscured our view of the oncoming car. [The sentence says that the sun was driving along the highway.]

How to Correct Dangling Modifiers

To eliminate a dangling modifier, you may *rewrite the sentence by adding to the modifying phrase the word being described* (as in the first corrected example that follows). Or you may *rewrite the sentence so that the word being modified becomes the sentence's subject* (as in the second corrected example):

Dangling Modifier	*While relaxing in my backyard hammock,* a neighbor's basketball hit me on the head. [The basketball was relaxing in the backyard?]
Correct	While *I* was relaxing in my backyard hammock, a neighbor's basketball hit me on the head.

or

Correct	While relaxing in my backyard hammock, *I* was hit on the head by my neighbor's basketball.

PRACTICE: CORRECTING PROBLEMS WITH MODIFICATION

Correct any misplaced, ambiguous, or dangling modifiers that you find in the following sentences. Be careful, though; not every sentence is incorrect.

1. While cooking dinner, the baby began to howl.

2. Swaying from the boughs of a tall tree, the children were intrigued by the ape's agility and grace.

3. When pondering her problems, it finally struck Laura that her life was filled with many pleasures.

4. At the end of the semester, I realized that I only needed tutoring in one course.

5. While waiting for the plumber, the hot-water tank began to leak all over the basement floor.

6. After swimming the entire length of the lake, the coach, much to his embarrassment, passed out.

7. Dogs and cats can scare small children wandering loose.

8. Faded and brittle with age, we read the old newspaper clipping with difficulty.

9. The reporters indicated that they only wanted a few minutes of the candidate's time.

10. With disgust, I threw the greasy hamburger into the trash can that had been dripping all over me.

11. Investigating the crime scene, the detectives made a surprising discovery.

12. An outfit that can only be worn once or twice a year isn't a practical investment.

13. Spinning wildly on the barn roof, the boys noticed an old copper weathervane.

14. We bought our dining room table at a discount store which cost less than one hundred dollars.

15. Pushing a shopping cart and muttering to herself, the homeless woman approached me warily.

PUNCTUATION

p

Correct **punctuation** is no trivial matter. Notice how a single comma alters the meaning of this sentence:

Their uncle would be the only visitor they feared.

Their uncle would be the only visitor, they feared.

The first sentence suggests that the uncle's visit is a source of anxiety; the second sentence suggests that the uncle is, unfortunately, the only person to pay a visit. So choose your punctuation carefully. Skillful punctuation helps you get your message across; careless punctuation can undermine your credibility and spoil an otherwise effective piece of writing.

In the pages ahead, we discuss, first, end punctuation (the period, question mark, and exclamation point) and then other punctuation marks (such as the comma, semicolon, and colon).

PERIOD (.)

The most frequent misuse of the **period** is at the end of a *fragment*—a word or group of words that doesn't constitute a full sentence, only part of one. (For more on sentence fragments, see pages 650–655 of the Handbook.) The correct uses of the period are outlined here.

1. At the end of full statements A period correctly completes any full sentence not worded as a question or exclamation:

> The dognappers were caught with three pets that they planned to sell to a medical laboratory.

> The campus senators asked when the college administrators would approve the new plan.

Although the second sentence reports that a question was asked, the sentence itself is a statement. For this reason, it ends with a period, not with a question mark.

2. With some abbreviations A period is also used to indicate a shortened form of a word; that is, an abbreviation:

Prof. (Professor)   Dec. (December)
Rev. (Reverend)   p.m. (*post meridiem*, Latin phrase meaning "after noon")

When an abbreviation ends a sentence, only one period is needed at the sentence's close:

> They didn't place the order until 3 a.m.

Some abbreviations, though, have no period at all. These include the abbreviated titles of organizations and government agencies, as well as the official U.S. Postal Service abbreviations for state names:

> NFL (National Football League)
> FDA (Food and Drug Administration)
> ME (Maine)

In addition, it is becoming increasingly acceptable to omit the periods in frequently used abbreviations—for example, *MTV* (Music Television) and *mph* (miles per hour). If you're in doubt whether to include a period in an abbreviation, consult a recent dictionary. Many dictionaries have a separate section that lists abbreviations.

3. In decimal numbers A period precedes the fractional portion of a decimal number:

> 5.38 (five and thirty-eight hundredths)

Since money is counted according to the decimal system, a period occurs between dollars and cents:

> $10.35

(For more information on writing numerals, see pages 703–704 of the Handbook.)

? QUESTION MARK (?)

1. At the end of direct questions   Just as a period concludes a statement, a **question mark** concludes a question:

> Where can a dorm resident find peace and solitude**?**
>
> The panelists debated the question, "Should drugs be legalized**?**"
>
> Did the consultants name their report "The Recycling Crisis"**?**

Notice that in the second example above, the actual question occurs only within the quotation marks. Therefore, the question mark is placed *before* the final quotation marks (and no final period is necessary). In the third example, though, the whole sentence is a question, so the question mark goes *after* the final quotation marks.

2. In parentheses, following an item of questionable accuracy   Whenever you're unable to confirm the accuracy of a name, date, or other item, indicate your uncertainty by following the item with a question mark enclosed in parentheses:

> The fraud, begun in 1977 **(?)**, was discovered only this year.

! EXCLAMATION POINT (!)

At the end of emphatic sentences   An **exclamation point** is placed at the end of a sentence to indicate strong emotion:

> That's the worst meal I've ever eaten**!**

Use exclamation points sparingly; otherwise, they lose their effectiveness.

, COMMA (,)

The **comma** is so frequent in writing that mastering its use is essential. By dividing a sentence into its parts, commas clarify meaning. Compare the following:

> As soon as we had won the contest was declared illegal.
>
> As soon as we had won**,** the contest was declared illegal.

The comma shows the reader where to pause in order to make sense of the sentence. The following pages discuss the correct use of the comma.

1. Between sentences joined by a coordinating conjunction When joining two complete sentences with a coordinating conjunction (*and, but, for, nor, or, so, yet*), place a comma *before* the coordinating conjunction:

My father loves dining out, *but* he is fussy about food.

It's permissible to omit the comma, though, if the two complete sentences are very short:

They lied *yet* they won the case.

☑ TWO CAUTIONS

☐ Don't, as in the sentences that follow, use a comma when the coordinating conjunction serves as the link between two verbs or nouns of equal weight.

Incorrect We *visit* the boardwalk, *and picnic* on the beach every summer. [delete comma between the verbs]

Incorrect The public *schools, and* the *banks* will be closed tomorrow. [delete comma between the nouns used as subjects]

Incorrect I gave him a *book, and* a *tie* for his birthday. [delete comma between the nouns used as direct objects]

☐ Don't, as in the following sentences, use a comma when a coordinating conjunction links words or phrases that cannot stand alone as sentences:

Incorrect Many people believe that herbal teas are medicinal, *and that drinking them will cure disease.* [delete comma]

Incorrect The summer house is beautiful, *but far from the beach.* [delete comma]

Incorrect We planned to paint the house white, *or beige.* [delete comma]

---

2. Between items in a series As the examples in the preceding box show, you do *not* use a comma between *two* items in a series. However, you *do* use a comma to separate *three or more* items in a series:

Bicycle racing requires practice, stamina, and determination.

It was a long, lonely, frightening drive to the cabin.

Notice that in both examples a comma appears before the last item in the series, whether or not this last item is preceded by *and* or *or.* (Although journalists and popular writers often omit the last comma in a series, its inclusion is expected in most other writing.)

However, if each item in the series is joined by *and* or *or*, do not place commas between them:

We didn't applaud *or* support *or* encourage the protesters.

3. Between adjectives of equal weight   A comma can substitute for the word *and* between adjectives of *equal weight* that describe the same noun:

Collecting exotic, colorful plants is one of my grandparents' hobbies.

In this sentence, the adjectives *exotic* and *colorful* contribute equally to the description of the noun *plants*. To test whether two adjectives have equal weight, reverse them or imagine the word *and* between them. If the sentence sounds fine, the adjectives have equal weight; thus, there should be a comma between them.

 CAUTION

☐ Don't, as in the sentence that follows, use a comma between adjectives of *unequal weight:*

Incorrect We bought a new, American-made stereo.

The fact that the stereo is *American-made* has more weight than the fact that it is *new*. Moreover, the sentence would sound strange if the adjectives were reversed or if *and* appeared between them. For these reasons, there should be no comma between *new* and *American-made*.

---

4. Setting off nonrestrictive word groups   When a word, phrase, or clause describes a noun but isn't crucial for identifying that noun, it is *set off* from the rest of the sentence *with a comma*. Such a word or group of words is considered **nonrestrictive,** or **nonessential.**

Here's an example:

The professor asked the class to read Twain's *Pudd'nhead Wilson*, a novel both droll and dark.

Because *Pudd'nhead Wilson* identifies the novel sufficiently, the phrase *a novel both droll and dark* is nonrestrictive and, thus, set off with a comma. If the nonrestrictive phrase appears midsentence, it is preceded and followed by commas:

The professor asked the class to read Twain's *Pudd'nhead Wilson,* a novel both droll and dark, by the end of the week.

In the next sentence, however, the book's title is *not set off by a comma* because the word group making up the title is **restrictive,** or **essential;** that is, it is needed for identification (Twain wrote more than one novel):

The professor asked the class to read Twain's droll and dark novel *Pudd'nhead Wilson.*

(For a discussion of restrictive and nonrestrictive clauses, turn to page 654 in the Handbook.)

5. Setting off words that precede the main body of the sentence   When introductory material precedes the sentence's main subject and verb, such material is usually followed by a comma:

Yes, I'll be happy to read the report.

Like most children, my little sister loves animals.

Because English Composition is a required course, sections are always filled.

If, however, the introductory material is very brief, you may often omit the comma:

Surely everyone has an urge to see exotic places.

6. Setting off words that follow the main body of the sentence   Material attached to the end of a sentence—after the main subject and verb—is preceded by a comma:

Many people think a walk is a waste of time, *like napping or daydreaming.*

You should start any new exercise program slowly, *making sure not to push yourself.*

7. Setting off interrupting words and phrases   Some words and phrases inserted into the body of a sentence can be removed without significant loss of meaning. Such *interrupting* elements are preceded and followed by commas when they occur midsentence:

Dr. Helen Rafton, *standing by the door and chatting with reporters,* is a celebrated botanist.

I told him, *when he mentioned the accident,* my version of what had happened.

The snowfall was heavy; classes, *however,* were held as usual.

☑ CAUTION

☐ Note that a *pair of commas* must be used to set off interrupting words or phrases that occur midsentence. A single comma, as in the following sentences, is *not* enough to set off interrupting elements:

Incorrect The high school reunion, scheduled for Memorial Day weekend should be well attended. [comma needed after *weekend*]

Incorrect They reported with considerable anxiety, the results of the test. [comma needed before *with*]

Incorrect The autumn day was surprisingly warm; we therefore, decided to go on a picnic. [comma needed before *therefore*]

In the last sentence, the transitional adverb *therefore* should be flanked by commas because it occurs *within* an independent clause. But when a transitional adverb comes *between* two independent clauses, it is preceded by a semicolon and followed by a comma (see page 658 in the Handbook).

---

8. Setting off words in direct address   Use a comma before and/or after the name of a person or group being addressed directly:

Ladies and gentlemen, the meeting is about to begin.

"Remember, Janet, to turn the thermostat down," my father always warned.

9. Between a short quotation and the phrase that indicates the quotation's source   Use a comma between a short quotation and a reference to its source or speaker:

My roommate remarked, "You remind me of a hungry bulldog."

"You can't block access to the building," the police informed the striking employees.

(For more on punctuating quotations, see pages 688–691 of the Handbook.)

10. Between the elements of a date or place   Use a comma to separate the nonnumerical portions of a mailing address, as well as the numbers in a date:

The witness testified that the package was delivered to 102 Glendale Road, Kirkwood, New Jersey 08043 on January 23, 1999.

Also, place a comma after the year if the date appears before the end of the sentence:

They were married on June 28, 1974, in New York City.

When you reverse the day and month in a date or give only the month and year or the month and day, do not use commas. Also, don't put a comma between a state and a ZIP code:

February 14, 1999
14 February 1999
February 1999
February 14
New York, NY 10022

PRACTICE: CORRECTING COMMA ERRORS

Where appropriate, provide or eliminate commas in the following sentences. Be careful, though; some of the commas belong just where they are.

   1. The local movie theater, despite efforts to attract customers finally closed its doors, and was purchased by a supermarket chain.
   2. As a little boy, I dreamed about wearing a plaid flannel shirt and, like Paul Bunyan, camping out underneath towering trees.
   3. Their parents, always risk takers divorced in August and remarried in February just six months later.
   4. Shaken by the threat of a hostile takeover, the board of directors, and the stockholders voted to sell the retail division which had been losing money for years.
   5. Despite my parents' objections I read Stephen King's novels *The Shining*, and *Carrie* when I was in junior high. The books terrified me; nevertheless, I couldn't put them down.
   6. We skimmed the chapter, looked quickly at the tables, and charts, realized we didn't know enough to pass the exam, and began to panic.
   7. After years of saving his money my brother bought a used car and then his problems started.
   8. I discovered last week, that my neighbors, whose friendship I had always treasured, intend to sue me.
   9. Late yesterday afternoon, I realized that Dan was lying, and had driven my car without permission.
10. Although it can be annoying, and frustrating, forgetting things usually isn't an early sign of Alzheimer's disease, as many people think.
11. "Going to New York" Maria said, "was like walking onto a movie set."
12. The long, pretentious report issued on May 11, 1992 neither analyzed the problem adequately, nor proposed reasonable solutions.
13. By going to a party alone a single person stands a better chance of meeting someone, and of having a good time.

14. Janet and Sandy her younger sister run three miles each day even in the winter.

15. Al pleaded "Let me borrow your notes and I'll never ask for anything again. I promise."

16. Mumbling under his breath, the man picked over the tomatoes, and cucumbers in the market's produce department.

17. All too often these days people assume that a bank statement is correct, and that there's no need to open the envelope, and examine the statement closely.

18. In the last two seconds of the game the quarterback seized the ball, and plunged across the goal line, scoring the game's winning point.

19. After the uprising was quelled, numerous dissidents were imprisoned but an unknown number remained at large, waiting for the right moment to stage a revolution.

20. Our psychology professor, who has an active, clinical practice, talked about the pressures, and rewards of being in a helping profession.

; | SEMICOLON (;)

1. Between independent clauses closely related in meaning   You may connect two independent clauses with a **semicolon,** rather than writing them as separate sentences. When you do, though, the clauses should be closely related in meaning. They might, for example, *reinforce* each other:

> Making spaghetti sauce is easy; most people can do it after only a few tries.

Or the clauses might *contrast* with each other:

> Many homebuyers harbor suspicious feelings about the real estate industry; most realtors, however, are honest and law-abiding.

Use of the semicolon is especially common when the *clauses* are *short:*

> Smile when you are introduced; nod or bow slightly to acknowledge applause; wait for silence; pause a second; then begin your speech.

You may also use a semicolon (instead of a period) between independent clauses linked by *transitions* (like *then* and *next*) or by *transitional adverbs* (such as *moreover* and *however*):

> We continually lost track of our sales; *finally,* a friend showed us a good accounting system.

> Customers kept requesting food items other than produce; *therefore,* the owners expanded their fruit and vegetable market into a general convenience store.

Note that when the second independent clause starts with a transitional expression, a comma is placed *after* the transition. However, if a comma is placed *before* the transition, a *comma splice* results (see pages 657–659 of the Handbook on ways to avoid comma splices).

2. Between items in a series, when any of the items contains a comma When individual items in a series have internal commas, another form of punctuation is needed to signal clearly where one item ends and another begins. For this purpose, use the semicolon:

> After dinner, we had to choose between seeing a movie classic, like *Casablanca, Rear Window,* or *It's a Wonderful Life;* playing Clue, Scrabble, or Monopoly; or working out at the gym.

3. Before coordinating conjunctions used to join independent clauses, when any of the clauses contains a comma Ordinarily, independent clauses joined by a coordinating conjunction (*and, but, for, nor, or, so, yet*) have a comma, not a semicolon, between them. However, when any such clause has internal commas, a semicolon is needed between the clauses:

> The mist settled in the valley, hiding the fields, the foliage, and the farms; and the pleasant road became a menace.

COLON (:)

1. To introduce an illustrative statement or list of examples Use a **colon** to introduce lengthy illustrative material—either a full statement or a number of examples—whenever that material is preceded by a full sentence:

> In the spring, the city has a special magic: Street musicians, jugglers, and ethnic festivals enthrall tourist and resident alike.

> Having nine brothers and sisters determined a number of my character traits: my love of solitude, my craving for attention, my resentment of anything secondhand.

As the first example shows, when the material following the colon can stand alone as a complete sentence, it begins with a capital letter (*Street*). Otherwise, as in the second example, the material after the colon starts with a lowercase letter (*my*).

2. To introduce a long quotation Use a colon when a complete sentence introduces a long quotation (five or more lines) that is set off in block (indented) form without quotation marks:

```
The witness to the accident told the police:
        I was walking to my car in the parking lot when I glanced
        over at the other side of the street. I saw the traffic
```

> light turn yellow, and a silver convertible started to
> slow down. Just then, a red station wagon came racing
> down the street. When the convertible stopped for the
> light, the station wagon kept going--right into the con-
> vertible's rear fender.

(See pages 583–586 in Chapter 21 for more information on the format for long and short quotations.)

3. After the opening of a business letter   Follow the opening of a business letter with a colon:

> Dear Ms. Goldwin:

Use a comma, however, in the salutation of a personal letter.

4. Between parts of certain conventional notations   A number of standard notations include colons. One example is time notation, with hours and minutes separated by a colon:

> 4:52 p.m.

In a ratio, a colon substitutes for the word *to:*

> By a ratio of 3:2, Americans prefer Glocko cleanser.

In a reference to the Bible, the colon separates chapter and verse numbers:

> Genesis 2:14

Titles and subtitles (of books, journal articles, short stories, works of art, films, and so on) are also separated by a colon:

> *Election Handbook: A Participant's Guide*

" "

QUOTATION MARKS (" ")

1. Direct quotations   A *direct quotation* reproduces exactly the wording, punctuation, and spelling of the source. It is also enclosed in *double* **quotation marks:**

> "Youngsters in elementary school should learn the importance of budgeting money,"
> the psychologist said.

A quotation within a quotation is enclosed in *single* (' ') quotation marks.

The psychologist said, "It was gratifying when my children told me, 'We're glad you taught us how to spend money sensibly.'"

 CAUTION

Indirect Quotations

☐ *Indirect quotations*—those referred to or paraphrased rather than reproduced word for word—*don't* get quotation marks:

Correct The psychologist said that even young children should be taught how to manage money wisely.

As in the preceding sentence, the word *that* is often used to introduce an indirect quotation. There is *no comma* before or after *that* in this case.

Use a comma between a short quotation and an identifying phrase like *they commented* or *he said*. Such phrases may be placed before, after, or within the quotation:

She argued, "They won't reject the plan."

"They won't reject the plan," *she argued*.

"They won't reject the plan," *she argued*, "if they understand its purpose."

When, as in the last example, the identifier interrupts the quotation midsentence, commas flank both sides of the identifier. But if the identifier comes between two quoted sentences, it is followed by a period:

"They won't reject the plan," *she argued*. "They understand its purpose."

 CAUTION

More on Punctuating Direct Quotations:

☐ Always place a period or comma *inside* the closing quotation marks:

Correct "You know what you meant to say," the instructor remarked, "but the reader doesn't."

☐ Always place a colon or semicolon *outside* the closing quotation marks:

Correct The article stated, "Rice is the major foodstuff of all Asian peoples"; in particular, the Japanese eat ten times more rice than Americans.

☐ Place question marks and exclamation points according to their context. If a quotation is itself a question or exclamation, the question mark or exclamation point goes *inside* the closing quotation marks. No other end punctuation is used:

Correct "Who's responsible for this decision?" the chief executive demanded. Each department head responded, "Not me!"

As the first sentence here shows, no comma is used when an identifying phrase follows a quoted question or exclamation.

If the entire sentence, not just the quotation, is a question or an exclamation, the question or exclamation mark goes *outside* the quotation marks, at the end of the entire sentence:

Correct

Who taught you to ask for things by saying "Gimme"**?**

I eagerly await the day when people will again say "Please" and "Thank you"**!**

☐ Use no punctuation other than quotation marks when a quotation is blended (with or without the word *that*) into the rest of a sentence:

Correct

People who believe that **"rules are made to be broken"** only substitute their own rules.

People who believe **"rules are made to be broken"** only substitute their own rules.

Capitalization in Direct Quotations

☐ Start a quotation with a capital letter if it is a full sentence:

Correct The author admitted, "**T**he classy-sounding pseudonym was a marketing strategy."

☐ Start a quotation with a lowercase letter if it is not a complete sentence, or if it is blended (with or without the word *that*) into the rest of your sentence:

Correct Using a "**c**lassy-sounding pseudonym" was, the author admitted, "**a** marketing strategy."

The author admitted that "**t**he classy-sounding pseudonym was a marketing strategy."

(For information on adding to or deleting from quotations, see pages 553–555 in Chapter 20.)

2. Titles of short works   Put quotation marks around the titles of short works—book chapters, poems, stories, articles, editorials, essays, individual episodes of a television or radio program—that are part of a larger work or series:

> The business professor spent almost two weeks discussing the chapter "Ethics in the Workplace."

> Kenneth Koch's poem "Mending Sump" parodies Robert Frost's "Mending Wall."

Titles of longer works are underlined or italicized (see pages 701–702 of the Handbook).

3. Calling attention to a word's use   To focus attention on a particular word or term, you may enclose it in quotation marks:

> The report started with a discussion of just what "sex education" signifies.

> People frequently say "between" when they should say "among."

Quotation marks also enclose words being used humorously or ironically:

> To celebrate their victory, the team members indulged in such "adult" behavior as pouring champagne over each other's heads.

> (See pages 701–703 of the Handbook on highlighting words with italics.)

ELLIPSIS (. . .)

An **ellipsis,** consisting of three spaced periods (. . .), indicates that *words* have been *omitted from quoted material.* To use the ellipsis correctly, follow the guidelines presented here.

1. When to use the ellipsis   You may use an ellipsis to shorten a quotation, as long as you don't distort its meaning:

Original

> The judge commented, "It won't surprise you to learn that this has been the most disturbing and the most draining case I have tried in all my years on the bench."

With Ellipsis

> The judge commented, "It won't surprise you to learn that this has been the most disturbing . . . case I have tried in all my years on the bench."

When you drop words from the end of a sentence or omit an entire sentence, the period that ends the sentence appears in its usual place, followed by the three spaced periods that signal the omission:

The judge commented, "It won't surprise you to learn that this has been the most disturbing and the most draining case I have tried. . . ."

Notice that in this case, there is no space between the last word in the sentence and the sentence's period.

2. When *not* to use the ellipsis   When you omit words from the beginning of a quotation, do not use an ellipsis; just begin your quotation at the point you've selected:

The judge commented, "This has been the most disturbing and the most draining case I have tried in all my years on the bench."

(For more on using the ellipsis, see pages 554–555, and 578–580.)

APOSTROPHE (')

1. In place of omitted letters   In standard contractions, an **apostrophe** replaces any omitted letters:

can't, don't, I'm, it's, she's, we've

Apostrophes also replace any letters dropped for the purpose of reproducing casual speech or slang:

"Keep singin' an' marchin'!" he shouted.

2. To indicate possession   To show the possessive form of most *singular nouns,* add *'s:*

The singer**'s** debut was a disaster.

Several of Salinger**'s** books have been banned from high school libraries.

The boss**'s** office was small and poorly lit.

For *plural nouns* ending in *s,* add only an apostrophe to show possession:

Students**'** grades improved after computer-assisted instruction.

Plural nouns that do *not* end in *s* need both an apostrophe and an *s* to show possession:

The children**'s** school was set on fire.

To show *joint possession* (two or more owners of the same thing), make only the last noun possessive:

Lubin and Wachinsky's firm handled the defense.

To show *individual possession* of more than one thing, make each noun possessive:

The girl**'s** and the boy**'s** parents urged them to date other people.

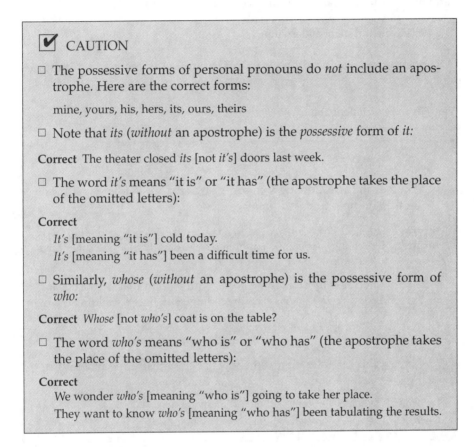

☑ CAUTION

□ The possessive forms of personal pronouns do *not* include an apostrophe. Here are the correct forms:

mine, yours, his, hers, its, ours, theirs

□ Note that *its* (*without* an apostrophe) is the *possessive* form of *it*:

Correct The theater closed *its* [not *it's*] doors last week.

□ The word *it's* means "it is" or "it has" (the apostrophe takes the place of the omitted letters):

Correct
It's [meaning "it is"] cold today.
It's [meaning "it has"] been a difficult time for us.

□ Similarly, *whose* (*without* an apostrophe) is the possessive form of *who*:

Correct *Whose* [not *who's*] coat is on the table?

□ The word *who's* means "who is" or "who has" (the apostrophe takes the place of the omitted letters):

Correct
We wonder *who's* [meaning "who is"] going to take her place.
They want to know *who's* [meaning "who has"] been tabulating the results.

Amounts (of time, money, weight, and so on) should also be written in possessive form when appropriate:

Employees can accumulate a maximum of a month's sick leave.

We could buy only five dollars' worth of gas.

3. To indicate some plurals   When a letter, symbol, or word treated as a word is made plural, an apostrophe often precedes the final *s*:

I got mostly C**'s** my first semester of college.

Her letters seem to shout; they contain so many !**'s**.

He uses too many *and***'s** to connect one thought to another.

However, common abbreviations such as *VCR, ESP,* and *SAT* don't take the apostrophe in the plural:

The local television station reported that residents sighted three *UFO*s last summer.

When you refer to a decade, you may omit the apostrophe:

The 1960**s** were turbulent and exciting.

An apostrophe is required only to replace omitted numerals that indicate the century:

The '60s were turbulent and exciting.

 CAUTION

☐ Don't, as in the following sentences, use an apostrophe when forming the simple plural of a noun:

Incorrect The *plant's* (or *plants'*) need to be watered. [delete apostrophe]
Incorrect The young people played three *radio's* (or *radios'*) at the same time. [delete apostrophe]

This kind of error is most likely to occur with a noun that is short (*plant*) or that ends in a vowel (*radio*). The preceding sentences should read:

Correct The *plants* need to be watered.
Correct The young people played three *radios* at the same time.

☐ Don't, as in the following sentence, use an apostrophe when forming the third-person singular form of the verb:

Incorrect The television *blare's* all day in many homes.
Correct   The television *blares* all day in many homes.

( )

PARENTHESES ( )

Parentheses enclose subordinate but related ideas, facts, or comments—items that would unnecessarily interrupt the sentence if set off by commas. A parenthetic remark may be located anywhere in a sentence except at the beginning, but it should immediately follow the item to which it refers. The presence of parentheses does not otherwise affect a sentence's punctuation. Here are some guidelines to follow when using parentheses.

1. A parenthetic sentence between two other sentences or at the end of a paragraph If you place a parenthetic sentence between two other sentences or at the end of a paragraph, simply write the parenthetic sentence as you normally would; then enclose it in parentheses. The sentence in parentheses should begin with a capital letter and end with a period or other end punctuation:

> Writing home from summer camp is a chore most youngsters avoid. (Some camps have children write home once a week.) Most parents, though, eagerly await letters from their kids.

2. At the end of a sentence   Material that extends or illustrates a sentence should be inserted in parentheses at the end of the sentence *before* the closing period. Such parenthetic material shouldn't start with a capital letter. Also, the parenthetic material doesn't have its own period.

> It is a cruel irony that everything I am allergic to is wonderful (like chocolate, roses, and dogs).

> It is a cruel irony that everything I am allergic to is wonderful (for example, I can't get enough of chocolate, roses, and dogs).

3. A parenthetic sentence inside another sentence   When parenthetic material that can stand alone as a full statement occurs within another sentence, the parenthetic material should *not* begin with a capital letter or end with a period:

> Watering a garden the right way (yes, there's a wrong way) is important.

If, however, the parenthetic material is a question, do end it with a question mark:

> Watering a garden the right way (you didn't think there was a wrong way?) is important.

4. After a word that would be followed by a comma   When you insert a parenthetic comment after a word that would otherwise be followed by a comma, move the comma to the end of the parenthetic element:

Original   Without sufficient water, the trees started to lose their leaves in July.

Parenthetic   Without sufficient water (only half an inch the whole month), the trees started to lose their leaves in July.

5. Enclosing numbers or letters assigned to items in a series   Use parentheses to enclose the numbers or letters assigned to items in a series. The items in a series are followed by commas:

> Before making a drastic change in your life, you should (1) discuss it with friends, (2) seek the advice of people who have had a similar change, and (3) determine whether a less dramatic change would be sufficient.

> Research indicates that (a) 58% of hospitalized patients improve, (b) 20% stay the same, and (c) 22% get worse.

6. Enclosing inserted dates and organizations' abbreviations When you add information such as dates and abbreviations to an otherwise complete sentence, enclose this information in parentheses:

Frank Lloyd Wright (1869–1959) was one of America's foremost architects.

Angry commuters founded Students for the Abolition of Privileged Parking (SAPP) and vowed to eliminate faculty-only lots.

BRACKETS [ ]

[ ]

1. To clarify a quotation When, for the purpose of clarification or correction, you insert your own words into a quotation, enclose them within **brackets:**

"In its entire history, the mining company [founded 1858] has never experienced a strike," the owner said.

"Research done at that laboratory [Sci-Tech] is suspect," the physician testified.

Use parentheses, not brackets, to insert a comment within your *own* sentence or paragraph.

2. To signal a linguistic irregularity within a quotation Quotations sometimes contain linguistic irregularities—such as colloquialisms or errors in spelling, grammar, or usage. In such cases, you may want to follow the irregularity with the Latin term *sic* in brackets, thus indicating that the questionable word or expression appears exactly as used by the quoted writer or speaker:

"None of the tenents [sic] complained about the building," the landlord wrote in a letter to the housing authority.

Note: When omitting words from a quotation, you should insert an ellipsis enclosed within brackets to indicate that *you*, rather than the original author, are inserting the ellipsis. (For information about the use of brackets when quoting material in a research paper, see page 554. For more on quotations, see pages 553–555, 578–586, and 688–690.)

HYPHEN (-)

-

A **hyphen** consists of one short line (and should not be confused with the dash—see page 698).

1. To break a word A word that is too long to fit at the end of a typed line may be divided between two syllables, with a hyphen indicating the break. (Check the dictionary if you're uncertain where the syllables begin and end.)

Once a clear contest between good and evil, between right and wrong, television wrestling now features stereotype-defying and ambiguous protagonists.

Most word-processing programs automatically either break long words at the end of lines or move them to the next line (called "word wrapping").

2. To combine words into an adjective or noun   When you combine two or more words to form a new adjective or noun, use hyphens between the original words:

The question is whether this country should maintain first-strike capability.

The only exception is a compound adjective that contains an adverb ending in *ly.* In this case, don't place a hyphen after the *ly:*

The poorly constructed VCR jammed within the week.

In a series of hyphenated compound adjectives or nouns all having the same final word, write that word only at the end of the series:

First-, second-, and third-year students must take one semester of gym.

3. Between a combined number and word   Hyphenate a numeral combined with a word:

The new car has a 2.6-liter engine.

4. After certain prefixes   Compound words beginning with *self* or *ex* take a hyphen after the prefix:

My ex-roommate is self-employed as a computer consultant.

So do words that, without the hyphen, would be misread as other words.

A growing number of young professionals live in co-ops.

5. To write certain numbers   Use a hyphen when writing most numbers composed of two words:

The zoning ordinance outlines twenty-one restrictions.

Note, however, that two-word numbers like *one hundred* and *two thousand* don't take a hyphen.

A hyphen is required when a fraction is used as a compound modifier:

The class was almost one-half empty.

(For more on writing numbers, see pages 703–704 of the Handbook.)

Dash (--)

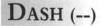

A **dash** (—) is composed of two (or three) typed hyphens (-- or ---). Don't leave a space between the hyphens or between the words that precede or follow the dash.

To highlight a thought or idea   A dash *signals* an *added* or *interrupting thought* and, unlike parentheses, highlights that thought. When the added thought occurs at the sentence's end, it is preceded by a single dash:

The package finally arrived--badly damaged.

When the added thought occurs midsentence, it receives two sets of two dashes, one set before the added thought and another after:

The ambassador--after serving for more than two decades--suddenly resigned her post.

PRACTICE: CORRECTING PROBLEMS WITH PUNCTUATION

Correct any punctuation problems that you find in the following sentences. Be careful, though; some of the punctuation marks belong just where they are.

1. The New Madrid fault, which lies in the central part of the country will be the site of a major earthquake within the next thirty years.

2. In the children's story, the hero carries a fresh, yellow rose rather than a sword.

3. I asked "Wasn't Uncle Pete drafted into the army in 1943?"

4. "Branch offices, and drive-in windows," the bank president announced, "will be closed January 4, the day of the governors funeral".

5. Some people avoid physical work; others seek out, and enjoy it. But, probably no one likes it all the time.

6. The scientists said that "they wondered how anyone could believe stories of outer-space visitors."

7. On one of the office's paneled wall's the executive had a framed copy of the poem, *If.*

8. Many children collect stamps according to a theme, like wildlife, aeronautics, or sports, but adults usually prefer to collect on the basis of stamps' rarity.

9. Shoplifters often believe they are doing no harm; nevertheless shoplifting is stealing and therefore, illegal.

10. The young people fell in love with the house, that stood next to a clear cold stream.

11. The kennel owner sent birthday cards' and small gifts to all the dog's she had boarded during the year.

12. The polished floor in the hallway, and dining room lost it's sheen after only a week.

13. According to the lawyer, the property is clearly ours' and not the other family's.

14. The celebration was loud, and unruly; finally police arrived at the scene around 11:00 p.m.

15. The parents know it's too early to tell whose children will need tutoring.

16. Did the visiting journalist make her speech, "Preserving a Source's Confidentiality?"

17. In the student handbook, the Dean wrote, "A student may be suspended for any of the following; using drugs, plagiarizing papers, cheating on exams, vandalizing college property . . ."

18. They asked us what courses we planned to take during the summer?

19. In the closet, (which hadn't been opened for years) we found three baseball bats, and half a dozen badminton sets.

20. Who's notes will you borrow to study for tomorrows exam.

MECHANICS

cap

CAPITALIZATION

Always capitalize the pronoun *I* and the first word of a sentence. Following are other **capitalization** guidelines.

1. Proper names   Whether they appear in noun, adjective, or possessive form, proper names are always capitalized. **Proper names** include the following: names of individuals; countries, states, regions, and cities; political, racial, and religious groups; languages; institutions and organizations; days, months, and holidays; historical periods; product brand names; fully specified academic degrees (Master of Science in Chemistry); and particular academic courses. Here are some examples:

> *Representative O'Dwyer*, a *Democrat* from the *Midwest*, introduced several bills in *Congress* last *March*.

> According to my *Marketing 101* professor, *Cuddles Cat Chow* set new sales records in the *Southwest*.

> All *Buddhists* are vegetarians.

> *Latin* and *Greek* regained widespread popularity during the *Renaissance*.

Do not capitalize the names of ideologies and philosophies, such as *communism* and *idealism* (unless the name is derived from that of an individual—for example, *Marxism*). Similarly, avoid capitalizing compass directions, unless the direction serves as the name of a region (the *West*, the *Northeast*) or is attached to the name of a continent, country, or city (*North America, South Angola, West Philadelphia*).

Finally, don't capitalize the following: seasons; animal breeds (unless part of the name is derived from that of a place—such as *French poodle* and *Labrador retriever*); types of academic degrees (*bachelor's, master's, doctorate*); or academic subjects and areas (*sociology, mathematics*), unless they're part of a course title or department name (*Sociology I, Mathematics Department*). Here are some more examples:

> On one side of the Continental Divide, rivers flow *east*; on the other, they flow *west*.
>
> In San Francisco, there is little temperature variation between *spring* and *summer*.
>
> Only one professor in the Psychology Department doesn't have a *doctorate*.

2. Titles of literary and other artistic works   When writing a title, capitalize the first word and all other words, except articles (*a, an, the*), conjunctions (*and, but*), and prepositions (*on, to*) of fewer than five letters.

> In *The Structure of Scientific Revolutions*, Thomas Kuhn discusses the way the scientific establishment resists innovation. However, Anna Stahl disputes Kuhn's argument in *The Controversy Over Scientific Conservatism*.

3. Official and personal titles   Capitalize official and personal titles when they precede a name or are used in place of the name of a specific person:

> Only *Reverend* Zager could stretch a sermon to an hour and a half.
>
> *President* Bush met with the Japanese delegation.
>
> Weeks before Father's Day, the stores start featuring gifts for *Dad*.

Do not capitalize such titles otherwise:

> The *reverend* encouraged the congregation to donate food and clothing to the poor.
>
> Citizens elect the *president* of the United States every four years.
>
> His *dad* writes for the local paper.

UNDERLINING AND ITALICS

ital

In machine-printed text, ***italicizing*** (*slanted type*) serves the same purposes as **underlining**.

1. Titles of individual works   Underline or italicize the titles of works that are published individually—not as part of a magazine, anthology, or other collection. Such works are often lengthy—entire books, magazines, journals, newspapers, movies, television programs, musical recordings, plays, and so on. They may, however, also be works of visual art, such as paintings and sculptures. Here are some examples:

> When I was a child, my favorite book was At the Back of the North Wind.

> The movie critic panned Friday the 13th, Part 83.

> Titled The Lost, the sculpture looks like a giant staple.

However, titles of certain historical documents and major religious writings, such as the books of the Bible, are neither italicized nor enclosed in quotation marks, but important words begin with a capital letter:

the Bible	Declaration of Independence
Song of Solomon	Bill of Rights
Old Testament	U.S. Constitution
the Koran	Monroe Doctrine

(See page 691 of the Handbook for ways to designate the titles of short works like poems and short stories.)

2. Foreign terms   Foreign words not fully incorporated into mainstream English should be underlined or italicized:

> Before protesters knew what was happening the legislation was a fait accompli.

3. For emphasis   Underline or italicize words you wish to stress, but do so sparingly because too many italicized words actually weaken emphasis:

> The campaign staff will never allow the candidate to appear in an open forum.

4. Letters and numbers referred to as words   Underline or italicize letters or numbers when they function as words:

> In the local high school, teachers give A's and B's only to outstanding students.

5. Calling attention to a word's use   To call attention to the way a word is being used, you may underline or italicize it:

> Why use conflagration when a simple word like fire will do?

> The most common prepositions are at, for and to.

(See page 701 of the Handbook for another way to highlight words.)

6. Vehicles of transportation   Underline or italicize the names of ships, planes, trains, and spacecraft:

A design flaw led to the explosion of the space shuttle <u>Challenger</u>.

NUMBERS

1. When to use words   Generally, *words* instead of numerals are used for **numbers** that can be written out in *one* or *two words*. When written out, numbers between 21 and 99 (except round numbers) are hyphenated (*twenty-one; ninety-nine*). If the number requires *three or more words,* use *numerals;* a hyphenated number counts as one word. Also use words for any number that occurs at the start of a sentence:

The store manager came up with *three* fresh ideas for attracting more customers.

They retired when they were only *forty-five.*

The paper reported that more than *six hundred* birds died in the forest fire.

Two hundred forty-eight people were on the hijacked plane.

You may prefer to rephrase a sentence that begins with a long number, so that you can use numerals instead of words:

The hijacked plane had *248* people on board.

2. When to use numerals   Numerals are generally used to indicate measurements:

The office was approximately *10 feet, 8 inches* wide.

Dates, times, addresses, page numbers, decimals, and percentages are also usually given as numerals. When a date includes the day as well as the month and year, give only the numeral to identify the day (for example, write *March 4,* not *March 4th; May 2,* not *May 2nd*):

The builder claims that the wood delivered on *August 3, 1989,* was defective.

Use numerals when a time reference contains *a.m.* or *p.m.* or specifies the minutes as well as the hour:

We set the alarm for *5 a.m.* and left the house by *5:45.*

However, use words with *o'clock:*

My roommate has trouble getting up before *eleven o'clock* in the morning.

In addresses, the house or building number is always given in numerals:

Last weekend, I visited my childhood home at *80 Manemet Road.*

For a numbered street, use numerals unless the number is less than ten or the building and street numbers would be written next to each other—a potential source of confusion:

The shelter moved from 890 East 47th Street to *56 Second Avenue*.

Always give page numbers as numerals. It's also standard to give percentages and decimal amounts in numerals:

Sales increased *5%* last year.

More than *2.5 million* boxes of oat bran were sold last year.

He lost *0.007 pound* on the supposedly miraculous new diet.

ab

ABBREVIATIONS

1. Personal and professional titles   The **abbreviations** for some personal titles appear *before* the person's name:

Dr. Tony Michelin   *Ms.* Carla Schim

Others come *after:*

Houston J. Marshall, *Esq.*   Nora Rubin, *MD*

Professional titles such as *Professor, Senator,* and *Governor* may be abbreviated only before a full name:

Prof. Eleanor Cross   Rep. George M. Dolby

Professor Cross   Representative Dolby

2. Common terms and organizations   Use the standard initials for common terms and widely known organizations:

VCR	MTV	AIDS
CIA	UFO	ESP
FBI	NATO	AT&T

Notice that these abbreviations do not include periods.

The first time you refer to a less familiar organization, give its full name, followed by the abbreviation in parentheses. Thereafter, you may refer to the organization with only the abbreviation. If the organization uses an ampersand (&) for *and* or abbreviations for terms such as *Incorporated* (Inc.) and *Company* (Co.), you may use them as well.

3. Time   Use the Latin abbreviations *a.m.* (*ante meridiem*) and *p.m.* (*post meridiem*) for time of day:

> They started work at *4 a.m.* and got home at *6:15 p.m.*

Use numerals with the abbreviations *AD* (*anno Domini*—"in the year of the Lord"), *BC* ("before Christ"), *CE* (the common era), and *BCE* (before the common era), unless you refer to centuries rather than specific years. In that case, write out the century before the abbreviation:

> The pottery was made around *AD 56,* but the tools date back to the *third century BC.*

Note that the year precedes BC (*684 BC*) but follows AD (*AD 1991*).

4. Latin terms   If you use the Latin abbreviations *i.e.* (for "that is") and *e.g.* (for "for example"), remember that they should be followed by a comma and used parenthetically:

> Employees are enthusiastic about recent trends in the business world (**e.g.,** the establishment of on-site day-care programs and fitness centers).

Whenever possible, however, replace these abbreviations with their English equivalents.

In addition, try to avoid *etc.* ("and so on") by citing all examples you have in mind, instead of leaving them up to the reader's imagination.

5. Names of regions   Except in addresses, don't abbreviate geographic regions:

> With a student rail pass, you can tour *Great Britain* [not *G.B.*] at discount rates.

Exceptions to this rule include *Washington, D.C.,* and *U.S.* when it is used as a modifier (*U.S. policy,* for example).

In addresses, states' names are abbreviated according to the postal designations—with two capital letters and no periods:

> NY   RI   NJ

6. Units of measure   Don't abbreviate common units of measure:

> The bedroom was *15 feet, 9-1/2 inches* wide.

> Among other extravagances, the couple offered guests *ten pounds* of imported caviar.

However, do abbreviate such technical units of measure as millimeters (*mm.*) and revolutions per minute (*rpm*).

(Turn to page 709 for a practice exercise on mechanics.)

SPELLING

SPELLING

Spelling need not be a mystery. For reference, always have on hand a recent standard dictionary or a spelling dictionary. If you use a word processor, an automatic "spell check" program may be valuable (though not always foolproof). Another strategy is to keep a personal inventory of the words you misspell or need to look up repeatedly (see page 134 for instructions). Finally, knowing about basic spelling rules and commonly misspelled words can help you minimize spelling errors. Here are some guidelines you should find helpful.

1. When *i* and *e* are adjacent Do you remember the rhyme for spelling a word with an adjacent *i* and *e*?

i before e	*except after c*	**or when pronounced like *a* as in *neighbor* and *weigh***
ach**ie**ve	c**ei**ling	b**ei**ge
p**ie**ce	conc**ei**ted	fr**ei**ght
th**ie**f	dec**ei**ve	r**ei**gn
y**ie**ld	rec**ei**ve	th**ei**r

The rule does *not* apply if the *i* and *e* are in separate syllables: *science, society*. It also does not apply to the following exceptions:

caff**ei**ne	inv**ei**gle	s**ei**ze
either	l**ei**sure	sl**ei**ght
financ**ie**r	n**ei**ther	spec**ie**s
for**ei**gn	prot**ei**n	w**ei**rd

2. Doubling the final consonant   This rule applies to words that satisfy the following conditions:

- The word's last three letters must be consonant, vowel, consonant *and*
- The word must be either one syllable (*plan*) or accented on the final syllable (*control*).

In such cases, double the final consonant before adding an ending that begins with a vowel (such as *-ed, -er, -al,* and *-ing*):

plan/plan**ned**	control/control**ler**
refer/refer**ral**	begin/begin**ning**

However, do *not* double the final consonant in the following cases:

- Words that end in a silent *e* (*pave/paved, mope/moping*)[5]
- Words ending in two vowels and a consonant or in two consonants (*appear/appearance, talk/talking*)
- Words whose accent is not on the final syllable (*develop/developing*)
- Words that no longer are accented on the final syllable when the ending is added (*refer/reference, prefer/preferable*). An exception is the word *questionnaire*, which does contain a double *n*.

3. Dropping the final silent *e*   For a word that ends in a silent (not pronounced separately) *e*, drop the *e* before adding an ending that begins with a vowel:

cope/cop**ing**	receive/receiv**able**
cute/cut**est**	guide/guid**ance**

But keep the *e* before an ending beginning with a consonant:

sincere/sincer**ely**	base/bas**ement**
definite/definit**ely**	nine/nin**ety**

Exceptions include the following: *truly, awful, argument; dyeing* and *singeing* (to avoid confusion with *dying* and *singing*); *changeable, courageous, manageable, noticeable,* and similar words where the final *e* is needed to keep the sound of the *g* or *c* soft.

---

[5]An exception is *write/written*. Note, however, that the *-ing* form of *write* is *writing*, not *writting*.

4. Adding to words that end in *y* For most words ending in *y*, change the *y* to *ie* before adding an *s:*

city/cit**ies**   study/stud**ies**   story/stor**ies**

Change the *y* to *i* before all other endings, except *-ing:*

copy/cop**ies**   cry/cr**ies**   study/stud**ies**

The *y* remains when the ending is *-ing:*

copy**ing**   cry**ing**   study**ing**

The *y* also stays when it is preceded by a vowel:

delay/dela**ys**/dela**yed**/dela**ying**

5. Words ending in *-f* and *-fe* Words ending in *-f* and *-fe* normally change to *-ves* in the plural:

leaf/lea**ves**   life/li**ves**
knife/kni**ves**   wife/wi**ves**

An exception is *roof,* whose plural simply adds an *-s.*

6. Common spelling errors **Homonyms** are words that sound alike but have different spellings and meanings. (A spelling dictionary will provide a complete list of homonyms and other commonly confused words.) If you're not sure of the differences in meaning between any of the homonym pairs listed, check your dictionary. Here are a few of the most troublesome:

accept/except	knew/new	their/there/they're
affect/effect	lose/loose	to/too/two
complement/compliment	principal/principle	whose/who's
its/it's	than/then	your/you're

Cognates are words with the same root. However, they may not always have the same spelling:

curious/curiosity   disaster/disastrous
generous/generosity   four/forty

Some words contain *silent* (or nearly silent) *letters* that are often erroneously omitted when the word is spelled:

environment   suppose**d** to
February   sophomore
government   use**d** to

Finally, avoid *nonexistent forms* of words. For example, there is no such word as *its'*; *a lot* is two words, not one; and few instructors consider *alright* an acceptable variant of *all right.*

Correct any mechanics or spelling problems that you find in the following sentences. Be careful, though; not every sentence contains an error, and some sentences may contain more than one.

1. "Emerging Nations in today's World," one of the supplementary texts in Modern History I, is on reserve at the libary.

2. Last year, while visiting my parents in central Florida, I took a disastrous coarse in Sociology.

3. The analysts of the election-eve pole concluded, "Its a toss-up."

4. For some reason, Spring tends to have a depressing affect on me.

5. Rev. Astor's teeth chattered at my brother's outdoor wedding, held in March in Northern Massachusetts.

6. Weighing in at 122 lbs. was Tim Fox, a sophmore from a community college in Ala.

7. In the fall, when the foliage is at it's peek, many people pack their hiking gear and head for the country.

8. 300 students signed up for the experimental seminar that Prof. Julia Cruz plans to offer through the Business Department. The class is scheduled to meet at eight a.m. on Monday.

9. Senator Miller, who was suppose to end the press conference once the subject of the enviroment came up, got embroiled in an arguement with several reporters.

10. Listen to nutritionists; many of them contend that their are advantages to limiting the amount of protein in you're diet.

11. My roommate, who's native language is French, recieved an award for writting a provocative series of articles on student pressures.

12. The President of the company distributed to key management 30 copies of the book How To win in Business. Many employees, though, are offended by the books emphasis on what it calls economic opportunism.

13. My parents always reminded me to watch my p's and q's. Not surprisingly, they were frequently complemented on my good behavior.

14. In the South during the summer months, it is light well after nine o'clock in the evening.

15. Prof. Mohr excepts no if's, and's, or but's when a student tries to hand in a paper past it's due date.

ACKNOWLEDGMENTS

Angelou, Maya. "Sister Flowers." From *I Know Why the Caged Bird Sings* by Maya Angelou. Copyright © 1969 and renewed 1997 by Maya Angelou. Reprinted by permission of Random House, Inc.

Barry, Dave, "The Ugly Truth about Beauty." From *The Miami Herald*, copyright © 1998 by Tribune Media Services, Inc. All Rights Reserved. Reprinted with permission.

Bryson, Bill, "Your New Computer." From *I'm a Stranger Here Myself* by Bill Bryson, copyright © 1999 by Bill Bryson. Used by permission of Broadway Books, a division of Random House, Inc.

Cole, Diane. "Don't Just Stand There." From *The New York Times*, 1982. Reprinted by permission of the author.

Cole, K. C. "Entropy." From *The New York Times*, March 18, 1982. Copyright © 1982 by The New York Times Company. Reprinted by permission.

Darley, John M., and Bibb Latané. "Why People Don't Help in a Crisis." From *Psychology Today*, December 1968. Reprinted with permission from Psychology Today Magazine, Copyright © 1968 (Sussex Publishers, Inc.).

Douglas, Susan. "Managing Mixed Messages." From *Where the Girls Are* by Susan Douglas. Copyright © 1994 by Susan J. Douglas. Reprinted by permission of Times Books, a division of Random House, Inc.

Frost, Robert. "Out, Out—" Copyright © 1916 by Holt, Rinehart, and Winston. Reprinted by permission of Henry Holt & Company, Inc.

Garity, Joyce. "Is Sex All That Matters?" Reprinted by permission of Joyce Garity.

Gleick, James, "Life As Type A." From *Faster* by James Gleick. Copyright © 1999 by James Gleick. Reprinted by permission of Pantheon Books, a division of Random House, Inc.

Goodman, Ellen. "Family Counterculture." From *The Boston Globe*, August 16, 1991 © 1991, The Boston Globe Newspaper Co./Washington Post Writers Group. Reprinted with permission.

Hughes, Langston. "Early Autumn." From *Short Stories* by Langston Hughes. Copyright © 1996 by Ramona Bass and Arnold Rampersad. Reprinted by permission of Hill and Wang, a division of Farrar, Straus & Giroux, Inc.

Jacoby, Susan, "Common Decency." Copyright © 1991 by Susan Jacoby. Originally appeared in *The New York Times*. Reprinted by permission of Georges Borchardt, Inc. on behalf of the author.

Johnson, Beth, "Bombs Bursting in Air." Reprinted by permission of the author. Beth Johnson lives in Lederach, PA.

King, Stephen, "Why We Crave Horror Movies." Originally appeared in *Playboy*, 1982. Reprinted by permission. © Stephen King. All rights reserved.

Leo, John. "Absolutophobia." From *U.S. News & World Report*, July 21, 1997. Copyright, July 21, 1997, *U.S. News & World Report*.

Liu, Sophronia, "So Tsi-Fai." First published in *Hurricane Alice 2*, No. 4 (Fall 1986). Copyright © 1986 by Sophronia Liu. Reprinted by permission of the author.

Lorde, Audre. "The Fourth of July." Reprinted with permission from *Zami: A New Spelling of My Name* by Audre Lorde. © 1982. Published by The Crossing Press: Santa Cruz, CA.

Lutz, William, "Doublespeak." From *Dourblespeak* by William Lutz. Copyright © 1989 by Blonde Bear, Inc. Reprinted by permission of HarperCollins Publishers, Inc.

McClintock, Ann. "Propaganda Techniques in Today's Advertising." Reprinted by permission of the author.

Morrison, Toni. "A Slow Walk of Trees." From *The New York Times*, July 4, 1976. Reprinted by permission of International Creative Management, Inc. Copyright © 1976 by Toni Morrison.

Orwell, George. "Shooting an Elephant." From *Shooting an Elephant and Other Essays* by George Orwell, copyright 1950 by Sonia Brownell Orwell and renewed 1978 by Sonia Pitt-Rivers, reprinted by permission of Harcourt, Inc.

Paglia, Camille, "Rape: A Bigger Danger Than Feminists Know." Reprinted by permission of the author.

Parks, Gordon, "Flavio's Home." From *Voices in the Mirror* by Gordon Parks. Copyright © 1990 by Gordon Parks. Used by permission of Doubleday, a division of Random House.

Rhodes, Richard. "Watching the Animals." Copyright © 1971 by Richard Rhodes. Originally published in *Harper's*. Reprinted by permission of the author.

Schlesinger, Arthur, Jr. "The Cult of Ethnicity: Good and Bad." From *Time*, July 8, 1991. © 1991 Time Inc. Reprinted by permission.

Sherry, Mary, "In Praise of the 'F' Word." From *Newsweek*, May 6, 1991. Reprinted with permission of the author.

Staples, Brent. "Black Men and Public Space." Reprinted by permission of the author.

Stoll, Clifford. "Why Computers Don't Belong in the Classroom." From *High-Tech Heretic* by Clifford Stoll, copyright © 1999 by Clifford Stoll. Used by permission of Doubleday, a division of Random House, Inc.

Suina, Joseph. "And Then I Went to School." From *Linguistic and Cultural Influences on Learning Mathematics* by Cocking and Mestre. Reprinted by permission of Joseph Suina and Lawrence Erlbaum Associates, Inc.

Tannen, Deborah. "But What Do You Mean?" From *Talking from 9 to 5* by Deborah Tannen. Copyright © 1994 by Deborah Tannen. Reprinted by permission of HarperCollins Publishers, Inc.

White, E. B. "Once More to the Lake." From *One Man's Meat*, text copyright © 1941 by E. B. White. Reprinted by permission of Tilbury House Publishers, Gardiner, Maine.

Woolf, Virginia. "The Death of the Moth." From *The Death of the Moth and Other Essays* by Virginia Woolf, copyright 1942 by Harcourt Brace & Company and renewed 1970 by Marjorie T. Parsons, Executrix, reprinted by permission of the publisher.

Yahoo! home page and Disability Legal Issues page. Reproduced with permission of Yahoo! Inc. © 2000 by Yahoo! Inc. YAHOO! and the YAHOO! logo are trademarks of Yahoo! Inc.

Yuh, Ji-Yeon. "Let's Tell the Story of All America's Cultures." From the *Philadelphia Inquirer,* June 30, 1991. Reprinted with permission from *The Philadelphia Inquirer.*

INDEX

BRIEF CONTENTS

Taken from: *Workplace Communications: The Basics,* Second Edition by George J. Searles

APPENDICES

BUSINESS
COMMUNICATIONS
APPENDICES

A

The Keys to Successful Communication: Purpose, Audience, and Tone

Learning Objective When you complete this chapter you'll be able to identify your communication purpose and your audience, thereby achieving the appropriate tone in every workplace writing situation.

- Purpose
- Audience
- Tone
- Exercises

Every instance of workplace writing occurs for a specific reason and is intended for a particular individual or group. Much the same is true of spoken messages, whether delivered in person or over the telephone. Therefore, there is always both a purpose and an audience to take carefully into account, to ensure that the tone of the exchange will be appropriate to the situation. Although this may seem obvious, awareness of purpose, audience, and tone is the single most crucial factor determining whether your communication will succeed. This opening chapter concentrates on these fundamental concerns, presents a brief overview of the basic principles involved, and provides exercises in their application.

Purpose

Nearly all workplace writing is done for one or more of three purposes: to create a record, to request or provide information, or to persuade. A caseworker in a social services agency, for example, might interview an applicant for public assistance to gather information that will then be reviewed in determining the applicant's eligibility. Clearly, such writing is intended both to provide information and to create a record. The purchasing director of a manufacturing company, on the other hand, might write a letter inquiring whether a particular supplier can provide materials more cheaply than the current vendor. The supplier will likely reply promptly. Obviously, the primary purpose of both letters is to exchange information. In yet another setting, a probation officer composes a pre-sentencing report intended to influence the court to grant probation to the offender or impose a jail sentence. The officer may recommend either, and the report will become part of the offender's record, but the primary purpose of this example of workplace writing is to persuade.

The first step in the writing process is to consciously identify which of the three categories of purpose applies. You must ask yourself, "Am I writing primarily to create a record, to request or provide information, or to persuade?" Once you make this determination, the question becomes, "Summarized in one sentence, what am I trying to say?" To answer, you must zoom in on your subject matter, focusing on the most important elements. A helpful strategy is to employ the "Five W's" that journalists use to structure the opening sentences of newspaper stories: Who, What, Where, When, Why. Just as they do for reporters, the Five W's will enable you to get off to a running start. Consider, for example, how the Five W's technique applies in each of the following situations:

- *Caseworker writing to provide information and create a record*

  WHO   WHAT   WHERE

  Carolyn Matthews visited the downtown office of the County

            WHEN WHY

  Social Services Department on May 15 to apply for public assistance.

- *Purchasing director writing to request information*

          WHO   WHAT

  I'd like to know whether you can provide gaskets for less than

             WHERE   WHEN

  $100/dozen, shipped to my company on a monthly basis,

      WHY

  because I am seeking a new supplier.

- *Probation officer writing to persuade*

      WHO   WHAT

  Jerome Farley should be denied probation and sentenced to

   WHERE   WHEN   WHY

  state prison, effective immediately, because he is a repeat offender.

Audience

Next ask yourself, "Who will read what I have written?" This is a crucial aspect of the communications process. To illustrate, consider these introductory paragraphs from two articles on the subject of breast cancer. The first excerpt is from *Good Housekeeping*, a popular monthly magazine, while the second is from *Cancer*, the medical journal of the American Cancer Society.

> In the last five years or so, we've made a great deal of progress in breast cancer prevention. While we still have more questions than answers, the questions themselves are significant—and we're closer to the answers than we've ever been.
>
> The issues of prevention are growing more important as we're becoming more able to identify people who have hereditary and genetic breast cancer. That isn't theoretical risk, but actual risk. The hope is that someday we'll be able to say, for example, "You have a fifty percent risk by age forty and an eighty percent risk by age eighty." Once someone knows that, she's really going to want to find some form of prevention.

From Susan Love, M.D., "Your Best Self-Defense Against Breast Cancer," *Good Housekeeping* May 1995: 72.

To be useful, breast-conserving therapy must provide not only survival equivalent to mastectomy but also low rates of local recurrence, satisfactory cosmetic results, and a low risk of complications. Prospective randomized trials have established that breast-conserving therapy and mastectomy provide equivalent survival rates. The precise criteria required to assure a low rate of local recurrence, however, are still controversial. Various factors have been identified that affect the rate of recurrence in the breast after breast-conserving therapy. Among these, the major factors are the presence or absence of carcinoma at the inked margins of resection (margins), the volume of excision, and the presence or absence of an extensive intraductal component (EIC).

From Irene Gage, M.D., *et al.*, "Pathologic Margin Involvement and the Risk of Recurrence in Patients Treated with Breast-Conserving Therapy," *Cancer* 78.9 (1 November 1996): 1921–1928.

Anyone can immediately recognize the differences between these two pieces of writing. Obviously, the *Good Housekeeping* coverage is general in nature, employs simple vocabulary and no technical terms, and is therefore easy to follow. The *Cancer* article, on the other hand, with its highly specialized content and terminology, is much more challenging. Even the *titles* of the two articles reflect these contrasts. The reason for the differences is that a popular magazine like *Good Housekeeping* is intended for the general public, while a professional journal like *Cancer* is written specifically for highly educated experts. Both articles were written by recognized authorities (the author of the first article was also a co-author of the second), and the purpose of both articles is to inform. But the two publications are targeted at entirely different audiences, hence the dramatic dissimilarity between the two excerpts. This dissimilarity makes sense. For the *Good Housekeeping* piece to be significantly more sophisticated, or for the *Cancer* piece to be any less so, would be inappropriate. Each is well suited to its readership.

Workplace communications are governed by this same dynamic. A memo, letter, report, or oral presentation must be tailored to its intended audience; otherwise, it probably will not achieve the desired results. Therefore, ask yourself the following questions before attempting to prepare any sort of formal communication:

- Am I writing to one person or more than one?
- What are their job titles and/or areas of responsibility?
- What is the level of their education and/or technical expertise?
- What do they already know about the topic?
- Why do they need this information?

- What do I want them to do as a result of receiving it?
- What factors may influence their response?

Obviously, these questions are closely related, so the answers will sometimes overlap. Nevertheless, by profiling your readers or listeners in this way, you'll come to see the subject of your planned communication from the viewpoint of your audience as well as from your own. You'll be better able to state the purpose of your communication, provide necessary details, cite meaningful examples, achieve the correct level of formality, and avert possible misunderstandings, thereby achieving your desired outcome.

In identifying your audience, remember that workplace communications fall into four broad categories:

- ***Upward communication:*** Intended for those above you in the workplace hierarchy.

- ***Lateral communication:*** Intended for those at your own level.

- ***Downward communication:*** Intended for those below you in the hierarchy.

- ***Outward communication:*** Intended for those outside your workplace.

These differences will influence your communications in many ways, particularly by determining format. For in-house communications (the first three categories) the memo has traditionally been the preferred medium and is now almost always electronically generated by in-house computer networks. For outward communication, such as correspondence with clients, customers, or the general public, the standard business letter has been the norm. Business letters are either mailed or transmitted by a fax machine. If, however, you're corresponding with another workplace with which you're linked via computer network, e-mail is obviously the fastest, most efficient choice.

 # Tone

Your hierarchical relationship to your reader will play a major role in determining the *tone* of your communication as well. This is especially true when you're attempting to convey "bad news" (the denial of a request from an employee whom you supervise, for example) or to suggest that staff members adopt some new or different procedure. Although such messages can be phrased in a firm, straightforward manner, a harsh voice or belligerent attitude is seldom productive.

The workplace is essentially a set of individuals and relationships, busy people working together to accomplish a common goal: the mission of the business, organization, or agency. A high level of cooperation and collective commitment is needed for this to happen. Ideally, each person exerts a genuine effort to foster a climate of shared enthusiasm and commitment. When co-workers become defensive or resentful, morale problems inevitably develop, undermining productivity. In such a situation, everyone loses.

Therefore, do not try to sound tough or demanding when writing memos about potentially sensitive issues. Instead, appeal to the reader's sense of fairness and cooperation. Phrase your sentences in a nonthreatening way, emphasizing the reader's point of view by using a reader-centered (rather than a writer-centered) perspective. For obvious reasons, this approach should govern your correspondence intended for readers outside the workplace.

Here are some examples of how to create a reader-centered perspective by means of creative revision:

Writer-Centered Perspective	Reader-Centered Perspective
If I can answer any questions, I'll be happy to do so.	If you have any questions, please ask.
We shipped the order this morning.	Your order was shipped this morning.
I'm happy to report that . . .	You'll be glad to know that . . .

Notice the use of *you* and *your* to personalize the communication, which we'll refer to as the "you" approach. Always remember *please, thank you,* and other polite terms.

Now consider Figures 1.1 and 1.2. Both memos have the same purpose, to change a specific behavior, and both address the same audience. But the first version adopts a writer-centered approach and is harshly combative. The reader-centered revision, on the other hand, is diplomatic and therefore much more persuasive. The first is almost certain to create resentment and hard feelings, while the second is far more likely to achieve the desired results.

EASTERN MANUFACTURING, INC.

MEMORANDUM

DATE: March 11, 2003

TO: All Employees

FROM: Brian Johnson, Supervisor
             Maintenance

SUBJECT: Littering

For some time now, smoking has been strictly prohibited inside the Main Building. Do NOT smoke anywhere indoors!

Some of you still insist on smoking and have been doing so outside. As a result, the areas near the rear exit and around the picnic tables are constantly littered with smoking-related debris (filter tips, half-smoked cigarettes, matchbooks, etc.), creating an eyesore and making more work for my staff, who have to keep cleaning up this mess.

Starting Monday, sand buckets will be provided outside the rear doors and in the picnic area. Use them!

FIGURE 1.1   Original Memo

In most settings you can adopt a somewhat more casual manner with your equals and with those below you than you can with those above you in the chain of command or with persons outside the organization. But in any case avoid an excessively conversational style. Even when the situation is not particularly troublesome, and even when your

EASTERN MANUFACTURING, INC.
MEMORANDUM

DATE: March 11, 2003

TO: All Employees

FROM: Brian Johnson, Supervisor
             Maintenance

SUBJECT: Outdoor Ashtrays

Because the Main Building is a No Smoking zone, some of you have been taking your breaks outdoors.

We appreciate your compliance with company regulations and wish to minimize your inconvenience. As of Monday, sand bucket "ashtrays" will be provided for your use outside the rear doors and near the picnic tables. This will help maintain a more pleasant atmosphere for us all by minimizing litter behind the building.

Again, thanks very much for your cooperation!

FIGURE 1.2   **Revised Memo**

reader is well known to you, remember that "business is business." Although you need not sound stuffy, it is important to maintain a certain level of formality. Accordingly, you should never allow personal matters to appear in workplace correspondence. Consider, for example, Figure 1.3, a memo in which the writer has obviously violated this rule. Although the writer's tone toward his supervisor is appropriately respect-

Tech Tips

A slangy, vernacular style is out of place in workplace writing, as are expletives and any coarse or vulgar language. Something that may seem clever or humorous to you may not amuse your reader and will probably appear foolish to anyone reviewing the correspondence later on. Keep this in mind when sending computer-generated messages via e-mail, a medium that seems to encourage a looser, more playful manner of interaction. Typical of this are e-mail emoticons, silly "faces" created by combinations of punctuation marks, like these:

:-)   :-(;-)
Smile   Frown   Wink

Briefly popular when first devised, they now distract or annoy most serious readers, undermining the writer's credibility.

In a similar vein you should avoid overdependence on abbreviations and acronyms (words composed of the initial letters of a phrase or expression). Probably the best-known examples are ASAP (as soon as possible), FYI (for your information), and NRN (no reply necessary). Although these acronyms are universally recognized and therefore useful, a great many others—far less familiar—have become popular in Internet chat rooms and other informal on-line settings. Most are inappropriate for the workplace because they may not be readily understood. Here are 10 examples:

BTW: by the way   IRL: in real life
FAQ: frequently asked questions   OTOH: on the other hand
FWIW: for what it's worth   TMOT: trust me on this
IMHO: in my humble opinion   TTYTT: to tell you the truth
IOW: in other words   WADR: with all due respect

Although such constructions may seem appealing at first glance, they can easily create confusion. As with emoticons, stay away from them.

ful, the content of his memo should be far less detailed. The revised version in Figure 1.4 is therefore much better.

A sensitive situation awaits you when you must convey unpleasant information or request assistance or cooperation from superiors. Although you may sometimes yearn for a more democratic arrangement, every workplace has a pecking order that you must take into account as you choose your words. Hierarchy exists because some individuals—by virtue of greater experience, education, or access to information—are in

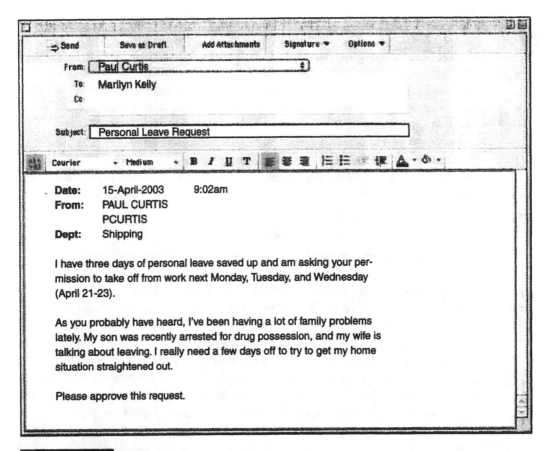

FIGURE 1.3   Original Memo

fact better positioned to lead. Although this system sometimes functions imperfectly, the supervisor, department head, or other person in charge will respond better to subordinates whose communications reflect an understanding of this basic reality. Essentially, the rules for writing to a person higher on the ladder are the same as for writing to someone on a lower rung. Be focused and self-assured, but use the "you" approach, encouraging the reader to see the advantage in accepting your recommendation or granting your request.

An especially polite tone is advisable when addressing those who outrank you. Acknowledge that the final decision is theirs and that you are fully willing to abide by that determination. This can be achieved either through "softening" words and phrases ("perhaps," "with your per-

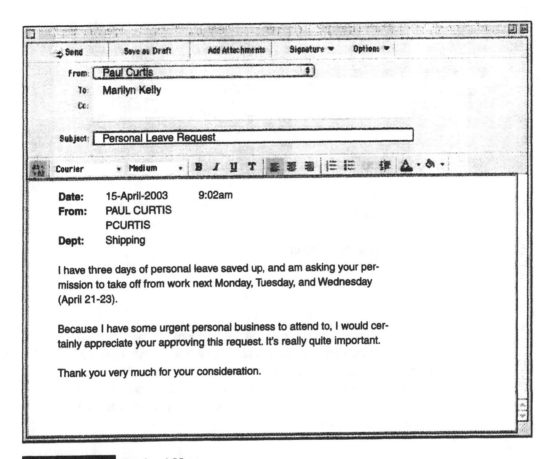

FIGURE 1.4   **Revised Memo**

mission," "if you wish") or simply by stating outright that you'll accept whatever outcome may develop. Consider, for example, the memos in Figures 1.5 and 1.6. Although both say essentially the same thing, the first memo is completely inappropriate in tone, so much so that it would likely result in negative personal consequences for the writer. The second memo would be much better received because it properly reflects the nature of the professional relationship between writer and reader.

Communicating with customers or clients also requires a great deal of sensitivity and tact. When justifying a price increase, denying a claim, or apologizing for a delay, you will probably create an unpleasant climate unless you present the facts in an unantagonistic manner. Always strive for the most upbeat, reader-centered wording you can devise. Here

Western Trucking, Inc.

MEMORANDUM

DATE: May 19, 2004

TO: Anne Scott, Supervisor
            Dispatching

FROM: Thomas Kearney, Driver

SUBJECT: Drug Testing

Just wanted to let you know that you'd better forget about the random drug-testing policy you announced in your memo yesterday. It's a dumb idea that will never work. All the drivers are angry about it, and there are a lot of questions that your memo left completely unanswered! From what I hear, people in other departments have a lot of questions too. Better clear some of this stuff up or nobody's ever going to hold still for it.

| FIGURE 1.5 | Original Memo |

---

are some examples of how to rephrase negative content in more positive, reader-centered terms:

Negative Wording	Positive Wording
We cannot process your claim because the necessary forms have not been completed.	Your claim can be processed as soon as you complete the necessary forms.

Western Trucking, Inc.

MEMORANDUM

DATE: May 19, 2004

TO: Anne Scott, Supervisor
            Dispatching

FROM: Thomas Kearney, Driver

SUBJECT: Drug Testing

There is some confusion about the new drug testing policy that was announced yesterday. Probably as a result of that misunderstanding, there also appears to be some resistance to the plan.

If you'll permit me a suggestion, it might be a good idea to schedule a brief meeting with the employees to offer information, address their concerns, and clarify some of the more troubling features of the policy.

Thank you for considering this idea, and please let me know if I can assist in any way.

FIGURE 1.6   **Revised Memo**

Negative Wording	Positive Wording
We do not take phone calls after 3:00 p.m. on Fridays.	You may reach us by telephone until 3:00 p.m. on Fridays.
We closed your case because we never received the information requested in our letter of April 2.	Your case will be reactivated as soon as you provide the information requested in our April 2 letter.

When the problem has been caused by an error or oversight on your part, be sure to apologize. However, do not state specifically what the mistake was, or your letter may be used as evidence against you should a lawsuit ensue. Simply acknowledge that a mistake has occurred, express regret, explain how the situation will be corrected, and close on a conciliatory note. Consider, for example, the letter in Figure 1.7. The body and conclusion are fine, but the introduction practically invites legal action. Here's a suggested revision of the letter's opening paragraph, phrased in less incriminating terms:

> Thank you for purchasing our product and for taking the time to contact us about it. We apologize for the unsatisfactory condition of your Superior microwave dinner.

Moreover, given the serious nature of the complaint, the customer services representative should certainly have made a stronger effort to establish a tone of sincerely apologetic concern. As it stands, this letter seems abrupt and rather impersonal—certainly not what the context requires. (For a much better handling of this kind of situation, see the adjustment letter in Figure 2.10.)

By determining your purpose and carefully analyzing your intended audience, you will achieve the correct tone for any communication situation. As we have seen, this is crucial when dealing with potentially resistive readers (especially those above you in the workplace hierarchy) and when rectifying errors for which you are accountable. In all instances, however, a courteous, positive, reader-centered approach gets the best results.

Superior Foods, Inc.

135 Grove St., Atlanta, GA 30300 • (324) 555-1234

October 12, 2003

Mr. Philip Updike
246 Alton St.
Atlanta, GA 30300

Dear Mr. Updike:

We are sorry that you found a piece of glass in your Superior microwave dinner. Please accept our assurances that this is a very unusual incident.

Here are three coupons redeemable at your local grocery market for complimentary Superior dinners of your choice.

We hope you will continue to enjoy our fine products.

Sincerely,

John Roth

John Roth
Customer Services Dept.

Enclosures (3)

FIGURE 1.7   **Letter to Customer**

Exercises

■ **EXERCISE 1.1**

Revise each of the following three memos to achieve a tone more appropriate to the purpose and audience.

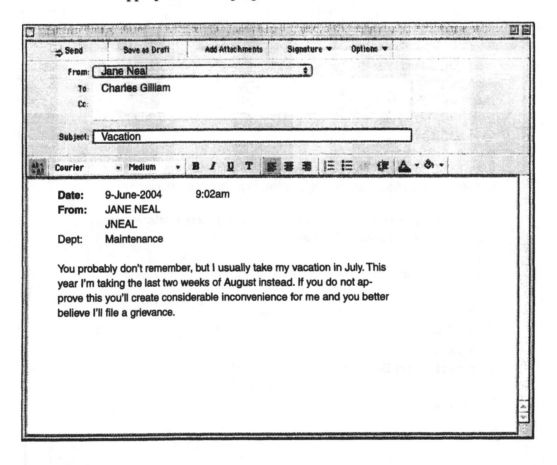

■ **EXERCISE 1.1**   **Continued**

COUNTY DEPARTMENT OF SOCIAL SERVICES

MEMO

DATE: March 17, 2003

TO: All Caseworkers

FROM: Cheryl Alston, Case Supervisor

SUBJECT: Goofing Off

A lot of you seem to think that this is a country club and are spending entirely too much time in the break room! As you well know, you're entitled to one 15-minute break in the morning and another in the afternoon. The rest of the time you're supposed to be AT YOUR DESK unless signed out for fieldwork.

■ **EXERCISE 1.1**   **Continued**

County Community College

MEMORANDUM

DATE: May 5, 2004

TO: All Employees

FROM: Charles Rigney, Chief
            Security

SUBJECT: Burglarized Vehicles

Recently, there's been a rash of burglaries in the faculty/staff parking lot. Items such as tape decks, cellular phones, and even a personal computer have been reported missing from vehicles.

After investigating, however, we've learned that several of these vehicles had been left unlocked. Don't be stupid! Always lock your car or else be prepared to get ripped off. My staff can't be everywhere at once, and if you set yourself up to be victimized, it's not our fault.

Revise each of the following three letters to achieve a tone more appropriate to the purpose and audience.

Bancroft's in the Mall

The Turnpike Mall • Turnpike East • Augusta, Maine 04330

February 17, 2003

Ms. Barbara Wilson
365 Grove St.
Augusta, ME 04330

Dear Ms. Wilson:

Your Bancroft's charge account is $650.55 overdue. We must receive a payment immediately.

If we do not receive a minimum payment of $50 within three days, we will refer your account to a collection agency and your credit rating will be permanently compromised.

Send a payment at once!

Sincerely,

Michael Modoski

Michael Modoski
Credit Department

■ EXERCISE 1.2   **Continued**

Southeast Insurance Company

Southeast Industrial Park   Tallahassee, FL 32301
Telephone: (904) 555-0123   FAX: (904) 555-3210

November 4, 2004

Mr. Francis Tedeschi
214 Summit Avenue
Tallahassee, FL 32301

Dear Mr. Tedeschi:

This is to acknowledge receipt of your 10/30/04 claim.

Insured persons entitled to benefits under the Tallahassee Manufacturing Co.
plan effective December 1, 1996, are required to execute statements of claims
for medical-surgical expense benefits only in the manner specifically mandated in your certificate holder's handbook.

Your claim has been quite improperly executed, as you have neglected to pro-
cure the Physician's Statement of Services Rendered. The information contained therein is prerequisite to any consideration of your claim.

Enclosed is the necessary form. See that it's filled out and returned to us without delay, or your claim cannot be processed.

Yours truly,

Ann Jurkiewicz

Ann Jurkiewicz
Claims Adjustor

Enclosure

■ **EXERCISE 1.2**   **Continued**

DEPARTMENT OF SOCIAL SERVICES

County Administration Building   Easton, NJ 07300
                                                (201) 555-0123

November 10, 2003

Easton Savings Bank
36 Bank Street
Easton, NJ 07300

Re: Charles Mangan (Social Security # 000-00-0000)

To Whom It May Concern:

The above individual has applied for Medical Assistance. This Department requires that a 30-month banking history accompany all such applications. You must send us the necessary information immediately.

Provide a listing of each month's average balance for the period of March 1, 2001, to November 1, 2003, along with verification of all closed or transferred accounts during that period.

This directive is made pursuant to New Jersey State Law, which mandates that all banking organizations must furnish such information to authorized representatives of the Department of Social Services to verify eligibility for any form of Public Assistance.

Sincerely,

Mary Louise Martin

Mary Louise Martin
Caseworker

■ EXERCISE 1.3

Revise each of the following three memos to eliminate inappropriate tone and/or content.

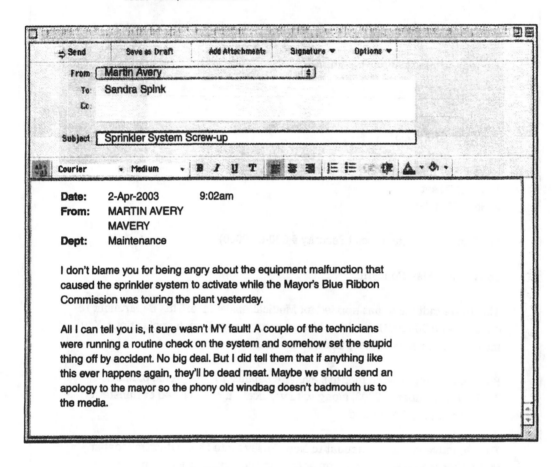

↵ Send	Save as Draft	Add Attachments	Signature ▼	Options ▼

From: Martin Avery   ◆
To: Sandra Spink
Cc:

Subject: Sprinkler System Screw-up

Courier   ▼   Medium   ▼   **B** *I* <u>U</u> **T**   ☰ ☰ ☰   ☷ ☷   🔗   A ▾ ◇ ▾

Date: 2-Apr-2003   9:02am
From: MARTIN AVERY
       MAVERY
Dept: Maintenance

I don't blame you for being angry about the equipment malfunction that caused the sprinkler system to activate while the Mayor's Blue Ribbon Commission was touring the plant yesterday.

All I can tell you is, it sure wasn't MY fault! A couple of the technicians were running a routine check on the system and somehow set the stupid thing off by accident. No big deal. But I did tell them that if anything like this ever happens again, they'll be dead meat. Maybe we should send an apology to the mayor so the phony old windbag doesn't badmouth us to the media.

■ EXERCISE 1.3   Continued

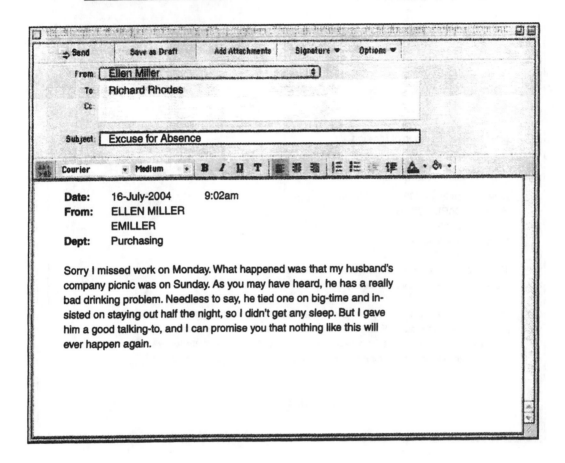

Date: 16-July-2004   9:02am
From: ELLEN MILLER
         EMILLER
Dept: Purchasing

Sorry I missed work on Monday. What happened was that my husband's company picnic was on Sunday. As you may have heard, he has a really bad drinking problem. Needless to say, he tied one on big-time and insisted on staying out half the night, so I didn't get any sleep. But I gave him a good talking-to, and I can promise you that nothing like this will ever happen again.

■ EXERCISE 1.3   Continued

Send	Save as Draft	Add Attachments	Signature ▼	Options ▼

From: Carl Roberts .... ♦

To: Marketing Department

Cc:

Subject: Rescheduling of Meeting

| Courier | ▼ Medium ▼ | B I U T | ≡ ≡ ≡ | ≣ ≣ | ⟂ 斐 | △ ▼ ♦ ▼ |

Date: 18-Nov-2003   9:01am
From: CARL ROBERTS
           CROBERTS
Dept: Marketing

The Friday afternoon department meeting has been rescheduled for Monday at
9 a.m., as I have to leave work early on Friday.

My son's high school football team (the mighty 7 & 0 Centerton Lions—rah! rah!)
have an out-of-state game Friday night against another undefeated team, in Illinois.
From what I understand, they're a real powerhouse, but I'm sure Centerton will beat
them, especially since Carl Junior's averaging nearly fourteen yards per carry!

:-) :-) :-) :-) :-) :-) :-)

GO, LIONS!!!

■ EXERCISE 1.4

Revise each of the following three letters to eliminate wording that might create legal liability.

Fin & Feather Pet Supplies

133 Court Street   Olympia, WA 98501

January 14, 2004

Mr. Robert Ryan
352 Stegman Street
Olympia, WA 98501

Dear Mr. Ryan:

We have received your letter of January 3, and we regret that the heating unit we sold you has malfunctioned, killing $1,500 worth of your tropical fish.

Since the unit was purchased more than three years ago, however, our storewide warranty is no longer in effect, and we are therefore unable to accept any responsibility for your loss. Nevertheless, we are enclosing a Fin & Feather discount coupon good for $10 toward the purchase of a replacement unit or another product of your choice.

We look forward to serving you in the future!

Sincerely,

Sandra Kouvel

Sandra Kouvel
Store Manager

Enclosure

■ EXERCISE 1.4   **Continued**

TELEVISION WORLD

521 Scott Street   Ames, Iowa 50010   (515) 555-1234

February 20, 2003

Ms. Christine Nguyen
230 Fairview Street
Ames, Iowa 50010

Dear Ms. Nguyen:

Thank you for your recent letter about the faulty wiring in the television set you purchased at Television World. We are glad to hear that the fire it caused resulted in only minor damages to your apartment.

If you will bring the television in we'll gladly exchange it for a more reliable set. Customer satisfaction is our #1 priority!

We are happy to assist you with all your video needs.

Yours truly,

Peter Keane

Peter Keane
Store Manager

HIGH ROLLER BIKES & BOARDS

516 Bridge Street ■ Phoenix, AZ 85000

August 18, 2004

Mr. Patrick Casey
252 Sheridan Street
Phoenix, AZ 85000

Dear Mr. Casey:

We are sorry that the bicycle tire we sold you burst during normal use, causing personal injury resulting in lingering lower back pain.

Certainly we will install a replacement tire free of charge if you simply bring your bicycle into our shop any weekday during the hours of 9 a.m. to 5 p.m.

Thank you for purchasing your bicycle supplies at High Roller!

Sincerely,

Monica Lamb

Monica Lamb
Store Manager

B

Correspondence: Memos and Letters

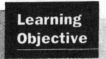
Learning Objective When you complete this chapter you will be able to use basic format and organization patterns to write effective memos and letters.

 Memos
Format
E-mail
Checklist: Evaluating a Memo

Exercises

 Letters
Formats
Checklist: Evaluating a Letter

Exercises

Of all the forms of written communication used in the workplace, memos (including e-mail) and business letters are by far the most common. Any large corporation, agency, or other organization generates thousands of such documents daily. And even in a small setting, they are fundamental to office procedure. Focusing on both format and content, and exploring some of the effects of recent technological advances, this chapter explains how to handle these routine but essential forms of correspondence.

Memos

Traditionally, the memo has been a vehicle for internal or "intramural" communication—a message from someone at Company X to someone else at Company X. The memo may be written to one person or to a group, but until fairly recently it has almost always been a form of in-house correspondence.

In such a situation the writer and reader(s) may be well acquainted. They may have seen one another moments before or even had lunch together. Indeed, the contents of the memo may already be known to all parties involved in the exchange. Although the usual purpose of a memo is to inform, often its function is to create a written record of a request or other message previously communicated in person, over the telephone, or through the grapevine.

Accordingly, a memo is usually quite direct in approach. Although an introductory sentence or two may be helpful to orient the reader, you should come to the point quickly and not ramble on. A common error is to obscure the central issue by confusing the reader with irrelevant details. A good memo focuses sharply, zooming in on what the reader needs to know. Depending on the subject, you should certainly be able to accomplish this in three or four short paragraphs, and one is often enough.

Format

A memo has essentially one basic format. Although minor variations do indeed exist, practically all memos—including e-mail generated on the computer—share certain standard features in formatting:

- The word *Memo, Memorandum,* or some equivalent term at or near the top of the page or screen.

- The TO line, enabling the memo to be "addressed," and the FROM line, allowing it to be "signed." When creating a memo on *paper*, always use the full name, title, and/or department of the person to whom you're writing. This not only ensures that the memo will reach its intended destination but also creates a more complete record for anyone reviewing the file later. For the same reason, use your own full name, title, and/or department in the FROM line. When you're creating an e-mail memo, however, the TO and FROM lines are handled somewhat differently. Depending on the characteristics of the system you're using, the TO line may include only the receiver's name (or e-mail address), omitting the receiver's title and/or department. This is because an e-mail message is electronically transmitted (rather than being physically delivered) to the intended reader, appearing on the appropriate screen the moment you send it. And *your* name (or e-mail address) is automatically activated as soon as you log onto the system, thereby eliminating the need for you to type it in on each document you create. Be aware also that the TO and FROM lines eliminate the need for a letter-style salutation ("Dear Ms. Bernstein") or complimentary close ("Yours truly"); although some writers like to use these devices as a way of making their memos less impersonal, they are better omitted. But note this exception: If your e-mail address does not reveal your name, you must provide it in a complimentary close or in the text of the memo to inform the reader of your identity.

■ The DATE line (provided automatically on e-mail, along with the exact *time* of transmission).

■ The SUBJECT line, identifying the topic. Like a newspaper headline, but even more concisely, the SUBJECT line orients and prepares the reader for what is to follow. To write a good subject line, answer this question: "In no more than three words, what is this memo really about?"

■ And, of course, the message or content of the memo. As explained earlier, three or four paragraphs should be sufficient: a concise introduction, a middle paragraph or two conveying the details, and perhaps a brief conclusion. If the message is quite simple, however, you should get to the point quickly. Some memos are as short as one paragraph, or even one sentence. Like so many other features of workplace communication, memo length is determined by purpose and audience.

The memo in Figure 2.1 embodies all these features and provides an opportunity to explore further the principle of *tone* introduced in Chapter 1.

CITY MANUFACTURING CO.
MEMORANDUM

DATE: May 12, 2003

TO: All Employees

FROM: Susan Lemley, Manager
             Personnel Department

SUBJECT: James Mahan

As many of you already know, James Mahan of the Maintenance Department
was admitted to Memorial Hospital over the weekend and is scheduled to
undergo surgery on Tuesday.

Although Jim will not be receiving visitors or phone calls for a while, you may
want to send him a "Get Well" card to boost his spirits. He's in Room 325.

We'll keep you posted about Jim's progress.

FIGURE 2.1   Basic Memo format

The personnel manager has picked her words carefully to avoid
sounding bossy. She says "You *may want* to send him a . . . card," not "You
should send him a . . . card," even though that's what she really means. As
discussed in Chapter 1, a tactful writer can soften a recommendation, a
request, or even a command simply by phrasing it in a diplomatic way. In
this situation an employee's decision whether to send a card is strictly a
matter of personal choice, so the memo's gentle tone is particularly appropriate. But the same strategy can also be used when conveying important
directives you definitely expect the reader to follow.

E-Mail

As mentioned in Chapter 1, e-mail messages (composed and read on
computer screens rather than on paper) have become a common feature

of today's workplace. Typically, the writer logs on by typing his or her user name and a confidential password or code that prevents unauthorized access. A few additional procedures cause a memo form (called a template) to appear on the screen. The writer simply fills in the blanks, as if typing on a preprinted memo form. When the message is completed, a click of the mouse will immediately send it to as many other users of the system as the writer wishes—one or everyone. The memo is also stored in the writer's electronic mailbox and kept there indefinitely for future reference. To read incoming memos, a similar procedure is used. After logging on, the reader clicks the mouse to access each new message. Depending on the reader's preferences, each can then be deleted, filed for future reference, printed, answered, or forwarded—or a combination of these options. Like the e-mail you've already seen in Chapter 1, Figure 2.2 is a typical e-mail memo.

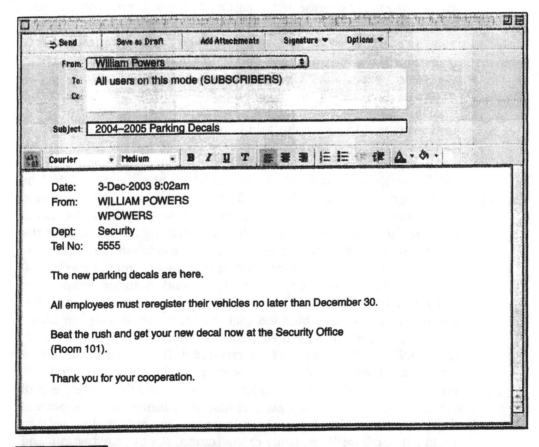

FIGURE 2.2   **E-Mail Memorandum**

There are important advantages to electronic information technology. On the most obvious level, e-mail is incomparably faster than conventional correspondence. In the past, communicating by memo involved at least five distinct steps:

1. Writing
2. Typing by a secretary
3. Proofreading and initialing by the writer
4. Photocopying for the writer's file
5. Routing to the intended reader(s)

Depending on office workload and clerical staffing levels, this could be a very time-consuming process. With e-mail, however, all five steps are compressed into one, permitting instantaneous communication.

Unfortunately, however, e-mail can also present some problems. One major drawback is that the very ease with which e-mail can be generated encourages overuse. In the past a writer would not bother to send a memo without good reason; there was too much time and effort involved to do otherwise. Now, however, much needless correspondence is produced. Yesterday's writers would wait until complete information on a given topic had been received and organized before passing it along to others. But today it's not uncommon for many memos to be written on the same subject, doling out the information in bits and pieces, sometimes within a very short time span. The resulting fragmentation wastes the energies of writer and reader alike and increases the possibility of confusion, not to mention the likelihood of premature response.

Similarly, memos about sensitive issues are often dashed off in "the heat of battle" without sufficient reflection. In the past the writer always had some time to reconsider a situation before actually sending a memo and had the option of revising or simply destroying the memo if, at the proofreading stage, it had come to seem a bit too insistent or otherwise inappropriate. The inherently rapid-fire nature of e-mail, however, all but eliminates any such opportunity for second thoughts. In addition, hasty composition causes a great many keyboarding miscues, omissions, and other fundamental blunders that must then be corrected in subsequent memos, creating the inefficient phenomenon of "e-mail about e-mail." Indeed, the absence of a secretarial "filter" has given rise to a great deal of embarrassingly bad writing in the workplace. You risk ridicule and loss of credibility unless you closely proofread every e-mail message before sending it. Make sure that the information is correct and that all pertinent details have been included. Be particularly careful to avoid typos, misspellings, faulty capitalization, sloppy punctuation, and basic grammatical errors.

Tech Tips

Despite its seemingly informal, spontaneous nature, e-mail is no less "official" and permanent than a memo printed on paper. It's important, therefore, to use this medium carefully, thoughtfully, and efficiently. These guidelines will help:

- Use e-mail only when necessary. Many situations—those requiring a back and forth exchange, for example—are better served by the telephone or by face-to-face conversation.

- Send e-mail only to the person(s) needing it; resist the urge to mass mail. Similarly, when *replying* to a mass mailing, do not click on "Reply All" unless there's a valid reason to do so. Reply only to the sender.

- Remember that in sensitive situations, e-mail is only partially able to convey "tone of voice." For this reason, voice-mail is often preferable, allowing your attitude and feelings to be perceived more accurately. (Regardless of your medium, however, never attempt to communicate when you're angry.)

- Follow the normal rules governing capitalization, spelling, punctuation, and grammar. There's a mistaken notion that writing becomes easier to read if "unrestricted" by conventional standards. In actuality, the exact opposite is true. Because of its unaccustomed appearance, nontraditional text is actually much more difficult for the reader to process efficiently.

- If no response is required from your reader, say so. In a related vein, you should not feel obligated to reply to every routine message you receive.

- When sending an attachment along with an e-mail memo, always provide a one- or two-sentence summary of the attachment right in the text of the memo. This allows your reader to decide whether it's worth the bother of opening the attachment.

- Understand that e-mail is not private. Recent court decisions have established that employers are within their rights to monitor workers' e-mail accounts (and Internet surfing) for impropriety and excessive personal use. Indeed, it's not uncommon for workers to be fired for stepping over the line in this regard. A good rule of thumb is, "Don't put it in an e-mail unless you'd have no problem with it appearing on the front page of your local paper."

- Observe the standard rules of e-mail etiquette. For example, avoid "flaming" (openly hostile or abusive comments, whether directed at the reader or at a third party). The fact that you're communicating electronically does not exempt you from the accepted norms of workplace courtesy.

As mentioned in Chapter 1, the company e-mail network is no place for personal messages or an excessively conversational style. Many employers provide a separate e-mail "bulletin board" on which workers can post and access announcements about garage or vehicle sales, carpooling, theater tickets, and the like. Such matters are appropriate only as bulletin board content. For more information on e-mail etiquette (sometimes called "netiquette"), you can consult these Web sites:

- http://www.fau.edu/netiquette/net/culture.html
- http://www.linfield.edu/policy/netiquette.html
- http://www.hotwired.com/webmonkey/guides/email/lists_page2.html

Now that so many organizations are linked via computer networks, the memo is no longer just an intramural communications medium. Since the memo format is the most common format used on-line, it's be-

---

✓ Checklist   Evaluating a Memo

A good memo

___ follows standard memo format;

___ includes certain features:

  ☐ DATE line (appears automatically in e-mail)

  ☐ TO line, which includes the name and often the title and/or department of the receiver

  ☐ FROM line, which includes the name (appears automatically in e-mail) and often the title and/or department of the sender

  ☐ SUBJECT line, which is a clear, accurate, but brief statement of what the memo is about

___ is organized into paragraphs (one is often enough) covering the subject fully in an orderly way;

___ includes no inappropriate content;

___ uses clear, simple language;

___ maintains an appropriate tone, neither too formal nor too conversational;

___ contains no typos or mechanical errors in spelling, capitalization, punctuation, and grammar.

ginning to rival the business letter as the major form of correspondence across company boundaries. Clearly, tone takes on even greater importance in e-mail memos sent to readers at other locations. Since the writer and the reader are usually not personally known to each other, a higher level of courteous formality is in order. In addition, the subject matter is often more involved than that of in-house correspondence, so memos sent outside one's workplace are commonly longer and more fully developed than those intended for co-workers. In all other aspects, however, they're essentially the same. Whether in-house or not, whether electronically generated or not, all memos are subject to the principles outlined in the checklist on the previous page.

 # Exercises

■ EXERCISE 2.1

You're the assistant to the personnel manager of a metals fabrication plant. Monday is Labor Day, and most of the 300 employees will be given a paid holiday. The company is under pressure, however, to meet a deadline. Therefore, a skeleton force of 40—all in the production department—will be needed to work the holiday. Those who volunteer will have the option of being paid overtime at the standard time-and-a-half rate or receiving two vacation days. If fewer than 40 volunteer, others will be assigned to work on the basis of seniority, with the most recently hired employees chosen first. The personnel manager has asked you to alert affected employees. Write a memo.

■ EXERCISE 2.2

You're a secretary at a regional office of a state agency. Normal working hours for civil service employees in your state are 8:30 a.m. to 4:30 p.m., with a lunch break from 12:00 to 12:30 p.m. During the summer, however, the hours are 8:30 a.m. to 4:00 p.m., with lunch unchanged. Summer hours are in effect from July 1 to September 2. It is now mid-June, and the busy office supervisor has asked you to remind employees of the summer schedule. Write a memo.

■ EXERCISE 2.3

You work in the lumberyard of a building supplies company. Every year on the July 4 weekend, the town sponsors the Liberty Run, a 10K (6.2-mile) road race. This year, for the first time, local businesses have been invited to enter five-member teams to compete for the Corporate Cup. The team with the best combined time takes the trophy. There will be no prize money involved but much good publicity for the winners. Since you recently ran the Boston Marathon, the company president wants you to recruit and organize a team. It's now April 20. Better get started. Write a memo.

■ EXERCISE 2.4

You're an office worker at a large paper products company that has just installed an upgraded computer system. Many employees are having difficulty with the new software. The manufacturer's representatives will be on-site all next week to provide training. Since you are studying computer technology, you've been asked to serve as liaison. You must inform your co-workers about the training, which will be delivered in Conference Room 3 from Monday through Thursday in eight half-day sessions (9:00 a.m. to 12:00 p.m. and 1:00 to 4:00 p.m.), organized alphabetically by workers' last names, as follows: A–B, C–E, F–I, J–M, N–P, Q–SL, SM–T, and U–Z. Workers unable to attend must sign up for one of two make-up sessions that will be held on Friday. You must ensure that everyone understands all these requirements. Write a memo.

■ EXERCISE 2.5

You're the manager of the employee cafeteria at a printing company. For many years the cafeteria has provided excellent service, offering breakfast from 7:00 to 8:30 a.m. and lunch from 11:00 a.m. to 2:00 p.m. It also serves as a break room, selling coffee, soft drinks, and snacks all day. But the cafeteria is badly in need of modernization. Work is scheduled to begin next Wednesday. Naturally, the cafeteria will have to be closed while renovations are in progress. Employees will still be able to have lunch and breaks, however, because temporary facilities are being set up in Room 101 of Building B, a now-vacant area formerly used for storage. The temporary cafeteria will provide all the usual services except for breakfast. Obviously, employees need to know about the situation. Write a memo.

■ EXERCISE 2.6

You're the security chief at a manufacturing company that makes small metal hand tools. The plant employs roughly 100 people. Management has told you that many tools have disappeared. According to company records, the plant produces approximately 50,000 per day, but far fewer are actually being shipped out. After double-checking the figures to ensure their accuracy, you have concluded that pilferage is the only possible explanation. A metal detector positioned at the employee exit near the time clock would catch anyone trying to smuggle tools out of the factory. Because the purchase cost of a metal detector is prohibitive, you have decided to rent one. Anyone caught stealing will immediately be fired, and a note to that effect will become part of the individual's personnel file. You don't want to create an atmosphere of hostility, but you do need to inform the employees about these developments. Write a memo.

■ EXERCISE 2.7

You're a caseworker at a new county agency that assists troubled youths by placing them in group homes run by the agency. There are five boys or girls per home, supervised by specially trained counselors. You find this job rewarding, although it involves more paperwork than you'd prefer. Yesterday, for example, the agency psychiatrist recommended a medication change for a boy who resides at Group Home #6. The boy has been diagnosed as hyperactive and has been receiving a daily dosage of 30 mg of Ritalin (one 10-mg tablet in the morning, one at noon, and one at bedtime). The doctor has decided to increase the dosage to 35 mg daily, by adding a 5-mg morning tablet. You have no reason to question the doctor's judgment, but you must inform the boy's counselors. Write a memo.

■ EXERCISE 2.8

You're the United Way representative at your place of employment, and must therefore encourage everyone to contribute. While no one can be required to donate, your own supervisor has publicly stated that the company goal is 100 percent participation, and you know from past experience that she is intolerant of failure. It's in your own interest, then, to persuade all your co-workers to contribute but without appearing to pressure them. Write a memo.

■ EXERCISE 2.9

You're the production manager for a computer parts manufacturer. Last month four machines had excessive downtime. The company's production of Part #Z43 has dropped. Two of your best customers have complained about late shipments of Part #Z43. One customer has canceled a standing order and is now buying the part from your principal competitor. For the past two months the company's production of Part #Y01 has also been declining. To discuss the situation, all production supervisors will meet in Conference Room G, in the west wing of the main building, at 10:00 a.m. next Monday. Each should bring to the meeting up-to-date figures on costs, equipment, personnel, and so on. You must inform the production supervisors about the meeting. Write a memo.

■ EXERCISE 2.10

Proofread and rewrite the following memo, correcting all typos and mechanical errors.

Memorial Hospital

MEMORANDUM

DATE: September 8, 2003

TO: All Employes

FROM: Roger Sammon, Clerk
             Medical Recrods Department

SUBJECT: Patricia Klosek

As many of you allready know. Patricia Klosik from the Medical records Depratment is retiring next month. After more then thirty years of faithfull service to Memorial hospital.

A party is being planed in her honor. It will be at seven oclock on friday October 24 at big Joes Resturant tickets are $30 per person whitch includes a buffay diner and a donation toward a gift.

If you plan to atend please let me no by the end of this week try to get you're check to me by Oct 10

Letters

Unlike memos, business letters are typically used for *external* communication, a message from someone at Company X to someone elsewhere—a customer or client, perhaps, or a counterpart at Company Y. But there are some similarities between the memo and the letter: The writer and the reader may or may not be acquainted, the message may or may not be news to the reader, and sometimes the objective is simply to create a written record. Usually, however, there's a more immediate purpose. Literally millions of letters are written every day, for an enormous variety of reasons. Some of the more typical purposes of a letter are to

- ask for information (inquiry);
- sell a product or service (sales);
- purchase a product or service (order);
- request payment (collection);
- voice a complaint (claim);
- respond to a complaint (adjustment);
- thank someone (acknowledgment).

Figures 2.4 through 2.13 provide examples of all these.

Formats

Notice that, regardless of purpose, a letter can be formatted in a variety of ways. The three most common styles are the modified block style with indented paragraphs, the modified block style, and the full block style.

Modified Block Style with Indented Paragraphs

As shown in Figures 2.4, 2.5, and 2.9, the date line, the complimentary close, and the writer's identification all begin at the center of the page. The first line of each paragraph is indented five spaces. All other lines are flush with the left margin.

Modified Block Style

As shown in Figures 2.6 through 2.8, the date line, the complimentary close, and the writer's identification all begin at the center of the page. All other lines (including the first line of each paragraph) are flush with the left margin.

Full Block Style

As shown in Figures 2.10 through 2.13, every line (including the first line of each paragraph) is flush with the left margin.

The three styles share several features: all are single-spaced through-out (except between the separate elements, where double-spacing is used), are centered on the page, and are framed by margins of 1 to 1½ inches. All three styles are in common use, with the modified block style with indented paragraphs considered the most traditional format (and a bit old-fashioned). Full block format, on the other hand, is the most con-temporary. As the template included with popular word processing soft-ware such as WordPerfect and Microsoft Word, it's rapidly becoming the norm. Regardless of format, however, every letter includes certain essen-tial components that are set forth on the page in the following sequence:

1. Writer's address (sometimes preprinted on letterhead) at the top of the page

2. Date (like e-mail memos, letters sent by fax are automatically im-printed with the exact time of transmission as well)

3. Inside address (the full name, title, and address of the receiver)

4. Salutation, followed by a colon (avoid gender-biased salutations such as "Dear Sir" or "Gentlemen")

5. Body of the letter, using the three-part approach outlined below

6. Complimentary close ("Sincerely" is best), followed by a comma

7. Writer's signature

8. Writer's name and title, beneath the signature

9. Enclosure line, if necessary, to indicate item(s) accompanying the letter

Along with these standard components, all business letters—irrespective of format—also embrace the same three-part pattern of organization:

1. A brief introductory paragraph establishing context (by referring to previous correspondence, perhaps, or by orienting the reader in some other way) and stating the letter's purpose concisely

2. A middle section (as many paragraphs as needed) conveying the content of the message by providing all necessary details, pre-sented in the most logical sequence

3. A brief concluding paragraph politely requesting action, thanking the reader, or providing any additional information pertinent to the situation

Tech Tips

Letters and other documents are often sent by a fax machine, basically a scanner with a modem that converts documents into digital data that is then transmitted over telephone lines to the receiver's fax machine, which prints out hard copy. As with e-mail, the obvious advantage of this technology is speed; a letter that might take two or three days to arrive by conventional mail can now be received instantaneously.

But whenever you fax anything, you must fax a cover memo along with it. In this memo you should include any additional information that might be necessary to orient the reader, and indicate how many pages (including the cover memo itself) you have included in the transmission so the reader will know if there's anything that was sent but not received. You should also include your fax number, telephone number, and e-mail address, so that the reader has the option of replying. Here's an example:

DONROC, INC.

36 Clinton St., Collegeville, NY 13323

FAX

DATE: November 12, 2003 (3:15 P.M.)

TO: John Lapinski, Main Office Comptroller (FAX #1234567)

FROM: George Searles, Branch Office Manager (FAX #8910111)
            Telephone 555-2595, e-mail gsrls@sarge.com

SUBJECT: Cosgrove Letter

PAGES: 2

Here's Michael Cosgrove's letter of November 10. Let's discuss this at Thursday's meeting.

Although the "fax machine to fax machine" scenario is the most common, computer software now permits interface between fax machines and computers. Another option, of course, is to send the cover memo as e-mail, with the accompanying document scanned in as an attachment. With so many workplace computers equipped with scanners, fax machines may eventually be rendered obsolete, especially since computers' printers produce better hard copy. At least for now, though, the fax machine remains a very useful device.

A fairly recent development is the open punctuation system in which the colon after the salutation and the comma after the complimentary close are omitted. Figure 2.12 illustrates this variation, which is gaining widespread acceptance. A more radical change is the trend toward a fully abbreviated, "no punctuation/all capitals" approach to the inside address (see Figure 2.13). This derives from the U.S. Postal Service recommendation that envelopes be so addressed to facilitate computerized scanning and sorting. As the inside address has traditionally matched the address on the envelope, such a feature may well become standard, at least for letters sent by conventional mail rather than by electronic means. Indeed, most companies using "window" envelopes have already adopted this style. For a list of standard abbreviations used in letter writing and formatting, see Figure 2.3.

Alabama	AL	Kentucky	KY	Ohio	OH
Alaska	AK	Louisiana	LA	Oklahoma	OK
Arizona	AZ	Maine	ME	Oregon	OR
Arkansas	AR	Maryland	MD	Pennsylvania	PA
California	CA	Massachusetts	MA	Puerto Rico	PR
Colorado	CO	Michigan	MI	Rhode Island	RI
Connecticut	CT	Minnesota	MN	South Carolina	SC
Delaware	DE	Mississippi	MS	South Dakota	SD
District of	DC	Missouri	MO	Tennessee	TN
Columbia		Montana	MT	Texas	TX
Florida	FL	Nebraska	NE	Utah	UT
Georgia	GA	Nevada	NV	Vermont	VT
Hawaii	HI	New Hampshire	NH	Virginia	VA
Idaho	ID	New Jersey	NJ	Washington	WA
Illinois	IL	New Mexico	NM	West Virginia	WV
Indiana	IN	New York	NY	Wisconsin	WI
Iowa	IA	North Carolina	NC	Wyoming	WY
Kansas	KS	North Dakota	ND		
Avenue	AVE	Expressway	EXPY	Parkway	PKWY
Boulevard	BLVD	Freeway	FWY	Road	RD
Circle	CIR	Highway	HWY	Square	SQ
Court	CT	Lane	LN	Street	ST
Turnpike	TPKE				
North	N	West	W	Southwest	SW
East	E	Northeast	NE	Northwest	NW
South	S	Southeast	SE		
Room	RM	Suite	STE	Apartment	APT

FIGURE 2.3 **Standard Abbreviations**

Source: U.S. Postal Service.

The Weekly News

P.O. Box 123
Littleton, New York 13300
Telephone (315) 555-1234 • Fax (315) 555-4321

February 24, 2002

Chief Joseph Kealy
Littleton Police Department
911 Main Street
Littleton, NY 13300

Dear Chief Kealy:

It is our understanding that a Littleton resident, Mr. Alex Booth, is the subject of an investigation by your department, with the assistance of the county district attorney. In keeping with the provisions of the New York Freedom of Information Law, I am requesting information about Mr. Booth's arrest.

This information is needed to provide our readership with accurate news coverage of the events leading to Mr. Booth's current situation. The Weekly News prides itself on fair, accurate, and objective reporting, and we are counting on your assistance as we seek to uphold that tradition.

Since the police blotter is by law a matter of public record, we will appreciate your full cooperation.

Sincerely,

Nancy Muller

Nancy Muller, Reporter

FIGURE 2.4   Inquiry Letter in Modified Block Style with Indented Paragraphs

Fashion First

254 Sunset Blvd, Weston, CA 95800   •   telephone (916) 555-1234

March 3, 2003

Ms. Sarah Levy
643 Glenwood Avenue
Weston, CA 95800

Dear Ms. Levy:

As a preferred customer and holder of our special Gold Card, you won't want to miss our annual Savings Spectacular.

All the fine clothing pictured in the enclosed brochure has been marked down a full 25%! To take advantage of these incredible bargains, you need only complete the order form on the back cover of the brochure. Or if you prefer, you may simply telephone your order. Our operators are standing by.

Purchases totaling $300 or more are entitled to another 10% off! But you must act quickly! The sale—open to Gold Card customers exclusively—ends on March 10. Order now!

Sincerely,

Jorgé Figueroa

Jorgé Figueroa, Manager
Customer Services Department

Enclosure

FIGURE 2.5   **Sales Letter in Modified Block Style with Indented Paragraphs**

Southton High School

62 Academy Street, Southton, GA 30300
Telephone (404) 555-1234 · Fax (404) 555-4321

July 10, 2004

Value-Rite Office Supplies
462 Decatur Street
Atlanta, GA 30300

Dear Value-Rite:

It's time once again for Southton High to order a shipment of custom-printed, spiral-bound notebooks for use by our students.

You may charge the following order to our account (#2468).

Catalog #	Quantity	Description	Unit Cost	Total
471	300	100 pages	$1.00	$300
472	200	250 pages	2.00	400
473	100	350 pages	3.00	300
			Subtotal	$1,000
			Tax (5%)	50
			Shipping	30
			Total	$1,080

Please provide blue covers with the gold SHS logo (which you have on file) and ship as promptly as possible.

Sincerely,

Karl Bradbury

Karl Bradbury, Vice Principal

FIGURE 2.6   **Order Letter In Modified Block Style**

Greene's

New Acres Mall   Tallahassee, FL 32301

June 16, 2003

Mr. William Britton
55-A Jackson Road
Tallahassee, FL 32301

Dear Mr. Britton:

We appreciate your continued patronage of Greene's. We note, however, that
your charge account is now $565.31 overdue, and that we have not received
your monthly payment since April.

If you have recently sent in your payment, please ignore this friendly
reminder. If not, we would appreciate a minimum remittance of $50.00
at your earliest convenience.

If you have any questions about your account, please call us at 555-0123,
Ext. 123.

Sincerely,

Heather Sutcliffe

Heather Sutcliffe
Credit Services Department

FIGURE 2.7   **Collection Letter in Modified Block Style**

Jane's Homestyle Restaurants, Inc.

239 Northrop Square   Seattle, WA 98100   (206) 555-1234

October 28, 2004

Mr. Joseph Chen, Director
Sales & Service Department
Ace Technologies Corporation
1168 Crosstown Turnpike
Seattle, WA 98100

Dear Mr. Chen:

I purchased the Ace Cash Register System 2000 for my three restaurants in
December 2003 and have experienced continuous problems with the video
monitors since then.

As recently as September of this year, another of the monitors had to be sent
in for repairs. Yesterday afternoon that same unit failed again. This occurrence
is not uncommon, as you can see by the nine repair invoices I have enclosed
for your reference.

Given the many problems we have had with these monitors, I am requesting
that you replace them, free of charge. Please call me about this as soon as
possible.

Sincerely,

Jane Pelham

Jane Pelham, Owner

Enclosures

FIGURE 2.8   **Corporate Claim Letter in Modified Block Style**

41 Allan Court
Tucson, AZ 86700
June 30, 2003

Consumer Relations Department
Superior Foods, Inc.
135 Grove Street
Atlanta, GA 30300

Dear Superior Foods:

Superior microwave dinners are excellent products that I have purchased regularly for many years. Recently, however, I had an unsettling experience with one of these meals.

While enjoying a serving of Pasta Alfredo, I discovered in the food what appeared to be a thick splinter of wood. I'm sure this is an isolated incident, but I thought your quality control department would want to know about it.

I've enclosed the splinter, taped to the product wrapper, along with the sales receipt for the dinner. May I please be reimbursed $4.98 for the cost?

Sincerely,

George Eaglefeather

George Eaglefeather

Enclosures

FIGURE 2.9   **Consumer Claim Letter in Modified Block Style with Indented Paragraphs**

Superior Foods, Inc.

135 Grove St., Atlanta, GA 30300   •   (324) 555-1234

July 7, 2003

Mr. George Eaglefeather
41 Allan Court
Tucson, AZ 86700

Dear Mr. Eaglefeather:

Thank you for purchasing our product and for taking the time to contact us about it. We apologize for the unsatisfactory condition of your Pasta Alfredo dinner.

Quality is of paramount importance to all of us at Superior Foods, and great care is taken in the preparation and packaging of all our products. Our quality assurance staff has been notified of the problem you reported. Although Superior Foods does not issue cash refunds, we have enclosed three complimentary coupons redeemable at your grocery for complimentary Superior dinners of your choice.

We appreciate this opportunity to be of service, and we hope you will continue to enjoy our products.

Sincerely,

John Roth

John Roth
Customer Services Department

Enclosures (3)

FIGURE 2.10   Adjustment Letter in Full Block Style

VALUE-RITE OFFICE SUPPLIES

462 Decatur Street • Atlanta, GA 30300 • (404) 555-1234

March 19, 2003

Ms. Helen Reynard, Owner
Reynard's Auto Palace
Central Highway
Atlanta, GA 30300

Dear Ms. Reynard:

For the past 10 years, Value-Rite Office Supplies has purchased all our delivery
vans from your dealership, and we have relied on your service department for
routine maintenance and necessary repairs. During that time I have been
repeatedly impressed by the professionalism of your employees, especially
Jarel Carter, who staffs the service desk.

Both in person and on the telephone, Jarel has always been exceptionally
knowledgeable, helpful, and courteous and is always willing to go the
extra mile to ensure customer satisfaction. Just last week, for example, he
interrupted his lunch break to get me some information about a part that has
been on back-order.

If you can continue to attract employees of Jarel's caliber, you shouldn't have
any difficulty remaining the area's #1 dealership. Be sure to keep him in mind
the next time you're considering merit raises!

Sincerely,

Gary Richie

Gary Richie, Owner

FIGURE 2.11   Acknowledgment Letter in Full Block Style

VALUE-RITE OFFICE SUPPLIES

462 Decatur Street • Atlanta, GA 30300 • (404) 555-1234

March 19, 2003

Ms. Helen Reynard, Owner
Reynard's Auto Palace
Central Highway
Atlanta, GA 30300

Dear Ms. Reynard

For the past 10 years, Value-Rite Office Supplies has purchased all our delivery vans from your dealership, and we have relied on your service department for routine maintenance and necessary repairs. During that time I have been repeatedly impressed by the professionalism of your employees, especially Jarel Carter, who staffs the service desk.

Both in person and on the telephone, Jarel has always been exceptionally knowledgeable, helpful, and courteous and is always willing to go the extra mile to ensure customer satisfaction. Just last week, for example, he interrupted his lunch break to get me some information about a part that has been on back-order.

If you can continue to attract employees of Jarel's caliber, you shouldn't have any difficulty remaining the area's #1 dealership. Be sure to keep him in mind the next time you're considering merit raises!

Sincerely

Gary Richie

Gary Richie, Owner

FIGURE 2.12   **Acknowledgment Letter in Full Block Style with Open Punctuation**

VALUE-RITE OFFICE SUPPLIES

462 Decatur Street • Atlanta, GA 30300 • (404) 555-1234

March 19, 2003

MS HELEN REYNARD
REYNARDS AUTO PALACE
CENTRAL HIGHWAY
ATLANTA GA 30300

Dear Ms. Reynard:

For the past 10 years, Value-Rite Office Supplies has purchased all our delivery vans from your dealership, and we have relied on your service department for routine maintenance and necessary repairs. During that time I have been repeatedly impressed by the professionalism of your employees, especially Jarel Carter, who staffs the service desk.

Both in person and on the telephone, Jarel has always been exceptionally knowledgeable, helpful, and courteous and is always willing to go the extra mile to ensure customer satisfaction. Just last week, for example, he interrupted his lunch break to get me some information about a part that has been on back-order.

If you can continue to attract employees of Jarel's caliber, you shouldn't have any difficulty remaining the area's #1 dealership. Be sure to keep him in mind the next time you're considering merit raises!

Sincerely,

Gary Richie

Gary Richie, Owner

FIGURE 2.13   Acknowledgment Letter in Full Block Style with Capitalized Inside Address

As mentioned earlier, more and more companies are communicating with each other by e-mail and other forms of electronic messaging rather than by business letter. The letter is still preferred, however, for more formal exchanges, especially those in which speed of delivery is not a major factor. And in situations involving individual customers and clients (many of whom still rely on conventional mail), the business letter remains the best bet. At least for the immediate future, therefore, the letter will continue to be a major form of workplace correspondence, although its role will almost certainly undergo further redefinition as various forms of electronic communication become increasingly widespread.

Like all successful communication, a good letter must employ an appropriate tone. Obviously, a letter is a more formal kind of communication than an in-house memo because it's more public. Accordingly, a letter should uphold the image of the sender's company or organization by reflecting a high degree of professionalism. But although a letter's style should be somewhat more polished than that of an in-house memo, the language should be no less natural and easy to understand. The key to achieving a readable style—in a letter or in anything else you write—is to understand that writing should not sound pompous or "official." Rather, it should sound much like ordinary speech—shined up just a bit. Whatever you do, avoid stilted, old-fashioned business clichés. Strive instead for direct, conversational phrasing. Here's a list of common overly bureaucratic constructions, paired with "plain English" alternatives:

Cliché	Alternative
As per your request	As you requested
Attached please find	Here is
At this point in time	Now
In lieu of	Instead of
In the event that	If
Please be advised that X	X
Pursuant to our agreement	As we agreed
Until such time as	Until
We are in receipt of	We have received
We regret to advise you that X	Regrettably, X

If you have a clear understanding of your letter's purpose and have analyzed your audience, you should experience little difficulty achieving the appropriate tone for the situation. If, in addition, your letter has been formatted in accordance with one of the standard layout styles and is written in clear, accessible, and mechanically correct language, the correspondence will likely accomplish its objectives. As noted earlier, you must scrupulously avoid typos and mechanical errors in memos. This is even more important when you compose letters intended for outside readers, who will take their business elsewhere if they perceive you as careless or incompetent. Always proofread carefully, making every effort to ensure that your work is error-free, and consult the following checklist.

✓ Checklist   Evaluating a Letter

A good letter

___ follows a standard letter format (full block is best);

___ includes certain features:

- ☐ Sender's complete address
- ☐ Date
- ☐ Receiver's full name and complete address
- ☐ Salutation, followed by a colon
- ☐ Complimentary close ("Sincerely" is best), followed by a comma
- ☐ Sender's signature and full name
- ☐ Enclosure notation, if necessary

___ is organized into paragraphs, covering the subject fully in an orderly way:

- ☐ First paragraph establishes context and states the purpose
- ☐ Middle paragraphs provide all necessary details
- ☐ Last paragraph politely achieves closure

___ includes no inappropriate content;

___ uses clear, simple language;

___ maintains an appropriate tone, neither too formal nor too conversational;

___ contains no typos or mechanical errors in spelling, capitalization, punctuation, and grammar.

Exercises

■ EXERCISE 2.11

For 10 days, save all the business letters you receive. Even though the bulk of them will be junk mail, make a list identifying the *purpose* of each. Prepare a brief oral presentation explaining which letter is the best and which is the worst, and why. (It may be helpful to create overhead transparencies or distribute photocopies to the class, assuming the letters do not contain confidential information.)

■ EXERCISE 2.12

A consumer product that you especially like is suddenly no longer available in retail stores in your area. Write the manufacturer an inquiry letter requesting information about the product and how to place an order.

■ EXERCISE 2.13

Proceeding as if you've received the information requested in Exercise 2.12, write a letter ordering the product.

■ EXERCISE 2.14

Pretend you've received the product ordered in Exercise 2.13 but it's somehow unsatisfactory. Write the manufacturer a claim letter expressing dissatisfaction and requesting an exchange or a refund.

■ EXERCISE 2.15

Team up with a classmate, exchange the claim letters you each wrote in response to Exercise 2.14, and write adjustment letters to each other.

■ EXERCISE 2.16

Write a claim letter expressing dissatisfaction with some product or service that you have actually been disappointed with in the recent past. After the letter has been returned to you with your instructor's corrections, you should then actually mail your claim letter, and see if you receive a reply or perhaps even some form of compensation.

■ **EXERCISE 2.17**

Write an acknowledgment letter to the editor of either your campus newspaper or a regional daily, expressing your approval of some meaningful contribution made by a local person or organization.

■ **EXERCISE 2.18**

The writer of this form letter appears to have no knowledge of standard styles of letter layout. Rewrite the letter, adjusting and correcting irregularities.

Centerton High School

100 School Street   Centerton, Iowa 50300

January 14, 2003

Dear Classmate,

Remember when the Centerton football team beat City Vocational 7–6 for the County Championship in '92? Or when the Honors Math Club went all the way to the finals in statewide competition? Or when Mr. Fisk lost his eyeglasses and accidentally went into the women's lavatory at the highway rest area during the class trip? It's hard to believe, but this spring will mark the 10th anniversary of our graduation from good old Centerton High! To celebrate this landmark, a Class of '93 committee—myself included—is working on a special reunion event starting at 6:00 p.m. on Saturday, May 10, at the Union Hall on Main Street. Husbands, wives, and "dates" are of course welcome in addition to the grads. Cost is $50 per person, which includes buffet dinner, cash bar, reunion T-shirt and a DJ playing all our favorite songs from the good old days. Mr. Fisk and many of our other teachers—some now retired—are also being invited to attend (free of charge). Please try to make it—the reunion won't be the same without you. You can complete the enclosed preregistration form indicating your intention to attend and your T-shirt size. We'd also like payment (or at least a $25/person deposit) at this time. Hope to see you at the reunion!

Yours truly, *Jane Hermanski (Class of '93)*, CHS Guidance Counselor

■ **EXERCISE 2.19**

The writer of this letter has adopted a highly artificial and pretentious style. Rewrite the letter to convey the message in "plain English."

COUNTY DEPARTMENT OF SOCIAL SERVICES

County Building, Northton, MN 55100

November 10, 2004

Ms. Sally Cramdon
359 Roberts Road
Northton, MN 55100

Dear Ms. Cramdon:

We are in receipt of your pay stubs and your letter of 5 November 2004 and have ascertained a determination re: your application for food stamp eligibility.

Enclosed please find photocopy of food stamp budget sheet prepared by this office on above date, counterindicating eligibility at this point in time. Per county eligibility stipulations, it is our judgment that your level of fiscal solvency exceeds permissible criteria for a household the size of your own (four persons).

In the subsequent event that your remuneration should decrease, and remain at the decreased level for a period of thirty (30) calendar days or more, please do not hesitate to petition this office for a reassessment of your eligibility status at that juncture.

Very truly yours,

William Hanlon

William Hanlon
Casework Aide

■ **EXERCISE 2.20**

The writer of this letter has committed a great many fundamental blunders, typos, and mechanical errors. Rewrite the letter, fixing all problems.

20/20 Optical Supply, Inc.

North Side Plaza   Northweston, WA 98501

August 11, 1003

Service Manger
Northweston Plumbing
23 Reynolds street
Northweston, Wa 98501

Dear Northwesern Plumbing;

Last week your worker's installed a new 50-gallon hot water heater in the basement of are North Side Plazza retail store, now the heater is leaking all over the floor.

Every time I call your phone number I get a recording thet say's you will return my call but you never do. As this has been going on for more than a weak I must ensist that you either call imediatley or send a service person. I'm getting tried of moping up water!!!

Please see to this at your very earlyest convience!

Your's truely

Robert Creech

Robert Creech
Store Manger

Short Reports: Page Design, Formats, and Types

Learning Objective

When you complete this chapter, you will be able to apply the basic principles of page design and format to write effective short reports of various kinds.

- **Page Design**
- **Report Formats: Memo, Letter, and Booklet**
- **Types of Reports**
  Incident Report
  Progress Report
  Recommendation Report
  Travel Report
  Checklist: Evaluating a Memo Report
  Checklist: Evaluating a Letter Report
  Checklist: Evaluating a Booklet Report

Exercises

Like memos and letters, reports are an important form of on-the-job communication, can be internal or external documents, and follow certain standard conventions. In several respects, however, reports are quite different from memos and letters.

For example, a report is rarely just a written account of information the reader already knows. Nearly always, the report's subject matter is new information. The reader may be acquainted with the general outline of the situation the report explores but not with the details. Very often, in fact, the reader will have specifically requested the report to get those details. Indeed, reports exist for that very purpose, to communicate needed information that's too complicated for a memo or letter. Stated in the simplest terms, there are essentially two kinds of reports: short and long. This chapter focuses on the former, discussing basic principles of page design, short report formats, and several common types of short reports.

Page Design

As we have seen, the physical characteristics of memos and letters are largely determined by established guidelines that vary only slightly. But reports, while also subject to certain conventions, are to a much greater degree the creation of individual writers who determine not only their content but also their physical appearance. This is significant because our ability to comprehend what we read is greatly influenced by its arrangement on the page or screen. A report, therefore, should never *look* difficult or intimidating. Consider, for example, Figure 4.1, which has been adapted from a safety manual for railroad employees.

Obviously, the passage is nearly unreadable in its present state. To make it more visually appealing, the first step is to insert more space between the lines and use both uppercase and lowercase letters (see Figure 4.2).

Certainly, the revised page is far more legible. It can be improved still further, however, by organizing the content into paragraphs and adopting a ragged right margin (see Figure 4.3).

The use of varied spacing, lists, and boldface headings, as well as some minor editing, will make the content emerge even more clearly. Obviously, Figure 4.4 is easier to read than the earlier versions. Certainly such revision is worthwhile and not particularly difficult if the following fundamental principles of effective page design are observed.

ELECTRIC SHOCK

ELECTRIC SHOCK IS NOT ALWAYS FATAL, AND RARELY IS IT IMMEDIATELY FATAL. IT MAY ONLY STUN THE VICTIM AND MOMENTARILY ARREST BREATHING. IN CASES OF ELECTRIC SHOCK, BREAK CONTACT, RESTORE THE VICTIM'S BREATHING BY MEANS OF ARTIFICIAL RESPIRATION, AND MAINTAIN WARMTH. TO AVOID RECEIVING A SHOCK YOURSELF, EXERCISE EXTREME CAUTION WHEN ATTEMPTING TO RELEASE THE VICTIM FROM CONTACT WITH A LIVE CONDUCTOR. MANY PERSONS, BY THEIR LACK OF KNOWLEDGE OF SUCH MATTERS, HAVE BEEN SEVERELY SHOCKED OR BURNED WHEN ATTEMPTING TO RESCUE A CO-WORKER. TO RELEASE A VICTIM FROM CONTACT WITH LIVE CONDUCTORS KNOWN TO BE 750 VOLTS OR LESS, DO NOT TOUCH THE CONDUCTOR, AND DO NOT TOUCH THE VICTIM OR THE VICTIM'S BARE SKIN IF THE VICTIM IS IN CONTACT WITH THE LIVE CONDUCTOR. INSTEAD, USE A PIECE OF DRY, NONCONDUCTING MATERIAL SUCH AS A PIECE OF WOOD, ROPE, OR RUBBER HOSE TO PUSH OR PULL THE LIVE CONDUCTOR AWAY FROM THE VICTIM. THE LIVE CONDUCTOR CAN ALSO BE HANDLED SAFELY WITH RUBBER GLOVES. IF THE VICTIM'S CLOTHES ARE DRY, THE VICTIM CAN BE DRAGGED AWAY FROM THE LIVE CONDUCTOR BY GRASPING THE CLOTHES—NOT THE BARE SKIN. IN SO DOING, THE RESCUER SHOULD STAND ON A DRY BOARD AND USE ONLY ONE HAND. DO NOT STAND IN A PUDDLE OR ON DAMP OR WET GROUND. TO RELEASE A VICTIM FROM CONTACT WITH LIVE CONDUCTORS OF UNKNOWN VOLTAGE OR MORE THAN 750 VOLTS . . .
[text continues]

FIGURE 4.1   Poor Page Design

■ Legible Type. Although many different typefaces and type sizes exist, most readers respond best to 12-point type using both uppercase and lowercase letters, like this text. Anything smaller or larger is difficult to read, as is the all-capitals approach; such options are useful only in major headings or to emphasize a particular word or phrase.

ELECTRIC SHOCK

Electric shock is not always fatal, and rarely is it immediately fatal. It may only stun the victim and momentarily arrest breathing. In cases of electric shock, break contact, restore the victim's breathing by means of artificial respiration, and maintain warmth. To avoid receiving a shock yourself, exercise extreme caution when attempting to release the victim from contact with a live conductor. Many persons, by their lack of knowledge of such matters, have been severely shocked or burned when attempting to rescue a co-worker. To release a victim from contact with live conductors known to be 750 volts or less, do not touch the conductor, and do not touch the victim or the victim's bare skin if the victim is in contact with the live conductor. Instead, use a piece of dry, nonconducting material such as a piece of wood, rope, or rubber hose to push or pull the live conductor away from the victim. The live conductor can also be handled safely with rubber gloves. If the victim's clothes are dry, the victim can be dragged away from the live conductor by grasping the clothes—not the bare skin. In so doing, the rescuer should stand on a dry board and use only one hand. Do not stand in a puddle or on damp or wet ground. To release a victim from contact with live conductors of unknown voltage or more than 750 volts . . . .

FIGURE 4.2   **Revised Page**

- Generous Margins. Text should be centered on the page and framed by white space. The top and bottom margins should both be at least 1 inch and the side margins 1.25 inches. If the report is to be bound, the left margin should be 2 inches. (If the report is to

ELECTRIC SHOCK

Electric shock is not always fatal, and rarely is it immediately fatal. It may only stun the victim and momentarily arrest breathing. In cases of electric shock, break contact, restore the victim's breathing by means of artificial respiration, and maintain warmth. To avoid receiving a shock yourself, exercise extreme caution when attempting to release the victim from contact with a live conductor. Many persons, by their lack of knowledge of such matters, have been severely shocked or burned when attempting to rescue a co-worker.

To release a victim from contact with live conductors known to be 750 volts or less, do not touch the conductor, and do not touch the victim or the victim's bare skin if the victim is in contact with the live conductor. Instead, use a piece of dry, nonconducting material such as a piece of wood, rope, or rubber hose to push or pull the live conductor away from the victim. The live conductor can also be handled safely with rubber gloves. If the victim's clothes are dry, the victim can be dragged away from the live conductor by grasping the clothes—not the bare skin. In so doing, the rescuer should stand on a dry board and use only one hand. Do not stand in a puddle or on damp or wet ground.

To release a victim from contact with live conductors of unknown voltage or more than 750 volts . . . .

FIGURE 4.3   **Second Revision**

be duplicated back-to-back before binding, then the 2-inch margin should be on the *right* side of the even-numbered pages.) The right margin should not be justified but should run ragged; this improves legibility by creating greater contrast from line to line.

ELECTRIC SHOCK

Electric shock is not always fatal, and is rarely immediately fatal. It may only stun the victim and momentarily arrest breathing. In cases of electric shock, do three things:

1. Break contact;
2. Restore breathing by artificial respiration;
3. Maintain warmth.

To avoid receiving a shock yourself, exercise extreme caution when attempting to release the victim from contact with a live conductor. Many persons, lacking knowledge of such matters, have been severely shocked or burned attempting to rescue a co-worker.

Release of victim from contact with live conductors known to be 750 volts or less:

- Do not touch the live conductor.
- Do not touch the victim or the victim's bare skin while the victim is in contact with the live conductor.
- Instead, use a piece of DRY, nonconducting material such as a piece of wood, rope, or rubber hose to push or pull the live conductor away from the victim. The live conductor may be handled safely with rubber gloves.
- If the victim's clothes are dry, the victim can be dragged away from the live conductor by grasping the clothing—not the bare skin. In so doing, the rescuer should stand on a dry board and . . . .

FIGURE 4.4   **Third Revision**

- Textual Divisions. Long, unbroken passages of text are very difficult to follow with attention, which is why the practice of dividing text into paragraphs was adopted centuries ago. In most workplace writing, paragraphs should not exceed five or six sentences and should be plainly separated by ample white space. If the paragraphs are single-spaced, insert double-spacing between them; if the paragraphs are double-spaced, use triple-spacing between them. To further organize content, group related paragraphs within a report into separate sections that logically reflect the internal organization of the report's information. Like the individual paragraphs, these sections should be plainly separated by proportionately greater spacing.

- Headings. Separate sections of text should be labeled with meaningful headings that further clarify content and allow the reader to skim the report for specific aspects of its subject matter. Ordinarily, a heading consists of a word or phrase, *not* a complete sentence. (Instructional materials, however, sometimes use *questions* as headings.) The position of a heading is determined by its relative importance. A major heading is set in boldface caps and centered,

LIKE THIS

A secondary heading is set either in uppercase letters or in both uppercase and lowercase, is flush with the margin, and can be underlined or set in boldface print (though not both),

Like This

or

Like This

A subtopic heading is run into the text, separated by a period or a colon, and is sometimes indented. Set in both uppercase and lowercase letters, it can be underlined or set in bold print (though not both),

Like This. These recommendations are based on those in *The Gregg Reference Manual*, considered the most widely recognized authority on such matters.

Obviously, these principles are flexible, and various approaches to heading design and placement are used, some of them quite elaborate. Among the most helpful recommendations in *Gregg* is to limit a report to no more than three levels of heads.

Tech Tips

Thanks to computerized word processing, nearly every workplace writer now has access to many page design features that in the past were available only through commercial print shops. As we've already seen, options such as varied spacing and type size, boldface print, capitalization, and underlining can make your documents appear much more professional. In addition, pages can be formatted in columns or other spatial arrangements.

Used selectively, these features enhance the design of a page not only by signaling major divisions and subdivisions within the content but also by creating emphasis with highlighted key words and phrases. In addition, many software packages are equipped with ready-made report templates and other features such as headers and automatic page numbering for multipage documents, and these can be adapted to the individual writer's needs.

Even more versatile are the many DTP (desktop publishing) programs now available. These programs take electronic word-processing to the next level and are therefore ideal for creating documents that are more elaborate, such as newsletters, brochures, and manuals. By imitating traditional print-shop techniques, which required a drafting table, scissors, paste, rulers, compasses, and the like, DTP programs enable you to draw complex layouts right on the page. You can rotate bits of text to any angle, curve text, and wrap text around irregularly shaped graphics. Graphics can be enlarged, reduced, or cropped. In addition, DTP programs provide a vast range of fonts and permit very tiny gradations in spacing and type size. Interfaced with standard word-processing and graphics-design software, a good optical scanner, and a high-resolution laser printer, a desktop publishing program such as Quark XPress or Aldus Pagemaker can produce excellent, professional-quality results.

But remember to exercise restraint and maintain consistency in using these tools. Keep your page design relatively simple. It's very easy to get carried away and end up creating a messy and confusing document, especially if you're still relatively new to this technology. Like visual elements, page design options should never function simply as decoration but as aids to your reader's understanding. The key is to experiment with your software and thoroughly familiarize yourself with its capabilities. Soon you'll develop a more accurate sense of which page design features might genuinely help your reader.

- Lists. Sometimes a list is more effective than a conventional paragraph. If the purpose of the list is to indicate a definite order of importance, the items in the list should be *numbered* in descending order, with the most important item first, least important last. Similarly, if the list's purpose is to indicate a chronological sequence of events or actions (as in a procedures manual), the items should be numbered in sequential order. Numbers are not necessary, however, in a list of approximately equal items. In those cases, "bullets" (solid black dots, like those used in this section), asterisks, or dashes will suffice.

Report Formats: Memo, Letter, and Booklet

Many companies and organizations prepare short reports using the fill-in-the-blanks approach typified by the forms reproduced in Figures 4.5 and 4.6. As we have seen, however, computer technology now enables individual writers to personally design the pages of their reports. A customized report can usually be categorized into one of three report formats: memo, letter, or booklet.

Typically used for in-house purposes, the **memo report** is similar to the conventional memo but is longer (two pages or more) and is therefore divided into labeled sections. The **letter report**—typically sent to an outside reader—is formatted like a conventional business letter, except that the letter report is divided into labeled sections, much like a memo report. The **booklet report** resembles a short term paper and includes a title page. It too is divided into labeled sections. It is also accompanied by a cover memo (for in-house reports) or cover letter (for reports sent to outside readers). Much like the opening paragraph of a memo report or letter report, this cover document serves to orient the reader by establishing context and explaining the purpose and scope of the booklet report.

Both memo reports and booklet reports often contain visuals; letter reports sometimes do. Figures 4.7, 4.8, and 4.9 illustrate the three formats. Written by a fictitious health inspector and his supervisor, these examples use easily understood subject matter. These three formats can be adapted to any workplace situation, however, simply by changing the headings to suit the context at hand.

EMPLOYEE ACCIDENT/FORM A

TO BE COMPLETED BY EMPLOYEE

Name _____ Home address _____

Social security no._____ Date of birth _____

Sex __M__ __F__ Department in which you work _____

Accident date _____ Day of week _____ Time _____ a.m. _____ p.m.

Date accident was reported _____ To whom _____

Location of accident _____ Witnesses _____

Description of accident (what was employee doing, what equipment was
being used, etc.)

_____

_____

_____

Description of injury (include nature of injury and body part)

_____

_____

_____

Did you receive medical care on premises? _____ Describe _____

_____

_____

If employee is being treated:

Name and address of physician: _____

Name and address of hospital: _____

Do you have a second job? _____

EMPLOYEE'S SIGNATURE _____ Date: _____

TO BE COMPLETED BY COMPANY NURSE

Above employee came to me on _____ regarding the above injury.

Comments:

_____

_____

_____

NURSE'S SIGNATURE _____ Date: _____

FIGURE 4.5 **Employee Accident Form**

CHESTER J. FULTZ
MAYOR

CITY OF WHALEN

DEPARTMENT OF PARKS
1 Cornelius Plaza, Whalen, New York
315-555-1234

HAROLD SCHROEDER
Parks Commissioner

EQUIPMENT FAILURE REPORT

Reported By: _____

Equipment Affected:	Date:	Time:

Description of Trouble:

Interim Measures Taken:

Description of Maintenance Performed:
(LIST ALL PARTS USED)

Date Restored to Service:	By:	Time:

FIGURE 4.6   **Equipment Failure Report Form**

Monroe County Health Department

MEMORANDUM

DATE: February 3, 2003

TO: Marjorie Witkowski, Supervisor

FROM: Richard Vaughan, Senior Inspector

SUBJECT: Restaurant Inspections

As you requested, here are the results of last week's inspections of food service establishments in the county, along with a week-by-week statistical summary of inspections during January.

UNSATISFACTORY

The following establishments were found to be in substantial violation of the sanitary code.

Big Daddy's Steak House
431 Grand Avenue, Conover Falls
Inspected January 27, 2003

Toxic chemicals (antifreeze, can of ant/roach killer) found on premises. Potentially hazardous foods not kept at or above 140 degrees F during hot holding. Food not protected—buckets of food stored on floor in cooler, food not covered in coolers. Raw meat stored over prepared foods in cooler. Food

FIGURE 4.7   Memo Report, Page 1

2

build-up in storage room refrigerator. Canned goods in poor condition (dented, rusted). Bowl used as flour scoop. Box of paper towels improperly stored on floor. Nonfood contact surfaces not easily cleanable. Cardboard used as liner on food storage shelves. Restroom missing hand wash sign. Light fixture missing shield and end caps. Kitchen ceiling tiles missing. No 2003 permit on display.

Employee Cafeteria, Paragon Insurance Co.
Airport Road, Cedarville
Inspected January 28, 2003

Potentially hazardous foods not kept at or below 45 degrees F during cold holding. Potentially hazardous foods not kept at or above 140 degrees F during hot holding. Single-service napkins stored on kitchen floor.

Roma Pizzeria
38 Crowley Street, Dunkirk
Inspected January 29, 2003

Worker serving pizza slices with bare hands. Potentially hazardous foods not kept at or above 140 degrees F during hot holding. Food not protected—uncovered food in freezer, salt bucket not labeled. Hair improperly restrained—hats, nets/visors required. In-use utensils stored on paper plate. Employee (delivery driver) smoking in kitchen.

SATISFACTORY

The following establishments were found to be in essential compliance with the sanitary code, although some violations were noted.

Imperial Wok
618 Rogers Street, Cooperton
Inspected January 30, 2003

Potentially hazardous foods not kept at or above 140 degrees F during hot holding. Food not protected—jars of juice stored on kitchen floor. Improper use of utensils—scoop stored handle down in flour.

FIGURE 4.7   **Memo Report, Page 2**

3

Cuzzie's Pub
39 Railroad Street, Monroe
Inspected January 31, 2003

Unshielded light fixture in walk-in cooler. No hand soap in restroom.

NO VIOLATIONS

The following establishments were found to be in full compliance with the sanitary code.

Conover Falls Coffee House
17 Village Green East, Conover Falls
Inspected January 27, 2003

Mister Eight Ball
49 Clinton Street, Dunkirk
Inspected January 29, 2003

SUMMARY OF JANUARY 2003 INSPECTIONS

	Unsatisfactory	Satisfactory	No Violations
Jan. 6–10	3	2	2
Jan. 13–17	5	0	1
Jan. 20–24	2	3	2
Jan. 27–31	3	2	2
Totals	13	7	7

FIGURE 4.7   Memo Report, Page 3

Monroe County Health Department

County Office Building ✦ **Court House Square**
Monroe, Wyoming 82001 ✦ **(307) 555-1200**

February 5, 2003

Mr. Daniel Runninghorse, Editor
The Monroe Daily Observer
687 Harpur Street
Monroe, WY 82001

Dear Mr. Runninghorse:

As you may know, the County Health Department conducts ongoing, unannounced inspections of food service establishments to ensure their compliance with state codes, rules, and regulations. Since the findings of these inspections are a matter of public record, The Monroe Daily Observer has in the past printed that information in its entirety. Now that you have become the editor of the Observer, we would like you to continue this practice, which we regard as a valuable service to the community and a validation of our efforts here at the department.

Here are the results of last week's inspections, as well as a week-by-week statistical summary of all inspections during January.

UNSATISFACTORY

The following establishments were found to be in substantial violation of the sanitary code.

Big Daddy's Steak House
431 Grand Avenue, Conover Falls
Inspected January 27, 2003

Toxic chemicals (antifreeze, can of ant/roach killer) found on premises. Potentially hazardous foods not kept at or above 140 degrees F during hot holding. Food not protected—buckets of food stored on floor in cooler, food not

---

FIGURE 4.8 **Letter Report, Page 1**

2

covered in coolers. Raw meat stored over prepared foods in cooler. Food build-up in storage room refrigerator. Canned goods in poor condition (dented, rusted). Bowl used as flour scoop. Box of paper towels improperly stored on floor. Nonfood contact surfaces not easily cleanable. Cardboard used as liner on food storage shelves. Restroom missing hand wash sign. Light fixture missing shield and end caps. Kitchen ceiling tiles missing. No 2003 permit on display.

Employee Cafeteria, Paragon Insurance Co.
Airport Road, Cedarville
Inspected January 28, 2003

Potentially hazardous foods not kept at or below 45 degrees F during cold holding. Potentially hazardous foods not kept at or above 140 degrees F during hot holding. Single-service napkins stored on kitchen floor.

Roma Pizzeria
38 Crowley Street, Dunkirk
Inspected January 29, 2003

Worker serving pizza slices with bare hands. Potentially hazardous foods not kept at or above 140 degrees F during hot holding. Food not protected— uncovered food in freezer, salt bucket not labeled. Hair improperly restrained—hats, nets/visors required. In-use utensils stored on paper plate. Employee (delivery driver) smoking in kitchen.

SATISFACTORY

The following establishments were found to be in essential compliance with the sanitary code, although some violations were noted.

Imperial Wok
618 Rogers Street, Cooperton
Inspected January 30, 2003

Potentially hazardous foods not kept at or above 140 degrees F during hot holding. Food not protected—jars of juice stored on kitchen floor. Improper use of utensils—scoop stored handle down in flour.

FIGURE 4.8   **Letter Report, Page 2**

3

Cuzzie's Pub
39 Railroad Street, Monroe
Inspected January 31, 2003

Unshielded light fixture in walk-in cooler. No hand soap in restroom.

NO VIOLATIONS

The following establishments were found to be in full compliance with the sanitary code.

Conover Falls Coffee House
17 Village Green East, Conover Falls
Inspected January 27, 2003

Mister Eight Ball
49 Clinton Street, Dunkirk
Inspected January 29, 2003

SUMMARY OF JANUARY 2003 INSPECTIONS

	Unsatisfactory	Satisfactory	No Violations
Jan. 6–10	3	2	2
Jan. 13–17	5	0	1
Jan. 20–24	2	3	2
Jan. 27–31	3	2	2
Totals	13	7	7

Please feel free to call me at your convenience if you have questions regarding these inspections or any other matters relating to the Monroe County Health Department. Unless I hear otherwise, I will continue to provide inspection results on a weekly basis.

Sincerely,

Marjorie Witkowski

Marjorie Witkowski
Supervisor

FIGURE 4.8   Letter Report, Page 3

Monroe County Health Department

MEMORANDUM

DATE: February 10, 2003

TO: Janet Butler, Commissioner

FROM: Marjorie Witkowski, Supervisor

SUBJECT: Inspections Report

As you requested, here is a complete report on the results of Richard Vaughan's inspections of food service establishments in the county during the last week of January, along with a week-by-week statistical summary of his inspections during that month.

FIGURE 4.9   **Booklet Report, Cover Memo**

INSPECTIONS OF FOOD SERVICE ESTABLISHMENTS
IN MONROE COUNTY, WYOMING
JANUARY 27–31, 2003

Report Submitted to

Janet Butler
Commissioner of Public Health

by

Marjorie Witkowski
Supervisor, County Health Department

February 10, 2003

FIGURE 4.9   **Booklet Report, Title Page**

INTRODUCTION

In keeping with its mandate to safeguard the public welfare, the Monroe County Health Department conducts ongoing, unannounced inspections of the county's food service establishments to ensure their compliance with state codes, rules, and regulations. This report provides the results of seven inspections conducted by Senior Inspector Richard Vaughan during the period of January 27–31 of this year, along with a week-by-week statistical summary of Mr. Vaughan's 27 total inspections during January.

UNSATISFACTORY

The following establishments were found to be in substantial violation of the sanitary code.

Big Daddy's Steak House
431 Grand Avenue, Conover Falls
Inspected January 27, 2003

Toxic chemicals (antifreeze, can of ant/roach killer) found on premises. Potentially hazardous foods not kept at or above 140 degrees F during hot holding. Food not protected—buckets of food stored on floor in cooler, food not covered in coolers. Raw meat stored over prepared foods in cooler. Food build-up in storage room refrigerator. Canned goods in poor condition (dented, rusted). Bowl used as flour scoop. Box of paper towels improperly stored on floor. Nonfood contact surfaces not easily cleanable. Cardboard used as liner on food storage shelves. Restroom missing hand wash sign. Light fixture missing shield and end caps. Kitchen ceiling tiles missing. No 2003 permit on display.

Employee Cafeteria, Paragon Insurance Co.
Airport Road, Cedarville
Inspected January 28, 2003

Potentially hazardous foods not kept at or below 45 degrees F during cold holding. Potentially hazardous foods not kept at or above 140 degrees F during hot holding. Single-service napkins stored on kitchen floor.

FIGURE 4.9   Booklet Report, Page 1

2

Roma Pizzeria
38 Crowley Street, Dunkirk
Inspected January 29, 2003

Worker serving pizza slices with bare hands. Potentially hazardous foods
not kept at or above 140 degrees F during hot holding. Food not protected—
uncovered food in freezer, salt bucket not labeled. Hair improperly restrained—
hats, nets/visors required. In-use utensils stored on paper plate. Employee
(delivery driver) smoking in kitchen.

SATISFACTORY

The following establishments were found to be in essential compliance with
the sanitary code, although some violations were noted.

Imperial Wok
618 Rogers Street, Cooperton
Inspected January 30, 2003

Potentially hazardous foods not kept at or above 140 degrees F during hot
holding. Food not protected—jars of juice stored on kitchen floor. Improper use
of utensils—scoop stored handle down in flour.

Cuzzie's Pub
39 Railroad Street, Monroe
Inspected January 31, 2003

Unshielded light fixture in walk-in cooler. No hand soap in restroom.

NO VIOLATIONS

The following establishments were found to be in full compliance with the
sanitary code.

Conover Falls Coffee House
17 Village Green East, Conover Falls
Inspected January 27, 2003

FIGURE 4.9   **Booklet Report, Page 2**

3

Mister Eight Ball
49 Clinton Street, Dunkirk
Inspected January 29, 2003

SUMMARY OF JANUARY 2003 INSPECTIONS

	Unsatisfactory	Satisfactory	No Violations
Jan. 6–10	3	2	2
Jan. 13–17	5	0	1
Jan. 20–24	2	3	2
Jan. 27–31	3	2	2
Totals	13	7	7

FIGURE 4.9   Booklet Report, Page 3

Types of Reports

Like memos and letters, workplace reports are written in all kinds of situations for an enormous variety of reasons. Many reports are in a sense unique because they are written in response to one-time occurrences. On the other hand, it's not uncommon for a given report to be part of an ongoing series of weekly, monthly, or annual reports on the same subject. Most reports can be classified into several broad categories. Some of the most common are as follows:

- Incident report: explains the circumstances surrounding a troublesome occurrence such as an accident, fire, equipment malfunction, or security breach.

- Progress report: outlines the status of an ongoing project or undertaking.

- Recommendation report: urges that certain procedures be adopted (or rejected).

- Travel report: identifies the purpose and summarizes the results of business-related travel.

Of course, an individual report can serve more than one purpose; overlap is not uncommon. An incident report, for example, may well conclude with a recommendations section intended to minimize the likelihood of recurrence. In every situation, the writer must consider the purpose and intended audience for the report. Content, language, tone, degree of detail, and overall approach must be appropriate to the circumstances, and the report headings, formatting, visuals, and other features must suit the role of the particular report. The following pages discuss the four common report types in detail.

Incident Report

An incident report creates a written record of a troublesome occurrence. The report is written either by the person involved in the incident or by the person in charge of the area where it took place. Such a report may be needed to satisfy government regulations, to guard against legal liability, or to draw attention to unsafe or otherwise unsatisfactory conditions in need of correction. Accordingly, an incident report must provide a thorough description of the occurrence and, if possible, an explanation of the cause(s). In addition, it often includes a section of recommendations for corrective measures.

When describing the incident, always provide complete details:

- Names and job titles of all persons involved, including onlookers
- Step-by-step narrative description of the incident
- Exact location of the incident
- Date and exact time of each major development
- Clear identification of any equipment or machinery involved
- Detailed description of any medical intervention required, including names of ambulance services and personnel, nurses, physicians, hospitals, or clinics
- Reliable statements (quotation or paraphrase) from persons involved
- Outcome of the incident

To avoid liability when discussing possible causes, use qualifiers such as *perhaps, maybe, possibly,* and *it appears.* Do not report the comments of witnesses and those involved as if those observations were verified facts; often they are grossly inaccurate. Attribute all such comments to their sources, and identify them as speculation only. Furthermore, exclude any comments unrelated to the immediate incident. Although you're ethically required to be as complete and accurate as possible, don't create an unnecessarily suspicious climate by relying on secondhand accounts or reporting verbatim the remarks of persons who are obviously angry or distraught, as in this example:

> Ronald Perkins suffered a severed index finger when his left hand became caught in a drill press after he tripped on some wood that another employee had carelessly left on the floor near the machine. According to Perkins, this was "pretty typical of how things are always done around here."

A more objective phrasing might look something like this:

> Ronald Perkins suffered a severed index finger when his left hand became caught in a drill press. Perkins said he had tripped on wood that was lying on the floor near the machine.

Similarly, the recommendations section of an incident report should not seek to assign blame or highlight incompetence but to encourage the adoption of measures that will decrease the likelihood of repeated problems. Consider, for example, the incident report in Figure 4.10, prepared in memo report format.

Southeast Insurance Company

MEMORANDUM

DATE: October 14, 2004

TO: Jonathan Purdy
            Physical Plant Supervisor

FROM: Bonnie Cardillo
            Nurse

SUBJECT: Incident Report

John Fitzsimmons, a claims adjuster, slipped and fell in the front lobby of the building, striking his head and momentarily losing consciousness.

DESCRIPTION OF INCIDENT

At approximately 2:55 p.m. on Thursday, October 8, Fitzsimmons was returning from his break when he slipped and fell in the front lobby, striking his head on the stone floor and momentarily losing consciousness. According to Beverly Barrett, the receptionist, the floor had just been mopped and was still wet. She paged Mike Moore, the security officer, who in turn paged me. When I arrived at approximately 3:00 p.m., Fitzsimmons had revived. I immediately checked his vital signs, which were normal. He refused further medical attention and returned to work. I advised him to contact me if he experienced any subsequent discomfort, but to my knowledge there has been none.

FIGURE 4.10   Incident Report (Memo Format), Page 1

2

RECOMMENDATIONS

Two ideas come to mind.

Perhaps we should remind all employees to contact me first (rather than Security) in situations involving personal injury. The sooner I'm contacted, the sooner I can respond. Obviously, time can be an important factor if the problem is serious.

To prevent other occurrences of this nature, perhaps the maintenance staff should be provided with large, brightly colored warning signs alerting employees and public alike to the presence of wet floors. I see these signs in use at the mall, the hospital, and elsewhere, and they do not appear expensive. I have noted also that many are bilingual, bearing both the English warning "Caution: Wet Floor" and the Spanish "Cuidado: Piso Mojado." No doubt they can be ordered from any of the catalogs regularly received by your office.

FIGURE 4.10 **Incident Report (Memo Format), Page 2**

Progress Report

A progress report provides information about the status of an ongoing project or activity that must be monitored to ensure successful completion within a specified period. Sometimes called status reports or periodic reports, progress reports are submitted either upon completion of key stages of a project or at regular, preestablished intervals—quarterly, monthly, weekly, or sometimes as often as every day. They are written by the individual(s) directly responsible for the success of the undertaking. The readers of these reports are usually in the management sector of the organization, however, and may not be familiar with the technical details of the situation. Rather, their priority is successful completion of the project within established cost guidelines. Therefore, the information in a progress report tends to be more general than specific, and the language tends to be far less technical than that of other kinds of reports.

Most progress reports include the following components:

- Introduction: provides context and background, identifying the project, reviewing its objectives, and alerting the reader to any new developments since the previous progress report.

- Work completed: summarizes accomplishments to date. This section can be organized in either of two ways: If the report deals with one major task, a chronological approach is advisable; if it deals with several related projects, then subdivisions by task are better.

- Work remaining: summarizes all uncompleted tasks, emphasizing what is expected to be accomplished first.

- Problems: identifies any delays, cost overruns, or other unanticipated difficulties. If all is well, or if the problems are of no particular consequence, this section may be omitted.

- Conclusion: summarizes the status of the project and recommends solutions to any major problems.

If properly prepared and submitted promptly, progress reports can be invaluable in enabling management to make necessary adjustments to meet deadlines, avert crises, and prevent unnecessary expense. Figure 4.11 depicts a progress report on capital projects, prepared in booklet report format with a transmittal memo.

WESTON INDUSTRIES, INC.

MEMORANDUM

DATE: November 10, 2003

TO: Judith Ayres
            Accounting Department

FROM: John Daly
            Physical Plant

SUBJECT: Progress Report on Capital Projects

As requested, here is the progress report on the five capital projects identified as high-priority items at last spring's long-range planning meeting:

- Replacement of front elevator in Main Building
- Replacement of all windows in Main Building
- Installation of new fire alarm system in all buildings
- Installation of emergency lighting system in all buildings
- Renovation of "B" Building basement

Please contact me if you have any questions.

FIGURE 4.11 **Progress Report (Booklet Format), Transmittal Memo**

WESTON INDUSTRIES, INC.

PROGRESS REPORT

on

CAPITAL PROJECTS

by

John Daly
Physical Plant

Submitted to

Judith Ayres
Accounting Department

November 10, 2003

FIGURE 4.11   Progress Report (Booklet Format), Title Page

INTRODUCTION

Weston Industries, Inc. is currently involved in several major capital projects that were identified as high-priority items at last spring's long-range planning meeting: replacement of the front elevator and all windows in the Main Building, installation of a new fire alarm system and emergency lighting system in all buildings, and renovation of the "B" Building basement. Progress has been made on all of these projects, although there have been a few problems.

WORK COMPLETED

Elevator Replacement

Equipment has been ordered from Uptown Elevator. The pump has arrived and is in storage. We have asked Uptown for a construction schedule.

Window Replacement

Entrance and window wall: KlearVue Window Co. has completed this job, but it is unsatisfactory. See "Problems" section below. Other windows: Architect has approved submittal package, and Cavan Glass Co. is preparing shop drawings. Architect has sent Cavan Glass Co. a letter stating that work must begin no later than April 1, with completion in July.

Fire Alarm System

First submittal package from Alert-All, Ltd. was reviewed by architect and rejected. A second package was accepted. The alarm system is on order.

Emergency Lighting System

BriteLite, Inc. has begun installation in the Main Building. They will proceed on a building-by-building basis, completing one before moving onto another.

Basement Renovation

First submittal package from Innovation Renovation was reviewed by architect and rejected. Innovation Renovation is preparing a second package to reduce HVAC costs. Work will begin in June.

FIGURE 4.11   Progress Report (Booklet Format), Page 1

2

WORK REMAINING

Elevator Replacement
Construction schedule must be received from Uptown Elevator. Work must begin.

Window Replacement
Entrance and window wall: Problems with KlearVue Window Co. must be resolved. See "Problems" section below. Other windows: Shop drawings must be received from Cavan Glass Co. and approved. Work must begin.

Fire Alarm System
System must be received. Work must begin. Work will be completed during downtime (10 p.m. to 6 a.m.) to minimize disruption.

Emergency Lighting System
BriteLite, Inc. must complete installation in the Main Building, then move on to other buildings. Bulk of this work will be done during downtime.

Basement Renovation
Final submittal package must be received from Innovation Renovation and approved. Work must begin.

PROBLEMS

Window Replacement
Entrance and window wall: KlearVue Window Co. is still responsible for replacing one window that has a defect in the glass. In addition, the architect refuses to accept three of the five large panes in the window wall due to excessive distortion in the glass. The architect has sent several letters to KlearVue but has received no response. The remaining balance on this contract ($17,750) is therefore being held, pending resolution of these problems.

CONCLUSION

Although none of the five capital projects targeted at the spring meeting has in fact been satisfactorily completed, all but one are moving forward through expected channels. The one troublesome item—the unsatisfactory windows—should be resolved. If KlearVue continues to ignore the architect's inquiries, perhaps our attorneys should attempt to get a response.

FIGURE 4.11   **Progress Report (Booklet Format), Page 2**

Recommendation Report

A recommendation report assesses a troublesome or unsatisfactory situation, identifies a solution to the problem, and persuades decision makers to pursue a particular course of action that will improve matters. Such reports are sometimes unsolicited. Generally, however, a recommendation report is written by a knowledgeable employee who has been specifically assigned the task. As with most kinds of reports, the content can vary greatly depending on the nature of the business or organization and on the nature of the situation at hand. In nearly all cases, however, recommendation reports are intended to enhance the quality of products or services, to maximize profits, to reduce costs, or to improve working conditions.

In the case of a solicited report, the writer should attempt to get a written request from the individual who wants the report and then carefully study it to determine the exact parameters of the situation in question. If unsure of any aspect of the assignment, the writer should seek clarification before continuing. As discussed in Chapter 1, it's vital to establish a firm sense of purpose and audience before you attempt to compose any workplace writing. A clear and focused written request—or the discussion generated by the lack of one—will provide guidance in this regard.

Since recommendation reports are persuasive in nature, they are in several respects trickier to write—and to live with afterward—than reports intended primarily to record factual information. Tact is of great importance. Since your report essentially is designed to bring about an improvement in existing conditions or procedures, you should guard against appearing overly critical of the present circumstances. Focus more on what *will be* than on what *is*. Emphasize solutions rather than problems. Do not assign blame for present difficulties except in the most extreme cases. A very helpful strategy in writing recommendation reports is to request input from co-workers, whose perspective may give you a more comprehensive understanding of the situation you're assessing.

Recommendation reports are structured in various ways, but almost all include three basic components:

- Problem: identifies not only the problem itself but also, if possible, its causes and its relative urgency.

- Solution: sets forth a recommendation and explains how it will be implemented and clearly states its advantages, including relevant data on costs, timing, and the like.

■ Discussion: summarizes briefly the report's key points and politely urges the adoption of its recommendation.

Figure 4.12, prepared in letter report format, depicts a recommendation report designed to enable a feed manufacturing company to avert fiscal problems by cutting costs at one of its mills.

Travel Report

There are two kinds of travel reports: field reports and trip reports. The purpose of both is to create a record of—and, by implication, justification for—an employee's work-related travel. The travel may be directly related to the performance of routine duties (a field visit to a customer or client, for example) or it may be part of the employee's ongoing professional development (such as a trip to a convention, trade show, or off-site training session). Submitted to the employee's immediate supervisor, a travel report not only describes the employee activity made possible by traveling but also assesses the activity's value and relevance to the organization.

Travel reports are usually structured as follows:

■ Introduction: provides all basic information, including destination, purpose of travel, arrival and departure dates and time, and mode of travel (personal car, company car, train, plane).

■ Description of activity/service performed: not an itinerary but rather a selectively detailed account. The degree of detail is greater if readers other than the supervisor will have access to the report and expect to learn something from it. In the case of a field report, any problems encountered should be detailed, along with corrective actions taken.

■ Cost accounting: usually required for nonroutine travel. The employee accounts for all money spent, especially if it is to be reimbursed by the employer.

■ Discussion: an assessment of the usefulness of the travel and, if applicable, includes recommendations regarding the feasibility of other such travel in the future. In the case of a field report, suggestions are sometimes made based on the particulars of the situation.

Figures 4.13 and 4.14, both in memo report format, depict the two kinds of travel reports.

COOPER & SONS FEED COMPANY

"Serving Livestock Breeders Since 1932"

Des Moines Mill   •   State Highway, Des Moines, IA 50300   •   (515) 555-1234

February 10, 2004

Ms. Mary Cooper, CEO
Cooper & Sons Feed Company
Main Office
427 Cosgrove Street
Des Moines, IA 50300

Dear Ms. Cooper:

Here is the report you requested, outlining a proposed expense management
plan that will enable the Des Moines Mill to cut costs.

PROBLEM

Because of the recent closings of several large family-run farms in the
surrounding area, our profit margin has shrunk. We must therefore reduce
the Des Moines Mill's annual operating budget by at least $70,000 for it to
remain viable.

SOLUTION

<u>Inventory Reduction</u>
Reduce inventory by $50,000, thereby creating savings on 10% interest expense.
Saving: $5,000.

<u>Elimination of Hourly Position</u>
Based on seniority, eliminate one customer service position, distributing re-
sponsibilities between the two remaining employees.
Saving: $10,500 in wages plus $2,100 in benefits; total, $12,600.

FIGURE 4.12   **Recommendation Report (Letter Format), Page 1**

2

Elimination of Salaried Position
Eliminate plant manager position, distributing responsibilities between the
two assistant managers.

Saving: $36,320 in salary plus $7,264 in benefits; total, $43,584.

Reduction of Remill Costs
Each load returned from farm for remill costs an average of $165 and creates
3.5 hours of overtime work. Lowering our error rate from 2 per month to 1 per
month will save $1,980 annually. In addition, this will raise the ingredient
value we capture on these feeds by 50% (6 ton/month × 12 months × $100
increased value) or $7,200.

Saving: total, $9,200.

DISCUSSION

Adoption of the above measures will result in a total annual savings of
$70,384. This is within the requirements.

The principal negative impact will be on personnel, and we regret the necessity
of eliminating the two positions. It should be noted, however, that the situation
could be much worse. The hourly customer service employee can be rehired
after the scheduled retirement of another customer service worker next year.
Also, the retrenched plant manager can be offered a comparable position at
the Cooper & Sons mill in Northton, where business is booming and several
openings currently exist.

Therefore, the above measures should be implemented as soon as possible to
ensure the continued cost-effectiveness of the Des Moines Mill.

Thank you for considering these recommendations. I appreciate having the
opportunity to provide input that may be helpful in the company's decision-
making process.

Sincerely,

John Svenson

John Svenson
Operations Assistant

FIGURE 4.12 **Recommendation Report (Letter Format), Page 2**

ACE TECHNOLOGIES CORP.

MEMORANDUM

DATE: November 12, 2003

TO: Joseph Chen, Director
             Sales & Service

FROM: Thomas Higgins
             Service Technician

SUBJECT: Travel to Jane's Homestyle Restaurant (Account #2468)

INTRODUCTION

On Monday, November 11, I traveled by company truck to Jane's Homestyle
Restaurant in Seattle to investigate the owner's complaint regarding
malfunctioning video monitors (Ace Cash Register System 2000). I left the
plant at 9:00 a.m. and was back by 10:30.

SERVICE PERFORMED

All three video monitors were functioning erratically. When I examined them,
however, the problem turned out to be very simple. Because of how the
Jane's Homestyle Restaurant counter area is designed, the keypad must be
positioned farther away from the monitor than usual. As a result, the 15" cable
(part #012) that creates interface between the two units is not quite long
enough to stay firmly in place, making the connection unstable.

After explaining the problem to the restaurant manager, I provided a
temporary "quick fix" by duct-taping the connections. When I returned to the
plant, I instructed the shipping department to send the restaurant three
20" replacement cables (part #123) by overnight delivery.

DISCUSSION

This incident demonstrates the need for more thorough testing of our systems
when they are initially installed, taking fully into account all features of the
environments in which they will be used. We might check with the other System 2000 accounts to determine whether any other customers have experienced similar difficulties. Maybe all System 2000 units should routinely be installed with the longer cable.

FIGURE 4.13   **Field Report (Memo Format)**

ACE TECHNOLOGIES CORP.

MEMORANDUM

DATE: November 12, 2003

TO: Floyd Danvers, Director
            Human Resources

FROM: Thomas Higgins
            Service Technician

SUBJECT: Travel to Northweston Marriott for Seminar

INTRODUCTION

On Thursday, November 6, and Friday, November 7, I traveled by company car to the Northweston Marriott to attend a seminar entitled "Workplace Communications: The Basics," presented by a corporate training consultant, Dr. George J. Searles. I left the plant at 8 a.m. and was back by 5 p.m. both days.

ACTIVITIES

The seminar consisted of four half-day sessions, as follows:

- Workplace Communications Overview (Thursday a.m.)
- Review of Mechanics (Thursday p.m.)
- Memos and Letters (Friday a.m.)
- Reports (Friday p.m.)

There were 21 participants from a variety of local businesses and organizations, and the sessions were a blend of lecture and discussion, with emphasis on clear, concise writing. The instructor distributed numerous handouts that illustrated the points under consideration.

COSTS

The program cost $600, paid by the company. Aside from two days' lunch allowance ($20 total) and use of the company car (38 miles total), there were no other expenses.

DISCUSSION

This was a very worthwhile program. I learned a lot from it. Since it would be quite difficult, however, to summarize the content here, I've appended a complete set of the handouts distributed by the instructor. As you will see when you examine these materials, the whole focus of the program was quite practical and hands-on. I recommend that other employees be encouraged to attend the next time this program is offered in our area.

FIGURE 4.14   **Trip Report (Memo Format)**

✓ Checklist   **Evaluating a Memo Report**

A good memo report

____ follows standard memo report format;

____ includes certain features:

- ☐ TO line, which provides the name and often the title and/or department of the receiver
- ☐ FROM line, which provides the name (provided automatically on e-mail) and often the title and/or department of the sender
- ☐ DATE line (provided automatically on e-mail)
- ☐ SUBJECT line, which provides a clear, accurate, but brief indication of what the memo report is about

____ is organized into separate, labeled sections, covering the subject fully in an orderly way;

____ includes no inappropriate content;

____ uses clear, simple language;

____ maintains an appropriate tone, neither too formal nor too conversational;

____ employs effective visuals—tables, graphs, charts, and the like—where necessary to clarify the text;

____ contains no typos or mechanical errors in spelling, capitalization, punctuation, and grammar.

Exercises

■ EXERCISE 4.1

Write a report either to your supervisor at work or to the campus safety committee at your college fully describing the circumstances surrounding an accident or injury you've experienced at work or at college and the results of that mishap. Include suggestions about how similar situations might be avoided in the future. Use the memo report format and include visuals if appropriate.

✓ Checklist   Evaluating a Letter Report

A good letter report

___ follows a standard letter format (full block is best);

___ includes certain features:

- ☐ Sender's complete address
- ☐ Date
- ☐ Receiver's full name and complete address
- ☐ Salutation, followed by a colon
- ☐ Complimentary close ("Sincerely" is best), followed by a comma
- ☐ Sender's signature and full name
- ☐ Enclosure notation, if necessary

___ is organized into paragraphs, covering the subject fully in an orderly way:

- ☐ First paragraph establishes context and states the purpose
- ☐ Middle paragraphs constitute the report, separated into labeled sections that provide all necessary details
- ☐ Last paragraph politely achieves closure

___ includes no inappropriate content;

___ uses clear, simple language;

___ maintains an appropriate tone, neither too formal nor too conversational;

___ employs effective visuals—tables, graphs, charts, and the like—where necessary to clarify the text;

___ contains no typos or mechanical errors in spelling, capitalization, punctuation, and grammar.

■ EXERCISE 4.2

Write a report to the local police department, studying the rush-hour traffic patterns at a major intersection near campus. Observe for one hour during either the morning or evening rush period on one typical weekday. Record the number and kinds of vehicles (car, truck, bus, motorcycle) and the directions in which they were traveling, along with an estimate of pedestrian traffic. Also record, of course, any accidents that occur. Evaluate the layout of the intersection (including lights, signs, and so forth) in terms of safety, and suggest improvements. Use the booklet report format and include visuals.

■ EXERCISE 4.3

Write a report to your communications instructor, outlining your progress in class. List attendance, grades, and any other pertinent information, including an objective assessment of your performance so far and the final grade you anticipate receiving. Use the memo report format and include visuals.

■ EXERCISE 4.4

Write a report to the academic dean, urging that a particular college policy be modified. Be specific about the reasons for your proposal. Justify the change and provide concrete suggestions about possible alternative policies. Use the memo report format and include visuals if appropriate.

■ EXERCISE 4.5

Write a report to your instructor, discussing any recent vacation trip you have taken. Summarize your principal activities during the trip, and provide an evaluation of how successful the vacation was. Use the letter report format and include visuals.

■ EXERCISE 4.6

Write a report to a classmate, outlining the performance of your favorite sports team over the past three years. Using statistical data, be as factual and detailed as your knowledge of the sport will permit. Attempt to explain the reasons for the team's relative success or lack of it. Use the booklet report format and include visuals.

■ EXERCISE 4.7

Write a report to the student services director or the physical plant director at your college, evaluating a major campus building with respect to accessibility to the physically challenged. Discuss the presence or absence of special signs, doors, ramps, elevators, restroom facilities, and the like. Suggest additional accommodations that should be provided if such needs exist. Use the booklet report format and include visuals.

✓ Checklist   **Evaluating a Booklet Report**

A good booklet report

_____ is accompanied by a transmittal document (memo or letter);

_____ includes a title page that contains the following:

- ☐ Title of the report
- ☐ Name(s) of author(s)
- ☐ Name of company or organization
- ☐ Name(s) of person(s) receiving the report
- ☐ Date

_____ is organized into separate, labeled sections, covering the subject fully in an orderly way;

_____ includes no inappropriate content;

_____ uses clear, simple language;

_____ maintains an appropriate tone, neither too formal nor too conversational;

_____ employs effective visuals—tables, graphs, charts, and the like—where necessary to clarify the text;

_____ contains no typos or mechanical errors in spelling, capitalization, punctuation, and grammar.

■ EXERCISE 4.8

Team up with a classmate of the opposite sex, and write a report to the physical plant director analyzing the differences, if any, between the men's and women's restroom facilities in the main building on your campus. Suggest any changes or improvements you think might be necessary. Use the booklet report format and include visuals.

■ EXERCISE 4.9

Have you ever been the victim of or witness to a minor crime on campus? Write a report to the college security director, relating the details of that experience and offering suggestions about how to minimize the likelihood of similar occurrences in the future. Use the letter report format and include visuals if appropriate.

■ EXERCISE 4.10

Write a report to your classmates in which you evaluate three nearby restaurants featuring similar cuisine (for example, seafood, Chinese, or Italian) or three nearby stores that sell essentially the same product (for example, athletic shoes, books and music, or clothing). Discuss such issues as selection, quality, price, and service. Use the booklet report format and include visuals.

■ EXERCISE 4.11

Each of Exercises 4.1 through 4.10 could be described as belonging to one (or more) of the report categories discussed in this chapter: incident, progress, recommendation, and travel. Write your instructor a report in which you categorize each of the exercises, providing reasons for your choices. Use the memo report format.

■ EXERCISE 4.12

The writer of the fictitious letter report depicted on the following pages has overused the design options afforded by the computer, creating an extremely confusing report that's almost impossible to comprehend. Fix it.

■ EXERCISE 4.12   **Continued**

Social Security Administration
Supplemental Security Income
Important Information

Date: November 10, 2004

Claim Number: 123-45-6789 DI

COUNTY DSS FOR
PETER WOOD
NORTHTON MN 55100

Type of Payment
Individual—Disabled

We are writing to tell you about changes in Peter Wood's Supplemental Security Income record.

INFORMATION ABOUT Peter Wood's PAYMENTS

This information does not change his current payment amount.

PETER WOOD'S Payment Is Based on These Facts

He has monthly income which must be considered in figuring his eligibility as follows:

••• His other unearned income of $157.30 for April 2004 on.
••• His wages of $75.00 or less for April 2004 on.

Things to Remember

This information is also being sent to Peter Wood.

■ **EXERCISE 4.12**   **Continued**

Do you disagree with the Decision???

If you disagree with the decision, you have the right to appeal. We will review your case and consider any new facts you have.

- You have 60 days to ask for an appeal.
- The 60 day period starts the day AFTER you get this letter.
- You must have GOOD REASON for waiting more than 60 days.

   TO APPEAL YOU MUST FILL OUT A FORM CALLED "REQUEST FOR RECONSIDERATION." THE FORM NUMBER IS SSA-561. TO GET THIS FORM CONTACT ONE OF OUR OFFICES. WE CAN HELP YOU FILL OUT THE FORM.

HOW TO APPEAL

There are two ways to appeal. You can pick the one you want. If you meet with us in person, it may help us decide your case.

* CASE REVIEW: *You have a right to review the facts in your file. You can give us more facts to add to your file. Then we'll decide your case again. You won't meet with the person who decides your case. This is the only kind of appeal you can have to appeal a medical decision.*

* INFORMAL CONFERENCE: *You'll meet with the person who decides your case. You can tell that person why you think you're right. You can give us more facts to help prove you're right. You can bring other people to help explain your case.*

If you want help with your appeal

YOU CAN HAVE A FRIEND, LAWYER, OR SOMEONE ELSE HELP YOU. THERE ARE GROUPS THAT CAN HELP YOU FIND A LAWYER OR GIVE YOU FREE LEGAL SERVICES IF YOU QUALIFY. THERE ARE ALSO LAWYERS WHO DO NOT CHARGE UNLESS YOU WIN YOUR APPEAL. YOUR LOCAL SOCIAL SECURITY OFFICE HAS A LIST OF GROUPS THAT CAN HELP WITH YOUR APPEAL. IF YOU GET SOMEONE TO HELP YOU, YOU SHOULD LET US KNOW. IF YOU HIRE SOMEONE, WE MUST APPROVE THE FEE.

■ EXERCISE 4.12   **Continued**

IF YOU HAVE ANY QUESTIONS

If you have any questions, you may call us toll-free at 1-800-555-1234, or call your local Social Security Office at 1-612-555-1234. We can answer most questions over the phone. You can also write or visit any Social Security office. The office that serves your area is located at:

BRANCH OFFICE
123 NORTHTON AVE
NORTHTON, MN 55100

If you do call or visit an office, please have this letter with you. It will help us answer your questions. Also, if you plan to visit an office, you may call ahead to make an appointment. This will help us serve you more quickly when you arrive at the office.

Sincerely,

Neil Perrault

Neil Perrault

Supplemental Security Administrator

D

Oral Presentations: Preparation and Delivery

Learning Objective When you complete this chapter, you'll be able to prepare and deliver successful oral presentations.

Preparation
Preliminaries
Rehearsal

Delivery
Introductions and Conclusions
Vocal Factors
Physical Factors
Eye Contact
Audiovisuals
Enthusiasm
Checklist: Evaluating a Public Speaker

Exercises

Most people dread the prospect of having to stand in front of an audience and make a speech. They feel unsure of themselves, and fear they'll appear awkward or foolish. Nevertheless, you should make a real effort to overcome such misgivings. The ability to present your ideas clearly and forcefully to a group of listeners is a valuable skill that equips you for leadership in the workplace, where it is often necessary to address groups of supervisors, co-workers, clients, or customers. The skill is also quite useful in community contexts, such as club gatherings, town meetings, school board hearings, and other public forums. It's certainly helpful in the college setting, too, where oral reports are becoming a requirement in more and more courses.

A good speech is the result of three elements: preparation, composure, and common sense. If that sounds familiar, it should; in Chapter 8 the same was said of the employment interview. In many respects, the two endeavors are similar. Both are examples of oral communication, both are fairly formal speaking situations, and both place essentially the same demands on you. The main difference, of course, is that in a job interview you're usually speaking to one or two listeners, whereas an oral presentation generally involves addressing a group. After reading this chapter, you should be able to prepare and deliver successful oral presentations.

Preparation

A successful oral presentation nearly always is based on thorough preparation. This involves some preliminary activities followed by actual rehearsal of the speech.

Preliminaries

Preparing for an oral presentation is much like preparing to write. Just as if you were about to compose a memo, letter, or written report, you must first identify your purpose. Are you simply trying to inform your listeners, or are you attempting to entertain them? Are you perhaps seeking to persuade them of something or motivate them to action? In any case, you need a plan that enables you to achieve your goal.

It's crucial to assess your audience. What are your listeners' backgrounds and interests? How about their perspective on your topic? In short, what might influence their expectations or responses? Unless you gear your remarks to your audience, you probably won't connect satisfactorily with your listeners. For example, a mayoral candidate addressing a gathering of senior citizens would be foolish to focus a campaign speech on long-range outcomes the listeners may never live to see. Such a group would respond better to a presentation of the candidate's short-term goals, particularly those related to that audience's immediate concerns—crime prevention, perhaps, or health care. Just as you do in written communications, you must always bear in mind the nature of your audience when preparing your remarks.

It's also helpful to get a look in advance at the room where you will be speaking. This ensures that you'll be somewhat more at ease during the presentation, because you'll be on familiar turf. If you're planning to use audiovisual equipment, you should acquaint yourself with it as well. Nothing is more embarrassing than launching a speech and suddenly discovering that there's no convenient electrical outlet for your slide projector, or that the bulb in the transparency projector is burned out. Guard against such setbacks by checking the equipment when you visit the site beforehand.

And of course you must be thoroughly familiar with your subject matter. Gather information about the topic and assemble an arsenal of facts, figures, and examples to support your statements. This requires some research and homework—an essential part of your preparation. You must know not only how to approach and organize the material but also how to *develop* it. Nobody wants to listen to a speaker who has nothing to say or who rambles on and on with no apparent direction or focus.

Therefore, the opening of your speech must include a clear statement of purpose, informing the audience about what to expect. From there you must follow a logical path, covering your material in coherent, step-by-step fashion, dealing with one main idea at a time, in orderly sequence. And you should provide effective transitions to facilitate progress from point to point. For all this to happen, you must write out your entire speech ahead of time. Since it's best, however, to actually *deliver* the speech from notes or note cards, a finely polished, letter-perfect piece of writing is not absolutely necessary. But you do need to have a well-developed and well-organized draft from which you can select key points and supporting details for your notes or note cards. You must also ensure that your notes or cards are plainly legible so you can glance down and easily see them on the lectern as you deliver the speech. Prepare your notes or cards using a bold, felt-tipped pen, and write substantially larger than you normally do. It's very damaging to your presentation if you have to pause to decipher your own handwriting, or if you have to bend over or pick up your notes or cards to see them clearly. Figure 9.1 is a page from the draft of an oral presentation about various applications of radar technology. Figure 9.2 shows notes based on that same information, and Figure 9.3 depicts note cards.

As we have seen, radar has obvious military value and has been used to detect and track enemy planes, submarines, missiles, and so on. Permanent Ballistic Missile Early Warning Systems (BMEWS) are in place at various strategic locations around the globe: Clear, Alaska; Thule, Greenland; Fylingdale Moor, England; and elsewhere. An impressive recent development is Relocatable Over-the-Horizon Radar (ROTHR), which can bounce high-frequency signals in the 5–28 MHz range off the ionosphere to scan an area from 500 to 1,800 nautical miles away. But radar has many nonmilitary applications as well.

Radar permits astronomers to measure interplanetary distances precisely and to collect much data that otherwise might be unavailable, by obtaining radar echoes from the major bodies of the solar system . . . and deriving as much information as possible from them. Since radar can ascertain surface textures and details and can find objects as small as insects or as large as mountains, it's obviously very useful in making maps of distant, restricted, or otherwise inaccessible places—even planets.

Obviously, radar can be nearly as useful to civilian aviators as it is to the military, by detecting storms and other aircraft and by determining location and altitude. Indeed, one of the first applications of radar was in radio altimeters. And, of course, air traffic controllers use radar extensively to prevent "runway incursions" and other mishaps.

FIGURE 9.1   **Draft Page of an Oral Presentation**

Permanent Ballistic Missile Early
Warning Systems (BMEWS):
   Clear, Alaska
       Thule, Greenland
           Fylingdale Moor, England

Relocatable Over-the-Horizon Radar (ROTHR): bounces
high-frequency signals off ionosphere; can scan areas
500–1,800 nautical miles away.

Astronomers: measure interplanetary distances, collect
solar system data.

Cartographers: make maps—even of planets; can find
objs as small as insects or as large as mts.

Aviators: detect storms, other planes; determine location,
altitude; air traffic control, prevent "runway incursions."

FIGURE 9.2   **Example of Oral Presentation Notes**

Permanent Ballistic Missile Early Warning
Systems (BMEWS):
  Clear, Alaska
    Thule, Greenland
      Fylingdale Moor, England

Relocatable Over-the-Horizon Radar (ROTHR):
bounces high-frequency signals off ionosphere;
can scan areas 500–1,800 naut. miles away.

FIGURE 9.3   Examples of Note Cards

Rehearsal

Important as the preliminaries are, rehearsal is the most important part of
your preparation. Many people skip this step, figuring they'll wing it when
the time comes and rely on their wits. Unless you're a very experienced
speaker, however, this almost never works. Before attempting to deliver an
oral presentation, you *must* practice it. You need not recruit a practice audience (although it certainly helps), but you must at least recite the speech
aloud several times. This reveals which parts of the presentation seem the
most difficult to deliver and establishes how *long* the speech really is. You
do not want to run noticeably shorter or longer than the allotted time,

since this violates the audience's expectations. Remember that speeches tend to run shorter in actuality than in rehearsal, because the pressures of live performance generally speed up the delivery. If aiming for a 5-minute presentation, you need 7 or 8 minutes in rehearsal. If you're expected to speak for half an hour, your rehearsal might take 40 to 45 minutes.

In addition to preparing your speech, you must prepare *yourself*. All the commonsense advice presented in Chapter 8 concerning the employment interview applies equally here. Get a good night's sleep. Shower. Eat, but do not consume any alcoholic beverages. Dismiss any troubling thoughts from your mind. Wear clothing appropriate for the occasion. All this preparation will contribute to your general sense of confidence and well-being, thereby helping you develop composure and deliver the presentation to the best of your ability.

Delivery

The key to successfully delivering your oral presentation in public is to relax. Admittedly, this is more easily said than done but not as difficult as it may seem. Most audiences are at least reasonably receptive, so you need not fear them. In the classroom setting, for example, all your listeners will soon be called on to present their own orals or will have done so already. This usually makes them sympathetic and supportive. It's simply not true that everyone in the room is scrutinizing your every word and gesture, hoping you'll perform poorly. (At any given moment, in fact, a certain percentage of the audience is probably not paying attention at all!) Nevertheless, there are several areas of concern you may wish to consider when delivering an oral presentation.

Introductions and Conclusions

Since first impressions are so important, a good oral presentation must begin with an effective introduction. Here are four useful strategies for opening your speech.

- ■ *Ask the audience a pertinent question.* This is an effective introduction because it immediately establishes a connection between you and your listeners—especially if somebody responds. But even if no one does, you can provide the answer yourself, thereby leading smoothly into your discussion. In a presentation titled "Tourist Attractions in New York City," for example, you might open with the query, "Does anyone here know the name of the street the Empire State Building is on?"

- **Describe a situation.** There's something in human nature that makes us love a story, especially if it involves conflict. The enduring appeal of fairy tales, myths and legends, and even soap operas and sentimental country-western lyrics proves the point. You can capitalize on this aspect of your listeners' collective psychology by opening your presentation with a brief story that somehow relates to your subject. A speaker attempting to explore the dangers of tobacco, for example, might begin like this: "My friend Jane, a wonderful young woman with a bright future, had been smoking a pack a day since tenth grade. Finally, at age 25, she had decided to quit. But when she went to the doctor for her annual physical, she learned that it was already too late. Tragically, Jane died of lung cancer less than a year later."

- **Present an interesting fact or statistic.** This will help you grab the audience's attention by demonstrating that you're familiar with your topic. The annual edition of *World Almanac and Book of Facts* is an excellent source of statistical information on diverse topics, but there are many other resources. Any qualified librarian can direct you to government documents, corporate reports, computer databases, and other useful resources. Even though statistics can be deceptive, people like what they perceive as the hard reality of such data and therefore find numbers quite persuasive. A speech intended to demonstrate the need for stricter gun control legislation, for example, might open with the observation, "In 1996 alone, there were more than 10,000 handgun-related murders in the United States." A useful Internet site is Statistical Resources on the Web at http://www.lib.umich.edu/govdocs/stats.html. Others are Infonation at http://www.un.org/Pubs/CyberSchoolBus/infonation/e_infonation.htm and Statistical Sites on the World Wide Web at http://www.bls.gov/bls/other.htm.

- **Use a quotation.** Get a "Big Name"—Shakespeare, Martin Luther King, the Bible—to speak for you. Find an appropriate saying that will launch your own remarks with flair. Many useful books of quotations exist, but *Bartlett's Familiar Quotations* (available in virtually any good bookstore or library) is the best known, and for good reason. Bartlett includes nearly 100 quotes on the subject of "money" alone, for example. *Bartlett's* is available—along with *Simpson's Contemporary Quotations*—on the Web at http://www.bartleby.com/. Another good source of quotations is The Quotation Ring at http://www.gunnar.cc/webring/quotes.html.

The conclusion to your talk is as important as the introduction. Always sum up when you reach the end of an oral presentation. Repeat your key points and show clearly how they support your conclusion. But like an airplane rolling smoothly to a stop on the runway rather than crashing to the ground after reaching its destination, you should not end abruptly. You can accomplish this by returning the audience to the starting point. When you reach the end of your speech, refer to the question, scenario, fact, statistic, or quote with which you opened. This creates in your listeners the satisfying sense of having come full circle, returning them to familiar territory.

Another common concluding tactic is to ask whether members of your audience have any questions. If so, you can answer them, and then your work is done. If no questions are forthcoming, the audience has in effect ended the speech for you. Since this creates the sense of a letdown, however, you can instead have an accomplice or two in the audience ask questions to which you have prepared responses in advance. Although staged, this is a common practice among professional speakers. Whatever form of conclusion you choose, always close by thanking the audience for their time and attention.

Vocal Factors

Obviously, the *voice* is the principal instrument of any oral presentation. Therefore, pay attention to your vocal qualities. Speak at a normal rate of speed, neither too fast nor too slow, and at a normal volume, neither too loud nor too soft. Pronounce clearly, so the audience can understand your every word without undue effort. When using a microphone, be sure it's approximately one foot away from your mouth—any farther, it may not pick up your voice adequately; any closer, your overly amplified *b*s and *p*s may create an annoyingly explosive sound. In addition, try to maintain the normal rhythms of everyday conversation. Nothing is more boring than listening to a speech delivered in an unvarying monotone. Conversely, it's irritating to be subjected to an overly theatrical delivery characterized by elaborate gestures or exaggerated vocal effects. The key is to be natural, as if you were speaking to one or two people rather than a whole group.

At the same time, however, an oral presentation is certainly a more formal speaking situation than a social conversation. Therefore, you should provide more examples and illustrations than you ordinarily might, along with more transitional phrases than usual. In addition, make a conscious effort to minimize verbal "ticks," those distracting little mannerisms that characterize everyday speech: "um," "y'know," "okay?" "right?" and the like. Listening to a tape recording of your oral presentation enables you to assess the degree to which you need to work on this. While you don't want to sound stiffly artificial, you should stay away from the more colorful vernacular. Avoid slang, expletives, and conspicuously substandard—"I ain't got no"—grammar. Achieving the right level of formality can be challenging, but practicing the presentation a few times helps.

Physical Factors

Although your voice is obviously important, your audience *sees* you as well as hears you. They respond to your body language as much as to your words. As you would in an employment interview, you must create a favorable physical impression. Get rid of any chewing gum or tobacco long before stepping up to the lectern. Stand up straight behind the lectern; don't slump or lean over it. Control your hand motions. Do not fold your arms, drum with your fingertips, click a ballpoint pen, or cling rigidly to the lectern with a stiff-armed, white-knuckled grip. Refrain from touching your face or hair, tugging at your clothes, or scratching your body. You can gesture occasionally to make a point, but only if such movements are spontaneous, as in casual conversation. In short, your hands should not distract the audience from what you're saying. Your feet, too, can create problems. Resist the tendency to tap your feet, shift from one leg to the other, or stray purposelessly from the lectern. Plant your feet firmly on the floor and stay put.

In the academic setting, your professors (much like many workplace supervisors) may impose certain regulations concerning proper attire for oral presentations. Baseball caps, for example, are sometimes prohibited, along with various other style and dress affectations such as those mentioned in the "Interview" section of Chapter 8. Whether in a college classroom or on the job, you should observe any such guidelines, even if you feel they're overly restrictive.

Eye Contact

As much as possible, *look* at your audience. This is probably the hardest part of public speaking. But it's imperative. Unless you maintain eye contact with audience members, you'll lose their attention. Keep your head up and your eyes focused forward. If you find it impossible to actually look at your listeners, fake it. Look instead at desk tops, chair legs, or the back wall. But you must create at least the *illusion* of visual contact.

Holding your listeners' attention is one—although certainly not the only—reason why you should absolutely avoid the dreadful error of simply reading to your audience from the text of your speech. Few practices are more boring, more amateurish, or more destructive of audience-speaker rapport. As mentioned in the section on preparation, you should deliver your presentation from notes or note cards rather than from a polished text to force yourself to adopt a more conversational manner. But keep your papers or cards out of sight, lying flat on the lectern. Do not distract the audience by nervously shuffling them.

Audiovisuals

To greatly enhance your oral presentation, consider using audiovisual aids in conjunction with the variety of visuals (tables, graphs, charts, pictures) discussed in Chapter 3. Audiovisual tools can be very helpful to both you and your audience by illustrating key points throughout your talk. If the room where you are speaking is equipped with a chalkboard, take advantage of it as appropriate. A flip chart—a giant, easel-mounted pad of paper that you write on with felt-tip markers—is another useful option. You may also choose to use large display posters prepared in advance, but you must remember to bring along tape or thumbtacks to secure them for viewing.

Whether using a chalkboard, flip chart, or poster to make your point, remember to position yourself *next to* it, not in front; you must not block the audience's view. Remember to face the audience rather than the display. Be sure your writing is plainly legible from a distance; write in large, bold strokes, using color for emphasis and incorporating the other design principles outlined in Chapter 4. Make sure your drawings and text are easy to see even from the back of the room. Follow this rule of thumb: The image must be at least one-sixth as large as the distance from which it will be seen. For example, a graph viewed from 30 feet should be 5 feet wide.

For lettering, use the following chart:

Distance	Size of Lettering
Up to 10 ft.	¾ in.
20 ft.	1 in.
30 ft.	1¼ in.
40 ft.	1½ in.
50 ft.	1¾ in.
60 ft.	2 in.

Although they require more preparation time, you may want to create slides or transparencies that can be projected onto a screen. They lend your presentation a great deal of credibility by making it much more professional and polished. One advantage is that you can control the size of the images on the screen, enlarging them as necessary to create displays that are easily visible even in a relatively big room. Particularly helpful are the computerized presentation software packages that have become increasingly affordable—and versatile—in recent years. With this software, you can create visuals of unprecedented sophistication, incorporating photographs as well as original images, a tremendous range of colors, three-dimensional effects, and other options.

The best known of these packages is Microsoft PowerPoint, which offers a wide range of creative options. You can choose from a variety of typefaces, templates, and clip art and can easily customize the appearance of the projected image using bulleted lists, columns, and other readily available layout features.

The slide shown in Figure 9.4—from a presentation to factory supervisors learning to spot potentially troubled employees—is an example of PowerPoint's basic capabilities. Notice the "gears" motif on the left, an appropriate design for the manufacturing environment. The bulleted items were projected one at a time to permit unhurried discussion of each point before the next was superimposed. Additional slides identified specific aspects of each of these "warning signs," again presented one at a time.

Clearly, PowerPoint can greatly facilitate the creation of transparencies and 35 mm slides for use with projectors. But this software is

FIGURE 9.4   **PowerPoint Slide**

really at its best when images are displayed by a projection device connected to a computer controlled by the person delivering the presentation. Such an arrangement allows for the most distinctive aspects of this software: animation effects, including an array of transition strategies for moving from one slide to the next. Incorporating techniques borrowed from Hollywood filmmakers, PowerPoint can cause text to "fly in" or "dissolve," for example, and can also incorporate various sound effects to accompany the visual images.

Here are some basic guidelines to bear in mind when using audio-visual media in conjunction with an oral presentation:

■ Make certain beforehand that your slides are properly inserted in their tray. They must not be reversed, upside down, or out of sequence.

■ Do not include too much information on a transparency; keep it simple. If a given transparency is unavoidably information rich, reveal only a section at a time, sliding a piece of paper downward to uncover each section when you're ready to discuss it. This technique causes the information on the screen to gradually expand in pace with your commentary, and your audience cannot read ahead and possibly miss your explanation. If you're using presentation software, this method can be applied electronically.

■ To draw the audience's attention to a detail on the screen, use a laser pointer rather than a yardstick or conventional pointer, which are effective only for pointing out details on chalkboards, posters, maps, and the like. If you don't have a laser pointer, highlight details by pointing to them on the transparency itself, but be sure to use a pen or freshly sharpened pencil rather than your finger, because the bulky shadow cast by your hand will block too much from view. Presentation software, of course, affords a variety of far more imaginative highlighting methods.

■ When adding notations on a transparency during your presentation, be sure to write legibly, using a marker designed for that purpose. Again, software greatly simplifies this procedure.

■ Avoid the glaring "empty white screen" effect; turn off your slide or transparency projector once you're done with it, or if you'll not be referring to it for more than a minute or two.

Depending on the length, scope, and topic of your speech, you may decide to supplement your remarks with videotape or sound

Tech Tips

Here are some basic guidelines for creating an effective PowerPoint presentation:

- Don't get "carried away" with all the options at your disposal; exercise restraint. As with so many aspects of workplace communications, less is often more.
- Do not allow a patterned, textured, or incompatibly colored background to obscure your text. Use a dark background with light text for projection in a lighted room; use a light background with dark text for projection in a darkened room.
- Use relatively large print for greater legibility: 30 to 34 point for text, 44 to 50 point bold for headings.
- Use consistent formatting features on all slides.
- Avoid large segments of running text. Use lists and outlines instead.
- Include no more than five items of information per slide.
- Include no more than 25 slides in any given presentation.
- Have a back-up plan to guard against technical difficulties. Prepare "hardcopy" handouts of your slides for distribution to the audience in case the computer or projector malfunctions.

recordings, provided they're of good quality. Relevant physical objects can also be displayed or passed around. If you were explaining how to tune a guitar, for example, you would certainly want to demonstrate the procedure on an actual instrument. Similarly, if you were explaining the workings of a particular tool or other device, ideally you would provide one (or more) for the audience to examine. However, these materials should *supplement*—not overshadow—your remarks. Much like visuals in written reports, audiovisual devices in oral presentations must always serve a useful purpose, enhancing without dominating, and should never be introduced simply for their own sake.

Enthusiasm

Try to deliver your oral presentations in a lively, upbeat, enthusiastic manner. This actually makes your job easier, since a positive attitude on your part will help to foster a more receptive attitude on the part of the audience. If your listeners sense that you'd rather be elsewhere, they tend to "tune out." When that occurs, you receive no encouraging feedback, and knowing you've lost your audience makes it even more difficult to continue. If you sense, however, that the audience is following along, this reinforcement in turn fuels your performance. But this cannot happen unless you project in an engaging way. From the start, *you* establish the tone. Therefore, it makes sense to adopt a positive attitude when giving an oral presentation, not only for the audience's sake but to serve your own purposes as well.

The many factors we've examined that contribute to a good delivery may seem like a lot to keep track of. If you're like most speakers, however, you probably have real difficulty in only one or two areas. An especially useful strategy is to videotape your rehearsal to determine what you should work on to improve your delivery. As stated at the outset, a successful oral presentation is the result of preparation, composure, and common sense. If you take seriously the recommendations offered in this chapter and practice the strategies and techniques suggested, your performance as a public speaker will improve greatly.

✓ Checklist   Evaluating a Public Speaker

A good public speaker

___ opens with an interesting, attention-getting introduction;

___ follows a clear and logical pattern of organization;

___ provides enough detail to fully develop the subject;

___ closes with a smooth, satisfying conclusion;

___ speaks in a firm, clear, expressive voice;

___ makes frequent eye contact with the audience;

___ appears physically relaxed and composed, with no distracting mannerisms;

___ maintains an appropriate level of formality, neither too casual nor too solemn;

___ delivers in an alert, engaging manner;

___ satisfies but does not exceed the appropriate length for the presentation.

Exercises

■ **EXERCISE 9.1**

Prepare and deliver a 5- to 10-minute oral presentation on one of the following autobiographical topics:

- A Childhood Memory
- My Brush with Danger
- My Angriest Moment
- My Most Satisfying Accomplishment
- My Career Goals
- What I Expect My Life to Be Like in Ten Years

■ **EXERCISE 9.2**

Prepare and deliver a 5- to 10-minute oral presentation that summarizes a book, article, lecture, film, or television broadcast related to your field of study or employment (see Chapter 5).

■ **EXERCISE 9.3**

Prepare and deliver a 5- to 10-minute oral presentation that provides a specific mechanism description related to your field of study or employment. Present an actual example of such a mechanism, along with any audiovisual aids that may be helpful to your audience (see Chapter 6).

■ **EXERCISE 9.4**

Prepare and deliver a 5- to 10-minute oral presentation describing a process related to your field of study or employment. Present any audiovisual aids that may be helpful to your audience (see Chapter 6).

■ **EXERCISE 9.5**

Prepare and deliver a 5- to 10-minute oral presentation describing a procedure related to your field of study or employment. Present any audiovisual aids that may be helpful to your audience (see Chapter 6).

■ EXERCISE 9.6

Prepare and deliver a 5- to 10-minute oral presentation providing instructions related to your field of study or employment. Present any audiovisual aids that may be helpful to your audience (see Chapter 7).

■ EXERCISE 9.7

Prepare and deliver a 5- to 10-minute oral presentation based on Exercise 4.10. Present any audiovisual aids that may be helpful to your audience.

■ EXERCISE 9.8

Prepare and deliver a 5- to 10-minute oral presentation based on Exercise 6.18. Present any audiovisual aids that may be helpful to your audience.

■ EXERCISE 9.9

Prepare and deliver a 5- to 10-minute oral presentation based on Exercise 7.8. Present any audiovisual aids that may be helpful to your audience.

■ EXERCISE 9.10

Prepare and deliver a 5- to 10-minute oral presentation based on Exercise 8.4. Present any audiovisual aids that may be helpful to your audience.

E

Long Reports: Format, Collaboration, and Documentation

Learning Objective

When you complete this chapter, you'll be able to create well-designed long reports, whether working independently or with others, and to correctly document the sources of your information.

Format

Transmittal Document
Title Page
Abstract
Table of Contents
List of Illustrations
Glossary
Text
Visuals
Pagination

Collaboration

Documentation

Bibliography
Parenthetical Citations
Checklist: Evaluating a Long Report

Exercises

n business, industry, and the professions, important decisions are made every day. Some concern routine matters while others are more complicated, involving considerable risk and expense. Suppose, for example, that a hospital administration is debating whether to add a new wing to the main building. Or perhaps a police department wants to switch to a different kind of patrol car, or a successful but relatively new business venture must decide whether to expand now or wait a few years. Each situation requires in-depth study before a responsible decision can be reached. The potential advantages and drawbacks of each alternative have to be identified and examined, as well as the long-range effects. This is where the long report comes into play. This chapter discusses how to prepare such a report, explaining its formatting components, the dynamics of group-written reports, and some standard procedures for documenting sources.

Format

Obviously, both the subject matter and the formatting of long reports will vary from one workplace to another, and in the academic context, from one discipline to another and even among instructors. Nevertheless, most long reports share the components described in the following paragraphs.

Transmittal Document

Prepared according to standard memo or business letter format (see Chapter 2), the transmittal document accompanies a long report, conveying it from whoever wrote it to whoever requested it. The transmittal document says, in effect, "Here's that report you wanted," and very briefly summarizes its content. The memo format is used for transmitting in-house reports, whereas the letter format is used for transmitting reports to outside readers. Often the transmittal document serves as a "cover sheet," although sometimes it's positioned immediately after the title page of the report. See Figure 10.1 for a sample transmittal memo.

Title Page

In addition to the title itself, this page includes the name(s) of whoever prepared the report, the name(s) of whoever requested it, the names of the companies or organizations involved, and the date. In an academic context, the title page includes the title, the names of the student author(s)

PARAMOUNT MANUFACTURING, INC.

MEMORANDUM

DATE: December 1, 2002

TO: Rosa Sheridan
             Director of Human Resources

FROM: William Congreve
             Administrative Assistant

SUBJECT: Drug Testing Report

As you may recall, we decided last month that I should compile a report on the current status of drug testing programs in the American workplace, so that we might explore the feasibility of introducing such a program here at Paramount Manufacturing. Here is the report. If you have any questions, I would be happy to provide further details.

FIGURE 10.1 Drug Testing Report, Transmittal Memo

and the instructor who assigned the report, the course name (along with the course number and section number), the college, and the date. See Figure 10.2 for a sample title page prepared for a workplace context.

Abstract

Sometimes called an executive summary, this is simply a brief synopsis—a greatly abbreviated version of the report (see Chapter 5). An effective abstract captures the essence of the report, including its major findings and recommendations. In the workplace, the function of an abstract is to assist those who may not have time to read the entire report but need to know what it says. Sometimes the abstract is positioned near the front of the report; other times it appears at the end. For a 10- or 20-page report, the abstract should not be longer than one page and can be formatted as one long paragraph. Figure 10.3 offers an example of a concise abstract.

Table of Contents

As in a book, the table of contents for a long report clearly shows each numbered section of the report, along with its title and the page on which it appears. Many also show subdivisions within sections. When fine-tuning a report before submitting it, check to ensure that the section numbers, titles, and page numbers used in the table of contents are consistent with those in the report itself (see Figure 10.4).

List of Illustrations

This list resembles the table of contents, but rather than referring to text sections, it lists tables, graphs, charts, and all other visuals appearing in the report—each numbered and titled—and their page numbers. As with the table of contents, always check to ensure that your illustrations list accurately reflects the visual contents of the report and their labeling/captions (see Figure 10.5).

Glossary

A "mini-dictionary," the glossary defines all potentially unfamiliar words, expressions, or symbols in your report. Not all reports need a glossary; it depends on the topic and the intended audience. But if you are using specialized vocabulary or symbols that may not be well known, it's best to include a glossary page with terms alphabetized for easy reference and symbols listed in the order in which they appear in the text (see Figure 10.6).

DRUG TESTING
IN THE WORKPLACE

by

William Congreve
Administrative Assistant

Submitted to

Rosa Sheridan
Director of Human Resources

Paramount Manufacturing, Inc.
Mission Viejo, California

December 1, 2002

FIGURE 10.2   **Drug Testing Report, Title Page**

ii

ABSTRACT

Paramount Manufacturing, Inc. is considering introducing a mandatory drug testing program. Although intended to reduce the costs associated with workplace substance abuse, drug testing is quite controversial. Some experts argue that the extent of workplace drug abuse has been greatly exaggerated and that drug programs—first introduced in large numbers in the 1980s—are a needless violation of employees' privacy. Most drug testing programs rely on EMIT, a test that often yields inaccurate results, thus necessitating the use of confirmatory GC/MS tests to reduce the possibility of false positives (and false negatives). Drug testing appears to be least problematic when used to screen applicants for employment rather than established employees. To avoid costly lawsuits and other setbacks, progressive companies observe several key features of successful drug testing protocol: a clear-cut policy statement, strict guidelines for specimen collection, use of NIDA-certified laboratories, confirmation of all positive test results, and employee assistance services. For Paramount to introduce a testing program, the best path may be to begin by testing job applicants only, rather than the existing workforce. In any case, more study is needed, preferably with the assistance of an outside (NIDA) consultant.

FIGURE 10.3   **Drug Testing Report, Abstract**

iii

TABLE OF CONTENTS

FIGURE 10.4 Drug Testing Report, Table of Contents

iv

LIST OF ILLUSTRATIONS

FIGURE 10.5   **Drug Testing Report, List of Illustrations**

GLOSSARY

antibodies: Protein substances developed by the body, usually in response to the presence of antigens (bacteria, for example).

assay: Analysis of a substance to determine its constituents and the relative proportions of each.

enzymes: Organic catalyst produced by living cells but capable of acting independently; complex colloidal substances that can induce chemical changes in other substances without undergoing change themselves.

false negative: Test result that incorrectly indicates the absence of the substance(s) tested for.

false positive: Test result that incorrectly indicates the presence of the substance(s) tested for.

mass spectrum: Identifiable pattern of electromagnetic energy given off by a substance under specific test conditions.

metabolites: Products of metabolism.

silica: Silicon dioxide, SiO_2.

FIGURE 10.6 Drug Testing Report, Glossary

Text

One major difference between a long report and an academic term paper is that a report is divided into sections, usually numbered, and each with its own title. As mentioned previously, it's important that these divisions within the text be accurately reflected in the table of contents.

Every long report also includes an introduction and a conclusion. The introduction provides an overview of the report, identifying its purpose and scope, and explaining the procedures used and the context in which it was written. The conclusion summarizes the main points in the report and lists recommendations, if any.

Visuals

A major feature of many reports, visuals (see Chapter 3) sometimes appear in a separate section—an appendix—at the end of a report. A better approach, however, is to integrate them into the text, as this is more convenient for the reader. Either way, you should draw the reader's attention to pertinent visuals (stating, for example, "See Figure 5"), and every visual must be properly numbered and titled, with its source identified. The numbering/titling system must be the same system used in the list of illustrations.

Pagination

Number your report pages correctly. There are several pagination systems in use. Generally, page numbers (1, 2, 3, and so on) begin on the introduction page and continue until the last page of the report. Front-matter pages (abstract, table of contents, list of illustrations, glossary, and anything else that precedes the introduction) are numbered with lowercase Roman numerals (i, ii, iii, iv, and so on). There is no page number on the transmittal document or the title page, although the latter "counts" as a front-matter page, so the page immediately following the title page is numbered as ii. The best position for page numbers is in the upper-right corner, because that location enables the reader to find a particular page simply by thumbing through the report. Notice the page numbering throughout the sample report in this chapter (Figures 10.3 through 10.18).

Collaboration

A memo, letter, or short report nearly always is composed by one person working individually. This is sometimes true of long reports as well. However, since the subject matter of long reports is often complex and multifaceted, they are often written collaboratively. This kind of team-work is very common in the workplace because it provides certain obvious advantages. For example, a group that works well together can produce a long report *faster* than one person working alone. In addition, the team possesses a broader perspective and a greater range of knowledge and expertise than an individual. To slightly amend the old saying, two heads—or more—are obviously better than one. And, with the development of *groupware* (word-processing and document design programs designed for collaborative use), teamworking has become easier and faster than ever.

Nevertheless, collaboration can sometimes be problematic because the members of a given group may find it difficult to interact smoothly. Real teamwork requires everyone involved to exercise tact, courtesy, and responsibility. The following factors are essential to successful, rewarding collaboration.

1. Everyone on the team must fully understand the purpose and goals of the project and agree to set aside individual preferences in favor of the group's collective judgment.

2. There must be a team leader in charge of the project—someone whom the other members are willing to recognize as the coordinator. Therefore, this leader should be *elected* from within the group. The leader must, of course, be knowledgeable and competent but must also be a "people person" with excellent interpersonal skills. Once the group has clearly identified the goals and scope of the project, the leader firmly enforces the agreed-on rules, negotiates and resolves conflicts, and holds the whole effort together.

3. The team next assigns clearly defined roles to the other members, designating responsibilities according to everyone's talents and strengths. For example, the group's most competent researcher takes charge of information retrieval. Someone trained in drafting or computer-assisted design formats the report and creates visuals. The member with the best keyboarding skills (or clerical support) produces the actual document. The best writer is the overall editor, making final judgments on matters of organization, style, mechanics, and the like. If an oral presentation is required, the group's most confident public speaker assumes that responsibility. A given individual may play more than one role, but everyone must feel satisfied that the work has been fairly distributed.

4. Once the project is under way, the team meets regularly to assess each other's progress, prevent duplication of effort, and resolve any

problems that may arise. All disagreements or differences of opinion are reconciled in a productive manner. In any group undertaking, a certain amount of conflict is inevitable and indeed necessary to achieve consensus. But this interplay should be a source of creative energy, not antagonism. Issues must be dealt with on an objectively intellectual level, not on a personal or emotional level. To this end, the group should adopt a code of interaction designed to minimize conflict and maximize the benefits of collaboration. Each team member should

- make a real effort to be calm, patient, reasonable, flexible—in short, *helpful*;
- voice all reservations, misgivings, and resentments rather than let them smolder;
- direct criticism at the *issue*, not the person—"There's another way of looking at this" rather than "You're only looking at this one way"—and try not to interpret criticism personally;
- avoid interrupting others who are speaking;
- paraphrase others' remarks—"What you're saying, then, is . . ."— to make certain of their meaning;
- suggest rather than command—"Maybe we should try it this way" instead of "Do it this way!"—and offer rather than demand—"If you'd like, I'll . . . ," instead of "I'm going to . . .";
- accentuate the positive rather than the negative—"Now that we've agreed on the visuals, we can move on" instead of "We can't seem to agree on anything but the visuals."

5. All members of the group must complete their fair share of the work in a conscientious fashion and observe all deadlines. Nothing is more disruptive to a team's progress than an irresponsible member who fails to complete work punctually, or "vanishes" for long periods of time. To contact one another between regularly scheduled meetings of the group, members should exchange telephone numbers and/or e-mail addresses. Indeed, the team leader should monitor the members' progress, reminding them of upcoming deadlines and meetings.

The group can handle the actual writing of the report in any of several ways:

- The whole team writes the report collectively, and then the editor revises the draft and submits it to the group for final approval or additional revisions.

- One person writes the entire report, and then the group—led by the editor—revises it collectively.
- Each team member writes one part of the report individually, and then the editor revises each part and submits the complete draft to the whole group for final approval or additional revisions.

Of these alternatives, the first is the most truly collaborative but is also extremely difficult and time-consuming, requiring uncommon harmony within the group. The second method is preferable, but places too great a burden on one writer. The third approach, therefore, is usually the best, provided the editor seeks clarification from individuals whenever necessary during the editing process. Note, however, that in every case the whole group gets to see and comment on the report in its final form. Since everyone's name will be on it, there should be no surprises when the finished product is released. Collaboration should be precisely that, producing a polished report approved by all members of the team.

Documentation

Documentation is simply a technical term for the procedure whereby writers identify the sources of their information. In the workplace and in popular periodicals, this is often accomplished by inserting the pertinent information directly into the text, as in this example:

> As railway historian William D. Middleton explains in his article "High-Speed Rail's 1835 Underpinning" in the Spring 2001 issue of *Invention and Technology*, the state-of-the-art Acela Express trains introduced in 1999 "travel over a civil-engineering infrastructure that owes much to the skills and foresight of engineers of the very early twentieth, and even the nineteenth, century" (52).

This straightforward approach eliminates the need for a bibliography (list of sources) at the end of the piece. Documentation in academic writing, however, nearly always includes both a bibliography and parenthetical citations identifying the origin of each quotation, statistic, paraphrase, or visual within the text.

Bibliography

There are several standard ways to format a list of citations. The Modern Language Association (MLA) format, which titles the list "Works Cited," and the American Psychological Association (APA) format, which titles the list "References," are the most commonly taught in college courses. A typical bibliography entry under each system would look like this:

MLA   Baron, Naomi S. *Alphabet to Email: How Written English Evolved and Where It's Heading.* London: Routledge, 2000.

APA   Baron, N. S. (2000). *Alphabet to email: How written English evolved and where it's heading.* London: Routledge.

Notice the differences between the two formats. Perhaps the most obvious is the placement of the date of publication. But variations also exist with respect to capitalization, punctuation, and abbreviation. In both systems, however, double-spacing is used throughout, and book titles—like the titles of newspapers, magazines, journals, and other periodicals—are italicized. (MLA style is a bit more flexible in this regard, allowing titles to be either italicized or underlined.) In both formats, entries appear in alphabetical order by authors' last names or, in the case of an anonymous work, by the first significant word of the title.

There are many other kinds of sources besides a single-author book, however, and each requires a slightly different handling. Some of the most common citations are as follows.

Book by Two Authors

MLA   Willis, Tracey R., and Gemma C. Siringo. *Academic Advisement for the 21st Century.* Washington: NEA, 2003.

APA   Willis, T. R., & Siringo, G. C. (2003). *Academic advisement for the 21st century.* Washington, DC: National Education Association.

Book by Three Authors

MLA   Whitman, William C., William M. Johnson, and John A. Tomczyk. *Refrigeration & Air Conditioning Technology.* 4th ed. Albany: Delmar, 2000.

APA   Whitman, W. C., Johnson, W. M., & Tomczyk, J. A. (2000). *Refrigeration & air conditioning technology* (4th ed.). Albany: Delmar.

Book by a Corporate Author

MLA   American Welding Society. *Welding Inspection Handbook.* 3rd ed. Miami: AWS, 2000.

APA   American Welding Society. (2000). *Welding inspection handbook* (3rd ed.). Miami: Author.

Edited Book of Articles

MLA   Fraser, Mark W., ed. *Risk and Resilience in Childhood: An Ecological Perspective.* Washington: NASW, 1997.

APA   Fraser, M. W. (Ed.). (1997). *Risk and resilience in childhood: An ecological perspective.* Washington, DC: National Association of Social Workers.

Article in an Edited Book of Articles

MLA   Dedmon, S. Rachel. "Attention Deficiency and Hyperactivity." *Risk and Resilience in Childhood: An Ecological Perspective.* Ed. Mark W. Fraser. Washington: NASW, 1997. 73–94.

APA   Dedmon, S. R. (1997). Attention deficiency and hyperactivity. In M. W. Fraser (Ed.), *Risk and resilience in childhood: An ecological perspective* (pp. 73–94). Washington, DC: National Association of Social Workers.

Article in a Newspaper

MLA   Richtel, Matt. "Defending a Merger: Hewlett-Packard and Compaq React to Critics." *New York Times* 5 Sept. 2001: C1.

APA   Richtel, M. (2001, September 5). Defending a merger: Hewlett-Packard and Compaq react to critics. *The New York Times,* p. C1.

Anonymous Article in a Newspaper

MLA   "EBay Chooses IBM Software for Auction Site." *Wall Street Journal* 6 Sept. 2001: B10.

APA   EBay chooses IBM software for auction site. (2001, September 6). *The Wall Street Journal,* p. B10.

Article in a Weekly or Biweekly Magazine

MLA   Scott, William B. "Australian Training Yields Top-Notch Fighter Pilots." *Aviation Week & Space Technology* 3 Sept. 2001: 90–93.

APA   Scott, W. B. (2001, September 3). Australian training yields top-notch fighter pilots. *Aviation Week & Space Technology, 155,* 90–93.

Article in a Monthly or Bimonthly Magazine

MLA   Komando, Kim. "Reinvigorate Your PC." *Popular Mechanics* June 2001: 68–71.

APA   Komando, K. (2001, June). Reinvigorate your PC. *Popular Mechanics, 178,* 68–71.

Anonymous Article in a Magazine

MLA   "The Internet's New Borders." *The Economist* 11 August 2001: 9–10.

APA   The Internet's new borders. (2001, August 11). *The Economist 360*, 9–10.

Article in a Trade Journal or Academic Journal

MLA   Jacobson, Wendy B. "Beyond Therapy: Bringing Social Work Back to
           Human Services Reform." *Social Work* 46.1 (2001): 51–61.

APA   Jacobson, W. B. (2001). Beyond therapy: Bringing social work back to
           human services reform. *Social Work 46*(1), 51–61.

Entry in an Encyclopedia or Other Reference Work

MLA   Gran, Richard J. "Magnetic Levitation Train." *World Book Encyclo-
           pedia.* 1998 ed.

APA   Gran, R. J. (1998). Magnetic levitation train. In *The World Book
           Encyclopedia* (Vol. 13, pp. 55–56). Chicago: World Book, Inc.

Entry in a Portable Electronic Encyclopedia or Other Reference Work

MLA   Engelhardt, A. G., and M. Kristiansen. "Ohm's Law." *Grolier Multime-
           dia Encyclopedia for Windows.* CD-ROM. Danbury: Grolier, 2002.

APA   Engelhardt, A. G., & Kristiansen, M. (2002). Ohm's law. *Grolier Multi-
           media Encyclopedia for Windows* [CD-ROM]. Danbury: Grolier.

Personal Interview

MLA   Britton, William. Personal interview. 10 Nov. 2002.

APA   In APA style, all personal communications (conversations, interviews,
           and the like) are excluded from the list of references. Such sources
           are documented only within your text, like this:

           Financial officer William Britton (personal communication, November
           10, 2002) stated that the "total cost of the project may be well over a
           million dollars."

Material from an On-Line Electronic Source

MLA   United States Sentencing Commission. *1977 Sourcebook of Federal
           Sentencing Statistics.* n.d. 8 Dec. 1999 <http://www.ussc.gov/
           annrpt/1997/sbtoc97.htm>.

APA   United States Sentencing Commission. (n.d.). *1997 sourcebook of
           federal sentencing statistics.* Retrieved December 8, 1999, from
           http://www.ussc.gov/annrpt/1997/sbtoc97.htm

The above examples follow the basic formats recommended by the MLA and the APA for documenting on-line sources. As you can see, both styles provide essentially the same information used to identify print sources: the author's name (if known), the title of the work, and—by way of publication data—the date the material was accessed and the URL or Web "address" at which it appeared. But electronic sources are of many different kinds, not all of which easily lend themselves to the above formats. For a more complete explanation of how electronic (and print) sources are handled, you should consult the two organizations' handbooks, readily available in most libraries:

> Gibaldi, Joseph, ed. *MLA Handbook for Writers of Research Papers.* 5th ed. New York: MLA, 1999.

> American Psychological Association. (2001). *Publication Manual of the American Psychological Association* (5th ed.). Washington, DC: Author.

As the *MLA Handbook* says, "recommendations on citing electronic works . . . will doubtless change as technology, scholarly uses of electronic materials, and electronic publication practices evolve" (179). Accordingly, both the MLA and the APA maintain Web sites that you can consult for up-to-date information on documentation and other matters:

MLA   http://mla.org/

APA   http://www.apastyle.org/

Parenthetical Citations

Every time you use one of your sources within the body of a report, whether quoting directly or paraphrasing in your own words, you must identify the source by inserting parentheses. The contents and positioning of these parentheses vary somewhat depending on whether you're using MLA or APA style. Here are examples of how to cite quotations:

MLA   "E-mail has emerged as a medium that allows communication in situations where neither speech nor writing can easily substitute" (Baron 259).

APA   "E-mail has emerged as a medium that allows communication in situations where neither speech nor writing can easily substitute" (Baron, 2000, p. 259).

Tech Tips

The Modern Language Association (MLA) Handbook says it quite well:

> Assessing Internet resources is a particular challenge. Whereas the print
> publications that researchers depend on are generally issued by reputable
> publishers, like university presses, that accept responsibility for the quality
> and reliability of the works they distribute, relatively few electronic publica-
> tions currently have comparable authority.

Consequently, you must exercise great selectivity when gathering information on-line. Here are some questions to ask when evaluating electronic
sources:

- Who has posted or sponsored the site? An individual? An organization?
  A special interest or advocacy group? What are their credentials or
  qualifications? The final suffix in the URL indicates a site's origins:

.com	Commercial enterprise
.org	Nonprofit organization
.edu	College, university, or other educational institution
.gov	Government agency
.mil	Military group
.net	Network

  Sometimes it's helpful to enter the individual's or group's name in
  a search engine to see what related sites emerge. This often reveals
  affiliations and biases that have an impact on credibility.

- Does the site itself provide links to related sites? Does it credit its own
  sources?

- Is the information presented in a reasonably objective fashion, or
  does the site seem to favor or promote a particular viewpoint or
  perspective?

- Does the site provide an e-mail address or other contact information
  that you can use to seek more information?

- What is the date of the posting? Is the information current?

- How well written is the site? How well designed? In short, does it seem
  to be the work of professionals or amateurs?

If you mention the author's name in your own text, neither MLA nor APA requires that the name appear in the parentheses, although the APA system then requires *two* parenthetical insertions:

MLA   As Baron observes, "E-mail has emerged as a medium that allows communication in situations where neither speech nor writing can easily substitute" (259).

APA   As Baron (2000) observes, "E-mail has emerged as a medium that allows communication in situations where neither speech nor writing can easily substitute" (p. 259).

When you're paraphrasing, the differences between the two styles are the same as when you're quoting.

MLA   E-mail is sometimes more practical than speech or writing (Baron 259).

APA   E-mail is sometimes more practical than speech or writing (Baron, 2000, p. 259).

MLA   As Baron observes, e-mail is sometimes more practical than speech or writing (259).

APA   As Baron (2000) observes, e-mail is sometimes more practical than speech or writing (p. 259).

To credit a quote or a paraphrase from an unsigned source (such as the "Anonymous Article" example shown on page 249), parenthesize the title (or a shortened version of it), along with the page number.

MLA   During the mid-1990s, "it was widely believed that the Internet would help undermine authoritarian regimes, reduce governments' abilities to levy taxes, and circumvent all kinds of local regulation" ("The Internet's" 9).

APA   During the mid-1990s, "it was widely believed that the Internet would help undermine authoritarian regimes, reduce governments' abilities to levy taxes, and circumvent all kinds of local regulation" ("The Internet's," 2001, p. 9).

The purpose of parenthetical citations is to enable readers to find your sources on the Works Cited or References page, in case they wish to consult those sources in their entirety.

Obviously, proper documentation is an important part of any report or other paper that has drawn on sources beyond the writer's own prior knowledge. On the following pages is a correctly prepared report, "Drug Testing in the Workplace," with documentation prepared according to MLA guidelines. As mentioned earlier, actual reports written in the workplace may employ other styles of documentation. But certainly the *format* of this report is fairly typical of the kind used in the workplace and in most college courses focusing on workplace communications. Once you've mastered this format, you can adapt it to a wide range of situations, whatever documentation system you may be using.

✓ Checklist   **Evaluating a Long Report**

An effective long report

____ is accompanied by a transmittal document (memo or letter);

____ includes certain components:

  ☐ Title page that includes the title of the report, name(s) of author(s), name of company or organization, name(s) of person(s) receiving the report, and the date

  ☐ Abstract that briefly summarizes the report

  ☐ Table of contents, with sections numbered and titled and page numbers provided

  ☐ List of illustrations, each numbered and titled, with page numbers provided

  ☐ Glossary, if necessary

____ is organized into sections numbered and titled in conformity with the table of contents, covering the subject fully in an orderly way;

____ is clear, accurate, and sufficiently detailed to satisfy the needs of the intended audience;

____ uses plain, simple language;

____ maintains an appropriate tone, neither too formal nor too conversational;

____ employs effective visuals—tables, graphs, charts, and the like— each numbered and titled in conformity with the list of illustrations;

____ includes full documentation (bibliography and parenthetical citations) prepared according to MLA or APA format;

____ contains no typos or mechanical errors in spelling, capitalization, punctuation, and grammar.

I - INTRODUCTION

Since the founding of the company in 1952, Paramount Manufacturing, Inc. has always sought to achieve maximum productivity while providing a safe, secure, and conducive work environment for our employees. In keeping with those goals, management has determined that it may now be time for Paramount to take a more active role in the war against drugs by adopting measures to ensure a drug-free workplace. One such measure that has been suggested is the creation of a mandatory drug testing policy for all new and established employees, and this idea is currently under consideration.

Because drug testing is somewhat controversial, however, there is need for further study and careful deliberation before a determination is reached. This report, compiled after an in-depth review of recent professional literature on the subject, is intended as a first step in that process.

II - BACKGROUND

Various estimates of the annual costs of workplace drug abuse differ greatly, but all the numbers are in the billions. In 1994 the National Safety Council put the figure at $111 billion, broken down into six main categories, as shown in Table 1.

Table 1   Work-Injury Costs

Wage and productivity losses	$59.9 billion
Medical costs	20.7 billion
Administrative expenses	14.4 billion
Employer costs	9.7 billion
Damage to motor vehicles	4.1 billion
Fire losses	3.1 billion
Total	$111.9 billion

Source: "An Alternative to Drug Testing?," p. 1.

According to Mark A. deBernardo, executive director of the Institute for a Drug-Free Workplace and a senior partner at a Washington law firm, "People who use drugs are one-third less productive and are 2.5 times more likely to have absences of eight days or more. People who use drugs are 3.6 times more likely to injure themselves or another person in a workplace accident. . . . Also, people who use drugs are 5 times more likely to file a workers comp claim" (Fletcher 1).

FIGURE 10.7   Drug Testing Report, Page 1

But several recent studies contend that the majority of workplace injuries are attributable to causes other than substance abuse. As shown in Table 2, "Dangerous working conditions, noise and dirt on-the-job, and conflicts at work appear to be the greatest predictors of job injuries. Sleeping problems, which may be exacerbated by shift work, also seem likely to be another direct cause of job injuries" (Macdonald 718). In addition, other reports maintain that substance abuse in society at large—and, by implication, in the workplace—is actually decreasing even while the issue becomes ever more exaggerated, a claim that would seem to be supported by data in Table 3. "At a national and local level, politicians, government agencies, law enforcement agencies, and the media directly benefit from concern over drugs and . . . find it in their best interests to sensationalize drug abuse" (Crow and Hartman 928).

Table 2 Percentage of Total Job Injuries Associated with Each Variable

Variable		Injuries [% (N)]	Total N	Injuries Associated with Variable
Trouble sleeping	No	5.7 (12)	210	77.8
	Yes	15.4 (42)	273	
Noise and dirt	No	6.2 (20)	324	62.3
	Yes	22.0 (33)	150	
Danger	No	6.8 (26)	380	50.9
	Yes	28.1 (27)	96	
Shift work	No	8.2 (31)	365	41.5
	Yes	21.8 (22)	101	
Worry	No	9.0 (35)	387	34.0
	Yes	19.8 (18)	91	
Boredom	No	9.1 (37)	408	28.8
	Yes	21.7 (15)	69	
Conflict	No	9.1 (42)	419	28.3
	Yes	25.0 (15)	60	
Illicit drug use	No	9.8 (43)	440	20.4
	Yes	25.6 (11)	43	

Source: Macdonald, p. 711.

In any case, workplace drug testing programs are quite common. A large number of these programs were introduced in the 1980s, a period of sharply increasing drug use (Konovsky and Cropanzano 698). One response to that

FIGURE 10.8 **Drug Testing Report, Page 2**

3

Table 3 Percentage of Employees Self-Reporting Use of Substances
in the Last 30 Days by Age and Employment Status, 1985, 1988, and 1990

	1985			1988			1990		
	18–25	26–34	35+	18–25	26–34	35+	18–25	26–34	35+
Cocaine									
Full-time	7.6	6.8	1.0	5.0	2.5	—	2.5	1.9	—
Part-time	3.9	6.9	—	3.6	—	—	—	—	—
Marijuana									
Full-time	23.5	17.7	3.7	16.9	11.2	1.3	12.6	7.4	2.9
Part-time	15.2	19.5	2.4	14.2	9.8	2.7	12.0	12.8	—
Psychotherapeutic[a]									
Full-time	6.1	4.9	2.2	4.0	2.3	0.8	2.0	1.3	1.2
Part-time	5.2	4.4	—	2.7	—	—	3.3	—	—
Alcohol									
Full-time	76.3	74.2	69.9	73.1	69.2	59.9	71.2	68.0	58.1
Part-time	66.0	71.3	60.6	65.4	54.6	62.7	58.9	54.6	57.9
Heavy Alcohol[b]									
Full-time	N/A	N/A	N/A	11.2	8.1	3.9	13.9	8.4	4.0
Part-time	N/A	N/A	N/A	12.0	4.4	—	9.2	5.2	3.1

[a]Illicit use of prescription-type stimulants, sedatives, tranquilizers, and/or analgesics.
[b]Drinking 5 or more drinks per occasion on 5 or more of the past 30 days.
Note:"—" means less than 0.05%. "N/A" means that data are not available.
Source: Martin, p. 17.

increase was the report from the President's Commission on Organized Crime, *America's Habit: Drug Abuse, Drug Trafficking and Organized Crime* (1986), which recommended that "Government and private sector employers who do not already require drug testing of job applicants and current employees should consider the appropriateness of such a testing program" (Glantz 1427). Accordingly, the American Management Association (AMA) found that testing increased from 21.5% of companies in 1986 to 81% in 1996; in a 1999 AMA poll, 83% of employers responding said they believed that drug testing deters employee drug use (Penttila 160).

In 1986, President Reagan signed Executive Order 12564, which mandated drug testing for federal employees in "safety sensitive" positions (law enforcement, public health and safety, and national security, for example) and for federally regulated industries such as transportation and nuclear power (Payson and Rosen 25). State and local governments soon followed suit, especially in the police and corrections sectors, as did private employers. This trend continued under President George H. W. Bush's National Drug Control

FIGURE 10.9 Drug Testing Report, Page 3

4

Strategy and his White House mandate for "fair but tough drug-free workplace programs in the private sector" (Brookler 132). Not everyone has been supportive, however, and some drug testing cases have been challenged on Constitutional grounds, specifically the Fourth Amendment protection against unreasonable search and seizure (Hukill 75). "In a white paper published in September 1999, the American Civil Liberties Union labeled drug testing a bad investment, an expensive effort that does not deter drug use, that harms workplace morale, that lowers company productivity, and that, in short, is unnecessary" (Beck 69).

According to Gerald L. Maatman Jr., a partner and chairman of the employment law practice group at Baker & McKenzie in Chicago, drug testing can be "a recipe for disaster" if it's not "crafted carefully or administered carefully" (Fletcher 1). One major problem is that privacy laws vary greatly from state to state. In Wisconsin and Minnesota, mechanical contractors and union plumbers are subject to a mandatory, statewide drug and alcohol testing and treatment program (Mader 1). Illinois, too, is very pro-employer. But California is very pro-employee. Indeed, the city of San Francisco (among others) has an ordinance prohibiting private sector employers from administering drug tests except under specific conditions, with no random or companywide screening permitted (Payson and Rosen 30).

Because of these variations, large companies with sites all over the country must tailor their policies to match local laws. Layne Thome, director of associate services for Home Depot, Inc. of Atlanta, handles drug testing and rehabilitation for the chain: "Where we run into problems are in the differences between state laws. We have a consistent policy that we follow, and wherever the state differs, we try to accommodate our policy to match . . . state requirements." As Maatman puts it, "Because there is no federal law that governs the privacy issue, you, in essence, have employers subject to very much a patchwork quilt of common law claims" (Fletcher 1).

III - TECHNICAL ASPECTS

Widespread drug testing first became possible in the 1970s, with the development of a relatively low-cost chemical assay called EMIT (enzyme multiplied immunoassay test), which can be used to detect the presence of a broad spectrum of drugs (alcohol, steroids, stimulants, sedatives, opiates,

FIGURE 10.10 **Drug Testing Report, Page 4**

hallucinogens, and others) in a single specimen of urine (West and Ackerman 579). Originally used only by crime laboratories, treatment centers, and the military, this technology quickly spread to the business and manufacturing sector (O'Keefe 34), where it is used to screen both prospective and current employees for evidence of substance abuse.

As Table 4 illustrates, an obvious advantage of urine testing is that it detects drugs for a relatively long time after their actual use.

Table 4   Approximate Duration of Detectability of Selected Drugs in Urine

Drugs	Approximate Duration of Detectability
Amphetamines	2 days
Barbiturates	1–7 days
Benzodiazepines	3 days
Cocaine metabolites	2–3 days
Methadone	3 days
Codeine	2 days
PCP	8 days
Cannabinoids	
Single use	3 days
Moderate smoker (4 times/week)	5 days
Heavy smoker (daily)	10 days
Chronic heavy smoker	21 days

Source: Rothstein, p. 294.

As Zimmer and Jacobs explain, urinalysis detects not the actual drug consumed but the metabolites created by its processing in the system. The EMIT technique introduces into the urine specimen a sample of the metabolite being sought, with a detectable enzyme "tag" attached to each of its molecules. Antibodies that bind to the metabolites are also added. If the specimen was originally free of drug metabolites, the antibodies will bond to the tagged ones, creating a new substance in which the "tag" is no longer detectable. But if the specimen does contain drug metabolites, some of those molecules will bind to the antibodies, leaving a surplus of tagged molecules that are unattached and therefore detectable (Zimmer and Jacobs 4–5).

FIGURE 10.11 Drug Testing Report, Page 5

6

A valuable feature of this technique is its adaptability to automation. Using sophisticated equipment such as the Olympus AU-500, a laboratory technician is able to analyze 4,000 urine samples in an hour. Hitachi's model 736-50 can almost double that pace (Zimmer and Jacobs 5). Therefore, employers can expect relatively fast turnaround, always an important consideration in personnel matters.

For a variety of reasons, however, test results are often inaccurate. One study conducted by the Centers for Disease Control (CDC) found accuracy rates as low as 33 percent, while a Northwestern University study reported 25 percent of the positive findings resulting from the EMIT technique were in fact false positives. One reason for inaccuracies is that many legal substances can cross-react with drugs the tests are designed to detect (see Table 5). Indeed, EMIT's manufacturer recommends that all positive findings be confirmed by means of more sophisticated follow-up tests (Chineson 91).

Table 5   Legal Substances That Cross-React with Tested-For Drugs

Type of Drug	Cross-Reactants
Amphetamines	1. Over-the-counter cold medications (decongestants) 2. Over-the-counter and prescription dietary aids 3. Asthma medications 4. Anti-inflammatory agents
Barbiturates	1. Anti-inflammatory agents 2. Phenobarbital (used to treat epilepsy)
Cocaine	1. Herbal teas (made from coca leaves)
Marijuana (cannabinoids)	1. Nonsteroidal anti-inflammatory agents 2. Ibuprofen (Advil, Motrin, Nuprin)
Morphine, opiates	1. Codeine 2. Prescription analgesics and antitussives 3. Poppy seeds 4. Over-the-counter cough remedies
Phencyclidine (PCP)	1. Prescription cough medicines 2. Valium

Source: Rothstein, p. 298

FIGURE 10.12   **Drug Testing Report, Page 6**

7

Among the most reliable of the confirmatory tests is a method known as gas chromatography/mass spectrometry (GC/MS). In this procedure, the urine sample is vaporized and then forced through a silica-coated tube. Because silica slows down substances at different rates, they exit the tube individually. Ion bombardment of the exiting substances causes them to fragment in patterns that can then be matched to the known mass spectrum of each drug. Although expensive, the GC/MS procedure is very accurate. "Routine GC/MS confirmation eliminates most false positives and allows laboratories to set immunoassay cutoff levels lower, thereby also reducing the number of false-negative results" (Zimmer and Jacobs 6–7).

IV - LEGAL AND ETHICAL ASPECTS

Despite drug testing's obvious appeal to employers wishing to rid the workplace of controlled substances, a number of legal and ethical problems surround its use. The practice is sometimes seen as "demeaning and intrusive" (Glantz 1427) and, as mentioned earlier, has been contested on Fourth Amendment grounds. The courts have been inconsistent, sometimes ruling in favor of the plaintiff, sometimes not. "The question is always, how far should the balance tip away from the right to be free from . . . intrusion— how weighty must the public interest be to abridge their rights?" (Glantz 1428).

Clearly, this is a difficult question that can be decided only on a case-by-case basis. There is no denying, however, that mandatory drug testing typically requires "individuals to submit to a highly intrusive test to vindicate . . . innocence. Such a presumption of guilt is contrary to the Constitution" (Glantz 1428). In addition, the tests constitute a serious invasion of workers' medical privacy, for urinalysis can reveal not only substance abuse, but also pregnancy, asthma, and the fact that an individual is being treated for heart disease, manic depression, epilepsy, diabetes, and "a host of other physical and mental conditions" (O'Keefe 38).

On the other hand, mandatory drug testing—especially of job applicants—can be an effective means of weeding out those whose use of controlled substances will almost certainly have a negative impact on job performance. Several studies have substantiated this. A Postal Service experiment screened 5,465 job applicants (of whom 4,375 were hired) at 21 participating sites,

FIGURE 10.13 Drug Testing Report, Page 7

8

testing for a variety of drugs. The results were not immediately released, and therefore had no impact on hiring decisions. But follow-ups revealed that those who had tested positive were about 1.5 times more likely to be fired and were more than 1.75 times more prone to absenteeism. In the case of cocaine specifically, users were twice as likely to be fired and more than 3 times as likely to be absent (West and Ackerman 586–587).

In view of such findings, it is hardly surprising that many major companies such as Coors, Georgia Power, and 3M conduct aggressive anti-drug campaigns targeting not only applicants but established employees ("Drug abuse at work," 72). Similarly, "despite the opposition of the AMA . . . physicians at Johns Hopkins Hospital in Baltimore and at Columbia-Presbyterian Medical Center in New York are . . . required to undergo random . . . screening" (West and Ackerman 589).

In cases of positive test results, employers' responses vary from workplace to workplace, as might be expected. According to one survey, "twenty-five percent of companies . . . automatically fire employees who use drugs" (Chineson 91). Others are less punitive. At many companies, a first offense will result in suspension and/or referral to a treatment program, with termination only for a second offense. From a legal standpoint, however, the worst-case scenario is that of the employee who sues the company after being incorrectly terminated or referred; "even when employers . . . verify positive results, employees who turn out to be drug-free upon retesting will be . . . stigmatized" (O'Keefe 35). The consequences of such errors can be quite costly indeed. "The average jury award for wrongful termination of employment is $750,000 and the average legal costs are $125,000, win or lose" (Brookler 128–129). To guard against such outcomes, employers must design their drug testing programs very carefully.

V - CHARACTERISTICS OF AN EFFECTIVE DRUG TESTING PROGRAM

Employers agree that for any drug testing program to succeed, every effort must be made to safeguard against error (and attendant liability) and to minimize any potentially negative impact on employee morale. To this end, most progressive companies design their programs according to the guide-lines published by the National Institute on Drug Abuse (NIDA). Some key features of a successful program are as follows:

FIGURE 10.14 **Drug Testing Report, Page 8**

9

- Clear-cut Policy Statement

  Using input from human resources, employee relations, union and legal department representatives, and employees themselves, a clear, comprehensive policy statement must be written. The statement should spell out the company's standards of employee conduct, details of how and under what circumstances testing will occur, and what steps will be taken in response to a positive test result.

- Strict Guidelines for Specimen Collection

  A company may choose to collect specimens in house (usually at the company's health or medical facility) or off site, at a hospital or clinic, or at a facility specializing in such procedures. In any case, it is absolutely crucial that collection be conducted according to the strictest NIDA standards. "Because the first few links in the chain of custody are forged here . . . many experts feel that choosing your collection site merits greater attention than choosing your lab" (Brookler 130).

- NIDA-Certified Laboratory

  To become NIDA certified, a lab must meet the most stringent standards of accuracy and protocol, especially regarding the chain of custody governing the handling of specimens. In short, NIDA-certified laboratories are the most reliable and certainly the most persuasive in court.

- Confirmation of Positive Results

  Positive test results should be confirmed by means of a GC/MS follow-up test. "Without the GC/MS confirmation, you aren't legally defensible" (Brookler 129). In the event of a positive confirmation, the case must then be referred to the company's medical review officer (MRO), a licensed physician knowledgeable about substance abuse, who searches for alternative medical explanations for the positive test result before providing final confirmation. The MRO may refer the case back to management only after the employee has been given the opportunity to meet with the MRO. (At most companies, the MRO is a contract employee.)

FIGURE 10.15 Drug Testing Report, Page 9

10

- Employee Assistance Program

  Since substance abuse is now recognized as a disease, many employers have begun to provide employee assistance programs. Rather than being terminated, employees who test positive may instead be referred for counseling. In such instances, the rehabilitation option is usually presented as a condition of continued employment.

CONCLUSION

Clearly, the whole subject of drug testing in the workplace is quite complicated. If Paramount Manufacturing is to introduce a testing program, perhaps the way to begin would be to require testing of job *applicants* only—at least at first. This would enable us to become gradually acquainted with the procedures and problems involved, without the risk of alienating employees already on board. We might expand the program at a later date, but not in the form of random testing, which has been shown to engender resentment and legal challenges. Any testing of the established workforce should be done only on a for-cause basis—in response to sudden absenteeism, erratic behavior, on-the-job accidents, and the like. And certainly we should establish provisions for an employee assistance program before any testing occurs. All this, however, is by way of suggestion only. The next step should be to call in an outside consultant, preferably from NIDA, to provide additional input before any final decision is made.

FIGURE 10.16 Drug Testing Report, Page 10

WORKS CITED

"An Alternative to Drug Testing?" *Inc.* April 1995: 112.

Beck, Evelyn. "Is the Time Right for Impairment Testing?" *Workforce* Feb. 2001: 69.

Brookler, Rob. "Industry Standards in Workplace Drug Testing." *Personnel Journal* April 1992: 128–132.

Chineson, Joel. "Mandatory Drug Testing: An Invasion of Privacy?" *Trial* Sept. 1986: 91–95.

Crow, Stephen M., and Sandra J. Hartman. "Drugs in the Workplace: The Problems and the Cures." *Journal of Drug Issues* 22 (1992): 923–937.

"Drug Abuse at Work." *The Economist* 30 Sept. 1989: 72.

Fletcher, Lee. "Employer Drug Testing Has Pitfalls." *Business Insurance* 23 Oct. 2000: 1.

Glantz, Leonard H. "A Nation of Suspects: Drug Testing and the Fourth Amendment." *American Journal of Public Health* 79. 10 (1989): 1427–1431.

Hukill, Craig. "Significant decisions in labor cases: Employee drug testing." *Monthly Labor Review* Nov. 1989: 75–77.

Konovsky, Mary A., and Russell Cropanzano. "Perceived Fairness of Employee Drug Testing as a Predictor of Employee Attitudes and Job Performance." *Journal of Applied Psychology* 76 (1991): 698–707.

Macdonald, Scott. "The Role of Drugs in Workplace Injuries: Is Drug Testing Appropriate?" *Journal of Drug Issues* 25 (1995): 703–722.

Mader, Robert P. "Drug-Test Accord." *Contractor* July 2000: 1.

Martin, Jack K., Joan M. Kraft, and Paul M. Roman. "Extent and Impact of Alcohol and Drug Use Problems in the Workplace: A Review of the Empirical Evidence." *Drug Testing in the Workplace: Research Advances in Alcohol and Drug Problems.* Vol. 11. Eds. Scott Macdonald and Paul Roman. New York: Plenum, 1994. 3–31.

FIGURE 10.17 Drug Testing Report, Works Cited

12

O'Keefe, Anne Marie. "The Case Against Drug Testing." *Psychology Today* June 1987: 34–38.

Payson, Martin F., and Philip B. Rosen. "Substance Abuse: A Crisis in the Workplace." *Trial* July 1987: 25–33.

Penttila, Chris. "Testy, Testy." *Entrepreneur* June 2000: 160.

Rothstein, Mark A. "Drug Testing in the Workplace: The Challenge to Employment Relations and Employment Law." *Ethical Theory and Business*. Eds. Tom L. Beauchamp and Norman E. Bowie. Upper Saddle River: Prentice, 1997. 292–309.

West, Louis Jolyon, and Deborah L. Ackerman. "The Drug-Testing Controversy." *Journal of Drug Issues* 23 (1993): 579–595.

Zimmer, Lynn, and James B. Jacobs. "The Business of Drug Testing: Technological Innovation and Social Control." *Contemporary Drug Problems* 19.1 (1992): 1–26.

FIGURE 10.18 Drug Testing Report, Works Cited (continued)

 **Exercises**

■ EXERCISE 10.1

Rewrite the transmittal memo (Figure 10.1) and the title page (Figure 10.2), as if the report were your own work submitted as an assignment in your Workplace Communications course.

■ EXERCISE 10.2

Rewrite the Works Cited in Figure 10.17 and 10.18, using APA format.

■ EXERCISE 10.3

Consult the MLA Web site at http://www.mla.org to determine how to handle documentation for the following kinds of on-line sources:

- Article in a reference database
- E-mail
- FTP (file transfer protocol), telnet, or gopher site
- Personal Web site
- Posting to a discussion list (listserv or newsgroup)
- Synchronous communication (MOOs, MUDs, and IRCs)

■ EXERCISE 10.4

Guided by the table of contents on the following page, team up with two or three other students to write a collaborative report entitled "Radar: History, Principles, Applications."

■ EXERCISE 10.5

Practically all Workplace Communications courses include a long report assignment at some point during the semester, usually near the end. Specific features of the project, however, vary greatly from instructor to instructor. Write a long report designed to satisfy your instructor's course requirements.

TABLE OF CONTENTS